BRIEF CONTENTS

CONTENTS

© KATIV/ISTOCKPHOTO.COM

KURHAN/SHUTTERSTOCK.COM

RITU MANOJ JETHANI/SHUTTERSTOCK.COM

APPENDICES

LAWRENCE J. GITMAN is an emeritus professor of finance at San Diego State University. He received his bachelor's degree from Purdue University, his M.B.A. from the University of Dayton, and his Ph.D. from the University of Cincinnati. Professor Gitman is a prolific textbook author and has more than 50 articles appearing in *Financial Management, The Financial Review,* the *Journal of Financial Planning,* the *Journal of Risk and Insurance,* the *Financial Services Review,* the *Journal of Financial Research, Financial Practice and Education,* the *Journal of Financial Education,* and other scholarly publications.

His major textbooks include *The Future of Business,* Sixth Edition, and *The Future of Business: The Essentials,* Fourth Edition, both of which are co-authored with Carl McDaniel; and *Fundamentals of Investing,* Twelfth Edition, which is co-authored with Michael D. Joehnk and Scott B. Smart. Gitman and Joehnk also wrote *Investment Fundamentals: A Guide to Becoming a Knowledgeable Investor,* which was selected as one of 1988's ten best personal finance books by *Money* magazine; *Principles of Managerial Finance,* Sixth Brief Edition, and *Principles of Managerial Finance,* Thirteenth Edition, both co-authored with Chad J. Zutter; *Foundations of Managerial Finance,* Fourth Edition; and *Introduction to Finance,* co-authored with Jeff Madura.

An active member of numerous professional organizations, Professor Gitman is past president of the Academy of Financial Services, the San Diego Chapter of the Financial Executives Institute, the Midwest Finance Association, and the FMA National Honor Society. In addition, he is a Certified Financial Planner® (CFP®). Gitman formerly served as a director on the CFP® Board of Governors, as vice-president–financial education for the Financial Management Association, and as director of the San Diego MIT Enterprise Forum. Gitman has two grown children and lives with his wife in La Jolla, California, where he is an avid bicyclist.

MICHAEL D. JOEHNK is an emeritus professor of finance at Arizona State University. In addition to his academic appointments at ASU, Professor Joehnk spent a year (1999) as a visiting professor of finance at the University of Otago in New Zealand. He received his bachelor's and Ph.D. degrees from the University of Arizona and his M.B.A. from Arizona State University. A Chartered Financial Analyst (CFA), he has served as a member of the Candidate Curriculum Committee and of the Council of Examiners of the Institute of Chartered Financial Analysts. He has also served as a director of the Phoenix Society of Financial Analysts and as secretary-treasurer of the Western Finance Association, and he was elected to two terms as a vice-president of the Financial Management Association. Professor Joehnk is the author or co-author of some 50 articles, five books, and numerous monographs. His articles have appeared in *Financial Management,* the *Journal of Finance,* the *Journal of Bank Research,* the *Journal of Portfolio Management,* the *Journal of Consumer Affairs,* the *Journal of Financial and Quantitative Analysis,* the *AAII Journal,* the *Journal of Financial Research,* the *Bell Journal of Economics,* the *Daily Bond Buyer, Financial Planner,* and other publications.

In addition to co-authoring several books with Lawrence J. Gitman, Professor Joehnk was the author of a highly successful paperback trade book, *Investing for Safety's Sake.* Dr. Joehnk was also the editor of *Institutional Asset Allocation,* which was sponsored by the Institute of Chartered Financial Analysts and published by Dow Jones–Irwin. He was a contributor to the *Handbook for Fixed Income Securities* and to *Investing and Risk Management,* Volume 1 of the Library of Investment Banking. In addition, he served a six-year term as executive co-editor of the *Journal of Financial Research.* He and his wife live in Flagstaff, Arizona, where they enjoy hiking and other activities in the nearby mountains and canyons.

RANDALL S. BILLINGSLEY is a finance professor at Virginia Tech. He received his bachelor's degree in economics from Texas Tech University and received both an M.S. in economics and a Ph.D. in finance from Texas A&M University. Professor Billingsley holds the Chartered Financial Analyst (CFA), Financial Risk Manager (FRM), and Certified Rate of Return Analyst (CRRA) professional designations. An award-winning teacher at the undergraduate and graduate levels, his research, consulting, and teaching focus on investment analysis and issues relevant to practicing financial advisors. Formerly a vice president at the Association for Investment Management and Research (now the CFA Institute), Professor Billingsley's published equity valuation case study of Merck & Company was assigned reading in the CFA curriculum for several years. In 2006, the Wharton School published his book,

Understanding Arbitrage: An Intuitive Approach to Financial Analysis. In addition, his research has been published in refereed journals that include the *Journal of Portfolio Management,* the *Journal of Banking and Finance, Financial Management,* the *Journal of Financial Research,* and the *Journal of Futures Markets.* Professor Billingsley advises the Student-Managed Endowment for Educational Development (SEED) at Virginia Tech, which manages an equity portfolio of about $4 million on behalf of the Virginia Tech Foundation.

Professor Billingsley's consulting to date has focused on two areas of expertise. First, he has acted extensively as an expert witness on financial issues. Second, he has taught seminars and published materials that prepare investment professionals for the CFA examinations. This has afforded him the opportunity to explore and discuss the relationships among diverse areas of investment analysis. His consulting endeavors have taken him across the United States and to Canada, Europe, and Asia. A primary goal of Professor Billingsley's consulting is to apply the findings of academic financial research to practical investment decision making and personal financial planning.

PART 1

FOUNDATIONS OF FINANCIAL PLANNING

1

UNDERSTANDING THE FINANCIAL PLANNING PROCESS

LEARNING GOALS

LG1 Identify the benefits of using personal financial planning techniques to manage your finances.

LG2 Describe the personal financial planning process and define your goals.

LG3 Explain the life cycle of financial plans, the role they play in achieving your financial goals, how to deal with special planning concerns, and the use of professional financial planners.

LG4 Examine the economic environment's influence on personal financial planning.

LG5 Evaluate the impact of age, education, and geographic location on personal income.

LG6 Understand the importance of career choices and their relationship to personal financial planning.

How Will This Affect Me? The heart of financial planning is making sure your values line up with how you spend and save. That means knowing where you are financially and planning on how to get where you want to be in the future no matter what life throws at you. For example, how should your plan handle the projection that Social Security costs may exceed revenues by 2017? And what if the government decides to raise marginal tax rates to help cover the federal deficit? An informed financial plan should reflect such uncertainties and more.

This chapter reviews the financial planning process and explains its context. Topics include how financial plans change to accommodate your current stage in life and the role that financial planners can play in helping you achieve your objectives. After reading this chapter you will have a good perspective on how to organize your overall personal financial plan.

1-1 The Rewards of Sound Financial Planning

LG1 What does living "the good life" mean to you? Does it mean having the flexibility to pursue your dreams and goals in life? Is it owning a home in a certain part of town, starting a company, being debt free, driving a particular type of car, taking luxury vacations, or having a large investment portfolio? Today's complex, fast-paced world offers a bewildering array of choices. Rapidly changing economic, political, technological, and social environments make it increasingly difficult to develop solid financial strategies that will improve your lifestyle consistently. Moreover, the recent financial crisis dramatizes the need to plan for financial contingencies. No matter how you define it, the good life requires sound planning to turn financial goals into reality.

The best way to achieve financial objectives is through *personal financial planning*, which helps define our financial goals and develop appropriate strategies to reach them. We should not solely depend on employee or government benefits—such as steady salary increases or adequate funding from employer-paid pensions or Social Security—to retire comfortably. Creating

After you read the chapter, explore the STUDY TOOLS listed on page 24.

flexible plans and regularly revising them is the key to building a sound financial future. Successful financial planning also brings rewards that include greater flexibility, an improved standard of living, wise spending habits, and increased wealth. Of course, planning alone does not guarantee success; but having an effective, consistent plan can help you use your resources wisely. Careful financial planning increases the chance that your financial goals will be achieved and that you will have sufficient flexibility to handle such contingencies as illness, job loss, and even financial crises.

The goal of this book is to remove the mystery from the personal financial planning process and replace it with the tools you need to take charge of your personal finances and your life. To organize this process, the text is divided into six parts as follows.

- **Part 1:** Foundations of Financial Planning
- **Part 2:** Managing Basic Assets
- **Part 3:** Managing Credit
- **Part 4:** Managing Insurance Needs
- **Part 5:** Managing Investments
- **Part 6:** Retirement and Estate Planning

Each part explains a different aspect of personal financial planning, as shown in Exhibit 1.1. This organizational scheme revolves around financial decision making that's firmly based on an operational set of financial plans. We believe that sound financial planning enables individuals to make decisions that will yield their desired results.

1-1a Improving Your Standard of Living

With personal financial planning we learn to acquire, use, and control our financial resources more efficiently. It allows us to gain more enjoyment from our income and thus to improve our **standard of living**—the necessities, comforts, and luxuries we have or desire.

Americans view standards of living, and what constitute necessities or luxuries, differently depending on their level of affluence. For example, 45 percent of Americans consider a second or vacation home the ultimate symbol of affluence, while others see taking two or more annual vacations or living in an exclusive neighborhood as an indicator of wealth.

standard of living
The necessities, comforts, and luxuries enjoyed or desired by an individual or family.

3

Exhibit 1.1 Organizational Planning Model

This text emphasizes making financial decisions regarding assets, credit, insurance, investments, and retirement and estates.

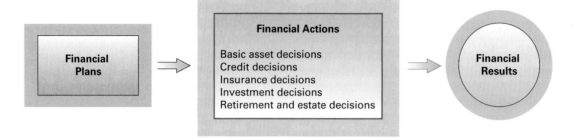

Financial Plans → **Financial Actions**
- Basic asset decisions
- Credit decisions
- Insurance decisions
- Investment decisions
- Retirement and estate decisions

→ **Financial Results**

average propensity to consume The percentage of each dollar of income, on average, that a person spends for current needs rather than savings.

So our quality of life is closely tied to our standard of living. Although other factors—geographic location, public facilities, local cost of living, pollution, traffic, and population density—also affect quality of life, wealth is commonly viewed as a key determinant. Material items such as a house, car, and clothing as well as money available for health care, education, art, music, travel, and entertainment all contribute to our quality of life. Of course, many so-called wealthy people live "plain" lives, choosing to save, invest, or support philanthropic organizations with their money rather than indulge themselves with luxuries.

One trend with a profound effect on our standard of living is the *two-income family*. What was relatively rare in the early 1970s has become commonplace today, and the incomes of millions of families have risen sharply as a result. About 75 percent of married adults say that they and their mate share all their money, while some partners admit to having a secret stash of cash. Two incomes buy more, but they also require greater responsibility to manage the money wisely.

1-1b Spending Money Wisely

Using money wisely is a major benefit of financial planning. Whatever your income, you can either spend it now or save some of it for the future. Determining your current and future spending patterns is an important part of personal money management. The goal, of course, is to spend your money so that you get the most satisfaction from each dollar.

Current Needs

Your current spending level is based on the necessities of life and your **average propensity to consume**, which is the percentage of each dollar of income, on average, that is spent for current needs rather than savings. A minimum level of spending would allow you to obtain only the necessities of life: food, clothing, and shelter. Although the quantity and type of food, clothing, and shelter purchased may differ among individuals depending on their wealth, we all need these items to survive.

Some people with high average propensities to consume earn low incomes and spend a large portion of it on basic necessities. On the other hand, individuals earning large amounts quite often have low average propensities to consume, in part because the cost of necessities represents only a small portion of their income.

Still, two people with significantly different incomes could have the same average propensity to consume because of differences in their standard of living. The person making more money may believe it is essential to buy better-quality items or more items and will thus, on average, spend the same percentage of each dollar of income as the person making far less.

Future Needs

A carefully developed financial plan should set aside a portion of current income for deferred, future spending. Placing these funds in various savings and investment vehicles

Financial Road Sign

Be SMART in Planning Your Financial Goals

Success is most likely if your goals are:

Specific: What do I want to achieve? What is required of me, and what are my constraints?

Measurable: How much money is needed? How will I know if I am succeeding?

Attainable: How can I do this? Is this consistent with my other financial goals?

Realistic: Am I willing and able to do this?

Timely: What is my target date? What short-term goals must be achieved along the way to achieve my longer-term goals?

Inspired by Paul J. Meyer's, *Attitude Is Everything*, The Meyer Resource Group, 2003.

allows you to generate a return on your funds until you need them. For example, you may want to build up a retirement fund to maintain a desirable standard of living in your later years. Instead of spending the money now, you defer actual spending until the future when you retire. Nearly 35 percent of Americans say retirement planning is their most pressing financial concern. Other examples of deferred spending include saving for a child's education, a primary residence or vacation home, a major acquisition (such as a car or home entertainment center), or even a vacation.

The portion of current income we commit to future needs depends on how much we earn and also on our average propensity to consume. About 45 percent of affluent Americans say they need at least $2.5 million to feel rich. The more we earn and the less we devote to current spending, the more we can commit to meeting future needs. In any case, some portion of current income should be set aside regularly for future use. This practice creates good saving habits.

1-1c Accumulating Wealth

In addition to using current income to pay for everyday living expenses, we often spend it to acquire assets such as cars, a home, or stocks and bonds. Our assets largely determine how wealthy we are. Personal financial planning plays a critical role in the accumulation of wealth by directing our financial resources to the most productive areas.

One's **wealth** depends on the total value of all the items that the individual owns. Wealth consists of financial and tangible assets. **Financial assets** are intangible, paper assets, such as savings accounts and securities (stocks, bonds, mutual funds, and so forth). They are *earning assets* that are held for the returns they promise. **Tangible assets**, in contrast, are physical assets, such as real estate and automobiles. These assets can be held for either consumption (e.g., your home, car, artwork, or jewelry) or investment purposes (e.g., a duplex purchased for rental income). In general, the goal of most people is to accumulate as much wealth as possible while maintaining current consumption at a level that provides the desired standard of living. To see how you compare with the typical American in financial terms, check out the statistics in Exhibit 1.2.

1-2 The Personal Financial Planning Process

LG2 Many people mistakenly assume that personal financial planning is only for the wealthy. However, nothing could be further from the truth. Whether you have a lot of money or not enough, you still need personal financial planning. If you have enough money, planning can help you spend and invest it wisely. If your income seems inadequate, taking steps to plan your financial activities will lead to an improved lifestyle. **Personal financial planning** is a systematic process that considers the important elements of an individual's financial affairs and is aimed at fulfilling his or her financial goals.

Everyone—including recent college graduates, young married couples, and others—needs to develop a personal financial plan. Knowing what you need to accomplish financially, and how you intend to do it, gives you an edge over someone who merely reacts to financial events as they unfold. Just think of the example provided by the recent financial crisis. Do you think that a financial plan would have helped in weathering the financial storm?

wealth The total value of all items owned by an individual, such as savings accounts, stocks, bonds, home, and automobiles.

financial assets Intangible assets, such as savings accounts and securities, that are acquired for some promised future return.

tangible assets Physical assets, such as real estate and automobiles, that can be held for either consumption or investment purposes.

personal financial planning A systematic process that considers important elements of an individual's financial affairs in order to fulfill financial goals.

 Knowing what you need to accomplish financially, and how you intend to do it, gives you an edge...

Exhibit 1.2 The Average American, Financially Speaking

This financial snapshot of the "average American" gives you an idea of where you stand in terms of income, net worth, and other measures. It should help you set some goals for the future.

	Income and Assets
What Do We Earn? (*median*)	
All families	$ 49,800
What Are We Worth? (*median*)	
All families	$ 96,000
Home Ownership (*median*)	
Value of primary residence	$176,000
Mortgage on primary residence	112,000
How Much Savings Do We Have? (*median*)	
Pooled investment funds (excluding money market)	$ 47,000
Individual stocks	12,000
Bonds	50,000
Bank accounts/CDs	24,000
Retirement accounts	48,000

Source: Adapted from Jesse Bricker, Brian K. Bucks, Arthur B. Kennickell, Traci L. Mach, and Kevin B. Moore, "Surveying the Aftermath of the Storm: Changes in Family Finances from 2007 to 2009," *Finance and Economics Discussion 2011–7,* Board of Governors of the Federal Reserve System, Washington, DC, (March 2011, data is for 2009.), http://federalreserve.gov/econresdata/scf/scf_2009p.htm, Tables 5 and 9, accessed February 2012.

financial goals
Results that an individual wants to attain, such as buying a home, building a college fund, or achieving financial independence.

1-2a Steps in the Financial Planning Process

If you take a closer look at financial planning, you'll see that the process translates personal financial goals into specific financial plans, which then help you implement those goals through financial strategies. The financial planning process involves the six steps shown in Exhibit 1.3. As you can see, the financial planning process runs full circle. You start with financial goals, formulate and implement financial plans and strategies to reach them, monitor and control progress toward goals through budgets, and use financial statements to evaluate the plan and budget results. This leads you back to redefining your goals so that they better meet your current needs and to revising your financial plans and strategies accordingly.

Let's now look at how goal setting fits into the planning process. In Chapters 2 and 3, we'll consider other information essential to creating your financial plans: personal financial statements, budgets, and taxes.

1-2b Defining Your Financial Goals

Financial goals are the results that an individual wants to attain. Examples include buying a home, building a college fund, and achieving financial

LES AND DAVE JACOBS/CULTURA/CORBIS

Exhibit 1.3 The Six-Step Financial Planning Process

The financial planning process translates personal financial goals into specific financial plans and strategies, implements them, and then uses budgets and financial statements to monitor, evaluate, and revise plans and strategies as needed. This process typically involves the six steps shown in sequence here.

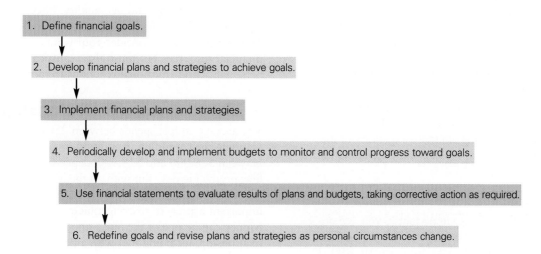

1. Define financial goals.

2. Develop financial plans and strategies to achieve goals.

3. Implement financial plans and strategies.

4. Periodically develop and implement budgets to monitor and control progress toward goals.

5. Use financial statements to evaluate results of plans and budgets, taking corrective action as required.

6. Redefine goals and revise plans and strategies as personal circumstances change.

© Cengage Learning

independence. What are your financial goals? Have you spelled them out? It's impossible to effectively manage your financial resources without financial goals. We need to know where we are going, in a financial sense, to effectively meet the major financial events in our lives. Your financial goals or preferences must be stated in monetary terms because money and the satisfaction it can bring are an integral part of financial planning.

The Role of Money

About 80 percent of Americans believe that money is power, and about 75 percent say that it is freedom. **Money** is the medium of exchange used to measure value in financial transactions. It would be difficult to set specific personal financial goals and to measure progress toward achieving them without the standard unit of exchange provided by the dollar. Money, as we know

money The medium of exchange used as a measure of value in financial transactions.

BEHAVIOR MATTERS

Practicing Financial Self-Awareness

Are you aware of your financial behavior, its causes, and its consequences? For example, are you routinely relying too heavily on your credit card debt? Are you saving enough to buy a new car or to fund your retirement? And the bottom line: Are you continuing the same financial behavior you have in the past and yet expecting different results?

The first decisive step in taking control of your life is to simply think about what you're thinking, feeling, and doing. Be financially self-aware: observe your own thoughts, feelings, and behavior concerning your finances. Take notes on things that affect how you feel and what you do about financial decisions. Watch yourself and be honest about your feelings concerning money and your future.

Then ask yourself two critically important questions:

- **Is the way I spend money consistent with what I say I believe?** Financial planning that works is taking the time to develop a plan that purposely lines up your values and your use of money.
- **Have I clearly stated the financial goals that are important to me and, if so, what am I doing today to make sure I achieve them?** The heart of financial planning is determining where you are today and where you want to be in the future. This implies the need for a financial plan: limited resources sometimes bring painful trade-offs.

Source: Adapted from Carl Richards, "Practicing Radical Self-Awareness," Behaviorgap.com, accessed February 2012.

utility The amount of satisfaction received from purchasing certain types or quantities of goods and services.

it today, is the key consideration in establishing financial goals. Yet it's not money, as such, that most people want. Rather, we want the **utility**, which is the amount of satisfaction received from buying quantities of goods and services of a given quality, that money makes possible. People may choose one item over another because of a special feature that provides additional utility. The added utility may result from the actual usefulness of the special feature or from the "status" it's expected to provide or both. Regardless, people receive varying levels of satisfaction from similar items, and their satisfaction isn't necessarily directly related to the cost of the items. We therefore need to consider utility along with cost when evaluating alternative qualities of life, spending patterns, and forms of wealth accumulation.

Go to Smart Sites

Is getting the lowest price important to you? Where can you search for the best prices? For more online resources, whenever you see "*Go to Smart Sites*" in this chapter, visit CourseMate for PFIN 3. Log in at www.cengagebrain.com. ●

The Psychology of Money

Money and its utility are not only economic concepts; they're also closely linked to the psychological concepts of values, emotion, and personality. Your personal value system—the important ideals and beliefs that guide your life—will also shape your attitude toward money and wealth accumulation. If you place a high value on family life, you may choose a career that offers regular hours and less stress or choose an employer who offers flextime rather than a higher-paying position that requires travel and lots of overtime. You may have plenty of money but choose to live frugally and do things yourself rather than hire someone to do them for you. Or if status and image are important to you, you may spend a high proportion of your current income on acquiring luxuries. Financial goals and decisions should be consistent with your personal values. You can formulate financial plans that provide the greatest personal satisfaction and quality of life by identifying your values.

Money is a primary motivator of personal behavior because it has a strong effect on self-image. Each person's unique personality and emotional makeup determine the importance and role of money in his or her life. You should become aware of your own attitudes toward money because they are the basis of your "money personality" and money management style. Check out the Bonus Exhibits to explore your attitude toward money. (Visit CourseMate for PFIN 3. Log in at **www.cengagebrain.com.**)

Some questions to ask yourself include: How important is money to me? Why? What types of spending give me satisfaction? Am I a risk taker? Do I need large financial reserves to feel secure? Knowing the answers to these questions is a prerequisite for developing realistic and effective financial goals and plans. Trade-offs between current and future benefits are strongly affected by values, emotions, and personality. Effective financial plans are both economically and psychologically sound. They must not only consider your wants, needs, and financial resources but must also realistically reflect your personality and emotional reactions to money.

1-2c Money and Relationships

The average couple spends between 250 and 700 hours planning their wedding in addition to an average of between $26,000 and $28,000, depending on where they live, on the big day. But with all the hoopla surrounding the wedding day, many couples overlook one of the most important aspects of marriage: financial compatibility. Money can be one of the most emotional issues in any relationship, including that with a partner, your parents, or children. Most people are uncomfortable talking about money matters and avoid such discussions, even with their partners. However, differing opinions on how to spend money may threaten the stability of a marriage or cause arguments between parents and children. Learning to communicate with your partner about money is a critical step in developing effective financial plans.

The best way to resolve money disputes is to be aware of your partner's financial style, keep the lines of communication open, and be willing to compromise. It's highly unlikely that you can change your partner's style (or your own, for that matter), but you can work out your differences. Financial planning is an especially important part of the conflict resolution process. To gain a better understanding of your differences, work together to establish a set of financial goals that takes into account each person's needs and values.

1-2d Types of Financial Goals

Financial goals cover a wide range of financial aspirations: controlling living expenses, meeting retirement needs, setting up a savings and investment program, and minimizing your taxes. Other important financial goals include having enough money to live as well as possible,

being financially independent, sending children to college, and providing for retirement.

Financial goals should be defined as specifically as possible. Saying that you want to save money next year is not a specific goal. How much do you want to save, and for what purpose? A goal such as "save 10 percent of my take-home pay each month to start an investment program" states clearly what you want to do and why.

Because they are the basis of your financial plans, your goals should be realistic and attainable. If you set a savings goal too high—for example, 25 percent of your take-home pay when your basic living expenses already account for 85 percent of it—then your goal is unattainable and there's no way to meet it. But if savings goals are set too low, you may not accumulate enough for a meaningful investment program. If your goals are unrealistic, they'll put the basic integrity of your financial plan at risk and be a source of ongoing financial frustration.

It's important to involve your immediate family in the goal-setting process. When family members "buy into" the goals, it eliminates the potential for future conflicts and improves the family's chances for financial success. After defining and approving your goals, you can prepare appropriate cash budgets. Finally, you should assign priorities and a time frame to financial goals. Are they short-term goals for the next year, or are they intermediate or long-term goals that will not be achieved for many more years? For example, saving for a vacation might be a medium-priority short-term goal, whereas buying a larger home may be a high-priority intermediate goal and purchasing a vacation home a low-priority long-term goal. Normally, long-term financial goals are set first, followed by a series of corresponding short-term and intermediate goals.

1-2e Putting Target Dates on Financial Goals

Financial goals are most effective when they are set with goal dates. **Goal dates** are target points in the future when you expect to have achieved or completed certain financial objectives. They may serve as progress checkpoints toward some longer-term financial goals and/or as deadlines for others. One goal may be to purchase a boat in 2016 (the goal date), another to accumulate a net worth of $200,000 by 2030. In the latter case, goal dates of 2017 and 2022 could be set for attaining a net worth of $10,000 and $110,000, respectively.

goal dates Target dates in the future when certain financial objectives are expected to be completed.

Long-Term Goals

Long-term financial goals should indicate wants and desires for a period covering about 6 years out to the next 30 or 40 years. Although it's difficult to pinpoint exactly what you will want 30 years from now, it's useful to establish some tentative long-term financial goals. However, you should recognize that long-term goals will change over time and that you'll need to revise them accordingly. If the goals seem too ambitious, you'll want to make them more realistic. If they're too conservative, you'll want to adjust them to a level that encourages you to make financially responsible decisions rather than squander surplus funds.

Short-Term Goals and Intermediate Goals

Short-term financial goals are set each year and cover a 12-month period. They include making substantial, regular contributions to savings or investments in order

Set financial goals carefully and realistically, because they form the basis for your personal financial plans. Each goal should be clearly defined and have a priority, time frame, and cost estimate.

Personal Financial Goals

Name(s) _Rick and Beth Fletcher_   Date _December 27, 2015_

Short-Term Goals (1 year or less)

Goal	Priority	Target Date	Cost Estimate
Buy new tires and brakes for Ford Focus	High	Feb. 2016	$ 500
Buy career clothes for Beth	High	May 2016	1,200
Take Colorado ski trip	Medium	Mar. 2016	1,800
Replace stereo components	Low	Sept. 2016	1,100
Buy new work cloths for Tim	Medium	June 2016	750

Intermediate Goals (2 to 5 years)

Goal	Priority	Target Date	Cost Estimate
Start family	High	2017	–
Repay all loans except mortgage	High	2018	$ 7,500
Trade Focus and buy larger car	High	2018	10,500
Buy new bedroom furniture	Low	2020	4,000
Take 2-week Hawaiian vacation	Medium	2017 – 18	5,000
Review insurance needs	High	2018	–
Accumulate $100,000 net worth	High	2020	–

Long-Term Goals (6+ years)

Goal	Priority	Target Date	Cost Estimate
Begin college fund for children	High	2021	? /year
Diversify/increase investment portfolio	High	2022	Varies
Buy larger home	High	2025	$ 250,000
Take European vacation	Low	2023	$ 10,000
Retire from jobs	High	2048	?
Increase college fund contributions	High	2023	–

© Cengage Learning

to accumulate your desired net worth. Intermediate goals bridge the gap between short- and long-term goals; and of course, both intermediate and short-term goals should be consistent with your long-term goals. Short-term goals become the key input for the cash budget, a tool used to plan for short-term income and expenses. To define your short-term goals, consider your immediate goals, expected income for the year, and long-term goals. Short-term planning should also include establishing an emergency fund with at least

6 months' worth of income. This special savings account serves as a safety reserve in case of financial emergencies such as a temporary loss of income.

Unless you attain your short-term goals, you probably won't achieve your intermediate or long-term goals. It's tempting to let the desire to spend now take priority over the need to save for the future. But by making some short-term sacrifices now, you're more likely to have a comfortable future. Worksheet 1.1 is a convenient way to summarize your personal financial goals. It groups them by time frame (short-term, intermediate, or long-term) and lists a priority for each goal (high, medium, or low), a target date to reach the goal, and an estimated cost.

We have filled out the form showing the goals that Rick and Beth Fletcher set in December 2015. The Saunders were married in 2011, own a condominium in a Midwestern suburb, and have no children. Because Rick and Beth are 28 and 26 years old, respectively, they have set their longest-term financial goal 33 years from now, when they want to retire. Rick has just completed his fifth year as a marketing representative for a large auto products manufacturer. Beth, a former elementary school teacher, finished her MBA in May 2014 and began working at a local advertising agency. Rick and Beth love to travel and ski. They plan to start a family in a few years, but for now they want to develop some degree of financial stability and independence. Their goals include purchasing assets (clothes, stereo, furniture, and car), reducing debt, reviewing insurance, increasing savings, and planning for retirement.

1-3 From Goals to Plans: A Lifetime of Planning

LG3 How will you achieve the financial goals you set for yourself? The answer, of course, lies in the financial plans you establish. Financial plans provide the road map for achieving your financial goals. The six-step financial planning process (introduced in Exhibit 1.3) results in separate yet interrelated components covering all the important financial elements in your life. Some elements deal with the more immediate aspects of money management, such as preparing a budget to help manage spending. Others focus on acquiring major assets, controlling borrowing, reducing financial risk, providing for emergency funds and future wealth accumulation, taking advantage of and managing employer-sponsored benefits, deferring and minimizing taxes, providing for financial security when you stop working, and ensuring an orderly and cost-effective transfer of assets to your heirs.

> ## As you move through different stages of your life, your needs and goals will change.

In addition to discussing your financial goals and attitudes toward money with your partner, you must allocate responsibility for money management tasks and decisions. Many couples make major decisions jointly and divide routine financial decision making on the basis of expertise and interest.

Others believe it is important for their entire family to work together as a team to manage the family finances. They hold family financial meetings once every few months to help their children understand how the household money is spent.

1-3a The Life Cycle of Financial Plans

Financial planning is a dynamic process. As you move through different stages of your life, your needs and goals will change. Yet certain financial goals are important regardless of age. Having extra resources to fall back on in an economic downturn or period of unemployment should be a priority whether you are 25, 45, or 65. Some changes—a new job, marriage, children, moving to a new area—may be part of your original plan.

REEFER/DREAMSTIME

More often than not, you'll face unexpected "financial shocks" during your life: loss of a job, a car accident, divorce or death of a spouse, a long illness, or the need to support adult children or aging parents. With careful planning, you can get through tough times and prosper in good times. You need to plan ahead and take steps to weather life's financial storms successfully. For example, setting up an emergency fund or reducing monthly expenses will help protect you and your family financially if a setback occurs.

As we move from childhood to retirement age, we traditionally go through different life stages. Exhibit 1.4 illustrates the various components of a typical *personal financial planning life cycle* as they relate to these different life stages. This exhibit presents the organizing framework of the entire financial planning process. We will refer to it throughout the book—and we suggest that you do so for the rest of your life. As we pass from one stage of maturation to the next, our patterns of income, home ownership, and debt also change. From early childhood, when we rely on our parents for support, to early adulthood, when we hold our first jobs and start our families, we can see a noticeable change in income patterns. For example, those in the 45–64 age group tend to have higher income than those younger than age 45. Thus, as our emphasis in life changes, so do the kinds of financial plans we need to pursue.

Exhibit 1.4 **The Personal Financial Planning Life Cycle**

As you move through life and your income patterns change, you'll typically have to pursue a variety of financial plans. For instance, after graduating from college, your focus likely will likely be on buying a car and a house, and you'll be concerned about health and automobile insurance to protect against loss.

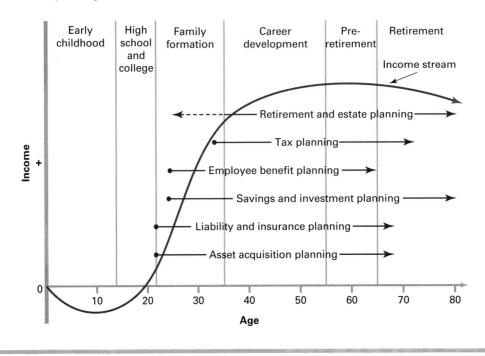

Today, new career strategies—planned and unplanned job changes, or several different careers over a lifetime, for example—are common and may require that financial plans be revised. Many young people focus on their careers and building a financial base before marrying and having children. The families of women who interrupt their careers to stay home with their children, whether for six months or six years, will experience periods of reduced income. A divorce, a spouse's death, or remarriage can also drastically change your financial circumstances. Many people in their 30s, 40s, and 50s find themselves in the "sandwich generation": supporting their elderly parents while still raising their own children and paying for college. And some people must cope with reduced income due to jobs lost because of corporate downsizing or early retirement.

1-3b Plans to Achieve Your Financial Goals

Financial goals can range from short-term goals, such as saving for a new sound system, to long-term goals, such as saving enough to start your own business. Reaching your particular goals requires different types of financial planning.

Asset Acquisition Planning

One of the first categories of financial planning we typically encounter is asset acquisition. We accumulate *assets*—things we own—throughout our lives. These include *liquid assets* (cash, savings accounts, and money market funds) used to pay everyday expenses, *investments* (stocks, bonds, and mutual funds) acquired to earn a return on our money, *personal property* (movable property such as automobiles, household furnishings, appliances, clothing, jewelry, home electronics, and similar items), and *real property* (immovable property; land and anything fixed to it, such as a house). Chapters 4 and 5 focus on important considerations for managing liquid assets and other major assets such as automobiles and housing.

Liability and Insurance Planning

Another category of financial planning is liability planning. A *liability* is something we owe, which is measured by the amount of debt we incur. We create liabilities by borrowing money. By the time most of us graduate from college, we have debts of some sort or another—examples include education loans, car loans, credit card balances, and so on. Our borrowing needs typically increase as we acquire assets like a home, furnishings, and appliances. Whatever the source of credit, such transactions have one thing in common: *the debt must be repaid at some future time.* How we manage our debt burden is just as important as how we manage our assets. Managing credit effectively requires careful planning, which is covered in Chapters 6 and 7.

Obtaining adequate *insurance coverage* is also essential. Like borrowing money, obtaining insurance is generally something that's introduced relatively early in our life cycle (usually early in the family formation stage). Insurance is a way to reduce financial risk and protect both income (life, health, and disability insurance) and assets (property and liability insurance). Most consumers regard insurance as absolutely essential—and for good reason. One serious illness or accident can wipe out everything you have accumulated over many years of hard work. But having the wrong amount of insurance can be costly. We'll examine how to manage your insurance needs in Chapters 8, 9, and 10.

Savings and Investment Planning

As your income begins to increase, so does the importance of savings and investment planning. Initially, people save to establish an emergency fund for meeting unexpected expenses. Eventually, however, they devote greater attention to investing excess income as a means of accumulating wealth, either for major expenditures such as a child's college education or for retirement. Individuals build wealth through savings and the subsequent investing of funds in various investment vehicles: common or preferred stocks, government or corporate bonds, mutual funds, real estate, and so on. The higher the returns on the investment of excess funds, the greater the wealth they accumulate.

Exhibit 1.5 shows the impact of alternative rates of return on accumulated wealth. The graph shows that if you had $1,000 today and could keep it invested at 4 percent, then you would accumulate

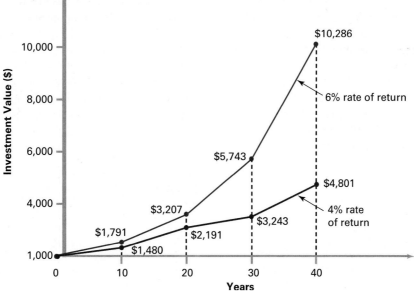

Exhibit 1.5 How a $1,000 Investment Grows over Time

Four or 6 percent: How big a deal is a 2 percent difference? The deal is more than twice the money over a 40-year period! Through the power of compound interest, a higher return means dramatically more money as time goes on.

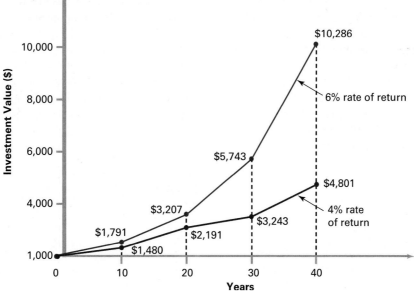

a considerable sum of money over time. For example, at the end of 40 years, you'd have $4,801 from your original $1,000. Earning a higher rate of return has even greater rewards. Some might assume that earning, say, 2 percentage points more (i.e., 6 percent rather than 4 percent) would not matter a great deal. But it certainly would! Observe that if you could earn 6 percent over the 40 years then you'd accumulate $10,286 or more than twice as much as you'd accumulate at 4 percent. This powerful observation is important to keep in mind when comparing competing investment and savings alternatives. For as we'll explore in Part 5 on managing investments, apparently small differences in various investment management fees can also translate into significant differences in net investment returns over long periods of time. The length of time you keep your money invested is just as important as the rate of return you earn on your investments. You can accumulate more than twice as much capital by investing for 40 rather than 30 years with either rate of return (4 percent or 6 percent). This is the magic of compound interest, which explains why it's so important to create strong savings and investment habits early in life. We'll examine compounding more fully in Chapter 2, savings in Chapter 4, and investments in Chapters 11, 12, and 13.

ICONCEPT/SHUTTERSTOCK.COM

Employee Benefit Planning

Your employer may offer a wide variety of employee benefit plans, especially if you work for a large firm. These could include life, health, and disability insurance; tuition reimbursement programs for continuing education; pension, profit-sharing, and 401(k) retirement plans; flexible spending accounts for child care and health care expenses; sick leave, personal time, and vacation days; and other miscellaneous benefits such as employee discounts and subsidized cafeterias or parking.

Managing your employee benefit plans and coordinating them with your other plans is an important part of the overall financial planning process. Especially in today's volatile labor market, you can no longer assume that you'll be working at the same company for many years. If you change jobs, your new company may not offer the same benefits. So your personal financial plans should include contingency plans to replace employer-provided benefits as required. We'll discuss employee benefits in greater detail in Chapters 2 (planning); 3 (taxes); 8, 9, and 10 (insurance); and 14 (retirement).

Tax Planning

Despite all the talk about tax reform, our tax code remains highly complex. Income can be taxed as active (ordinary), portfolio (investment), passive, tax-free, or tax-deferred. Then there are tax shelters, which use various aspects of the tax code (such as depreciation expenses) to legitimately reduce an investor's

tax liability. Tax planning considers all these factors and more. It involves looking at your current and projected earnings and then developing strategies that will defer and minimize taxes. Tax plans are closely tied to investment plans and will often specify certain investment strategies. Although tax planning is most common among individuals with high incomes, people with lower incomes can also obtain sizable savings. We'll examine taxes and tax planning in Chapter 3.

Retirement and Estate Planning

While you're still working, you should be managing your finances to attain those goals you feel are important after you retire. These might include maintaining your standard of living, extensive travel, visiting children, frequent dining at better restaurants, and perhaps a vacation home or boat. Retirement planning should begin long before you retire. As a rule, most people don't start thinking about retirement until well into their 40s or 50s. This is unfortunate, because it usually results in a substantially reduced level of retirement income. The sooner you start, the better off you'll be. Take, for instance, the IRA (individual retirement account), whereby certain wage earners were allowed to invest up to $6,000 per year in 2012. If you start investing for retirement at age 40, and put only $2,000 per year in an IRA earning 5 percent for 25 years, then your account will grow to $95,454 at age 65. However, if you start your retirement program 10 years earlier (at age 30), your IRA will grow to a whopping $180,641 at age 65! Although you're investing only $20,000 more ($2,000 per year for an extra 10 years), your IRA will nearly double in size. We'll look at IRAs and other aspects of retirement planning in Chapter 14.

Accumulating assets to enjoy in retirement is only part of the long-term financial planning process. As people grow older, they must also consider how they can most effectively pass their wealth on to their heirs, an activity known as *estate planning*. We'll examine this complex subject—which includes such topics as wills, trusts, and the effects of gift and estate taxes—in Chapter 15.

1-3c Special Planning Concerns

Students may not think that they need to spend much time on financial planning—not yet, anyway. However, the sooner you start, the better prepared you'll be to adapt your plans to changing personal circumstances. Such changes include changing or losing a job, relocating to a new state, getting married, having children, being in a serious accident, getting a chronic illness, losing a spouse through divorce or death, retiring, or taking responsibility for dependent parents. These and other stressful events are "financial shocks" that require reevaluation of your financial goals and plans.

Go to Smart Sites

Would you like to know about free educational programs and tutorials on financial planning? The Federal Reserve Bank of Chicago has compiled a number of resources for self-help on many topics. ●

Managing Two Incomes

As a general rule, partners in two-income households need to approach discussions on financial matters with an open mind and be willing to compromise. Spouses need to decide together how to allocate income to household expenses, family financial goals, and personal spending goals. Will you use a second income to meet basic expenses, afford a more luxurious lifestyle, save for a special vacation, or invest in retirement accounts? You may need to try several money management strategies to find the one that works best for you. Some couples place all income into a single joint account. Others have each spouse contribute *equal* amounts into a joint account to pay bills but retain individual discretion over remaining income. Still others contribute a *proportional* share of each income to finance joint expenses and goals. In any case, both spouses should have money of their own to spend without accountability. For an example of managing two incomes, see Worksheet 2.5 in Chapter 2 or get it online at CourseMate for PFIN 3. Log in at **www.cengagebrain.com**.

Managing Employee Benefits

If you hold a full-time job, then your employer probably provides various employee benefits, ranging from health and life insurance to pension plans. These are valuable benefits, which can have a major financial impact on family income. Most American families depend solely on employer-sponsored group plans for their health insurance coverage and also for a big piece of their life insurance coverage and retirement needs.

Today's employee benefits packages cover a full spectrum of benefits that may include:

- Health and life insurance
- Disability insurance
- Long-term care insurance
- Pension and profit-sharing plans
- Supplemental retirement programs, such as 401(k) plans
- Dental and vision care
- Child care, elder care, and educational assistance programs
- Subsidized employee food services

Each company's benefit package is different. Some companies and industries are known for generous benefit plans; others offer far less attractive packages. In general, large firms can afford more benefits than small ones can. Because employee benefits can increase your total compensation by 30 percent or more, you should thoroughly investigate your employee benefits to choose those appropriate for your personal situation. Be sure to coordinate your benefits with your partner's to avoid paying for duplicate coverage. Companies change their benefit packages often and today are shifting more costs to employees. Although an employer may pay for some benefits in full, typically employees pay for part of the cost of group health insurance, supplemental life insurance, long-term care insurance, and participation in voluntary retirement programs.

Due to the prevalence of two-income families and an increasingly diverse workforce, many employers today are replacing traditional programs, where the company sets the type and amount of benefits, with **flexible-benefit (cafeteria) plans**. In flexible-benefit programs, the employer allocates a certain amount of money to each employee and then lets the employee "spend" that money for benefits that suit his or her age, marital status, number of dependent children, level of income, and so on. These plans usually cover everything from child care to retirement benefits, offer several levels of health and life insurance coverage, and have some limits on the minimum and maximum amounts of coverage. Within these constraints, you can select the benefits that do you the most good. In some

flexible-benefit (cafeteria) plans The employer allocates a certain amount of money to each employee and then lets the employee "spend" that money for benefits that suit his or her age, marital status, number of dependent children, and level of income.

© GEOPAUL/ISTOCKPHOTO

plans, you can even take part of the benefits in the form of more take-home pay or extra vacation time!

Managing Your Finances in Tough Economic Times

Tough economic times can be due to broad macroeconomic trends like a recession, or they can be brought on by more personal, local developments. The effects of recessions and financial crises divide people into three groups: (1) those who are directly and severely hurt through job loss, (2) those who are marginally hurt by reduced income, and (3) those who are not directly hurt. If you are in either of the first two groups, then you must make significant lifestyle changes to reduce spending. Even if you are in the last group, a recession affects you indirectly. For example, retirement accounts typically drop in value and financial plans must be revised. And everyone's expectations are at least temporarily affected, which causes most people to be more cautious about their expenditures during a recession or crisis.

The financial crisis of 2008 and 2009 and the subsequent long period of high employment was a macroeconomic challenge of historic global proportions. It drives home the benefits of having a sound financial plan—and dramatized the cost of not having one. The precipitous decline in stock and home prices and the many people laid off from their jobs made everyone think a lot more about financial planning in general and how to survive a financial crisis in particular. Although we all hope that such broad crises will be rare, it is important to plan for a possible recurrence.

All of the financial planning principles explained in this book remained valid during the recent global financial crisis and should continue to serve us well in any future similar situations. But the breadth of the recent crisis posed some special planning issues.

So how do you best plan to survive a broad-based financial crisis? First, you remind yourself of the key principles of financial planning presented in this book:

- Spend less than you earn.
- Keep investing so your money continues to work toward your goals.
- Know where you are and plan for the unexpected. You cannot know where you are financially unless you carefully—and frequently—update your family's budget. And it is important to set aside money for an emergency fund. As discussed earlier in this chapter, you should set aside enough cash to last at least 6 months.

Second, don't panic when financial markets crash! This means that you shouldn't try to time the market by buying when the experts say it's at a low or by selling when they say it's at a high. Continue to invest for the long term but keep in mind how close you are to achieving your financial objectives. For example, if you pull all of your money out of the stock market when it has fallen, you will not be positioned to take advantage of its eventual recovery. Recessions and financial crises can be challenging. A financial plan that considers such contingencies will help you weather the storm. Part 5 of the book focuses on investment management.

1-3d Using Professional Financial Planners

Most financial planners fall into one of two categories based on how they are paid: commissions or fees. *Commission-based planners* earn commissions on the financial products they sell, whereas *fee-only planners* charge fees based on the complexity of the plan they prepare. Many financial planners take a hybrid approach and charge fees and collect commissions on products they sell, offering lower fees if you make product transactions through them. For a guide to some of the different planning designations, see the Chapter 1 Bonus Exhibits. (Visit CourseMate for PFIN 3. Log in at **www.cengagebrain.com**.)

1-4 The Planning Environment

LG4 Financial planning takes place in a dynamic economic environment created by the actions of government, business, and consumers. Your purchase, saving, investment, and retirement plans and decisions are influenced by both the present and future states of the economy. Understanding the economic environment will allow you to make better financial decisions.

Consider that a strong economy can lead to high returns in the stock market, which in turn can positively affect your investment and retirement programs. The economy also affects the interest rates you pay on your mortgage and credit cards as well as those you earn on savings accounts and bonds. Periods of high inflation can lead to rapid price increases that make it difficult to make ends meet. Here we look at two important aspects of the planning environment: the major financial planning players and the economy.

1-4a The Players

The financial planning environment contains various interrelated groups of players, each attempting to fulfill certain goals. Although their objectives are not necessarily incompatible, they do impose some constraints on one another. There are three vital groups: government, business, and consumers. Exhibit 1.6 shows the relationships among these groups.

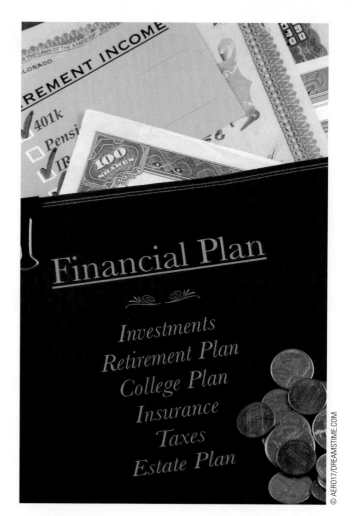

Government

Federal, state, and local governments provide us with many essential public goods and services, such as police and fire protection, national defense, highways, public education, and health care. The federal government plays a major role in regulating economic activity. Government is also a customer of business and an employer of consumers, so it's a source of revenue for business and of wages for consumers. The two major constraints from the perspective of personal financial planning are taxation and regulation.

Business

As Exhibit 1.6 shows, business provides consumers with goods and services and in return receives payment in the form of money. Firms must hire labor and use land and financial capital (economists call these *factors of production*) to produce those goods and services. In return, firms pay out wages, rents, interest, and profits to the various factors of production. Thus, businesses are an important part of the circular flow of income that sustains our free enterprise system. In general, they create a competitive environment in which consumers may select from an array of goods and services. All businesses are limited in some way by federal, state, and local laws.

Exhibit 1.6   The Financial Planning Environment

Government, business, and consumers are the major players in our economic system. They interact with one another to produce the environment in which we carry out our financial plans.

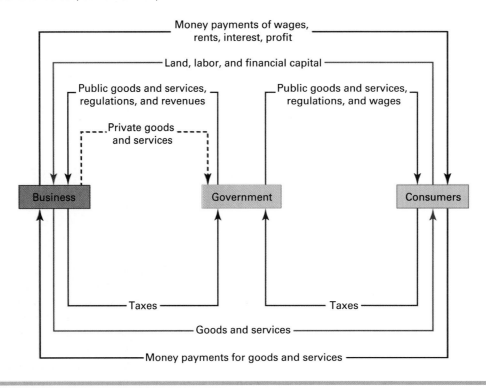

Money payments of wages, rents, interest, profit

Land, labor, and financial capital

Public goods and services, regulations, and revenues

Public goods and services, regulations, and wages

Private goods and services

Business   Government   Consumers

Taxes   Taxes

Goods and services

Money payments for goods and services

© Cengage Learning

Consumers

The consumer is the central player in the financial planning environment. Consumer choices ultimately determine the kinds of goods and services that businesses will provide. The consumer's choice of whether to spend or save also has a direct impact on present and future circular flows of money. Cutbacks in consumer spending are usually associated with a decline in economic activity, whereas increases in consumer spending help the economy to recover.

1-4b The Economy

Our economy is influenced by interactions among government, business, and consumers as well as by world economic conditions. Through specific policy decisions, the government's goal is to manage the economy to provide economic stability and a high level of employment. Government decisions have a major impact on the economic and financial planning environment. The federal government's *monetary policy*—programs for controlling the amount of money in circulation (the money supply)—is used to stimulate or moderate economic growth. For example, increases

in the money supply tend to lower interest rates. This typically leads to a higher level of consumer and business borrowing and spending that increases overall economic activity. The reverse is also true. Reducing the money supply raises interest rates, which reduces consumer and business borrowing and spending and thus slows economic activity. The historically low interest rates in the wake of the financial crisis of 2008 and 2009 and beyond reflect the efforts of the Federal Reserve (Fed) to bolster the sagging economy and decrease unemployment.

The government's other principal tool for managing the economy is *fiscal policy*—its programs of spending and taxation. Increased spending for social services, education, defense, and other programs stimulates the economy, whereas decreased spending slows economic activity. Increasing taxes, on the other hand, gives businesses and individuals less to spend and, as a result, negatively affects economic activity. Conversely, decreasing taxes stimulates the economy. The importance of fiscal policy is illustrated by the government's massive spending to stimulate the U.S. economy in 2008 and 2009 as a way to address the greatest financial crisis since the Great Depression of the 1930s in the United States.

Economic Cycles

Although the government uses monetary and fiscal policy to manage the economy and provide economic stability, the level of economic activity changes constantly. The upward and downward movement creates *economic cycles* (also called *business cycles*), which vary in length and in extent. An economic cycle typically contains four stages: *expansion, peak, contraction,* and *trough.*

Exhibit 1.7 shows how each of these stages relates to real gross domestic product (GDP), which is an important indicator of economic activity. The stronger the economy, the higher the levels of real GDP and employment. During an **expansion,** real GDP increases until it hits a **peak,** which usually signals the end of the expansion and the beginning of a **contraction.** During a contraction (also known as a recession), real GDP falls into a **trough,** which is the end of a contraction and the beginning of an expansion. For about 75 years, the government has been reasonably successful in keeping the economy out of a depression, although we have experienced periods of rapid expansion and high inflation followed by periods of deep recession. And some would argue that the financial crisis of 2008 and 2009 came close to precipitating a depression.

expansion The phase of the economic cycle when real GDP increases until it hits a peak.

peak The phase of the economic cycle when an expansion ends and a contraction begins.

contraction The phase of the economic cycle when real GDP falls.

trough The phase of the economic cycle when a contraction ends and an expansion begins.

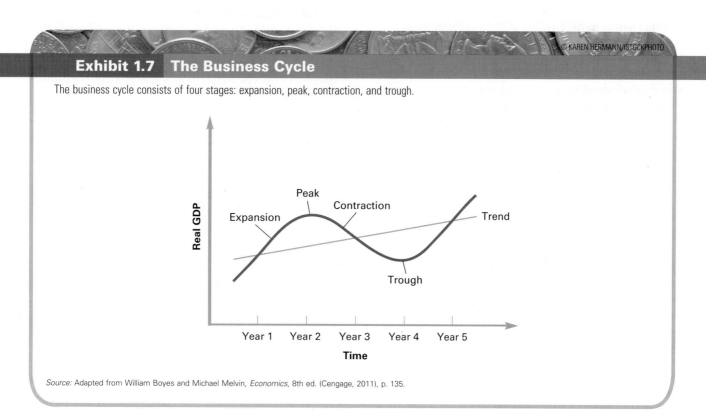

Exhibit 1.7 The Business Cycle

The business cycle consists of four stages: expansion, peak, contraction, and trough.

Source: Adapted from William Boyes and Michael Melvin, *Economics,* 8th ed. (Cengage, 2011), p. 135.

inflation A state of the economy in which the general price level is increasing.

consumer price index (CPI) A measure of inflation based on changes in the cost of consumer goods and services.

purchasing power The amount of goods and services that each dollar buys at a given time.

Inflation, Prices, and Planning

As we've discussed, our economy is based on the exchange of goods and services between businesses and their customers—consumers, government, and other businesses—for a medium of exchange called money. The mechanism that facilitates this exchange is a system of *prices*. Technically speaking, the price of something is *the amount of money the seller is willing to accept in exchange for a given quantity of some good or service*—for instance, $3 for a pound of meat or $10 for an hour of work. The economy is said to be experiencing a period of **inflation** when the general level of prices *increases* over time. The most common measure of inflation, the **consumer price index (CPI)**, is based on changes in the cost of consumer goods and services. At times, the rate of inflation has been substantial. In 1980, for instance, prices went up by a whopping 13.6 percent. Fortunately, inflation has dropped dramatically in this country, and the annual rate of inflation has remained below 5 percent every year since 1983, except in 1990, when it was 5.4 percent. Since 2000, the rate of inflation has ranged between 1.6 percent and 3.8 percent.

Inflation is of vital concern to financial planning. It affects not only what we pay for our goods and services but also what we earn in our jobs. Inflation tends to give an illusion of something that doesn't exist. That is, though we seem to be making more money, we really aren't. As prices rise, we need more income because our **purchasing power**—the amount of goods and services that each dollar buys at a given time—declines. For example, assume that you earned $48,000 in 2015 and received annual raises so that your salary was $52,000 by 2018. That represents an annual growth rate of 2.7 percent. However, if inflation averaged 2.3 percent per year, then your purchasing power would have decreased, even though your income rose: you'd need $52,451 just to keep pace with inflation. So be sure to look at what you earn in terms of its purchasing power, not simply in terms of absolute dollars.

Inflation also directly affects interest rates. High rates of inflation drive up the cost of borrowing money as lenders demand compensation for their eroding purchasing power. Higher interest rates mean higher mortgage payments, higher monthly car payments, and so on. High inflation rates also have a detrimental effect on stock and bond prices. Finally, sustained high rates of inflation can have devastating effects on retirement plans and other long-term financial goals. Indeed, for many people, they can put such goals out of reach.

1-5 What Determines Your Personal Income?

LG5, LG6 An obvious and important factor in determining how well we live is the amount of income we earn. In the absence of any inheritance or similar financial windfall, your income will largely depend on such factors as your age, marital status, education, geographic location, and choice of career. Making a lot of money isn't easy, but it can be done! A high level of income—whether derived from your job, your own business, or your investments—is within your reach if you have the dedication, commitment to hard work, and a well-thought-out set of financial plans. The data in Exhibit 1.8 show how income changes with age and education. For example, people with low incomes typically fall into the very young or very old age groups. Heads of households who have more formal education earn higher annual incomes than do those with lesser degrees.

> **Your income will largely depend on such factors as your age, marital status, education, geographic location, and choice of career.**

1-5a Where You Live

Geographic factors can also affect your earning power. Salaries vary regionally, tending to be higher in the Northeast and West than in the South. Typically, your salary will also be higher if you live in a large metropolitan area rather than a small town or rural area.

DENIS RAEV/PHOTOS.COM

Financial Planning Tips: Potential Financial Advisor Conflicts of Interest

When interviewing a prospective financial advisor, you should be aware of potential conflicts of interest:

How is the advisor compensated? Financial advisors can be compensated by product sale commissions and/or by client-paid fees. Client-paid fees can include an hourly fee, an annual retainer, a fee that is based on the amount invested with the advisor, or a flat fee for each service provided. And some advisors are paid using a combination of commissions and fees.

Conflicts of interest. While most advisors are honest, opportunities for conflicts of interest abound. Advisors who get a commission have an incentive to sell you the products that generate the most money for them, but those are not necessarily the best products for you. Advisors who are paid an hourly fee have an incentive to add hours to your bill. And advisors who earn a fee based on the amount of assets under management tend to encourage you to invest more with them.

Good questions to ask. Ask a prospective advisor how they are compensated. If an advisor receives commissions, ask for a description of the commissions on their products. Alternatively, ask a fee-paid advisor for a schedule of fees for each type of service provided. It would be helpful to use the questionnaire provided on the National Association of Personal Financial Advisors (NAPFA) website, which is **www.napfa.org.** The questionnaire has good questions to ask when interviewing a prospective advisor and provides a form that your advisor can use to disclose the commissions that he or she receives.

Source: Adapted from Jennifer Lane, CFP, with Bill Lane, "Advisor Fees and Conflicts," http://www.netplaces.com/money-for-40s-50s/do-you-need-an-advisor/advisor-fees-and-conflicts.htm, accessed February 2012.

MKABAKOV/SHUTTERSTOCK.COM

© KAREN HERMANN/ISTOCKPHOTO

Exhibit 1.8   How Age and Education Affect Annual Income

The amount of money you earn is closely tied to your age and education. Generally, the closer you are to middle age (45–65) and the more education you have, the greater your income will be.

ANNUAL INCOME (HEAD OF HOUSEHOLD)*

Age	Median Income ($)
25–34	42,800
35–44	60,800
45–54	64,800
55–64	54,800
65–74	41,000
75 or older	24,500

Education	Median Income ($)*
No high school diploma	27,380
High school diploma	30,627
Bachelor's degree	56,665
Master's degree	73,738
Professional degree	127,803
Dr. degree	103,054

*Age of head of household in 2007; income in 2009.

Source: Adapted from Jesse Bricker, Brian K. Brooks, Arthur B. Kennickell, Traci L. Mach, and Kevin B. Moore, "Surveying the Aftermath of the Storm: Changes in Family Finances from 2007 to 2009," *Finance and Economics Discussion 2011–7*, Board of Governors of the Federal Reserve System, Washington, D.C., http://federalreserve.gov/econresdata/scf/scf_2009p.htm, Table 9, accessed February 2012; and U.S. Census Bureau, Statistical Abstract of the U.S: 2012, http://nces.ed.gov/programs/digest/d10/tables/dt10_392.asp, Table 392, accessed February 2012.

Such factors as economic conditions, labor supply, and industrial base also affect salary levels in different areas. Living costs also vary considerably throughout the country. You'd earn more in Los Angeles than in Memphis, Tennessee, but your salary would probably not go as far owing to the much higher cost of living in Los Angeles.

1-5b Your Career

A critical determinant of your lifetime earnings is your career. The career you choose is closely related to your level of education and your particular skills, interests, lifestyle preferences, and personal values. Social, demographic, economic, and technological trends also influence your decision as to what fields offer the best opportunities for your future. Although not a prerequisite for many types of careers (e.g., sales, service, and certain types of manufacturing and clerical work), a formal education generally leads to greater decision-making responsibility—and consequently increased income potential—within a career. Exhibit 1.9 presents a list of average salaries for various careers.

 Go to Smart Sites

One of the first steps in the job search process is to assess your personality. Link to the Keirsey Temperament Sorter®-11 as a starting point. ●

1-5c Planning Your Career

Career planning and personal financial planning are closely related activities, so the decisions you make in one area affect the other. Like financial planning, career planning is a lifelong process that includes short- and long-term goals. Since your career goals are likely to change several times, you should not expect to stay in one field, or to remain with one company, for your whole life.

 Go to Smart Sites

The U.S. News & World Report Career Center has material on a variety of career topics ranging from internships and résumés to the hottest careers and benefits. ●

The average American starting a career today can expect to have at least 10 jobs with five or more employers, and many of us will have three, four, or even more careers during our lifetimes. Some of these changes will be based on personal decisions; others may result from layoffs or corporate downsizing. For example, a branch manager for a regional bank who feels that bank mergers have reduced her job prospects in banking may buy a quick-print franchise and become her own boss. Job security is practically a thing of the past, and corporate loyalty has given way to a more self-directed career approach that requires new career strategies.

© KAREN HERMANN/ISTOCKPHOTO

Exhibit 1.9	Representative Salaries for Selected Careers

Professional and managerial workers, who typically have a college degree, tend to earn the highest salaries.

Career	Average Annual Salary ($)
Accountants and auditors	68,690
Architects and engineers	75,550
Computer programmer	74,900
Family and general practice physicians	173,860
Financial analyst	86,040
Human resources manager	108,600
Lawyer	129,440
Paralegal	49,640
Pharmacist	109,380
Police officer	55,620
Psychologist	167,610
Registered nurse	67,720
Teacher, elementary school	54,330

Source: "Occupational Employment and Wages, May 2010," U.S. Department of Labor, Bureau of Labor Statistics, http://www.bls.gov/oes, accessed February 2012.

Through careful career planning, you can improve your work situation to gain greater personal and professional satisfaction. Some of the steps are similar to the financial planning process described earlier.

- Identify your interests, skills, needs, and values.
- Set specific long- and short-term career goals.
- Develop and use an action plan to achieve those goals.
- Review and revise your career plans as your situation changes.

A personal portfolio of skills, both general and technical, will protect your earning power during economic downturns and advance it during prosperous times. Employers need flexible, adaptable workers as companies restructure and pare down their operations. It's important to keep your skills current with on-the-job training programs and continuing education.

Good job hunting skills will serve you well throughout your career. Learn how to research new career opportunities and investigate potential jobs, taking advantage of online resources as well as traditional ones. Develop a broad base of career resources, starting with your college placement office, the public library, and personal contacts such as family and friends. Know how to market your qualifications to your advantage in your résumé and cover letters, on the phone, and in person during a job interview.

FINANCIAL PLANNING EXERCISES

LG1

1. How can using personal financial planning tools help you improve your financial situation? Describe changes you can make in at least three areas.

LG2, 3

2. *Use Worksheet 1.1.* Fill out Worksheet 1.1, "Summary of Personal Financial Goals," with goals reflecting your current situation and your expected life situation in 5 and 10 years. Discuss the reasons for the changes in your goals and how you'll need to adapt your financial plans as a result.

LG2

3. Recommend three financial goals and related activities for someone in each of the following circumstances:
   a. A Junior in college
   b. A 30-year-old computer programmer who plans to earn an MBA degree
   c. A couple in their 30s with two children, ages 5 and 9
   d. A divorced 42-year-old man with a 16-year-old child and a 72-year-old father who is ill

LG3

4. Explain the life cycle of financial plans and their role in achieving your financial goals.

LG4

5. Summarize current and projected trends in the economy with regard to GDP growth, unemployment, and inflation. How should you use this information to make personal financial and career planning decisions?

LG5

6. Evaluate the impact of age, education, and geographic location on personal income.

LG6

7. Assume that you graduated from college with a major in marketing and took a job with a large consumer products company. After three years, you are laid off when the company downsizes. Describe the steps you'd take to "repackage" yourself for another field.

PFIN Student Study Tools—Visit CourseMate for PFIN 3. Log in at **www.cengagebrain.com**. Check out the bonus exercises and exhibits, interactive worksheets, Smart Sites, Critical Thinking Cases, Money Online, Kiplinger videos, quizzing, and more.

Cool Apps—Look for this new feature on CourseMate for PFIN 3. Cool Apps navigates the growing world of apps that are available for personal financial planning and tracking.

2

USING FINANCIAL STATEMENTS AND BUDGETS

$ 10,737,418.24

LEARNING GOALS

LG1 Understand the relationship between financial plans and statements.

LG2 Prepare a personal balance sheet.

LG3 Generate a personal income and expense statement.

LG4 Develop a good record-keeping system and use ratios to evaluate personal financial statements.

LG5 Construct a cash budget and use it to monitor and control spending.

LG6 Apply time value of money concepts to put a monetary value on financial goals.

How Will This Affect Me? Recent polls show that 57 percent of households have no budget, and 50 percent of Americans have less than one month of savings set aside for emergencies.* These are scary numbers … and this chapter shows you what you can do to avoid being part of that alarming statistic.

Everyone knows that it's hard to get where you need to go if you don't know where you are. Financial goals describe your destination, and financial statements and budgets are the tools that help you determine exactly where you are in the journey. This chapter helps you define your financial goals and explains how to gauge your progress carefully over time.

2-1 Mapping Out Your Financial Future

LG1 On your journey to financial security, you need navigational tools to guide you to your destination: namely, the fulfillment of your financial goals. Operating without a plan is like traveling without a road map. Financial plans, financial statements, and budgets provide direction by helping you work toward specific financial goals. *Financial plans* are the roadmaps that show you the way, whereas *personal financial statements* let you know where you stand financially. *Budgets*, detailed short-term financial forecasts that compare estimated income with estimated expenses, allow you to monitor and control expenses and purchases in a manner that is consistent with your financial plans. All three tools provide control by bringing the various dimensions of your personal financial affairs into focus.

2-1a The Role of Financial Statements in Financial Planning

Before you can set realistic goals, develop your financial plans, or effectively manage your money, you must take stock of your current financial

*Monster.com poll and Harris Financial Literacy Study, 2009.

After you read the chapter, explore the STUDY TOOLS listed on page 47.

situation. You'll also need tools to monitor your progress. **Personal financial statements** are planning tools that provide an up-to-date evaluation of your financial well-being, help you identify potential financial problems, and help you make better-informed financial decisions. They measure your financial condition so you can establish realistic financial goals and evaluate your progress toward those goals. Knowing how to prepare and interpret personal financial statements is a cornerstone of personal financial planning.

> ## "Personal financial statements provide an up-to-date evaluation of your financial well-being and help you make better-informed financial decisions. "

The **balance sheet** describes your financial position—the assets you hold, less the debts you owe, equal your net worth (general level of wealth)—at a *given point in time*. In contrast, the **income and expense statement** measures financial performance *over* time. **Budgets**, another type of financial report, are *forward* looking; they allow you to monitor and control spending because they are based on expected income and expenses. Exhibit 2.1 summarizes the various financial statements and reports and their relationship to each other in the personal financial planning process. Note that *financial plans* provide direction to annual budgets.

2-2 The Balance Sheet: How Much Are You Worth Today?

LG2 Preparing a personal *balance sheet*, or *statement of financial position*, helps you get a handle on your financial well-being. Think of a

personal financial statements *Balance sheets* and *income and expense statements* that serve as planning tools that are essential to developing and monitoring personal financial plans.

balance sheet A financial statement that describes a person's financial position at a *given point* in time.

income and expense statement A financial statement that measures financial performance *over* time.

budget A detailed financial report that looks *forward*, based on expected income and expenses.

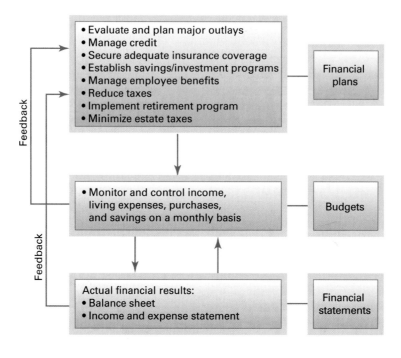

Exhibit 2.1 The Interlocking Network of Financial Plans and Statements

Personal financial planning involves a network of financial reports that link future goals and plans with actual results. Such a network provides direction, control, and feedback.

Feedback

- Evaluate and plan major outlays
- Manage credit
- Secure adequate insurance coverage
- Establish savings/investment programs
- Manage employee benefits
- Reduce taxes
- Implement retirement program
- Minimize estate taxes

Financial plans

Feedback

- Monitor and control income, living expenses, purchases, and savings on a monthly basis

Budgets

Actual financial results:
- Balance sheet
- Income and expense statement

Financial statements

---

assets Items that one owns.

liquid assets Assets that are held in the form of cash or can readily be converted to cash with little or no loss in value.

investments Assets such as stocks, bonds, mutual funds, and real estate that are acquired in order to earn a return rather than provide a service.

balance sheet as a snapshot taken of your financial position on one day out of the year.

A balance sheet has three parts that, taken together, summarize your financial picture:

- **Assets:** What you own
- **Liabilities, or debts:** What you owe
- **Net worth:** The difference between your assets and liabilities

The accounting relationship among these three categories is called the *balance sheet equation* and is expressed as follows:

Total assets = Total liabilities + Net worth

or

Net worth = Total assets − Total liabilities

Let's now look at the components of each section of the balance sheet.

2-2a Assets: The Things You Own

Assets are the items you own. An item is classified as an asset whether it was purchased with cash or financed using debt. A useful way to group assets is on the basis of their underlying characteristics and uses. This results in four broad categories: liquid assets, investments, real property, and personal property.

- **Liquid assets:** Low-risk financial assets held in the form of cash or instruments that can readily be converted to cash readily and quickly, with little or no loss in value. Cash on hand or in a checking or savings account, money market deposit accounts, money market mutual funds, or certificates of deposit that mature within 1 year are all examples of liquid assets.

- **Investments:** Assets acquired to earn a return rather than provide a service. These assets are mostly intangible *financial assets* (stocks, bonds, mutual funds, and other types of securities), typically acquired to achieve long-term personal financial goals. Business ownership, the cash value of life insurance and pensions, retirement funds such

as IRAs and 401(k) plans, and other investment vehicles such as commodities, financial futures, and options represent still other forms of investment assets.

- **Real and personal property:** Tangible assets that we use in our everyday lives. **Real property** refers to immovable property: land and anything fixed to it, such as a house. Real property generally has a relatively long life and high cost, and it may *appreciate*, or increase in value. **Personal property** is movable property, such as automobiles, recreational equipment, household furnishings, and similar items. The left side of Worksheet 2.1 lists some of the typical assets you'd find on a personal balance sheet.

In personal financial analysis, it is important for all assets, regardless of category, to be recorded on the balance sheet at their current **fair market value**, which may differ considerably from their original purchase price. Fair market value is either the actual value of the asset (such as money in a checking account) or the price for which the asset can reasonably be expected to sell in the open market (as with a used car or a home). Under generally accepted accounting principles (GAAP), the accounting

profession's guiding rules, assets appear on a company's balance sheet at *cost*, not *fair market value*.

2-2b Liabilities: The Money You Owe

Liabilities represent an individual's or a family's debts. They could result from department store charges, bank credit card charges, installment loans, or mortgages on housing and other real estate. A liability, regardless of its source, is something that you owe and must repay in the future.

Liabilities are generally classified according to maturity.

- **Current, or short-term, liabilities:** Any debt currently owed and due within 1 year of the date of the balance sheet. Examples include charges for consumable goods, utility bills, rent, insurance premiums, taxes, medical bills, repair bills, and total **open account credit obligations**— the outstanding balances against established credit lines (usually through credit card purchases).

- **Long-term liabilities:** Debt due 1 year or more from the date of the balance sheet. These liabilities typically include real estate mortgages, most consumer installment loans, education loans, and margin loans used to purchase securities.

Although most loans will fall into the category of long-term liabilities, *any loans, or any portion thereof, that come due within a year should be shown as current liabilities.* Examples of short-term loans include a six-month, single-payment bank loan and a nine-month consumer installment loan for a refrigerator. Regardless of the type of loan, *only the latest outstanding loan balance should be shown as a liability on the balance sheet*, because at any given time, it is the balance still due that matters, not the initial loan balance. Another important and closely related point is that *only the outstanding principal portion of a loan or mortgage should be listed as a liability on the balance sheet*. You'll find the most common categories of liabilities on Worksheet 2.1.

real property
Tangible assets that are immovable: land and anything fixed to it, such as a house.

personal property
Tangible assets that are movable and used in everyday life.

fair market value
The actual value of an asset, or the price for which it can reasonably be expected to sell in the open market.

liabilities Debts, such as credit card charges, loans, and mortgages.

current (short-term) liability Any debt due within 1 year of the date of the balance sheet.

open account credit obligations Current liabilities that represent the balances outstanding against established credit lines.

long-term liability Any debt due 1 year or more from the date of the balance sheet.

A balance sheet is set up to show what you own on one side (your assets) and how you paid for them on the other (debt or net worth). As you can see, the Saunders have more assets than liabilities.

BALANCE SHEET

Name(s) _Rick and Beth Fletcher_   Date _December 31, 2015_

ASSETS			LIABILITIES		
Liquid Assets			**Current Liabilities**		
Cash on hand	$	150	Utilities	$	175
In checking		575	Rent		
Savings accounts		760	Insurance premiums		
Money market funds and deposits		800	Taxes		
			Medical/dental bills		125
Certificates of deposit			Repair bills		
Total Liquid Assets	$	2,285	Bank credit card balances		425
			Dept. store credit card balances		165
Investments			Travel and entertainment card balances		135
Stocks		3,750	Gas and other credit card balances		
Bonds Corp.		1,000	Bank line of credit balances		
Certificates of deposit			Other current liabilities		45
Mutual funds		2,250	**Total Current Liabilities**	$	1,070
Real estate					
Retirement funds, IRA		4,000	**Long-Term Liabilities**		
Other			Primary residence mortgage	$160,000	
Total Investments	$	11,000	Second home mortgage		
			Real estate investment mortgage		
Real Property			Auto loans		4,350
Primary residence	$225,000		Appliance/furniture loans		800
Second home			Home improvement loans		
Other			Single-payment loans		
Total Real Property	$	225,000	Education loans		3,800
			Margin loans		
Personal Property			Other long-term loans (from parents)		4,000
Auto(s): '10 Toyota Corolla	$	13,600	**Total Long-Term Liabilities**	$	172,950
Auto(s): '08 Ford Focus		9,400	**(II) Total Liabilities**	$	174,020
Recreational vehicles					
Household furnishings		3,700			
Jewelry and artwork		1,500			
Other					
Other					
Total Personal Property	$	28,200	**Net Worth [(I) − (II)]**	$	92,465
(I)Total Assets	$266,485				
			Total Liabilities and Net Worth	$	266,485

net worth An individual's or family's actual wealth; determined by subtracting total liabilities from total assets.

equity The actual ownership interest in a specific asset or group of assets.

2-2c Net Worth: A Measure of Your Financial Worth

Now that you've listed what you own and what you owe, you can calculate your **net worth**, the amount of actual wealth or **equity** that an individual or family has in its owned assets. It represents the amount of money you'd have left after selling all your owned assets at their estimated fair market values and paying off all your liabilities (assuming there are no transaction costs). Rearranging this equation, we see that net worth equals total assets minus total liabilities. If net worth is less than zero, the family is *technically insolvent*. Although this form of

Financial Road Sign

Have Realistic Budget Plans

- **So what if it's on sale?** Don't buy it if you wouldn't have bought it anyway.
- **Spend less than you earn.** You'll need to pay off debt, design a realistic budget, and save some of your income each month.
- **Make more and buy less.** Make your own lunches, coffee, and even home goods if you know how.
- **Live one raise behind.** When you get a raise, continue living and spending as you did before and put that additional income into savings.
- **Make 30-day lists.** When you see something you really want to buy, put it on a 30-day list and only buy it if you still want it in 30 days.

Source: http://www.careeroverview.com/blog/2010/the-psychology-of-spending-money-25-tricks-you-need-to-know, accessed February 2012.

insolvency doesn't mean that the family will end up in bankruptcy proceedings, it likely shows insufficient financial planning. Net worth typically increases over the life cycle of an individual or family, as Exhibit 2.2 illustrates.

insolvency The financial state in which net worth is less than zero.

Go to Smart Sites

What's the fair market value of your car? The personal watercraft your uncle gave you? For more online resources, whenever you see "*Go to Smart Sites*" in this chapter, visit CourseMate for PFIN 3. Log in at **www.cengagebrain.com**. ●

2-2d Balance Sheet Format and Preparation

You should prepare your personal balance sheet at least once a year, preferably every three to six months. Here's how to do it, using the categories in Worksheet 2.1 as a guide:

Exhibit 2.2   Median Net Worth by Age

Net worth starts to build in the less-than-35 age bracket and continues to climb, peaking at around the 55–64 age bracket. It starts to decline once a person retires and begins to use assets to meet living expenses, usually around the age of 65. While not shown, net worth starts to decline once a person retires and begins to use assets to meet living expenses.

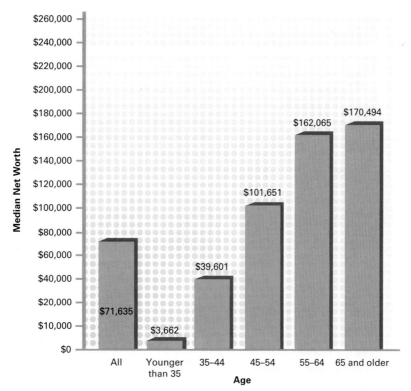

Source: Adapted from Brian K. Bucks, Arthur B. Kennickell, Traci L. Mach, and Kevin B. Moore, "Changes in U.S. Family Finances from 2004 to 2007: Evidence from the Survey of Consumer Finances," *Federal Reserve Bulletin*, Board of Governors of the Federal Reserve System, Washington, D.C., vol. 95 (February 2009), pp. A1–A55, http://www.federalreserve.gov/pubs/oss/oss2/2007/scf2007home.html, accessed March 2011.

cash basis A method of preparing financial statements in which only transactions involving actual cash receipts or actual cash outlays are recorded.

income Earnings received as wages, salaries, bonuses, commissions, interest and dividends, or proceeds from the sale of assets.

expenses Money spent on living expenses and to pay taxes, purchase assets, or repay debt.

1. **List your assets at their fair market value as of the date you are preparing the balance sheet.** You'll find the fair market value of liquid and investment assets on checking and savings account records and investment account statements. Estimate the values of homes and cars using published sources of information, such as advertisements for comparable homes and the *Kelley Blue Book* for used car values (see www.kbb.com).

2. **List all current and long-term liabilities.** Show all outstanding charges, *even if you haven't received the bill*, as current liabilities on the balance sheet.

3. **Calculate net worth.** Subtract your total liabilities from your total assets. This is your net worth, which reflects the equity you have in your total assets.

2-2e A Balance Sheet for Rick and Beth Fletcher

What can you learn from a balance sheet? Let's examine a hypothetical balance sheet as of December 31, 2015, prepared for Rick and Beth Fletcher the young couple (ages 28 and 26) we met in Chapter 1 (see Worksheet 2.1). Here's what this financial statement tells us about the Fletchers' financial condition.

- **Assets:** Given their ages, the Fletchers' asset position looks quite good. The dominant asset is their house. They also have $11,000 in investments, which include retirement funds, and appear to have adequate liquid assets to meet their bill payments and cover small, unexpected expenses.

- **Liabilities:** The Fletchers' primary liability is the $160,000 mortgage on their townhouse. Their equity, or actual ownership interest, in the townhouse is approximately $65,000 ($225,000 market value minus $160,000 outstanding mortgage loan). Their current liabilities are $1,070, with other debts of $12,950 representing auto, furniture, and education loans as well as a loan from their parents to help with the down payment on their home.

- **Net worth:** The Fletchers' net worth ($266,485 in total assets minus total liabilities of $174,020) is $92,465—considering their ages, a respectable amount that is well above the overall median shown in Exhibit 2.2 and enviably above that for their age group.

Comparing the Fletchers' total liabilities to their total assets gives a more realistic view of their current wealth position than looking at just assets or just liabilities.

2-3 The Income and Expense Statement: What We Earn and Where It Goes

LG3 When confronted with a lack of funds, the first question people ask themselves is, "Where does all the money go?" Preparing an *income and expense statement* would answer this question. Think of this statement as a motion picture that not only shows actual results over time but also lets you compare them with budgeted financial goals.

The income and expense statement has three major parts: *income*, *expenses*, and *cash surplus* (or *deficit*). A cash surplus (or deficit) is merely the difference between income and expenses. The statement is prepared on a **cash basis**, which means that *only transactions involving actual cash inflows or actual cash outlays are recorded*. The term *cash* is used in this case to include not only coin and currency but also checks and debit card transactions drawn against checking and certain types of savings accounts. Income and expense patterns change over the individual's or family's life cycle.

2-3a Income: Cash In

Common sources of **income** include earnings received as wages, salaries, self-employment income, bonuses, and commissions; interest and dividends received from savings and investments; and proceeds from the sale of assets such as stocks and bonds or a car. Other income items include pension, annuity, and social Security income; rent received from leased assets; alimony and child support; scholarships or grants; tax refunds; and miscellaneous types of income. Worksheet 2.2, Rick and Beth Fletcher's Income and Expense Statement, has general categories for recording income. Note also that the proper figure to use is *gross* wages, salaries, and commissions, which constitute the amount of income you receive from your employer *before* taxes and other payroll deductions.

Go to Smart Sites

For current surveys and trends on consumer spending, check out the Consumer Expenditure Survey at the Department of Labor's Bureau of Labor Statistics. ●

2-3b Expenses: Cash Out

Expenses represent money used for outlays. Worksheet 2.2, Rick and Beth Fletcher's Income and Expense Statement, categorizes them by the types of benefits they provide: (1) living expenses (such as housing, utilities, food, transportation,

© GEOPAUL/ISTOCKPHOTO

The income and expense statement shows what you earned, how you spent your money, and how much you were left with (or, if you spent more than you took in, how much you went "in the hole").

Name(s) __Rick and Beth Fletcher__

For the __Year__ _____ Ended __December 31, 2015__

INCOME

Wages and salaries	Name: Rick Fletcher	$	65,000
	Name: Beth Fletcher		18,350
	Name:		
Self-employment income			
Bonuses and commissions	Rick-sales commissions		3,050
Investment income	Interest received		195
	Dividends received		120
	Rents received		
	Sale of securities		
	Other		
Pensions and annuities			
Other income			
	(I) Total Income	$	86,715

EXPENSES

Housing	Rent/mortgage payment (include insurance and taxes, if applicable)	$	11,820
	Repairs, maintenance, improvements		1,050
Utilities	Gas, electric, water		1,750
	Phone		480
	Cable TV and other		240
Food	Groceries		2,425
	Dining out		3,400
Transportation	Auto loan payments		2,520
	License plates, fees, etc.		250
	Gas, oil, repairs, tires, maintenance		2,015
Medical	Health, major medical, disability insurance (payroll deductions or not provided by employer)		2,250
	Doctor, dentist, hospital, medicines		305
Clothing	Clothes, shoes, and accessories		1,700
Insurance	Homeowner's (if not covered by mortgage payment)		1,200
	Life (not provided by employer)		1,865
	Auto		1,780
Taxes	Income and social security		18,319
	Property (if not included in mortgage)		2,100
Appliances, furniture, and other major purchases	Loan payments		800
	Purchases and repairs		450
Personal care	Laundry, cosmetics, hair care		700
Recreation and entertainment	Vacations		2,000
	Other recreation and entertainment		2,630
Other items	Tuition and books: Beth		1,400
	Gifts		215
	Loan payments: Education loans		900
	Loan payments: Parents		600
	(II) Total Expenses	$	65,164
	CASH SURPLUS (OR DEFICIT) [(I) – (II)]	$	21,551

medical, clothing, and insurance), (2) tax payments, (3) asset purchases (such as autos, stereos, furniture, appliances, and loan payments on them), and (4) other payments for personal care, recreation and entertainment, and other expenses. Some are **fixed expenses**—usually contractual, predetermined, and involving

fixed expenses
Contractual, predetermined expenses involving equal payments each period.

variable expenses
Expenses involving payment amounts that change from one time period to the next.

cash surplus An excess amount of income over expenses that results in *increased* net worth.

cash deficit An excess amount of expenses over income, resulting in insufficient funds as well as in *decreased* net worth.

equal payments each period (typically each month). Examples include mortgage and installment loan payments, insurance premiums, and cable TV fees. Others (such as food, clothing, utilities, entertainment, and medical expenses) are **variable expenses**, because their amounts change from one time period to the next.

Exhibit 2.3 shows the average annual expenses by major category as a percentage of after-tax income. It's a useful benchmark to see how you compare with national averages. However, your own expenses will vary according to your age, lifestyle, and where you live. For example, it costs considerably more to buy a home in San Diego than in Charlotte. Similarly, if you live in the suburbs, your commuting expenses will be higher than those of city dwellers.

2-3c Cash Surplus (or Deficit)

The third component of the income and expense statement shows the net result of the period's financial activities. Subtracting total expenses from total income gives you the cash surplus (or deficit) for the period. At a glance, you can see how you did financially over the period. A positive figure indicates that expenses were less than income, resulting in a **cash surplus**. A value of zero indicates that expenses were exactly equal to income for the period, while a negative value means that your expenses exceeded income and you have a **cash deficit**.

GUNNAR PIPPEL/SHUTTERSTOCK.COM

Biggest Budgeting Mistakes

1. **Failing to plan for inevitable expenses.** While some expenses are unexpected, most aren't. Plan for your car to need maintenance and put it in your budget. Include property, auto, health and life insurance, taxes, clothing, and gifts.
2. **No emergency fund.** A real emergency—not just something unexpected—includes loss of income, severe illness, or death in the family.
3. **Living above your means.** If you are making the above budgeting mistakes, you may well spend more than you earn. A budget will help you prepare for the future without going deep into debt.

Source: Adapted from http://www.mydebt.co.za, accessed January 2012.

2-3d Preparing the Income and Expense Statement

As shown in Worksheet 2.2, the income and expense statement is dated to define the period covered. To prepare the statement, follow these steps:

1. **Record your income from all sources for the chosen period.**
2. **Establish meaningful expense categories.** Those shown on Worksheet 2.2 are a good starting point.

© KAREN HERMANN/ISTOCKPHOTO

Exhibit 2.3 | How We Spend Our Income

Almost three-quarters of expenditures made with pre-tax income fall into one of four categories: housing, transportation, food, and personal insurance and pensions.

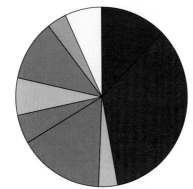

- Food—12.7%
- Housing—34.4%
- Apparel and services—3.5%
- Transportation—16.0%
- Entertainment—5.2%
- Health care—6.6%
- Personal insurance and pensions—11.2%
- Cash contributions—3.4%
- All other—7.0%

Source: "Consumer Expenditures—2010," Washington, D.C.: U.S. Department of Labor, Bureau of Labor Statistics, News Release, USDL-11-1395, Chart 1, "Shares of Average Annual Expenditures Spent on Major Components, 2010," September 27, 2011, p. 2.

3. **Subtract total expenses from total income to get the cash surplus (a positive number) or deficit (a negative number).** This "bottom line" summarizes the *net cash flow* resulting from your financial activities during the period.

Finally, when making your list of expenses for the year, remember to include the amount of income tax and Social Security taxes withheld from your paycheck as well as any other payroll deductions (health insurance, savings plans, retirement and pension contributions, and professional/union dues). These deductions (from gross wages, salaries, bonuses, and commissions) represent personal expenses, even if they don't involve a direct cash payment. You might be shocked when listing what's taken out of your paycheck. Even if you're in a fairly low federal income tax bracket, your paycheck could easily be reduced by more than 25 percent for taxes alone.

2-3e An Income and Expense Statement for Rick and Beth Fletcher

Rick and Beth Fletcher's balance sheet in Worksheet 2.1 shows us their financial condition as of December 31, 2015. Their income and expense statement for the year ending December 31, 2015, in Worksheet 2.2, was prepared using the background material presented earlier, along with the Fletchers' balance sheet. This statement shows how cash flowed into and out of their "pockets":

● **Income:** Total income for the year ending December 31, 2015, is $86,715. Rick's wages clearly represent the family's chief source of income, although Beth has finished her MBA and will now be making a major contribution.

Other sources of income include $195 in interest on their savings accounts and bond investments and $120 in dividends from their common stock holdings.

● **Expenses:** Total expenses for the year of $65,164 include their home mortgage, food, auto loan, clothing, and income and Social Security taxes. Other sizable expenses during the year include home repairs and improvements, gas and electricity, auto license and operating expenses, insurance, tuition, and education loan payments.

● **Cash surplus:** The Fletchers end the year with a cash surplus of $21,551 (total income of $86,715 minus total expenses of $65,164). The Fletchers can use their surplus to increase savings, invest in stocks, bonds, or other vehicles, or make payments on some outstanding debts. If they had a cash deficit, the Fletchers would have to withdraw savings, liquidate investments, or borrow an amount equal to the deficit to meet their financial commitments (that is, to "make ends meet"). With their surplus of $21,551, the Fletchers have made a positive contribution to their net worth.

2-4 Using Your Personal Financial Statements

LG4 Whether you're just starting out and have a minimal net worth or are further along the path toward achieving your goals, your balance sheet and income and expense statement provide insight into your current financial status. You now have the information you need to examine your financial position, monitor your financial activities, and track the progress you're making toward your financial goals. Let's now look at ways to help you create better personal financial statements and analyze them to better understand your financial situation.

2-4a Keeping Good Records

Although record keeping doesn't rank high on most "to do" lists, a good record-keeping system helps you manage and control your personal financial affairs. It's best to prepare your personal financial statements at least once each year, ideally when drawing up your budget. Many people update their financial statements every three or six months. You may want to keep a *ledger*, or financial record book, to summarize all your financial transactions. The ledger has sections for assets, liabilities, sources of income, and expenses; these sections contain separate accounts for each item.

Managing Your Financial Records

Your system doesn't have to be fancy to be effective. Start by taking an inventory. Make a list of everything you own and owe. Check it at least once a year to make sure it's up to date and to review your financial progress. Then, record transactions manually in your ledger or with financial planning software. You'll want to set up separate files for tax-planning records, with one for income (paycheck stubs, interest on savings accounts, and so on) and another for deductions, as well as for individual mutual fund and brokerage account records.

2-4b Tracking Financial Progress: Ratio Analysis

Each time you prepare your financial statements, you should analyze them to see how well you're doing on your financial goals. For example, with an income and expense statement, you can compare actual financial results with budgeted figures to make sure that your spending is under control. Likewise, comparing a set of financial plans with a balance sheet will reveal whether you're meeting your savings and investment goals, reducing your debt, or building up a retirement reserve. You can compare current performance with historical performance to find out if your financial situation is improving or getting worse.

Calculating certain financial ratios can help you evaluate your financial performance over time.

What's more, if you apply for a loan, the lender probably will look at these ratios to judge your ability to carry additional debt. Four important money management ratios are (1) solvency ratio, (2) liquidity ratio, (3) savings ratio, and (4) debt service ratio. The first two are associated primarily with the balance sheet; the last two relate primarily to the income and expense statement. Exhibit 2.4 defines these ratios and illustrates their calculation for Rick and Beth Fletcher.

Balance Sheet Ratios

When evaluating your balance sheet, you should be most concerned with your net worth at a given time. The **solvency ratio** shows, as a percentage, your degree of exposure to insolvency, or how much "cushion" you have as a protection against insolvency. Rick and Beth's solvency ratio is 35.1 percent, which means that they could withstand about a 35 percent decline in the market value of their assets before they would be insolvent. Consider that the stock market, as measured by the S&P 500 index, fell about 37 percent during the financial crisis of 2008. Also, the average home's value fell about 18 percent during that crisis year, as measured by the S&P/Case-Shiller U.S. National Home Price Index. The value of Rick and Beth's solvency ratio suggests that they are in good shape but may want to consider increasing it a bit in the future to manage a potential decline in the value of their assets even better.

Although the solvency ratio indicates the potential to withstand financial problems, it does not deal directly with the ability to pay current debts. This issue is addressed by the **liquidity ratio**, which shows how long you could continue to pay current debts (any

---

Exhibit 2.4	Ratios for Personal Financial Statement Analysis	
Ratio	**Formula**	**2015 Calculation for the Fletchers**
Solvency ratio	$\dfrac{\text{Total net worth}}{\text{Total assets}}$	$\dfrac{\$93,535}{\$266,485} = 0.351$, or 35.1%
Liquidity ratio	$\dfrac{\text{Total liquid assets}}{\text{Total current debts}}$	$\dfrac{\$2,285}{\$17,710^{(a)}} = 0.129$, or 12.90%
Savings ratio	$\dfrac{\text{Cash surplus}}{\text{Income after taxes}}$	$\dfrac{\$21,551}{\$86,715 - \$18,319} = \dfrac{\$21,551}{\$68,396}$ 0.315, or 31.5%
Debt service ratio	$\dfrac{\text{Total monthly loan payments}}{\text{Monthly gross (before-tax) income}}$	$\dfrac{\$1,387^{(b)}}{\$7,226^{(c)}} = 0.192$, or 19.2%

(a) You'll find the Saunders' total liquid assets ($2,285) and total current liabilities ($1,070) on Worksheet 2.1. The total current debt totals $17,710: current liabilities of $1,070 (from Worksheet 2.1) plus loan payments due within 1 year of $16,640 (from Worksheet 2.2). Note that loan payments due within 1 year consist of $11,820 in mortgage payments, $2,520 in auto loan payments, $800 in furniture loan payments, $900 in education loan payments, and $600 in loan payments to parents.

(b) On an annual basis, the Fletchers' debt obligations total $16,640 ($11,820 in mortgage payments, $2,520 in auto loan payments, $800 in furniture loan payments, $900 in education loan payments, and $600 in loan payments to parents; all from Worksheet 2.2). The Fletchers' total monthly loan payments are about $1,387 ($16,640 ÷ 12 months).

(c) Dividing the Fletchers' annual gross income (also found in Worksheet 2.2) of $86,715 by 12 equals $7,226 per month.

---

bills or charges that must be paid *within 1 year*) with existing liquid assets in the event of income loss.

The calculated liquidity ratio indicates that the Fletchers can cover only about 13 percent of their existing 1-year debt obligations with their current liquid assets. In other words, they have about 1Ã months of coverage (a month is one-twelfth, or 8.3 percent, of a year). If an unexpected event cut off their income, their liquid reserves would quickly be exhausted. Although there's no hard-and-fast rule for what this ratio should be, it seems too low for the Fletchers. They should consider strengthening it along with their solvency ratio. They should be able to add to their cash surpluses now that Beth is working full-time.

The amount of liquid reserves will vary with your personal circumstances and "comfort level." Another useful liquidity guideline is to have a reserve fund equal to at least six months of after-tax income available to cover living expenses. The Fletchers' after-tax income for 2015 was $5,700 per month ([$86,715 total income − $18,319 income and Social Security taxes] ÷ 12). Therefore, this guideline suggests they should have at least $34,200 in total liquid assets—considerably more than the $2,285 on their latest balance sheet. In troubled economic times, you may want to keep even more than six months of income in this fund as protection in case you lose your job.

Income and Expense Statement Ratios

When evaluating your income and expense statement, you should be concerned with the bottom line, which shows the cash surplus (or deficit) resulting from the period's activities. You can relate the cash surplus (or deficit) to income by calculating a **savings ratio**, which is done most effectively with after-tax income.

Rick and Beth saved about 31 percent of their after-tax income, which is excellent. (American families, on average, save about 5 percent to 8 percent). How much to save is a personal choice.

Although maintaining an adequate level of savings is obviously important to personal financial planning, so is the ability to pay debts promptly. In fact, debt payments have a higher priority. The **debt service ratio** allows you to make sure you can comfortably meet your debt obligations. This ratio excludes current liabilities and considers only mortgage, installment, and personal loan obligations.

Monthly loan payments account for about 19 percent of Rick and Beth's monthly gross income. This relatively low debt service ratio indicates that the Fletchers should have little difficulty in meeting their monthly loan payments. In your financial planning, try to keep your debt service ratio somewhere under 35 percent or so, because that's generally viewed as a manageable level of debt. Of course, the lower the debt service ratio, the easier it is to meet loan payments as they come due.

2-5 Cash In and Cash Out: Preparing and Using Budgets

LG5 Many of us avoid budgeting as if it were the plague. Yet preparing, analyzing, and monitoring your personal budget are essential steps for successful personal financial planning.

After defining your short-term financial goals, you can prepare a cash budget for the coming year. Recall that a *budget* is a short-term

savings ratio Cash surplus divided by net income (after tax); indicates relative amount of cash surplus achieved during a given period.

debt service ratio Total monthly loan payments divided by monthly gross (before-tax) income; provides a measure of the ability to pay debts promptly.

cash budget A budget that takes into account estimated monthly cash receipts and cash expenses for the coming year.

> ## Just as your goals will change over your lifetime, so too will your budget as your financial situation becomes more complex.

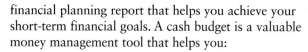

financial planning report that helps you achieve your short-term financial goals. A cash budget is a valuable money management tool that helps you:

1. Maintain the necessary information to monitor and control your finances
2. Decide how to allocate your income to reach your financial goals
3. Implement a system of disciplined spending—as opposed to just existing from one paycheck to the next
4. Reduce needless spending so you can increase the funds allocated to savings and investments
5. Achieve your long-term financial goals

Just as your goals will change over your lifetime, so too will your budget as your financial situation becomes more complex. Typically, the number of income and expense categories increases as you accumulate more assets and debts and have more family responsibilities. For most people this process does not become simpler until retirement.

2-5a The Budgeting Process

Like the income and expense statement, *a budget should be prepared on a cash basis*; thus, we call this document a **cash budget** because it deals with estimated cash receipts and cash expenses, including savings and investments, that are expected to occur in the coming year.

The cash budget preparation process has three stages: estimating income, estimating expenses, and finalizing the cash budget. When you're estimating income and expenses, take into account any anticipated changes in the cost of living and their impact on your budget components. If your income is fixed—not expected to change over the budgetary period—then increases in various expense items will probably decrease the purchasing power of your income. Worksheet 2.3, the Fletchers' "Annual Cash Budget by Month," has separate sections to record income (cash receipts) and expenses (cash expenses) and also lists the most common categories for each.

Estimating Income

The first step in preparing your cash budget is to estimate your income for the coming year. Include all income expected for the year: the take-home pay of both spouses, expected bonuses or commissions, pension or annuity income, and investment income—interest, dividend, rental, and asset (particularly security) sale income. Unlike the income and expense statement, in the cash budget you should use *take-home pay* (rather than gross income). Your cash

Worksheet 2.3 The Fletchers' Annual Cash Budget by Month

The annual cash budget shows several months in which substantial cash deficits are expected to occur; they can use this information to develop plans for covering those monthly shortfalls.

ANNUAL CASH BUDGET BY MONTH

Name(s) Rick and Beth Fletcher

For the Year   Ended December 31, 2016

	Jan.	Feb.	Mar.	April	May	June	July	Aug.	Sep.	Oct.	Nov.	Dec.	Total for the Year
INCOME													
Take-home pay	$4,800	$4,800	$4,800	$4,800	$4,800	$5,200	$5,200	$5,200	$5,200	$5,200	$5,200	$5,200	$60,400
Bonuses and commissions						1,350						1,300	2,650
Pensions and annuities													
Investment income		50				50			50			50	200
Other income													
(I) Total Income	$4,800	$4,800	$4,850	$4,800	$4,800	$6,600	$5,200	$5,200	$5,250	$5,200	$5,200	$6,550	$63,250
EXPENSES													
Housing (rent/mtge, repairs)	$1,185	$1,485	$1,185	$1,185	$1,185	$1,185	$1,185	$1,185	$1,185	$1,185	$1,185	$1,185	$14,520
Utilities (phone, elec., gas, water)	245	245	245	175	180	205	230	245	205	195	230	250	2,650
Food (home and away)	696	696	1,200	696	696	696	696	696	696	696	696	696	8,856
Transportation (auto/public)	375	620	375	355	375	375	575	375	375	425	375	375	4,975
Medical/dental, incl. insurance	50	50	50	50	50	75	50	50	50	50	50	50	625
Clothing	150	150	670	200	200	200	300	600	200	300	300	300	3,570
Insurance (life, auto, home)				660	1,598					660	1,598		4,516
Taxes (property)		550							550				1,100
Appliances, furniture, and other (purchases/loans)	60	60	60	60	60	60	60	60	60	60	60	60	720
Personal care	100	100	100	100	100	100	100	100	100	100	100	100	1,200
Recreation and entertainment	250	300	3,200	200	200	400	300	200	200	200	200	2,050	7,700
Savings and investments	575	575	575	575	575	575	575	575	575	575	575	575	6,900
Other expenses	135	200	175	135	510	180	135	235	235	135	405	325	2,805
Fun money	200	200	230	130	200	200	200	200	200	200	200	230	2,390
(II) Total Expenses	$4,021	$5,231	$8,065	$4,521	$5,929	$4,251	$4,406	$5,071	$4,081	$4,781	$5,974	$6,196	$62,527
CASH SURPLUS (OR DEFICIT) [(I)-(II)]	$779	($431)	($3,215)	$279	($1,129)	$2,349	$794	$129	$1,169	$419	($774)	$354	$723
CUMULATIVE CASH SURPLUS (OR DEFICIT)	$779	$348	($2,867)	($2,588)	($3,717)	($1,368)	($574)	($445)	$724	$1,143	$369	$723	$723

budget focuses on those areas that you can control—and most people have limited control over things like taxes withheld, contributions to company insurance and pension plans, and the like. In effect, take-home pay represents the amount of *disposable income* you receive from your employer.

Estimating Expenses

The second step in the cash budgeting process is by far the most difficult: preparing a schedule of estimated expenses for the coming year. This is commonly done using actual expenses from previous years (as found on income and expense statements and in supporting information for those periods) along with predetermined short-term financial goals.

Whether or not you have historical information, when preparing your budget, *be aware of your expenditure patterns and how you spend money*. After tracking your expenses over several months, study your spending habits to see if you are doing things that should be eliminated. For example, you may become aware that you are going to the ATM too often or using credit cards too freely. You'll probably find it easier to budget expenses if you group them into several general categories rather than trying to estimate each item. Worksheet 2.3 is an example of one such grouping scheme, patterned after the categories used in the income and expense statement.

Don't forget an allowance for "fun money," which family members can spend as they wish. This gives each person some financial independence and helps form a healthy family budget relationship.

Finalizing the Cash Budget

After estimating income and expenses, finalize your budget by comparing projected income to projected expenses. Show the difference in the third section as

a surplus or deficit. In a *balanced budget*, the total income for the year equals or exceeds total expenses. If you find that you have a deficit at year end, you'll have to *go back and adjust your expenses*. If you have several months of large surpluses, you should be able to cover any shortfall in a later month, as explained later. Budget preparation is complete once all monthly deficits are resolved and the total annual budget balances.

2-5b Dealing with Deficits

Even if the annual budget balances, in certain months expenses may exceed income, causing a monthly budget deficit. Likewise, a budget surplus occurs when income in some months exceeds expenses. Two remedies exist:

- Shift expenses from months with budget deficits to months with surpluses (or, alternatively, transfer income, if possible, from months with surpluses to those with deficits).
- Use savings, investments, or borrowing to cover temporary deficits.

Because the budget balances for the year, the need for funds to cover shortages is only temporary. In months with budget surpluses, you should return funds taken from savings or investments or repay loans. Either remedy is feasible for curing a monthly budget deficit in a balanced annual budget, although the second is probably more practical.

What can you do if your budget shows an *annual budget deficit* even after you've made a few expense adjustments? Here you have three options, as follows.

- **Liquidate enough savings and investments or borrow enough to meet the total budget shortfall for the year.** Obviously, this option is not preferred because it violates the objective of budgeting: to set expenses at a level that allows you to enjoy a reasonable standard of living *and* progress toward achieving your long-term goals.
- **Cut low-priority expenses from the budget.** This option is clearly preferable to the first one. It balances the budget without using external funding sources by eliminating expenses associated with your least important short-term goals, such as flexible or discretionary expenses for nonessential items (e.g., recreation, entertainment, and some types of clothing).
- **Increase income.** Finding a higher-paying job or perhaps a second, part-time job is the most difficult option; it takes more planning and may result in significant lifestyle changes. However, people who can't liquidate savings or investments or borrow funds to cover necessary expenses may have to choose this route to balance their budgets.

2-5c A Cash Budget for Rick and Beth Fletcher

Using their short-term financial goals (Worksheet 1.1 in Chapter 1) and past financial statements (Worksheets 2.1 and 2.2), Rick and Beth Fletcher have prepared their cash budget for the 2016 calendar year. Worksheet 2.3 shows the Fletchers' estimated total 2016 annual income and expenses by month as well as the monthly and annual cash surplus or deficit.

The Fletchers list their total 2016 take-home income of $63,250 by source for each month. By using take-home pay, they eliminate the need to show income-based taxes, Social Security payments, and other payroll deductions as expenses. The take-home pay reflects Rick and Beth's expected salary increases.

© MONKEY BUSINESS IMAGES/SHUTTERSTOCK.COM

In estimating annual expenses for 2016, the Fletchers anticipate a small amount of inflation and have factored some price increases into their expense projections. They have also allocated $6,900 to savings and investments, a wise budgeting strategy, and included an amount for fun money to be divided between them.

During their budgeting session, Rick and Beth discovered that their first estimate resulted in expenses of $63,877, compared with their estimated income of $63,250. To eliminate the $627 deficit in order to balance their budget and to allow for unexpected expenses, Rick and Beth made these decisions:

- Omit some low-priority goals: spend less on stereo components; take a shorter Hawaiian vacation instead of the Colorado ski trip shown in Worksheet 1.1.

- Reschedule some of the loan repayment to their parents.

- Reduce their fun money slightly.

These reductions lower Rick and Beth's total scheduled expenses to $62,527, giving them a surplus of $723 ($63,250 − $62,527) and balancing the budget on an annual basis with some money left over. Of course, the Fletchers can reduce other discretionary expenses to further increase the budget surplus and have a cushion for unexpected expenses.

The Fletchers' final step is to analyze monthly surpluses and deficits and determine whether to use savings, investments, or borrowing to cover monthly shortfalls. The bottom line of their annual cash budget lists the cumulative, or running, totals of monthly cash surpluses and deficits. Despite their $723 year-end cumulative cash surplus, they have cumulative deficits from March to August, primarily because of their March Hawaiian vacation and insurance payments. To help cover these deficits, Rick and Beth have arranged an interest-free loan from their parents. If they had dipped into savings to finance the deficits, they would have lost some interest earnings, which are included as income. They could also delay clothing and recreation and entertainment expenses until later in the year to reduce the deficits more quickly. If they weren't able to obtain funds to cover the deficits, they would have to reduce expenses further or increase income. At year end, they should use their surplus to increase savings or investments or to repay part of a loan.

2-5d Using Your Budgets

In the final analysis, a cash budget has value only if (1) you use it and (2) you keep careful records of actual income and expenses. These records show whether you are staying within your budget limits.

At the beginning of each month, record the budgeted amount for each category and enter income received and money spent on the appropriate pages. At month's end, total each account and calculate the surplus or deficit. Except for certain income accounts (such as salary) and fixed expense accounts (such as mortgage or loan payments), most categories will end the month with a positive or negative variance, indicating a cash surplus or deficit. You can then transfer your total spending by category to a **budget control schedule** that compares actual income and expenses with the various budget categories and shows the variances.

This monthly comparison makes it easy to identify major budget categories where income falls far short of—or spending far exceeds—desired levels (variances of 5 percent to 10 percent or more). After pinpointing these areas, you can take corrective action to keep your budget on course. Don't just look at the size of the variances. Analyze them, particularly the larger ones, to discover *why* they occurred. Only in exceptional situations should you finance budget adjustments by using savings and investments or by borrowing.

Looking at the Fletchers' budget control schedule for January, February, and March 2016, on Worksheet 2.4, you can see that actual income and expense levels are reasonably close to their targets and

have a positive variance for the months shown (their surpluses exceed the budgeted surplus amounts). The biggest variances were in food and transportation expenses, but neither was far off the mark. Thus, for the first three months of the year, the Fletchers seem to be doing a good job of controlling their income and expenses. In fact, by cutting discretionary spending, they have achieved a cumulative cash surplus of $349 for the year-to-date variance.

2-6 The Time Value of Money: Putting a Dollar Value on Financial Goals

LG6 Assume that one of your financial goals is to buy your first home in six years. Your first question is how much you want to spend on that home. Let's say you've done some "window shopping" and feel that, taking future inflation into consideration, you can buy a nice condominium for about $200,000 in six years. Of course, you won't need the full amount, but assuming that you'll make a 20 percent down payment of $40,000 (.20 × $200,000 = $40,000) and pay $5,000 in closing costs, you need $45,000. You now have a fairly well-defined long-term financial goal: *To accumulate $45,000 in six years to buy a home costing about $200,000.*

The next question is how to get all that money. You can easily estimate how much to save or invest each year if you know your goal and what you expect to earn on your savings or investments. In this case, if you have to start from scratch (that is, if nothing has already been saved) and estimate that you can earn about 5 percent on your money, you'll have to save or invest about $6,616 per year for each of the next six years to accumulate $45,000 over that time. Now you have another vital piece of information: *You know what you must do over the next six years to reach your financial goal.*

How did we arrive at the $6,616 figure? We used a concept called the **time value of money**, the idea that a dollar today is worth more than a dollar received in the future. With time value concepts, we can correctly compare dollar values occurring at different points in time. So long as you can earn a positive rate of return (interest rate) on your investments (ignoring taxes and other behavioral factors), in a strict financial sense you should always prefer to receive equal amounts of money sooner rather than later. The two key time value concepts, future value and present value, are discussed separately next. (*Note:* The time

budget control schedule A summary that shows how actual income and expenses compare with the various budget categories and where variances (surpluses or deficits) exist.

time value of money The concept that a dollar today is worth more than a dollar received in the future.

© KEITH WEBBER JR./ISTOCKPHOTO

The budget control schedule provides important feedback on how the actual cash flow is stacking up relative to the forecasted cash budget. If the variances are significant enough and/or continue month after month, the Fletchers should consider altering either their spending habits or their cash budget.

BUDGET CONTROL SCHEDULE

Name(s) Rick and Beth Fletcher

For the 3   Months Ended March 31, 2016

	Month: January				Month: February				Month: March			
	Budgeted Amount	Actual	Monthly Variance	Year-to-Date Variance	Budgeted Amount	Actual	Monthly Variance	Year-to-Date Variance	Budgeted Amount	Actual	Monthly Variance	Year-to-Date Variance
INCOME	(1)	(2)	(3)	(4)	(1)	(2)	(3)	(4)	(1)	(2)	(3)	(4)
Take-home pay	$4,800	$4,817	$17	$17	$4,800	$4,817	$17	$34	$4,800	$4,817	$17	$51
Bonuses and commissions			0	0								0
Pensions and annuities			0	0								0
Investment income			0	0					50	46	(4)	(4)
Other income			0	0								0
(I) Total Income	$4,800	$4,817	$17	$17	$4,800	$4,817	$17	$34	$4,850	$4,863	$13	$47
EXPENSES												0
Housing (rent/mtge, repairs)	$1,185	1,185	0	0	$1,485	1,485	0	0	$1,185	1,185	0	0
Utilities (phone, elec., gas, water)	245	237	(8)	(8)	245	252	7	(1)	245	228	(17)	(18)
Food (home and away)	696	680	(16)	(16)	696	669	(27)	(43)	1,200	1,325	125	82
Transportation (auto/public)	375	385	10	15	620	601	(19)	(4)	375	310	(65)	(69)
Medical/dental, incl. insurance	50	0	(50)	(30)	50	45	(5)	(35)	50	0	(50)	(85)
Clothing	150	190	40	40	150	135	(15)	25	670	650	(20)	5
Insurance (life, auto, home)	0	0	0	0	0	0	0	0	0	0	0	0
Taxes (property)	0	0	0	0	550	550	0	0				
Appliances, furniture, and other (purchases/loans)	60	60	0	0	60	60	0	0	60	60	0	0
Personal care	100	85	(15)	(15)	100	120	20	5	100	75	(25)	(20)
Recreation and entertainment	250	210	(40)	(40)	300	250	(50)	(90)	3,200	3,285	85	(5)
Savings and investments	575	575	0	0	575	575	0	0	575	575	0	0
Other expenses	135	118	(17)	(17)	200	150	(50)	(67)	175	150	(25)	(92)
Fun money	200	200	0	(30)	200	225	25	(5)	230	130	(100)	(105)
(II) Total Expenses	$4,021	$3,925	($96)	($101)	$5,231	$5,117	($114)	($210)	$8,065	$7,973	($92)	($302)
											0	0
CASH SURPLUS (OR DEFICIT) [(I)-(II)]	$779	$892	$113	$118	($431)	($300)	$131	$244	($3,215)	($3,110)	$105	$349
CUMULATIVE CASH SURPLUS (OR DEFICIT)	$779	$892		$118	$348	$592		$244	($2,867)	($2,518)		$349

Key: Col. (3) = Col. (2) − Col. (1); Col. (7) = Col. (6) − Col. (5); Col. (11) = Col. (10) − (Col. (9); Col. (4) = Col. (3); Col. (8) = Col. (4) + Col. (7); Col. (12) = Col. (8) + Col. (11).

© Cengage Learning

future value The value to which an amount today will grow if it earns a specific rate of interest over a given period.

value discussions and demonstrations initially rely on the use of financial tables. As an alternative, Appendix E explains how to use financial calculators, which determine the interest factors internally to conveniently make time value calculations. The calculator keystrokes for each calculation are shown in the text margin near the related discussion.)

2-6a Future Value

To calculate how much to save to buy the $200,000 condominium, we used **future value**, the value to which an amount today will grow if it earns a specific rate of interest over a given period. Assume, for example, that you make annual deposits of $2,000 into a savings account that pays 5 percent interest per year. At the end of 20 years, your deposits would total $40,000 (20 × $2,000). If you made no withdrawals, your account balance would have increased to $66,132! This growth in value occurs not only because of earning interest but also because of **compounding**—the interest earned each year is left in the account and becomes part of the balance (or principal) on which interest is earned in subsequent years.

Future Value of a Single Amount

To demonstrate future value, let's return to the goal of accumulating $45,000 for a down payment to buy a home in six years. The correct way to approach this problem is to use the *future value* concept. For instance, if you can invest $100 today at 5 percent, you will have $105 in a year. You will earn $5 on your investment (.05 × $100 = $5) and get your original $100 back. Once you know the length of time and rate of return involved, you can find the future value of any investment by using the following simple formula:

Future value = Amount invested × Future value factor

Tables of future value factors simplify the computations in this formula (see Appendix A). The table is easy to use; simply find the factor that corresponds to a given year and interest rate. Referring to Appendix A, you will find the future value factor for a six year investment earning 5 percent is 1.340 (the factor that lies at the intersection of six years and 5 percent).

Returning to the problem at hand, let's say you already have accumulated $5,000 toward the purchase of a new home. To find the future value of that investment in six years earning 5 percent, you can use the preceding formula as follows:

Future value = $5,000 × 1.340
= $6,700

In six years, then, you will have $6,700 if you invest the $5,000 at 5 percent. Because you feel you are going to need $45,000, you are still $38,300 short of your goal.

Future Value of an Annuity

How are you going to accumulate the additional $38,300? You'll again use the future value concept, but this time you'll use the *future value annuity factor*. An **annuity** is a fixed sum of money that occurs annually; for example, a deposit of $1,000 per year for each of the next five years, with payment to be made at the end of each year. To find out how much you need to save each year in order to accumulate a given amount, use this equation:

$$\text{Yearly savings} = \frac{\text{Amount of money desired}}{\text{Future value annuity factor}}$$

When dealing with an annuity you need to use a different table of factors, such as that in Appendix B. Note that it's very much like the table of future value factors and, in fact, is used in exactly the same way: the proper future value annuity factor is the one that corresponds to a given year *and* interest rate. For example, you'll find in Appendix B that the future value annuity factor for six years and 5 percent is 6.802. Using this factor in the previous equation, you can find out how much to save each year to accumulate $38,300 in six years, given a 5 percent rate of return, as follows:

Yearly savings = $38,300 / 6.802 = $5,630.70

> **compounding** When interest earned each year is left in the account and becomes part of the balance (or principal) on which interest is earned in subsequent years.
>
> **annuity** A fixed sum of money that occurs annually.

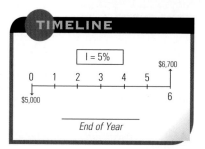

TIMELINE

I = 5%

0 1 2 3 4 5 $6,700

$5,000   6

End of Year

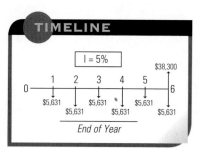

CALCULATOR

Inputs	Functions
5000	PV
6	N
5	I
	CPT
	FV
	Solution
	6,700.48

SEE APPENDIX E FOR DETAILS.

TIMELINE

I = 5%

$38,300

0   1   2   3   4   5   6

$5,631 $5,631 $5,631 $5,631 $5,631 $5,631

End of Year

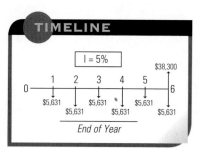
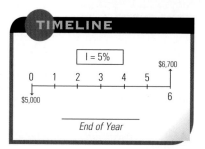

© TATIANAPOPOVA/SHUTTERSTOCK

present value The value today of an amount to be received in the future; it's the amount that would have to be invested today at a given interest rate over a specified time period to accumulate the future amount.

discounting The process of finding present value; the inverse of *compounding* to find future value.

You'll need to save about $5,630.70 a year to reach your goal. Note in this example that you must add $5,630.70 each year to the $5,000 you initially invested in order to build up a pool of $45,000 in six years. At a 5 percent rate of return, the $5,630.70 per year will grow to $38,300 and the $5,000 will grow to $6,700, so in 6 years, you'll have $38,300 and the $5,000

TIMELINE

I = 5%

$45,000

0 — 1 — 2 — 3 — 4 — 5 — 6

$6,616 $6,616 $6,616
  $6,616 $6,616 $6,616

End of Year

will grow to $6,700, so in six years, you'll have $38,300 + $6,700 = $45,000.

How much, you may ask, would you need to save each year if you didn't have the $5,000 to start with? In this case, your goal would still be the same (to accumulate $45,000 in six years), but because you'd be starting from scratch, the full $45,000

would need to come from yearly savings. Assuming you can still earn 5 percent over the six-year period, you can use the same future value annuity factor (6.802) and compute the amount of yearly savings as follows:

Yearly savings = $45,000 / 6.802 = $6,615.70

or approximately $6,616. Note that this amount corresponds to the $6,616 figure cited at the beginning of this section.

2-6b Present Value

Lucky you! You've just won $100,000 in your state lottery. You want to spend part of it now, but because you're 30 years old, you also want to use part of it for your retirement fund. Your goal is to accumulate $300,000 in the fund by the time you're age 55 (25 years from now). How much do you need to invest if you estimate that you can earn 5 percent annually on your investments during the next 25 years?

Using **present value**, the value today of an amount to be received in the future, you can calculate the answer. It represents the amount you'd have to invest today at a given interest rate over

the specified time period to accumulate the future amount. The process of finding present value is called **discounting**, which is the inverse of *compounding* to find future value.

Present Value of a Single Amount

Assuming that you wish to create the retirement fund (future value) by making a single lump-sum deposit today, you can use this formula to find the amount that you need to deposit:

Present value = Future value × Present value factor

HOCUS-FOCUS/ISTOCKPHOTO

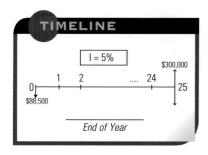

TIMELINE

I = 5%

$300,000

0   1   2   24   25

$88,500

End of Year

Tables of present value factors make this calculation easy (see Appendix C). First, find the present value factor for a 25-year investment at a 5 percent discount rate (the factor that lies at the intersection of 25 years and 5 percent) in Appendix C; it is 0.295. Then, substitute the future value of $300,000 and the present value factor of 0.295 into the formula as follows:

Present value = $300,000 × 0.295 = $88,500

The $88,500 is the amount you'd have to deposit today into an account paying 5 percent annual interest in order to accumulate $300,000 at the end of 25 years.

Present Value of an Annuity

You can also use present value techniques to determine how much you can withdraw from your retirement fund each year over a specified time horizon. This calls for the *present value annuity factor*. Assume that at age 55, you wish to begin making equal annual withdrawals over the next 30 years from your $300,000 retirement fund. At first, you might think you could withdraw $10,000 per year ($300,000/30 years). However, the funds still on deposit would continue to earn 5 percent annual interest. To find the amount of the equal annual withdrawal, you again need to consider the time value of money. Specifically, you would use this formula:

$$\text{Annual withdrawal} = \frac{\text{Initial deposit}}{\text{Present value annuity factor}}$$

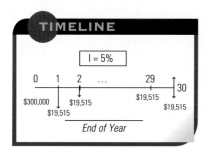

TIMELINE

I = 5%

0   1   2   ...   29   30

$300,000 $19,515

$19,515 $19,515 $19,515

End of Year

Use the present value annuity factors in Appendix D for this calculation. Substituting the $300,000 initial deposit and the present value annuity factor for

30 years and 5 percent of 15.732 (from Appendix D) into the preceding equation, we get:

$$\text{Annual withdrawal} = \frac{\$300,000}{15.732} = \$19,514.73$$

Therefore, you can withdraw $19,514.73 each year for 30 years. This value is clearly much larger than the $10,000 annual withdrawal mentioned earlier.

CALCULATOR

Inputs	Functions
300000	PV
30	N
5	I
	CPT
	PMT
	Solution
	19,515.43

SEE APPENDIX E FOR DETAILS.

Other Applications of Present Value

You can also use present value techniques to analyze investments. Suppose you have an opportunity to purchase an annuity investment that promises to pay $700 per year for five years. You know that you'll receive

> **Future and present value concepts allow you to place monetary values on long-term financial goals.**

© ILINSERGEY/SHUTTERSTOCK.COM

a total of $3,500 ($700 × 5) over the five-year period. However, you wish to earn a minimum annual return of 5 percent on your investments. What's the most you should pay for this annuity today? You can answer this question by rearranging the terms in the formula to get:

Initial deposit = Annual withdrawal × Present value annuity factor

Adapting the equation to this situation, "initial deposit" represents the maximum price to pay for the annuity, and "annual withdrawal" represents the annual annuity payment of $700. The present value annuity factor for five years and 5 percent (found in Appendix D) is 4.329. Substituting this into the equation, we obtain:

Initial deposit = $700 × 4.329 = $3,030.30

The most you should pay for the $700, five year annuity, given your 5 percent annual return, is about $3,030. At this price, you'd earn 5 percent on the investment.

Using the present value concept, you can easily determine the present value of a sum to be received in the future, equal annual future withdrawals available from an initial deposit, and the initial deposit that would generate a given stream of equal annual withdrawals. These procedures, like future value concepts, allow you to place monetary values on long-term financial goals.

Planning Over a Lifetime: Budgeting

While budgeting is important across all stages of the life cycle, here are some key considerations in each stage.

Independent Lifestyle (20s)	Family and Career Development (30–45)	Mature Lifestyle (45–65)	Retirement (65 and beyond)
Develop financial record-keeping system.	Revise budget in light of family and career financial changes.	Revise budget to reflect typically higher income relative to expenses.	Revise budget to adapt to retirement living expenses, health costs, insurance needs and income.
Develop a budget and carefully track expenses.	Budget amount for children's education.	Evaluate projected expenses and housing for retirement planning.	Draw on retirement income sources and accumulated assets.
Budget savings each month and build up an emergency fund.	Determine and set aside retirement contribution.	More aggressively budget to increase retirement contributions.	Spend to meet previously determined long-term financial goals.
Develop personal balance sheet, income statement, and calculate net worth at least annually.	Spend to meet previously determined short- and medium-term financial goals.	Spend to meet previously determined medium-term financial goals.	Update personal balance sheet, income statement, and calculate net worth at least annually.
Develop short-, medium-, and long-term financial goals	Update personal balance sheet, income statement, and calculate net worth at least annually.	Update personal balance sheet, income statement, and calculate net least annually.	

FINANCIAL PLANNING EXERCISES

LG2, 3

1. **Scott Bennett is preparing his balance sheet and income and expense statement for the year ending June 30, 2016. He is having difficulty classifying six items and asks for your help. Which, if any, of the following transactions are assets, liabilities, income, or expense items?**
   a. Scott rents a house for $1,350 a month.
   b. On June 21, 2016, Scott bought diamond earrings for his wife and charged them using his MasterCard. The earrings cost $900, but he hasn't yet received the bill.
   c. Scott borrowed $3,500 from his parents last fall, but so far, he has made no payments to them.
   d. Scott makes monthly payments of $225 on an installment loan; about half of it is interest, and the balance is repayment of principal. He has 20 payments left, totaling $4,500.
   e. Scott paid $3,800 in taxes during the year and is due a tax refund of $650, which he hasn't yet received.
   f. Scott invested $2,300 in some common stock.

LG5

2. **Stan and Elizabeth Carpenter are preparing their 2016 cash budget. Help the Carpenters reconcile the following differences, giving reasons to support your answers.**
   a. Their only source of income is Stan's salary, which amounts to $5,000 a month before taxes. Elizabeth wants to show the $5,000 as their monthly income, whereas Stan argues that his take-home pay of $3,917 is the correct value to show.
   b. Elizabeth wants to make a provision for *fun money*, an idea that Stan cannot understand. He asks, "Why do we need fun money when everything is provided for in the budget?"

LG6

3. **Use future or present value techniques to solve the following problems.**
   a. If you inherited $45,000 today and invested all of it in a security that paid a 7 percent rate of return, how much would you have in 25 years?
   b. If the average new home costs $275,000 today, how much will it cost in 10 years if the price increases by 5 percent each year?
   c. You think that in 15 years, it will cost $214,000 to provide your child with a 4-year college education. Will you have enough if you take $75,000 *today* and invest it for the next 15 years at 4 percent?
   d. If you can earn 4 percent, how much will you have to save *each year* if you want to retire in 35 years with $1 million?

LG6

4. **Greg Fredericks wishes to have $800,000 in a retirement fund 20 years from now. He can create the retirement fund by making a single lump-sum deposit today.**
   a. If upon retirement in 20 years, Greg plans to invest $800,000 in a fund that earns 4 percent, what is the maximum annual withdrawal he can make over the following 15 years?
   b. How much would Greg need to have on deposit at retirement in order to withdraw $35,000 annually over the 15 years if the retirement fund earns 4 percent?
   c. To achieve his annual withdrawal goal of $35,000 calculated in part b, how much more than the amount calculated in part a must Greg deposit today in an investment earning 4 percent annual interest?

PFIN Student Study Tools—Visit CourseMate for PFIN 3. Log in at **www.cengagebrain.com**. Check out the bonus exercises and exhibits, interactive worksheets, Smart Sites, Critical Thinking Cases, Money Online, Kiplinger videos, quizzing, and more.

Cool Apps—Look for this new feature on CourseMate for PFIN 3. Cool Apps navigates the growing world of apps that are available for personal financial planning and tracking.

3

PREPARING YOUR TAXES

LEARNING GOALS

LG1 Discuss the basic principles of income taxes and determine your filing status.

LG2 Describe the sources of gross income and adjustments to income, differentiate between standard and itemized deductions and exemptions, and calculate taxable income.

LG3 Prepare a basic tax return using the appropriate tax forms and rate schedules.

LG4 Explain who needs to pay estimated taxes, when to file or amend your return, and how to handle an audit.

LG5 Know where to get help with your taxes and how software can make tax return preparation easier.

LG6 Implement an effective tax planning strategy.

HOW WILL THIS AFFECT ME? There's an old joke that people who complain about taxes can be divided into two groups: men and women. This chapter helps you pursue the tax-planning goal of maximizing the money that you get to keep by legally minimizing the taxes you have to pay. Income, various adjustments to income, deductions, and credits are considered in computing taxes. The chapter walks through the steps in completing representative tax returns. The impact of Social Security taxes and tax shelters are considered. And a framework for choosing a professional tax preparer or tax preparation software is provided. After reading this chapter you should be able to prepare your own taxes or to better understand and evaluate how your taxes are prepared by software or a tax professional.

3-1 Understanding Federal Income Tax Principles

LG1 Taxes are dues that we pay for membership in our society; they're the cost of living in this country. Federal, state, and local tax receipts fund government activities and a wide variety of public services, from national defense to local libraries. Administering and enforcing federal tax laws is the responsibility of the Internal Revenue Service (IRS), a part

PAUL MAGUIRE/ALAMY

JAMIE DUPLASS/SHUTTERSTOCK.COM

After you read the chapter, explore the STUDY TOOLS listed on page 72.

of the U.S. Department of Treasury.

Because federal income tax is generally the largest tax you'll pay, you are wise to make tax planning an important part of personal financial planning. A typical American family currently pays *more than one-third of its gross income in taxes:* federal income and Social Security taxes as well as numerous state and local income, sales, and property taxes. You should make tax planning a year-round activity and always consider tax consequences when preparing and revising your financial plans and making major financial decisions.

> ❝ **Make tax planning a year-round activity and always consider tax consequences when preparing and revising your financial plans and making major financial decisions.** ❞

The overriding objective of tax planning is simple: *to maximize the amount of money that you can legally keep legally by minimizing the amount of taxes you pay.* So long as it's done honestly and within the tax codes, there is nothing immoral, illegal, or unethical about trying to minimize your tax bill. Here we concentrate on *income taxes paid by individuals*—particularly the federal income tax, the largest and most important tax for most taxpayers. To give you a good understanding of your future tax situation, we use a mid-career couple to demonstrate the key aspects of individual taxation.

 Go to Smart Sites

How long does the average American have to work this year to pay federal, state, and local taxes? Find this year's date of "Tax Freedom Day" at the Tax Foundation Web site. You'll also find information there about tax policy, tax rates, tax collections, and the economics of taxation. For more online resources, whenever you see "*Go to Smart Sites*" in this chapter, visit CourseMate for PFIN 3. Log **www.cengagebrain.com**. ●

© GEOPAUL/ISTOCKPHOTO

taxes The dues paid for membership in our society; the cost of living in this country.

income taxes A type of tax levied on taxable income by the federal government and by many state and local governments.

progressive tax structure A tax structure in which the larger the amount of taxable income, the higher the rate at which it is taxed.

marginal tax rate The tax rate you pay on the next dollar of taxable income.

average tax rate The rate at which each dollar of taxable income is taxed on average; calculated by dividing the tax liability by taxable income.

In addition to federal income tax, there are other forms of taxes to contend with—for example, federal self-employment taxes and state and local sales, income, property, and license taxes. Thus, a person saving to purchase a new automobile costing $25,000 should realize that the state and local sales taxes, as well as the cost of license plates and registration, may add 10 percent or more to the total cost of the car.

Here we present key tax concepts and show how they apply to common situations. The tax tables, calculations, and sample tax returns presented in this chapter are based on the tax laws applicable to the calendar year 2011. *Although tax rates and other provisions will change, the basic procedures will remain the same.*

3-1a The Economics of Income Taxes

Income taxes are the major source of revenue for the federal government. Personal income taxes are scaled on progressive rates. To illustrate how this **progressive tax structure** works, consider the following data for *single taxpayers* filing 2011 returns:

Taxable Income	Tax Rate (%)
$1 to $8,500	10
$8,501 to $34,500	15
$34,501 to $83,600	25
$83,601 to $174,400	28
$174,401 to $379,150	33
Over $379,151	35

Of course, any nontaxable income can be viewed as being in the 0 percent tax bracket. As taxable income moves from a lower to a higher bracket, the higher rate applies *only to the additional taxable income in that bracket* and not to the entire taxable income. For example, consider two single brothers Scott and Nathan, whose taxable incomes are $45,000 and $90,000, respectively (see table below).

Note that Scott pays the 25 percent rate only on that portion of the $45,000 in taxable income that exceeds $34,000. Because this scale is progressive, the more money you make, the progressively more you pay in taxes: although Nathan's taxable income is twice that of Scott's, his income tax is about 2½ times higher than his brother's.

The tax rate for each bracket—10 percent, 15 percent, 25 percent, 28 percent, 33 percent, and 35 percent—is called the **marginal tax rate**, or the rate applied to the next dollar of taxable income. When you relate the tax liability to the level of taxable income earned, the tax rate, called the **average tax rate**,

Name	Taxable Income	Tax Calculation	Tax Liability
Scott	$45,000	= [($45,000 − $34,500) × 0.25]	
		+ [($34,500 − $8,500) × 0.15]	
		+ [$8,500 × 0.10]	
		= $2,625 + $3,900 + $850 =	$7,375
Nathan	$90,000	= [($90,000 − $83,600) × 0.28]	
		+ [($83,600 − $34,500) × 0.25]	
		+ [($34,500 − $8,500) × 0.15]	
		+ [$8,500 × 0.10]	
		= $1,792 + $12,275 + $3,900 + $850 =	$18,817

drops considerably. Scott's average tax rate, calculated by dividing the tax liability by taxable income, is about 16.4 percent ($7,375/$45,000). Nathan's average tax rate is about 20.9 percent ($18,817/$90,000). Clearly, taxes are still progressive, but the average size of the bite is not as bad as the stated tax rate might suggest.

3-1b Your Filing Status

The taxes you pay depend in part on your *filing status*, which is based on your marital status and family situation on the last day of your tax year (usually December 31). There are five different filing status categories.

- **Single taxpayers:** Unmarried or legally separated from their spouses by either a separation or final divorce decree.

- **Married filing jointly:** Married couples who combine their income and allowable deductions and file one tax return.

- **Married filing separately:** Each spouse files his or her own return, reporting only his or her income, deductions, and exemptions.

- **Head of household:** A taxpayer who is unmarried and pays more than half of the cost of keeping up a home for himself or herself and an eligible dependent child or relative.

- **Qualifying widow or widower with dependent child:** A person whose spouse died within two years of the tax year (for example, in 2009 or 2010 for the 2011 tax year) and who supports a dependent child may use joint return tax rates and is eligible for the highest standard deduction.

Every individual or married couple who earns a specified level of income is required to file a tax return. For example, for those under 65, a single person who earned more than $9,500 and a married couple with a combined income of more than $19,000 must file a tax return (for 2011). Like the personal tax rates, these minimums are adjusted annually based on the annual rate of inflation. Regardless, even if your income falls below the current minimum level, you must file a tax return in order to receive a refund of any income tax withheld during the year.

3-1c Your Take-Home Pay

Most of us actually pay taxes as we earn income throughout the year. Under this *pay-as-you-go* system, your employer withholds (deducts) a portion of your income every pay period and sends it to the IRS to be credited to your own tax account. Self-employed persons must also prepay their taxes by forwarding part of their income to the IRS at four dates each year (referred to as quarterly estimated tax payments).

After the close of the taxable year, you calculate the actual taxes you owe and file your tax return. When you file, you receive full credit for the amount of taxes withheld (including estimated tax payments) from your income during the year and either (1) receive a refund from the IRS (if too much tax was withheld from your paycheck and/or prepaid in estimated taxes) or (2) have to pay additional taxes (if the amount withheld/prepaid didn't cover your tax liability). Your employer normally withholds funds not only for federal income taxes but also for FICA (Social Security) taxes and, if applicable, state and

federal withholding taxes Taxes—based on the level of earnings and the number of withholding allowances claimed—that an employer deducts from the employee's gross earnings each pay period.

Federal Insurance Contributions Act (FICA) or Social Security tax The law establishing the combined old-age, survivor's, disability, and hospital insurance tax levied on both employer and employee.

taxable income The amount of income subject to taxes; it is calculated by subtracting adjustments, the larger of itemized or standard deductions, and exemptions from gross income.

gross income The total of all of a taxpayer's income (before any adjustments, deductions, or exemptions) subject to federal taxes; it includes active, portfolio, and passive income.

local income taxes (which may be deductible on federal returns). Other payroll deductions include life and health insurance, savings plans, retirement programs, professional or union dues, and charitable contributions—all of which lower your take-home pay. Your *take-home pay* is what you're left with after subtracting the amount withheld from your *gross earnings*.

Federal Withholding Taxes

The amount of **federal withholding taxes** deducted from your gross earnings each pay period depends on both the level of your earnings and the number of withholding allowances you have claimed on a form called a *W-4*, which you must complete for your employer. Withholding allowances reduce the amount of taxes withheld from your income. A taxpayer is entitled to one allowance for himself or herself, one for a nonworking spouse (if filing jointly), and one for each dependent claimed (children or parents being supported mainly by the taxpayers). In addition, you may qualify for a *special allowance* or *additional withholding allowances* under certain circumstances. Taxpayers may have to change their withholding allowances during the tax year if their employment or marital status changes.

self-employed persons pay the full 13.3 percent tax but can deduct 50 percent of it on their tax returns. Further, in 2011, a special tax provision reduced the Social Security portion for the individual taxpayer by 2 percentage points, from 6.2 percent to 4.2 percent in an attempt to compensate for the recession. This 2 percent reduction did not apply to the employer paid portion, so in 2011, the payment was not evenly split. This special tax provision was extended to 2012 taxes in early 2012.

Most states have their own income taxes, which differ from state to state. Some cities assess income taxes as well. These state and local income taxes will also be withheld from earnings. They are deductible on federal returns, but deductibility of federal taxes on the state or local return depends on state and local laws.

3-2 It's Taxable Income That Matters

LG2 Calculating your income taxes is a complex process involving several steps and many computations. Exhibit 3.1 depicts the procedure to compute your **taxable income** and total tax liability owed. It looks simple enough—just subtract certain adjustments from your gross income to get your adjusted gross income; then subtract either the standard deduction or your itemized deductions and your total personal exemptions to get taxable income; and finally, compute your taxes, subtract any tax credits from that amount, and add any other taxes to it to get your total tax liability. This isn't as easy as it sounds, however! As we'll see, some problems can arise in defining what you may subtract.

 Calculating your income taxes is a complex process involving several steps and many computations.

FICA and Other Withholding Taxes

All employed workers (except certain federal employees) must pay a combined old-age, survivor's, disability, and hospital insurance tax under provisions of the **Federal Insurance Contributions Act (FICA)**. Known more commonly as the **Social Security tax**, it is paid equally by employer and employee. In 2011, the total Social Security tax rate was 13.3 percent, allocating 10.4 percent to Social Security and 2.9 percent to Medicare. The 10.4 percent applies only to the first $106,800 of an employee's earnings (this number rises with national average wages), whereas the Medicare component is paid on all earnings. In 2011,

3-2a Gross Income

Gross income essentially includes any and all income subject to federal taxes. Here are some common forms of gross income:

- Wages and salaries
- Bonuses, commissions, and tips
- Interest and dividends received
- Alimony received
- Business and farm income
- Gains from the sale of assets
- Income from pensions and annuities

Exhibit 3.1 **Calculating Your Taxable Income and Total Tax Liability Owed**

To find taxable income, you must first subtract all adjustments to gross income and then subtract deductions and personal exemptions. Your total tax liability owed includes tax on this taxable income amount, less any tax credits, plus other taxes owed.

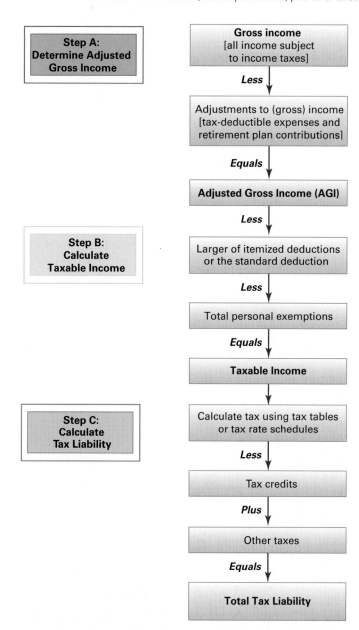

Step A: Determine Adjusted Gross Income

Gross income [all income subject to income taxes]

Less

Adjustments to (gross) income [tax-deductible expenses and retirement plan contributions]

Equals

Adjusted Gross Income (AGI)

Step B: Calculate Taxable Income

Less

Larger of itemized deductions or the standard deduction

Less

Total personal exemptions

Equals

Taxable Income

Step C: Calculate Tax Liability

Calculate tax using tax tables or tax rate schedules

Less

Tax credits

Plus

Other taxes

Equals

Total Tax Liability

© Cengage Learning

- Income from rents and partnerships
- Prizes, lottery, and gambling winnings

In addition to these sources of income, others—such as child-support payments and municipal bond interest—are considered *tax exempt* and as such are excluded (totally or partially) from gross income.

Three Kinds of Income
Individual income falls into one of three basic categories.

- **Active income:** Income *earned* on the job, such as wages and salaries, bonuses, and tips; also includes most other forms of *noninvestment* income, such as pension income and alimony

- **Portfolio income:** Earnings—interest, dividends, and capital gains (profits on the sale of investments)—generated from most types of investment holdings; includes savings accounts, stocks, bonds, mutual funds, options, and futures

adjustments to (gross) income Allowable deductions from gross income, including certain employee, personal retirement, insurance, and support expenses.

● **Passive income**: A special category that includes income derived from real estate, limited partnerships, and other forms of tax shelters

These categories limit the amount of deductions and write-offs that taxpayers can take. Specifically, the amount of allowable, deductible expenses associated with portfolio and passive income *is limited to the amount of income derived from these two sources.* For deduction purposes, you cannot combine portfolio and passive income with each other or with active income. *Investment-related expenses can be used only with portfolio income*, and with a few exceptions, *passive investment expenses can be used only to offset the income from passive investments.* All the other allowances and deductions that we'll describe later are written off against the total amount of *active* income the taxpayer generates.

Capital Gains

Technically, a *capital gain* occurs whenever an asset (such as a stock, a bond, or real estate) is sold for more than its original cost. So, if you purchased stock for $50 per share and sold it for $60, you'd have a capital gain of $10 per share.

Capital gains are taxed at different rates, depending on the holding period. Exhibit 3.2 shows the different holding periods and applicable tax rates based on the 2011 tax brackets.

Although there are no limits on the amount of capital gains taxpayers can generate, the IRS imposes some restrictions on the amount of capital losses (only on the sale of income-producing assets) taxpayers can take in a given year. Specifically, a taxpayer can write off capital losses, dollar for dollar, against any capital gains. After that, he or she can write off a maximum of $3,000 in additional capital losses against active income. Thus, if a taxpayer had $10,000 in capital gains and $18,000 in capital losses in 2011, only $13,000 could be written off on 2011 taxes: $10,000 against the capital gains generated

in 2011 and another $3,000 against active income. The remainder—$5,000 in this case—will have to be written off in later years, in the same order as just indicated: first against any capital gains and then up to $3,000 against active income.

Go to Smart Sites

Fairmark Press offers a guide to Capital *Gains and Losses* to help you understand the tax treatment of securities sales. It's just one of many tax guides you'll find at the site's *Tax Guide for Investors.* ●

SELLING YOUR HOME: A SPECIAL CASE. Homeowners receive special tax treatment on the sale of a home. Single taxpayers can exclude from income the first $250,000 of gain ($500,000 for married taxpayers) on the sale of a principal residence. To qualify, the taxpayer must own and occupy the residence as a principal residence for at least two of the five years prior to the sale. For example, the Lazards (married taxpayers) just sold their principal residence, which they purchased four years earlier for $325,000, for $475,000. They may exclude their $150,000 gain ($475,000 − $325,000) from their income because they occupied the residence for more than two years, and the gain is less than $500,000.

This exclusion is available on only one sale every two years. A loss on the sale of a principal residence is not deductible. Generally speaking, this law is quite favorable to homeowners.

3-2b Adjustments to (Gross) Income

Now that you've totaled your gross income, you can deduct your **adjustments to (gross) income.** These are allowable deductions from gross income, including certain employee, personal retirement, insurance, and support expenses. Most of these deductions are nonbusiness in nature. Here are some items that can be treated as adjustments to income:

Exhibit 3.2	**Capital Gains Tax Categories as of 2011**

Capital gains tax rates are as low as 0 percent for low-income levels or 15 percent for higher-income levels, so long as the holding period is over 12 months.

Holding Period	Tax Brackets (2011)	Tax on Capital Gains
Less than 12 months	All (10%, 15%, 25%, 28%, 33%, and 35%)	Same as ordinary income
Over 12 months	10%, 15%	0%
	25%, 28%, 33%, 35%	15%

© Cengage Learning

- Educator expenses (limited)
- Higher education tuition costs (limited)
- IRA contributions (limited)
- Self-employment taxes paid (limited to 50 percent of the amount paid)
- Self-employed health insurance payments
- Penalty on early withdrawal of savings
- Alimony paid
- Moving expenses (some limits)

[*Note*: The limitations on deductions for self-directed retirement plans, such as individual retirement accounts (IRAs) and Simplified Employee Pensions (SEPs), are discussed in Chapter 14.]

After subtracting the total of all allowable adjustments to income from your gross income, you're left with **adjusted gross income (AGI)**. AGI is an important value, because it's used to calculate limits for certain itemized deductions.

3-2c Deductions: Standard or Itemized?

As shown in Exhibit 3.1, the next step in calculating your taxes is to subtract allowable deductions from your AGI. This may be the most complex part of the tax preparation process. You have two options: take the *standard deduction*, a fixed amount that depends on your filing status, or list your *itemized deductions* (specified tax-deductible personal expenses). Obviously, you should use the method that results in larger allowable deductions.

Standard Deduction

Instead of itemizing personal deductions, a taxpayer can take the **standard deduction**, a blanket deduction that includes the various deductible expenses that taxpayers normally incur. People whose total itemized deductions are too small take the standard deduction, which varies depending on the taxpayer's filing status (single, married filing jointly, and so on), age (65 or older), and vision (blind). In 2011, the standard deduction ranged from $5,800 to $16,200. For single filers it is $5,800, and for married people filing jointly it is $11,600. Those over 65 and those who are blind are eligible for a higher standard deduction. Each year, the standard deduction amounts are usually adjusted annually to any changes in the cost of living.

adjusted gross income (AGI) The amount of income remaining after subtracting all allowable adjustments to income from gross income.

standard deduction A blanket deduction that depends on the taxpayer's filing status, age, and vision and that can be taken by a taxpayer whose total itemized deductions are too small.

Financial Planning Tips: Don't Overlook These Ways to Reduce Your Taxes

It is all too common for some taxpayers to overlook tax deductions and credits that would decrease their tax bill. While there are qualifications and limitations on these tax deductions and credits, it's worth your time to be aware of these opportunities.

- **Medical travel expenses.** The costs of traveling to visit health care providers to receive medical care are deductible if the visits are recommended by a doctor. There is a standard mileage deduction if you drive, and you can deduct direct expenses like taxis, parking fees, and tolls.
- **Health insurance and medical expenses.** Health insurance premiums are deductible—and that includes long-term-care insurance. Similarly, the cost of prescriptions and separate charges for medical coverage included in a dependent child's college fees are deductible. Medical bills that you pay for a person who is your dependent are also deductible.
- **Real estate taxes and home sale costs.** Real estate taxes paid are deductible, as are any "point" fees associated with a mortgage. Annual maintenance fees for a condo also may be deducted because they are your share of the overall property's real estate taxes.

- **Volunteer and donation-related expenses.** When you donate to a charity or volunteer your time, the associated expenses are tax-deductible. For example, if you donate cookies to be sold by a charity, you can deduct the cost of baking them. Transportation costs can also be deducted.
- **Job search expenses.** The costs associated with looking for a new job are generally deductible. So you can write off employment placement agency fees, resume printing costs, and related travel expenses.
- **Tax and investment-related expenses.** The expenses paid for preparing your tax return are deductible. Further, any expenses associated with managing your investments are generally deductible. For example, you can write off financial advisors' fees and investment publication subscription costs.
- **College tuition tax credit.** You can get up to a $2,500 tax credit in college tuition for family members if your adjusted gross income falls within certain limits.

MKABAKOV/SHUTTERSTOCK.COM

Itemized Deductions

Itemized deductions allow taxpayers to reduce their AGI by the amount of their allowable personal expenditures. Some of the more common ones allowed by the IRS include:

- Medical and dental expenses (*in excess* of 7.5 percent of AGI)

- State, local, and foreign income and property taxes; state and local personal property taxes

- Residential mortgage interest and investment interest (limited)

- Charitable contributions (limited to 50 percent, 30 percent, or 20 percent of AGI depending on certain factors)

- Casualty and theft losses (in excess of 10 percent of AGI; reduced by $100 per loss)

- Job and other expenses (in excess of 2 percent of AGI)

- Moving expenses (some restrictions; also deductible for those who don't itemize)

Choosing the Best Option

Your decision to take the standard deduction or itemize deductions may change over time. Taxpayers who find they've chosen the wrong option and paid too much may recalculate their tax using the other method and file an *amended return (Form 1040X)* to claim a refund for the difference. For example, suppose that you computed and paid your taxes, which amounted to $2,450, using the standard deduction. A few months later you discover that, had you itemized your deductions, your taxes would have been only $1,950. Using the appropriate forms, you can file for a $500 refund ($2,450 − $1,950). To avoid having to file an amended return, it is best to estimate your deductions using both the standard and itemized deduction amounts and then choose the one that results in lower taxes.

3-2d Exemptions

Deductions from AGI based on the number of persons supported by the taxpayer's income are called **exemptions**. A taxpayer can claim an exemption for himself or herself, his or her spouse, and any *dependents*—children or other relatives earning less than a stipulated level of income ($3,700 in 2011)—for whom the *taxpayer provides more than half* of their total support. This income limitation is waived for dependent children under the age of 24 (at the end of the calendar year) who are full-time students. So a college student, for example, could earn $8,000 and still be claimed as an exemption by her parents, so long as

© OLJ STUDIO/SHUTTERSTOCK

all other dependency requirements are met. In 2011, each exemption claimed was worth $3,700, an amount tied to the cost of living and adjusted annually.

A personal exemption can be claimed only once. If a child is *eligible* to be claimed as an exemption by her parents, then she doesn't have the choice of using a personal exemption on her own tax return regardless of whether the parents use her exemption. In 2011, a family of four could take total exemptions of $14,800—that is, 4 × $3,700. Subtracting the amount claimed for itemized deductions (or the standard deduction) and exemptions from AGI results in the amount of *taxable income*, which is the basis on which taxes are calculated. A taxpayer who makes $50,000 a year may have only, say, $25,000 in taxable income after adjustments, deductions, and exemptions. It is the *lower*, taxable income figure that determines how much tax an individual must pay.

3-3 Calculating and Filing Your Taxes

LG3 To calculate the amount of taxable income, we consider: (1) tax rates, (2) tax credits, (3) tax forms and schedules, and (4) the procedures for determining tax liability.

3-3a Tax Rates

To find the amount of *taxable income*, we subtract itemized deductions (or the standard deduction for non-itemizers) *and* personal exemptions from AGI. *Both itemizers and non-itemizers* use this procedure, which is a key calculation in determining your tax liability. It is *reported taxable income* that determines the amount of income subject to federal income taxes. Once you know the amount of your taxable income, you can refer to *tax rate tables* (or to the *tax rate schedules* if taxable income is greater than $100,000) to find the amount of taxes you owe.

Tax rates vary not only with the amount of reported taxable income but also with filing status. Thus, different tax rate schedules apply to each filing category; two schedules are shown in Exhibit 3.3. The vast majority of taxpayers fall into the first three brackets and are subject to tax rates of either 10 percent, 15 percent, or 25 percent.

To see how the tax rates in Exhibit 3.3 work, consider two single taxpayers: one has taxable income

© KAREN HERMANN/ISTOCKPHOTO

Exhibit 3.3 Sample Tax Rate Schedules

Tax rates levied on personal income vary with the amount of reported taxable income and the taxpayer's filing status.

2011
Tax Rate
Schedules

Schedule X—If your filing status is **Single**

If your taxable income is: Over—	But not over—	The tax is:	of the amount over—
$0	$8,500	------ 10%	$0
8,500	34,500	$850.00 + 15%	8,500
34,500	83,600	4,750.00 + 25%	34,500
83,600	174,400	17,025.00 + 28%	83,600
174.400	379,500	42,449.00+ 33%	174,400
379,150	------	110,016.50 + 35%	379,150

Schedule Y-1—If your filing status is **Married filing jointly** or **Qualifying widow(er)**

If your taxable income is: Over—	But not over—	The tax is:	of the amount over—
$0	$17,000	------ 10%	$0
17,000	69,000	$1,700.00 + 15%	17,000
69,000	139,350	9,500.00 + 25%	69,000
139,350	212,300	27,087.50 + 28%	139,350
212,300	379,150	47,513.50 + 33%	212,300
379,150	------	102,574.00 + 35%	379,150

Schedule Y-2—If your filing status is **Married filing separately**

If your taxable income is: Over—	But not over—	The tax is:	of the amount over—
$0	$8,500	------ 10%	$0
8,500	34,500	$850.00 + 15%	8,500
34,500	69,675	4,750.00 + 25%	34,500
69,675	106,150	13,543.75+ 28%	69,675
106,150	189.575	23,756.75 + 33%	106,150
189,575	------	51,287.00 + 35%	189,575

Schedule Z—If your filing status is **Head of household**

If your taxable income is: Over—	But not over—	The tax is:	of the amount over—
$0	$12,150	------ 10%	$0
12,150	46,250	$1,215.00 + 15%	12,150
46,250	119,400	6,300.00 + 25%	46,260
119,400	193,350	24,617.50 + 28%	119,400
193,350	379,150	45,323.50 + 33%	193,350
379,150	------	106,637.50 + 35%	379,150

Source: Internal Revenue Service.

of $12,500; the other, $35,600. Here's how we would calculate their respective tax liabilities:

- For taxable income of $12,500: $850 + [($12,500 − $8,500) × 0.15] = $850 + $600 = $1,450

- For taxable income of $35,600: $4,750 + [($35,600 − $34,500) × 0.25] = $4,750 + $275 = $5,025

The income of $12,500 is partially taxed at the 10 percent rate and partially taxed at the 15 percent rate. The first $8,500 of the $35,600 is taxed at 10 percent, the next $26,000 at 15 percent, and the remaining $1,100 at 25 percent. Keep in mind that taxpayers use the same procedures at this point whether they itemize or not. To show how the amount of tax liability will vary with the level of taxable income, Exhibit 3.4 lists the taxes due on a range of taxable incomes, from $1,500 to $400,000, for individual and joint returns.

Returning to our example involving the taxpayer with an income of $35,600, we see that this individual had an average tax rate of 14.1 percent ($5,025/$35,600), which is considerably less than the stated tax rate of 25 percent. Actually, the 25 percent represents the taxpayer's *marginal tax rate*—the rate at which the next dollar of taxable income is taxed. Notice in our calculations that the marginal 25 percent tax rate applies only to that portion of the single person's income that exceeds $34,500, or $1,100 in this example.

Some taxpayers are subject to the *alternative minimum tax (AMT)*, currently 26 percent of the first $175,000 and 28 percent of the excess. A taxpayer's tax

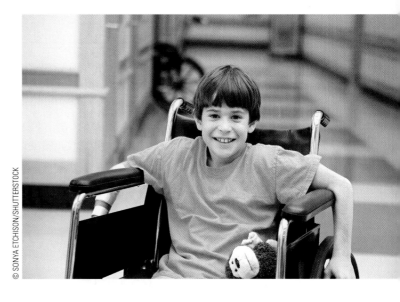

© SONYA ETCHISON/SHUTTERSTOCK

liability is the higher of the AMT or the regular tax. The AMT is designed to ensure that high-income taxpayers with many deductions and tax shelter investments that provide attractive tax write-offs are paying their fair share of taxes. The AMT includes in taxable income certain types of deductions otherwise allowed, such as state and local income and property taxes, miscellaneous itemized deductions, unreimbursed medical expenses, and depreciation. Therefore, taxpayers with moderate levels of taxable income, including those living in states with high tax rates and self-employed persons with depreciation deductions, may be subject to the AMT calculation and additional tax.

© KAREN HERMANN/ISTOCKPHOTO

Exhibit 3.4   Taxable Income and the Amount of Income Taxes Due (2011)

Given the progressive tax structure used in this country, it follows that the larger your income, the more you can expect to pay in taxes.

Taxable Income	Taxes Due (rounded)	
	Individual Returns	Joint Returns
$ 1,500	$ 150[a]	$ 150[a]
8,000	800[a]	800[a]
15,000	1,825[b]	1,500[a]
30,000	4,075[b]	3,650[b]
60,000	11,125[c]	8,150[b]
100,000	21,125[d]	17,250[c]
180,000	44,297[e]	38,470[d]
400,000	117,314[f]	109,872[f]

[a] Income is taxed at 10%.
[b] 15% tax rate now applies.
[c] 25% tax rate now applies.
[d] 28% tax rate now applies.
[e] 33% tax rate now applies.
[f] 35% tax rate now applies.

© Cengage Learning

3-3b Tax Credits

After determining the amount of taxes you owe, some taxpayers are allowed to take certain deductions, known as **tax credits**, directly from that amount. A tax credit is much more valuable than a deduction or an exemption because it directly reduces, dollar for dollar, the amount of *taxes due*, whereas a deduction or an exemption merely reduces the amount of *taxable income*. An often-used tax credit is for *child and dependent care expenses*. This credit is based on the amount spent for dependent care while a taxpayer (and spouse, if married) works or goes to school. An *adoption tax credit* of up to $12,360 is available for the qualifying costs of adopting a child under age 18. Other common tax credits include: credit for the elderly or the disabled, foreign tax credit, credit for prior year minimum tax, mortgage interest credit, and credit for a qualified electric vehicle. To receive any of these credits, the taxpayer must file a return along with a separate schedule in support of the tax credit claimed.

Go to Smart Sites

Need a tax form or instructions on how to fill it out? At the IRS Web site you can download tax forms, instructions, IRS publications, and regulations. Once there, you can also click on "More Online Tools" to access the IRS withholding calculator–you can use it to make sure you aren't having too much or too little withheld from your paycheck. ●

3-3c Tax Forms and Schedules

The IRS requires taxpayers to file their returns using specified tax forms. These forms and various instruction booklets on how to prepare them are available to taxpayers free of charge. Tax forms and instructions can be downloaded from **http://www.irs.gov**. Check out the Bonus Exhibits for a list of commonly used tax forms and schedules. (Visit CourseMate for PFIN 3. Log in at **www.cengagebrain.com**.)

Variations of Form 1040

All individuals use some variation of Form 1040 to file their tax returns. *Form 1040EZ* is a simple, one-page form. You qualify to use this form if you are single or married filing a joint return; under age 65 (both if filing jointly); not blind; do not claim any dependents; have taxable income of less than $100,000 from only wages, salaries, tips, or taxable scholarships or grants; have interest income of less than $1,500; and do not claim any adjustments to income, itemize deductions, or claim any tax credits. Worksheet 3.1 shows the Form 1040EZ filed in 2011 by Hiro Tanaka, a full-time graduate student at State University. His sources of income include a $12,500 scholarship, of which $4,900 was used for room and board; $7,600 earned from part-time and summer jobs; and $50 interest earned on a savings account deposit. Because scholarships used for tuition and fees are not

taxed, he should include as income only the portion used for room and board. He had a total of $495 withheld for federal income taxes during the year. Although Hiro would also complete a Salaries & Wages Report form, it is omitted for simplicity because it lists only the $4,900 of his scholarship that went toward his room and board, his part-time income of $7,600, and the details of his withholdings.

To use *Form 1040A*, a two-page form, your income must be less than $100,000 and be derived only from specified sources. Using this form, you may deduct certain IRA contributions and claim certain tax credits, but you cannot itemize your deductions. If your income is over $100,000 or you itemize deductions, you must use the standard *Form 1040* along with any applicable schedules.

Despite detailed instructions that accompany the tax forms, taxpayers still make a lot of mistakes when filling them out. Common errors include missing information and arithmetic errors. So check and recheck your forms *before submitting them to the IRS*. Tax software to assist with computations is available free of charge at **http://www.irs.gov**.

3-3d The 2011 Tax Return of James and Rose Sullivan

Let's now put all the pieces of the tax preparation puzzle together to see how James and Rose Sullivan calculate and file their income taxes. The Sullivans own their own home and are both 35 years old. Married for 11 years, they have three children—Michael (age 9), Keith (age 7), and Katie (age 3). James is a manager for an insurance company headquartered in

tax credits
Deductions from a taxpayer's tax liability that directly reduce his or her *taxes due* (rather than reducing *taxable income*).

Form 1040EZ is easy to use, and most of the instructions are printed on the form itself. Hiro Tanaka qualifies to use it because he is single, under age 65, not blind, and meets its income and deduction restrictions.

Department of the Treasury—Internal Revenue Service

Form 1040EZ

Income Tax Return for Single and Joint Filers With No Dependents (99)   **2011**

OMB No. 1545-0074

Your first name and initial	Last name	Your social security number
Hiro	Tanaka	1 2 3 4 5 6 7 8 9

If a joint return, spouse's first name and initial | Last name | Spouse's social security number

Home address (number and street). If you have a P.O. box, see instructions. | Apt. no.
1000 State University Drive | 201-B

▲ Make sure the SSN(s) above are correct.

City, town or post office, state, and ZIP code. If you have a foreign address, also complete spaces below (see instructions).
Anytown, Anystate 10001

Presidential Election Campaign
Check here if you, or your spouse if filing jointly, want $3 to go to this fund. Checking a box below will not change your tax or refund.   ☑ You   ☐ Spouse

Foreign country name | Foreign province/county | Foreign postal code

Income

Attach Form(s) W-2 here.

Enclose, but do not attach, any payment.

1	Wages, salaries, and tips. This should be shown in box 1 of your Form(s) W-2. Attach your Form(s) W-2.	1	12500
2	Taxable interest. If the total is over $1,500, you cannot use Form 1040EZ.	2	50
3	Unemployment compensation and Alaska Permanent Fund dividends (see instructions).	3	
4	Add lines 1, 2, and 3. This is your **adjusted gross income.**	4	12550
5	If someone can claim you (or your spouse if a joint return) as a dependent, check the applicable box(es) below and enter the amount from the worksheet on back. ☑ You ☐ Spouse If no one can claim you (or your spouse if a joint return), enter $9,500 if **single;** $19,000 if **married filing jointly.** See back for explanation.	5	9500
6	Subtract line 5 from line 4. If line 5 is larger than line 4, enter -0-. This is your **taxable income.** ▶	6	3050

Payments, Credits, and Tax

7	Federal income tax withheld from Form(s) W-2 and 1099.	7	495
8a	**Earned income credit (EIC)** (see instructions).	8a	
b	Nontaxable combat pay election. 8b		
9	Add lines 7 and 8a. These are your **total payments and credits.** ▶	9	495
10	**Tax.** Use the amount on **line 6 above** to find your tax in the tax table in the instructions. Then, enter the tax from the table on this line.	10	305

Refund

Have it directly deposited! See instructions and fill in 11b, 11c, and 11d or Form 8888.

11a	If line 9 is larger than line 10, subtract line 10 from line 9. This is your **refund.** If Form 8888 is attached, check here ▶ ☐	11a	190
▶ b	Routing number	▶ c Type: ☐ Checking ☐ Savings	
▶ d	Account number		

Amount You Owe

12	If line 10 is larger than line 9, subtract line 9 from line 10. This is the **amount you owe.** For details on how to pay, see instructions. ▶	12	

Third Party Designee

Do you want to allow another person to discuss this return with the IRS (see instructions)? ☐ **Yes.** Complete below.   ☐ **No**

Designee's name ▶ | Phone no. ▶ | Personal identification number (PIN) ▶

Sign Here

Joint return? See instructions.

Keep a copy for your records.

Under penalties of perjury, I declare that I have examined this return and, to the best of my knowledge and belief, it is true, correct, and accurately lists all amounts and sources of income I received during the tax year. Declaration of preparer (other than the taxpayer) is based on all information of which the preparer has any knowledge.

Your signature	Date	Your occupation	Daytime phone number
Hiro Tanaka	4/14/12	Student	(555) 555-1212

Spouse's signature. If a joint return, **both** must sign. | Date | Spouse's occupation

If the IRS sent you an Identity Protection PIN, enter it here (see inst.)

Paid Preparer Use Only

Print/Type preparer's name | Preparer's signature | Date | Check ☐ if self-employed | PTIN

Firm's name ▶ | Firm's EIN ▶
Firm's address ▶ | Phone no.

For Disclosure, Privacy Act, and Paperwork Reduction Act Notice, see instructions.   Cat. No. 11329W   Form **1040EZ** (2011)

© Cengage Learning

their hometown. Rose works part-time as a sales clerk in a retail store. During 2011, James's salary totaled $60,415, while Rose earned $9,750. James's employer withheld taxes of $6,260, and Rose's withheld $1,150. During the year, the Sullivans earned $800 interest on their joint savings account and realized $1,250 in capital gains on the sale of securities that they had owned for 11 months. In addition, James kept the books for his brother's car dealership, from which he netted $5,800 during the year. Because no taxes were withheld from any of their outside income, during the year they made estimated tax payments totaling $1,000. The Sullivans' records indicate that they had $14,713 of potential itemized deductions during the year. Finally, the Sullivans plan to contribute $4,000 to Rose's traditional IRA account. Beginning in 2011, the Sullivans plan to switch Rose's account to a Roth IRA (see Chapter 14 for more information about that topic).

Finding the Sullivans' Tax Liability: Form 1040

Looking at the Sullivans' 2011 tax return (Worksheet 3.2), we can get a feel for the basic calculations required in the preparation of a Form 1040. Although we don't include the supporting schedules here, we illustrate the basic calculations that they require. The Sullivans have detailed records of their income and expenses, which they use not only for tax purposes but as an important input to their budgeting process. Using this information, the Sullivans intend to prepare their 2011 tax return so that their total tax liability is as low as possible. Like most married couples, the Sullivans file a *joint return*.

GROSS INCOME. The Sullivans gross income in 2011 amounted to $78,015—the amount shown as "total income" on line 22 of their tax return. They have both active income and portfolio income, as follows:

ACTIVE INCOME

James's earnings	$60,415
Rose's earnings	9,750
James's business income (net)	5,800
Total active income	$75,965

PORTFOLIO INCOME

Interest from savings account	$ 800
Capital gains realized*	1,250
Total portfolio income	$ 2,050
Total income ($75,965 + $2,050)	$78,015

* Because this gain was realized on stock held for less than 12 months, the full amount is taxable as ordinary income.

They have no investment expenses to offset their portfolio income, so they'll be liable for taxes on the full amount of portfolio income. Although they have interest income, the Sullivans don't have to file Schedule B (for interest and dividend income) with the Form 1040, because the interest is less than $1,500 and they earned no dividends. (If they receive dividends on stock in the future, they will have to complete a Qualified Dividends and Capital Gains Tax Worksheet, provided in the Form 1040 instruction booklet. Qualified dividends are taxed at the lower capital gains rates.) In addition, James will have to file Schedule C, detailing the income earned and expenses incurred in his bookkeeping business, and Schedule D to report capital gains income.

ADJUSTMENTS TO GROSS INCOME. The Sullivans have only two adjustments to income: Rose's IRA contribution and 50 percent of the self-employment tax on James's net business income. Since Rose isn't covered by a retirement plan and since James's and her combined modified AGI is below $169,000 (this amount moves to $173,000 for 2012) they can deduct her entire $4,000 contribution (the maximum contribution to an IRA is $5,000 or, depending on age, $6,000 in 2011) to an IRA account even though James is already covered by a company-sponsored retirement program (see Chapter 14). Using 2011 rates, James's self-employment tax will be 15.3 percent of his $5,800 net business income, and he will be able to deduct one-half that amount—$443.70 [(0.153 × $5,800)/2]— on line 27.

ADJUSTED GROSS INCOME. After deducting the $443.70 self-employment tax and Rose's $4,000 IRA contribution from their gross income, the Sullivans are left with an AGI of $73,571.30, as reported on line 37.

ITEMIZED DEDUCTIONS OR STANDARD DEDUCTION? The Sullivans are filing a joint return, and neither is over age 65 or blind; so, according to the box on page 2 of Form 1040, they are entitled to a standard deduction of $11,600. However, they want to evaluate their itemized deductions before deciding which type of deduction to take. Of course they'll take the higher deduction because it will result in the lowest amount of taxable income and thus keep their tax liability to a minimum. Their preliminary paperwork resulted in the following deductions:

Medical and dental expenses	$ 1,223
State income and property taxes paid	2,560
Mortgage interest	7,893
Charitable contributions	475
Job and other expenses	2,522
Total	$14,673

Because they itemize deductions, the Sullivans use standard Form 1040 to file their tax return. When filed with the IRS, their return will include not only Form 1040 but also other schedules and forms detailing many of their expenses and deductions.

Form **1040**   Department of the Treasury—Internal Revenue Service   (99)

U.S. Individual Income Tax Return   2011   OMB No. 1545-0074   IRS Use Only—Do not write or staple in this space.

For the year Jan. 1–Dec. 31, 2011, or other tax year beginning _____ , 2011, ending _____ , 20 ____   See separate instructions.

Your first name and initial	Last name	Your social security number
James T.	Sullivan	1 2 3 4 5 6 7 8 9

If a joint return, spouse's first name and initial	Last name	Spouse's social security number
Rose D.	Sullivan	9 8 7 6 5 4 3 2 1

Home address (number and street). If you have a P.O. box, see instructions.   Apt. no.

1234 Success Circle

▲ Make sure the SSN(s) above and on line 6c are correct.

City, town or post office, state, and ZIP code. If you have a foreign address, also complete spaces below (see instructions).

Anytown, Anystate 10001

Presidential Election Campaign
Check here if you, or your spouse if filing jointly, want $3 to go to this fund. Checking a box below will not change your tax or refund.   ☑ You   ☐ Spouse

Foreign country name	Foreign province/county	Foreign postal code

Filing Status

Check only one box.

1 ☐ Single
2 ☑ Married filing jointly (even if only one had income)
3 ☐ Married filing separately. Enter spouse's SSN above and full name here. ▶
4 ☐ Head of household (with qualifying person). (See instructions.) If the qualifying person is a child but not your dependent, enter this child's name here. ▶
5 ☐ Qualifying widow(er) with dependent child

Exemptions

6a ☑ **Yourself.** If someone can claim you as a dependent, **do not** check box 6a . . . . .
b ☑ **Spouse** . . . .

c **Dependents:** (1) First name Last name	(2) Dependent's social security number	(3) Dependent's relationship to you	(4) ✓ if child under age 17 qualifying for child tax credit (see instructions)
Michael R. Sullivan	0 6 5 0 1 2 3 4 7	son	☑
Keith O. Sullivan	0 1 2 3 4 5 6 7 8	son	☑
Katie C. Sullivan	0 3 4 6 5 1 2 3 4	Daughter	☑

If more than four dependents, see instructions and check here ▶ ☐

d   Total number of exemptions claimed . . . .

Boxes checked on 6a and 6b   2
No. of children on 6c who:
• lived with you   3
• did not live with you due to divorce or separation (see instructions) ____
Dependents on 6c not entered above ____
Add numbers on lines above ▶   5

Income

Attach Form(s) W-2 here. Also attach Forms W-2G and 1099-R if tax was withheld.

If you did not get a W-2, see instructions.

Enclose, but do not attach, any payment. Also, please use Form 1040-V.

7	Wages, salaries, tips, etc. Attach Form(s) W-2	7	70,165
8a	**Taxable** interest. Attach Schedule B if required	8a	800
b	**Tax-exempt** interest. **Do not** include on line 8a . . .	8b		
9a	Ordinary dividends. Attach Schedule B if required	9a	
b	Qualified dividends	9b		
10	Taxable refunds, credits, or offsets of state and local income taxes . . .	10	
11	Alimony received	11	
12	Business income or (loss). Attach Schedule C or C-EZ	12	5,800
13	Capital gain or (loss). Attach Schedule D if required. If not required, check here ▶ ☐	13	1,250
14	Other gains or (losses). Attach Form 4797	14	
15a	IRA distributions .	15a	b Taxable amount . . .	15b	
16a	Pensions and annuities	16a	b Taxable amount . . .	16b	
17	Rental real estate, royalties, partnerships, S corporations, trusts, etc. Attach Schedule E	17	
18	Farm income or (loss). Attach Schedule F	18	
19	Unemployment compensation	19	
20a	Social security benefits	20a	b Taxable amount . . .	20b	
21	Other income. List type and amount _____	21	
22	Combine the amounts in the far right column for lines 7 through 21. This is your **total income** ▶	22	78,015

Adjusted Gross Income

23	Educator expenses	23	
24	Certain business expenses of reservists, performing artists, and fee-basis government officials. Attach Form 2106 or 2106-EZ	24	
25	Health savings account deduction. Attach Form 8889 .	25	
26	Moving expenses. Attach Form 3903	26	
27	Deductible part of self-employment tax. Attach Schedule SE .	27	443	70
28	Self-employed SEP, SIMPLE, and qualified plans . .	28	
29	Self-employed health insurance deduction	29	
30	Penalty on early withdrawal of savings	30	
31a	Alimony paid **b** Recipient's SSN ▶	31a	
32	IRA deduction	32	4000
33	Student loan interest deduction	33	
34	Tuition and fees. Attach Form 8917	34	
35	Domestic production activities deduction. Attach Form 8903	35	
36	Add lines 23 through 35	36	4,443	70
37	Subtract line 36 from line 22. This is your **adjusted gross income** . . . . . ▶	37	73,571	30

For Disclosure, Privacy Act, and Paperwork Reduction Act Notice, see separate instructions.   Cat. No. 11320B   Form **1040** (2011)

Form 1040 (2011)   Page **2**

Tax and Credits	38	Amount from line 37 (adjusted gross income)	38	73,571	30
	39a	Check { ☐ **You** were born before January 2, 1947, ☐ **Blind.** } **Total boxes** if: { ☐ **Spouse** was born before January 2, 1947, ☐ **Blind.** } **checked ▶ 39a**			
Standard Deduction for—	b	If your spouse itemizes on a separate return or you were a dual-status alien, check here ▶ **39b**☐			
• People who check any box on line 39a or 39b **or** who can be claimed as a dependent, see instructions.	40	**Itemized deductions** (from Schedule A) **or** your **standard deduction** (see left margin) . .	40	11,979	
	41	Subtract line 40 from line 38	41	61,592	30
	42	**Exemptions.** Multiply $3,700 by the number on line 6d.	42	18,500	
	43	**Taxable income.** Subtract line 42 from line 41. If line 42 is more than line 41, enter -0- . . .	43	43,092	73
	44	**Tax** (see instructions). Check if any from: **a** ☐ Form(s) 8814 **b** ☐ Form 4972 **c** ☐ 962 election	44	5,613	91
• All others: Single or Married filing separately, $5,800	45	**Alternative minimum tax** (see instructions). Attach Form 6251	45		
	46	Add lines 44 and 45 . . . . ▶	46		
	47	Foreign tax credit. Attach Form 1116 if required	47		
Married filing jointly or Qualifying widow(er), $11,600	48	Credit for child and dependent care expenses. Attach Form 2441	48		
	49	Education credits from Form 8863, line 23	49		
	50	Retirement savings contributions credit. Attach Form 8880	50		
	51	Child tax credit (see instructions)	51	3000	
Head of household, $8,500	52	Residential energy credits. Attach Form 5695	52		
	53	Other credits from Form: **a** ☐ 3800 **b** ☐ 8801 **c** ☐	53		
	54	Add lines 47 through 53. These are your **total credits**	54	3,000	
	55	Subtract line 54 from line 46. If line 54 is more than line 46, enter -0- . . . . . . ▶	55	2,613	91
Other Taxes	56	Self-employment tax. Attach Schedule SE	56	887	40
	57	Unreported social security and Medicare tax from Form: **a** ☐ 4137 **b** ☐ 8919 . .	57		
	58	Additional tax on IRAs, other qualified retirement plans, etc. Attach Form 5329 if required . .	58		
	59a	Household employment taxes from Schedule H	59a		
	b	First-time homebuyer credit repayment. Attach Form 5405 if required	59b		
	60	Other taxes. Enter code(s) from instructions _____	60		
	61	Add lines 55 through 60. This is your **total tax** . . . . ▶	61	3,501	31
Payments	62	Federal income tax withheld from Forms W-2 and 1099	62	7,410	
	63	2011 estimated tax payments and amount applied from 2010 return	63	1,000	
If you have a qualifying child, attach Schedule EIC.	64a	**Earned income credit (EIC)**	64a		
	b	Nontaxable combat pay election	**64b**		
	65	Additional child tax credit. Attach Form 8812	65		
	66	American opportunity credit from Form 8863, line 14 . .	66		
	67	First-time homebuyer credit from Form 5405, line 10 . . .	67		
	68	Amount paid with request for extension to file . . .	68		
	69	Excess social security and tier 1 RRTA tax withheld . . .	69		
	70	Credit for federal tax on fuels. Attach Form 4136 . . .	70		
	71	Credits from Form: **a** ☐ 2439 **b** ☐ 8839 **c** ☐ 8801 **d** ☐ 8885	71		
	72	Add lines 62, 63, 64a, and 65 through 71. These are your **total payments** . . . . . ▶	72	8,410	
Refund	73	If line 72 is more than line 61, subtract line 61 from line 72. This is the amount you **overpaid**	73	4,908	69
	74a	Amount of line 73 you want **refunded to you.** If Form 8888 is attached, check here . ▶ ☐	74a	4,908	69
Direct deposit? See instructions. ▶	b	Routing number [ ] ▶ c Type: ☐ Checking ☐ Savings			
	d	Account number [ ]			
	75	Amount of line 73 you want **applied to your 2012 estimated tax ▶**	75		
Amount You Owe	76	**Amount you owe.** Subtract line 72 from line 61. For details on how to pay, see instructions ▶	76		
	77	Estimated tax penalty (see instructions)	77		

Third Party Designee	Do you want to allow another person to discuss this return with the IRS (see instructions)? ☐ **Yes.** Complete below. ☐ **No**
	Designee's name ▶ _____ Phone no. ▶ _____ Personal identification number (PIN) ▶ _____

Sign Here	Under penalties of perjury, I declare that I have examined this return and accompanying schedules and statements, and to the best of my knowledge and belief, they are true, correct, and complete. Declaration of preparer (other than taxpayer) is based on all information of which preparer has any knowledge.

	Your signature	Date	Your occupation	Daytime phone number
Joint return? See instructions. Keep a copy for your records.	James T. Sullivan	4/10/12	Manager	(555) 555-1234
	Spouse's signature. If a joint return, **both** must sign.	Date	Spouse's occupation	If the IRS sent you an Identity Protection PIN, enter it here (see inst.)
	Rose D. Sullivan.	4/10/12	Sales Clerk	

Paid Preparer Use Only	Print/Type preparer's name	Preparer's signature	Date	Check ☐ if self-employed	PTIN
	Firm's name ▶			Firm's EIN ▶	
	Firm's address ▶			Phone no.	

Form **1040** (2011)

© Cengage Learning

© MORGAN LANE PHOTOGRAPHY/SHUTTERSTOCK.COM

The taxes, mortgage interest, and charitable contributions are deductible in full and so, at the minimum, the Sullivans will have itemized deductions amounting to $10,928 ($2,560 + $7,893 + $475). However, to be deductible, the medical and dental expenses and the job and other expenses must exceed stipulated minimum levels of AGI—only that portion exceeding the specified minimum levels of AGI can be included as part of their itemized deductions. For medical and dental expenses the minimum is 7.5 percent of AGI, and for job and other expenses it is 2 percent of AGI. Because 7.5 percent of the Sullivans' AGI is $5,517.85 (0.075 × $73,571.30), they fall short of the minimum and cannot deduct any medical and dental expenses. In contrast, because 2 percent of their AGI is $1,471.43 (0.02 × $73,571.30), they can deduct any job and other expenses exceeding that amount, or $2,522 − $1,471.43 = $1,050.57. Adding that amount to their other allowable deductions ($10,928) results in total itemized deductions of $11,979. This amount exceeds the standard deduction of $11,600, so the Sullivans should strongly consider itemizing their deductions. They would enter the details of these deductions on Schedule A and attach it to their Form 1040. (The total amount of the Milroys' itemized deductions is listed on line 40 of Form 1040.)

The Sullivans are entitled to claim two exemptions for themselves, and another three for their three dependent children, for a total of five (see line 6d). Because each exemption is worth $3,700, they receive a total personal exemption of $18,500 (5 × $3,700); this amount is listed on line 42 of their Form 1040.

THE SULLIVANS' TAXABLE INCOME AND TAX LIABILITY. Taxable income is found by subtracting itemized deductions and personal exemptions from AGI. In the Sullivans' case, (rounded) taxable income amounts to $73,571.30 − $11,978.57 − $18,500 = $43,092.73, as shown on line 43. Given this information, the Sullivans can now refer to the tax rate schedule (like the one in Exhibit 3.3) to find their appropriate tax rate and, ultimately, the amount of taxes they'll

have to pay. (Because the Sullivans' taxable income is less than $100,000, they could use the *tax tables* [not shown in this chapter] to find their tax. For clarity and convenience, we use the schedules here.) As we can see, the Sullivans' $43,092 in taxable income places them in the 15 percent marginal tax bracket. Using the schedule in Exhibit 3.3, they calculate their tax as follows: $1,700 + [0.15 × ($43,092.73 − $17,000)] = $5,613.90. They enter this amount on line 44.

The Sullivans also qualify for the child tax credit: $1,000 for each child under age 17. They enter $3,000 on lines 51 and 54 and subtract that amount from the tax on line 46, entering $2,613.91 on line 55. In addition, the Sullivans owe self-employment (Social Security) tax on James's $5,800 net business income. This will increase their tax liability by $887 (0.153 × $5,800) and would be reported on Schedule SE and entered on line 56 of Form 1040. (Recall that the Sullivans deducted 50 percent of this amount, or $443.70, on line 27 as an adjustment to income.) The Sullivans enter their total tax liability on line 61: $3,501.31 ($2,613.91 + $887.40).

GUNNAR PIPPEL/SHUTTERSTOCK.COM

Preparing for Tax Time

Planning for tax time can ease the burden substantially. The following tips will help you get organized:

- **Collect expense receipts, bank statements, and income documents.** This is the most time-consuming part of preparing for tax time. Rely as much as possible on online sources for simplicity. Classify everything as either income or a tax-deductible expense. And make sure to look over retirement, mortgage, and property tax statements. Ideally, it's best to use a system all year for keeping track of tax-related information. Spreadsheets, a Web-based program like Mint.com, or financial software like Quicken are helpful tools.

- **Decide whether you want to do your taxes yourself or get help.** If you don't want to go it completely alone, consider tax preparation software like TurboTax, H&R Block, or TaxACT. If you want to delegate tax preparation to someone else, make sure that that person is qualified to take on this big responsibility. A good tax preparer can save you a lot of money. Consider certified public accountants (CPAs), tax attorneys, and enrolled agents (EAs). Interviewing a prospective tax preparer is a good idea, and the recommendation of a friend, family member, or a colleague at work is worth a lot, too. Asking around is a good start; asking lots of straightforward questions leads to a good finish.

DO THEY GET A TAX REFUND? The total amount of taxes withheld is $7,410 ($6,260 from James's salary and $1,150 from Rose's wages, combined on line 61); they also made estimated tax payments of $1,000 (shown on line 62) for a subtotal of $8,410. This brings the total payments shown on line 72 to $8,410, which exceeds their tax liability. As a result, they are entitled to a refund of $4,908.69: the $9,210 withholding less their $3,501.31 tax liability. (About 65 percent of all taxpayers receive refunds each year.) Instead of paying the IRS, they'll be getting money back. (Generally, it takes 1 to 2 months after a tax return has been filed for a refund check to be mailed.)

All the Sullivans have to do now is sign and date their completed Form 1040 and send it, along with any supporting forms and schedules, to the nearest IRS district office on or before April 17, 2012.

One reason for the Sullivans' large refund was the child tax credit. With such a sizable refund, the Sullivans may want to stop making estimated tax payments because their combined withholding more than covers the amount of taxes they owe. Another option is to change their withholding to reduce the amount withheld.

Note that if total tax payments had been less than the Sullivans' tax liability, they would have owed the IRS money—the amount owed is found by subtracting total tax payments made from the tax liability. If they owed money, they would include a check in the amount due with Form 1040 when filing their tax return.

3-4 Other Filing Considerations

LG4, LG5 Other considerations related to tax filing include the need to pay estimated taxes, file for extensions, or amend the return; the possibility of a tax audit; and whether to use a tax preparation service or computer software to assist you in preparing your return.

3-4a Estimates, Extensions, and Amendments

Like James Sullivan, who provided accounting services to his brother's business, you may have income that's not subject to withholding. You may need to file a declaration of estimated taxes with your return and to pay quarterly taxes. Or perhaps you are unable to meet the normal April 15 filing deadline or need to correct a previously filed return. Let's look at the procedures for handling these situations.

Estimated Taxes

Because federal withholding taxes are regularly taken only from employment income, such as that paid in the form of wages or salaries, the IRS requires certain people to pay **estimated taxes** on income earned from other sources. Estimated tax payments are most commonly required of investors, consultants, lawyers, business owners, and various other professionals who are likely to receive income that is not subject to withholding.

The declaration of estimated taxes (Form 1040-ES) is normally filed with the tax return. Estimated taxes must be paid in four installments, which are usually on April 15, June 15, and September 15 of the current year, and January 15 of the following year. Failure to estimate and pay these taxes in accordance with IRS guidelines can result in a penalty levied by the IRS.

Go to Smart Sites

Looking for a tax preparer who is also an authorized e-file provider in your area? Many tax professionals are also authorized to file your return electronically—the IRS has a authorized e-file provider locator on its Web site. ●

April 15: Usual Filing Deadline

As we've seen from the Sullivan family example, at the end of each tax year, those taxpayers required to file a return must determine the amount of their *tax liability*—the amount of taxes they owe due to the past year's activities. The tax year corresponds to the calendar year and covers the period January 1 through December 31. Taxpayers may file their returns any time after the end of the tax year and *must* file no later than April 15 of the year immediately following the tax year (or by the first business day after that date if it falls on a weekend or federal holiday). If you have a computer, an Internet connection, and tax preparation software, you can probably use the IRS's *e-file* and *e-pay* to file your return and pay your taxes electronically either by using a credit card or by authorizing an electronic withdrawal from your checking or

filing extension An extension of time beyond the usual April 15 deadline during which taxpayers, with the approval of the IRS, can file their returns without incurring penalties.

amended return A tax return filed to adjust for information received after the filing date of the taxpayer's original return or to correct errors.

tax audit An examination by the IRS to validate the accuracy of a given tax return.

savings account. You can use an "Authorized *e-file* Provider," who may charge a fee to file for you, or do it yourself using commercial tax preparation software.

Depending on whether the total of taxes withheld and any estimated tax payments is greater or less than the computed tax liability, the taxpayer either receives a refund or must pay additional taxes. Taxpayers can pay their taxes using a credit card; however, because the IRS cannot pay credit card companies an issuing fee, taxpayers must call a special provider and pay a service charge to arrange for the payment.

Filing Extensions and Amended Returns

It's possible to receive an extension of time for filing your federal tax return. You can apply for an automatic six-month **filing extension**, which makes the due date October 15, simply by submitting Form 4868. In filing for an extension, however, the taxpayer must estimate the taxes due and remit that amount with the application. The extension does *not* give taxpayers more time to pay their taxes.

After filing a return, you may discover that you overlooked some income or a major deduction or made a mistake, so that you paid too little or too much in taxes. You can easily correct this by filing an **amended return** (Form 1040X) showing the corrected amount of income or deductions and the amount of taxes you should have paid, along with the amount of any tax refund or additional taxes owed. You generally have three years from the date you file your original return or two years from the date you paid the taxes, whichever is later, to file an amended return.

3-4b Audited Returns

Because taxpayers themselves provide the key information and fill out the necessary tax forms, the IRS has no proof that taxes have been correctly calculated. In addition to returns that stand out in some way and warrant further investigation, the IRS also randomly selects some returns for a **tax audit**—an examination to validate the return's accuracy. The odds of being audited are actually quite low; the IRS audits about 1 percent of returns. Despite the traditionally scary aura that surrounds the audit concept, the outcome of an audit is not always additional tax owed to the IRS. In fact, about 5 percent of all audits result in a refund to the taxpayer, and in 15 percent of all audits, the IRS finds that returns are correctly prepared.

Financial Planning Tips: Watch out for Tax Audit Red Flags

While it's true that the IRS typically only audits about 1 percent of tax returns, there are clearly some practices that increase your chance of being audited. It's wise to be aware of the following possible triggers:

- **High income.** The more income you make, the more likely you are to experience an audit. For example, if you make more than $200,000, you chance is about 4 percent, and if you make $1 million or more, your chance rises to about 12 percent. (That doesn't necessarily mean you shouldn't try to make as much money as you can—just be aware of this risk. Note that if you file your taxes honestly and keep good records, an audit isn't really such a terrible event.)
- **Unreported taxable income.** If your 1099s and W-2s add up to more than the income reported on your tax return, expect a bill from the IRS—and a possible audit.
- **Higher-than-average deductions.** If your deductions are large relative to your income, the IRS can flag your return for a potential audit. Make sure that you know the IRS regulations for donations and keep all supporting documents and receipts.
- **Home office deductions.** A home office is supposed to be used exclusively for business. The IRS has found

that this requirement is frequently not met, and the deduction is consequently denied. Thus, this is a red flag for an audit. If you take this deduction, be ready to prove it.
- **Business meals, travel, and entertainment.** IRS experience shows that the self-employed are responsible for most of the underreporting of income and overstating of deductions. Large deductions for meals, travel, and entertainment are an audit flag. Make sure to keep good records if you plan to take these kinds of deductions.
- **Business use of a vehicle.** Claiming 100 percent business use of a car is a red flag to the IRS because it's rare for an individual to really use a car exclusively for business. Make sure that you keep detailed mileage logs.
- **Unreported foreign bank account.** You are required to disclose offshore accounts. If the IRS finds an unreported account, it's an audit flag.

Source: Adapted from Joy Taylor, "IRS Audit Red Flags: The Dirty Dozen," http://www.kiplinger.com/features/archives/12-audit-red-flags-the-irs-looks-for.html, accessed June 2012.

MKABAKOV/SHUTTERSTOCK.COM

Typically, audits question (1) whether all income received has been properly reported and (2) whether the deductions claimed are legitimate and for the correct amount. The IRS can take as many as three years—and in some cases, six years—from the date of filing to audit your return, so you should retain records and receipts used in preparing returns for about seven years. Severe financial penalties, even prison sentences, can result from violating tax laws.

In sum, you should take advantage of all legitimate deductions to minimize your tax liability, but you must also be sure to properly report all items of income and expense as required by the Internal Revenue Code.

3-4c Tax Preparation Services: Getting Help on Your Returns

Many people with simple tax situations prepare their own tax returns. Some taxpayers with quite complicated financial affairs may also invest their time in preparing their own returns. The IRS offers many informational publications with step-by-step instructions to help you prepare your tax return. You can order them directly from the IRS by mail, download them from the IRS Web site (http://www.irs.gov), or order them by calling the IRS toll-free number (800-829-3676, or special local numbers in some areas). An excellent (and free) comprehensive tax preparation reference book is IRS *Publication 17, Your Federal Income Tax*. Other IRS information services are *TeleTax*, which provides recorded phone messages on selected tax topics via a toll-free number (800-829-4477), and *FaxBack*, which will fax many forms and instructions to you when you call 703-368-9694.

Help from the IRS

The IRS, in addition to issuing various publications for use in preparing tax returns, also provides direct assistance to taxpayers. The IRS will compute taxes for those whose taxable income is less than $100,000 and who do not itemize deductions. Persons who use this IRS service must fill in certain data, sign and date the return, and send it to the IRS on or before April 15 of the year immediately following the tax year. The IRS attempts to calculate taxes that result in the "smallest" tax bite. It then sends taxpayers a refund (if their withholding exceeds their tax liability) or a bill (if their tax liability is greater than the amount of withholding). People who either fail to qualify for or do not want to use this total tax preparation service can still obtain IRS assistance in preparing their returns from a toll-free service. Consult your telephone directory for the toll-free number of the IRS office closest to you.

Private Tax Preparers

More than half of all taxpayers prefer to use professional *tax preparation services* to improve accuracy and minimize their tax liability. The fees charged by

professional tax preparers can range from at least $100 for simple returns to $1,000 or more for complicated returns. You can select from the following types of tax preparation services.

- **National and local tax services**: These include national services such as H&R Block and independent local firms. These services are best for taxpayers with relatively common types of income and expenditures.
- **Certified public accountants (CPAs)**: Tax professionals who prepare returns and can advise taxpayers on planning.
- **Enrolled agents (EAs)**: Federally licensed individual tax practitioners who have passed a difficult, two-day, IRS-administered exam. They are fully qualified to handle tax preparation at various levels of complexity.
- **Tax attorneys**: Lawyers who specialize in tax planning.

Always check your own completed tax returns carefully before signing them. Remember that *taxpayers themselves must accept primary responsibility for the accuracy of their returns*. The IRS requires professional tax preparers to sign each return as the preparer, enter their own Social Security number and address, and give the taxpayer a copy of the return being filed. Tax preparers with the necessary hardware and software can electronically file their clients' tax returns so that eligible taxpayers can receive refunds more quickly.

There's no guarantee that your professional tax preparer will correctly determine your tax liability. Even the best preparers may not have all the answers at their fingertips. In a recent *Money* magazine annual tax return test, none of the 45 experienced tax preparers who were contacted prepared the tax return for a fictional family correctly; and only 24 percent of them calculated a tax liability that was within $1,000 of the correct amount. To reduce the chance of error, you should become familiar with the basic tax principles and regulations, check all documents (such as *W-2s* and *1099s*) for accuracy, maintain good communication with your tax preparer, and request an explanation of any entries on your tax return that you don't understand.

3-4d Computer-based Tax Returns

Many people use their personal computers to help with tax planning and preparing tax returns. Several good tax software packages will save hours when you're filling out the forms and schedules involved in filing tax returns. The programs often identify tax-saving opportunities you might otherwise miss. These computer programs aren't for everyone, however. Simple returns, like the 1040EZ, don't require them.

And for complex returns, there's no substitute for the skill and expertise of a tax accountant or attorney. Tax preparation software will be most helpful for taxpayers who itemize deductions but don't need tax advice.

There are two general kinds of software: tax planning and tax preparation. Planning programs such as Quicken let you experiment with different strategies to see their effects on the amount of taxes you must pay. The other category of tax software focuses on helping you complete and file your tax return. These programs take much of the tedium out of tax preparation, reducing the time you spend from days to hours. If you file the long Form 1040 and some supporting forms, invest in the stock market, own real estate, or have foreign income or a home-based business, you'll probably benefit from using tax preparation programs.

The two major software players are Intuit's TurboTax and Block H&R Block's TaxCut, both available for either Windows or Macintosh. TurboTax also has a Web-based version that lets you work on your returns from any computer. Both major companies also offer an add-on program that accurately assigns fair market value to the household items most commonly donated to charity. Both programs feature a clean interface and guide you through the steps in preparing your return by asking you the questions that apply to your situation. In addition to the primary tax-form preparation section, they include extensive resources and links to additional Web references, video clips to make tricky concepts easier to understand, tax planning questionnaires, deduction finders, and more. They may warn you if a number you've typed looks incorrect. State tax return packages cost more. Both TurboTax and TaxCut guarantee their calculations and will pay any penalties you incur that are due to program errors. All major software providers have free online versions for preparing federal taxes for people who meet specific requirements which vary by provider. See http://apps.irs.gov/app/freeFile/jsp/index.jsp for a listing of providers of free federal software with their individual restrictions. More of the specifics of TurboTax are covered in the Cool Apps feature—visit CourseMate for PFIN 3 at **www.cengagebrain.com**.

The IRS recently introduced "fill-in forms," which allow you to enter information while the form is displayed on your computer by Adobe Acrobat Reader (free software readily available on the Web). After entering the requested information, you can print out the completed form. Fill-in forms give you a cleaner, crisper printout for your records and for filing with the IRS. Unlike tax preparation software, these fill-in forms have no computational capabilities, so you must do all your calculations before starting. In addition, you should be ready to enter all the data at once, because Acrobat Reader doesn't save your completed forms. These forms are labeled "Fill-in forms" at the IRS Web site.

3-5 Effective Tax Planning

LG6 *Tax planning* is a key ingredient of your overall personal financial planning. The overriding objective of effective tax planning is to maximize total after-tax income by reducing, shifting, and deferring taxes to as low a level as legally possible. By all means, don't confuse tax avoidance with tax evasion, which includes such illegal activities as omitting income or overstating deductions. **Tax evasion**, in effect, involves a failure to accurately report income or deductions and, in extreme cases, a failure to pay taxes altogether. Persons found guilty of tax evasion are subject to severe financial penalties and even prison terms. **Tax avoidance**, in contrast, focuses on reducing taxes in ways that are legal and compatible with the intent of Congress.

> " **The idea behind deferring taxes is to reduce or eliminate your taxes today by postponing them to some time in the future when you may be in a lower tax bracket.** "

3-5a Fundamental Objectives of Tax Planning

Tax planning basically involves the use of various investment vehicles, retirement programs, and estate distribution procedures to (1) reduce, (2) shift, and (3) defer taxes. You can *reduce* taxes, for instance, by using techniques that create tax deductions or credits or that receive preferential tax treatment—such as investments that produce depreciation (such as real estate) or generate tax-free income (such as municipal bonds). You can *shift* taxes by using gifts or trusts to transfer some of your income to other family members who are in lower tax brackets and to whom you intend to provide some level of support anyway, such as a retired, elderly parent.

The idea behind *deferring* taxes is to reduce or eliminate your taxes today by postponing them to some

time in the future when you may be in a lower tax bracket. Perhaps more important, *deferring taxes gives you use of the money that would otherwise go to taxes*—thereby allowing you to invest it to make even more money. Deferring taxes is usually done through various types of retirement plans, such as IRAs, or by investing in certain types of annuities, variable life insurance policies, or even Series EE bonds (U.S. savings bonds).

The fundamentals of tax planning include making sure that you take all the deductions to which you're entitled and also take full advantage of the various tax provisions that will minimize your tax liability. Thus, comprehensive tax planning is an ongoing activity with both an immediate and a long-term perspective. Tax planning is closely interrelated with many financial planning activities, including investment, retirement, and estate planning.

3-5b Some Popular Tax Strategies

Many tax strategies are fairly simple and straightforward and can be used by the average middle-income taxpayer. You certainly don't have to be in the top income bracket to enjoy the benefits of many tax-saving ideas and procedures. For example, the interest income on Series EE bonds is free from state income

tax evasion The illegal act of failing to accurately report income or deductions and, in extreme cases, failing to pay taxes altogether.

tax avoidance The act of reducing taxes in ways that are legal and compatible with the intent of Congress.

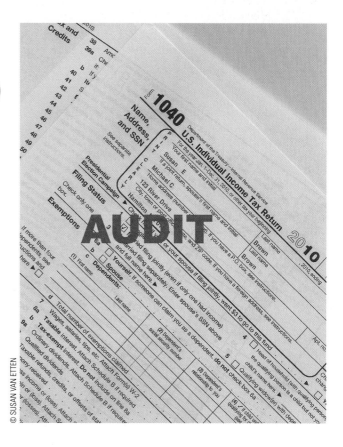

© SUSAN VAN ETTEN

tax, and the holder can elect to delay payment of federal taxes until (1) the year the bonds are redeemed for cash or (2) the year in which they finally mature, whichever occurs first. This feature makes Series EE bonds an excellent vehicle for earning tax-deferred income.

There are other strategies that can cut your tax bill. Accelerating or bunching deductions into a single year may permit itemizing deductions. Shifting income from one year to another is one way to cut your tax liability. If you expect to be in the same or a higher income tax bracket this year than you will be next year, defer income until next year and shift expenses to this year so you can accelerate your deductions and reduce taxes this year.

Maximizing Deductions

Review a comprehensive list of possible deductions for ideas, because even small deductions can add up to big tax savings. Accelerate or bunch deductions into one tax year if this allows you to itemize rather than take the standard deduction. For example, make your fourth-quarter estimated state tax payment before December 31 rather than on January 15 to deduct it in the current taxable year. Group miscellaneous expenses—and schedule unreimbursed elective medical procedures—to fall into one tax year so that they exceed the required "floor" for deductions (2 percent of AGI for miscellaneous expenses; 7.5 percent of AGI for medical expenses). Increase discretionary deductions such as charitable contributions.

Income Shifting

One way of reducing income taxes is to use a technique known as **income shifting**. Here the taxpayer shifts a portion of his or her income, and thus taxes, to relatives in lower tax brackets. This can be done by creating trusts or custodial accounts or by making outright gifts of income-producing property to family members. For instance, parents with $125,000 of taxable income (28 percent marginal tax rate) and $18,000 in corporate bonds paying $2,000 in annual interest might give the bonds to their 15-year-old child—with the understanding that such income is to be used ultimately for the child's college education.

The $2,000 would then belong to the child, who would probably be assumed to be able to pay $105 (0.10 × [$2,000 − $950 minimum standard deduction for a dependent]) in taxes on this income while the parents' taxable income would be reduced by $2,000, reducing their taxes by $560 (0.28 × $2,000).

Unfortunately, this strategy is not as simple as it might seem. A number of restrictions surround the strategy for children under 19, so it's possible to employ such techniques with older children (and presumably with other older relatives, such as elderly parents). Parents also need to recognize that shifting assets into a child's name to save taxes could affect the amount of college financial aid for which the child qualifies. Additional tax implications of gifts to dependents are discussed in Chapter 15.

Tax-Free and Tax-Deferred Income

Some investments provide tax-free income; in most cases, however, the tax on the income is only deferred (or delayed) to a later day. Although there aren't many forms of tax-free investments left today, probably the best example would be the *interest* income earned on *municipal bonds*. Such income is free from federal income tax and possibly state income taxes. (Tax-free municipal bonds are discussed in Chapter 12.) Earnings on money put into a Roth IRA are also tax-free. Income that is **tax deferred**, in contrast, only delays the payment of taxes to a future date. Yet until that time arrives, tax-deferred investment vehicles allow you to *accumulate tax-free earnings*. This results in much higher savings than would occur in a taxed account. A good example of tax-deferred income would be income earned in a *traditional IRA*. Chapter 14 provides a detailed discussion of this and other similar arrangements.

Most any wage earner can open an IRA and contribute up to $5,000 (or possibly $6,000, depending on an age qualification) each year to the account (in 2011). *All the income you earn in your IRA accumulates tax free.* This is a *tax-deferred* investment and so you'll eventually have to pay taxes on these earnings, but not until you start drawing down your account. In addition to IRAs, tax-deferred income can also be obtained from other types of pension and retirement plans and annuities. Chapter 14 provides more information on these financial products and strategies.

Planning Over a Lifetime: Tax Preparation and Planning

Here are some key considerations for life insurance use in each stage of the life cycle.

Pre-family Independence: 20s	Family Formation/Career Development: 30–45	Pre-Retirement: 45–65	Retirement: 65 and Beyond
✓ Manage your withholding amount so that it is about equal to your tax bill. Avoid large amounts owed or refunded.	✓ When you marry and/or have family changes, revise your withholding amount accordingly.	✓ As your income grows, consider tax-exempt investments like municipal bonds.	✓ Estimate Social Security benefits and plan when you will start receiving payments.
✓ Maintain a careful record of income and tax-deductible expenses.	✓ Acquire tax shelters like a mortgage, which has tax-deductible interest expenses.	✓ Consider increasing your average contributions to tax-sheltered retirement plans.	✓ Plan orderly withdrawals from tax-sheltered retirement accounts and associated tax bill.
✓ Consider using tax preparation software.	✓ Make regular contributions to your employer's tax-sheltered retirement plan and consider IRAs.	✓ Consider "catch up" larger retirement plan contributions.	✓ Consider the use of life insurance to manage potential taxes on estate. This is covered in more detail in Chapter 15.

FINANCIAL PLANNING EXERCISES

LG2, 3

1. Mary Watson is 24 years old and single, lives in an apartment, and has no dependents. Last year she earned $45,000 as a sales assistant for Focused Business Analytics: $3,910 of her wages was withheld for federal income taxes. In addition, she had interest income of $142. Estimate her taxable income, tax liability, and tax refund or tax owed.

LG2

2. Debra Ferguson received the items and amounts of income shown in the chart to the right during 2011. Help her calculate (a) her gross income and (b) that portion (dollar amount) of her income that is tax exempt.

Salary	$33,500
Dividends	800
Gift from mother	500
Child support from ex-husband	3,600
Interest on savings account	250
Rent	900
Loan from bank	2,000
Interest on state government bonds	300

LG2

3. If Amy Phillips is single and in the 28 percent tax bracket, calculate the tax associated with each of the following transactions. (Use the IRS regulations for capital gains in effect in 2011.) Treat each of the following cases as independent of the others.
   a. She sold stock for $1,200 that she purchased for $1,000 5 months earlier.
   b. She sold bonds for $4,000 that she purchased for $3,000 3 years earlier.
   c. She sold stock for $1,000 that she purchased for $1,500 15 months earlier.

LG3

4. *Use Worksheets 3.1 and 3.2.* Qiang Gao graduated from college in 2011 and began work as a systems analyst in July of that year. He is preparing to file his income tax return for 2011 and has collected the financial information shown in the table to the right for that calendar year.

Tuition, scholarships, and grants	$ 5,750
Scholarship, room, and board	1,850
Salary	30,250
Interest income	185
Deductible expenses, total	3,000
Income taxes withheld	2,600

   a. Prepare Qiang's 2011 tax return, using a $5,700 standard deduction, a personal exemption of $3,650, and the tax rates given in Exhibit 3.3. Which tax form should Qiang use, and why?
   b. Prepare Qiang's 2011 tax return using the data in part a along with the following information:

IRA contribution	$5,000
Cash dividends received	150

   Which tax form should he use in this case? Why?

LG3

5. Demonstrate the differences resulting from a $1,000 tax credit versus a $1,000 tax deduction for a single taxpayer in the 25 percent tax bracket with $40,000 of pre-tax income.

LG4

6. Steve and Beth Compton have been notified that they are being audited. What should they do to prepare for the audit?

PFIN Student Study Tools—Visit CourseMate for PFIN 3. Log in at **www.cengagebrain.com**. Check out the bonus exercises and exhibits, interactive worksheets, Smart Sites, Critical Thinking Cases, Money Online, Kiplinger videos, quizzing, and more.

Cool Apps—Look for this new feature on CourseMate for PFIN 3. Cool Apps navigates the growing world of apps that are available for personal financial planning and tracking.

MANAGING BASIC ASSETS

NEW PLAN

Memo No.
Date

4

MANAGING YOUR CASH AND SAVINGS

LEARNING GOALS

LG1 Understand the role of cash management in the personal financial planning process.

LG2 Describe today's financial services marketplace, both depository and nondepository financial institutions.

LG3 Select the checking, savings, electronic banking, and other bank services that meet your needs.

LG4 Open and use a checking account.

LG5 Calculate the interest earned on your money using compound interest and future value techniques.

LG6 Develop a cash management strategy that incorporates a variety of savings plans.

How Will This Affect Me? Finding the best mix of alternative cash management accounts and assets requires careful cost/benefit analysis in light of personal objectives and constraints.

This chapter presents a variety of different alternatives and focuses on key characteristics that include liquidity, minimum balances, interest rate returns and costs, and safety. Cash management alternatives examined include checking and savings accounts as well as money market deposit accounts, certificates of deposit, money market mutual funds, U.S. Treasury bills, U.S. and U.S. Series I bonds. This chapter will prepare you to design an effective cash management strategy, which is an integral part of a comprehensive financial plan.

4-1 The Role of Cash Management in Personal Financial Planning

LG1 Establishing good financial habits involves managing cash as well as other types of assets. In this chapter, we focus our attention on **cash management**—the routine, day-to-day administration of cash and near-cash resources, also known as *liquid assets*. These assets are considered liquid because they're either held in cash or can be readily converted into cash with little or no loss in value.

In addition to cash, there are several other kinds of liquid assets, including checking accounts, savings accounts, money market deposit accounts, money market mutual funds, and other short-term investment vehicles. Exhibit 4.1 briefly describes some popular types of liquid assets and the representative rates of return they earned in the spring of 2012. The rates reflect the Federal Reserve's (the Fed's) policy goal of keeping rates low to help stimulate the economy during the fragile period following the global financial crisis of 2008–2009. As a rule, near-term needs are met using cash on hand, and unplanned or future needs are met using some type of savings or short-term investment vehicle.

In personal financial planning, efficient cash management ensures adequate funds for both household use and an effective savings program. Write checks only at certain times of the week or month and, just as important, avoid carrying your checkbook (or debit card) when you might be tempted to spend money for unplanned purchases. If you're going shopping, set a maximum spending limit beforehand—an amount consistent with your cash budget. This system not only helps you avoid frivolous, impulsive expenditures but also documents how and where you spend your money.

> " **A good way to keep your spending in line is to make all household transactions using a tightly controlled checking account.** "

Another aspect of cash management is establishing an ongoing savings program, which is an important part of personal financial planning. Savings are not only a cushion against financial emergencies but also a way to accumulate funds to meet future financial goals. You may want to put money aside so that you can go back to school in a few years to earn a graduate degree, or buy a new home, or take a vacation. Savings will help you meet these specific financial objectives.

4-1a The Problem with Low Interest Rates

Just how low did interest rates fall in the wake of the financial crisis under the Fed's policies? Consider how some key interest rates in the spring of 2012 compare with their historical averages from April 1980 to April 2012. The average interest rates on 5- and 10-year Treasury bonds over this time period were 6.46 percent and 6.88 percent, respectively. In April 2012, these rates had fallen to only 0.89 percent and 2.05 percent! And a prudent saver looking for a short-term return on a 3-month negotiable CD could only get 0.29 percent, while the historical average was 4.70 percent!

These massive drops in interest rates have important implications for your personal finances. For a sense of the significance of the drop in interest rates, consider the effect of investing $25,000 for 5 years at the low rate of

cash management
The routine, day-to-day administration of cash and near-cash resources, also known as *liquid assets*, by an individual or family.

After you read the chapter, explore the STUDY TOOLS listed on page 96.

© DARIUSZ URBANCZYK/SHUTTERSTOCK.COM

Exhibit 4.1 — Representative Rates of Return

Type	Spring 2012	Description
Cash	0%	Pocket money; the coin and currency in one's possession.
Checking account	0%–0.47%	A substitute for cash. Offered by commercial banks and other financial institutions such as savings and loans and credit unions.
Savings account/ Money market deposit	0.05%–0.90%	Savings accounts are available at any time, but funds cannot be withdrawn by check. Money market deposit accounts (MMDAs) require a fairly large (typically $1,000 or more) minimum deposit, and offer check-writing privileges.
Certificate of deposit (CD)	0.15%–1.15% (1-year)	A savings instrument where funds are left on deposit for a stipulated period (1 week to 1 year or more); imposes a penalty for withdrawing funds early. Market yields vary by size and maturity; no check-writing privileges.
U.S. Treasury bill (T-bill)	0.085% (3-month)	Short-term, highly marketable security issued by the U.S. Treasury (originally issued with maturities of 13 and 26 weeks); smallest denomination is $100.
U.S. savings bond (EE)	0.60%	Issued at a discount from face value by the U.S. Treasury; rate of interest is tied to U.S. Treasury securities. Long a popular savings vehicle (widely used with payroll deduction plans). Matures to face value in approximately 5 years; sold in denominations of $25 and more.

© Cengage Learning

only 0.089 percent in April 2012 vs. investing at the historical average rate of 6.46 percent. After 5 years, you would have earned about $34,188 at the average rate and only about $26,132 at the lower rate.

There are benefits and costs to the unprecedentedly low interest rates that have persisted since the financial crisis of 2008–2009. Whether they are a net benefit or a net cost depends on your perspective. In 2012, the Fed committed to keeping interest rates low for at least the next two years. While financial markets generally reacted positively to this low rate policy by pushing up asset prices, low interest rates also tend to signal sluggish economic growth and the risk of deflation. The benefits of lower interest rates include the reduced costs of financing the massive federal budget deficit, which is a significant savings given that interest on the federal debt was $454 billion in 2011. And lower rates have helped support the "too big to fail" banks. Indeed, the Fed's low interest rate policy has allowed banks to pay less than 1 percent interest on savings. But the costs are equally impressive. Low interest rates reduce income to retirees and to pension funds. This means that some retirees will have to dip into their principal, which could put more stress on welfare programs for the elderly and may prompt the government to increase its financial support of underfunded pension funds.

The recent extremely low interest rates favor borrowers and dampen the incentive to save. While keeping big banks afloat has advantages, many argue that low interest rates have helped protect banks from absorbing the consequences of their actions and redistribute wealth away from prudent savers. Indeed, the inflation-adjusted real interest rate has been negative, which means that savers are not keeping up with

inflation and will either have to tap into their principal or cut their spending. This is bad for retirees and for the overall economy. People are also giving less to charity as they seek to cover income shortfalls resulting from lower interest rates. The percentage of savings out of income is decreasing. From 1999 to 2009, the number of taxpayers grew by more than 13 million, while those earning any taxable interest fell from 67.2 million to 57.8 million. Thus, the percentage of taxpayers earning interest dropped dramatically, from 52.9 percent to 44.1 percent, over this time period.

Low interest rates also create economic distortions, especially when real, inflation-adjusted interest rates are negative. Low interest rates encourage the substitution of capital for labor, which is important because about 70 percent of economic activity in developed economies is due to consumption. This substitution consequently reduces overall aggregate demand as employment and income levels drop. The lower borrowing costs also encourage the substitution of debt for equity in corporate capital structures, which increases financial risk. Low rates discourage savings and discourage the reduction of overall debt levels in the economy. Consider the impact of interest rates on saving for retirement. A drop in interest rates from 5 percent to 4 percent requires an 18 percent increase in the amount saved each year in order to reach the same goal over 30 years. Similarly, for every 1 percent decline in rates, pension fund liabilities increase by about $180 billion. Low interest rates also encourage investors to search for investments that pay income, which increases the demand for stocks paying high dividends and for lower-grade, riskier bonds. Low interest rates imply low opportunity costs for holding assets that pay no income. Investors consequently hope for asset price increases, which push up demand for commodities like gold and alternative assets (such as art) and can encourage the mispricing of risk and thereby create asset bubbles. Unfortunately, low interest rates do not seem to have increased the supply of credit. Being fearful of taking much risk during and after the financial crisis, banks have tended to invest more in government securities and less in risky loans.

So what's a prudent saver to do in such a low-interest-rate environment? Unfortunately, the search for higher current returns has led many people to make investments of questionable risk. Some have moved into higher-quality corporate bonds. But when rates are so low, they are likely to go up. And bond prices fall when rates rise, which poses substantial risk to longer-term bonds. More moderate strategies involve buying stocks that pay higher dividends and buying preferred stocks, which will be discussed more in Chapter 12. But stocks are generally riskier than bonds, so the pursuit of higher returns in a low-interest-rate environment must be tempered by careful consideration of the suitability of the likely higher risk.

4-2 Today's Financial Services Marketplace

LG2 Sonia Whitehead Beth White hasn't been inside her bank in years. Her company deposits her salary into her checking account each month, and she regularly does all her banking from her home computer: with the click of a mouse, she can check her account balances, pay her bills, even search for the best rates on savings instruments. And by making a few simple entries, she is able to withdraw money from her U.S. bank account using an automated teller machine (ATM) in Zurich!

The financial services industry continues to evolve, thanks in large part to advanced technology and changing regulations. Today, consumers can now choose from many different types of financial institutions, all competing for their business. No longer must you go to one place for your checking account, another for credit cards or loans, and yet another for brokerage services. Instead, financial institutions are expanding services and competitively pricing their products by bundling different accounts. For example, if you have $25,000 worth of funds in several Bank of America accounts, you're eligible for reduced or zero-cost commissions on stock trades, free checking, free bill-pay, a credit card, and free ATM debit card transactions. And online banking gives you easy access to all of these services.

The *financial services industry* as we know it today comprises all institutions that market various kinds of *financial products* (such as checking and savings

accounts, credit cards, loans and mortgages, insurance, and mutual funds) and *financial services* (such as financial planning, securities brokerage, tax filing and planning, estate planning, real estate, trusts, and retirement). What 20–25 years ago were several distinct (though somewhat related) industries is now, in essence, one industry in which firms are differentiated more by organizational structure than by name or product offerings.

4-2a Types of Financial Institutions

Financial institutions can be classified into two broad groups—depository and nondepository—based on whether or not they accept deposits as traditional banks do.

BEHAVIOR MATTERS

Why Can't I Seem to Save More— and What Can I Do About It?

There's a well-worn joke about meaning to read a book about procrastination . . . but you just can't get around to it. Similarly, procrastination is a common behavioral bias that often keeps us from saving more because we just keep putting it off. There is evidence that people procrastinate when they have to make decisions that are perceived as complex. For example, if you view the saving decision more broadly as a set of subsequent complex investment decisions, you're more likely to put off the decision to save more. So what is the best way to proceed if you want to save more? Simplify the decision by adopting an easy plan like saving 10 percent of your income by filling out the bank paperwork that will automatically transfer the money each month from your checking to savings account. Putting basic decisions like this on autopilot combats our natural tendency to procrastinate. That's a start that you can build on before approaching more complex investing decisions. But no savings means nothing to invest . . . it's best to act now and not worry about specific savings decisions every month.

 Go to Smart Sites

Looking for a fee-free Internet bank? PC Magazine has five good ones to choose from, and why. For more online resources, whenever you see *"Go to Smart Sites"* in this chapter, visit CourseMate for PFIN 3. Log in at **www.cengagebrain.com.** ●

© GEOPAUL/ISTOCKPHOTO

Depository Financial Institutions

The vast majority of financial transactions take place at *depository financial institutions*—commercial banks (both brick-and-mortar and Internet), savings and loan associations (S&Ls), savings banks, and credit unions.

Exhibit 4.2 Depository Financial Institutions

Depository financial institutions differ from their nonbank counterparts, such as stock brokerages and mutual funds, in their ability to accept deposits. Most consumers use these institutions to meet their checking and savings account needs.

Institution	Description
Commercial bank	Offers checking and savings accounts and a full range of financial products and services; the only institution that can offer *non-interest-paying checking accounts (demand deposits)*. The most popular of the depository financial institutions. Most are traditional *brick-and-mortar banks*, but **Internet banks**—online commercial banks—are growing in popularity because of their convenience, lower service fees, and higher interest paid on account balances.
Savings and loan association (S&L)	Channels the savings of depositors primarily into mortgage loans for purchasing and improving homes. Also offers many of the same checking, saving, and lending products as commercial banks. Often pays slightly higher interest on savings than do commercial banks.
Savings bank	Similar to S&Ls, but located primarily in the New England states. Most are *mutual* associations—their depositors are their owners and thus receive a portion of the profits in the form of interest on their savings.
Credit union	A nonprofit, member-owned financial cooperative that provides a full range of financial products and services to its *members*, who must belong to a common occupation, religious or fraternal order, or residential area. Generally small institutions when compared with commercial banks and S&Ls. Offer interest-paying checking accounts—called **share draft accounts**—and a variety of saving and lending programs. Because they are run to benefit their members, they pay higher interest on savings and charge lower rates on loans than do other depository financial institutions.

© Cengage Learning

Internet bank An online commercial bank.

share draft account An account offered by credit unions that is similar to interest-paying checking accounts offered by other financial institutions.

Although they're regulated by different agencies, depository financial institutions are commonly referred to as "banks" because of their similar products and services. What sets these institutions apart from others is their ability to accept deposits; most people use them for their checking and savings account needs. These depository financial institutions are briefly described in Exhibit 4.2.

Nondepository Financial Institutions

Other types of financial institutions that offer banking services, *but don't accept deposits like traditional banks*, are considered *nondepository institutions*. Today you can hold a credit card issued by a stock brokerage firm or have an account with a mutual fund that allows you to write a limited number of checks.

4-2b How Safe Is Your Money?

Almost all commercial banks, S&Ls, savings banks, and credit unions are federally insured by U.S. government agencies. The few that are not federally insured usually obtain insurance through

either a state-chartered or private insurance agency. Most experts believe that these privately insured institutions have less protection against loss than those that are federally insured. Exhibit 4.3 lists the insuring agencies and the maximum insurance amounts provided under the various federal deposit insurance programs.

DMITRIY SHIRONOSOV/SHUTTERSTOCK.COM

© KAREN HERMANN/ISTOCKPHOTO

Exhibit 4.3 Federal Deposit Insurance Programs

Insurance on checking and savings accounts at federally insured institutions covers up to $250,000.

Savings Institution	Insuring Agency	Basic Insurance Amounts
Commercial bank	Federal Deposit Insurance Corporation (FDIC)	$250,000/depositor through the Bank Insurance Fund (BIF)
Savings and loan association	FDIC	$250,000/depositor through the Savings Association Insurance Fund (SAIF)
Savings bank	FDIC	$250,000/depositor through the Bank Insurance Fund (BIF)
Credit union	National Credit Union Administration (NCUA)	$250,000/depositor through the National Credit Union Share Insurance Fund (NCUSIF)

Deposit insurance protects the funds you have on deposit at banks and other depository institutions against institutional failure. In effect, the insuring agency stands behind the financial institution and guarantees the safety of your deposits up to a specified maximum amount. The Dodd-Frank Wall Street Reform and Consumer Protection Act was signed into law in late 2010 and increased the maximum deposit insurance amount from $100,000 to $250,000.

It's important to understand that deposit insurance is provided to the *depositor* rather than to a *deposit account*. Thus, the checking *and* savings accounts of each depositor are insured and, *so long as the maximum insurable amount is not exceeded,* the depositor can have any number of accounts and still be fully protected. This is an important feature to keep in mind because many people mistakenly believe that the maximum insurance applies to *each* of their accounts. For example, a depositor with a checking account balance of $15,000 at a branch office of First National Bank, an MMDA of $135,000 at First National Bank's main office, and a $50,000 CD issued by the same First National Bank is entirely covered by the FDIC's deposit insurance amount of $250,000 per depositor. If the CD were for $150,000, however, then the total for this depositor would be $300,000 and thus not entirely covered under the plan. However, purchasing the CD *from another bank*, which also provides $250,000 of deposit insurance, would fully protect all of this depositor's funds.

Now that banks are offering a greater variety of products, including mutual funds, it's important to remember that only deposit accounts, including CDs, are covered by deposit insurance. *Securities purchased through your bank are not protected by any form of deposit insurance.*

As a depositor, it's possible to increase your $250,000 of traditional deposit insurance if necessary by opening accounts in different depositor names at the same institution. For example, a married couple can obtain as much as $1,500,000 in coverage by setting up several accounts:

- One in the name of each spouse ($500,000 in coverage)
- A *joint account* in both names (good for another $500,000, which is $250,000 per account owner)
- *Separate trust or self-directed retirement (IRA, Keogh, etc.) accounts* in the name of each spouse (good for an additional $250,000 per spouse)

In this case, each depositor name is treated as a separate legal entity, receiving full insurance coverage—the husband alone is considered one legal entity, the wife another, and the husband and wife as a couple a third. The trust and self-directed retirement accounts are also viewed as separate legal entities.

deposit insurance
A type of insurance that protects funds on deposit against failure of the institution; can be insured by the FDIC and the NCUA.

4-3 A Full Menu of Cash Management Products

LG3 As a student on a tight budget, working his way through college, Scott Schaeffer knew how important it was to plan his saving and spending, and Scott wanted to make the correct decisions about managing his financial resources. By using a checking account comparison chart, like the one in Exhibit 4.4, Scott could compare information on daily balance requirements, service fees, interest rates, and the services his bank offers to college students and others.

Exhibit 4.4   Checking Accounts Comparison Chart

Most banks offer a variety of checking account options, which are typically differentiated by minimum balances, fees, and other services.

Representative Bank USA

Features	College Checking	Custom Checking	Advantage Checking	Advantage Plus Checking
Minimum daily balance (to waive monthly service fee)	None	$750 in checking	$5,000 in checking	$7,500 combined balance
Monthly service fee	$5.95	$9 with direct deposit	$11 without direct deposit; no fee with Homeowner's Option	$12 ($2 discount with direct deposit)
Interest	No	No	Yes	Yes
Online statements	Free	Free	Free	Free
Check safekeeping	Free	Free	Free	Free
Monthly check return	$3.00	$3.00	$3.00	Free
ATM and check card	Free	Free	Free	Free
Bank by phone	Free automated calls	Free automated calls	Free automated calls	Free banker-assisted calls
Overdraft protection	Credit card	Credit card	Credit card, line of credit account, and select deposit accounts	Credit card, line of credit account, and select deposit accounts
Direct deposit advance service	Not available	Yes, with a direct deposit of $100 a month or more	Yes, with a direct deposit of $100 a month or more	Yes, with a direct deposit of $100 a month or more

© Cengage Learning

demand deposit An account held at a financial institution from which funds can be withdrawn on demand by the account holder; same as a *checking account.*

4-3a Checking and Savings Accounts

People hold cash and other forms of liquid assets, such as checking and savings accounts, for the convenience that they offer in making purchase transactions, meeting normal living expenses, and providing a safety net, or cushion, to meet unexpected expenses. Because of the federal *Truth in Savings Act of 1993,* all depository financial institutions must clearly disclose fees, interest rates, and terms on both checking and savings accounts. In addition, banks must use a standard *annual percentage yield (APY)* formula that takes compounding (discussed later) into account when stating the interest paid on accounts. This makes it easier for consumers to compare each bank's offerings. The law also requires banks to pay interest on a customer's full daily or monthly average deposit balance. And it strictly prohibits them from paying interest on only the lowest daily balance or paying no interest if the account balance falls below the minimum balance for just 1 day. In addition,

banks must notify customers 30 days in advance before lowering rates on deposit accounts or CDs.

Checking Accounts

A checking account held at a financial institution is known as a **demand deposit**, meaning that the bank must permit these funds to be withdrawn whenever the account holder demands. You put money into your checking account by *depositing* funds; you withdraw it by *writing a check, using a debit card,* or *making a cash withdrawal.* So long as you have sufficient funds in your account, the bank, when presented with a valid check or an electronic debit, must immediately pay the amount indicated by deducting it from your account.

Regular checking is the most common type of checking account. Traditionally, it pays no interest, but any service charges can be waived if you maintain a minimum balance (usually between $500 and $1,500), though many banks are moving away from such minimum balance requirements. Technically, only commercial banks can offer non-interest-paying regular checking accounts. Savings banks, S&Ls, and credit unions also offer checking accounts; but these accounts, which must pay interest, are called *NOW (negotiable order of withdrawal) accounts* or, in the case of credit unions, *share draft accounts*.

Savings Accounts

A savings account is another form of liquid asset available at commercial banks, S&Ls, savings banks, credit unions, and other types of financial institutions. Savings deposits are referred to as **time deposits**, since they are expected to remain on deposit for longer periods of time than demand deposits. Because savings deposits earn higher rates of interest, they are typically preferable to checking accounts when the depositor's goal is to accumulate money for a future expenditure or to maintain balances for meeting unexpected expenses. Most banks pay higher interest rates on larger savings account balances. For example, a bank might pay 0.65 percent on balances up to $2,500, 0.65 percent on balances between $2,500 and $10,000, and 0.75 percent on balances of more than $10,000. In addition to withdrawal policies and deposit insurance, the stated interest rate and the method of calculating interest paid on savings accounts are important considerations when choosing the financial institution in which to place your savings. As noted above, current interest rates are extremely low by historical standards due to the Fed's post-crisis policy initiatives.

Interest-Paying Checking Accounts

Depositors can choose from NOW accounts, money market deposit accounts, and money market mutual funds.

NOW ACCOUNTS. Negotiable order of withdrawal (NOW) accounts are checking accounts on which the financial institution pays interest. There is no legal minimum balance for a NOW, but many institutions impose their own requirement, often between $500 and $1,000. Some pay interest on any balance in the account, but most institutions pay a higher rate of interest for balances above a specified amount.

MONEY MARKET DEPOSIT ACCOUNTS. Money market deposit accounts (MMDAs) are offered at banks and other financial institutions and compete with money market mutual funds for deposits. MMDAs are popular with savers and investors because of their convenience and safety and because deposits in MMDAs (unlike those in money funds) are *federally insured*. Most banks require a minimum MMDA balance of $1,000 or more.

Depositors can use check-writing privileges or ATMs to access MMDA accounts. They receive a limited number (usually six) of free monthly checks and transfers but pay a fee on additional transactions. Although this reduces the flexibility of these accounts, most depositors view MMDAs as savings and so do not consider these restrictions to be a serious obstacle. Moreover,

MMDAs pay the highest interest rate of any bank account on which checks can be written.

MONEY MARKET MUTUAL FUNDS. Money market mutual funds have become the most successful type of mutual fund ever offered. A **money market mutual fund (MMMF)** pools the funds of many small investors to purchase high-return, short-term marketable securities offered by the U.S. Treasury, major corporations, large commercial banks, and various government organizations. (Mutual funds are discussed in detail in Chapter 13.)

MMMFs have historically paid interest at rates of 1 percent to 3 percent above those paid on regular savings accounts. Moreover, investors have instant access to their funds through check-writing privileges, although these must be written for a stipulated minimum amount (often $500). The checks look like, and are treated like, any other check drawn on a demand deposit account. And as with all interest-bearing checking accounts, you continue to earn interest on your money while the checks make their way through the banking system.

Asset Management Accounts

Perhaps the best example of a banking service also offered by a nondepository financial institution is the **asset management account (AMA)**, or *central asset account*. The AMA is a comprehensive deposit account that combines checking, investing, and borrowing activities and is offered primarily by brokerage houses and mutual funds. AMAs appeal to investors because they can consolidate most of their financial transactions at one institution and on one account statement.

A typical AMA account includes an MMDA with unlimited free checking, a Visa or MasterCard debit card, use of ATMs, and brokerage and loan accounts. Annual fees and account charges (e.g., a per-transaction charge for ATM withdrawals) vary, so it pays to shop around. The distinguishing feature of these accounts is that they automatically "sweep" excess balances—for example, amounts over $500—into a higher-return MMMF on a daily or weekly basis. When the account holder needs funds to purchase securities or cover checks written on the MMDA, the funds are transferred back to the MMDA. And if the amount of securities purchased or checks presented for payment

time deposit A savings deposit at a financial institution; remains on deposit for a longer time than a demand deposit.

negotiable order of withdrawal (NOW) account A checking account on which the financial institution pays interest; NOWs have no legal minimum balance.

money market deposit account (MMDA) A federally insured savings account, offered by banks and other depository institutions, that competes with money market mutual funds.

money market mutual fund (MMMF) A mutual fund that pools the funds of many small investors and purchases high-return, short-term marketable securities.

asset management account (AMA) A comprehensive deposit account; offered primarily by brokerage houses and mutual funds.

electronic funds transfer systems (EFTSs) Systems using the latest telecommunications and computer technology to electronically transfer funds into and out of customers' accounts.

debit cards Specially coded plastic cards used to transfer funds from a customer's bank account to the recipient's account to pay for goods or services.

automated teller machine (ATM) A remote computer terminal that customers of depository institutions can use to make basic transactions 24 hours a day, 7 days a week.

exceeds the account balance, the needed funds are supplied automatically through a loan.

Although AMAs are an attractive alternative to a traditional bank account, they do have some drawbacks. For example, compared with banks, there are fewer "branch" locations. However, AMAs are typically affiliated with ATM networks, making it easy to withdraw funds. Yet ATM transactions are more costly; checks can take longer to clear; and some bank services may not be offered. Moreover, AMAs are not covered by deposit insurance, although these deposits are protected by the *Securities Investor Protection Corporation* and the firm's private insurance.

4-3b Electronic Banking Services

The fastest-changing area in cash management today is *electronic banking services*. Whether you're using an ATM or checking your account balance online, electronic banking services make managing your money easier and more convenient. Electronic funds transfer systems allow you to conduct many types of banking business at any hour of the day or night.

Electronic Funds Transfer Systems

Electronic funds transfer systems (EFTSs) allow depositors to conduct a variety of different types of bank transactions at any time by using the latest telecommunications and computer technology to electronically transfer funds into and out of their accounts. For example, your employer may use an EFTS to electronically transfer

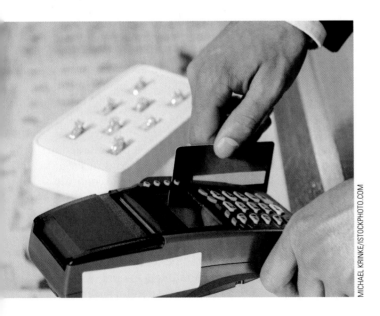

your pay from the firm's bank account directly into your personal bank account at the same or a different bank. This eliminates the employer's need to prepare and process checks and the employee's need to deposit them. Electronic transfer systems make possible such services as debit cards and ATMs, preauthorized deposits and payments, bank-by-phone accounts, and online banking.

DEBIT CARDS AND AUTOMATED TELLER MACHINES. This form of EFTS uses specially coded plastic cards, called **debit cards**, to transfer funds from the customer's bank account (a debit) to the recipient's account. A debit card may be used to make purchases at any place of business set up with the point-of-sale terminals required to accept debit card payments. The personal identification number (PIN) issued with your debit card verifies that you are authorized to access the account.

Visa and MasterCard issue debit cards linked to your checking account that give you even more flexibility. In addition to using the card to purchase goods and services, you can use it at ATMs, which have become a popular way to make banking transactions. **Automated teller machines (ATMs)** are remote computer terminals that customers of a bank or other depository institution can use to make deposits, withdrawals, and other transactions such as loan payments or transfers between accounts—24 hours a day, 7 days a week. Most banks have ATMs outside their offices, and some place free-standing ATMs in shopping malls, airports, and grocery stores; at colleges and universities; and in other high-traffic areas to enhance their competitive position. If your bank belongs to an EFTS network, such as Cirrus, Star, or Interlink, then you can get cash from the ATM of any bank in the United States or overseas that is a member of that network. (In fact, the easiest way to get foreign currency when you travel overseas is through an ATM on your bank's network! It also gives you the best exchange rate for your dollar.) Banks charge an average per-transaction fee of $2.40 for using the ATM of another bank, and some also charge when you use your ATM card to pay certain merchants. However, to be more competitive some banks now reimburse the fees associated with using the ATMs of other banks.

Debit card use is increasing because these cards are convenient both *for retailers*, who don't have to worry about bounced checks, and *for consumers*, who don't have to write checks. These cards are so popular, in fact, that the total dollar volume of purchases made using Visa's branded debit cards actually surpassed their credit-card purchases in 2008. Indeed, the convenience of debit cards may be their biggest drawback: *they make it easy to overspend*. To avoid such problems, make sure you record all debit card purchases immediately in your checkbook ledger and deduct them from your checkbook balance. Also be aware that, if there's a problem with a purchase, you can't stop payment—an action you could take if you had paid by check or credit card.

How to Use Online Banking Effectively

- **Confirm that the online bank site is legitimate.** Watch out for fake Web sites that use a name or Internet address similar to, but not the same as, that of your bank. These sites try to trick you into entering their Web site and providing your account number and password. Make sure that you have typed the correct Internet address for your specific bank before entering any account information. Read the "About Us" section that describes the institution and confirm that its deposits are insured by the FDIC. Look for the FDIC logo or "Member FDIC." It is wise to check the FDIC's online database of insured institutions, which is found by searching "Bank Find" at http://www2.fdic.gov/idasp/main_bankfind.asp.

- **Protect your personal Information.** Banks are required to inform you of their privacy policy. This describes what personal information the bank keeps and what information, if any, it shares with other companies. When logging onto a bank site, make sure that the Web site is encrypted. This is indicated by a browser icon that looks like a "lock" or a "key," and "https" should be in the address line as well. Passwords or PINs should be used, unique to you, and changed regularly.

Source: Adapted from "Safe Internet Banking," http://www.fdic.gov/bank/individual/online/safe.html, July 15, 2010, accessed March 2012.

as obtaining an account balance, finding out what checks have cleared, transferring funds to other accounts, and dispatching payments to participating merchants. To encourage banking by phone, many banks today charge no fee on basic account transactions or allow a limited number of free transactions per month. However, online banking options are replacing bank-by-phone accounts.

Online Banking and Bill Payment Services
The Pew Internet & American Life Project recently found that nearly 45 percent of Internet users rely on some form of *online banking* services. This percentage has grown steadily as banks make online services easier to use and as people become more comfortable using the Internet for financial transactions. Many individuals do little more than check their balances, but more than half use the Internet to transfer funds as well. Today, most banks aggressively compete for your online banking business because it's in their best financial interests to do so. A recent study showed that the cost of a full-service teller transaction is about $1.00, an ATM transaction is less than 30 cents, and an Internet transaction is less than 1 cent.

> ## Today, most banks aggressively compete for your online banking business.

Although a computer-based bank-at-home system doesn't replace the use of an ATM to obtain cash or deposit money, it can save both time and postage when you're paying bills. Other benefits include convenience and the potential to earn higher interest rates and pay lower fees. While some banks still charge for online banking services, it's free at most banks. But online banking doesn't always live up to its promises. You can't make cash deposits, checks may get lost in the mail, and you don't know when the funds will reach your account. The *Money in Action* on the next page provides more information to help you decide if online banking is right for you.

4-3c Regulation of EFTS Services

The federal *Electronic Fund Transfer Act of 1978* describes your rights and responsibilities as an EFTS user. Under this law, you cannot stop payment on a defective or questionable purchase, although individual banks and state laws often have more lenient provisions. If there's an error, you must notify the bank within 60 days of its occurrence. The bank must

PREAUTHORIZED DEPOSITS AND PAYMENTS. Two related EFTS services are *preauthorized deposits and payments*. They allow you to receive automatic deposits or make payments that occur regularly. For example, you can arrange to have your paycheck or monthly pension or Social Security benefits deposited directly into your account. Regular, fixed-amount payments, such as mortgage and consumer loan payments or monthly retirement fund contributions, can be preauthorized to be made automatically from your account. You can also preauthorize regular payments of varying amounts such as monthly utility bills.

BANK-BY-PHONE ACCOUNTS. Bank customers can make various types of transactions by telephone, either by calling a customer service operator who handles the transaction or by using the keypad on a touch-tone telephone to instruct the bank's computer. After the customer provides a secret code to access the account, the system provides the appropriate prompts to perform various transactions, such

then investigate and advise you of the results within 10 days. The bank can then take up to 45 more days to investigate the error but must return the disputed money to your account until the issue is resolved.

If you fail to notify the bank of an error within 60 days, the bank has no obligation under federal law to conduct an investigation or return your money. You must notify the bank immediately about the theft, loss, or unauthorized use of your EFTS card. Notification within 2 business days after you discover the card missing limits your loss to $50. After 2 business days, you may lose up to $500 (but never more than the amount that was withdrawn by the thief). If you don't report the loss within 60 days after your periodic statement was mailed, you can lose all the money in your account. When reporting errors or unauthorized transactions, it's best to notify your bank by telephone and follow up with a letter; then keep a copy of the letter in your file. These safeguards notwithstanding, *your best protection is to guard carefully the PIN used to access your accounts.* Don't write the PIN on your EFTS card, and be sure to check your statements for possible errors or unauthorized transactions.

© JASON STITT/SHUTTERSTOCK.COM

4-3d Other Bank Services

In addition to the services described earlier in this chapter, many banks offer other types of money management services, such as safe-deposit boxes and trust services.

- **Safe-deposit boxes:** A *safe-deposit box* is a rented drawer in a bank's vault. Boxes can be rented for an average of about $30 per year, depending on their size. When you rent a box, you receive one key to it and the bank keeps another key. The box can be opened only when both keys are used. This arrangement protects items in the box from theft and serves as an excellent storage place for jewelry, contracts, stock certificates, titles, and other important documents. Keeping valuables in a safe-deposit box may also reduce your homeowner's insurance by eliminating the "riders" that are often needed to cover such items.

- **Trust services:** Bank trust departments provide investment and estate planning advice. They manage and administer the investments in a trust account or from an estate.

4-4 Maintaining a Checking Account

LG4 By the time Jack Cramer started college, he had a thriving car-detailing business that earned him several hundred dollars per week. Some customers paid him in advance, some paid after the fact, and some forgot (or otherwise neglected) to pay at all. But by depositing each check or cash payment into his checking account, Jack was able to keep track of his earnings without complicated bookkeeping. A checking account is one of the most useful cash management tools you can have. It's a safe and convenient way to hold money and streamline point-of-sale purchases, debt payments, and other basic transactions. You can have regular or interest-paying checking accounts at commercial banks, S&Ls, savings banks, credit unions, and even brokerage houses through asset management accounts. For convenience, we'll focus on commercial bank checking accounts, although our discussion applies also to checking accounts maintained at other types of financial institutions.

IMAGE SOURCE/JUPITER IMAGES

4-4a Opening and Using Your Checking Account

Factors that typically influence the choice of where to maintain a checking account are convenience, services, and cost. Many people choose a bank based solely on convenience factors: location, business hours, number of drive-thru windows, and number and location of branch offices and ATMs. Ease of access is obviously an important consideration because most people prefer to bank near home or work. But in addition to convenience and safety, you should also consider the interest rates the bank offers, types of accounts (including special accounts that combine such features as credit cards, free checks, and reduced fees), structure and level of fees and charges, and quality of customer service.

The Cost of a Checking Account

Bank service charges have increased sharply for a variety of reasons, including the growth of interest-bearing checking accounts. Today few, if any, banks and other depository institutions allow unlimited free check-writing privileges. Most banks levy monthly and per-check fees when your checking account balance drops below a required minimum, and some may charge for checking no matter how large a balance you carry.

Some banks are moving away from minimum balance requirements, but a common requirement is to maintain a minimum balance of $500 to $1,000 or more to avoid service charges. Although some banks use the *average monthly* balance in an account to determine whether to levy a service charge, most use the *daily* balance procedure. This means that if your account should happen to fall just $1 below the minimum balance *just once* during the month, you'll be hit with the full service charge—even if your average balance is three times the minimum requirement. Service charges take two forms: (1) a base service charge of, say, $7.50 a month, and (2) additional charges of, say, 25 cents for each check you write and 10 cents for each ATM or bank-by-phone transaction.

In addition to the service charges on checking accounts, banks have increased most other check-related charges and raised the minimum balances required for free checking and waivers of specified fees. The average charge on a returned check is between $25 and $30, and stop-payment orders typically cost $20 to $35. Some banks charge fees for ATM or bank-by-phone transactions that exceed a specified number. Most also charge for using the ATM of another bank that is not a member of the same network. It's not surprising that smart consumers use cost as the single most important variable when choosing where to set up a checking account.

Individual or Joint Account?

Two people wishing to open a checking account may do so in one of three ways:

1. They can each open individual checking accounts (on which the other cannot write checks).

Financial Planning Tips

Choosing a New Bank

If you're looking for a new bank, here are some important factors to consider:

- **Convenient location and online services**. Find a bank that is conveniently located *and* has online services, because online service providing banks tend to pay more competitive savings rates.
- **Free checking and free money transfers.** "Free checking" usually means that you aren't required to keep a minimum balance in your account and can write as many checks a month as you like. Even if it isn't labeled as such, look for free checking. Also look for banks that let you transfer funds between different accounts for free.
- **Convenient ATMs.** The average fee for using the ATM of another bank is about $3. Although some banks are starting to refund such fees, by visiting only ATMs that belong to your bank, you can avoid all surcharges and the hassle of refunds. It is best to have an ATM close to your work and home.
- **Overdraft and FDIC protection.** Given that fees for bounced checks average about $30, it is important to know what the charges are and what kind of overdraft protection is offered. Also make sure that your deposits are insured by the FDIC.
- **Competitive interest income.** Find out if the bank pays interest on your balance. You can shop for the most competitive rates in your zip code at **www.bankingmyway.com**.

Source: Adapted from Farnoosh Torabi, ìBack to Basics: Choosing a New Bank,î http://www.mainstreet.com/article/moneyinvesting/savings/back-basics-choosing-new-bank, accessed March 2012; and ìHow to Choose the Best Checking Account,î http://www.mainstreet.com/article/money/investing/how-choose-best-checking-account, accessed March 2012.

2. They can open a joint account that requires both signatures on all checks.
3. They can open a joint account that allows either one to write checks (the most common type of joint account).

One advantage of the joint account over two individual accounts is lower service charges. In addition, the account has rights of survivorship: for a married couple, this means that if one spouse dies, the surviving spouse, after fulfilling a specified legal requirement, can draw checks on the account. If account owners are treated as tenants in common rather than having rights of survivorship, then the survivor gets only his or her share of the account. Thus, when you're opening a joint account, be sure to specify the rights you prefer.

General Checking Account Procedures

After you select the bank that meets your needs, it's a simple matter to open an account. The application form asks for basic personal information such as name, date of birth, Social Security number, address, phone, and place of employment. You'll also have to provide identification,

checkbook ledger
A booklet, provided with a supply of checks, used to maintain accurate records of all checking account transactions.

overdraft The result of writing a check for an amount greater than the current account balance.

overdraft protection An arrangement between the account holder and the depository institution wherein the institution automatically pays a check that overdraws the account.

stop payment An order made by an account holder instructing the depository institution to refuse payment on an already issued check.

sign signature cards, and make an initial deposit. The bank will give you a supply of checks to use until your personalized checks arrive.

After opening a checking account, follow these basic procedures:

- Always write checks in ink.
- Include the name of the person being paid, the date, and the amount of the check—written in both numerals and words for accuracy.
- Sign the check the same way as on the signature card you filled out when opening the account.
- Note the check's purpose on the check—usually on the line provided in the lower-left corner. This information is helpful for both budgeting and tax purposes.

Make sure to enter all checking account transactions—checks written, deposits, point-of-sale debit purchases, ATM transactions, and preauthorized automatic payments and deposits—in the **checkbook ledger** provided with your supply of checks. Then, *subtract* the amount of each check, debit card purchase, ATM cash withdrawal, or payment, and *add* the amount of each deposit to the previous balance to keep track of your current account balance. Good transaction records and an accurate balance prevent overdrawing the account.

Prepare a deposit slip with each deposit (such slips are generally included with your checks and also available at your bank) listing the currency, coins, and checks being deposited. List checks by the *transit ID number* printed on the check, usually at the top right. Also properly endorse all checks that you're depositing. To protect against possible loss of endorsed checks, it's common to use a special endorsement, such as "Pay to the order of XYZ Bank," or a restrictive endorsement, such as "For deposit only." When depositing checks, you may encounter a delay in funds' availability due to the time required for them to clear. To avoid overdrawing your account, know your bank's "hold" policy on deposits—as a rule, it generally takes between one and five business days for funds to become available.

Overdrafts

When a check is written for an amount greater than the current account balance, the result is an **overdraft**. If the overdraft is proven to be intentional, the bank can initiate legal proceedings against the account holder. The action taken by a bank on an overdraft depends on the strength of its relationship with the account holder and the amount involved. In the vast majority

of cases, the bank simply stamps the overdrawn check with the words "insufficient balance (or funds)" and returns it to the party to whom it was written. This is often called a "bounced check." The account holder is notified of this action, and the holder's bank deducts a penalty fee of as much as $20 to $25 or more from his checking account. The depositor of a "bad check" may also be charged as much as $15 to $20 by her bank, which explains why merchants typically charge bad check writers $15 to $25 per bounced check and often refuse to accept future checks from them.

When you have a strong relationship with your bank or arrange **overdraft protection**, the bank will pay a check that overdraws the account. In cases where overdraft protection has not been prearranged but the bank pays the check, the account holder is usually notified by the bank and charged a penalty fee for the inconvenience. However, the check does not bounce, and the check writer's creditworthiness is not damaged.

There are several ways to arrange overdraft protection. Many banks offer an overdraft line of credit that automatically extends a loan to cover the amount of an overdraft. In most cases, however, the loans are made only in specified increments, such as $50 or $100, and interest (or a fee) is levied against the loan amount, not the actual amount of the overdraft. This can be an expensive form of protection, particularly if you do not promptly repay the loan.

Another way to cover overdrafts is with an *automatic transfer program*, which automatically transfers funds from your savings account into your checking account in the event of an overdraft. Under this program, some banks charge both an annual fee and a fee on each transfer. Of course, *the best form of overdraft protection is to use good cash management techniques and regularly balance your checking account.*

Stopping Payment

Occasionally it's necessary to **stop payment** on a check if it was issued as part of a contract that was not carried out, or because a good or service paid for by check is found to be faulty (note that some states prohibit you from stopping payment on faulty goods or services). To stop payment on a check, you must notify the bank and fill out a form indicating the check number and date, amount, and the name of the party to whom it was written. You can initiate stop-payment orders online or by phone. Once you place a stop-payment order, the bank refuses payment on the affected check, and the check will be rejected if another bank presents it in the check-clearing process. Banks typically charge a fee ranging from $25 to $30 per check to stop payment. There's one big exception to all this, and that is, *if your checks or checkbook are lost or stolen, there's no need to stop payment on them* because you have no personal liability. Stopping payment in this case only incurs expense; it doesn't change your personal liability.

4-4b Monthly Statements

Once a month, your bank provides a statement—an itemized listing of all transactions in your checking account (checks written, ATM transactions, debit purchases, automatic payments, and deposits made). Also included are bank service charges and interest earned (see Jeremy Bentley's May 2015 bank statement in Exhibit 4.5). Some banks include your original canceled checks with your bank statement, although most are abandoning this practice as we move toward a "paperless" society. Banks that don't return canceled checks will provide photocopies of them on request, generally for a fee. Many banks now let you view canceled checks online, free of charge. It's important to review your monthly bank statement to verify the accuracy of your account records and to reconcile any differences between the statement balance and the balance shown in your checkbook ledger. The monthly statement is also a valuable source of information for your tax records.

Account Reconciliation

You should reconcile your bank account as soon as possible after receiving your monthly statement. The **account reconciliation** process, or *balancing the checkbook,* can uncover errors in recording checks or deposits, in addition or subtraction, and, occasionally, in the bank's processing of a check. It can also help you avoid overdrafts by forcing you to verify your account balance monthly. Assuming that neither you nor the bank has made any errors, discrepancies between your checkbook ledger account balance and your bank statement can be attributed to one of four factors:

1. Checks that you've written, ATM withdrawals, debit purchases, or other automatic payments subtracted from your checkbook balance haven't yet been received and processed by your bank and therefore remain outstanding.
2. Deposits that you've made and added to your checkbook balance haven't yet been credited to your account.
3. Any service (activity) charges levied on your account by the bank haven't yet been deducted from your checkbook balance.
4. Interest earned on your account (if it's a NOW or an MMDA account) hasn't yet been added to your checkbook balance.

For a list of the steps to reconcile your checkbook each month, see the Bonus Exhibit "Make that Checkbook Balance." (Visit CourseMate for PFIN 3. Log in at **www.cengagebrain.com**.) The reverse side of your bank statement usually provides a form for reconciling your account, along with step-by-step instructions. As an illustration, Worksheet 4.1 includes an account reconciliation form that Jeremy Bentley completed for the month of May 2015 using the reconciliation procedures described in "Make that Checkbook Balance."

You can use this form to reconcile either regular or interest-paying checking accounts such as NOWs or MMDAs.

4-4c Special Types of Checks

In some circumstances, sellers of goods or services may not accept personal checks because they can't be absolutely sure that the check is good. This is common for large purchases or when the buyer's bank is not located in the same area where the purchase is being made. A form of check that guarantees payment may be required instead; these include cashier's checks, traveler's checks, and certified checks.

- **Cashier's check**: Anyone can buy a **cashier's check** from a bank. These checks are often used by people who don't have checking accounts. They can be purchased for the face amount of the check plus a service fee of about $2, although occasionally they're issued at no charge to bank customers. The bank issues a check payable to a third party and drawn on itself, not you—the best assurance you can give that the check is good.

- **Traveler's check**: Some large financial organizations—such as Citibank, American Express, MasterCard, Visa, and Bank of America—issue **traveler's checks**, which can be purchased at commercial banks and most other financial institutions. They typically come in denominations ranging from $20 to $100, and any amount—in multiples of $20 to $100—can be purchased at a time. A fee of 1 percent or more can be charged on the purchase, which is often waived for good customers. Properly endorsed and countersigned traveler's checks are accepted by most U.S. businesses and can be exchanged for local currencies in most parts of the world. Because they're insured against loss or theft, they provide a safe, convenient, and popular form of money for travel.

- **Certified check**: A **certified check** is a personal check that the bank certifies, with a stamp, to guarantee that the funds are available. The bank immediately deducts the amount of the check from your account. There's usually only a minimal or no charge for this service if you are the bank's customer for this service.

account reconciliation Verifying the accuracy of your checking account balance in relation to the bank's records as reflected in the bank statement, which is an itemized listing of all transactions in the checking account.

cashier's check A check payable to a third party that is drawn by a bank on itself in exchange for the amount specified plus, in most cases, a service fee (of about $5).

traveler's check A check sold (for a fee of about 1.5 percent) by many large financial institutions, typically in denominations ranging from $20 to $100, that can be used for making purchases and exchanged for local currencies in most parts of the world.

certified check A personal check that is guaranteed (for a fee of $10 to $15 or more) by the bank on which it is drawn.

Exhibit 4.5 **A Bank Statement**

Each month, you receive a statement from your bank or depository financial institution that summarizes the month's transactions and shows your latest account balance. This sample statement for May 2015 for Jeremy Bentley not only shows the checks that have been paid, it also lists all ATM transactions, point-of-sale transactions using his ATM card (the Interlink payments at Lucky Stores), and direct payroll deposits.

```
    YOUR BANK                        #240
    P.O. BOX 516   ANY CITY, USA   90000-0000

      JEREMY A. BENTLEY
      1765 SHERIDAN DRIVE              N        CALL (800) 222-0000
      YOUR CITY, STATE 12091          21        24 HOURS/DAY, 7 DAYS/WEEK
                                                FOR ASSISTANCE WITH
                                                YOUR ACCOUNT.

PAGE 1 OF 1      THIS STATEMENT COVERS: 4/30/2015 THROUGH 5/29/2015
```

PREMIUM ACCOUNT	SUMMARY			
	PREVIOUS BALANCE	473.68	MINIMUM BALANCE	21.78
0123-45678	DEPOSITS	1,302.83+		
	WITHDRAWALS	1,689.02-		
	SERVICE CHARGES	7.50-		
	DIRECT DEPOSIT DISCOUNT	1.00+		
	NEW BALANCE	80.99		

CHECKS AND WITHDRAWALS	CHECK	DATE PAID	AMOUNT	CHECK	DATE PAID	AMOUNT
	203	5/01	10.00	213	5/08	40.00
	204	4/30	15.00	214	5/09	9.58
	205	5/10	635.00	215	5/20	66.18
	206	5/08	25.00	216	5/20	64.92
	207	5/07	19.00	217	5/21	25.03
	208	5/07	50.00	218	5/21	37.98
	209	5/08	15.00	219	5/22	35.00
	210	5/10	83.00	220	5/22	105.00
	211	5/10	10.00	222*	5/22	100.00
	212	5/08	70.00	223	5/21	40.00
				224	5/29	40.82

ATM TRANSACTIONS		DATE	AMOUNT
	PREMIUM ACCOUNT FEE LESS $1.00 DISCOUNT	4/30	6.50
	INTERLINK PURCHASE #572921 ON 04/30 AT LUCKY STORE NO 043	5/01	50.00
	WITHDRAWAL #08108 AT 00165A ON 05/04	5/06	20.00
	INTERLINK PURCHASE #807409 ON 05/11 AT LUCKY STORE NO 056	5/13	12.51
	WITHDRAWAL #01015 AT 00240C ON 05/17	5/17	20.00
	WITHDRAWAL #04792 AT 00167C ON 05/20	5/20	20.00
	WITHDRAWAL #04386 AT 00240D ON 05/21	5/21	40.00
	INTERLINK PURCHASE #880318 ON 05/28 AT LUCKY STORE #043	5/29	30.00

DEPOSITS		DATE POSTED	AMOUNT
	AVS RNT CAR SYST PAYROLL G2 000000035382	5/03	618.69
	AVS RNT CAR SYST PAYROLL G2 000000035382	5/17	83.39
	AVS RNT CAR SYST PAYROLL G2 000000035382	5/17	600.75

ATM LOCATIONS USED	
	00165A: 249 PRIMROSE RD, ANY CITY, USA
	00240C: 490 BROADWAY, ANY CITY, USA
	00167C: 1145 BROADWAY, ANY CITY, USA
	00240D: 490 BROADWAY, ANY CITY, USA

© KAREN HERMANN/ISTOCKPHOTO

© Cengage Learning

Jeremy Bentley used this form to reconcile his checking account for the month of May 2015. Because line A equals line B, he has fully reconciled the difference between the $80.99 bank statement balance and his $339.44 checkbook balance. Accounts should be reconciled each month—as soon as possible after receiving the bank statement.

CHECKING ACCOUNT RECONCILIATION

For the Month of ___May___ , 20 _15_

Accountholder Name (s) ___Jeremy Bentley___

Type of Account ___Regular Checking___

1. Ending balance shown on bank statement _____ $ 80.99

Add up checks and withdrawals still outstanding:

Check Number or Date	Amount	Check Number or Date	Amount
221	$ 81.55		$
225	196.50		
Lucky—5/28	25.00		
ATM—5/29	40.00		
	TOTAL	$ 343.05	

2. Deduct total checks/withdrawals still outstanding from bank balance _____ – $343.05

Add up checks and withdrawals still outstanding:

Date	Amount	Date	Amount
5/29/15	595.00		
	TOTAL	$ 595.00	

3. Add total deposits still outstanding to bank balance _____ + $595.00

A **Adjusted Bank Balance (1 – 2 + 3)** _____ $332.94

4. Ending balance shown in checkbook _____ $339.44

5. Deduct any bank service charges for the period __(–$7.50 + $1.00)__ – $ 6.50

6. Add interest earned for the period _____ + $ 0

B **New Checkbook Balance (4 – 5 + 6)** _____ $332.94

Note: Your account is reconciled when line A equals line B.

4-5 Establishing a Savings Program

LG5, LG6 Almost 94 percent of American families have some form of savings, making it clear that most of us understand the value of saving for the future. In the wake of the recent financial crisis, the U.S. personal saving rate increased to an average of almost 6 percent of after-tax income after hitting a low of around 1 percent in 2005. The act of saving is a deliberate, well-thought-out activity designed to preserve the value of money, ensure liquidity, and earn a competitive rate of return. Almost by definition, *smart savers are smart investors*. They regard saving as more than putting loose change into a piggy bank; rather, they recognize the importance of saving and know that savings must be managed as astutely as any security. After all, what we normally think of as "savings" is really a form of investing—albeit in short-term, highly liquid, low-risk investment. Establishing and maintaining an ongoing savings program is a vital element of personal financial planning. To get the most from your savings, however, you must understand your options and how different savings vehicles pay interest.

4-5a Starting Your Savings Program

Careful financial planning dictates that you hold a portion of your assets to meet liquidity needs and accumulate wealth. Although opinions differ as to how much you should keep as liquid reserves, the post-crisis consensus is that most families should have an amount equal to at least six months of after-tax income. Therefore, if you take home $3,000 a month, you should have about $18,000 in liquid reserves. If your employer has a strong salary continuation program covering extended periods of illness, or if you have a sizable line of credit available, then a somewhat lower amount is probably adequate.

A specific savings plan should be developed to accumulate funds. Saving should be a priority item in your budget, not something that occurs only when income happens to exceed expenditures. Some people manage this by arranging to have savings directly withheld from their paychecks. Not only do direct deposit arrangements help your savings effort, they also enable your funds to earn interest sooner. Or you can transfer funds on a regular basis to other financial institutions, such as commercial banks, savings and loans, savings banks, credit unions, and even mutual

funds. But the key to success is to establish a *regular* pattern of saving.

You should make it a practice to set aside an amount you can comfortably afford *each month*, even if it's only $50 to $100. (Keep in mind that $100 monthly deposits earning 4 percent interest will grow to more than $36,500 in 20 years.) For a listing of some strategies you can use to increase your savings and build a nest egg, check out the Bonus Exhibits. (Visit CourseMate for PFIN 3. Log in at **www.cengagebrain.com**.)

You must also decide which savings vehicles best meet your needs. Many savers prefer to keep their emergency funds in a regular savings or money market deposit account at an institution with federal deposit insurance. Although these accounts are safe, convenient, and highly liquid, they tend to pay relatively low rates of interest. Other important considerations include your risk preference, the length of time you can leave your money on deposit, and the level of current and anticipated interest rates.

Suppose that one year from now, you plan to use $5,000 of your savings to make the down payment on a new car, and you expect interest rates to drop during that period. In such a case, you might want to lock in today's higher rate by purchasing a 1-year certificate of deposit (CD). On the other hand, if you're unsure about when you'll actually need the funds or believe that interest rates will rise, you may be better off with an MMDA or MMMF because their rates change with market conditions, and you can access your funds at any time without penalty.

Many financial planning experts recommend keeping a minimum of 10 percent to 25 percent of your investment portfolio in savings-type instruments, in addition to the six months of liquid reserves noted earlier. Thus, someone with $50,000 in investments should probably have a minimum of $5,000 to $12,500—and possibly more—in short-term vehicles such as MMDAs, MMMFs, or CDs. At times, the amount invested in short-term vehicles could far exceed the recommended minimum, approaching 50 percent or more of the portfolio. This generally depends on expected interest rate movements. If interest rates are relatively high and you expect them to fall, you would invest in long-term vehicles in order to lock in the attractive interest rates. On the other hand, if rates are relatively low and you expect them to rise, you might invest in short-term vehicles so that you can more quickly reinvest when rates do rise.

You should make it a practice to set aside an amount you can comfortably afford each month.

4-5b Earning Interest on Your Money

Interest earned is the reward for putting your money in a savings account or short-term investment vehicle, and it's important for you to understand how that interest is earned. Unfortunately, even in the relatively simple world of savings, not all interest rates are created equal.

The Effects of Compounding

Interest can be earned in one of two ways. First, some short-term investments are sold on a *discount basis*. This means the security is sold for a price that's lower than its redemption value; the difference between the purchase price and redemption value is the amount of interest earned on the investment. Treasury bills, for instance, are issued on a discount basis. Another way to earn interest on short-term investments is by *direct payment*, which occurs when interest is applied to a regular savings account. That is, the amount of interest earned is added to the amount invested, so at maturity you get your money back, plus whatever you earned in interest. Although this is a relatively simple process, determining the actual rate of return can be complicated.

The first complication is in the method used to determine the amount and rate of **compound interest** earned annually. You've probably read or seen advertisements by banks or other depository institutions declaring that they pay daily, rather than annual, interest. Consider an example to understand what this means. Assume that you invest $1,000 in a savings account advertised as paying annual **simple interest** at a rate of 5 percent; that means the interest is paid only on the initial amount of the deposit. Thus, if you leave the $1,000 on deposit for one year, you'll earn $50 in interest, and the account balance will total $1,050 at year's end. In this case, the **nominal (stated) rate of interest** is 5 percent. In contrast, the **effective rate of interest** is the annual rate of return that's *actually earned* (or *charged*) during the period the funds are held (or borrowed). You can calculate it with the following formula:

$$\text{Effective rate of interest} = \frac{\text{Amount of interest earned during the year}}{\text{Amount of money invested or deposited}}$$

In our example, because $50 was earned during the year on an investment of $1,000, the effective rate is $50/$1,000 or 5 percent, which is the same as the nominal rate of interest. (Notice in the preceding formula that it's interest earned during the *year* that matters; if you wanted to calculate the effective rate of interest on an account held for six months, you'd double the amount of interest earned.)

But suppose you can invest your funds elsewhere at a 5 percent rate, *compounded semiannually*.

Because interest is applied to your account at midyear, you'll earn *interest on interest* for the last six months of the year, thereby increasing the total interest earned for the year. The actual dollar earnings are determined as follows:

First 6 months' interest = $1,000 × 0.05 × 6/12 =	$25.00
Second 6 months' interest = $1,025 × 0.05 × 6/12 =	$25.63
Total annual interest	$50.63

Interest is generated on a larger investment in the second half of the year because the amount of money on deposit has increased by the amount of interest earned in the first half ($25). Although the nominal rate on this account is still 5 percent, the effective rate is 5.06 percent ($50.63/$1,000). As you may have guessed, *the more frequently interest is compounded, the greater the effective rate for any given nominal rate*. Exhibit 4.6 shows these relationships for a sample of interest rates and compounding periods. Note that with a 7 percent nominal rate, daily compounding adds one-fourth of a percent to the total return—not a trivial amount.

Compound Interest Generates Future Value

Compound interest is consistent with the *future value* concept introduced in Chapter 2. You can use the procedures described there to find out how much an investment or deposit will grow over time at a compounded rate of interest. For example, using the future value formula and the future value factor from Appendix A (if you need a reminder on that, see Chapter 2), you can find out how much $1,000 will

compound interest When interest earned in each subsequent period is determined by applying the *nominal (stated) rate of interest* to the sum of the initial deposit and the interest earned in each prior period.

simple interest Interest that is paid only on the initial amount of the deposit.

nominal (stated) rate of interest The promised rate of interest paid on a savings deposit or charged on a loan.

effective rate of interest The annual rate of return that is actually earned (or charged) during the period the funds are held (or borrowed).

© BIORAVEN/SHUTTERSTOCK.COM

Exhibit 4.6 The Magic of Compounding

The effective rate of interest you earn on a savings account will exceed the nominal (stated) rate if interest is compounded more than once a year (as are most savings and interest-paying accounts).

	Effective Rate				
Nominal Rate (%)	Annually (%)	Semiannually (%)	Quarterly (%)	Monthly (%)	Daily (%)
3	3.00	3.02	3.03	3.04	3.05
4	4.00	4.04	4.06	4.07	4.08
5	5.00	5.06	5.09	5.12	5.13
6	6.00	6.09	6.14	6.17	6.18
7	7.00	7.12	7.19	7.23	7.25
8	8.00	8.16	8.24	8.30	8.33
9	9.00	9.20	9.31	9.38	9.42
10	10.00	10.25	10.38	10.47	10.52
11	11.00	11.30	11.46	11.57	11.62
12	12.00	12.36	12.55	12.68	12.74

© Cengage Learning

certificate of deposit (CD) A type of savings instrument issued by certain financial institutions in exchange for a deposit; typically requires a minimum deposit and has a maturity ranging from seven days to as long as seven or more years.

be worth in four years if it's deposited into a savings account that pays 5 percent interest, compounded annually:

Future value = Amount deposited × Future value factor
= $1,000 × 1.216
= $1,216

You can use the same basic procedure to find the future value of an *annuity,* except you'd use the future value annuity factor from Appendix B (see Chapter 2). For instance, if you put $1,000 a year into a savings account that pays 5 percent per year compounded annually, in four years you will have:

Future value = Amount deposited yearly × Future value annuity factor
= $1,000 × 4.310
= $4,310

CALCULATOR

Inputs	Functions
1000	PV
4	N
5	I
	CPT
	FV
	Solution
	$1,215.51

SEE APPENDIX E FOR DETAILS.

© GEOPAUL/ISTOCKPHOTO

Go to Smart Sites

If you're not satisfied with the CD rate at your local bank, go to Bankrate.com. There you'll find not only the highest rates on CDs nationwide but also the checking and savings account fees at banks in your city. ●

4-5c A Variety of Ways to Save

During the past decade or so, there has been a huge growth of savings and short-term investment vehicles, particularly for people of modest means. Today, investors can choose from savings accounts, money market deposit accounts, money market mutual funds, NOW accounts, CDs, U.S. Treasury bills, Series EE bonds, Series I savings bonds, and asset management accounts. We examined several of these savings vehicles earlier in this chapter. Let's now look at the four remaining types of deposits and securities.

Certificates of Deposit

Certificates of deposit (CDs) differ from the savings instruments discussed earlier in that CD funds (except for CDs purchased through brokerage firms) must remain on deposit for a specified period (from seven days to as long as seven or more years). Although it's possible to withdraw funds prior to maturity, an

Financial Road Sign

Determining How Much Interest You Will Earn

Before opening a deposit account, investigate the following factors that determine the amount of interest you'll earn on your savings or interest-bearing checking account:

- Frequency of compounding. The more often interest is compounded, the higher your return.
- Balance on which interest is paid. For balances that qualify to earn interest, most banks now use the actual balance, or day of deposit to day of withdrawal, method. The actual balance method is fairest because it pays depositors interest on all funds on deposit for the actual amount of time they remain there.
- Interest rate paid. The Truth in Savings Act standardized the way that banks calculate the rate of interest they pay on deposit accounts. This makes it easy to compare each bank's annual percentage yield (APY) and to choose the bank offering the highest APY.

interest penalty usually makes withdrawal somewhat costly. The bank or other depository institution is free to charge whatever penalty it likes, but most require you to forfeit some interest. Banks, S&Ls, and other depository institutions can offer any rate and maturity CD they wish. As a result, a wide variety of CDs are offered by most banks, depository institutions, and other financial institutions such as brokerage firms. Most pay higher rates for larger deposits and longer periods of time. CDs are convenient to buy and hold because they offer attractive and highly competitive yields plus federal deposit insurance protection.

Go to Smart Sites

At the T-bill page of Treasury Direct's Web site, you can learn about T-bills and then buy them online. ●

U.S. Treasury Bills

The **U.S. Treasury bill (T-bill)** is considered the ultimate safe haven for savings and investments. T-bills are issued by the U.S. Treasury as part of its ongoing process of funding the national debt. They are sold on a discount basis in minimum denominations of $100 and are issued with 1-month (4-week), 3-month (13-week), 6-month (26-week), or 1-year (52-week) maturities. The bills are auctioned off every Monday.

Backed by the full faith and credit of the U.S. government, T-bills pay an attractive and safe return that is free from state and local income taxes.

T-bills are almost as liquid as cash because they can be sold at any time (in a very active secondary market) with no interest penalty. However, should you have to sell before maturity, you may lose some money on your investment if interest rates have risen, and you'll have to pay a broker's fee. Treasury bills pay interest on a *discount basis* and thus are different from other savings or short-term investment vehicles—that is, their interest is equal to the difference between the purchase price paid and their stated value at maturity. For example, if you paid $980 for a bill that will be worth $1,000 at maturity, you'll earn $20 in interest ($1,000 – $980).

An individual investor may purchase T-bills directly by participating in the weekly Treasury auctions or indirectly through a commercial bank or a securities dealer who buys bills for investors on a commission basis. T-bills may now be purchased over the Internet (**www.treasurydirect.gov**) or by using a touch-tone phone (call 800-722-2678 and follow the interactive menu to complete transactions).

Series EE Bonds

Although they are issued by the U.S. Treasury on a discount basis and are free of state and local income

U.S. Treasury bill (T-bill) A short-term (3-, 6-, or 12-month maturity) debt instrument issued at a discount by the U.S. Treasury in its ongoing process of funding the national debt.

Series EE bond A savings bond issued in various denominations by the U.S. Treasury.

I savings bond A savings bond issued at face value by the U.S. Treasury; its practically fixed rates provides some inflation protection.

taxes, **Series EE bonds** are quite different from T-bills. Savings bonds are *accrual-type securities,* which means that interest is paid when they're cashed in or before maturity, rather than periodically during their lives. Also known as "Patriot Bonds"—in honor of September 11, 2001—Series EE bonds are backed by the full faith and credit of the U.S. government and can be replaced without charge in case of loss, theft, or destruction. You can purchase them at banks or other depository institutions or through payroll deduction plans. Issued in denominations from $25 through $10,000, their purchase price is a uniform 50 percent of the face amount (thus a $100 bond will cost $50 and be worth $100 at maturity).

Series EE savings bonds earn interest at a fixed rate for 30 years. Their long life lets investors use them for truly long-term goals like education and retirement. The higher the rate of interest being paid, the shorter the time it takes for the bond to accrue from its discounted purchase price to its maturity value. Bonds can be redeemed any time after the first 12 months, although redeeming EE bonds in less than 5 years results in a penalty of the last 3 months of interest earned. The interest rate is set every 6 months in May and November and changes with prevailing Treasury security market yields. EE bonds increase in value every month and the stipulated interest rate is compounded semiannually.

In addition to being exempt from state and local taxes, Series EE bonds give their holders an appealing tax twist: *Savers need not report interest earned on their federal tax returns until the bonds are redeemed.* A second attractive tax feature—available to qualified bond holders—allows partial or complete tax avoidance of EE bond earnings when proceeds are used to pay education expenses, such as college tuition, for the bond purchaser, a spouse, or another IRS-defined dependent.

I Savings Bonds

I savings bonds are similar to Series EE bonds in several ways. For starters, both are issued by the U.S. Treasury, they're both accrual-type securities, and interest on both of them compounds semi-annually over a 30-year period. And like Series EE bonds, I savings bonds' interest remains exempt from state and local income taxes but does face state and local estate, inheritance, gift, and other excise taxes. In addition, interest earnings are subject to federal income tax but

© MOSHIMOCHI/SHUTTERSTOCK.COM

may be excluded when used to finance education, with some limitations.

There are some major differences between the two savings vehicles, however. For one, I bonds are available in smaller denominations (between $25 and $10,000), and while Series EE bonds are sold at a discount, I bonds are sold at face value. I savings bonds also differ from Series EE bonds in that their annual interest rate combines a fixed rate that remains the same for the life of the bond with a semiannual inflation rate that changes with the Consumer Price Index for all Urban Consumers (CPI-U). In contrast, the rate on Series EE bonds is based on the 6-month averages of 5-year Treasury security market yields. Thus, *the key difference between Series EE bonds and I bonds is that I bond returns are adjusted for inflation.* Note in particular that the earnings rate cannot go below zero and that the value of I bonds cannot drop below their redemption value.

Planning Over a Lifetime: Managing Cash and Savings

Here are some key considerations for managing your cash and savings in each stage of the life cycle.

Pre-family Independence: 20s	Family Formation/Career Development: 30–45	Pre-Retirement: 45–65	Retirement: 65 and Beyond
✓ Build up savings in general and emergency fund in particular.	✓ Increase savings to fund future financial goals.	✓ Maintain emergency fund.	✓ Maintain list of bank accounts that are easily accessible by spouse and family.
✓ Pay off any outstanding college loans.	✓ Broaden variety of cash management vehicles and reliance on financial planners for strategy development.	✓ Relate savings strategies more directly to retirement planning.	✓ Take advantage of bank accounts with senior discounts on fees.
✓ Find best mix of financial institution accounts based on fees, returns, and convenience. Make comparisons across banks.	✓ Carefully relate savings program to funding childrens' future educational needs.	✓ Start being sensitive to the presence of "senior" discounts.	✓ Integrate cash management and savings with retirement spending and estate plan.
		✓ Get an estimate of your Social Security benefits based on your expected retirement date.	

FINANCIAL PLANNING EXERCISES

LG1

1. Your parents are retired and have expressed concern about the really low interest rates they're earning on their savings. They've been approached by an advisor who says he has a "sure-fire" way to get them higher returns. What would you tell your parents about the low-interest-rate environment, and how would you advise them to view the advisor's new prospective investments?

LG3

2. Suppose that someone stole your ATM card and withdrew $950 from your checking account. How much money could you lose (according to federal legislation) if you reported the stolen card to the bank: (a) the day the card was stolen, (b) 6 days after the theft, (c) 65 days after receiving your periodic statement?

LG2, 3, 4

3. You're getting married and are unhappy with your present bank. Discuss how you should go about choosing a new bank and opening an account. Consider the factors that are important to you in selecting a bank—such as the type and ownership of new accounts and bank fees and charges.

LG4

4. Determine the annual net cost of these checking accounts:
   a. Monthly fee $4, check-processing fee of 20 cents, average of 23 checks written per month
   b. Annual interest of 2.5 percent paid if balance exceeds $750, $8 monthly fee if account falls below minimum balance, average monthly balance $815, account falls below $750 during four months

LG5, 6

5. If you put $6,000 in a savings account that pays interest at the rate of 4 percent, compounded annually, how much will you have in five years? (Hint: Use the future value formula.) How much interest will you earn during the five years? If you put $6,000 each year into a savings account that pays interest at the rate of 4 percent a year, how much would you have after five years?

LG6

6. Describe some of the short-term investment vehicles that can be used to manage your cash resources. What factors would you focus on if you were concerned that the government deficits associated with the recent financial crisis will lead to a significant increase in future inflation?

PFIN Student Study Tools—Visit CourseMate for PFIN 3. Log in at **www.cengagebrain.com**. Check out the bonus exercises and exhibits, interactive worksheets, Smart Sites, Critical Thinking Cases, Money Online, Kiplinger videos, quizzing, and more.

Cool Apps—Look for this new feature on CourseMate for PFIN 3. Cool Apps navigates the growing world of apps that are available for personal financial planning and tracking.

USE THE TOOLS.

- Rip out the Review Cards in the back of your book to study.

Or Visit CourseMate to:

- Read, search, highlight, and take notes in the Interactive eBook
- Review Flashcards (Print or Online) to master key terms
- Test yourself with Auto-Graded Quizzes
- Bring concepts to life with Games, Videos, and Animations!

Go to CourseMate for **PFIN** to begin using these tools.
Access at **www.cengagebrain.com**

Complete the Speak Up
survey in CourseMate at
www.cengagebrain.com

Follow us at
www.facebook.com/4ltrpress

5

MAKING AUTOMOBILE AND HOUSING DECISIONS

LEARNING GOALS

LG1 Design a plan to research and select a new or used automobile.

LG2 Decide whether to buy or lease a car.

LG3 Identify housing alternatives, assess the rental option, and perform a rent-or-buy analysis.

LG4 Evaluate the benefits and costs of homeownership and estimate how much you can afford to pay for a home.

LG5 Describe the home-buying process.

LG6 Choose mortgage financing that meets your needs.

How Will this Affect Me? A home is typically the largest single investment you'll ever make and a car is usually the second largest. The decisions to buy and finance these assets are consequently important, personal, and complicated.

This chapter presents frameworks for deciding when to buy a first home, how to finance a home, and when to rent rather than to purchase a home. It also discusses how to best go about buying a new or a used car and how to decide between leasing and purchasing a car. Given the large costs of such assets, this chapter provides frameworks that will significantly affect your short- and long-term financial well-being.

5-1 Buying an Automobile

LG1 Buying an automobile is probably the first major expenditure that many of us make. The car purchase is second only to housing in the amount of money the typical consumer spends. Because you'll buy a car many times during your life—most people buy one every two to five years—a systematic approach to selecting and financing a vehicle can mean significant savings. Before making any major purchase—whether it's a car, house, or large appliance—consider some basic guidelines to wise purchasing decisions.

- *Research* your purchase thoroughly, considering not only the market but also your personal needs.
- *Select* the best item for your needs.
- *Buy* the item after negotiating the best price and arranging financing on favorable terms. Be sure you understand all the terms of the sale before signing any contracts.
- *Maintain* your purchase and make necessary repairs promptly.

Exhibit 5.1 summarizes the steps in the new car-buying process.

5-1a Choosing a Car

Hybrid, diesel, or gas? Sport utility vehicle (SUV) or pickup truck? Sedan, convertible, or coupe? Car buyers today have more choices than ever before, so being an informed buyer is more important than ever. A good place to start your research is by

JUPITER IMAGES

After you read the chapter, explore the STUDY TOOLS listed on page 126.

tapping into the many available sources of information about cars, their prices, features, and reliability. Industry resources include manufacturers' brochures and dealer personnel. Car magazines, such as *Car and Driver*, *Motor Trend*, and *Road and Track*, and consumer magazines, such as *Consumer Reports* and *Consumer Guide*, regularly compare and rate cars. In addition, *Consumer Reports* and *Kiplinger's Personal Finance* magazine publish annual buying guides that include comparative statistics and ratings on most domestic and foreign cars.

The Internet has made it especially easy to do your homework before ever setting foot in a dealer's showroom. It's so easy today to visit one of the many comprehensive Web sites for car shoppers, where you'll find pricing and model information, as well as links to other useful sites. Don't forget the Web sites of the automobile

> " Car buyers today have more choices than ever before, so being an informed buyer is more important than ever. "

companies themselves; for example, Ford Motor Company is online at **http://www.ford.com**, Toyota is at **http://www.toyota.com**, and so on.

Go to Smart Sites

With Edmunds.com's auto loan calculators, you can evaluate auto financing options and check rates to find the lowest auto loan rates in your area. For more online resources, whenever you see "*Go to Smart Sites*" in this chapter, visit CourseMate for PFIN 3. Log in at **www.cengagebrain.com**. ●

© GEOPAUL/ISTOCKPHOTO

5-1b Affordability

Before shopping for a car, determine how much you can afford to spend. You'll need to calculate two numbers unless you plan to pay cash for the entire cost of the car.

- **Amount of down payment:** This money will likely come from savings, so be sure not to deplete your emergency fund.

Exhibit 5.1 — Key Steps in Buying a New Car

These steps summarize the car-buying process discussed in this chapter.

- Research which car best meets your needs and determine how much you can afford to spend on it. Choose the best way to pay for your new car—cash, financing, or lease. Ask your insurance agent for annual premium quotes for insuring various cars, as auto insurance is another significant expense of owning a car.

- Check Web sites like Edmunds.com and TV and newspapers for incentives and rebates on the car you would like to buy. This could include a cash rebate or low-cost financing.

- Decide on a price based on dealer's cost for the car and options, plus a markup for the dealer's profit, minus rebates and incentives.

- Find the exact car for you in terms of size, performance, safety, and styling. Choose at least three "target cars" to consider buying. Get online quotes from multiple car dealers.

- Test-drive the car—and the car salesperson. Test-drive the car at least once, both on local streets and on highways. Determine if the car salesperson is someone you want to do business with. Is he or she relaxed, open, and responsive to your questions?

- If you are trading in your old car, you are not likely to get as high a price as if you sell it yourself. Look up your car's trade-in value at Edmunds.com or kbb.com. Get bids from several dealers.

- Negotiate the lowest price on your new car by getting bids from at least three dealers. Hold firm on your target price before closing the deal.

- Close the deal after looking not just at the cost of the car but also the related expenses. Consider the sales tax and various fees. Get the salesperson to fax you a worksheet and invoice before you go to the dealership.

- Review and sign the paperwork. If you have a worksheet for the deal, the contract should match it. Make sure the numbers match and there are no additional charges or fees.

- Inspect the car for scratches and dents. If anything is missing—like floor mats, for example—ask for a "Due Bill" that states it in writing.

Source: Adapted from Philip Read, "10 Steps to Buying a New Car," http://www.edmunds.com/car-buying/10-steps-to-buying-a-new-car.html, accessed March 2011.

- **Size of the monthly loan payment you can afford:** Carefully consider the amount of money you have available and the amount you can afford to spend, along with your basic transportation needs. Don't forget to include insurance. And remember: your monthly car payment should be no more than 20 percent of your monthly net income.

Crunching the Numbers

You can also use the down payment and monthly payment amounts to calculate the total amount that you can afford for a car. For example, suppose that you have $3,000 for a down payment, you can pay $500 a month, and your bank is offering 4-year (48-month) car loans at 6 percent annual (6%/12 = .5%, monthly) interest. How much of a loan can you afford? Using a financial calculator and the keystrokes shown in the margin, you'll find that you can take out a loan of about $21,300. Add that to the $3,000 down payment, and you'll be able to afford a car costing $24,300.

Operating Costs

The out-of-pocket cost of operating an automobile includes not only car payments but also insurance, license, fuel, oil, tires, and other operating and maintenance outlays. Some of these costs are *fixed* regardless of how much you drive; others are *variable*, depending on the number of miles you drive. The biggest fixed cost is likely to be the *installment payments* associated with the loan (or lease) used to acquire the car; the biggest variable cost will probably be fuel.

CALCULATOR

Inputs	Functions
48	N
.5	I
500	PMT
	CPT
	PV
	Solution
	21,290.16

SEE APPENDIX E FOR DETAILS.

Another significant cost is **depreciation**, which is the loss in value that occurs over the period of ownership. In effect, depreciation is the difference between the price you paid for the car and what you can sell it for. If you paid $20,000 for an automobile that can be sold three years later for $14,000, the car will cost you $6,000 in depreciation. Although depreciation may not be a recurring out-of-pocket cost, it's an important operating expense that shouldn't be overlooked.

Gas, Diesel, or Hybrid?

One thing that's becoming increasingly important in car buying is the type of fuel you prefer to use in your car. If you're a "green" who's concerned about the environmental impact of the fuel your car uses, you may be interested only in a hybrid car. In this case, price differences may not matter. Although you'll want to consider fuel economy when car shopping, comparable gas-fueled, internal combustion engines and diesel-powered cars tend to have similar fuel economy. Generally, diesels are a bit noisier, have less acceleration but more power, and have longer engine lives than do traditional gas-powered cars.

Hybrids, which blend gas and battery power, have experienced rapid sales growth due to high gas prices, improved technology and availability, and greater public awareness of environmental issues. Although they're more economical and less polluting than gas- and diesel-powered vehicles, hybrids do have some disadvantages: high cost of battery replacement, more sluggish acceleration, generally higher repair costs, and typically higher initial purchase price. It's important to consider the differences between the costs and performance of differently fueled vehicles and decide on the vehicle you want before shopping for a specific new or used car.

New, Used, or "Nearly New"?

One decision you must make is whether to buy a new, used, or "nearly new" car. If you can't afford to buy a new car, the decision is made for you. Some people who can afford to buy a new car choose to buy a used car so they can have a better model—a used luxury car such as a BMW, Lexus, or Mercedes—rather than a less-expensive brand of new car, such as a Ford. With the increasing popularity of used cars, car dealers are trying to dispel the negative image associated with buying a used, or "pre-owned," car. For some sound advice, see the Bonus Exhibit "Pros and Cons of Buying a Used Car." (Visit CourseMate for PFIN 3. Log in at **www.cengagebrain.com**.)

Once you know what you want, shop at these places:

- **Franchise dealerships:** Offer the latest-model used cars, provide financing, and will negotiate on price.

- **Superstores:** AutoNation, CarMax, and similar dealers offer no-haggle pricing and a large selection. They certify their cars and may offer a limited short-term warranty.

- **Independent used car lots:** Usually offer older (four- to six-year-old) cars and have lower overhead than franchise dealers. There are no industry standards, so be sure to check with the Better Business Bureau before buying.

- **Private individuals:** Generally cost less because there's no dealer overhead; may have maintenance records. Be sure that the seller holds the title to the car.

> **depreciation** The loss in the value of an asset such as an automobile that occurs over its period of ownership; calculated as the difference between the price initially paid and the subsequent sale price.

Size, Body Style, and Features

Your first consideration should be what type of car you need. More than one style category may work for you. For example, a family of five can buy a mid-size or full-size sedan, station wagon, minivan, or compact or full-size SUV. When considering size, body style, and features, think about your needs, likes, and dislikes as well as the cost. In most cases there's a direct relationship between size and cost: In general, the larger the car, the more expensive it will be to purchase and to operate. Also consider performance, handling, appearance, fuel economy, reliability, repair problems, and the resale value of the car. And don't try to adapt your needs to fit the car you want—a two-passenger sports car may not be appropriate if you need the car for business or if you have children.

By listing all of the options you want before shopping for a new car, you can avoid paying for features you really don't need. Literally hundreds of options—ranging in price from a few dollars up to $2,000 or more—are available, including automatic transmission, a bigger engine, air conditioning, high-performance brakes, an iPod/MP3 player, clock, power windows, power seats, electric door locks, leather seats, navigation systems, a rear window defroster, and special suspension. Some appearance-related options are two-tone or metallic paint, electric sunroof, special tires, sport wheels, and various interior and exterior trim packages. On new cars, window stickers detail each option and its price; in contrast, you're usually on your own with used cars.

© RITU MANOJ JETHANI/SHUTTERSTOCK.COM

anchor A behavioral bias in which an individual tends to allow an initial estimate (of value or price) to dominate the subsequent assessment (of value or price) regardless of new information to the contrary.

Other Considerations

Here are some other factors that affect affordability:

- **Trading in or selling your existing car**: Although trading in is convenient, it's generally more financially advantageous to sell your old car outright. If you're willing to take the time, you can usually sell your car for more than the wholesale price typically offered by a dealer on a trade-in.

- **Fuel economy**: The *Environmental Protection Agency (EPA) mileage ratings* are especially useful on new vehicles, which carry a sticker indicating the number of miles per gallon each model is expected to get for both city and highway driving.

- **Safety features**: Government regulations ensure that these features are likely to be similar in new cars, but older used cars may not have some features such as side-impact airbags. And don't forget to include the cost of *auto insurance*.

5-1c The Purchase Transaction

Once you've determined what you can afford to spend and the features that you want, you're ready to begin car shopping. If you plan to buy a new car, visit all dealers with cars that meet your requirements. Look the cars over and ask questions—but don't make

BEHAVIOR MATTERS

Watch Out for "Anchoring": The Case of the Used Car Salesperson Strategy

While we try to be logical and objective in making purchases, psychologists find that people make estimates of the appropriate price of an item by starting from an initial estimate of value. We tend to make biased decisions because we often **anchor** on that initial value and have a hard time moving away from it in negotiating transactions.

Consider a common strategy of used car salespeople. Why do you think that they start negotiating with a high price and then work their way down? Salespeople are trying to get the consumer anchored on the initial high price so that when a lower price is offered, the consumer tends to view the lower price as a good value, even if that is not the case. Combine this behavioral bias with our tendency to be a bit too overconfident about our negotiating skills, and you have a potential problem.

So what should you do in light of the anchoring behavioral bias? Recognize the tendency, do your homework about a reasonable price for a used car or any other item you want to buy, and take into account the used car salesperson's strategy.

any offers until you've found two or three cars with the desired features that are priced within your budget. Also, if you can be flexible about the model and options you want, you can sometimes negotiate a better deal than if you're determined to have a particular model and options. Be sure to do some comparison shopping, because a dealer selling the same brand as another may give you a better deal. And watch out for something called lowballing, where the salesperson quotes a low price to get you to make an offer, and then negotiates the price upward prior to your signing the sales contract. Exhibit 5.2 lists some other factors to consider once you begin looking at cars.

Negotiating Price

Choosing among various makes, models, and options can make comparisons difficult. The price you pay for a car, whether new or used, can consequently vary widely. The more you narrow your choices to a particular car, the easier it is to get price quotes from dealers to make an "apples-to-apples" comparison.

The "sticker price" on a new car represents the manufacturer's *suggested retail price* for that particular car with its listed options. This price means very little. The key to negotiating a good price is knowing the *dealer's cost* for the car. The easiest and quickest way to find the dealer's invoice cost is going to the Edmunds (**http://www.edmunds.com**) or Kelley Blue Book (**http://www.kbb.com**) Web sites. Try to negotiate the lowest acceptable markup above dealer invoice (3 percent to 4 percent for cars priced under $20,000; 6 percent to 7 percent for higher-priced models), then push for a firm quote, and make it clear that you are comparison shopping.

If you want to avoid negotiating entirely, you can buy your car through a buying service, either by phone or over the Internet. These include independent companies—such as AutoVantage (**http://www.autovantage.com**), Autobytel (**http://www.autobytel.com**), and AutoWeb (**http://www.autoweb.com**)—or

ZHANG YI BJ/AP PHOTOS

Exhibit 5.2 Finding the Best Car for You

Start by inspecting the key points of the car. Don't overlook the obvious:

- *How easy is it to get people and things into and out of the car?*

  Do the doors open easily?

  Is the trunk large enough for your needs?

  Does the car offer a pass-through or fold-down rear seat to accommodate larger items?

- *Comfort and visibility:*

  Are the seats comfortable?

  Can you adjust the driver's seat and steering wheel properly?

  What are the car's blind spots for a person of your height?

  Can you see all the gauges clearly?

  Can you reach the controls for the radio, iPod/MP3 player, heater, air conditioner, and other features easily while driving?

  Does it have the options you want?

Then take the car for a test drive.

- Set aside at least 20 minutes and drive it on highways and local roads.

- To test acceleration, merge into traffic getting onto the freeway and try passing another car.

- If possible, drive home and make sure the car fits into your garage—especially if you're interested in a larger SUV or truck!

- For a used car, test the heater and air conditioner. Then turn the fan off and listen for any unusual engine noises.

- Check out overall handling. Parallel park, make a U-turn, brake hard, and so on. Do the gears shift smoothly? If testing a standard transmission, try to determine if the clutch is engaging too high or too low, which might indicate excessive wear or a problem.

As soon as you return to the car lot, take notes on how well the car handled and how comfortable you felt driving it. This is especially important if you are testing several cars.

services offered through credit unions, motor clubs, and discount warehouses such as Costco. Buying services work in a variety of ways. They may have an arrangement with a network of dealers to sell cars at a predetermined price above invoice, provide you with competitive bids from several local dealers, find the car you want and negotiate the price with the dealer, or place an order with the factory for a made-to-order car. The price for these services ranges from about $55 for a Costco membership to as much as $600, and results vary. You'll get a good price through a service—although you can't assume that it will be the best price.

It's best not to discuss your plan to finance the purchase or the value of your trade-in until you've settled the question of price. These should be separate issues. Salespeople will typically want to find out how much you can afford monthly and then offer financing deals with payments close to that amount. In the case of trade-ins, the dealer might offer you a good price for your old car and raise the price of the new car to compensate. The dealer may offer financing terms that sound attractive, but be sure to compare them with the cost of bank loans. Sometimes dealers increase the price of the car to

make up for a low interest rate, or attractive financing may apply only to certain models. If you're interested in dealer financing, make sure the monthly payment quoted by the dealer's finance manager is just for the loan. Often financing charges include unneeded extras such as credit life insurance, accident insurance, an extended warranty, or a service package.

Manufacturers and dealers often offer buyers special incentives, such as rebates and cut-rate financing, particularly when car sales are slow. In some cases, you may have a choice between a rebate and low-cost financing. To determine which is the better deal, calculate the difference between the monthly payments on a market-rate bank loan and the special dealer loan for the same term. Multiply the payment difference by the loan maturity, in months, and compare it with the rebate. For example, assume that the dealer offers either a $1,000 rebate or a 4 percent interest rate on a $10,000, 4-year loan. Your monthly payments would be $226 with dealer financing and $234 on a 6 percent bank loan with similar terms. The payment savings over the life of the loan are $384 ($8 per month × 48 months), which is less than the $1,000 rebate. So in this case you would be better off with the rebate.

sales contract An agreement to purchase an automobile that states the offering price and all conditions of the offer; when signed by the buyer and seller, the contract legally binds them to its terms.

lease An arrangement in which the lessee receives the use of a car (or other asset) in exchange for making monthly lease payments over a specified period.

closed-end lease The most popular form of automobile lease; often called a *walk-away lease*, because at the end of its term the lessee simply turns in the car (assuming the preset mileage limit has not been exceeded and the car hasn't been abused).

open-end (finance) lease An automobile lease under which the estimated *residual value* of the car is used to determine lease payments; if the car is actually worth less than this value at the end of the lease, the lessee must pay the difference.

residual value The remaining value of a leased car at the end of the lease term.

capitalized cost The price of a car that is being leased.

money factor The financing rate on a lease; similar to the interest rate on a loan.

Closing the Deal

Whether you're buying a new or used car, to make a legally binding offer you must sign a **sales contract** that specifies the offering price and all the conditions of your offer. The sales contract also specifies whether the offer includes a trade-in. If it does, the offering price will include both the payment amount and the trade-in allowance. Because this agreement contractually binds you to purchase the car at the offering price, be sure that you want and can afford the car before signing the agreement. You may be required to include a deposit of around $200 or more with the contract to show that you're making an offer in good faith.

Once the dealer accepts your offer, you complete the purchase transaction and take delivery of the car. If you're not paying cash for the car, you can arrange financing through the dealer, at your bank, a credit union, or a consumer finance company. The key aspects of these types of installment loans, which can be quickly negotiated if your credit is good, are discussed in Chapter 7.

5-2 Leasing a Car

LG2 Don't worry about temperamental engines or transmissions—just get a new car every few years using a leasing arrangement. Put a small amount down, make easy payments. No wonder leasing is popular, accounting for 15 percent to 20 percent of all new vehicles delivered. When you **lease**, you (the lessee) receive the use of a car in exchange for monthly lease payments over a specified period of time, usually two to four years. Leasing appeals to a wide range of car owners, even though the total cost of leasing is generally more than buying a car with a loan, and at the end of the lease you have nothing. The car—and the money you paid to rent it—is gone. So why do so many car buyers lease their cars? Reasons include rising new car prices, the nondeductibility of consumer loan interest, lower monthly payments, driving a more expensive car for the same monthly payment, and minimizing the down payment to preserve cash.

With all the advertisements promising low monthly lease payments, it's easy to focus on only the payment.

Unlike a loan purchase, with a lease you're paying not for the whole car but only for its use during a specified period. Leasing is a more complex arrangement than borrowing money to buy a car. Until you understand how leasing works, and compare lease terms with bank financing, you won't know if leasing is the right choice for you.

5-2a The Leasing Process

The first step is the same for leasing as it is for purchasing: research car types and brands, comparison shop at several dealers, and find the car you want at the best price. Don't ask the dealer about leasing or any financing incentives until *after* you've negotiated the final price. Then compare the lease terms offered by the dealer to those of at least one independent leasing firm. As with a purchase, try to negotiate lower lease payments—a payment reduction of $20 a month saves nearly $1,000 on a four-year lease. And don't reveal what you can afford to pay per month; doing so can lead you to a poor lease deal.

The vast majority of car lessees choose the **closed-end lease**, often called the *walk-away lease*, because at the end of its term you simply turn in the car and walk away, assuming that you have neither exceeded the preset mileage limit nor abused the car. Under the less popular **open-end (or finance) lease**, if the car is worth less than the estimated **residual value**—the remaining value of the car at the end of the lease term—then you must pay the difference. These leases are used primarily for commercial business leasing.

A commonly cited benefit of leasing is the absence of a down payment. However, today most leases require a "capital cost reduction," which is a type of down payment that lowers the potential depreciation and therefore your monthly lease payments.

Given the one-time, up-front capital cost reduction payment, the size of the monthly lease payment is based on four variables:

1. The **capitalized cost** of the car (the price of the car you are leasing)
2. The forecast *residual value* of the car at the end of the lease
3. The **money factor**, or financing rate on the lease (similar to the interest rate on a loan)
4. The *lease term*

Terminating a lease early is often difficult and costly, so be reasonably certain that you can keep the car for the full lease term. The lease contract should outline any costs and additional fees associated with early termination. Early termination clauses also apply to cars that are stolen or totaled in an accident. Some leases require "gap insurance" to cover the lost lease payments that would result from early termination caused by one of these events.

Under most leases, you are responsible for insuring and maintaining the car. Also, be aware that at the end of the lease, you are obligated to pay for any "unreasonable wear and tear." A good lease contract should clearly define what is considered unreasonable. In addition, most leases require the lessee to pay a disposition fee of about $150 to $250 when the car is returned.

The annual mileage allowance—typically, about 10,000 to 15,000 miles per year for the lease term—is another important lease consideration. Usually the lessee must pay between 10 and 25 cents per mile for any miles over the limit. For example, if the lease allows 15,000 miles per year and you put 50,000 miles on a car over the three-year term of the lease, then you'd exceed the limit by 5,000 miles ($3 \times 15{,}000 = 45{,}000 < 50{,}000$); at 20 cents per mile, you'd be liable for $0.20 \times 5{,}000 = \$1{,}000$. Clearly, if you expect to exceed the allowable mileage, you would be wise to negotiate a more favorable rate for extra miles before signing the lease contract.

Most auto leases include a **purchase option** (either a fixed price, the market price at the end of the lease term, or the residual value of the car) that specifies the price at which the lessee can buy the car at the end of the lease term. A lower residual results in a lower purchase price but raises monthly payments.

© SHELLY AGAMI PHOTOAR/SHUTTERSTOCK.COM

purchase option A price specified in a lease at which the lessee can buy the car at the end of the lease term.

5-2b The Lease versus Purchase Analysis

To decide whether it is less costly to lease rather than purchase a car, you need to perform a *lease versus purchase analysis* to compare the total cost of leasing to the total cost of purchasing a car over equal periods. In this analysis, the purchase is assumed to be financed with an installment loan over the same period as the lease.

For example, assume that Stella Rather is considering either leasing or purchasing a new Toyota Prius costing $29,900. The four-year, closed-end lease that she is considering requires a $2,900 down payment (capital cost reduction), a $500 security deposit, and monthly payments of $440, including sales tax. If she purchases the car, she will make a $4,500 down payment and finance the balance with a four-year, 4 percent loan requiring monthly payments of about $576. She will also have to pay 5 percent sales tax ($1,500) on the purchase, and she expects the car to have a residual value of $16,500 at the end of four years. After filling in Worksheet 5.1, Stella concludes that purchasing is better because its *total cost* of $17,665.42 is $6,762.58 less than the $24,428.00 total cost of leasing—even though the monthly lease payment is about $136 lower. Clearly, all else being equal, the least costly alternative is preferred.

5-2c When the Lease Ends

At the end of the lease, you'll be faced with a major decision. Should you return the car and walk away, or should you buy the car? If you turn in the car and move on to a new model, you may be hit with "excess wear and damage" and "excess mileage" charges and disposition fees. If you can't return the car without high repair charges or greatly exceeded mileage allowances, you may come out ahead by buying the car. Whether the purchase option makes sense depends on the residual value. Sometimes, with popular cars, the residual value in your lease agreement is below the car's trade-in value. Buying the car then makes sense. Even if you want a different car, you can exercise the purchase option and sell the car on the open market and net the difference, which could be $1,000 or more. If the reverse is true and the residual is higher than the price of a comparable used car, just let the lease expire.

Financial Planning Tips

When Does it Make Sense to Lease a Car?

The most important question to ask yourself is why you need a new car every few years. While about 20 percent of retail consumers used to lease rather than buy cars, since the financial crisis of 2008–2009 that has fallen closer to 15 percent. This is, in part, because when interest rates are low, lease payments are not much cheaper than financing. When rates move back up, leasing is likely to become more popular again.

Leasing may make sense if:

- You value purchasing flexibility. A lease allows you to put off the purchasing decision while using the car. It's like having a test drive that lasts several years instead of a few minutes.
- You value the convenience of not having to deal with significant auto repairs.
- You're self-employed and can write off your leasing payment as a business expense.
- You want to drive a luxury car for less but you don't want to put up that much money.

The key is being honest about why you want to lease and being informed about the costs and benefits of a leasing arrangement.

Source: Adapted from "To Buy or to Lease?" http://www.cars.com/go/advice/Story.jsp?section=lease&subject=buy_lease&story=buyLease, accessed March 2012.

DBLIGHT/ISTOCKPHOTO.COM

This worksheet illustrates Stella Rather's lease versus purchase analysis for a new Toyota Prius costing $29,990. The 4-year closed-end lease requires an initial payment of $3,400 ($2,900 down payment + $500 security deposit) and monthly payments of $440. Purchasing requires a $4,500 down payment, sales tax of 5 percent ($1,499.50), and 48 monthly payments of $575.45. The trade-in value of the new car at the end of 4 years is estimated to be $16,500. *Because the total cost of leasing of $24,428 is greater than the $17,665.42 total cost of purchasing, Stella should purchase rather than lease the car.*

AUTOMOBILE LEASE VERSUS PURCHASE ANALYSIS*

Name _Stella Rather_ Date _Sep 11, 2015_

Item Description	Amount
LEASE	
1 Initial payment:	
a. Down payment (capital cost reduction): $ 2,900.00	
b. Security deposit: 500.00	$ 3,400.00
2 Term of lease and loan (years)*	4
3 Term of lease and loan (months) (Item 2 × 12)	48
4 Monthly lease payment	$ 440.00
5 Total payments over term of lease (Item 3 × Item 4)	$ 21,120.00
6 Interest rate earned on savings (in decimal form)	0.030
7 Opportunity cost of initial payment (Item 1 × Item 2 × Item 6)	$ 408.00
8 Payment/refund for market value adjustment at end of lease ($0 for closed-end leases) and/or estimated end-of-term charges	$ 0.00
9 Total cost of leasing (Item 1a + Item 5 + Item 7 + Item 8)	$ 24,428.00
PURCHASE	
10 Purchase price	$ 29,990.00
11 Down payment	$ 4,500.00
12 Sales tax rate (in decimal form)	0.50
13 Sales tax (Item 10 × Item 12)	$ 1,499.50
14 Monthly loan payment (Terms: _25,490.00_, _48_ months, _4_ %)	$ 575.54
15 Total payments over term of loan (Item 3 × Item 14)	$ 27,625.92
16 Opportunity cost of down payment (Item 2 × Item 6 × Item 11)	$ 540.00
17 Estimated value of car at end of loan	$ 16,500.00
18 Total cost of purchasing (Item 11 + Item 13 + Item 15 + Item 16 − Item 17)	$ 17,665.42

DECISION

If the value of Item 9 is less than the value of Item 18, leasing is preferred; otherwise, the *purchase alternative is preferred.*

*Note: This form is based on assumed equal terms (periods) for the lease and the installment loan, which is assumed to be used to finance the purchase.

© Cengage Learning

5-3 Meeting Housing Needs: Buy or Rent?

5-3a Housing Prices and the Recent Financial Crisis

LG3 Before considering how and when to buy or rent a home, it is important to consider the recent rough history of housing prices during and after the financial crisis of 2008–2009. After examining this context in which housing decisions are made, we'll consider how to know when you should buy your first home. There are many factors to consider before taking on such a large financial responsibility. In the remainder of this chapter, we'll explore some of these factors and discuss how to approach the home-buying and renting process.

The bubble in real estate prices had important side effects. It encouraged a massive increase in construction and the extraction of a lot of home equity through home equity loans and refinancings, about two-thirds of which went into increased consumption. Net worth increased with home prices as well. Yet those side effects went in the opposite direction during the financial crisis. Between 2007 and 2009, the crisis reduced the average family's net worth by about 23 percent and dampened consumption, which slowed the macroeconomy. Home **foreclosures**, the process whereby lenders attempt to recover loan balances from borrowers who have quit making payments by forcing the sale of the home pledged as collateral, increased from only 1.2 percent of homes in 2006 to 4.6 percent in 2010. While the number of bank-owned homes and foreclosures has decreased substantially, average net worth, consumption, and home prices remain depressed as of early 2012.

From early 2001 through 2006, home prices in the United States rose rapidly. The median nominal sales price of existing single-family homes rose from $147,800 to $221,900. In the third quarter of 2006, existing home prices started dropping and fell to a median price of $166,200 by the end of 2011. Prices had fallen because the real estate bubble had popped and the financial crisis of 2008–2009 had vastly depressed home sales. This period of recession was characterized by high unemployment, low consumer confidence, and tighter credit. Indeed, about 1 in 7 American homeowners had *negative equity* in their homes, meaning they owed more on their mortgage than their homes were worth.

foreclosure the process whereby lenders attempt to recover loan balances from borrowers who have quit making payments by forcing the sale of the home pledged as collateral.

5-3b What Type of Housing Meets Your Needs?

Knowing when to buy your first home is not always clear-cut. There are many factors to consider before taking on such a large financial responsibility. In the remainder of this chapter, we'll explore some of these factors and discuss how to approach the home-buying process.

Because you have your own unique set of likes and dislikes, the best way to start your search for housing is to list your preferences and classify them according to whether their satisfaction is essential, desirable, or merely a "plus." This exercise is important for three reasons. First, it screens out housing that doesn't meet your minimum requirements. Second, it helps you recognize that you may have to make trade-offs, because seldom will you find a single home that meets all your needs. Third, it will help you focus on those needs for which you are willing and able to pay.

Homeownership in America has always been viewed as a highly desirable financial objective—which explains in part why we have such a high ownership rate in this country. The home-ownership rate in the United States in 2011 was around 66 percent, which is the lowest since 1998 and far lower than the high of 69.2 percent in 2004. As a potential homeowner, one of the first decisions you'll have to make is the type of housing unit that you want and need. Several of the following may be suitable:

- **Single-family homes:** These are the most popular choice. They can be stand-alone homes on their own legally defined lots or *row houses* or *townhouses* that share a common wall. As a rule, single-family homes offer buyers privacy, prestige, pride of ownership, and maximum property control.

© KATI MOLIBN/SHUTTERSTOCK.COM

- **Condominiums:** The term **condominium**, or **condo**, describes a form of ownership rather than a type of building. Condominiums can be apartments, townhouses, or cluster housing. The condominium buyer receives title to an individual residential unit and joint ownership of common areas and facilities such as lobbies, swimming pools, lakes, and tennis courts. Buyers arrange their own mortgages and pay their own taxes for their units. They are assessed a monthly *homeowner's fee* for their proportionate share of common facility maintenance costs. Many home buyers are attracted to condominiums because they don't want the responsibility of maintaining and caring for a large property. The Bonus Exhibit "Condo Buyer's Checklist" lists some of the key things to check before buying a condominium. (Visit CourseMate for PFIN 3. Log in at **www.cengagebrain.com**.)

- **Cooperative apartments:** In a **cooperative apartment**, or **co-op**, building, each tenant owns a share of the nonprofit corporation that owns the building. Residents lease their units from the corporation and pay a monthly assessment in proportion to ownership shares, based on the space they occupy. These assessments cover the cost of services, maintenance, taxes, and the mortgage on the entire building, and they are subject to change depending on the actual costs of operating the building and the actions of the board of directors, which determines the corporation's policies.

- **Rental units:** Some individuals and families choose to *rent* or *lease* their place of residence rather than own it. They may be just starting out and have limited funds for housing, they may be uncertain as to where they want to live, or they just may prefer renting. Rental units range from duplexes, fourplexes, and even single-family homes to large, high-rise apartment complexes containing several hundred units. Renting does come with restrictions, however. For example, you may not be allowed to have a pet or make changes to the unit's appearance.

Gauging the General Attractiveness of Renting vs. Buying a Home

You can get a general sense of the relative cost of renting vs. buying a home by considering the so-called **rent ratio**, which is the ratio of the average house price to the

average annual rent in the area that you are considering. Given the bursting of the housing bubble in the late 2000s, the inflation-adjusted rent ratio as of early 2012 fell to around late-1990 levels. Thus, the relative attractiveness of renting has decreased in recent years. Exhibit 5.3 shows the nominal rent ratios for major U.S. cities, which differ significantly in the relative attractiveness of buying versus renting. It suggests that rent ratios between 31 and 35 indicate that it is more attractive to rent than to buy. At the other extreme, a rent ratio between 6 and 10 indicates that it is more attractive to rent than to buy. And a moderate rent ratio (between 16 and 20) suggests that while renting is expensive, it may still be better to buy. Exhibit 5.6 shows that in early 2012, New York City had a whopping rent ratio of 39, which implies that it was much cheaper to rent than to buy a home. On the other end of the spectrum, Las Vegas had a rent ratio of only 6, and Phoenix a ratio of only 7. Thus, it was quite attractive to buy rather than rent in those cities at that time. You may want to consider the rent ratio when considering where to relocate or to form some basic expectations if you've decided where to move.

Analyzing the Rent-or-Buy Decision

Many people choose to rent rather than buy their home. For example, young adults usually rent for one or more of the following reasons: (1) they don't have the funds for a down payment and closing costs, (2) they're unsettled in their jobs and family status, (3) they don't want the additional responsibilities associated with homeownership, or (4) they believe they can afford a nicer home later by renting now because housing market conditions or mortgage rates are currently unattractive. The economics of renting or buying a place to live depends on three main factors: (1) housing prices and mortgage interest rates, (2) tax write-offs for homeowners, and (3) the expected increase or decrease in home values over time.

To choose the lowest-cost alternative, compare the cost of renting with the cost of buying, as illustrated by the rent-or-buy analysis in Worksheet 5.2. Note that because the interest deduction nearly always exceeds the amount of the standard deduction ($5,900 for single and $11,900 for married filing jointly in 2012), the form assumes that the taxpayer will itemize deductions.

Suppose that you must decide between renting an apartment for $850 a month or buying a similar-sized condominium for $150,000. Purchasing the condo involves a $30,000 down payment; taking out a $120,000, 6 percent, 30-year mortgage

Inputs	Functions
120000	PV
360	N
6	÷
12	=
	I
	CPT
	PMT
	Solution
	719.46

CALCULATOR

SEE APPENDIX E FOR DETAILS.

Exhibit 5.3   Relative Attractiveness of Renting Versus Buying a House

The Trulia Rent vs. Buy Index portrays the average list price of homes versus the average annual rent on two-bedroom apartments, condos, and townhomes in America's 50 largest cities by population listed on Trulis.com.

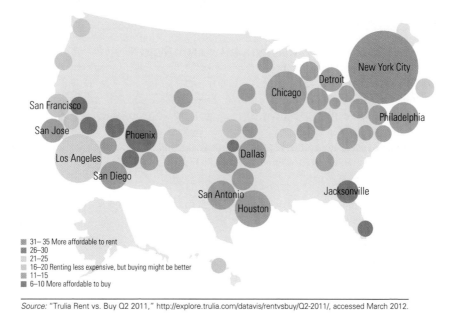

31– 35 More affordable to rent
26–30
21–25
16–20 Renting less expensive, but buying might be better
11–15
6–10 More affordable to buy

Source: "Trulia Rent vs. Buy Q2 2011," http://explore.trulia.com/datavis/rentvsbuy/Q2-2011/, accessed March 2012.

with monthly mortgage payments of $719; $4,500 in closing costs; and property taxes, insurance, and maintenance. With renting, the only costs are the $850 monthly rental payment and an annual renter's insurance premium of $600. Assume that you're in the 25 percent ordinary income tax bracket and that you'll itemize deductions if you purchase the home. Substituting the appropriate values into Worksheet 5.2 and making the required calculations results in the total cost of each alternative.

The cost of renting in Part A of Worksheet 5.2 is simply the annual rent (monthly rent multiplied by 12) plus the annual renter's insurance premium of $600, plus the $40 opportunity cost of the security deposit, all of which results in a total annual cost of $10,840. The annual cost of buying in Part B includes mortgage payments, property taxes, homeowner's insurance, annual maintenance, and closing costs to arrive at total costs of $14,964 in Item 6. Then, subtract the portion of the mortgage payment going to pay off the loan balance because it's not part of the interest cost. Subtract the tax savings derived from interest and property taxes to arrive at Item 11, which is the after-tax cost of homeownership of $10,980. But as a homeowner, you also enjoy the benefits of appreciation. Assuming a modest 2 percent inflation in the value of the home reduces the annual cost to $7,980. Thus, buying is better than renting because the total cost of renting is $2,860 ($10,840 – $7,980) a year more than the total cost of buying.

It's important not to base the rent-or-buy decision solely on the numbers. Your personal needs and the general condition of the housing market are also important considerations. If you think you may want

With this procedure for making the rent-or-buy decision, you should *rent* if the total cost of renting is less than the total cost of buying or *buy* if the total cost of renting is more than the total cost of buying. In this example, the rental option requires monthly payments of $850. The purchase option is a $150,000 condo, financed with a $30,000 down payment and a $120,000, 6 percent, 30-year mortgage, with additional closing costs of $4,500.

RENT-OR-BUY ANALYSIS

A. COST OF RENTING

1. Annual rental costs
   (12 × monthly rental rate of $ _850_) .... $ 10,200

2. Renter's insurance 600

3. Opportunity cost of security deposit: $ *1,000* × after-tax savings rate *0.040* 40
   Total cost of renting (line A.1 + line A.2 + line A.3) .... $ 10,840

B. COST OF BUYING

1. Annual mortgage payments (Terms: $ *120,000* , *360* months, *6* %) $ 8,634
   (12 × monthly mortgage payment of $ *719*)

2. Property taxes 3,000
   (*2.0*% of price of home)

3. Homeowner's insurance 750
   (*0.5*% of price of home)

4. Maintenance 1,200
   (*0.8*% of price of home)

5. After-tax cost of interest on down payment and closing costs 1,380
   ($ *34,500* × *4.0* % after-tax rate of return)

6. Total costs (sum of lines B.1 through B.5) .... $ 14,964

Less:

7. Principal reduction in loan balance (see note below) .... $ 1,434

8. Tax savings due to interest deductions* 1,800
   (Interest portion of mortgage payments $ *7,200* × tax rate of *25* %)

9. Tax savings due to property tax deductions* 750
   (line B.2 × tax rate of *25* %)

10. Total deductions (sum of lines B.7 through B.9) 3,984

11. Annual after-tax cost of homeownership .... $ 10,980
    (line B.6 − line B.10)

12. Estimated annual appreciation in value of home 3,000
    (*2* % of price of home)
    Total cost of buying (line B.11 − line B.12) .... $ 7,980

Note: Find monthly mortgage payments using a calculator or from Exhibit 5.5. An easy way to approximate the portion of the annual loan payment that goes to interest (line B.8) is to multiply the interest rate by the size of the loan (in this case, $120,000 × .06 = $7,200). Then, to find the principal reduction in the loan balance (line B.7), simply subtract the amount that goes to interest from total annual mortgage payments ($8,634 − $7,200 = $1,434).

*Tax shelter items.

© Cengage Learning

to move to a different city in a few years or if you're worried about job security, renting may make sense even if the numbers favor buying. Think of this as the intangible value of flexibility. Further, for some people, factors such as the need for privacy, the desire to personalize one's home, and the personal satisfaction gained from homeownership outweigh the financial considerations. In some housing markets, a relative surplus of rental properties causes the cost of renting to be lower than the cost of owning a comparable house or condominium. You should look at the rent-or-buy decision over a timeline of several years, using different assumptions regarding rent increases, mortgage rates, home appreciation rates in the area, and the rate of return that you can earn on the funds you could invest (if you rent) rather than use toward a down payment on a house (if you buy).

5-4 How Much Housing Can You Afford?

LG4 Buying a home obviously involves a lot of careful planning and analysis. Not only must you decide on the kind of home you want (its location, number of bedrooms, and other features), you must also consider its cost, what kind of mortgage to get, how large a monthly payment you can afford, what kind of homeowner's insurance coverage to have, and so forth.

Sound financial planning dictates caution when buying a home or any other major item. Spending too much for a home or automobile can have a detrimental effect not only on your budget and lifestyle but also on your savings and investment plans and possibly even your retirement plans. Knowing how much housing you can afford goes a long way toward helping you achieve balanced financial goals.

5-4a Benefits of Owning a Home

Homeownership offers the security and peace of mind derived from living in one's own home and the feeling of permanence and sense of stability. This so-called psychological reward is not the only reason people enjoy owning their home. There are also some significant financial payoffs from homeownership.

- **Tax shelter:** As noted in Chapter 3, you can deduct both mortgage interest and property taxes when calculating your federal and, in most states, state income taxes, thereby reducing your taxable income and thus your tax liability. The only requirement is that you itemize your deductions. This tax break is so good that people who have never itemized usually begin doing so after they buy their first house.

- **Inflation hedge:** Not only does homeownership offer a place to live, it also represents an investment that provides a valuable inflation hedge. That's because homes generally appreciate in value at a rate equal to or greater than the rate of inflation. For example, from 2001 through 2006, a home became one of the best investments that you could make, generating a far better return than stocks, bonds, or mutual funds. Indeed, many people bought homes simply for their investment potential. More subdued expectations in the wake of the financial crisis of 2009 are that housing prices will roughly keep pace with the rate of inflation for the foreseeable future.

5-4b The Cost of Homeownership

Although there definitely are some strong emotional and financial reasons for owning a home, there's still the question of whether you can afford to own one. There are two important aspects to consider when it comes to affordability: (1) you must be able to come up with the

down payment and other closing costs, and (2) you must be able to meet the cash-flow requirements associated with monthly mortgage payments and other home maintenance expenses. In particular, there are five types of costs to consider: the down payment, points and closing costs, mortgage payments, property taxes and insurance, and maintenance and operating expenses.

 Homeownership offers the security and peace of mind derived from living in one's own home and the feeling of permanence and sense of stability.

The Down Payment
The first major hurdle is the **down payment**. Most buyers finance a major part of the purchase price of the home, but they're required by lenders to invest money

down payment A portion of the full purchase price provided by the purchaser when a house or other major asset is purchased; often called *equity*.

loan-to-value ratio The maximum percentage of the value of a property that the lender is willing to loan.

private mortgage insurance (PMI) An insurance policy that protects the mortgage lender from loss in the event the borrower defaults on the loan; typically required by lenders when the down payment is less than 20 percent.

mortgage points Fees (one point equals 1 percent of the amount borrowed) charged by lenders at the time they grant a mortgage loan; they are related to the lender's supply of loanable funds and the demand for mortgages.

of their own, called *equity*. The actual amount of down payment required varies among lenders, mortgage types, and properties. To determine the amount of down payment required in specific instances, lenders use the **loan-to-value ratio**, which specifies the maximum percentage of the value of a property that the lender is willing to loan. For example, if the loan-to-value ratio is 80 percent, the buyer will have to come up with a down payment equal to the remaining 20 percent.

Generally, first-time home buyers must spend several years accumulating enough money to afford the down payment and other costs associated with a home purchase. You can best accumulate these funds if you plan ahead, using future value techniques to determine the monthly or annual savings necessary to have a stated amount by a specified future date. A detailed demonstration of this process is included in Chapter 11 (see Worksheet 11.1, Part B). A disciplined savings program is the best way to obtain the funds needed to come up with the down payment and other closing costs on a home.

If you don't have enough savings to cover the down payment and closing costs, you can consider several other sources. The Federal National Mortgage Association ("Fannie Mae") has programs to help buyers who have limited cash for a down payment and closing costs. The "Fannie 3/2" Program is available from local lenders to limit required down payments for qualified buyers. "Fannie 97" helps the home buyer who can handle monthly mortgage payments but doesn't have cash for the down payment. It requires only a 3 percent down payment from the borrower's own funds, and the borrower needs to have only one month's mortgage payment in cash savings, or reserves, after closing. Programs have also developed to help banks liquidate homes owned by Fannie Mae because of the foreclosures resulting from the financial crisis of 2009. The HomePath Mortgage Financing program is available from local and national lenders. Borrowers who meet certain income criteria may qualify for a 97 percent loan-to-value mortgage and may obtain their down payment from a gift, grant or loan from a nonprofit organization, state or local government, or employer. The HomePath Renovation Mortgage Financing program is a comparable program available only on homes that will be a primary residence and are in need of light renovations.

As a rule, when the down payment is less than 20 percent, the lender will require the buyer to obtain **private mortgage insurance (PMI)**, which protects the lender from loss if the borrower defaults on the loan. Usually PMI covers the lender's risk above 80 percent of the house price. Thus, with a 10 percent down payment, the mortgage will be a 90 percent loan, and mortgage insurance will cover 10 percent of the home's price. The cost of mortgage insurance can be included in your monthly payment, and the average cost ranges from about $40 to $70 per month. Under federal law, PMI on most loans made on or after July 29, 1999, ends automatically once the mortgage is paid down to 78 percent of the original value of the house.

Go to Smart Sites

Go online to find out how much more house you could afford with private mortgage insurance. ●

Points and Closing Costs

A second hurdle to homeownership relates to mortgage points and closing costs. **Mortgage points** are fees charged by lenders at the time that they grant a mortgage loan. Points are like interest in that they are a charge for borrowing money. They're related to the lender's supply of loanable funds and the demand for mortgages; the greater the demand relative to the supply, the more points you can expect to pay. One point equals 1 percent of the amount borrowed. Thus, if you borrow $100,000 and loan fees equal 3 points, the amount of money you'll pay in points is $100,000 × .03 = $3,000.

Lenders typically use points as an alternative way of charging interest on their loans. They can vary the interest rate along with the number of points they charge to create loans with comparable effective rates. For example, a lender might be willing to give

© ANDY DEAN PHOTOGRAPHY/SHUTTERSTOCK.COM

© GEOPAUL/ISTOCKPHOTO

you a 5 percent rather than an 6 percent mortgage if you're willing to pay more points; that is, you choose between a 6 percent mortgage rate with 1 point or a 5 percent mortgage rate with 3 points. If you choose the 5 percent loan, you'll pay a lot more *at closing* (although the amount of interest paid *over the life of the mortgage* may be considerably less).

Points increase the *effective rate of interest* or APR on a mortgage. The amount you pay in points and the length of time you hold a mortgage determine the increase in the effective interest rate. For example, on an 8 percent, 30-year, fixed-rate mortgage, each point increases the annual percentage rate by about 0.11 percent if the loan is held for 30 years or 0.17 percent if held 15 years. You pay the same amount in points regardless of how long you keep your home. So, the longer you hold the mortgage, the longer the period over which you amortize the points and the smaller the effect of the points on the effective annual interest rate.

According to IRS rulings, the points paid on a mortgage at the time a home is originally purchased are usually considered immediately tax deductible. However, the same points are *not* considered immediately tax deductible if they're incurred when *refinancing* a mortgage; in this case, the amount paid in points must be written off (*amortized*) over the life of the new mortgage loan.

Closing costs are all expenses that borrowers ordinarily pay when a mortgage loan is closed and they receive title to the purchased property. Closing costs are like down payments: they represent money that you must come up with *at the time you buy the house*. Closing costs are made up of such items as loan application and loan origination fees, mortgage points, title search and insurance fees, attorneys' fees, appraisal fees, and other miscellaneous fees. Exhibit 5.4 provides a list of these fees and shows that they can total 50 percent or more of the down payment amount. For example, as can be seen in the exhibit, with a 10 percent down payment on a $200,000 home, the closing costs are about 56 percent of the down payment, or $11,130.

closing costs All expenses (including mortgage points) that borrowers ordinarily pay when a mortgage loan is closed and they receive title to the purchased property.

Mortgage Payments

The monthly mortgage payment is determined using a standard but fairly detailed formula. Each mortgage payment is made up partly of principal repayment on the loan and partly of interest charges on the loan. However, as Exhibit 5.5 shows, for most of the life of the mortgage the vast majority of each monthly payment goes to *interest*. The loan illustrated

© KAREN HERMANN/ISTOCKPHOTO

Exhibit 5.4   Closing Costs: The Hidden Costs of Buying a Home

The closing costs on a home mortgage loan can be substantial—as much as 5 percent to 7 percent of the price of the home. Except for the real estate commission (generally paid by the seller), the buyer incurs the biggest share of the closing costs and must pay them—in addition to the down payment—when the loan is closed and title to the property is conveyed.

Item	Size of Down Payment	
	20%	10%
Loan application fee	$ 300	$ 300
Loan origination fee	1,600	1,800
Points	4,160	5,400
Mortgage and homeowner's insurance	—	675
Title search and insurance	665	665
Attorneys' fees	400	400
Appraisal fees	425	425
Home inspection	350	350
Mortgage tax	665	725
Filing fees	80	80
Credit reports	35	35
Miscellaneous	200	200
Total closing costs	$9,530	$11,130

Note: Typical closing costs for a $200,000 home—2.6 points charged with 20 percent down, 3 points with 10 percent down. Actual amounts will vary by lender and location.

© Cengage Learning

For most of the life of a mortgage loan, the vast majority of each monthly payment goes to interest and only a small portion goes toward repaying the principal. Over the 30-year life of the 5 percent, $100,000 mortgage illustrated here, the homeowner will pay about $93,255 in interest.

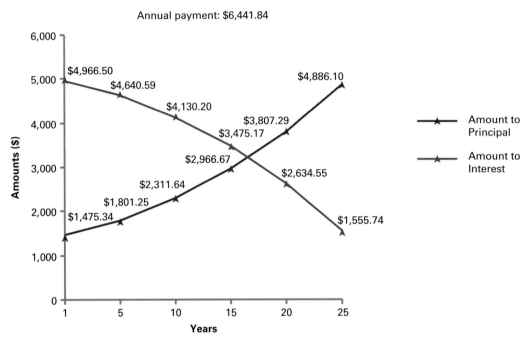

Annual payment: $6,441.84

Amount to Principal

Amount to Interest

Note: Dollar amounts noted on the graph represent the total amount of principal repaid and interest from the $6,441.84 annual payment made during the given year.

© Cengage Learning

in the exhibit is a $100,000, 30-year, 5 percent mortgage with monthly payments of $536.82, for a total of $6,441.84 per year. Note that it is not until the 16th year of this 30-year mortgage that the principal portion of the monthly loan payment exceeds the amount that goes to interest.

In practice, most mortgage lenders and realtors use their calculator to obtain monthly payments. Some of them still use *comprehensive mortgage payment tables,* which provide monthly payments for virtually any combination of loan size, interest rate, and maturity. Exhibit 5.6 provides an excerpt from one such comprehensive mortgage payment table (with values rounded to the nearest cent). It lists the *monthly payments* associated with a $10,000, fixed-rate loan for selected maturities of 10 to 30 years and for various interest

CALCULATOR	
Inputs	**Functions**
180000	PV
360	N
6	÷
12	=
	I
	CPT
	PMT
	Solution
	1,079.19

SEE APPENDIX E FOR DETAILS.

rates ranging from 5 percent to 10 percent. This table can be used to find the monthly payment for a loan of any size. For example, suppose that you'd like to find the monthly loan payment on a $180,000, 6 percent, 30-year mortgage. To do so, simply divide the amount of the loan ($180,000) by $10,000 and then multiply this factor (18.0) by the payment amount shown in Exhibit 5.5 for a 6 percent, 30-year loan ($59.96):

$180,000/$10,000 = 18.0 and 18.0 × $59.96 = $1,079.28

The resulting monthly mortgage payment is thus $1,079.28. The calculator keystrokes shown in the margin can be used with a financial calculator to more easily and precisely calculate mortgage payments. Note that the mortgage payment of $1,079.19 is a more accurate figure than the value calculated using the table.

AFFORDABILITY RATIOS. The key issue regarding mortgage payments is *affordability*: How large a monthly mortgage payment can you afford, given your budget? This amount determines how much you can borrow to finance the purchase of a home.

To obtain a mortgage, a potential borrower must be "qualified"—that is, demonstrate that he or she has

The monthly loan payments on a mortgage vary not only by the amount of the loan but also by the rate of interest and loan maturity.

Rate of Interest	Loan Maturity				
	10 Years	15 Years	20 Years	25 Years	30 Years
5.0%	$106.07	$ 79.08	$ 66.00	$ 58.46	$ 53.68
5.5	108.53	81.71	68.79	61.41	56.79
6.0	111.02	84.39	71.64	64.43	59.96
6.5	113.55	87.11	74.56	67.52	63.21
7.0	116.11	89.88	77.53	70.68	66.53
7.5	118.71	92.71	80.56	73.90	69.93
8.0	121.33	95.57	83.65	77.19	73.38
8.5	123.99	98.48	86.79	80.53	76.90
9.0	126.68	101.43	89.98	83.92	80.47
9.5	129.40	104.43	93.22	87.37	84.09
10.0	132.16	107.47	96.51	90.88	87.76

Instructions: (1) Divide amount of the loan by $10,000; (2) find the loan payment amount in the table for the specific interest rate and maturity; and (3) multiply the amount from step 1 by the amount from step 2.

Example: Using the steps just described, the monthly payment for a $98,000, 5.5 percent, 30-year loan would be determined as: (1) $98,000/$10,000 = 9.8; (2) the payment associated with a 5.5 percent, 30-year loan, from the table, is $56.79; (3) the monthly payment required to repay a $98,000, 5.5 percent, 30-year loan is 9.8 × $56.79 = $556.54.

© Cengage Learning

adequate income and an acceptable credit record to make scheduled loan payments reliably. Federal and private mortgage insurers and institutional mortgage investors have certain standards they expect borrowers to meet to reduce the borrower's risk of default.

The most important affordability guidelines relate both *monthly mortgage payments* and *total monthly installment loan payments* (including the monthly mortgage payment and monthly payments on auto, furniture, and other consumer installment loans) *to monthly borrower gross income.* Customary ratios for a *conventional mortgage* stipulate that monthly mortgage payments cannot exceed 25 percent to 30 percent of the borrower's monthly *gross* (before-tax) income, and the borrower's total monthly installment loan payments (including the mortgage payment) cannot exceed 33 percent to 38 percent of monthly gross income. Because both conditions stipulate a range, the lender has some leeway in choosing the most appropriate ratio for a particular loan applicant.

Let's look at how these affordability ratios work. Assume that your monthly gross income is $4,500. Applying the lower end of the ranges (that is, 25 percent and 33 percent), we see that this income level supports mortgage payments of $1,125 a month

($4,500 × .25 = $1,125) *so long as total monthly installment loan payments do not exceed $1,485* ($4,500 × .33 = $1,485). If your nonmortgage monthly installment loan payments exceeded $360 (the difference between $1,485 and $1,125), then your mortgage payment would have to be reduced accordingly or other installment loan payments would have to be reduced or paid off.

Property Taxes and Insurance

The standard mortgage payment often includes property taxes and homeowner's insurance. The mortgage payment therefore consists of *p*rincipal, *i*nterest, property *t*axes, and homeowner's *i*nsurance (or **PITI** for short). Actually, that portion of the loan payment that goes for taxes and insurance is paid into an *escrow account,* where it accumulates until the lender pays property taxes and homeowner insurance premiums are due.

Because they're local taxes levied to fund schools, law enforcement, and other local services, the level of **property taxes** differs from one community to

PITI Acronym that refers to a mortgage payment consisting of principal, interest, property taxes, and homeowner's insurance.

property taxes Taxes levied by local governments on the *assessed value* of real estate for the purpose of funding schools, law enforcement, and other local services.

another. In addition, within a given community, individual property taxes will vary according to the *assessed value* of the real estate—the larger and/or more expensive the home, the higher the property taxes, and vice versa.

As a rule, annual property taxes vary from less than 0.5 percent to more than 2 percent of a home's approximate market value. Thus the property taxes on a $100,000 home could vary from about $500 to more than $2,000 a year, depending on location and geographic area.

The other component of the monthly mortgage payment is **homeowner's insurance**. Its cost varies with such factors as the age of the house, location, materials used in construction, and geographic area. Homeowner's insurance is required by mortgage lenders and covers only the replacement value of the home and its contents, not the land. Annual insurance costs usually amount to approximately 0.25 percent to 0.5 percent of the home's market value, or from $500 to $1,000 for a $200,000 house.

Maintenance and Operating Expenses

In addition to monthly mortgage payments, homeowners will incur periodic maintenance and operating expenses. Maintenance costs should be anticipated even on new homes. Painting, mechanical and plumbing repairs, and lawn maintenance, for example, are inescapable facts of homeownership. Such costs are likely to be greater for larger, older homes. Thus, although a large, established home may have an attractive purchase price, a new, smaller home may be a better buy in view of its lower maintenance and operating costs. Also consider the cost of operating the home—specifically, the cost of utilities such as electricity, gas, water, and sewage. These costs have skyrocketed over the past 20 years and today are a large part of homeownership costs, so obtain estimates of utilities when evaluating a home for purchase.

5-4c Performing a Home Affordability Analysis

Worksheet 5.3 helps you determine the maximum price for a home purchase based on your monthly income and down payment amount after meeting estimated closing costs. In our example, Betsy and Ralph Compton have a combined annual income of $75,200 and savings of $30,000 for a down payment and closing costs. They estimate monthly property taxes and homeowner's insurance at $375 and expect the mortgage lender to use a 28 percent monthly mortgage payment affordability ratio, to lend at an average interest rate of 6 percent on a 30-year (360-month) mortgage, and to require a 10 percent minimum down payment. The Comptons' analysis shows that they can afford to purchase a home for about $201,000.

Worksheet 5.3 walks us through the steps that the Compton family took to reach this conclusion. The maximum purchase price is determined from two perspectives: the maximum based on monthly income and the maximum based on the minimum acceptable down payment. The lower of the two estimates determines the maximum purchase price. Based on their monthly income and the 28 percent affordability ratio, their monthly payment could be $1,755 ($6,267 × .28), shown as Item 4. After deducting taxes and insurance, the maximum monthly mortgage payment amount is $1,380 (Item 6). We can use the calculator keystrokes shown in the margin or the table in Exhibit 5.6 to find the Comptons' maximum loan. The calculator indicates a maximum purchase price of $230,172.43,

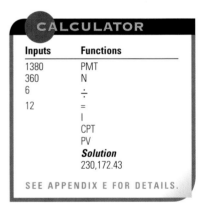

CALCULATOR

Inputs	Functions
1380	PMT
360	N
6	÷
12	=
	I
	CPT
	PV
	Solution
	230,172.43

SEE APPENDIX E FOR DETAILS.

GUNNAR PIPPEL/SHUTTERSTOCK.COM

When Is it Time to Buy a First Home?

The timing of when to buy a first home depends on your current and expected income and expenses, future plans, and your preferred lifestyle.

It's probably a good time to buy a home if you have the following:

- Reliable income and a good credit history, both of which you should be able to document.
- Ability to make at least a five percent down payment and to cover closing costs.
- The desire to build equity and to be eligible for homeowner tax breaks and credits.
- Ability to finance home-maintenance and improvement projects.
- Adequate savings and a cash reserve sufficient to handle the loss of your job or another financial challenge for at least a few months.
- The plan to stay in your home for at least four years.

Source: Adapted from http://www.freddiemac.com/homeownership/rent_or_buy/right_for_you.html, accessed March 2012.

Worksheet 5.3 Home Affordability Analysis for the Betsy and Ralph Compton Family

By using the following variables in the home affordability analysis form, the Comptons estimate a maximum home purchase price of $201,000: their combined annual income of $75,200; the $30,000 available for a down payment and paying all closing costs; estimated monthly property taxes and homeowner's insurance of $375; the lender's 28% monthly mortgage payment affordability ratio; an average interest rate of 6% and expected loan maturity of 30 years; and a minimum down payment of 10%.

HOME AFFORDABILITY ANALYSIS*

Name: Betsy and Ralph Compton   Date: August 14, 2015

Item	Description	Amount
1	Amount of annual income	$ 75,200
2	Monthly income (Item 1 ÷ 12)	$ 6,267
3	Lender's affordability ratio (in decimal form)	0.28
4	Maximum monthly mortgage payment (PITI) (Item 2 × Item 3)	$ 1,755
5	Estimated monthly prop tax and homeowner's insurance payment	$ 375
6	Maximum monthly loan payment (Item 4 − Item 5)	$ 1,380
7	Approximate average interest rate on loan	6%
8	Planned loan maturity (years)	30
9	Monthly mortgage payment per $10,000 (using Item 7 and Item 8 and Table of Monthly Mortgage Payments in Exhibit 5.11)	$ 59.96
10	Maximum loan based on monthly income ($10,000 × Item 6 ÷ Item 9)	$230,000
11	Funds available for making a down payment and paying closing costs	$ 30,000
12	Funds available for making a down payment (Item 11 × .67)	$ 20,100
13	Maximum purchase price based on available monthly income (Item 10 + Item 12)	$250,100
14	Minimum acceptable down payment (in decimal form)	0.10
15	Maximum purchase price based on down payment (Item 12 ÷ Item 14)	$201,000
16	Maximum home purchase price (lower of Item 13 and Item 15)	$201,000

*Note: This analysis assumes that one-third of the funds available for making the down payment and paying closing costs are used to meet closing costs and that the remaining two-thirds are available for a down payment. This means that closing costs will represent an amount equal to 50% of the down payment.

© Cengage Learning

which is more accurate than the approximation provided using Exhibit 5.6. Using Exhibit 5.6, a $10,000 loan for 30 years at 6 percent would result in a monthly payment of $59.96, as indicated in Item 9. Now, find out how much of a loan a payment of $1,380 would support:

$ 10,000 × $ 1,380/$ 59.96 = $ 230,153.44

With a down payment of $30,000 and monthly income of $6,267, the Compton family can afford a home costing $250,100 (Item 13). The Comptons then look at the maximum purchase price based on their $30,000 down payment, or $150,000 (Item 15). Their maximum home purchase price is the lower of Items 13 and 15, or $201,000 (Item 16), and is limited by the amount available for a down payment.

real estate short sale Sale of real estate property in which the proceeds are less than the balance owed on a loan secured by the property sold.

5-5 The Home-Buying Process

LG5 Buying a home requires time, effort, and money. You'll want to educate yourself about available properties and prevailing prices by doing a systematic search and careful analysis. You'll also need a basic understanding of the role of a real estate agent, the mortgage application process, the real estate sales contract, and other documents required to close a deal.

> You need to understand the role of a real estate agent, the mortgage application process, the real estate sales contract, and other documents required to close a deal.

5-5a Shop the Market First

Most people who shop the housing market rely on real estate agents for information, access to properties, and advice. Today, even with homes, it's becoming commonplace to shop via the Internet, visiting various real estate sites to learn about available properties. Going online, you can specify preferences such as location, price, and size and then obtain descriptions and color photos of all properties that meet your needs.

As noted earlier, you must begin your home search project by figuring out what *you* require for your particular lifestyle needs—in terms of living space, style, and other special features. The property's location, neighborhood, and school district are usually important considerations as well. It's helpful to divide your list into *necessary* features, such as the number of bedrooms and baths, and *optional*—but desirable—features, such as fireplaces, whirlpool tubs, and so on. And of course, an affordability analysis is a critical part of the housing search.

Keep an open mind as you start looking. You may find that you like a house that's far different from what you first thought you wanted. For example, you may begin your search looking for a one-story, contemporary ranch house with a pool but fall in love with a two-story colonial with wonderful landscaping, no pool, and all the other features you want. Be flexible and look at a variety of homes in your price range. This can be invaluable in helping to define your wants and needs more clearly.

Financial Planning Tips

Top Home Remodeling Projects

The National Association of Realtors found that the value of home remodeling projects declined by only about half as much as home prices during the recent financial crisis. While it's best to expect that you will not get all of your money back from home improvements when you sell your home, keep in mind that you will likely enjoy the improvements until that time and will probably recover most of the money. Here's a list of the top remodeling projects in terms of the percentage of the investment recovered at the sale of the home.

Project	Cost Recovered
Entry door replacement (steel)	73.0%
Attic bedroom	72.5%
Minor kitchen remodel	72.1%
Garage door replacement	71.9%
Deck addition (wood)	70.1%
Siding replacement (vinyl)	69.5%
Window replacement (vinyl)	68.0%
Window replacement (wood)	67.5%
Basement remodel	66.8%
Major kitchen remodel	65.7%
Deck addition (composite)	62.8%
Two-Story Addition	62.4%

Source: "Remodeling Cost vs. Value Report: 2011-12," *Remodeling Magazine*, http://www.remodeling.hw.net/2011/costvsvalue/article/entrydoorreplacementsteel.aspx, accessed March 2012.

DBLIGHT/ISTOCKPHOTO.COM

Real Estate Short Sales

The bursting of the real estate bubble associated with the financial crisis of 2008–2009 increased the use of real estate short sales. A **real estate short sale** is the sale of property in which *the proceeds are less than the balance owed on the mortgage* used to secure the property. This procedure is an effort by a mortgage lender to come to terms with homeowners who are about to default or are defaulting on their mortgage loans. A broker's price opinion or an appraisal is obtained to estimate the probable selling price of the property for the purposes of the short sale. The short sale typically occurs to prevent home foreclosure by finding the most economic means for the mortgage lender to recover as much of the loan balance owed on the property as possible. In contrast, in a foreclosure the borrower typically cannot make scheduled mortgage payments and the lender repossesses the property in an effort to recover the loan balance owed. Mortgage holders will agree to a short sale only if it believes that the proceeds generated by the sale will produce a smaller loss than foreclosing on the property. A real estate short sale may consequently be viewed as a negotiated effort to mitigate the losses of the mortgage lender.

While a short sale can reduce a lender's losses, *it can also be beneficial for the homeowner*. A real estate short sale will avoid having a foreclosure appear on the homeowner's credit history. Short sales should also help homeowners manage the costs that got them into trouble in the first place. Finally, a short sale is usually faster and cheaper for the homeowner than a foreclosure. However, a short sale will generally have the same negative effect on the homeowner's credit score as a foreclosure.

5-5b Using an Agent

Real estate agents are professionals who are in daily contact with the housing market. Once you describe your needs to an agent, he or she can begin to search for appropriate properties. Your agent will also help you negotiate with the seller, obtain satisfactory financing, and, although not empowered to give explicit legal advice, prepare the real estate sales contract. Most real estate firms belong to a local **Multiple Listing Service (MLS)**, a comprehensive listing, updated daily, of properties for sale in a given community or metropolitan area. A brief description of each property and its asking price are included; many of which are accompanied by photos of the property.

Buyers should remember that *agents typically are employed by sellers*. Unless you've agreed to pay a fee to a sales agent to act as a buyer's agent, a realtor's primary responsibility, by law, is to sell listed properties at the highest possible prices. Agents are paid only if they make a sale, so some might pressure you to "sign now or miss the chance of a lifetime." But most agents will listen to your needs and work to match you with the right property and under terms that will benefit both you and the seller. Good agents recognize that their interests are best served when all parties to a transaction are satisfied.

Real estate commissions generally range from 5 percent to 6 percent for new homes and 6 percent to 7 percent for previously occupied homes or *resales*. It may be possible to negotiate a lower commission with your agent or to find a discount broker, or one who charges a flat fee. Commissions are paid only by the seller, but because the price of a home is often inflated by the size of the real estate commission, the buyer probably absorbs some or even all of the commission.

5-5c Prequalifying and Applying for a Mortgage

Before beginning your home search, you may want to meet with one or more mortgage lenders to prearrange a mortgage loan. **Prequalification** can work to your advantage in several ways. You'll know ahead of time the specific mortgage amount that you qualify for—subject, of course, to changes in rates and terms—and can focus your search on homes within an affordable price range. Prequalification also provides estimates of the required down payment and closing costs for different types of mortgages. It identifies in advance any problems, such as credit report errors, that might arise from your application and allows you time to correct them. Finally, prequalification enhances your bargaining power with the sellers of a house by letting them know that the deal won't fall through because you can't afford the property or obtain suitable financing. And since you will have already gone through the mortgage application process, the time required to close the sale should be relatively short.

5-5d The Real Estate Sales Contract

After selecting a home to buy, you must enter into a sales contract. State laws generally specify that, to be enforceable in court, real estate buy–sell agreements must be in writing and contain certain information, including (1) the names of buyers and sellers, (2) a description of the property sufficient for positive identification, (3) specific price and other terms, and (4) usually the signatures of the buyers and sellers. Real estate sales transactions often take weeks and sometimes months to complete. Contract requirements help keep the facts straight and reduce the chance for misunderstanding, misrepresentation, or fraud.

Although these requirements fulfill the minimums necessary for court enforcement, in practice real estate sales contracts usually contain several other contractual clauses relating to earnest money deposits, contingencies, personal property, and closing costs. An **earnest money deposit** is the money that you pledge to show good faith when you make an offer. If, after signing a sales contract, you withdraw from the transaction without a valid reason, you might have to forfeit this deposit. A valid reason for withdrawal would be stated in the contract as a contingency clause. With a **contingency clause**, you can condition your agreement to buy on such factors as the availability of financing, a satisfactory termite inspection or other

Multiple Listing Service (MLS) A comprehensive listing, updated daily, of properties for sale in a given community or metropolitan area; includes a brief description of each property with a photo and its asking price but can be accessed only by realtors who work for an MLS member.

prequalification The process of arranging with a mortgage lender, in advance of buying a home, to obtain the amount of mortgage financing the lender deems affordable for the home buyer.

earnest money deposit Money pledged by a buyer to show good faith when making an offer to buy a home.

contingency clause A clause in a real estate sales contract that makes the agreement conditional on such factors as the availability of financing, property inspections, or obtaining expert advice.

physical inspection of the property, or the advice of a lawyer or real estate expert.

5-5e Closing the Deal

After you obtain financing and your loan is approved, the closing process begins. The **Real Estate Settlement Procedures Act (RESPA)** governs closings on owner-occupied houses, condominiums, and apartment buildings of four units or fewer. This act reduced closing costs by prohibiting kickbacks made to real estate agents and others from lenders or title insurance companies. It also requires clear, advance disclosure of all closing costs to home buyers. Exhibit 5.7 provides some tips to help you sail through the home-buying process in general and the closing process in particular.

5-6 Financing the Transaction

LG6 Earlier in this chapter, we saw that mortgage terms can dramatically affect the amount you can afford to spend on a home. The success of a real estate transaction often hinges on obtaining a mortgage with favorable terms. A **mortgage loan** is secured by the property: If the borrower defaults, the lender has the legal right to liquidate the property to recover the funds it is owed. Before you obtain such a loan, it's helpful to understand the sources and types of mortgages and their underlying economics.

© KAREN HERMANN/ISTOCKPHOTO

Exhibit 5.7 Common Home-Buying Mistakes

Keeping in mind the following advice will improve your chances of becoming a happy, successful homeowner.

- **Don't wipe out your savings.** While it makes sense to put down the largest down payment you can afford, it is important to keep your emergency reserves intact, hold money for closing costs, and set aside funds to handle possible repairs and future maintenance.

- **Pick the right neighborhood.** You've heard that the three most important factors in valuing real estate are location, location, and location. This is no joke. Drive through a neighborhood, ask the police department about crime statistics, and talk to neighbors before you buy. If they don't want to talk, that tells you something too!

- **Stay away from the most expensive home in the neighborhood.** While having the largest and most expensive home in the neighborhood might be appealing, it doesn't bode well for resale value. If you need three bedrooms, don't consider a five-bedroom that looks good but costs more and meets your needs less.

- **Interview your agent and ask hard questions.** Make sure that he or she is experienced. Consider signing a buyer's broker agreement, which gives both you and the broker responsibilities and reasonable performance expectations.

- **Rely on professional advice.** Pay attention to what your agent or mortgage broker tells you. Look up information on the Internet, read real estate books, and ask for a second opinion. Lawyers and accountants are excellent resources.

- **Use traditional financing.** One of the biggest lessons of the recent financial crisis is that real estate prices don't always go up. And what you don't know about your mortgage can hurt you! Don't sign off on your mortgage until you understand every detail. Terms like indexes, margins, caps, and negative amortization should make you nervous.

- **Don't change the financial picture before closing.** While waiting for loan funding, there is no need to buy a new car to match your new home. Your excellent credit report does not give you free rein to buy whatever you want. Borrowing too much more at this time could adversely affect the funding of a mortgage.

- **Be sure to do the home inspection.** Home inspections are *not* a waste of time and money. Qualified home inspectors can find problems that most of us would miss.

- **Be careful about taking on additional debt after closing.** After you become a homeowner, you'll be offered many deals on a home equity loan. Although it may be tempting to pull out all your equity and use this newfound money to buy all sorts of new toys, you should stick to a reasonable financial plan. It is critically important to cover the contingency of losing a job or an emergency by setting aside some money.

Source: Based on Elizabeth Weintraub, "Top 10 Ways to Lose Your Home," http://homebuying.about.com/od/buyingahome/tp/072007LoseHome.htm, accessed March 2011.

5-6a Sources of Mortgage Loans

The major sources of home mortgages today are commercial banks, thrift institutions, and mortgage bankers or brokers. Commercial banks are also an important source of *interim construction loans,* providing short-term financing during the construction phase for individuals who are building or remodeling a home. After the home is completed, the homeowner obtains *permanent financing*, in the form of a standard mortgage loan, and then uses the proceeds from it to repay the construction loan.

Another way to obtain a mortgage loan is through a mortgage banker or mortgage broker. Both solicit borrowers, originate loans, and place them with traditional mortgage lenders as well as life insurance companies and pension funds. Whereas **mortgage bankers** often use their own money to initially fund mortgages they later resell, **mortgage brokers** take loan applications and then seek lenders willing to grant the mortgage loans under the desired terms. Most brokers also have ongoing relationships with different lenders, thereby increasing your chances of finding a loan even if you don't qualify at a commercial bank or thrift institution. Brokers can often simplify the financing process by cutting through red tape, negotiating more favorable terms, and reducing the amount of time to close the loan. Mortgage brokers earn their income from commissions and origination fees paid by the lender, costs that are typically passed on to the borrower in the points charged on a loan. See Chapter 5's Bonus Exhibits for advice on finding a good mortgage broker. (Visit CourseMate for PFIN 3. Log in at **www. cengagebrain.com.**)

Shopping for the best mortgage rate and terms has become a lot easier thanks to the Internet. Many sites allow you to search for the best fixed-rate or adjustable-rate mortgage in your area. HSH Associates, a mortgage consulting firm with a Web site at **http:// www.hsh.com**, lists mortgages offered by banks, mortgage companies, and brokerage firms across the country along with information on prevailing interest rates, terms, and points. Bankrate, **http://www. bankrate.com,** and similar sites also offer mortgage comparisons.

Go to Smart Sites

Keep track of changes in the housing market as housing prices recover from the recent financial crisis. Zillow's Home Value Index is a good place to start. ●

5-6b Types of Mortgage Loans

For our purposes here, we'll group mortgages in two catagories based on (1) terms of payment and (2) whether they're conventional, insured, or guaranteed.

There are literally dozens of different types of home mortgages from which to choose. The most common types of mortgage loans made today are fixed-rate and adjustable-rate mortgages.

Fixed-Rate Mortgages

The **fixed-rate mortgage** still accounts for a large portion of all home mortgages. Both the rate of interest and the monthly mortgage payment are fixed over the full term of the loan. The most common type of fixed-rate mortgage is the *30-year fixed-rate* loan, although *10- and 15-year loans* are becoming more popular as homeowners recognize the advantages of paying off their loan over a shorter period of time. Because of the risks that the lender assumes with a 30-year loan, it's usually the most expensive form of home financing.

Becoming especially popular is the *15-year fixed-rate* loan. Its chief appeal is that it is repaid twice as fast (15 years versus 30) and yet the monthly payments don't increase all that

mortgage banker A firm that solicits borrowers, originates primarily government-insured and government-guaranteed loans, and places them with mortgage lenders; often uses its own money to initially fund mortgages it later resells.

mortgage broker A firm that solicits borrowers, originates primarily conventional loans, and places them with mortgage lenders; the broker merely takes loan applications and then finds lenders willing to grant the mortgage loans under the desired terms.

fixed-rate mortgage The traditional type of mortgage in which both the rate of interest and the monthly mortgage payment are fixed over the full term of the loan.

much. To pay off a loan in less time, the homeowner must pay more each month, but monthly payments don't have to be doubled to pay off the loan in half the time; rather, the monthly payment on a 15-year loan is generally only about 20 percent to 30 percent larger than the payment on a 30-year loan. The following table shows the difference in monthly payment and total interest paid for 30- and 15-year fixed-rate mortgages. In both cases the purchaser borrows $160,000 at a 5 percent fixed rate of interest.

Perhaps the most startling feature is the substantial difference in the total amount of interest paid over the term of the loan. Note in the example above that you can save *more than $81,000* just by financing your home with a 15-year mortgage rather than over the traditional 30 years! And keep in mind this savings is possible even though monthly payments differ by only about $406.

Adjustable-Rate Mortgages (ARMs)

Another popular form of home loan is the **adjustable-rate mortgage (ARM)**. In this case, the rate of interest, and therefore the size of the monthly payment, is adjusted based on market interest rate movements. The mortgage interest rate is linked to a specific *interest rate index* and is adjusted at specific intervals (usually once or twice a year) based on changes in the index. When the index moves up, so does the interest rate on the mortgage and, in turn, the size of the monthly mortgage payment increases. The new interest rate and monthly mortgage payment remain in effect until the next adjustment date.

The term of an ARM can be 15 or 30 years. Because the size of the monthly payments will vary with interest rates, there's no way to tell what your future payments will be. However, because the borrower assumes most or all of the interest rate risk

in these mortgages, the *initial rate of interest* on an adjustable-rate mortgage is normally well below—typically by 2 to 3 percentage points—the rate of a standard 30-year fixed-rate loan. Of course, whether the borrower actually ends up paying less interest depends on the behavior of market interest rates during the term of the loan.

FEATURES OF ARMS. It's important for home buyers to understand the basic features of an ARM:

- **Adjustment period:** Although the period of time between rate changes is typically six months to one year, adjustment periods can range from three months to three years or more.

- **Index rate:** A baseline rate that captures the movement in interest rates, usually tied to six-month U.S. Treasury securities, six-month CDs, or the average cost of funds to savings institutions.

- **Margin:** The percentage points that a lender *adds to the index* to determine the rate of interest on an ARM, usually a fixed amount over the life of the loan.

- **Interest rate caps:** Limits the amount the interest rate can increase over a given period. *Periodic caps* limit interest rate increases from one adjustment to the next (typically lenders cap annual rate adjustments at 1 to 2 percentage points), and *overall caps* limit the interest rate increase over the life of the loan (lifetime interest rate caps are typically set at 5 to 8 percentage points). Many ARMs have both periodic and overall interest rate caps.

- **Payment caps:** Limits on monthly payment increases that may result from a rate adjustment—usually a percentage of the previous payment. If your ARM has a 5 percent payment cap, your monthly payments can increase no more than 5 percent from one year to the next—regardless of what happens to interest rates.

Because most ARMs are 30-year loans (360 payments), you can determine the initial monthly payment in the same manner as for any other 30-year mortgage. For example, for an $100,000 loan at 6.5 percent (4.5 percent index rate + 2 percent margin), we can use a calculator as shown in the margin or Exhibit 5.5 to find the first-year monthly payments of $632.07. Assuming a 1-year adjustment period, if the index rate rises to 5.5 percent, then the interest rate for the second

CALCULATOR	
Inputs	Functions
100000	PV
360	N
6.5	÷
12	=
	I
	CPT
	PV
	Solution
	632.07

SEE APPENDIX E FOR DETAILS.

Term of Loan	Regular Monthly Payment	Total Interest Paid over Life of Loan
30 years	$ 858.91	$149,209.25
15 years	$1,265.27	$ 67,748.56

year will be 7.5 percent (5.5 percent + 2 percent = 7.5 percent). The size of the monthly payment for the next 12 months will then be adjusted upward to about $697.83. This process is repeated each year thereafter until the loan matures.

BEWARE OF NEGATIVE AMORTIZATION. Some ARMs are subject to **negative amortization**—that is, there's actually an increase in the principal balance of the loan resulting from *monthly loan payments that are lower than the amount of monthly interest being charged.* In other words, you could end up with a larger mortgage balance on the next anniversary of your loan than on the previous one. This occurs when the payment is intentionally set below the interest charge, or when the ARM has interest rates that are adjusted monthly—with monthly payments that adjust annually. In the latter case, when rates are rising on these loans, the current monthly payment can be less than the interest being charged, and the difference is added to the principal, thereby increasing the size of the loan. When considering an ARM, be sure to learn whether negative amortization could occur. Generally, loans without the potential for negative amortization are available, although they tend to have slightly higher initial rates and interest rate caps.

Here are a couple of other types of ARMs lenders may sometimes offer:

- **Convertible ARMs** allow borrowers to convert from an adjustable-rate to a fixed-rate loan during a specified time period, usually any time between the 13th and 60th month. Although these loans seldom provide the lowest initial rate, they allow the borrower to convert to a fixed-rate loan if interest rates decline. A conversion fee of about $500 is typical, and the fixed rate is normally set at 0.25 percent to 0.5 percent above the going rate on fixed-rate loans at the time you convert.

- **Two-step ARMs** have just two interest rates, the first for an initial period of 5 to 7 years and a higher one for the remaining term of the loan.

Fixed or Adjustable Rate?

Fixed-rate mortgages are popular with home buyers who plan to stay in their homes for at least 5 to 7 years and want to know what their payments will be. Of course, the current level of interest rates and your expectations about future interest rates will influence your choice of a fixed-rate or adjustable-rate mortgage. When the average interest rate on a 30-year mortgage loan is high, people often choose adjustable-rate mortgages to avoid being locked into prevailing high rates. In sharp contrast, when interest rates are low, many home buyers opt for fixed-rate mortgages to lock in these attractive rates. In such situations, many homeowners with adjustable-rate mortgages will often refinance them with fixed-rate loans to take advantage of the favorable fixed rates.

Other Mortgage Payment Options

In addition to standard fixed-rate and adjustable-rate mortgage loans, some lenders offer variations designed to help first-time home buyers.

- **Interest-only mortgages** are loans requiring the borrower to pay only the interest portion of the loan. Rather than amortizing the loan with equal monthly payments, the borrower merely pays the accrued interest each month—the option to pay interest only lasts for a specified period, often 5 to 10 years, after which time all future loan payments will also include principal. These mortgages allow the borrower to make lower payments (early on in the life of the loan) that are still fully tax deductible. Most interest-only mortgages are offered as ARMs.

- **Graduated-payment mortgages** are loans offering low payments for the first few years, gradually increasing until year 3 or 5, and then remaining fixed. The low initial payments appeal to people who are just starting out and expect their income to rise. If this doesn't occur, however, it could result in a higher debt load than the borrower can handle.

- **Growing-equity mortgages** are fixed-rate mortgages with payments that increase over a specific period. The extra funds are applied to the principal, so a conventional 30-year loan can be paid off in about 20 years.

- **Biweekly mortgages** are loans on which payments equal to half of a regular monthly payment are made every 2 weeks rather than once a month. Because you make 26 payments (52 weeks/2), which is the equivalent of 13 monthly payments, the principal balance declines faster and so you pay less interest over the life of the loan.

negative amortization When the principal balance on a mortgage loan increases because the monthly loan payment is lower than the amount of monthly interest being charged; some ARMs are subject to this undesirable condition.

convertible ARM An adjustable-rate mortgage loan that allows borrowers to convert from an adjustable-rate to a fixed-rate loan, usually at any time between the 13th and the 60th month.

two-step ARM An adjustable-rate mortgage with just two interest rates: one for the first 5 to 7 years of the loan, and a higher one for the remaining term of the loan.

interest-only mortgage A mortgage that requires the borrower to pay only interest; typically used to finance the purchase of more expensive properties.

graduated-payment mortgage A mortgage that starts with unusually low payments that rise over several years to a fixed payment.

growing-equity mortgage Fixed-rate mortgage with payments that increase over a specific period. Extra funds are applied to the principal so that the loan is paid off more quickly.

biweekly mortgage A loan on which payments equal to half the regular monthly payment that are made every 2 weeks.

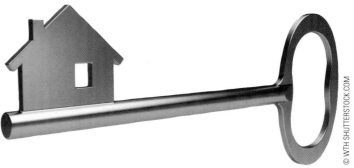
© WTH.SHUTTERSTOCK.COM

buydown Financing made available by a builder or seller to a potential new-home buyer at well below market interest rates, often only for a short period.

conventional mortgage A mortgage offered by a lender who assumes all the risk of loss; typically requires a down payment of at least 20 percent of the value of the mortgaged property.

FHA mortgage insurance A program under which the Federal Housing Administration (FHA) offers lenders mortgage insurance on loans having a high loan-to-value ratio; its intent is to encourage loans to home buyers who have very little money available for a down payment and closing costs.

VA loan guarantee A guarantee offered by the U.S. Veterans Administration to lenders who make qualified mortgage loans to eligible veterans of the U.S. Armed Forces and their unmarried surviving spouses.

● **Buydowns** are a type of seller financing sometimes offered on new homes. A builder, for example, arranges for mortgage financing with a financial institution at interest rates well below market rates; to illustrate, a builder may offer 5 percent financing when the market rate of interest is around 6 percent or 6.5 percent. Be careful, though, because the reduced rate may only be good for a short period, or the buyer may actually end up paying for the reduced interest in the form of a higher purchase price.

Conventional, Insured, and Guaranteed Loans

A **conventional mortgage** is a mortgage offered by a lender who assumes all the risk of loss. To protect themselves, lenders usually require a down payment of at least 20 percent of the value of the mortgaged property. For lower down payments, the lender usually requires *private mortgage insurance (PMI)*, as described earlier in the chapter. High borrower equity greatly reduces the likelihood of default on a mortgage and subsequent loss to the lender. However, a high down payment requirement makes home buying more difficult for many families and individuals.

The **FHA mortgage insurance** program helps people buy homes even when they have very little money available for a down payment and closing costs; these are known as *insured loans.* As of early 2012, the up-front mortgage insurance premium for a 15- or 30-year mortgage was 2.25 percent of the loan amount—paid by the borrower at closing or included in the mortgage—plus another 0.5 percent to 1.15 percent annual renewal premium, paid monthly, depending on the maturity of the loan and the amount of the down payment. Home buyers who want a 15-year mortgage and make a down payment greater than 10 percent of the purchase price pay only the up-front fee. The FHA agrees to reimburse lenders for losses up to a specified maximum amount if the buyer defaults. The minimum required down payment on an FHA loan is 3 percent of the sales price. The interest rate on an FHA loan is generally about 0.5 percent to

1 percent lower than that on conventional fixed-rate loans. The affordability ratios that are used to qualify applicants for these loans are typically less stringent than those used for conventional loans.

Guaranteed loans are similar to insured loans, but better—if you qualify. **VA loan guarantees** are provided by the U.S. Veterans Administration to lenders who make qualified mortgage loans to eligible veterans of the U.S. armed forces and their unmarried surviving spouses. This program, however, does not require lenders or veterans to pay a premium for the guarantee. In many instances, an eligible veteran must pay only closing costs; in effect, under such a program, a veteran can buy a home with no down payment. (This can be done *only once* with a VA loan.) The mortgage loan—subject to a usual maximum of about $417,000 (or more in high-cost counties) for a no-money-down loan (as of early 2012)—can amount to as much as 100 percent of a purchased property's appraised value. It is important to note that there are some regional differences in VA loan requirements. VA loans include a funding fee of about 2 percent on first-time, no-down-payment loans for regular military members (the fee is lower if the down payment is 10 percent or more). The VA sets the maximum interest rate, which (as with FHA loans) is usually about 0.5 percent *below* the rate on conventional fixed-rate loans. To qualify, the veteran must meet VA credit guidelines.

5-6c Refinancing Your Mortgage

After you've purchased a home and closed the transaction, interest rates on similar loans may drop. If rates drop by 1 percent to 2 percent or more, then you should consider the economics of refinancing after carefully comparing the terms of the old and new mortgages, the anticipated number of years you expect to remain in the home, any prepayment penalty on the old mortgage, and the closing costs associated with the new mortgage.

Worksheet 5.4 provides a form for analyzing the impact of refinancing. The data for the De Luca family's analysis is shown. Their original $80,000, 10-year-old, 8 percent mortgage has a current balance of $70,180 and monthly payments of $587 for 20 more years. If they refinance the $70,180 balance at the prevailing rate of 5 percent, then the monthly payment would drop to $463 over the remaining 20-year life of the current mortgage. The De Lucas

Using this form, the De Lucas find that—by refinancing the $70,180 balance on their 10-year-old, $80,000, 8 percent, 30-year mortgage (which has no prepayment penalty and requires payments of $587 per month) with a 5 percent, 20-year mortgage requiring $463 monthly payments and $2,400 in total after-tax closing costs—it will take 26 months to break even. Because the De Lucas plan to stay in their home for at least 60 more months, the refinancing is easily justified.

MORTGAGE REFINANCING ANALYSIS

Name _James and Angela De Luca_ Date _October 8, 2015_

Item	Description	Amount
1	Current monthly payment (Terms: $ 80,000, 8%, 30 years)	$ 587
2	New monthly payment (Terms: $ 70,180, 5%, 20 years)	463
3	Monthly savings, pretax (Item 1 − Item 2)	$ 124
4	Tax on monthly savings [Item 3 × tax rate (25 %)]	31
5	Monthly savings, after-tax (Item 3 − Item 4)	$ 93
6	Costs to refinance:	
	a. Prepayment penalty	$ 0
	b. Total closing costs (after-tax)	2,400
	c. Total refinancing costs (Item 6a + Item 6b)	$2,400
7	Months to break even (Item 6c ÷ Item 5)	26

© Cengage Learning

plan to live in their house for at least 5 more years. They won't have to pay a penalty for prepaying their current mortgage, and closing and other costs associated with the new mortgage are $2,400 after taxes. Substituting these values into Worksheet 5.4 reveals (in Item 7) that it will take the De Lucas 26 months to break even with the new mortgage. Because 26 months is considerably less than their anticipated minimum

5 years (60 months) in the home, *the economics easily support refinancing their mortgage under the specified terms.* Most families decide to refinance in order to lower their monthly mortgage payments—it is after all, almost like getting a raise in pay! In such cases, the analysis is relatively simple: determine how long it will take for the monthly savings to equal any closing costs (as spelled out in Worksheet 5.4).

Planning Over a Lifetime: Auto and Housing Decisions

Here are some key considerations in making auto and housing decisions in each stage of the life cycle.

Pre-family Independence: 20s	Family Formation/Career Development: 30–45	Pre-Retirement: 45–65	Retirement: 65 and Beyond
✓ Start saving for a downpayment on a house.	✓ Compare current mortgage rates with yours and evaluate the value of refinancing.	✓ Periodically re-evaluate the attractiveness of refinancing your mortgage.	✓ Re-evaluate housing choices and location. Consider downsizing but watch transactions costs.
✓ Compare renting vs. buying a house.	✓ Budget to make additional payments on your mortgage to gain greater financial flexibility in the future.	✓ Budget to pay-off your mortgage prior to retirement.	✓ Pay-off mortgage.
✓ Familiarize yourself with the various types of mortgages.	✓ Save to finance a replacement for your current car.	✓ Consider whether different type of car(s) appropriate.	✓ Consider whether more than one family car is needed in retirement.

FINANCIAL PLANNING EXERCISES

1. Debbie Snyder has just graduated from college and needs to buy a car to commute to work. She estimates that she can afford to pay about $450 per month for a loan or lease and has about $2,000 in savings to use for a down payment. Develop a plan to guide her through her first car-buying experience, including researching car type, deciding whether to buy a new or used car, negotiating the price and terms, and financing the transaction.

LG2

2. *Use Worksheet 5.1.* Damien Smart is trying to decide whether to lease or purchase a new car costing $18,000. If he leases, he'll have to pay a $600 security deposit and monthly payments of $450 over the 36-month term of the closed-end lease. On the other hand, if he buys the car, then he'll have to make a $2,400 down payment and will finance the balance with a 36-month loan requiring monthly payments of $515; he'll also have to pay a 6 percent sales tax ($1,080) on the purchase price, and he expects the car to have a residual value of $6,500 at the end of three years. Use the automobile lease versus purchase analysis form in Worksheet 5.1 to find the total cost of both the lease and the purchase and then recommend the best strategy for Damien.

LG3

3. Cliff Arthur has equally attractive job offers in Miami and Los Angeles. The rent ratios in the cities are 8 and 20, respectively. Cliff would really like to buy rather than rent a home after he moves. Explain how to interpret the rent ratio and what it tells Cliff about the relative attractiveness of moving to Miami rather than Los Angeles, given his stated goal.

LG4

4. Using the maximum ratios for a conventional mortgage, how big a monthly payment could the Taylor family afford if their gross (before-tax) monthly income amounted to $3,500? Would it make any difference if they were already making monthly installment loan payments totaling $750 on two car loans?

LG5

5. Find the *monthly* mortgage payments on the following mortgage loans using either your calculator or the table in Exhibit 5.5:
   a. $90,000 at 6.5 percent for 30 years
   b. $125,000 at 5.5 percent for 20 years
   c. $97,500 at 5 percent for 15 years

LG3, 4

6. *Use Worksheet 5.2.* Aurelia Montenegro is currently renting an apartment for $725 per month and paying $275 annually for renter's insurance. She just found a small townhouse she can buy for $185,000. She has enough cash for a $10,000 down payment and $4,000 in closing costs. Aurelia estimated the following costs as a percentage of the home's price: property taxes, 2.5 percent; homeowner's insurance, 0.5 percent; and maintenance, 0.7 percent. She is in the 25 percent tax bracket. Using Worksheet 5.2, calculate the cost of each alternative and recommend the least costly option—rent or buy—for Aurelia.

LG6

7. *Use Worksheet 5.4.* Miao Tian purchased a condominium 4 years ago for $200,000, paying $1,250 per month on her $162,000, 8 percent, 25-year mortgage. The current loan balance is $152,401. Recently, interest rates dropped sharply, causing Miao to consider refinancing her condo at the prevailing rate of 6 percent. She expects to remain in the condo for at least 4 more years and has found a lender that will make a 6 percent, 21-year, $152,401 loan, requiring monthly payments of $1,065. Although there is no prepayment penalty on her current mortgage, Miao will have to pay $1,500 in closing costs on the new mortgage. She is in the 15 percent tax bracket. Based on this information, use the mortgage refinancing analysis form in Worksheet 5.4 to determine whether she should refinance her mortgage under the specified terms.

PFIN Student Study Tools—Visit CourseMate for PFIN 3. Log in at **www.cengagebrain.com**. Check out the bonus exercises and exhibits, interactive worksheets, Cool Apps, Smart Sites, Critical Thinking Cases, Money Online, Kiplinger videos, quizzing, and more.

STOCKLITE/SHUTTERSTOCK.COM

6

USING CREDIT

LEARNING GOALS

LG1 Describe the reasons for using consumer credit and identify its benefits and problems.

LG2 Develop a plan to establish a strong credit history.

LG3 Distinguish among the different forms of open account credit.

LG4 Apply for, obtain, and manage open forms of credit.

LG5 Choose the right credit cards and recognize their advantages and disadvantages.

LG6 Avoid credit problems, protect yourself against credit card fraud, and understand the personal bankruptcy process.

How Will This Affect Me? The ability to borrow funds to buy goods and services is as convenient as it is seductive. It is important to understand how to get and maintain access to credit via credit cards, debit cards, lines of credit, and other means. This chapter reviews the common sources of consumer credit and provides a framework for choosing among them. It also discusses the importance of developing a good credit history, achieving and maintaining a good credit score, and protecting against identity theft and credit fraud. The chapter will help you understand the need to use credit intentionally, in a way that is consistent with your overall financial objectives.

6-1 The Basic Concepts of Credit

LG1, LG2 It's so easy—just slide that credit card through the reader and you can get gas for your car, buy a laptop at Staples, or furnish an apartment. It happens *several hundred million times a day* across the United States. Credit, in fact, has become an entrenched part of our everyday lives, and we as consumers use it in one form or another to purchase just about every type of good or service imaginable. Indeed, because of the ready availability and widespread use of credit, our economy is often called a "credit economy." And for good reason: by early 2012, individuals in this country had run up almost *$2.5 trillion* in consumer debt—and that doesn't even include home mortgages.

Consumer credit is important in the personal financial planning process because of the impact it can have on (1) attaining financial goals and (2) cash budgets. For one thing, various forms of consumer credit can help you reach your financial objectives by enabling you to acquire some of the more expensive items in a systematic fashion without throwing your whole budget into disarray. But there's another side to consumer credit: it has to be paid back! Unless credit is used intelligently, the "buy now, pay later" attitude can quickly turn an otherwise orderly budget into a budgetary nightmare and lead to some serious problems—even bankruptcy!

After you read the chapter, explore the STUDY TOOLS listed on page 152.

6-1a Why We Use Credit

People typically use credit as a way to pay for goods and services that cost more than they can afford to take from their current income. This is particularly true for those in the 25–44 age group, who simply have not had time to accumulate the liquid assets required to pay cash outright for major purchases and expenditures. As people begin to approach their mid-40s, however, their savings and investments start to build up and their debt loads tend to decline—which is really not too surprising when you consider that the median household net worth for those in the 45–54 age group is considerably higher than for those aged 35 to 44.

Whatever their age group, people tend to borrow for several major reasons.

- **To avoid paying cash for large outlays.** Rather than pay cash for large purchases such as houses and cars, most people borrow part of the purchase price and then repay the loan on some scheduled basis. Spreading payments over time makes big-ticket items more affordable, and consumers get the use of an expensive asset right away.

- **To meet a financial emergency.** For example, people may need to borrow to cover living expenses during a period of unemployment or to purchase plane tickets to visit a sick relative.

- **For convenience.** Merchants as well as banks offer a variety of charge accounts and credit cards that allow consumers to charge just about anything—from gas or clothes and stereos to doctor and dental bills and even college tuition. Further, in many places—restaurants, for instance—using a credit card is far easier than writing a check.

- **For investment purposes.** As we'll see in Chapter 11, it's relatively easy for an investor to partially finance the purchase of many different kinds of investments with borrowed funds. In fact, *margin loans*, as they're called, amounted more to than $289.4 billion toward the end of 2012.

The "buy now, pay later" attitude can quickly turn an otherwise orderly budget into a budgetary nightmare.

129

6-1b Improper Uses of Credit

Many people use consumer credit to live beyond their means. For some people, overspending becomes a way of life, and it is perhaps the biggest danger in borrowing—especially because it's so easy to do. And nowhere did that become more apparent than in the wake of *the credit crisis of 2007–2009.* Indeed, as credit became more readily available and easier to obtain, it also became increasingly clear that many consumers were, in fact, severely overusing it. Whether or not the consumer deserved the credit was really not an issue—the only thing that seemed to matter was that it was there for the taking! All this resulted in a credit meltdown unlike anything this country had ever seen.

Fact is, once hooked on "plastic," people use their credit cards to make even routine purchases and all too often don't realize they have overextended themselves until it's too late. Overspenders simply won't admit that they're spending too much. As far as they're concerned, they can afford to buy all those things because, after all, they still have their credit cards and can still afford to pay the minimum amounts each month. Unfortunately, such spending eventually leads to mounting bills. And by making only the minimum payment, borrowers pay a huge price in the long run. Look at Exhibit 6.1, which shows the amount of time and interest charges required to repay credit card balances if you make only minimum payments of 3 percent of the outstanding balance. For example, if you carry a $3,000 balance—which is about *one-fourth* the national average—on a card that charges 15.0 percent annually, then it would take you 14 years to retire the debt and your interest charges would total some $2,000—*or more than 66 percent of the original balance!*

Some cards offer even lower minimum payments of just 2 percent of the outstanding balance.

Although such small payments may seem like a good deal, clearly they don't work to your advantage and only increase the time and amount of interest required to repay the debt. Indeed, by making minimum 2 percent payments, it would take *more than 32 years* to pay off a $5,000 balance on a credit card that carries a 15 percent rate of interest. In contrast, that same $5,000 balance could be paid off in *just 16.4 years* if you had made 3 percent minimum payments. Just think, making an additional 1 percent payment can save you nearly 16 years of interest! That's why federal banking regulators have issued guidelines stating that minimum monthly credit card payments should cover at least 1 percent of the outstanding balance plus all monthly finance charges and any other fees.

The best way to steer clear of future repayment shock is to avoid using your credit card in the following situations:

1. to meet basic living expenses;
2. to make impulse purchases, especially expensive ones; and
3. to purchase nondurable (short-lived) goods and services.

Except in situations where credit cards are used occasionally for convenience, or where payments on recurring credit purchases are built into the monthly budget, a good rule to remember when considering the use of credit is that *the product purchased on credit should outlive the payments.*

Unfortunately, people who overspend eventually arrive at the point where they must choose to either become delinquent in their payments or sacrifice necessities, such as food and clothing. If payment obligations aren't met, the consequences are likely to be a damaged credit rating, lawsuits, or even personal bankruptcy. See the Bonus Exhibit, "Some Credit

© KAREN HERMANN/ISTOCKPHOTO

Exhibit 6.1 Minimum Payments Mean Maximum Years

Paying off credit card balances at the minimum monthly amount required by the card issuer will take a long time and cost you a great deal of interest, as this table demonstrates. *The calculations here are based on a minimum 3% payment and 15% annual interest rate.*

Original Balance	Years to Repay	Interest Paid	Total Interest Paid as Percentage of Original Balance
$5,000	16.4	$3,434	68.7%
4,000	15.4	2,720	68.0
3,000	14.0	2,005	66.8
2,000	12.1	1,291	64.5
1,000	8.8	577	57.7

© Cengage Learning

Danger Signs," which lists some common signals that indicate it may be time to stop buying on credit. (Visit CourseMate for PFIN 3. Log in at **www.cengagebrain.com**.) *Ignoring the telltale signs that you are overspending can only lead to more serious problems.*

6-1c Impact of the Credit Crisis on Borrowers

The majority of U.S. households' liabilities—up to 80 percent—are mortgages. As housing prices continued to grow rapidly until late in 2006, many households took on large mortgages because housing looked like such a great investment. However, as the economy slowed and unemployment increased during and in the wake of the financial crisis of 2007–2009, overly indebted households had trouble making their mortgage payments. In response, they drastically cut spending on housing and consumer durables and many also sold their houses to reduce their debt. This reduced overall economic activity, as measured by gross domestic product (GDP), and exacerbated the downward spiral in home prices. As consumers adapted to the financial crisis, their total indebtedness relative to disposable income fell from between 2008 and 2011. About two-thirds of the reduction is due to home and consumer loan defaults. Foreclosures currently in progress should reduce debt even further. Even though interest rates fell to historical lows, the decline in housing prices made it harder for households to refinance their mortgages.

The financial crisis created an increase in consumers' demand for cash and safe government securities while banks became more reluctant to make risky loans. Indeed, lenders also wanted to hold safer assets such as those of the government. Interestingly, much of the extra public borrowing required to help stimulate the economy during the crisis was financed by the increased demand by savers for safe assets. This is one of the reasons that government bond yields fell even as the government's indebtedness rose.

This "deleveraging" by consumers resulted, in part, from reduced use of and demand for installment and revolving credit and reduced the supply of credit by lenders. For example, lenders reduced credit card limits by about 28 percent during and after the crisis to reduce their exposure to credit risk. Thus, deleveraging was caused by both tightening credit conditions and voluntary household decisions. While debt continues to fall, reduced home equity will likely constrain consumer spending and thereby dampen GDP growth.

Consumer borrowing and spending have been changed by the recent financial crisis. Debt has been reduced both voluntarily and involuntarily, there is growing demand for more extensive disclosure and transparency in financial contracts in general and mortgage contracts in particular, and there is greater

focus on value purchases. Discount store and online sales have soared as consumers look for more bargains.

6-1d Establishing Credit

The willingness of lenders to extend credit depends on their assessment of your creditworthiness—that is, your ability to repay the debt promptly. Lenders look at various factors in making this decision, such as your present earnings and net worth. Equally important, they look at your current debt position and your credit history. Thus, it's worth your while to do what you can to build a strong credit rating.

First Steps in Establishing Credit
First, open checking and savings accounts. They signal stability to lenders and indicate that you handle your financial affairs in a businesslike way. Second, use credit: open one or two charge accounts and use them periodically, even if you prefer paying cash. You might pay an annual fee or interest on some (or all) of your account balances, but in the process, you'll build a record of being a reliable credit customer. Third, obtain a small loan, even if you don't need one. If you don't actually need the money, put it in a liquid investment, such as a money market account or certificate

© JASON STITT/SHUTTERSTOCK.COM

debt safety ratio The proportion of total monthly consumer credit obligations to monthly take-home pay.

of deposit. The interest you earn should offset some of the interest expense on the loan; you can view the difference as a cost of building good credit. You should repay the loan promptly, perhaps even a *little* ahead of schedule, to minimize the difference in interest rates. Keep in mind that your ability to obtain a large loan in the future will depend, in part, on how you managed smaller ones in the past.

Build a Strong Credit History

From a financial perspective, maintaining a strong credit history is just as important as developing a solid employment record! Don't take credit lightly, and don't assume that getting the loan or the credit card is the toughest part. It's not. That's just the first step; servicing it (i.e., making payments) in a prompt and timely fashion—month in and month out—is the really tough part of the consumer credit process. And in many respects, it's the most important element of consumer credit because it determines your creditworthiness. By using credit wisely and repaying it on time, you're establishing a *credit history* that tells lenders you're a dependable, reliable, and responsible borrower. When you take on credit, you have an *obligation* to live up to the terms of the loan, including how and when the credit will be repaid.

If you foresee difficulty in meeting a monthly payment, let the lender know. Usually arrangements can be made to help you

through the situation. This is especially true with installment loans that require fixed monthly payments. Don't just skip a payment, because that's going to put your account into a *late status until you make up the missed payment.* Instead, try to work out an extension with your lender. Here's what you do. Explain the situation to the loan officer and ask for an extension of one (or two) months on your loan. In most cases, so long as this hasn't occurred before, the extension is almost automatically granted. The maturity of the loan is formally extended for a month (or two), and the extra interest of carrying the loan for another month (or two) is either added to the loan balance or, more commonly, paid at the time the extension is granted (such an extension fee generally amounts to a fraction of the normal monthly payment). Then, in a month or two, you pick up where you left off and resume your normal monthly payments on the loan. This is the most sensible way of making it through those rough times because it doesn't harm your credit record. Just don't do it too often.

Go to Smart Sites

Are you living beyond your means? Investopedia has five signs to watch for. For more online resources, whenever you see "*Go to Smart Sites*" in this chapter, visit CourseMate for PFIN 3. Log in at **www.cengagebrain.com**. ●

Financial Road Sign

The 5 C's of Credit

Lenders often look to the "5 C's of Credit" as a way to assess the willingness and ability of a borrower to repay a loan.

1. **Character:** A key factor in defining the borrower's willingness to live up to the terms of the loan.
2. **Capacity:** The ability of the borrower to service the loan in a timely fashion.
3. **Collateral:** Something of value that's used to secure a loan and that the lender can claim in case of default.
4. **Capital:** The amount of unencumbered assets owned by the borrower, used as another indicator of the borrower's ability to repay the loan.
5. **Condition:** The extent to which prevailing economic conditions could affect the borrower's ability to service a loan.

How Much Credit Can You Handle?

Sound financial planning dictates that you need to have a good idea of how much credit you can comfortably tolerate. The easiest way to avoid repayment problems and ensure that your borrowing won't place an undue strain on your monthly budget is to *limit the use of credit to your ability to repay the debt!* A useful guideline (and one widely used by lenders) is to make sure your monthly repayment burden doesn't exceed 20 percent of your monthly *take-home pay.* Most experts, however, regard the 20 percent figure as the *maximum* debt burden and strongly recommend a **debt safety ratio** closer to 10 percent or 15 percent—perhaps even lower if you plan on applying for a new mortgage in the near future. Note that the monthly repayment burden here *does include* payments on your credit cards, but it *excludes* your monthly mortgage obligation.

To illustrate, consider someone who takes home $2,500 a month. Using a 20 percent ratio, she should have monthly consumer credit payments of no more than $500—that is, $2,500 × 0.20 = $500. This is the maximum amount of her monthly disposable income that she should need to pay off both personal loans and other forms of consumer credit (such as credit cards and education loans). This, of course, is not the maximum amount of consumer credit that she can have outstanding—in fact, her total consumer indebtedness can, and likely would, be considerably larger. The key factor is that with her income level, her *payments* on this type of debt should not exceed $500 a month. Exhibit 6.2 provides a summary of low (10 percent), manageable (15 percent), and maximum (20 percent) monthly credit payments for various income levels. Obviously, *the lower the debt safety ratio, the better shape you're in, creditwise, and the easier it should be for you to service your outstanding consumer debt.*

You can compute the debt safety ratio as follows:

$$\text{Debt safety ratio} = \frac{\text{Total monthly consumer credit payments}}{\text{Monthly take-home pay}}$$

This measure is the focus of Worksheet 6.1, which you can use for keeping close tabs on your own debt safety ratio. It shows the impact that each new loan you take out, or credit card you sign up for, can have on this important measure of creditworthiness. Consider, for example, Alan and Clarissa Simpson. As seen in Worksheet 6.1, they have five outstanding consumer loans and they're carrying balances on three credit cards. All totaled, these eight obligations require monthly payments of almost $740, which accounts for about one-fifth of their combined take-home pay and gives them a debt safety ratio of 18 percent. And note the information at the bottom of the worksheet that says if the Simpsons want to lower this ratio to, say, 15 percent, then they'll either have to reduce their monthly payments to $615 or increase their take-home pay to at least $4,927 a month.

6-2 Credit Cards and Other Types of Open Account Credit

LG3 Open account credit is a form of credit extended to a consumer in advance of any transactions. Typically, a retail outlet or bank agrees to allow the consumer to buy or borrow up to a specified amount on open account. Credit is extended so long as the consumer does not exceed the established **credit limit** and makes payments in accordance with the specified terms. Open account credit issued by a retail outlet, such as a department store or oil company, is usually usable only in that establishment or one of its locations. In contrast, open account credit issued by banks, such as *MasterCard* and *Visa* accounts, can be used to

open account credit A form of credit extended to a consumer in advance of any transaction.

credit limit A specified amount beyond which a customer may not borrow or purchase on credit.

© KAREN HERMANN/ISTOCKPHOTO

Exhibit 6.2   Credit Guidelines Based on Ability to Repay

According to the debt safety ratio, the amount of consumer credit you should have outstanding depends on the monthly payments you can afford to make.

Monthly Take-Home Pay	Monthly Consumer Credit Payments		
	Low Debt Safety Ratio (10%)	*Manageable* Debt Safety Ratio (15%)	*Maximum* Debt Safety Ratio (20%)
$1,000	$100	$150	$ 200
$1,250	$125	$188	$ 250
$1,500	$150	$225	$ 300
$2,000	$200	$300	$ 400
$2,500	$250	$375	$ 500
$3,000	$300	$450	$ 600
$3,500	$350	$525	$ 700
$4,000	$400	$600	$ 800
$5,000	$500	$750	$1,000

© Cengage Learning

A worksheet like this one will help a household stay on top of their monthly credit card and consumer loan payments as well as their *debt safety ratio*—an important measure of creditworthiness. The key here is to keep the debt safety ratio as low as (reasonably) possible, something that can be done by keeping monthly loan payments in line with monthly take-home pay.

MONTHLY CONSUMER LOAN PAYMENTS & DEBT SAFETY RATIO

Name _Alan and Clarissa Simpson_   **Date** _June 21, 2015_

■ Type of Loan*	Lender	Current Monthly (or Min.) Payment
• Auto and personal loans	1. Ford Motor Credit	$ 360.00
	2. Bank of America	115.00
	3.	
• Education loans	1. U.S. Dept. of Education	75.00
	2.	
• Overdraft protection line	1. Bank of America	30.00
• Personal line of credit		
• Credit cards	1. Bank of America Visa	28.00
	2. Fidelity MC	31.00
	3. JC Penney	28.00
	4.	
• Home equity line	1. Bank of America	72.00
TOTAL MONTHLY PAYMENTS		$ 739.00

*Note: List only those loans that require regular monthly payments.

■ Monthly Take-Home Pay	1. Alan	$ 1,855.00
	2. Clarissa	2,250.00
TOTAL MONTHLY TAKE-HOME PAY		$ 4,105.00

■ **Debt Safety Ratio:**

$$\frac{\text{Total monthly payments}}{\text{Total monthly take-home pay}} \times 100 = \frac{\$ \ 739.00}{\$4,105.00} \times 100 = \underline{18.0} \%$$

• **Changes needed to reach a new debt safety ratio**

   1. New (Target) debt safety ratio: _15.0 %_

   2. At current take-home pay of _$4,105.00_ ,
       total monthly payments must equal:

$$\text{Total monthly take-home pay} \times \text{Target debt safety ratio}^{**}$$

$$\underline{\$4,105.00} \times \underline{0.150} = \underline{\$ \ 615.75}$$
                                          New Monthly Payments

   OR

   3. With current monthly payments of _$739.00_ ,
       total take-home pay must equal:

$$\frac{\text{Total monthly payments}}{\text{New (target) debt safety ratio}} \times 100 = \frac{\$ \ 739.00}{0.150} = \underline{\$4,926.67}$$
                                                        New take-home pay

Note: Enter debt safety ratio as a decimal (e.g., 15% = 0.15).

© Cengage Learning

make purchases at a wide variety of businesses. Having open account credit is a lot like having your own personal line of credit—it's there when you need it.

Open account credit generally is available from two broadly defined sources:

1. financial institutions, and
2. retail stores/merchants.

Financial institutions issue general-purpose credit cards, as well as secured and unsecured revolving lines of credit and overdraft protection lines. *Retail stores and merchants* make up the other major source of open account credit. They provide this service as a way to promote the sales of their products, and their principal form of credit is the charge (or credit) card. Let's now take a look at these two forms of credit, along with *debit cards* and *revolving lines of credit*.

6-2a Bank Credit Cards

Probably the most popular form of open account credit is the **bank credit card**, issued by commercial banks and other financial institutions—Visa and MasterCard being the two dominant types. These cards allow their holders to charge purchases worldwide at literally millions of stores, restaurants, shops, and gas stations, as well as at state and municipal governments, colleges and universities, medical groups, and mail-order houses—not to mention the Internet, where they've become the currency of choice. They can be used to pay for almost anything—groceries, doctor bills, college tuition, airline tickets, and car rentals. They can also be used to borrow money.

In fact, by 2003, the amount of transactions completed with credit and debit cards had actually surpassed those made with cash or check.

RYASICK PHOTOGRAPHY/SHUTTERSTOCK

The recent financial crisis brought tougher credit standards and sharply reduced credit lines to the bank credit card business. Standards tend to tighten quickly in a crisis, and it can take several years before they move back to their pre-crisis levels. As a result, consumers are finding it harder to get new credit cards, and the limits on existing cards are often slashed. Many economists forecast that, this time, credit standards are likely to remain far more stringent than what existed prior to the crisis. Despite all this, bank credit cards can still be of great convenience and value to consumers. But to get the most from them, individuals who use these cards should be thoroughly familiar with their basic features.

Line of Credit

The **line of credit** provided to the holder of a bank credit card is set by the issuer. It's the maximum amount that the cardholder can owe at any given time. The size of the credit line depends on both the applicant's request and the results of the issuer's investigation of the applicant's credit and financial status. Lines of credit can reach $50,000 or more, but for the most part, they range from about $500 to $2,500. Although card issuers fully expect you to keep your credit within the specified limits, most won't take any real action until you extend your account balance by a certain percentage. For example, if you had a $1,000 credit limit, you probably wouldn't hear a peep out of the card issuer until your outstanding balance exceeded, say, $1,200 (i.e., 20 percent above the $1,000 line of credit). On the other hand, don't count on getting off scot-free, because most card issuers assess *over-the-limit* fees whenever you go over your credit limit (more on this later).

Cash Advances

In addition to purchasing merchandise and services, the holder of a bank credit card can obtain a **cash advance** from any participating bank. Cash advances are loans on which interest begins to accrue immediately. They're transacted in the same way as merchandise purchases, except that they take place at a commercial bank or some other financial institution and involve the receipt of cash (or a check) instead of goods and services. Another way to get a cash advance is to use the "convenience checks" that you receive from the card issuer to pay for purchases. You can even use your credit card to draw cash from an ATM, any time of the day or night. Usually, the size of the cash advance from an ATM is limited to some nominal

bank credit card A credit card issued by a bank or other financial institution that allows the holder to charge purchases at any establishment that accepts it.

line of credit The maximum amount of credit a customer is allowed to have outstanding at any point in time.

cash advance A loan that can be obtained by a bank credit cardholder at any participating bank or financial institution.

base rate The rate of interest a bank uses as a base for loans to individuals and small to midsize businesses.

grace period A short period of time, usually 20 to 30 days, during which you can pay your credit card bill in full and not incur any interest charges.

amount (a common amount is $500 or less), although the amount you can obtain from the teller window at a bank is limited only by the unused credit in your account.

Interest Charges

Generally speaking, *the interest rates on credit cards are higher than any other form of consumer credit. The average annual rate of interest* charged on bank credit cards was around 16.87 percent in early 2012. You'll find that most bank cards have one rate for merchandise purchases and a much higher rate for cash advances. For example, the rate on merchandise purchases might be 12 percent, while the rate on cash advances could be 19 percent or 20 percent. And when shopping for a credit card, watch out for those *special low introductory rates* that many banks offer. Known as "teaser rates," they're usually only good for the first 6 to 12 months. Then, just as soon as the introductory period ends, so do the low interest rates.

Most of these cards have variable interest rates that are tied to an index that moves with market rates.

NOEL HENDRICKSON/JUPITER IMAGES

The most popular is the prime or **base rate**: the rate a bank uses as a base for loans to individuals and small or midsize businesses. These cards adjust their interest rate monthly or quarterly and usually have minimum and maximum rates. To illustrate, consider a bank card whose terms are *prime plus 7.5 percent*, with a minimum of 10 percent and a maximum of 15.25 percent. If the prime rate is 3.25 percent, then the rate of interest charged on this card would be 3.25 percent + 7.5 percent = 10.75 percent.

Bank credit card issuers must disclose interest costs and related information to consumers *before* extending credit. In the case of purchases of merchandise and services, the specified interest rate may not apply to charges until after the **grace period**. During this short period, usually 20 to 30 days, you have historically been able to pay your credit card bill in full and avoid any interest charges. However, once you carry a balance—that is, when you don't pay your card in full during the grace period—the interest rate is usually applied to any unpaid balances carried from previous periods as well as to any new purchases made. Interest on cash advances, in contrast, *begins the day that the advance is taken out.*

Then There Are Those Other Fees

Besides the interest charged on bank credit cards, there are a few other fees you should be aware of. To begin with, many (though not all) bank cards charge *annual fees* just for the "privilege" of being able to use the card. In most cases, the fee is around $25 to $40 a year, though it can amount to much more for prestige cards. As a rule, the larger the bank or S&L, the more likely it is to charge an annual fee for its credit cards. What's more, many issuers also charge a *transaction fee* for each (non-ATM) cash advance; this fee usually amounts to about $5 per cash advance or 3 percent of the amount obtained in the transaction, whichever is more.

Historically, card issuers have come up with many ways to squeeze additional revenue from you. These have included late-payment fees, over-the-limit charges, foreign transaction fees, and balance transfer fees. For example, if you're a bit late in making your payment then some banks will hit you with a late-payment fee, which is really a redundant charge because you're already paying interest on the unpaid balance. Similarly, if you happened to go over your credit limit then you'd be hit with a charge for that, too (again, this is in addition to the interest you're already paying). Critics really dislike this fee because they maintain it's hard for cardholders to know when they've hit their credit ceilings. Some card issuers even went so far as to slap you with a fee for *not using your credit card*—one bank, for example, charged a $15 fee to customers (cardholders) who didn't use their credit cards in a six-month period. Given the widespread

136

Part 3 • Managing Credit

use of variable interest rates, bank cardholders should know that—just as falling rates bring down interest rates on credit cards—rising market rates are guaranteed to lead to much higher interest charges!

These onerous credit card issuer practices and extra fees led to the passage of the Credit Card Act of 2009.

6-2b Special Types of Bank Credit Cards

Bank credit cards sure aren't what they used to be. Today, in addition to standard, "plain vanilla" bank cards, you can obtain cards that offer rebates and special incentive programs, cards that are sponsored by nonprofit organizations, even credit cards aimed specifically at college students.

Reward Cards

One of the fastest-growing segments of the bank card market is the **reward (co-branded) credit card**, which combines features of a traditional bank credit card with an incentive: cash, merchandise rebates, airline tickets, or even investments. About half of credit cards are rebate cards, and new types are introduced almost every day. Here are some of the many incentive programs.

- **Frequent flyer programs.** In this program, the cardholder earns free frequent flyer miles for each dollar charged on his or her credit card. These frequent flyer miles can then be used with airline-affiliated programs for free tickets, first-class upgrades, and other travel-related benefits.

- **Automobile rebate programs.** Some credit cards allow the cardholder to earn annual rebates of up to 5 percent that can be used, up to specified limits, for new car purchases, leases, or auto maintenance programs. Indeed, most of the major car companies offer some kind of rewards-related credit card that can be used to buy a car or related items.

- **Other merchandise rebates.** An increasing number of companies are participating in bank card reward programs, including, for example, Norwegian Cruise Line, Harrah's casino, NASCAR, Starbucks, and Marriott Hotels. Several regional phone companies even offer rebates on phone calls. (A good site for finding information about rebate card offers is **http://www.cardtrak.com**.)

Are rebate cards a good deal? Well, yes and no. To see if they make sense for you, evaluate these cards carefully by looking at your usage patterns and working out the annual cost of the cards before and after the rebate. Don't get so carried away with the gimmick that you lose sight of the total costs. Most incentive cards carry higher interest rates than regular bank cards do. These cards generally work best for those can use the rebates, charge a lot, and don't carry high monthly balances.

Affinity Cards

"Credit cards with a cause" is the way to describe **affinity cards**. These cards are nothing more than standard Visa or MasterCards that are issued in conjunction with a sponsoring group—most commonly some type of charitable, political, or professional organization. So-named because of the bond between the sponsoring group and its members, affinity cards are sponsored by such nonprofit organizations as Mothers Against Drunk Driving (MADD), the American Wildlife Fund, AARP, and the Special Olympics. In addition, they are issued by college and university alumni groups, labor organizations, religious and fraternal groups, and professional societies. So, why even bother with one of these cards? Well, unlike traditional bank cards, affinity cards make money for the group backing the card because the sponsoring groups receive a share of the profits. But to cover the money that goes to the sponsoring organization, the issuer/bank usually charges higher fees or higher interest rates. Even so, some may view these cards as a great way to contribute to a worthy cause.

reward (co-branded) credit card A bank credit card that combines features of a traditional bank credit card with an additional incentive, such as rebates and airline mileage.

affinity cards A standard bank credit card issued in conjunction with some charitable, political, or other nonprofit organization.

Others, however, may feel it makes more sense to use a traditional credit card and then write a check to their favorite charity.

Secured Credit Cards

You may have seen the ads on TV where the announcer says that no matter how bad your credit, you can still qualify for one of their credit cards. The pitch may sound too good to be true; and in some respects, it is because there's a catch. Namely, the credit is "secured"—meaning you have to put up *collateral* in order to get the card! These are so-called **secured**, or **collateralized credit cards** where the amount of credit is determined by the amount of liquid collateral you're able to put up. These cards are targeted at people with no credit or bad credit histories, who don't qualify for conventional credit cards. Issued as Visa or MasterCard, they're like any other credit card except for the collateral. To qualify, a customer must deposit a certain amount (usually $500 or more) into a 12- to 18-month certificate of deposit that the issuing bank holds as collateral. The cardholder then gets a credit line equal to the deposit. If the customer defaults, the bank has the CD to cover its losses. By making payments on time, it's hoped that these cardholders will establish (or reestablish) a credit history that may qualify them for a conventional (unsecured) credit card. Secured credit cards normally carry annual fees and finance charges that are equal to, or greater than, those of regular credit cards.

Student Credit Cards

Some large banks, through their Visa and MasterCard programs, have special credit cards that specifically target college students. These **student credit** cards often come packaged with special promotional programs that are meant to appeal to this segment of the market—such as free music, movie tickets, and the like. Except for these features, there's really nothing unusual about these cards or their terms. Most simply require that you be enrolled in a two- or four-year college or university and have some source of income, whatever that may be. In particular, they usually *do not require* any parental or guardian guarantees, nor do they require that you hold a full-time (or even a part-time) job. From the student's perspective, these cards not only offer convenience but are also great for building up a solid credit history. Just *remember to use them*

responsibly; that's the way to get the most from these cards—or any other form of credit, for that matter!

6-2c Retail Charge Cards

Retail charge cards are issued by department stores, oil companies, car rental agencies, and so on. These cards are popular with merchants because they build consumer loyalty and enhance sales; consumers like them because they offer a convenient way to shop. These cards carry a preset credit limit—a line of credit—that varies with the creditworthiness of the cardholder. This form of credit is most common in department and clothing stores and other high-volume outlets, where customers are likely to make several purchases each month. Most large oil companies also offer charge cards that allow customers to buy gas and oil products, *but they're expected to pay for such purchases in full upon receipt of the monthly bill*. Interest on retail charge cards is typically fixed at 1.5 percent to 1.85 percent monthly, or about 18 percent to 22 percent per year—considerably more than what most bank cards charge.

6-2d Debit Cards

It looks like a credit card, it works like a credit card, it even has the familiar MasterCard and Visa credit card markings. But it's not a *credit* card—rather, it's a *debit* card. Simply put, a **debit card** provides direct access to your checking account and, thus, *works like writing a check*. That is, when you use a debit card to make a purchase, the amount of the transaction is charged directly to your checking account. Using a debit card isn't the same thing as buying on credit; it may appear that you're charging it, but actually *you're paying with cash*. Accordingly, there are no finance charges to pay.

Debit cards are becoming very popular, especially with consumers who want the convenience of a credit card but not the high cost of interest that comes with them. In fact, in 2006, debit card use exceeded credit card use for the first time. This is no small feat given there are more than 58 billion credit/debit card transactions each year in the United States. Debit cards are accepted at most establishments displaying the Visa or MasterCard logo but function as an alternative to writing checks. If you use a debit card to make a purchase at a department store or restaurant, the transaction will show up on your next monthly *checking account* statement. Needless to say, to keep your records straight, you should enter debit card transactions directly into your checkbook ledger as they occur and treat them as withdrawals, or checks, by subtracting them from your checking account balance. Debit cards can also be used to gain access to your account through 24-hour teller machines or ATMs—which is the closest thing to a cash advance that these cards have to offer.

A big disadvantage of a debit card, of course, is that it doesn't provide a line of credit. In addition, it can cause overdraft problems if you fail to make the proper entries to your checking account or inadvertently use it when you think you're using a credit card. Also, some debit card issuers charge a transaction fee or a flat annual fee; and some *merchants* may even charge you just for using your debit card. On the plus side, a debit card enables you to avoid the potential credit problems and high costs of credit cards. Further, it's as convenient to use as a credit card—in fact, if convenience is the major reason you use a credit card, you might want to consider switching to a debit card for at least some transactions, especially at outlets such as gas stations that give discounts for cash purchases and consider a debit card to be as good as cash.

6-2e Revolving Credit Lines

Revolving lines of credit are offered by banks, brokerage houses, and other financial institutions. These credit lines normally don't involve the use of credit cards. Rather, they're accessed by writing checks on regular checking accounts or specially designated credit line accounts. They are a form of open account credit and often represent a far better deal than credit cards, not only because they offer more credit but also because they can be a lot less expensive. And there may even be a tax advantage to using one of these other kinds of credit. These lines basically provide their users with ready access to borrowed money (that is, cash advances) through revolving lines of credit. The three major forms of open (non–credit card) credit are overdraft protection lines, unsecured personal lines of credit, and home equity credit lines.

Overdraft Protection

An **overdraft protection line** is simply a line of credit linked to a checking account that enables a depositor to overdraw his or her checking account up to a predetermined limit. These lines are usually set up with credit limits of $500 to $1,000, but they can be for as much as $10,000 or more. The consumer taps this line of credit by simply writing a check, and if that particular check happens to overdraw the account,

revolving line of credit A type of open account credit offered by banks and other financial institutions that can be accessed by writing checks against demand deposit or specially designated credit line accounts.

overdraft protection line A line of credit linked to a checking account that allows a depositor to overdraw the account up to a specified amount.

the overdraft protection line will automatically advance funds in an amount necessary to put the account back in the black. In some cases, overdraft protection is provided by *linking the bank's credit card to your checking account*. These arrangements act like regular overdraft lines except that, when the account is overdrawn, the bank automatically taps your credit card line and transfers the money into your checking account. It's treated as a cash advance from your credit card, but the result is the same as a regular overdraft protection line; it automatically covers overdrawn checks.

If you're not careful, you can quickly exhaust this type of credit by writing a lot of overdraft checks. As with any line of credit, there's a limit to how much you can obtain. Be extremely careful with such a credit line and by all means, *don't take it as a license to overdraw your account routinely!* Doing so on a regular basis is a signal that you're probably mismanaging your cash and/or living beyond your budget. It's best to view an overdraft protection line strictly as an *emergency* source of credit—and any funds advanced should be repaid as quickly as possible.

Unsecured Personal Lines

Another form of revolving credit is the **unsecured personal credit line**, which basically makes a line of credit available to an individual on an as-needed basis. In essence, it's a way of borrowing money from a bank, S&L, credit union, savings bank, or brokerage firm any time you wish but without going through all the hassle of setting up a new loan.

Here's how it works. Suppose that you apply for and are approved for a personal line of credit at your bank. Once you've been approved and the credit line is established, you'll be issued *checks* that you can write against it. If you need a cash advance, all you need to do is write a check (against your credit line account) and deposit it into your checking account. Or, if you need the money to buy some big-ticket item—say, an expensive stereo system—you can just make the credit line check out to the dealer and, when it clears, it will be charged against your unsecured personal credit line as an advance. Personal lines of credit are usually set up for minimums of $2,000 to $5,000 and often amount to $25,000 or more. As with an overdraft protection line, once an advance is made, repayment is set up on a monthly installment basis. Depending on the amount outstanding, repayment is normally structured over a period of two to five years; to keep the monthly payments low, larger amounts of debt are usually given longer repayment periods.

Although these credit lines do offer attractive terms to the consumer, they come with their share of problems, perhaps the biggest of which is how easily the cash advances can be obtained. These lines also normally involve *substantial* amounts of credit and are nearly as easy to use as credit cards. This combination can have devastating effects on a family's budget if it leads to overspending or excessive reliance on credit. As such, systematic repayment of the debt should be built into the budget, and every effort should be made to ensure that using this kind of credit will not overly strain the family finances.

Home Equity Credit Lines

Consider this: A couple buys a home for $285,000; some 10 years later, it's worth $365,000. The couple now has an asset worth $365,000 on which all they owe is the original mortgage, which may now have a balance of, say, $220,000. The couple clearly has built up a substantial amount of equity in their home: $365,000 − $220,000 = $145,000. But how can they tap that equity without having to sell their home? The answer is a **home equity credit line**. Such lines are much like unsecured personal credit lines except that they're *secured with a second mortgage on the home*. These lines of credit allow you to tap up to 100 percent (or more) of the equity in your home by merely writing a check. Although some banks and financial institutions allow their customers to borrow up to 100 percent of the *equity* in their homes—or, in some cases, even more—most lenders set their maximum credit lines at 75 percent to 80 percent *of the market value* of the home, which reduces the amount of money they'll lend.

Here's how these lines work. Recall the couple in our example that has built up equity of $145,000 in their home—equity against which they can borrow through a home equity credit line. Assuming that they have a good credit record and using a 75 percent loan-to-market-value ratio, a bank would be willing to lend

© HANNAMARIAH SHUTTERSTOCK.COM

up to $273,750; that is, 75 percent of the value of the house is $0.75 \times \$365,000 = \$273,750$. Subtracting the $220,000 still due on the first mortgage, we see that our couple could qualify for a home equity credit line of $53,750. Note, in this case, that if the bank had been willing to lend the couple *100 percent of the equity* in their home, then it would have given them a (much higher) credit line of $145,000, which is the difference between what the house is worth and what they still owe on it. Most lenders don't like to do this because it results in very large credit lines and, perhaps more important, it doesn't provide the lender with much of a cushion should the borrower default.

Home equity lines also have an attractive tax feature: the annual interest charges on such lines may be fully deductible for those who itemize. This is the only type of consumer loan that still qualifies for such tax treatment. According to the latest provisions of the tax code, a homeowner is allowed to *fully deduct the interest charges on home equity loans up to $100,000,* regardless of the original cost of the house or use of the proceeds. Indeed, the only restriction is that *the amount of total indebtedness on the house cannot exceed its fair market value,* which is highly unlikely because homeowners usually cannot borrow more than 75 percent to 80 percent of the home's market value anyway. In our preceding example, the homeowners could take out the full amount of their credit line ($53,750) and every dime that they paid in interest would be tax deductible. If they paid, say, $3,225 in interest and if they were in the 28 percent tax bracket, then this feature would reduce their tax liability by some $903 (i.e., $3,225 × 0.28)— assuming, of course, that they itemize their deductions.

Not only do home equity credit lines offer shelter from taxes, they're also among *the cheapest forms of consumer credit.* For example, while the average rate on standard credit cards in early 2012 was about 16.87 percent, the average rate on home equity credit lines was 5.22 percent. To see what that can mean to you as a borrower, assume you have $10,000 in consumer debt outstanding. If you had borrowed that money through a standard consumer loan at 16.87 percent, then you'd pay interest of $1,687 per year—none of which would be tax deductible. Borrow the same amount through a home equity credit line at 5.22 percent and you'll pay only $522 in interest. And because that's all tax deductible, if you're in the 28 percent tax bracket, then after-tax cost to you would be $522 × (1 − 0.28) = $375.84.

Home equity credit lines are offered by a variety of financial institutions, from banks and S&Ls to major brokerage houses. All sorts of credit terms and credit lines are available, and most of them carry repayment periods of 10 to 15 years or longer. Perhaps most startling, however, is the maximum amount of credit available under these lines—indeed, $100,000 figures are not at all unusual. And it's precisely because of the enormous amount of money available that this form of credit should be used with caution. *The fact that you have equity in your home does not necessarily imply that you have the cash flow necessary to service the debt that such a credit line allows.* Remember that your home serves as the collateral on this line of credit, and if you can't repay the loan, you could lose it!

6-3 Obtaining and Managing Open Forms of Credit

LG4 Consumers love to use their charge cards. In 2011, Visa and MasterCard handled about $6.8 trillion in transactions.

> **It's easy to see why consumer credit has become such a popular way of making relatively routine purchases.**

For the sake of convenience, people often maintain several different kinds of open credit. Nearly every household, for example, uses 30-day charge accounts to pay their utility bills, phone bills, and so on. In addition, most families have one or more retail charge cards and a couple of bank cards; some people, in fact, may have as many as 15 to 20 cards or more. And that's not all—families can also have revolving credit lines in the form of overdraft protection or a home equity line. When all these cards and lines are totaled together, a family conceivably can have tens of thousands of dollars of readily available credit. It's easy to see why consumer credit has become such a popular way of making relatively routine purchases.

6-3a Opening an Account

What do retail charge cards, bank credit cards, and revolving lines of credit all have in common? *Answer:* They all require you to go through a formal credit application. Let's now look at how you'd go about obtaining open forms of credit, including the normal credit application, investigation, and decision process. We'll couch our discussion in terms of credit cards, but keep in mind that similar procedures apply to other revolving lines of credit as well.

The Credit Application
With over 600 million credit cards in the hands of American consumers, you'd think that consumer credit is available to just about anyone. And it is—but you

credit investigation An investigation that involves contacting credit references or corresponding with a credit bureau to verify information on a credit application.

credit bureau An organization that collects and sells credit information about individual borrowers.

must apply for it. Applications are usually available at the store or bank involved. Sometimes they can be found at the businesses that accept these cards or obtained on request from the issuing companies. The type of information requested in a typical credit card application covers little more than personal/family matters, housing, employment and income, and existing charge accounts. Such information is intended to give the lender insight about the applicant's creditworthiness. In essence, the lender is trying to determine whether the applicant has the *character* and *capacity* to handle the debt in a prompt and timely manner.

The Credit Investigation

Once the credit application has been completed and returned to the establishment issuing the card—or more commonly today, submitted online—it is subject to a **credit investigation**. The purpose is to evaluate the kind of credit risk that you pose to the lender. So be sure to fill out your credit application carefully. Believe it or not, they really do look at those things pretty closely. The key items that lenders look at are how much money you make, how much debt you have outstanding and how well you handle it, and how stable you are (for example, your age, employment history, whether you own or rent a home, and so on). Obviously, the higher your income and the better your credit history, the greater the chance that your credit application will be approved. During the investigation, the lender will verify much of the information you've provided—obviously, false or misleading information will almost certainly result in outright rejection of your application.

The Credit Bureau

A **credit bureau** is a type of reporting agency that collects and sells information about individual borrowers. If, as is often the case, the lender doesn't know you personally, it must rely on a cost-effective way of verifying your employment and credit history. And that's where credit bureaus come into play, as they maintain basic credit files on current and potential borrowers.

Contrary to popular opinion, your credit file does *not* contain everything anyone would ever want to know about you—there's nothing on your lifestyle, friends, habits, or religious or political affiliations. Instead, most of the information is pretty dull stuff and covers such things as name, Social Security number, age, number of dependents, employment record and salary data, public records of bankruptcies, and the names of those who recently requested copies of your file.

Although one late credit card payment probably won't make much of a difference on an otherwise clean credit file, a definite pattern of delinquencies (consistently being 30 to 60 days late with your payments) or a personal bankruptcy certainly will. Unfortunately, poor credit traits will stick with you for a long time, because delinquencies remain on your credit file for as long as 7 years, and bankruptcies for 10 years. An example of an actual credit bureau report (or at least a part of one) is provided in Exhibit 6.3.

Local credit bureaus are established and mutually owned by local merchants and banks. They collect and store credit information on people living within the community and make it available, for a fee, to members who request it. Local bureaus are linked together nationally through one of the "big three" national bureaus—TransUnion, Equifax Credit Information Services, and Experian—each of which provides the mechanism for obtaining credit information from almost any place in the United States. Traditionally, credit bureaus did little more than collect and provide credit information; they neither analyzed the information nor used it to make final credit decisions. In 2006, however, the three major credit bureaus announced that they had jointly developed a new credit-scoring system, called *VantageScore*, that would incorporate data from all three bureaus—Equifax, Experian, and TransUnion. Thus, for the first time, each of the three national bureaus began assigning uniform credit ratings to individual credit files—though they're still obligated to report other credit scores, such as the widely used FICO scores.

Credit bureaus in the past were heavily criticized because of the large numbers of reporting errors they made and their poor record in promptly and efficiently correcting these errors. Fortunately, things have changed dramatically in recent years as the major bureaus have taken a more consumer-oriented approach. Even so, you should ensure that your credit report accurately reflects your credit history. The best way to do that is to obtain a copy of your own credit report—by law, you're entitled to receive *a free copy of your credit report once a year* (to get yours, go to the Web site set up by the Federal Trade Commission at **http://www.annualcreditreport.com**)—and then go through it carefully. If you do find a mistake, let the credit bureau know immediately—and by all means, put it writing; *then request a copy of the corrected file to make sure that the mistake has been eliminated.* Most consumer advisors recommend that you review your credit files annually.

Exhibit 6.3 **An Example of a Credit Bureau Report**

Credit bureau reports have been revised and are now easier to understand. Notice that, in addition to some basic information, the report deals strictly with credit information—including payment records, past-due status, and types of credit.

Your Credit Report as of 04/09/2015

This Credit Report is available for you to view for 30 days. If you would like a current Credit Report, you may order another from MyEquifax.

ID # XXXXXXXXXXXX

- *Personal Data*

  John Q. Public
  2351 N 85th Ave
  Phoenix, AZ 85037

  Social Security Number: 022-22-2222
  Date of Birth: 1/11/1965

- *Previous Address(es):*

  133 Third Avenue
  Phoenix, AZ 85037

- *Employment History*

	Location:	Employment Date:	Verified Date:
Cendant Hospitality FR	Phoenix, AZ	2/1/1994	1/3/2006
Previous Employment(s):			
SOFTWARE Support Hospitality Franch	Location: Atlanta, GA	Employment Date: 1/3/2006	Verified Date: 1/3/2006

- *Public Records*

  No bankruptcies on file
  No liens on file
  No foreclosures on file

- *Collection Accounts*

  No collections on file.

- *Credit Information*

Company Name	Account Number and Whose Account	Date Opened	Last Activity	Type of Account and Status	High Credit	Items as of Date Reported Terms Balance		Past Due	Date Reported
Americredit Financial Services	40404XXXX JOINT ACCOUNT	03/2005	03/2015	Installment REPOSSESSION	$16933	$430	$9077	$128	2/2015

  Prior Paying History
  30 days past due 07 times; 60 days past due 05 times; 90+ days past due 03 times
  INVOLUNTARY REPOSSESION AUTO

| Capital One | 412174147128XXXX INDIVIDUAL ACCOUNT | 10/2003 | 01/2015 | Revolving PAYS AS AGREED | $777 | 15 | $514 | | 01/2015 |

  Prior Paying History
  30 days past due 02 times; 60 days past due 1 times; 90+ days past due 00 times
  CREDIT CARD

| Desert Schools FCU | 423325003406XXXX INDIVIDUAL ACCOUNT | 07/2002 | 06/2012 | Revolving PAYS AS AGREED | $500 | | $0 | | 07/2012 |

  Prior Paying History
  30 days past due 02 times; 60 days past due 00 times; 90+ days past due 00 times
  ACCOUNT PAID   CLOSED ACCOUNT

- *Credit Inquiries*

  Companies that Requested your Credit File

  04/09/2014 EFX Credit Profile Online
  06/30/2014 Automotive
  01/18/2013 Desert Schools Federal C.U.
  07/02/2012 Time Life, Inc.

credit scoring A method of evaluating an applicant's creditworthiness by assigning values to such factors as income, existing debts, and credit references.

Here are the Web sites for the three national credit bureaus:

- Equifax Credit Information Services
  http://www.equifax.com
- TransUnion LLC Consumer Disclosure Center
  http://www.tuc.com
- Experian (formerly TRW) National Consumer Assistance Center
  http://www.experian.com

6-3b The Credit Decision

Using the data provided by the credit applicant, along with any information obtained from the credit bureau, the store or bank must decide whether to grant credit. Very likely, some type of **credit scoring** scheme will be used to make the decision. An overall credit score is developed for you by assigning values to such factors as your annual income, whether you rent or own your home, number and types of credit cards you hold, level of your existing debts, whether you have savings accounts, and general credit references. Fifteen or 20 different factors or characteristics may be considered, and each characteristic receives a score based on some

predetermined standard. For example, if you're 26 years old, single, earn $32,500 a year (on a job that you've had for only two years), and rent an apartment, you might receive the following scores:

1.	Age (25–30)	5 points
2.	Marital status (single)	−2 points
3.	Annual income ($30–$35 thousand)	12 points
4.	Length of employment (2 years or less)	4 points
5.	Rent or own a home (rent)	0 points
		19 points

Similar scores would be assigned to another 10 to 15 factors and other things being equal, the stronger your personal traits or characteristics, the higher the score you'll receive. Statistical studies have shown that certain personal and financial traits can be used to determine your creditworthiness. Indeed, the whole credit scoring system is based on extensive statistical studies that identify the characteristics to look at and the scores to assign.

The biggest provider of credit scores is, by far, Fair Isaac & Co.—the firm that produces the widely used *FICO scores*. Unlike some credit score providers, *Fair Isaac uses only credit information in its calculations*. There's nothing in them about your age, marital status, salary, occupation, employment history, or where you live. Instead, FICO scores are derived from the following five major components, which are listed along with their respective weights: payment history (35 percent), amounts owed (30 percent), length of credit history (15 percent), new credit (10 percent), and types of credit used (10 percent). FICO scores, which are reported by all three of the major credit bureaus, range from a low of 300 to a max of 850. These scores are meant to be an indication of a borrower's credit risk; the higher the score, the lower the risk. While few, if any, credit decisions are based solely on FICO scores, you can be sure that higher scores are likely to result in lower interest rates on loans and therefore lower loan payments.

Financial Road Sign

Keeping up your FICO Scores

Raising your FICO score is a lot like losing weight: It takes time and there's no quick fix. But here are some tips you might want to follow to reach a high score:

- Pay your bills on time.
- If you've missed payments, get current and stay current.
- If you're having trouble making ends meet, contact your creditors and work out a payment plan.
- Keep credit card balances low.
- Pay off debt rather than move it around.
- Don't open new credit cards just to increase your available credit.
- Reestablish your credit history if you've had problems in the past.

Source: Adapted from "How Can I Increase My FICO Score?," http://www.myfico.com/crediteducation/questions/increase-score.aspx, accessed May 2012. Copyright Notice: © 2002–2006 Fair Isaac Corporation. Copyright © Fair Isaac Corporation. Used with permission. Fair Isaac, myFICO, the Fair Isaac logos, and the Fair Isaac product and service names are trademarks or registered trademarks of Fair Isaac Corporation.

Go to Smart Sites

To learn more about FICO scores—including what's in your FICO score, what's not in it, and what you can do to improve it—visit the Fair Isaac & Co. Web site. ●

6-3c Computing Finance Charges

Because card issuers don't know in advance how much you'll charge on your account, they cannot specify the dollar amount of interest you will be charged. But they can—and must, according to the Truth in Lending Act—disclose the *rate of interest* that they charge and their method of computing finance charges. This is the **annual percentage rate (APR)**, the true or actual rate of interest paid, which must include all fees and costs and be calculated as defined by law. Remember, it's your right as a consumer to know—and it is the lender's obligation to tell you—the dollar amount of charges (where applicable) and the APR on any financing you consider.

The amount of interest you pay for open credit depends partly on the method the lender uses to calculate the balances on which they apply finance charges. Most bank and retail charge card issuers use one of two variations of the **average daily balance (ADB) method**, which applies the interest rate to the ADB of the account over the billing period. The most common method (used by an estimated 95 percent of bank card issuers) is the *ADB including new purchases*. An alternative is the ADB method *excluding new purchases*. Balance calculations under each of these methods are as follows:

- **ADB including new purchases**. For each day in the billing cycle, take the outstanding balance, including new purchases, and subtract payments and credits; then divide by the number of days in the billing cycle.

- **ADB excluding new purchases**. Same as the first method but *exclude* new purchases.

These different calculations can obviously affect a card's credit balance and therefore the amount of finance charges you'll have to pay. Also be aware that the finance charges on two cards with the same APR but different methods of calculating balances may differ dramatically. It's important to know the method your card issuer uses. As a rule, for active card users, the ADB procedure that *includes new purchases* will produce considerably more interest income for the issuer and, in turn, is *far more expensive* from the cardholder's perspective.

annual percentage rate (APR) The actual or true rate of interest paid over the life of a loan; includes all fees and costs.

average daily balance (ADB) method A method of computing finance charges by applying interest charges to the average daily balance of the account over the billing period.

Crunching the Numbers

Let's look at an example of how to calculate balances and finance charges under the most popular method, *the ADB including new purchases*. Assume that you have a FirstBank Visa card with a monthly interest rate of 1.5 percent.

Your statement for the billing period extending from October 10, 2015, through November 10, 2012—a total of 31 days—shows that your beginning balance was $1,582, you made purchases of $750 on October 15 and $400 on October 22, and you made a $275 payment on November 6. Therefore, the outstanding balance for the first 5 days of the period (October 11 through 15) was $1,582; for the next 7 days (October 16 through 22), it was $2,332 ($1,582 + $750); for the next 15 days (October 23 through November 6), it was $2,732 ($2,332 + $400); and for the last 4 days, it was $2,457 ($2,732 less the $275 payment), all of which is summarized in Exhibit 6.5.

We can now calculate the average daily balance using the procedure shown in Exhibit 6.5. Note that the outstanding balances are weighted by the number of days that the balance existed and then averaged (divided) by the number of days in the billing period. By multiplying the ADB of $2,420.71 by the 1.5 percent interest rate, we get a finance charge of $36.31.

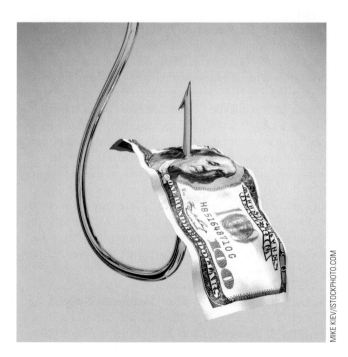

6-3d Managing Your Credit Cards

Congratulations! You have applied for and been granted a bank credit card, as well as a retail charge card from your favorite department store.

Exhibit 6.4 Finding the Average Daily Balance and Finance Charge

The ADB including new purchases is the method most widely used by credit card issuers to determine the monthly finance charge on an account.

	Number of Days (1)	Balance (2)	Calculation (1) × (2) (3)
	5	$1,582	$ 7,910
	7	$2,332	16,324
	15	$2,732	40,980
	4	$2,457	9,828
Total	31		$75,042

$$ADB = \frac{\$75,042}{31} = \$2,420.71$$

Finance charge: $2,420.71 × .015 = $36.31

© Cengage Learning

---

minimum monthly payment In open account credit, a minimum specified percentage of the new account balance that must be paid in order to remain current.

You carefully reviewed the terms of the credit agreement and have at least a basic understanding of how finance charges are computed for each account. Now you must manage your accounts efficiently, using the monthly statements to help you make the required payments on time, as well as to track purchases.

The Statement

If you use a credit card, you'll receive monthly statements similar to the sample bank card statement in Exhibit 6.5, showing billing cycle and payment due dates, interest rate, minimum payment, and all account activity during the current period. (Retail charge cards have similar monthly statements, but without a section for cash advances.) The statement summarizes your account activity: the previous balance (the amount of credit outstanding at the beginning of the month—not to be confused with past-due, or late, payments); new charges made (four, in this case) during the past month; any finance charges (interest) on the unpaid balance; the preceding period's payment; any other credits (such as those for returns); and the new balance (previous balance plus new purchases and finance charges, less any payments and credits). You should review your statements every month. Save your receipts and use them to verify statement entries for purchases and returns *before* paying. If you find any errors or suspect fraudulent use of your card, first use the issuer's toll-free number to report any problems;

then follow up *in writing* within 60 days of the post-mark on the bill.

Although merchandise and cash transactions are separated on the statement, the finance charge in each case is calculated at the rate of 1.5 percent per month (18 percent annually). This procedure works fine for illustration, but it's a bit out of the ordinary because most card issuers charge a higher rate for cash advances than for purchases.

Payments

Credit card users can avoid *future* finance charges by paying the total new balance shown on their statement each month. For example, if the $534.08 total new balance shown in Exhibit 6.5 is paid by the due date of September 21, 2015, then no additional finance charges will be incurred. (The cardholder, however, is still liable for the $4.40 in finance charges incurred to date.) If cardholders cannot pay the total new balance, they can pay any amount that is equal to or greater than the **minimum monthly payment** specified on the statement. If they do this, however, they will incur additional finance charges in the following months. Note that the account in Exhibit 6.5 has a minimum payment of 5 percent of the new balance, rounded to the nearest full dollar. As shown at the bottom of the statement, this month's minimum payment is $27.00 (i.e., $534.08 × 0.05 = $26.70 ≈ $27.00). This $27.00 includes a *principal payment* of $22.60; that is: $27.00 − $4.40 (in interest charges) = $22.60. That's actually about 4.25 percent of the "new balance." If the new balance had been less than $200, the bank would have required a payment of $10 (which is the absolute minimum dollar payment) or of the total

Exhibit 6.5 A Bank Credit Card Monthly Statement

Each month, a bank credit cardholder receives a statement that provides an itemized list of charges and credits as well as a summary of previous activity and finance charges.

Please detach the above portion and return it with your payment to insure proper credit.

Bank Card Statement

Retain this statement for your records.

Account Number 123-XYZ-45678	Name(s) Mr. Scott Lataste Mrs. Emily Lataste	8-24-15 Statement Date	09-21-15 Payment Due Date

ACCOUNT ACTIVITY

			FINANCE CHARGE CALCULATION			
Previous Balance	203.64	Credit Status	Amounts Subject to Finance Charge		This Month's Charge	
Payments –	119.89	Your Credit Limit is:	A. *Average			ENTIRE BAL.
Credits –	.00		Daily Balance	293.25	4.40	1.5% 18.00%
Subtotal	83.75		B. *Cash Advance	.00	.00	Monthly Nominal
New Transaction +	445.93	2000.00	C. *Loan Advance	.00	.00	Periodic Annual
Finance Charge +	4.40	Your Available Credit is:				Rate Rate
Late Charge +	.00				4.40 18.00%	
NEW BALANCE	534.08	1465.92	*Finance Charges explained on reverse side		Finance Charge	Annual Percentage Rate

Mail Billing Inquiries to: Post Office Box 7890, Van Niles, California, 85258, or call   800/000-0000
For Inquiries on Past Due Accounts, Overlimits or Credit Line Increase, call   800/000-0000

Posted Mo./Day	Transaction Description or Merchant Name and Location		Purchase Mo./Day	Bank Reference Number	Purchases/ Advances/Debits	Payments Credits
8-08	AMERICA WEST AIRLINES	LOS ANGELES	07-25	850000008823395192	42.00	
8-13	HACIENDA MOTORS	COSTA MESA	08-05	015400018537022316	166.86	
8-15	RICOS RESTAURANT	PALM SPRG	08-10	114500018856161722	132.47	
8-12	PAYMENT—THANK YOU		08-11	4501000182MD02139		119.89
8-24	RENEES RESTAURANT	NEWPORT	08-13	114500068201632483	104.60	

Notice See reverse side for important information

			Total Debits	Total Credits
MIN. PAYMENT: 27.00	NEW BALANCE: 534.08		445.93	119.89

© Cengage Learning

new balance, if less than $10. Cardholders who fail to make the minimum payment are considered to be in default on their account, and the bank issuing the card can take whatever action it deems necessary.

Go to Smart Sites

Use About.com's Credit Card Calculators to find out how interest rate changes affect your balance, if debt consolidation makes sense, and answers to similar questions. ●

6-4 Using Credit Wisely

LG5, LG6 As we've discussed, credit cards and revolving lines of credit can simplify your life financially. Unfortunately, you can also get into real trouble with these forms of credit unless you use them wisely! That's why you should carefully shop around to choose the right credit cards for your personal situation, understand the advantages and disadvantages of credit cards, learn how to resolve credit problems, and know how to avoid the ultimate cost of credit abuse—bankruptcy.

6-4a Shop Around for the Best Deal

They say it pays to shop around, and when it comes to credit cards, that's certainly true. With all the fees and high interest costs, it pays to get the best deal possible. So, where do you start? Most credit experts suggest the first thing you should do is step back and take a look at yourself. What kind of "spender" are you, and how do you pay your bills? The fact is, no single credit card is right for everyone. If you pay off your card balance each month, then you'll want a card that's different from the one that's right for someone who carries a credit balance from month to month and may only pay the minimum due. Regardless of which category you fall into, there are basically four card features to look for:

- Annual fees
- Rate of interest charged on account balance
- Length of the grace period
- Method of calculating balances

Now, if you normally pay your account balance in full each month, get a card with *no annual fees and a long grace period*. The rate of interest on the card is irrelevant because you don't carry account balances from month to month anyway. In sharp contrast, if you don't pay your account in full, then look for cards that charge *a low rate of interest on unpaid balances*. The length of the grace period isn't all that important here, but obviously, other things being equal, you're better off with low (or no) annual fees.

Sometimes, however, "other things aren't equal" and you have to decide between interest rates and annual fees. If you're not a big spender and don't build up big balances on your credit card, then *avoid* cards with annual fees and get one with as *low* a rate of interest as possible. (*Note*: This situation probably applies to most college students—or at least it should.) On the other hand, if you do carry big balances (say, $1,000 or more), then you'll probably be better off *paying an annual fee* (even a relatively high one) *to keep the rate of interest on the card as low as possible.*

The bottom line is: don't take the first credit card that comes along. Instead, get the one that's right for you. Learn as much as you can about the credit cards you've been offered or are considering. To do that, go to Web sites like **www.bankrate.com; www.creditcards.com;** or **www.cardtrak.com,** to mention just a few. These sites provide all sorts of information about fees, rates, credit terms, and so forth on a wide array of different types of credit cards. Another alternative is to go to publications like *Money* magazine and *Kiplinger's Personal Finance*. These magazines regularly publish information about banks and other financial institutions that offer low-cost credit cards nationally; see Exhibit 6.6 for an example.

6-4b Avoiding Credit Problems

Unfortunately, as the volume of credit card purchases has grown, so has the level of credit card debt. As a result, it's not unusual to find people using credit cards to solve cash-flow problems; even the most careful consumers occasionally find themselves with mounting credit card debt, especially after the year-end holiday buying season. The real problems occur when the situation is no longer temporary and the debt continues to increase. If overspending is not curtailed, then the size of the unpaid balance may seriously strain the budget. Essentially, people who let their credit balances build up are *mortgaging their future*. By using credit, they're actually committing a part of their future income to make payments on the debt. Unfortunately, the more income that has to go just to make payments on

Exhibit 6.6 Average Interest Rates for Different Types of Credit Cards

© KAREN HERMANN/ISTOCKPHOTO

Information about low-cost credit cards is readily available in the financial media. Pay particular attention to the *cards with the lowest rates* (probably best for people who regularly carry an account balance) and *no-fee cards with the lowest rates* (probably best for people who pay their accounts in full each month).

Type of Credit Card	Average Annual Percentage Rate (APR)
Balance transfer cards	16.51%
Cash back cards	16.41%
Low interest cards	10.62%
Rewards cards	15.41%

These rates are as of April 4, 2012; rates are adjustable. Banks sometimes offer lower introductory rates, many charge no annual fee, and the cards vary in credit score requirements. Most of these cards have variable rates. Data compiled from http://www.bankrate.com, accessed April 2012.

© Cengage Learning

charge cards (and other forms of consumer credit), the less there is available for other purposes.

The best way to avoid credit problems is to be disciplined when using credit. Reduce the number of cards you carry, and don't rush to accept the tempting preapproved credit card offers that you may get in the mail. A wallet full of cards can work against you in two ways. Obviously, the ready availability of credit can tempt you to overspend and incur too much debt. But there's another, less obvious, danger: when you apply for a loan, lenders look at the *total amount* of credit you have available, as well as at the outstanding balances on your credit cards. If you have a lot of unused credit capacity, it may be harder to get a loan because of lender concerns that you could become overextended. So think twice before accepting a new credit card. You really don't need three or four bank cards. Two is the most that financial advisors suggest you carry. And should you decide to start using a new card (because their offer was just too good to pass up), then *get rid of one of your old cards*—physically cut up the old card and inform the issuer in writing that you're canceling your account.

6-4c Credit Card Fraud

Despite all the efforts of law enforcement officials, there are still people out there who are doing their best to rip you off! In fact, plastic has become the vehicle of choice among crooks. No doubt about it: credit card crime is big business, with annual losses in the United States estimated to run in the billions of dollars a year. Basically, "it's us against them,"

and the first thing you have to understand is that the credit card you're carrying around is a powerful piece of plastic. Be careful with it. To reduce your chances of being defrauded, here are some suggestions you should follow:

- Never, ever, give your account number to people or organizations *who call you*. No matter how legitimate it sounds.
- It's okay to give your account number over the phone (if you initiated the call) when ordering or purchasing something from a major catalog house, airline, hotel, and so on.
- Use the same precautions *when purchasing something over the Internet with* your credit card—don't do it *unless* you're dealing with a major retailer who uses state-of-the-art protection against fraud and thievery.
- When paying for something *by check*, don't put your Social Security or credit card account number on the check, and don't let the store clerk do it.
- Don't put your phone number or address (and certainly not your Social Security number) on credit/charge slips, even if the merchant asks for it—they're not entitled to it.
- When using your card to make a purchase, *always keep your eye on it*; if the clerk wants to make another imprint, ask for the first one and tear it up on the spot.
- Always draw a line on the credit slip through any blank spaces above the total.

Financial Planning Tips: Protect Against Identity Theft

Watch out for the following methods that thieves use to get your information:

- **Dumpster diving.** Don't leave bills or anything with personal information in your trash.
- **Skimming.** Watch for unusual "additions" to credit and debit card readers that can steal your numbers.
- **Phishing.** Thieves can pretend to be financial institutions or companies and can use Web pop-ups or send e-mail messages that ask you to disclose personal information.
- **Changing your address.** Thieves can reroute your bills to them by completing a change of address form.
- **Old-fashioned stealing.** Simple still works. Thieves continue to steal wallets and purses, mail, and new checks or tax information. Also, they sometimes bribe employees to provide access to your personal information.
- **Pretexting.** Thieves can obtain your personal information from financial institutions, telephone companies, and other sources under false pretenses.

So what should you do? The FTC recommends the following:

- **Deter** thefts by protecting your information. Be aware of the abovementioned ways in which information is stolen.
- **Detect** suspicious activity by consistently checking your financial and billing statements.
- **Defend** against identity theft as soon as you suspect a possible problem. Place a "fraud alert" on your credit reports by contacting one of the consumer reporting companies noted earlier in this chapter (Experian, TransUnion, or Equifax). Contact the security departments of each company where an unauthorized account was opened.

Source: Adapted from http://www.ftc.gov/bcp/edu/microsites/idtheft/consumers/about-identity-theft.html, accessed April 2012.

- *Destroy* all old credit slips; and when you receive your monthly statement, be sure to *go over it promptly* to make sure there are no errors. If you find a mistake, call or send a letter immediately, detailing the error.

- If you lose a card or it's stolen, *report it to the card issuer immediately*—the most you're ever liable for with a lost or stolen card is $50 (per card), but if you report the loss before the card can be used, you won't be liable for any unauthorized charges.

- Destroy old cards or those you no longer use.

6-4d Bankruptcy: Paying the Price for Credit Abuse

It certainly isn't an overstatement to say that, during the 1980s and 1990s, *debt was in!* In fact, the explosion of debt that has occurred since 1980 is almost incomprehensible. The national debt rose from less than a trillion dollars when the 1980s began to about $15.6 trillion by early 2012. Businesses also took on debt rapidly. Not to be outdone, consumers were using credit like there was no tomorrow. So it should come as no surprise that when you couple this heavy debt load with a serious economic recession like that in 2009, you have all the ingredients of a real financial crisis. And that's just what happened, as personal bankruptcies soared—indeed, in 2011 alone, more than 1.35 million people filed for **personal bankruptcy.**

When too many people are too heavily in debt, a recession (or some other economic reversal) can come along and push many of them over the edge. But let's face it, the recession is not the main culprit here; the only way a recession can push you over the edge is if you're already sitting on it! The real culprit is excess debt. Some people simply abuse credit by taking on more than they can afford. Then, sooner or later, these debtors start missing payments and their credit rating begins to deteriorate. Unless corrective actions are taken, this is followed by repossession of property and, eventually, even bankruptcy. Two of the most widely used bankruptcy procedures (employed by well over 95 percent of those individuals who file for bankruptcy) are (1) the Wage Earner Plan and (2) straight bankruptcy.

CARO/ALAMY

Wage Earner Plan

The **Wage Earner Plan** (as defined in *Chapter 13* of the U.S. Bankruptcy Code) is a workout procedure involving some type of debt restructuring—usually by establishing a debt repayment schedule that's more compatible with the person's income. It may be a viable alternative for someone who has a steady source of income, not more than $1,081,400 in secured debt and $360,475 in unsecured debt, and a reasonably good chance of being able to repay the debts in three to five years. A majority of creditors must agree to the plan, and interest charges (along with late-payment penalties) are waived for the repayment period. Creditors usually will go along with this plan because they stand to lose more in a straight bankruptcy.

> ❝ **When too many people are too heavily in debt, a recession can push many of them over the edge.** ❞

Straight Bankruptcy

Straight bankruptcy, which is allowed under *Chapter 7* of the bankruptcy code, can be viewed as a legal procedure that results in "wiping the slate clean and starting anew." *About 70 percent of those filing personal bankruptcy choose this route.* However, straight bankruptcy does not eliminate all the debtor's obligations, nor does the debtor necessarily lose all of his or her assets. For example, the debtor must make certain tax payments and keep up alimony and child-support payments but is allowed to retain certain payments from Social Security, retirement, veterans', and disability benefits. The debtor also may retain the equity in a home, a car, and some other personal assets. Minimum values are established by federal regulations, though state laws are generally much more generous regarding the amount the debtor is allowed to keep.

Planning Over a Lifetime: Using Credit

Here are some key considerations for using credit in each stage of the life cycle.

Pre-family Independence: 20s	Family Formation/Career Development: 30–45	Pre-Retirement: 45–65	Retirement: 65 and Beyond
✓ Obtain a credit card to start building a credit history. Consider a secured card first.	✓ Watch consumer credit use carefully to avoid over-spending.	✓ Re-evaluate use of consumer credit in light of revised expenditures and income.	✓ Budget to eliminate reliance on consumer credit in retirement.
✓ Plan to pay all consumer credit bills in full.	✓ Periodically evaluate credit card costs, and change cards if you are not getting the best deal.	✓ Check your credit score periodically.	✓ Maintain credit score to assure credit access.
✓ Carefully monitor all charges and financial statements for unauthorized transactions.	✓ Continue to monitor all accounts for unauthorized transactions and possible identity theft.	✓ Continue to watch for unauthorized transactions and identity theft.	✓ Be particularly careful about releasing personal financial information.

FINANCIAL PLANNING EXERCISES

LG1 1. After graduating from college last fall, Jessica Stevens took a job as a consumer credit analyst at a local bank. From her work reviewing credit applications, she realizes that she should begin establishing her own credit history. Describe for Jessica several steps that she could take to begin building a strong credit record. Does the fact that she took out a student loan for her college education help or hurt her credit record?

LG2 2. Robert Denby has a monthly take-home pay of $1,685; he makes payments of $410 a month on his outstanding consumer credit (excluding the mortgage on his home). How would you characterize Robert's debt burden? What if his take-home pay were $850 a month and he had monthly credit payments of $150?

LG2 3. *Use Worksheet 6.1.* Rebecca Collins is evaluating her debt safety ratio. Her monthly take-home pay is $3,320. Each month, she pays $380 for an auto loan, $120 on a personal line of credit, $60 on a department store charge card, and $85 on her bank credit card. Complete Worksheet 6.1 by listing Rebecca's outstanding debts, and then calculate her debt safety ratio. Given her current take-home pay, what is the maximum amount of monthly debt payments that Rebecca can have if she wants her debt safety ratio to be 12.5 percent? Given her current monthly debt payment load, what would Rebecca's take-home pay have to be if she wanted a 12.5 percent debt safety ratio?

LG3 4. David and Joan Mead have a home with an appraised value of $180,000 and a mortgage balance of only $90,000. Given that an S&L is willing to lend money at a loan-to-value ratio of 75 percent, how big a home equity credit line can David and Joan obtain? How much, if any, of this line would qualify as tax-deductible interest if their house originally cost $200,000?

LG4 5. Isaac Primack recently graduated from college and is evaluating two credit cards. Card A has an annual fee of $75 and an interest rate of 9 percent. Card B has no annual fee and an interest rate of 16 percent. Assuming that Isaac intends to carry no balance and pay off his charges in full each month, which card represents the better deal? If Isaac expected to carry a significant balance from one month to the next, which card would be better? Explain.

LG4 6. Janine Waite has several credit cards, on which she is carrying a total current balance of $14,500. She is considering transferring this balance to a new card issued by a local bank. The bank advertises that, for a 2 percent fee, she can transfer her balance to a card that charges a 0 percent interest rate on transferred balances for the first nine months. Calculate the fee that Janine would pay to transfer the balance, and describe the benefits and drawbacks of balance transfer cards.

LG5 7. Lei Sung was reviewing her credit card statement and noticed several charges that didn't look familiar to her. Lei is unsure whether she should "make some noise," or simply pay the bill in full and forget about the unfamiliar charges. If some of these charges aren't hers, is she still liable for the full amount? Is she liable for any part of these charges—even if they're fraudulent?

PFIN Student Study Tools—Visit CourseMate for PFIN 3. Log in at **www.cengagebrain.com**. Check out the bonus exercises and exhibits, interactive worksheets, Smart Sites, Critical Thinking Cases, Money Online, Kiplinger videos, quizzing, and more.

Cool Apps—Look for this new feature on CourseMate for PFIN 3. Cool Apps navigates the growing world of apps that are available for personal financial planning and tracking.

WHY CHOOSE?

Every 4LTR Press solution comes complete with a visually engaging textbook in addition to an interactive eBook. Go to CourseMate for **PFIN** to begin using the eBook. Access at **www.cengagebrain.com**

Complete the Speak Up
survey in CourseMate at
www.cengagebrain.com

 Follow us at
www.facebook.com/4ltrpress

7

USING CONSUMER LOANS

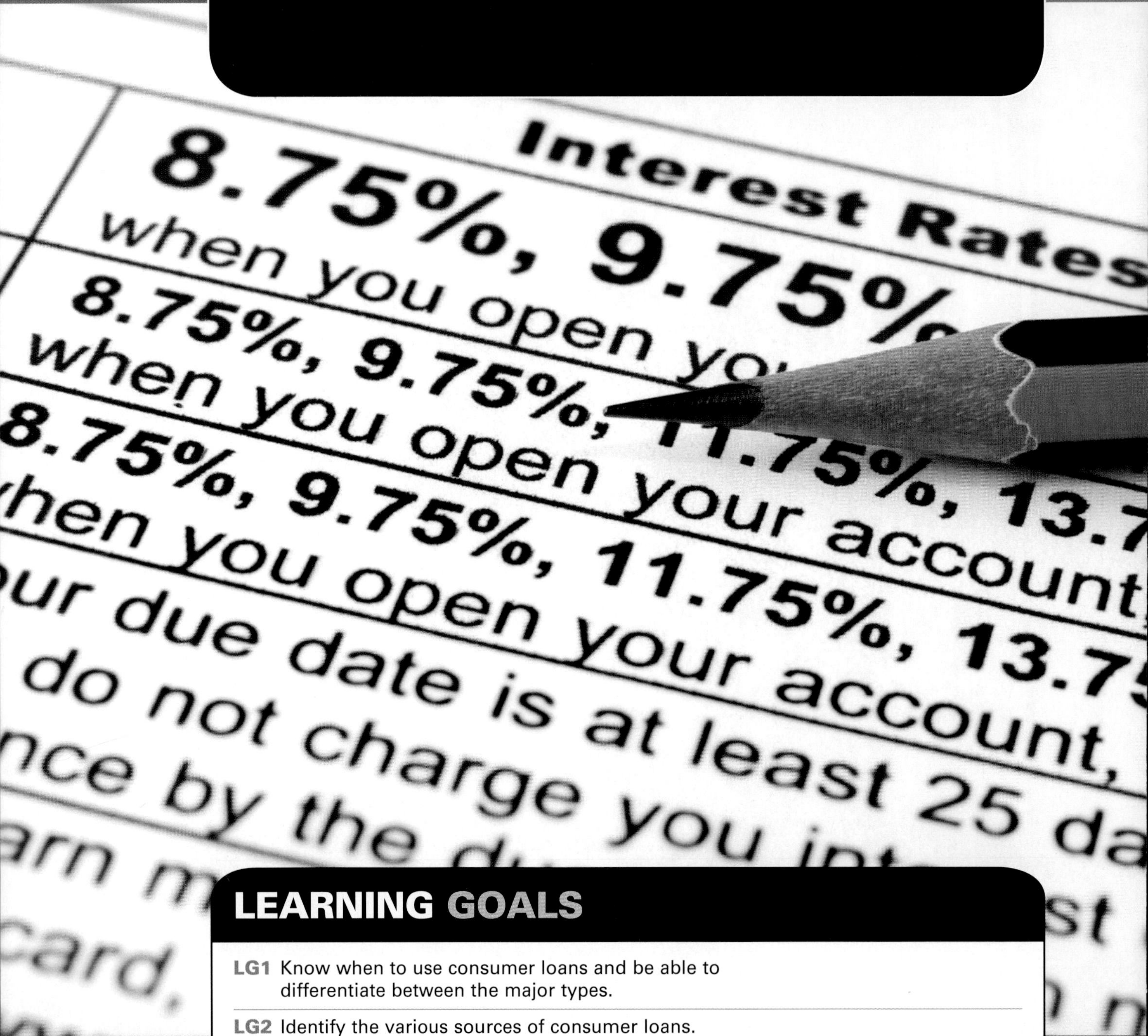

8.75%, Interest Rates
when you open you
8.75%, 9.75%,
when you open you
8.75%, 9.75%, 11.75%, 13.7
hen you open your account
8.75%, 9.75%, 11.75%, 13.7
hen you open your account,
ur due date is at least 25 da
do not charge you int
nce by the du
rn m
card,

LEARNING GOALS

LG1 Know when to use consumer loans and be able to differentiate between the major types.

LG2 Identify the various sources of consumer loans.

LG3 Choose the best loans by comparing finance charges, maturity, collateral, and other loan terms.

LG4 Describe the features of, and calculate the finance charges on, single-payment loans.

LG5 Evaluate the benefits of an installment loan.

LG6 Determine the costs of installment loans and analyze whether it is better to pay cash or to take out a loan.

How Will This Affect Me? Consumer loan sources abound and their terms vary significantly. The primary types are single-payment and installment consumer loans. It's important to understand when to use each credit source, to be able to calculate and compare their costs, and to determine the circumstances in which it is best to take out a loan or pay cash. Practical examples considered in this chapter include taking out a car loan and borrowing to pay for a college education. The chapter provides you with an applied framework for evaluating the best ways to choose among and obtain consumer loans.

7-1 Basic Features of Consumer Loans

LG1, LG2 In previous chapters, we've discussed the different types of financial goals that individuals and families can set for themselves. These goals often involve large sums of money and may include such things as a college education or the purchase of a new car. One way to reach these goals is to systematically save the money. Another is to use a loan to at least partially finance the transaction. Consumer loans are important to the personal financial planning process because they can help you reach certain types of financial goals. The key, of course, is to successfully manage the credit by keeping both the amount of debt used and the debt repayment burden *well within your budget!*

7-1a Using Consumer Loans

As we saw in Chapter 6, using open or revolving credit can be helpful to those who plan and live within their personal financial budgets. More important to the achievement of long-term personal financial goals, however, are *single-payment* and *installment loans*. These long-term

liabilities are widely used to finance the purchase of goods that are far too expensive to buy from current income, to help fund a college education, or to pay for certain nondurable items, such as expensive vacations.

They differ from open forms of credit in several ways, including the formality of their lending arrangements. That is, whereas open account credit results from a rather informal process, **consumer loans** are *formal, negotiated contracts* that specify both the terms for borrowing and the repayment schedule. Another difference is that an open line of credit can be used again and again, but consumer loans are one-shot transactions made for specific purposes. Because there's no revolving credit with a consumer loan, no more credit is available (from that particular loan) once it's paid off. Furthermore, no credit cards or checks are issued with this form of credit. Finally, whereas open account credit is used chiefly to make repeated purchases of relatively low-cost *goods and services*, consumer loans are used mainly to *borrow money* to pay for big-ticket items.

7-1b Different Types of Loans

Although they can be used for just about any purpose imaginable, most consumer loans fall into one of the following categories.

- **Auto loans**. Financing a new car, truck, SUV, or minivan is the single most common reason for borrowing money through a consumer loan. Indeed, auto loans account for about 35 percent of all consumer credit outstanding. Generally speaking, about 80 percent to 90 percent of the cost of a new vehicle (somewhat less with used cars) can be financed with credit. The buyer must provide the rest through a *down payment*.

> **consumer loans** Loans made for specific purposes using formally negotiated contracts that specify the borrowing terms and repayment.

Consumer loans are important to the personal financial planning process because they can help you reach certain types of financial goals.

After you read the chapter, explore the STUDY TOOLS listed on page 176.

The loan is *secured* with the auto, meaning that the vehicle serves as **collateral** for the loan and can be repossessed by the lender should the buyer fail to make payments. These loans generally have maturities ranging from 36 to 60 months.

- **Loans for other durable goods.** Consumer loans can also be used to finance other kinds of *costly durable goods*, such as furniture, home appliances, TVs, home computers, recreational vehicles, and even small airplanes and mobile homes. These loans are also secured by the items purchased and generally require some down payment. Maturities vary with the type of asset purchased: 9- to 12-month loans for less costly items, such as TVs and stereos, versus a 10- to 15-year loan for (say) a mobile home.

- **Education loans.** Getting a college education is another important reason for taking out a consumer loan. Such loans can be used to finance either undergraduate or graduate studies, and special government-subsidized loan programs are available to students and parents. We'll discuss student loans in more detail in the following section.

- **Personal loans.** These loans are typically used for nondurable expenditures, such as an expensive European vacation or to cover temporary cash shortfalls. Many personal loans are *unsecured*, which means there's no collateral with the loan other than the borrower's good name.

- **Consolidation loans.** This type of loan is used to straighten out an unhealthy credit situation, which often occurs when consumers overuse credit cards, credit lines, or consumer loans and can no longer promptly service the debt. By borrowing money from one source to pay off other forms of credit, borrowers can replace, say, five or six monthly payments that total $400 with one payment amounting to $250. *Consolidation loans are usually expensive, and people who use them must be careful to stop using credit cards and other forms of credit until they repay the loans. Otherwise, they may end up right back where they started.*

Student Loans

Today, the average annual cost of a college education ranges from about $13,000 at a state school to over $40,000 at some private colleges. Many families, even those who started saving for college when their children were young, are faced with higher-than-expected bills. Fortunately, there are many types of financial aid programs available, including some federal programs as well as state, private, and college-sponsored programs.

Certainly, paying for a college education is one of the most legitimate reasons for going into debt. Although you could borrow money for college through normal channels—that is, take out a regular consumer loan from your bank and use the proceeds to finance an education—there are better ways to go about getting education loans. Indeed, in 2010 Congress significantly modified the federal college funding system. The new legislation ends the bank-based student loan system by preventing private financial institutions from making profits as intermediaries between students and federal education aid dollars. All federal student loans must now go through a direct lending program, so private lending companies such as Sallie Mae are now out of that business. The federal government (and some state governments) have available several different types of subsidized educational loan programs. The federally sponsored programs are:

- Stafford loans (Direct and Federal Family Education Loans—FFEL)
- Perkins loans
- Parent Loans (PLUS)

The Stafford and Perkins loans have the best terms and are the foundation of the government's student loan program. In contrast, PLUS (which stands for *Parent Loans for Undergraduate Students*) loans are *supplemental loans* for *undergraduate students* who demonstrate a need but, for one reason or another, don't qualify for Stafford or Perkins loans or who need more aid than they're receiving. Under this program, parents can take out loans to meet or supplement the costs of their children's college education, *up to the full cost of attendance.* Whereas Stafford and Perkins loans are made directly to students, PLUS loans are made to the parents or legal guardians of college students.

© ANDRESR/SHUTTERSTOCK.COM

Probably the best place to look for information about these and other programs is the Internet. For example, look up FASTWEB (which stands for *Financial Aid Search Through the WEB*). This site, which is free, not only provides details on all the major, and some of the not-so-major, student loan programs but also has a service that matches individuals with scholarships and loans—even going so far as to provide form letters to use in requesting more information. (The address for this Web site is **http://www.fastweb.com**.)

Let's look at the Stafford loan program to see how student loans work. There are two types of Stafford loans. In the subsidized loan program, the U.S. Department of Education pays interest while the student is in school and also during certain grace and deferment periods. In the unsubsidized program, the borrower is responsible for all interest, whether in or out of school. Stafford loans carry low, government-subsidized interest rates. The whole process—which really is quite simple—begins with a visit to the school's financial aid office, where a financial aid counselor will help you determine your eligibility. To be eligible, you must demonstrate a *financial need*, where the amount of your financial need is defined as the cost of attending school *less* the amount that can be paid by you or your family. Thus, in these programs, students are expected to contribute something to their educational expense regardless of their income. You must also be making *satisfactory progress in your academic program*, and you cannot be in default on any other student loans. Each academic year, you'll have to fill out a Free Application for Federal Student Aid (FAFSA) statement to attest that these qualifications are being met (you can complete and submit the form on the Web at **http://www.fafsa.ed.gov**).

Go to Smart Sites

To find advice on financing college (loans and scholarships) and helpful online calculators, check out The Princeton Review's financing section. For more online resources, whenever you see "*Go to Smart Sites*" in this chapter, visit CourseMate for PFIN 3. Log in at **www.cengagebrain.com**. ●

OBTAINING A STUDENT LOAN. All you have to do to obtain a (Stafford) loan is complete a simple application form. The latest innovation in this procedure involves transmitting the application electronically to the necessary parties, thus reducing paperwork and speeding up the processing (see, for example, **http://www.staffordloan.com**).

Each program has specific loan limits. For example, with subsidized Stafford loans for *dependent* students, you can borrow up to $3,500 per academic year for first-year studies, $4,500 for the second year, and $5,500 per academic year thereafter, up to a subsidized loan maximum of $23,000 for undergraduate studies—you can obtain even more if you can show that you're no longer dependent on your parents; in other words, that you're an *independent* undergraduate student paying for your college education on your own. Graduate students can qualify for up to $8,500 per academic year for independent students. The maximum for both undergraduate and graduate subsidized loans combined is $65,000 (or $224,000 for health professionals). And there's no limit on the *number* of loans you can have, only on the maximum dollar amount that you can receive annually from each program. Exhibit 7.1 compares the major loan provisions of the three federally sponsored student loan programs: Stafford, Perkins, and PLUS loans.

Each year, right on through graduate school, a student can take out a loan from one or more of these government programs. Over time, that can add up to a lot of loans, and a substantial amount of debt—all of which must be repaid. But here's another nice feature of these loans: *loan repayment doesn't begin until after you're out of school* (for the Stafford and Perkins programs only; repayment on PLUS loans normally begins within 60 days of loan disbursement). In addition, except for PLUS loans, interest doesn't begin accruing until you get out of school. Once repayment begins, you start paying interest on the loans; this interest may be tax deductible, depending on your income.

Student loans are usually amortized with monthly (principal and interest) payments over a period of 5 to 10 years. To help you service the debt, if you have several student loans outstanding, you can *consolidate* the loans at a single blended rate and extend the repayment period to as long as 20 years. You also can ask for either: (1) an *extended repayment* for a longer term of up to 30 years; (2) a *graduated repayment schedule*, which will give you low payments in the early years and then higher payments later on; or (3) an *income-contingent repayment plan*, with payments that fluctuate annually according to your income and debt levels. But no matter what you do, *take the repayment provisions seriously because defaults will be reported to credit bureaus and become a part of your credit file!* What's more, according to recent legislation, you can't get out of repaying your student loans by filing for bankruptcy: whether you file under Chapter 7 or Chapter 13, *student loans are no longer dischargeable in a bankruptcy proceeding.*

ARE STUDENT LOANS "TOO BIG TO FAIL"? During the recent financial crisis, some banks were deemed "too big to fail" by virtue of their importance to the operation of the entire financial system. Their size consequently became the rationale for providing

Exhibit 7.1 **Federal Government Student Loan Programs at a Glance**

More and more college students rely on loans subsidized by the federal government to finance all or part of their educations. There are three types of federally subsidized loan programs, the basic loan provisions of which are listed here. These loans all have low interest rates and provide various deferment options and extended repayment terms. (*Note: Loan rates and terms shown here are for the 2012–2013 school year.*)

Loan Provisions	Type of Federal Loan Program		
	Stafford Loans*	Perkins Loans	PLUS Loans
Borrower	Student	Student	Parent
Interest rate	3.4%	5%	8.5%
Borrowing limits	*Dependent students:* $23,000 (undergrad); $65,000 (grad/professional) *Independent students:* $57,500 (undergrad) $65,000 (grad/professional)	$27,500 (undergrad) $60,000 (grad/professional)	*No total dollar limit:* Cost of attendance minus any other financial aid received
Loan fees	1% of loan origination fee (0.5% rebate up to July 2012)	None	Up to 4% of loan amount
Loan term	10–25 years	10 years	10 years

*Data are for subsidized Stafford loans, and interest rates are as of mid-2012. Stafford loans can be subsidized or unsubsidized and the lifetime limits can differ. Congress passed a bill keeping the rate at this lower rate for 2012– 2013, which is below the previously determined 6.8%. Subsidized Stafford loans also have annual borrowing limits ranging from $3,500 for the freshman year for dependent students to $8,500 per year in graduate/professional school for independent students; likewise, Perkins loans have annual limits of $5,500 per year of undergraduate study and $8,000 per year of graduate school.
Source: http://www.fastweb.com and http://www.staffordloan.com, accessed July 2012.

massive public financial assistance. Education is important to the economy, and, as discussed in this chapter, the federal government provides loans to finance undergraduate and graduate education. The financial crisis obviously put more pressure on households seeking to pay the increasing cost of college educations. So how large have student loans grown? Student loans now total more than $1 trillion! And students took out about $117 billion in student loans in 2011 alone. So the federal government has taken on a significant liability to support higher education that is important to the overall economy. This recently prompted a representative of the newly created Consumer Finance Protection Bureau (CFPB) to observe that the student loan program has possibly become "too big to fail" as well.

While this chapter discusses the limits on public loans, there is no limit on private student loans. The Federal Reserve Bank of New York estimates that the average student loan was about $12,800 in early 2012. However, the top 1 percent of student borrowers owes more than $150,000. And about 27 percent of all student borrowers have a past-due balance! These balances take on particular significance given that the average starting salary of a recent college graduate is about $41,700.

A recent survey by the Young Invincibles, a nonprofit group focusing on issues affecting 18- to 34-year-olds, found that about two-thirds of student borrowers with private loans did not understand the differences between public and private student loans. This is significant because public lenders are often more flexible than private lenders in providing financial relief when borrowers are under pressure. For example, federal programs provide public service loan forgiveness, income-based repayment, and loan repayment assistance programs. While the financial crisis has increased reliance on federal student loans, the U.S. Congress fortunately decided in mid-2012 not to double the interest rate on Stafford loans from 3.4 percent to 6.8 percent. So the 3.4 percent rate was maintained in 2012–2013.

STRATEGIES FOR REDUCING STUDENT LOAN COSTS It's important to borrow as little as possible to cover college costs. This common-sense goal can be quantified by borrowing in light of the student's expected future salary. Based on that expected future salary, figure out what monthly payment the student will be able to afford and then use a loan repayment calculator to determine the maximum amount that can be borrowed at the expected interest rate on the loan. For example, consider using the following online student loan calculator: **http://www.bankrate.com/ calculators/college-planning/loan-calculator.aspx.**

The analysis should also include looking for the lowest interest rate. Before borrowing, it makes sense to explore all possibly available grants and scholarships and to apply for federal student aid. And upon graduation it is wise to explore the Public Service Loan Forgiveness and Loan Repayment Assistance programs. There could also be the option to consolidate federal student loans and to participate in an income-based repayment program.

Single-Payment or Installment Loans

Consumer loans can also be broken into categories based on the type of repayment arrangement—single-payment or installment. **Single-payment loans** are made for a specified period, at the end of which time payment in full (principal plus interest) is due. They generally have maturities ranging from 30 days to a year or so. Sometimes single-payment loans are made to finance purchases or pay bills when the cash to be used for repayment is known to be forthcoming in the near future; in this case, they serve as a form of **interim financing**. In other situations, single-payment loans are used by consumers who want to avoid being strapped with monthly installment payments.

Installment loans, in contrast, are repaid in a series of fixed, scheduled payments rather than in one lump sum. The payments are almost always set up on a monthly basis, with each installment made up partly of principal and partly of interest. For example, out of a $75 monthly payment, $50 might be credited to principal and the balance to interest. These loans are typically made to finance the purchase of a good or service for which current resources are inadequate. The repayment period can run from six months to six years or more. Installment loans have become a way of life for many consumers. They're popular because they provide a convenient way to "buy now and pay later."

Fixed- or Variable-Rate Loans

Most consumer loans are made at fixed rates of interest—that is, the interest rate charged and the monthly payments remain the same over the life of the obligation. However, variable-rate loans are also being made with increasing frequency, especially on *longer-term installment loans*. As with an adjustable-rate home mortgage, the rate of interest charged on such loans changes periodically in keeping with prevailing market conditions. If market interest rates go up, the rate of interest on the loan goes up accordingly, as does the monthly loan payment. These loans have periodic adjustment dates (for example, monthly, quarterly, or semiannually), at which time the interest rate and monthly payment are adjusted as necessary. Once an adjustment is made, the new rate remains in effect until the next adjustment date

(sometimes the payment amount remains the same but the number of payments changes). Many variable-rate loans have caps on the maximum increase per adjustment period as well as over the life of the loan. Generally speaking, variable-rate loans are desirable *if interest rates are expected to fall* over the course of the loan. In contrast, fixed-rate loans are preferable *if interest rates are expected to rise*.

7-1c Where Can You Get Consumer Loans?

Consumer loans can be obtained from a number of sources, including commercial banks, consumer finance companies, credit unions, S&Ls, sales finance companies, and life insurance companies—even brokerage firms, pawnshops, or friends and relatives. *Commercial banks* dominate the field and provide nearly half of all consumer loans. Second to banks are *consumer finance companies* and then *credit unions*. Together, about 75 percent of all consumer loans are originated by these three financial institutions!

Commercial Banks

Because they offer various types of loans at attractive rates of interest, commercial banks are a popular source of consumer loans. One nice thing about commercial banks is that they typically charge lower rates than most other lenders, largely because they take only the best credit risks and are able to obtain relatively inexpensive funds from their depositors. The demand for their loans is generally high, and they can be selective in making consumer loans. Commercial banks usually lend only to customers with good credit ratings who can readily demonstrate an ability to repay a loan according to the specified terms. They also give preference to loan applicants who are account holders. Although banks prefer to make loans secured by some type of collateral, they also make unsecured loans to their better customers.

Consumer Finance Companies

Sometimes called *small loan companies*, **consumer finance companies** make secured and unsecured (signature) loans to qualified individuals. These companies do not accept deposits but obtain funds from their stockholders and through open market borrowing. Because they don't have the inexpensive sources of funds that banks and other deposit-type

single-payment loan A loan made for a specified period, at the end of which payment is due in full.

interim financing The use of a single-payment loan to finance a purchase or pay bills in situations where the funds to be used for repayment are known to be forthcoming in the near future.

installment loan A loan that is repaid in a series of fixed, scheduled payments rather than a lump sum.

consumer finance company A firm that makes secured and unsecured personal loans to qualified individuals; also called a *small loan company*.

sales finance company A firm that purchases notes drawn up by sellers of certain types of merchandise, typically big-ticket items.

captive finance company A sales finance company that is owned by a manufacturer of big-ticket merchandise. GMAC is a captive finance company.

cash value (of life insurance) An accumulation of savings in an insurance policy that can be used as a source of loan collateral.

institutions do, their interest rates are generally quite high. Actual rates charged by consumer finance companies are regulated by interest-rate ceilings (or usury laws) set by the states in which they operate. The maximum allowable interest rate may vary with the size of the loan, and the state regulatory authorities may also limit the length of the repayment period. Loans made by consumer finance companies typically are for $5,000 or less and are secured by some type of collateral. These lenders specialize in small loans to high-risk borrowers. As such, they are quite costly, but they may be the only alternative for people with poor credit ratings.

 Go to Smart Sites

America's Credit Unions provides information to help you find a credit union in your area. ●

Credit Unions

A credit union is a cooperative financial institution that is owned by the people ("members") who use its services. Only the members can obtain installment loans and other types of credit from these institutions, but credit unions can offer membership to just about anyone they want, not merely to certain groups of people. Because they are nonprofit organizations with minimal operating costs, credit unions charge relatively low rates on their loans. They make either unsecured or secured loans, depending on the size and type of loan requested. Generally speaking, membership in a credit union provides the most attractive borrowing opportunities available because their interest rates and borrowing requirements are usually more favorable than other sources of consumer loans.

Savings and Loan Associations

Savings and loan associations (S&Ls), as well as savings banks, primarily make mortgage loans. They aren't major players in the consumer loan field, but S&Ls are permitted to make loans on such consumer durables as automobiles, televisions, refrigerators, and other appliances. They can also make certain types of home improvement and mobile-home loans as well as some personal and educational loans. Rates of interest on consumer loans at S&Ls are fairly close to the rates charged by commercial banks; if anything,

they tend to be a bit more expensive. Like their banking counterparts, the rates charged at S&Ls will, in the final analysis, depend on such factors as type and purpose of the loan and the borrower's overall creditworthiness.

Sales Finance Companies

Businesses that sell relatively expensive items—such as automobiles, furniture, and appliances—often provide installment financing to their customers. Because dealers can't afford to tie up their funds in installment contracts, they sell them to a **sales finance company**. This procedure is often called "selling paper" because the merchants are, in effect, selling their loans to a third party. When the sales finance company purchases these notes, customers are usually notified to make payments directly to it.

The largest sales finance organizations are the **captive finance companies** owned by the manufacturers of big-ticket items. Ford Motor Credit Corporation (FMCC) and General Electric Credit Corporation (GECC) are just two examples of captive finance companies that purchase the installment loans made by the dealers of their products. Most commercial banks also act as sales finance companies by buying paper from auto dealers and other businesses. The cost of financing through a sales finance company is generally higher than the rates charged by banks and S&Ls, particularly when you let the dealer do all the work in arranging the financing (dealers normally get a cut of the finance income, so it's obviously in their best interest to secure as high a rate as possible).

Life Insurance Companies

Life insurance policyholders may be able to obtain loans from their insurance companies. That's because certain types of policies not only provide death benefits but also have a savings function, so they can be used as collateral for loans. Life insurance companies are required by law to make loans against the **cash value**—the amount of accumulated savings—of certain types of life insurance policies. The rate of interest on this type of loan is stated in the policy and usually carries a variable rate that goes up and down with prevailing market conditions. Although you'll be charged interest for as long as the policy loan is outstanding, these loans don't have repayment dates—in other words, *you don't have to pay them back*. When you take out a loan against the cash value of your life insurance policy, you're really borrowing from yourself. Thus, the amount of the loan outstanding, plus any accrued interest, is deducted from the amount of coverage provided by the policy—*effectively lowering your insurance coverage*. The chief danger in life insurance loans is that they don't have a firm maturity date, so *borrowers may lack the motivation to repay them*.

© GEOPAUL/ISTOCKPHOTO

The Paradox of Financial Choices

More choices are better than fewer choices, right? That sounds like common sense. Yet behavioral finance studies show that when presented with too many financial choices, people tend to get overwhelmed and fall back on what they already know or to just make the simplest choice by default. This is called the *paradox of choice*. Complexity can overwhelm the average consumer. Our brains are just not wired to analyze lots of choices. The best defense is to be financially literate: do your homework, develop a framework for making such decisions, and be prepared to ask for help.

Consider the complicated choice among various mortgage types and terms. You have to choose between 15- and 30-year maturities and between fixed and adjustable rate mortgages; decide on the amount of the down payment, the amount of "points" (percent of the loan amount) to pay in order to reduce your mortgage rate, and when to "lock in" your rate; and you must choose the best array of up-front mortgage-related fees. You'll also have the option of choosing conventional, Federal Housing Association (FHA), Veterans Association (VA), and "no-document" mortgages. Some consumers, when facing so many decisions, wind up making bad ones, borrowing too much and holding mortgages that are inconsistent with their best interests. And research shows that lower financial literacy and analytical abilities are directly related to higher mortgage default rates.

This book in general, and the chapters on managing credit in particular, should help prepare you to make these complicated financial decisions.

7-2 Managing Your Credit

LG3 Borrowing money to make major purchases—and, in general, using consumer loans—is a sound and perfectly legitimate way to conduct your financial affairs. From a financial planning perspective, you should ask yourself two questions when considering the use of a consumer loan: (1) Does making this transaction fit into your financial plans? and (2) Does the required debt service on the loan fit into your monthly cash budget? Indeed, when *full consideration is given not only to the need for the asset or item in question, but also to the repayment of the ensuing debt,* sound credit management is the result. In contrast, if the expenditure in question will seriously jeopardize your financial plans or if repaying the loan is likely to strain your cash budget, then you should definitely reconsider the purchase! Perhaps it can be postponed, or you can liquidate some other assets in order to come up with more down payment. Whatever route you choose, the key point is to make sure that the debt will be fully compatible with your financial plans and cash budget *before* the loan is taken out and the money spent.

When full consideration is given not only to the need for the asset or item in question, but also to the repayment of the ensuing debt, sound credit management is the result.

7-2a Shopping for Loans

Once you've decided to use credit, it's equally important that you shop around and evaluate the various costs and terms available. You may think the only thing you need do to make a sound credit decision is to determine which source offers the lowest finance charge. But this could not be farther from the truth—as we'll see below, finance charges are just one of the factors to consider when shopping for a loan.

KURHAN/SHUTTERSTOCK.COM

Before you lend money to family or friends, it's helpful to answer the following questions:

- **Has your friend or family member explored other funding sources?** Starting with a bank or a credit union makes sense. If that doesn't work, non-financial-institution peer-to-peer lending organizations like Prosper (http://prosper.com) or Lending Cub (http://lendingclub.com) are worth looking into. Every other resource should be exhausted before you consider giving a loan to friends or relatives.

- **Can you help other than with money?** For example, if a friend or relative is out of work, perhaps you could help by providing an introduction or by arranging an interview.

- **Will the loan be repaid?** It's a cliché for a reason: Don't lend any money that you can't afford to lose. If you really think repayment is unlikely, you may want to consider just offering cash as a gift, without any obligation to repay.

- **What will happen to your relationship if the loan isn't repaid?** How hard would you push your friend or relative for repayment, and how far would you be willing to go? Could you just forget about the money without bearing a grudge? Is the risk of losing a friend worth any interest that you might earn on the loan?

- **What if the loan is not used as you'd hoped?** Resist the urge to direct how the money is used. While you should be repaid, you have no control over how the money is used. Don't lend the money if you have concerns about how it will be used.

- **Is the interest rate fair?** It is sometimes awkward to charge interest to a relative or friend. If you do decide to do that, though, a good rule is to charge interest at a rate comparable to that on a high-yield savings account. If you didn't make the loan, it's likely you'd keep it in a savings account anyway. If you charge interest, it should be a fair, legal rate.

- **Should this be a formal, legal transaction?** Even though this is your friend or relative, it's wise to formalize the loan with a contract. A contract shows that you're serious about the arrangement and expect to be repaid. For less than $20, you can get a promissory note on the Web at http://www.nolo.com/products/promissory-note-for-personal-loan-installment-payments-with-interest-pr032.html. If you wouldn't consider taking legal action against a friend or a relative, consider just giving some money instead of extending a loan.

Source: Adapted from Flexo, "Lending Money to Friends and Family," Consumerism Commentary, http://www.consumerismcommentary.com/lending-money-to-friends-and-family/, accessed April 2012.

Finance Charges

What's it going to cost me? That's one of the first things most people want to know when taking out a loan. And that's appropriate because borrowers should know what they'll have to pay to get the money. Lenders are required by law to clearly state all finance charges and other loan fees. Find out the effective (or true) *rate* of interest you'll have to pay on the loan, as well as whether the loan carries a fixed or variable rate. In this regard, ask the lender what the *annual rate of interest* on the loan will be because it's easier (and far more relevant) to compare percentage rates on alternative borrowing arrangements than the dollar amount of the loan charges. This rate of interest, known as the *annual percentage rate (APR),* includes not only the basic cost of money but also any additional fees that might be required on the loan (APR is more fully discussed later). Also, if it's a variable-rate loan, find out what the interest rate is pegged to, how many "points" are added to the base rate, how often the loan rate can be changed, and if rate caps exist. Just as important is how the lender makes the periodic adjustments: will the *size* of the monthly payment change, or the *number* of monthly payments?

Loan Maturity

Try to make sure that the size and number of loan payments will fit comfortably into your spending and savings plans. As a rule, the cost of credit increases with the length of the repayment period. Thus, to lower your cost, you should consider shortening the loan maturity—but only to the point where doing so won't place an unnecessary strain on your cash flow. Although a shorter maturity may reduce the cost of the loan, it also increases the size of the monthly loan payment. Indeed, finding a monthly loan payment that you'll be comfortable with is a critical dimension of sound credit management.

Altering the loan maturity is just one way of coming up with an affordable monthly payment; fortunately, there are scores of Web sites where you can quickly run through all sorts of alternatives to find the monthly payment that will best fit your monthly budget. (The "tools" section of most major financial services sites on the Internet have "calculators" that enable you to quickly and easily figure interest rates and monthly loan payments for all sorts of loans; generally, all you need to do is plug in a few key pieces of information—such as the interest rate and loan term—and then hit "calculate" and let the computer do the rest. For example, go to the calculator page of **http://www.finaid.org** and try out their "Loan Calculator.")

Total Cost of the Transaction

When comparison shopping for credit, always look at the total cost of *both* the price of the item purchased *and* the price of the credit. Retailers often manipulate both sticker prices and interest rates, so you really won't know what kind of deal you're getting until you look at the total cost of the transaction. Along this line, comparing *monthly payments* is a good way to get a handle on total cost. It's a simple matter to compare total costs: *just add the amount put down on the purchase to the total of all the monthly loan payments*; other things being equal, the one with the lowest total is the one you should pick.

Collateral

Make sure you know up front what collateral (if any) you'll have to pledge on the loan and what you stand to lose if you default on your payments. Actually, if it makes no difference to you and if it's not too inconvenient, using collateral often makes sense because it may result in *lower* finance charges—perhaps half a percentage point or so.

Other Loan Considerations

In addition to following the guidelines just described, here are some questions that you should also ask: Can you choose a *payment date* that will be compatible with your spending patterns? Can you obtain the loan *promptly and conveniently*? What are the charges for late payments, and are they reasonable? Will you receive a refund on credit charges if you prepay your loan, or are there prepayment penalties? Taking the time to look around for the best credit deal will pay off, not only in reducing the cost of such debt but also in keeping the burden of credit in line with your cash budget and financial plans. In the long run, you're the one who has the most to gain (or lose). Thus *you should see to it that the debt you undertake does, in fact, have the desired effects on your financial condition.* You're paying for the loan, so you might as well make the most of it!

Financial Planning Tips

Is a 0 Percent APR Loan Really a Great Deal? Watch the Rebate ...

Many 0 percent APR loan deals also give you the alternative of a cash-back rebate. You can have one or the other, but not both. Taking the cash-back rebate means that you finance your loan at a normal interest rate. However, accepting the rebate will allow you to borrow less, although you pay a higher interest rate.

Consider an example in which you buy a car and finance $15,000 for 48 months at a 6.7 percent APR interest rate, which requires a monthly payment of $357.11. Your total payments over the life of the loan are $17,141. Interest is $17,141 − $15,000 = $2,141. Alternatively, a 0 percent APR loan deal for the same car at the same price would cost you only $312.50 per month, which is a savings of $2,141 over the life of the loan. Assume that both loans are for 48 months and that your downpayment is the same.

Now, assume that the car dealer offers a $2,000 cash-back rebate as an alternative to the 0 percent APR loan deal. This would reduce the loan amount to $13,000, which would mean a monthly payment of $309.49 at 6.7 percent APR. So the cash-back rebate provides a lower monthly payment than the 0 percent APR loan!

So what can we generalize from this example? If you have the choice, it is almost always better to accept a rebate than a 0 percent APR loan. This is especially the case if you don't have much down payment money, because the rebate effectively acts as a down payment.

Source: Adapted from "0% APR Loan Deals—Good Deal or Not?" http://best-car-deals.buyerreports.org/0-apr-loan-deals, accessed April 2012.

7-2b Keeping Track of Your Consumer Debt

To stay abreast of your financial condition, it's a good idea to periodically take inventory of the consumer debt you have outstanding. Ideally, you should do this every three or four months but at least once a year. To take inventory of what you owe, simply list all your outstanding consumer debt. Include *everything except your home mortgage*—installment loans, student loans, single-payment loans, credit cards, revolving credit lines, overdraft protection lines, even home equity credit lines.

Worksheet 7.1 should be helpful in preparing a list of your debts. To use it, simply list the current monthly payment and the latest balance due for each type of consumer credit outstanding; then, total both columns to see how much you're paying each month and how large a debt load you have built up. Hopefully, when you've totaled all the numbers, you won't be surprised to learn just how much you really do owe.

Use a worksheet like this one to keep track of your outstanding credit along with your monthly debt service requirements. Such information is a major component of sound credit management.

AN INVENTORY OF CONSUMER DEBT

Name ___Drew and Audrey Simmons___   Date ___June 14, 2015___

Type of Consumer Debt	Creditor	Current Monthly Payment*	Latest Balance Due
Auto loans	1. Ford	$ 342.27	$ 13,796.00
	2.		
	3.		
Education loans	1. U.S. Dept of Education	117.00	7,986.00
	2.		
Personal installment loans	1. Chase Bank	183.00	5,727.00
	2. Bank of America	92.85	2,474.00
Home improvement loan			
Other installment loans	1.		
	2.		
Single-payment loans	1.		
	2.		
Credit cards (retail charge cards, bank cards, T&E cards, etc.)	1. MBNA Visa	42.00	826.00
	2. Amex Blue	35.00	600.00
	3. Sears	40.00	1,600.00
	4.		
	5.		
	6.		
	7.		
Overdraft protection line	Hilands Schools Credit Union	15.00	310.00
Personal line of credit			
Home equity credit line	Wells Fargo	97.00	9,700.00
Loan on life insurance			
Margin loan from broker			
Other loans	1. Mom & Dad		2,500.00
	2.		
	3.		
	Totals	$ 964.12	$ 45,519.00

$$\text{Debt safety ratio} = \frac{\text{Total monthly payments}}{\text{Monthly take-home pay}} \times 100 = \frac{\$\ 964.12}{\$\ 5,200.00} \times 100 = \underline{18.5}\%$$

*Leave the space blank if there is *no* monthly payment required on a loan (e.g., as with a single-payment or education loan).

© Cengage Learning

An easy way to assess your debt position is to compute your *debt safety ratio* (we discussed this ratio in Chapter 6) by dividing the total monthly payments (from the worksheet) by your monthly take-home pay. If 20 percent or more of your take-home pay is going to monthly credit payments, then you're relying too heavily on credit; if your debt safety ratio works out to 10 percent or less, you're in a strong credit position. *Keeping track of your credit and holding the amount of outstanding debt to a reasonable level is the surest way to maintain your creditworthiness.*

7-3 Single-Payment Loans

LG4 Unlike most types of consumer loans, a single-payment loan is repaid in full with a single payment on a given due date. The payment usually consists of principal and all interest charges. Sometimes, however, interim interest payments must be made (for example, every quarter), in which case the payment at maturity is made up of principal plus any unpaid interest. Although installment loans are far more popular, single-payment loans still have their place in the consumer loan market.

Single-payment loans can be secured or unsecured and can be taken out for just about any purpose. They're perhaps most useful when the funds needed for a given purchase or transaction are temporarily unavailable but are expected to be forthcoming in the near future. By helping you cope with a temporary cash shortfall, these loans can serve as a form of interim financing until more permanent arrangements can be made.

7-3a Important Loan Features

When applying for either a single-payment or an installment loan, you must first submit a **loan application**, an example of which is shown in Exhibit 7.2. Basically, the loan application gives the lending institution information about the purpose of the loan, whether it will be secured or unsecured, and the applicant's financial condition. The loan officer uses this document, along with other information (such as a credit report from the local credit bureau and income verification) to determine whether you should be granted the loan. Here again, some type of *credit scoring* (as discussed in Chapter 6) may be used to make the decision. When applying for a loan, you should also consider various features of the debt, the three most important of which are loan collateral, loan maturity, and loan repayment.

Loan Collateral

Most single-payment loans are secured by certain specified assets. For *collateral*, lenders prefer items they feel are readily marketable at a price that's high enough to cover the principal portion of the loan—for example, an automobile, jewelry, or stocks and bonds. If a loan is obtained to purchase some personal asset, then that asset may be used to secure it. In most cases, lenders don't take physical possession of the collateral but instead file a **lien**, which is a legal claim that permits them to liquidate the collateral to satisfy the loan if the borrower defaults. If the borrowers maintain possession or title to *movable* property—such as cars, TVs, and jewelry—then the instrument that gives lenders title to the property in event of default is called a **chattel mortgage**. If lenders hold title to the collateral—or take possession

of it, as is often the case with stocks and bonds—then the agreement giving them the right to sell these items in case of default is a **collateral note**.

Loan Maturity

As indicated previously, the maturity (or term) on a single-payment loan is usually for a period of one year or less; it very rarely extends to two years or longer. When you request a single-payment loan, be sure that the term is long enough to allow you to obtain the funds for repaying the loans *but* not any longer than necessary. Don't stretch the maturity out too far because the amount of the finance charges paid will increase with time. Because the loan is retired in a single payment, the lender must be assured that you'll be able to repay it even if certain unexpected events occur in the future. So, the term of your single-payment loan must be reconciled with your budget, as well as with your ability to pay.

Loan Repayment

Repayment of a single-payment loan is expected at a single point in time: on its maturity date. Occasionally, the funds needed to repay this type of loan will be received prior to maturity. Depending on the lender, the borrower might be able to repay the loan early and thus reduce the finance charges. Many credit unions actually permit early repayment of these loans with *reduced* finance charges. However, commercial banks and other single-payment lenders may not accept early repayments or, if they do, may charge a **prepayment penalty** on them. This penalty normally amounts to a set percentage of the interest that would have been paid over the remaining life of the loan. The Truth in Lending Act requires lenders to disclose in the loan agreement whether, and in what amount, prepayment penalties are charged on a single-payment loan.

Occasionally, an individual will borrow money using a single-payment loan and then discover that he or she is short of money when the loan comes due. Should this happen to you, don't just let the payment go past due; instead, *inform the lender in advance so that a partial payment, loan extension, or some other arrangement can be made.* Under such circumstances, the lender will often agree to a **loan rollover**, in which case the original loan is paid off

Exhibit 7.2 **A Consumer Loan Credit Application**

© KAREN HERMANN/ISTOCKPHOTO

A typical loan application, like this one, contains information about the persons applying for the loan, including source(s) of income, current debt load, and a brief record of employment.

CONSUMER CREDIT APPLICATION

LOAN INFORMATION

Amount Requested $ | Purpose | Application Type ☐Individual ☐Joint

COLLATERAL INFORMATION

☐Motor Vehicle: Year_____ Make_____ Model_____ Miles_____
☐Personal Property   ☐Other (Describe)

APPLICANT INFORMATION

Name (Last, First, M.I.) | E-mail Address

Social Security # | Date of Birth | ☐Married ☐Unmarried ☐Separated | # of Dependents

CO-APPLICANT INFORMATION

Name (Last, First, M.I.) | E-mail Address

Social Security # | Date of Birth | ☐Married ☐Unmarried ☐Separated | # of Dependents

APPLICANT RESIDENCE INFORMATION

Address (Number, St, and Apt. or Lot # if applicable) | Telephone #

City, State, Zip Code | Time At Residence Years / Months

Previous Address | Time At Residence Years / Months

☐Rent ☐Live with Parents ☐Own ☐Other_____ | Landlord or Mortgage Holder Name: Phone #: | Monthly Payment $

CO-APPLICANT RESIDENCE INFORMATION

Address (Number, St, and Apt. or Lot # if applicable) | Telephone #

City, State, Zip Code | Time At Residence Years / Months

Previous Address | Time At Residence Years / Months

☐Rent ☐Live with Parents ☐Own ☐Other_____ | Landlord or Mortgage Holder Name: Phone #: | Monthly Payment $

APPLICANT EMPLOYMENT INFORMATION

Employer | Employer Telephone

Employer Address | Position

Gross Income: $ | ☐Weekly ☐Bi-weekly ☐Monthly | Time At Job Years / Months

Other Income: $ Source

Previous Employer & location | Previous Emp. Phone #

Position | Time At Job Years / Months

CO-APPLICANT EMPLOYMENT

Employer | Employer Telephone

Employer Address | Position

Gross Income: $ | ☐Weekly ☐Bi-weekly ☐Monthly | Time At Job Years / Months

Other Income: $ Source | Alimony, Child support, or separate maintenance income need not be revealed if you do not wish to have it considered as a basis for repaying this obligation.

Previous Employer & Location | Previous Emp. Phone #

Position | Time At Job Years / Months

APPLICANT CREDIT REFERENCES

Creditor	Payment	Balance

☐Checking Bank Name_____ Acct#_____
☐Savings Bank Name_____ Acct#_____

CO-APPLICANT CREDIT REFERENCES

Creditor	Payment	Balance

☐Checking Bank Name_____ Acct#_____
☐Savings Bank Name_____ Acct#_____

AUTHORIZATION AND SIGNATURES

By signing this application, you promise that all information provided is true and complete. You also promise that you have revealed any pending lawsuits or unpaid judgements against you. You intend the lender and/or assignee to rely upon these promises in deciding whether to extend credit to you. You authorize a full investigation of your credit record and your employment history. You also authorize the seller and/or assignee to release information about your credit experience with them. You understand that the lender will retain this application whether or not it is approved. I understand that if the application is for a secured loan additional information may be required.

Applicant Signature | Date

Co-Applicant Signature | Date

© Cengage Learning

by taking out another loan. The lender will usually require that all the interest and at least part of the principal be paid at the time of the rollover. So if you originally borrowed $5,000 for 12 months, then the bank might be willing to lend you a lower amount, such as $3,500 for another 6 to 9 months, as part of a loan rollover. In this case, you'll have to "pay down" $1,500 of the original loan, along with all interest due. However, you can expect the interest rate on a rollover loan to go up a bit; that's the price you pay for falling short on the first loan. Also, you should not expect to get more than one, or at the most two, loan rollovers—a bank's patience tends to grow short after a while!

7-3b Finance Charges and the Annual Percentage Rate

As indicated in Chapter 6, lenders are required to disclose both the dollar amount of finance charges and the APR of interest. A sample **loan disclosure statement** applicable to either a single-payment or installment loan can be seen in Exhibit 7.3. Note that such a statement discloses not only interest costs, but also other fees and expenses that may be tacked onto the loan. Although disclosures like this one allow you to compare the various borrowing alternatives, you still need to understand the methods used to compute finance charges because similar loans with the same *stated* interest rates may have different finance charges and APRs. The two basic procedures used to calculate the finance charges on single-payment loans are the *simple interest method* and the *discount method*.

Simple Interest Method

Interest is charged only on the *actual loan balance outstanding* in the **simple interest method**. This method is commonly used on revolving credit lines and installment loans made by commercial banks, S&Ls, and credit unions. To see how it's applied to a single-payment loan, assume that you borrow $1,000 for two years at an 8 percent annual rate of interest.

> **loan disclosure statement** A document, which lenders are required to supply borrowers, that states both the dollar amount of finance charges and the APR applicable to a loan.
>
> **simple interest method** A method of computing finance charges in which interest is charged on the actual loan balance outstanding.

DBLIGHT/ISTOCKPHOTO.COM

© STOCKLIFE/SHUTTERSTOCK.COM

Exhibit 7.3 A Loan Disclosure Statement

The loan disclosure statement informs the borrower of all charges (finance and otherwise) associated with the loan and the annual percentage rate (APR). It also specifies the payment terms as well as the existence of any balloon payments.

FEDERAL TRUTH IN LENDING DISCLOSURE STATEMENT

Creditor: YOUR FAVORITE MORTGAGE CORPORATION
Borrower(s):

Account Number: 1111111

ANNUAL PERCENTAGE RATE	FINANCE CHARGE	Amount Financed	Total of Payments
The cost of your credit as a yearly rate	The dollar amount the credit will cost you	The amount of credit provided to you or on your behalf	The amount you will have paid after you have made all payments as scheduled
7.337 %	$ 205,017.52	$ 138,796.50	$ 343,814.02

Your payment schedule will be:

NUMBER OF PAYMENTS	AMOUNT OF PAYMENTS	WHEN PAYMENTS ARE DUE
359	$955.05	Monthly beginning 09/01/15
1	951.07	Monthly beginning 08/01/46

Variable Rate: If checked, your loan contains a variable rate feature. Disclosures about the variable rate feature have been provided to you earlier.

Demand Feature: If checked, this obligation has a demand feature.

Insurance: You may obtain property insurance from anyone you want that is acceptable to the creditor.
   If checked, you can get insurance through Your Favorite Mortgage Corporation. You will pay $____ for 12 months hazard insurance coverage. You will pay $ ____for 12 months flood insurance coverage.

Security: You are giving a security interest in   property being purchased   property located at
1234 118TH STREET, NW, WASHINGTON, DC 20009
   Assignment of brokerage account and pledge of securities   Personal property: stocks and lease
   Assignment of life insurance policy   Other:
Late Charges: If a payment is late, you will be charged **5.000** % of the payment.

Prepayment: If you pay off early, you   may   will not have to pay a penalty. You   may   will not be entitled to a refund of part of the finance charge.

Assumption: Someone buying your house   may, subject to conditions, be allowed to   cannot assume the remainder of the mortgage on the original terms.

See your contract documents for any additional information about nonpayment, default, any required repayment in full before the scheduled date, prepayment refunds and penalties and assumption policy.

ACKNOWLEDGMENT

By signing below you acknowledge that you have received a completed copy of this Federal Truth in Lending Statement prior to the execution *of* any closing documents.

_____   _____
Borrower/Date of Acknowledgment   Borrower/Date of Acknowledgment

Source: Adapted from http://www.entitledirect.com/static/entitle/sampledocs/fed_truth_in_lending.pdf, accessed October 2012.

On a single-payment loan, the actual loan balance outstanding for the two years will be the full $1,000 because no principal payments will be made until this period ends. With simple interest, the finance charge, F_s, is obtained by multiplying the *principal* outstanding by the stated annual rate of interest and then multiplying this amount by the term of the loan:

$$F_s = P \times r \times t$$

where:

F_s = finance charge calculated using the simple interest method
P = principal amount of loan
r = stated annual rate of interest
t = term of loan, as stated in years (for example, t would equal 0.5 for a 6-month loan, 1.25 for a 15-month loan, and 2.0 for a 2-year loan)

Thus, substituting $1,000 for P, 0.08 for r, and 2 for t in the equation, we see that the finance charge F_s on our $1,000, 2-year loan would be: $160 (i.e., $1,000 × 0.08 per year × 2 years). With this type of credit arrangement, the size of the loan repayment is found by adding the finance charges to the principal amount of the loan, so you'd have to make a payment of $1,000 + $160 = $1,160 at maturity to retire this debt. To calculate the true, or annual, percentage rate on this loan, the average annual finance charge is divided by the average loan balance outstanding, as follows:

$$\text{APR} = \frac{\text{Average annual finance charge}}{\text{Average loan balance outstanding}}$$

In this case, the average annual finance charge is found by dividing the total finance charge by the life of the loan (in years). In our example, the result is $80 ($160/2). Because no principal payments are made on these loans, the outstanding loan balance is fixed at $1,000, as is the average loan balance. Dividing the $80 average annual finance charge by the $1,000 average loan balance, we obtain an APR of 8 percent. Note that the APR and the stated rate of interest are equivalent: they both equal 8 percent. *This will always be the case when the simple interest method is used to calculate finance charges, regardless of whether loans are single-payment or installment.*

Discount Method

The **discount method** calculates total finance charges on the full principal amount of the loan, *which is then subtracted from the amount of the loan.* The difference between the amount of the loan and the finance charge is then disbursed (paid) to the borrower—in

other words, finance charges are paid in advance and represent a discount from the principal portion of the loan. The finance charge on a single-payment loan using the discount method, F_d, is calculated in exactly the same way as for a simple interest loan:

$$F_d = F_s = P \times r \times t$$

Using the above formula, the finance charge F_d on the $1,000, 8 percent, two-year, single-payment loan is (of course) the same $160 that we calculated earlier. But, in sharp contrast to simple interest loans, the loan repayment with a discount loan is based on the original principal amount of the loan, P. Thus, for the $1,000 loan, the borrower will receive $840 ($1,000 less $160) and in two years will be required to pay back $1,000.

To find the APR on this loan, substitute the appropriate values into the APR equation shown previously. But in this case, although the average annual finance charge is the same $80 ($160/2), the borrower will receive only $840, which is the average amount of the loan. When these figures are used in the APR equation, we find the true rate for this 8 percent discount loan is closer to 9.52 percent ($80/$840). Clearly, the discount method yields a much higher APR on single-payment loans than does the simple interest method. The Bonus Exhibit "Finance Charges and APRs for a Single-Payment Loan ($1,000 Loan for Two Years at 8 Percent Interest)" contrasts the results from both methods for the single-payment loan example discussed here. (Visit CourseMate for PFIN 3. Log in at www.cengagebrain.com.)

7-4 Installment Loans

LG5, LG6 Installment loans differ from single-payment loans in that they require the borrower to repay the debt in a series of installment payments (usually monthly) over the life of the loan. Installment loans have long been one of the most popular forms of consumer credit—right up there with credit cards! Much of this popularity is due to how conveniently the loan repayment is set up; not surprisingly, most people find it easier on their checkbooks to make a series of small payments than to make one big payment.

 Go to Smart Sites

It's easier than ever to keep track of your debt, and do it wherever you are. Mint.com's free site can help you track all your cards and even features a free app. ●

7-4a A Real Consumer Credit Workhorse

As a financing vehicle, installment loans can be used to finance just about any type of big-ticket item imaginable. New car loans are the dominant type of installment loan, but this form of credit is also used to finance home furnishings, appliances and entertainment centers, camper trailers and other recreational vehicles, and even expensive vacations. Also, more and more college students are turning to this type of credit as one way to finance their education. Not only can installment loans be used to finance all sorts of things, they can also be obtained at many locations. You'll find them at banks and other financial institutions as well as at major department stores and merchants that sell relatively expensive products. Go into a home appliance store to buy a high-priced stereo, and chances are you'll be able to arrange for installment-loan financing right there on the spot. These loans can be taken out for just a few hundred dollars, or they can involve thousands of dollars—indeed, installment loans of $25,000 or more are not that uncommon. In addition, installment loans can be set up with maturities as short as six months or as long as 7 to 10 years or even 15 years.

> ## Installment loans have long been one of the most popular forms of consumer credit—right up there with credit cards!

Most installment loans are secured with some kind of collateral—for example, the car or home entertainment center you purchased with the help of an installment loan usually serves as collateral on the loan. Even personal loans used to finance things like expensive vacations can be secured; in these cases, the collateral could be securities, CDs, or some other type of financial asset. One rapidly growing segment of this market consists of installment loans secured by second mortgages. These so-called *home equity loans* are similar to the home equity credit lines discussed in Chapter 6, except they involve a set amount of money loaned over a set period of time (often as long as 15 years) rather than a revolving credit line from which you can borrow, repay, and reborrow. For example, if a borrower needs $25,000 to help pay for an expensive new boat, he can simply take out a loan in that amount and *secure it with a second mortgage on his home.* This loan would be like any

other installment loan in the sense that it'll be repaid over a set period of time in monthly installments. Besides their highly competitive interest rates, a big attraction of *home equity loans* is that the interest paid on them usually can be taken as a tax deduction. Thus, borrowers get the double benefit of *low interest rates and tax deductibility.*

7-4b Finance Charges, Monthly Payments, and the APR

Earlier, we discussed two ways of computing finance charges on single-payment loans. Here, we look at the two procedures—*simple and add-on interest*—that are normally used to compute finance charges and monthly payments on installment loans. To illustrate, we'll use an 8 percent, $1,000 installment loan that is to be paid off in 12 monthly payments. As in the earlier illustration for single-payment loans, we assume that interest is the only component of the finance charge; there are no other fees and charges.

Using Simple Interest

When simple interest is used with installment loans, interest is charged only on the outstanding balance of the loan. Thus, as the loan principal declines with monthly payments, the amount of interest being charged also decreases. Because finance charges change each month, the procedure used to find the interest expense is mathematically complex. Fortunately, this isn't much of a problem in practice because of the widespread use of computers, handheld financial calculators (which we'll illustrate later), and preprinted finance tables—an example of which is provided in Exhibit 7.4. The tables show the *monthly payment* that would be required to retire an installment loan carrying a given simple rate of interest with a given term to maturity. Because these tables (sometimes referred to as *amortization schedules*) have interest charges built right into them, the monthly payments shown cover both principal and interest.

Notice that the loan payments shown in Exhibit 7.4 cover a variety of interest rates (from 6 percent to 18 percent) and loan maturities (from 6 to 60 months). The values in the table represent the monthly payments required to retire a $1,000 loan. Although it's assumed that you're borrowing $1,000, you can use the table with any size loan. For example, if you're looking at a $5,000 loan, just multiply the monthly loan payment from the table by 5; or, if you have a $500 loan, multiply the loan payment by 0.5. In many respects, this table is just like the mortgage loan payment schedule introduced in Chapter 5, except we use much shorter loan maturities here than with mortgages.

Exhibit 7.4

A Table of Monthly Installment Loan Payments (to Repay a $1,000, Simple Interest Loan)

You can use a table like this to find the monthly payments on a wide variety of simple interest installment loans. Although it's set up to show payments on a $1,000 loan, with a little modification, you can easily use it with any size loan (the principal can be more or less than $1,000).

Rate of Interest	Loan Maturity						
	6 Months	12 Months	18 Months	24 Months	36 Months	48 Months	60 Months
6.0%	$169.60	$86.07	$58.23	$44.32	$30.42	$23.49	$19.33
6.5	169.84	86.30	58.46	44.55	30.65	23.71	19.57
7.0	170.09	86.53	58.68	44.77	30.88	23.95	19.80
7.5	170.33	86.76	58.92	45.00	31.11	24.18	20.05
8.0	170.58	86.99	59.15	45.23	31.34	24.42	20.28
8.5	170.82	87.22	59.37	45.46	31.57	24.65	20.52
9.0	171.07	87.46	59.60	45.69	31.80	24.89	20.76
9.5	171.32	87.69	59.83	45.92	32.04	25.13	21.01
10.0	171.56	87.92	60.06	46.15	32.27	25.37	21.25
11.0	172.05	88.50	60.64	46.73	32.86	25.97	21.87
12.0	172.50	88.85	60.99	47.08	33.22	26.34	22.25
13.0	173.04	89.32	61.45	47.55	33.70	26.83	22.76
14.0	173.54	89.79	61.92	48.02	34.18	27.33	23.27
15.0	174.03	90.26	62.39	48.49	34.67	27.84	23.79
16.0	174.53	90.74	62.86	48.97	35.16	28.35	24.32
17.0	175.03	91.21	63.34	49.45	35.66	28.86	24.86
18.0	175.53	91.68	63.81	49.93	36.16	29.38	25.40

© Cengage Learning

Calculator Keystrokes

Instead of using a table like the one in Exhibit 7.4, you could just as easily have used a handheld financial calculator to *find the monthly payments on an installment loan*. Here's what you'd do. First, set the payments per year (P/Y) key to 12 to put the calculator in a monthly payment mode. Now, to find the monthly payment needed to pay off an 8 percent, 12-month, $1,000 installment loan, use the keystrokes shown here, where

> N = length of the loan, *in months*
> I/Y = the *annual* rate of interest being charged on the loan
> PV = the amount of the loan, entered as a *negative* number

As seen, to pay off this installment loan, you will have to make payments of $86.99 per month for the next 12 months.

Here's how to use the table in Exhibit 7.4. Suppose that we want to find the monthly payment required on our $1,000, 8 percent, 12-month loan. Looking under the 12-month column and across from the 8 percent rate of interest, we find a value of $86.99; that is the monthly payment it will take to pay off the $1,000 loan in 12 months. When we multiply the monthly payments ($86.99) by the term of the loan in months (12), the result is total payments of $86.99 × 12 = $1,043.88. The difference between the total payments on the loan and the principal portion represents the *finance charges on the loan*—in this case, $1,043.88 − $1,000 = $43.88 in interest charges.

From each monthly payment (of $86.99),

CALCULATOR

Inputs	Functions
12	N
8	I/Y
−1000	PV
	CPT
	PMT
	Solution
	86.99

SEE APPENDIX E FOR DETAILS.

add-on method A method of calculating interest by computing finance charges on the original loan balance and then adding the interest to that balance.

rule of 78s (sum-of-the-digits method) A method of calculating interest that has extra-heavy interest charges in the early months of the loan.

a certain portion goes to interest and the balance is used to reduce the principal. Because the principal balance declines with each payment, the amount that goes to interest also *decreases*, while the amount that goes to principal *increases*.

Add-on Method

Some installment loans, particularly those obtained directly from retail merchants or made at finance companies and the like, are made using the **add-on method**. Add-on loans are very expensive. Indeed, they generally rank as one of the most costly forms of consumer credit, with APRs that are often well above the rates charged even on many credit cards. With add-on interest, the finance charges are calculated using the *original* balance of the loan; this amount (the total finance charges) is then added on to the original loan balance to determine the total amount to be repaid. The amount of finance charges on an add-on loan can be found by using the familiar simple interest formula:

$$F_s = P \times r \times t$$

Given the $1,000 loan that we've been using for illustrative purposes, the finance charges on an 8 percent, 1-year add-on loan would be

$$F_s = \$1,000 \times 0.08 \times 1 = \$80$$

Compared to the finance charges for the same loan on a simple interest basis ($43.88), *an add-on loan is a lot more expensive.* Keep in mind that both of these loans would be quoted as "8 percent" loans. Thus, you may think you're getting an 8 percent loan, but looks can be deceiving—especially when you're dealing with add-on interest!

To find the monthly payments on an add-on loan, all you need to do is add the finance charge ($80) to the *original* principal amount of the loan ($1,000) and then divide this sum by the number of monthly payments to be made. In the case of our $1,000, 1-year loan, this results in monthly payments of $90; that is, ($1,000 + $80)/12 = $1,080/12 = $90. As expected, these monthly payments are higher than the ones with the simple interest loan ($86.99). So, when you're taking out an installment loan, be sure to find out whether simple or add-on interest is being used to compute finance charges. And if it's add-on, you might want to consider looking elsewhere for the loan.

Because the actual rate of interest with an add-on loan is considerably higher than the stated rate, we must determine the loan's APR. That can easily be done with a financial calculator, as shown next. As you can see, the APR on this 8 percent add-on loan is more like 14.45 percent. Clearly, when viewed from an APR perspective, the add-on loan is an expensive

Calculator Keystrokes

Here's how you *find the APR on an add-in installment loan* using a financial calculator. First, make sure the payments per year (P/Y) key is set to 12 so that the calculator is in the monthly payment mode. Then, to find the APR on a $1,000, 12-month, 8 percent add-on installment loan, use the following keystrokes, where

N = Length of the loan, in months
PV = Size of the loan, entered as a negative number
PMT = Size of the monthly installment loan payments

You'll find that the APR on the 8 percent add-on loan is a whopping 14.45 percent!

form of financing! The reason is that, when add-on interest is applied to an installment loan, the interest included in each payment is charged on the *initial principal*, even though the outstanding loan balance is reduced as installment payments are made. A summary of comparative finance charges and APRs for simple interest and add-on interest methods is presented in Exhibit 7.5.

Federal banking regulations require that the exact APR (accurate to the nearest 0.25 percent) must be disclosed to borrowers. And note that not only interest, but also any other fees required to obtain a loan, are considered part of the finance charges and must be included in the computation of APR.

CALCULATOR

Inputs	Functions
12	N
−1000	PV
90	PMT
	CPT
	I/Y
	Solution
	14.45

SEE APPENDIX E FOR DETAILS.

Prepayment Penalties

Another type of finance charge that's often found in installment loan contracts is the *prepayment penalty,* which is an additional charge you may owe if you decide to pay off your loan prior to maturity. When you pay off a loan early, you may find that you owe quite a bit more than expected, especially if the lender uses the **rule of 78s** (or **sum-of-the-digits method**) to calculate the amount of interest paid and the principal balance to date. You might think that paying off a $1,000, 8 percent, 1-year loan at the end of six months would mean that you've paid about half of the principal and owe somewhere around $500 to the lender. Well, that's just not so with a loan that uses the rule of 78s! This method charges more interest in

| Exhibit 7.5 | **Comparative Finance Charges and APRs (Assumes a $1,000, 8 percent, 12-Month Installment Loan)** |

In sharp contrast to simple interest loans, the APR with add-on installment loans is much higher than the stated rate.

	Simple Interest	Add-on Interest
Stated rate on loan	8%	8%
Finance charges	$43.88	$80.00
Monthly payments	$86.99	$90.00
Total payments made	$1,043.88	$1,080.00
APR	8%	14.45%

the early months of the loan on the theory that the borrower has use of more money in the loan's early stages and so should pay more finance charges in the early months and progressively less later. There's nothing wrong with that, of course; it's how all loans operate. But what's wrong is that *the rule of 78s front-loads an inordinate amount of interest charges to the early months of the loan, thereby producing a much higher principal balance than you'd normally expect* (remember: the more of the loan payment that goes to interest, the less that goes to principal).

7-4c Buy on Time or Pay Cash?

When buying a big-ticket item, you often have little choice but to take out a loan—the item being purchased is just so expensive that you can't afford to pay cash. And even if you do have the money, you may still be better off using something like an installment loan *if the cash purchase would end up severely depleting your liquid reserves.* But don't just automatically take out a loan. Rather, take the time to find out if, in fact, that is the best thing to do. Such a decision can easily be made by using Worksheet 7.2, which considers the cost of the loan relative to the after-tax earnings generated from having your money in some type of short-term investment. Here, it's assumed that the consumer has an adequate level of liquid reserves and that these reserves are being held in some type of savings account. (Obviously, if this is not the case, then there's little reason to go through the exercise because you have no choice but to borrow the money.) Essentially, it all boils down to this: *If it costs more to borrow the money than you can earn in interest, then withdraw the money from your savings to pay cash for the purchase; if not, you should probably take out a loan.*

Consider this situation: You're thinking about buying a second car (a nice, low-mileage used vehicle), but after the normal down payment, you still need to come up with $12,000. This balance can be taken care of in one of two ways: (1) you can take out a

36-month, 8 percent installment loan (with a monthly payment of $376.04), or (2) you can pay cash by drawing the money from a money fund (paying 4 percent interest today and for the foreseeable future). We can now run the numbers to decide whether to buy on time or pay cash—see Worksheet 7.2 for details. In this case, we assume the loan is a standard installment loan (where the interest does not qualify as a tax deduction) and that you're in the 28 percent tax bracket. The worksheet shows that by borrowing the money you'll end up paying about $1,537 in interest (line 4), none of which is tax deductible. In contrast, by leaving your money on deposit in the money fund, you'll receive only $1,038 in interest, after taxes (see line 11). Taken together, we see the net cost of borrowing (line 12) is nearly $500—so you'll be paying $1,537 to earn only $1,038, which certainly doesn't make much sense! Clearly, it's far more cost-effective in this case to take the money from savings and pay cash for the car, because you'll save nearly $500.

Although $500 is a pretty convincing reason for avoiding a loan, sometimes the actual dollar spread between the cost of borrowing and interest earned is very small, perhaps only $100 or less. Being able to deduct the interest on a loan can lead to a relatively small spread, but it can also occur, for example, if the

Using a worksheet like this, you can decide whether to buy on time or pay cash by comparing the after-tax cost of interest paid on a loan with the after-tax interest income lost by taking the money out of savings and using it to pay cash for the purchase.

BUY ON TIME OR PAY CASH

Name _Caleb S. McComas_   Date _2/28/2015_

■ **Cost of Borrowing**		
1. Terms of the loan		
a. Amount of the loan	$ 12,000.00	
b. Length of the loan (in years)	3.00	
c. Monthly payment	$ 376.04	
2. Total loan payments made		
(monthly loan payment × length of loan in months)		
$ _376.04_ per month _36_ months		$ 13,537.44
3. Less: Principal amount of the loan		$ 12,000.00
4. Total interest paid over life of loan		
(line 2 − line 3)		$ 1,537.44
5. Tax considerations:		
• Is this a home equity loan (where interest expenses can be deducted from taxes)?	☐ yes ☑ no	
• Do you itemize deductions on your federal tax returns?	☑ yes ☐ no	
• If you answered yes to BOTH questions, then proceed to line 6; if you answered no to *either one* or *both* of the questions, then proceed to *line 8* and use *line 4* as the after-tax interest cost of the loan.		
6. What federal tax bracket are you in?		
(use either 10, 15, 25, 28, 33, or 35%)	_28_ %	
7. Taxes saved due to interest deductions		
(line 4 × tax rate, from line 6: $ _____ × _____%)		$ 0.00
8. Total after-tax interest cost on the loan (line 4 − line 7)		$ 1,537.44
■ **Cost of Paying Cash**		
9. Annual interest earned on savings (annual rate of interest earned on savings × amount of loan: _4_ % × _12,000.00_)		$ 480.00
10. Annual after-tax interest earnings (line 9 × [1 − tax rate] — e.g., 1 − 28% = 72%: $ _480.00_ × _72_ %)		$ 346.00
11. Total after-tax interest earnings over life of loan (line 10 × line 1b: $ _346.00_ × _3_ years)		$ 1,038.00
■ **Net Cost of Borrowing**		
12. Difference in cost of borrowing vs. cost of paying cash (line 8 − line 11)		$ 499.44

BASIC DECISION RULE: *Pay cash* if line 12 is positive; *borrow the money* if line 12 is negative.

Note: For simplicity, compounding is ignored in calculating *both* the cost of interest and interest earnings.

© KEITH WEBBER JR./ISTOCKPHOTO

© Cengage Learning

amount being financed is relatively small—say, you want $1,500 or $2,000 for a ski trip to Utah. In this case—and so long as the spread stays small enough—you may decide it's still worthwhile to borrow the money in order to maintain a higher level of liquidity. Although this decision is perfectly legitimate when very small spreads exist, it makes less sense as the gap starts to widen.

Planning Over a Lifetime: Using Consumer Loans

Here are some key considerations for using credit in each stage of the life cycle.

Pre-family Independence: 20s	Family Formation/Career Development: 30–45	Pre-Retirement: 45–65	Retirement: 65 and Beyond
✓ Make sure your emergency fund is adequate.	✓ Start selectively relying on savings rather than credit for large purchases.	✓ If you must make credit payments late, inform the lender.	✓ Consider a second mortgage or home equity line of credit to reduce borrowing costs.
✓ If you are married, maintain your individual credit history by not borrowing exclusively as a couple.	✓ Budget to keep credit account balances easy to pay each month.	✓ Monitor your credit card and bank statements for unauthorized transactions.	✓ Budget to limit dependence on consumer credit.
✓ Review your credit report at least once a year.	✓ Monitor your credit report at least once a year.	✓ Monitor your credit report at least once a year.	✓ Monitor your credit report at least once a year.

FINANCIAL PLANNING EXERCISES

LG1, 2

1. Bridget Morrow is a sophomore at State College and is running out of money. Wanting to continue her education, Bridget is considering a student loan. Explain her options. How can she best minimize her borrowing costs and maximize her flexibility?

LG3, 6

2. Assume that you've been shopping for a new car and intend to finance part of it through an installment loan. The car you're looking for has a sticker price of $18,000. Auto Boss has offered to sell it to you for $3,000 down and finance the balance with a loan that will require 48 monthly payments of $333.67 Four Wheel Specialists will sell you the exact same vehicle for $3,500 down, plus a 60-month loan for the balance, with monthly payments of $265.02. Which of these two finance packages is the better deal?

LG 3

3. *Use Worksheet 7.1.* Every six months, Brad Stengel takes an inventory of the consumer debts that he has outstanding. His latest tally shows that he still owes $4,000 on a home improvement loan (monthly payments of $125); he is making $85 monthly payments on a personal loan with a remaining balance of $750; he has a $2,000, secured, single-payment loan that's due late next year; he has a $70,000 home mortgage on which he's making $750 monthly payments; he still owes $8,600 on a new car loan (monthly payments of $375); and he has a $960 balance on his MasterCard (minimum payment of $40), a $70 balance on his Exxon credit card (balance due in 30 days), and a $1,200 balance on a personal line of credit ($60 monthly payments). Use Worksheet 7.1 to prepare an inventory of Brad's consumer debt. Find his debt safety ratio, given that his take-home pay is $2,500 per month. Would you consider this ratio to be good or bad? Explain.

LG5, 6

4. Using the simple interest method, find the monthly payments on a $3,000 installment loan if the funds are borrowed for 24 months at an annual interest rate of 6 percent.

LG4

5. Find the finance charges on a 6.5 percent, 18-month, single-payment loan when interest is computed using the simple interest method. Find the finance charges on the same loan when interest is computed using the discount method. Determine the APR in each case.

LG5, 6

6. Assuming that interest is the only finance charge, how much interest would be paid on a $5,000 installment loan to be repaid in 36 monthly installments of $166.10? What is the APR on this loan?

LG5, 6

7. Todd Kowalski is borrowing $10,000 for five years at 7 percent. Payments, which are made on a monthly basis, are determined using the add-on method.
   a. How much total interest will Todd pay on the loan if it is held for the full five-year term?
   b. What are Todd's monthly payments?
   c. How much higher are the monthly payments under the add-on method than under the simple interest method?

LG6

8. *Use Worksheet 7.2.* Constance Botin wants to buy a home entertainment center. Complete with a big-screen TV, DVD, and sound system, the unit would cost $4,500. Constance has over $15,000 in a money fund, so she can easily afford to pay cash for the whole thing (the fund is currently paying 5 percent interest, and Constance expects that yield to hold for the foreseeable future). To stimulate sales, the dealer is offering to finance the full cost of the unit with a 36-month installment loan at 4 percent, simple. Constance wants to know: Should she pay cash for the home entertainment center or buy it on time? (*Note:* Assume that Constance is in the 28 percent tax bracket and that she itemizes deductions on her tax returns.) Briefly explain.

PFIN Student Study Tools—Visit CourseMate for PFIN 3. Log in at **www.cengagebrain .com**. Check out the bonus exercises and exhibits, interactive worksheets, Cool Apps, Smart Sites, Critical Thinking Cases, Money Online, Kiplinger videos, quizzing, and more.

PART
4

MANAGING INSURANCE NEEDS

© ZIMMYTWS/SHUTTERSTOCK.COM

8

INSURING YOUR LIFE

LEARNING GOALS

LG1 Explain the concept of risk and the basics of insurance underwriting.

LG2 Discuss the primary reasons for life insurance and identify those who need coverage.

LG3 Calculate how much life insurance you need.

LG4 Distinguish among the various types of life insurance policies and describe their advantages and disadvantages.

LG5 Choose the best life insurance policy for your needs at the lowest cost.

LG6 Become familiar with the key features of life insurance policies.

How Will This Affect Me? Insurance should be used only to protect against potentially catastrophic losses, not for small risk exposures. It should cover losses that could derail your family's future. It balances the relatively small, certain loss of ongoing premiums against low-probability, high-cost risk exposures. This chapter focuses on how to go about buying life insurance. Premature death is clearly a catastrophic loss that could endanger your family's financial future. We start by explaining how to determine the amount of life insurance that is right for you. We also consider how to choose among key insurance products, which include term life, whole life, universal life, variable life, and group life policies. The key features of life insurance contracts are explained, and frameworks for choosing an insurance agent and an insurance company are presented. The chapter should prepare you to make informed life insurance decisions.

8-1 Basic Insurance Concepts

LG1 As most people discover, life is full of unexpected events that can have far-reaching consequences. Your car is sideswiped on the highway and damaged beyond repair. A family member falls ill and can no longer work. A fire or other disaster destroys your home. Your spouse dies suddenly. Although most people don't like to think about possibilities like this, protecting yourself and your family against unforeseen events is part of sound financial planning. Insurance plays a central role in providing that protection. *Life insurance* helps replace lost income if premature death occurs, providing funds so that your loved ones can keep their home, maintain an acceptable lifestyle, pay for education, and meet other special needs. *Health insurance* covers medical costs when you get sick or become disabled. Property insurance reimburses you if, for example, your car or home are destroyed or damaged.

All of these types of insurance are intended *to protect you and your family from the financial consequences of losing assets or income when an accident, illness, or death occurs*. By anticipating the potential risks to which your assets and income could be exposed and by weaving insurance protection into your financial plan, you lend a degree of certainty to your financial future. This chapter introduces important insurance concepts and then focuses on life insurance decisions.

8-1a The Concept of Risk

In insurance terms, *risk* is the chance of economic loss. Whenever you and your family have a financial interest in something—your life, health, home, car, or business—there's a risk of financial loss. To protect against such losses, you must employ strategies such as risk avoidance, loss prevention and control, risk assumption, and insurance.

Risk Avoidance
The simplest way to deal with risk is to avoid the act that creates it. For example, people who are afraid they might lose everything as a result of an automobile accident could avoid driving. Similarly, avid skydivers or bungee jumpers might want to choose another recreational activity. But **risk avoidance** has its costs. People who avoid driving experience considerable inconvenience, and the retired skydiver may suffer from stress-related health risks. Risk avoidance is attractive when the cost of avoidance is less than the cost of handling it some other way.

Loss Prevention and Control
Loss prevention is any activity that reduces the chance that a loss will occur (such as driving within the speed limit to lessen the chance

> **risk avoidance** Avoiding an act that would create a risk.
>
> **loss prevention** Any activity that reduces the probability that a loss will occur.

PHIL DATE/SHUTTERSTOCK.COM

> " **By anticipating the potential risks to which your assets and income could be exposed and by weaving insurance protection into your financial plan, you lend a degree of certainty to your financial future.** "

After you read the chapter, explore the STUDY TOOLS listed on page 201.

of being in a car accident). **Loss control**, in contrast, is any activity that lessens the severity of loss once it occurs (such as wearing a safety belt or buying a car with air bags). Loss prevention and control should be important parts of all risk management programs.

Risk Assumption

Risk assumption involves bearing the risk of loss. Risk assumption is an effective way to handle small exposures to loss when insurance is too expensive. For example, the risk of having your *PFIN* text stolen probably doesn't justify buying insurance. Risk assumption is also a reasonable approach for dealing with large, uninsurable risks, such as a nuclear holocaust. Unfortunately, people often assume risks while unaware of their exposure to loss or thinking that their insurance policy offers adequate protection when it doesn't.

Insurance

An **insurance policy** is a contract between you (the insured) and an insurance company (the insurer) under which the insurance company agrees to reimburse you for any losses you suffer according to specified terms. From your perspective, *you are transferring your risk of loss to the insurance company.* You pay a relatively small *certain* amount (the insurance premium) in exchange for the insurance company's promise that it will reimburse you if you suffer a covered loss.

Why are insurance companies willing to accept this risk? It's simple. They combine the loss experiences of large numbers of people and use statistical information, called *actuarial data*, to estimate the risk—frequency and magnitude—of loss for the given population. They set and collect premiums, which they invest and use to pay out losses and expenses. If they pay out less than the sum of the premiums and the earnings on them, they make a profit.

8-1b Underwriting Basics

Insurance companies take great pains in **underwriting**, deciding whom they will insure and the applicable premiums they will charge. Underwriters design rate-classification schedules so that people pay premiums that reflect their chance of loss. Through underwriting, insurance companies try to guard against *adverse selection*, which happens when only high-risk clients apply for and get insurance coverage. Insurers are always trying to improve their underwriting capabilities in order to set premium rates that will protect policyholders adequately and yet be attractive and

reasonable. Because underwriting practices and standards vary among insurance companies, you can often save money by shopping around for the company offering the most favorable underwriting policies for your specific characteristics and needs.

8-2 Why Buy Life Insurance?

LG2 Life insurance planning is an important part of every successful financial plan. Its primary purpose is to *protect your dependents from financial loss in the event of your untimely death.* Life insurance protects the assets that you've accumulated during your life and provides funds to help your family reach important financial goals, even after you die. The key idea is that life insurance protects your family from the potentially catastrophic financial damage caused by the premature death of the major breadwinner(s).

> **Life insurance protects the assets that you've accumulated during your life and provides funds to help your family reach important financial goals, even after you die.**

8-2a Benefits of Life Insurance

People don't like to talk about death or the things associated with it, so they often delay addressing their life insurance needs. Life insurance is

© SLAVOLJUB PANTELIC/SHUTTERSTOCK.COM

intangible, and its benefits typically occur after you die. The key benefits of life insurance include the following:

- **Financial protection for dependents**. If your family or loved ones depend on your income, will they be able to maintain their current lifestyle, stay in their home, or afford a college education after you die? The most important benefit of life insurance is providing financial protection for your dependents after your death.

- **Protection from creditors**. A life insurance policy can be structured so that death benefits are paid directly to a named beneficiary, which means that creditors cannot claim the cash benefits from your life insurance policy.

- **Tax benefits**. Life insurance proceeds paid to your heirs are not usually subject to state or federal income taxes, and under certain circumstances, they can pass to named beneficiaries free of any *estate* taxes.

- **Vehicle for savings**. Some types of life insurance policies can serve as a savings vehicle, particularly for those who are looking for safety of principal.

Just as with other other aspects of personal financial planning, life insurance decisions can be made easier by following a step-by-step approach. You will need answers to the following questions:

- Do you need life insurance?
- If so, how much life insurance do you need?
- Which type of life insurance is best, given your financial objectives?
- What factors should be considered in making the final purchase decision?

8-2b Do You Need Life Insurance?

In general, life insurance should be considered if you have dependents counting on you for financial support. Neither a single adult without children or other relatives to support nor a child typically needs life insurance. Life insurance requirements of married couples depend on their earning potential and assets—such as a house—that they want to protect. The need for life insurance increases with children because they will suffer the greatest financial hardship from the premature death of a parent. Even non–wage-earning parents often need life insurance to ensure that children are cared for adequately if the parent dies. As families accumulate assets, their life insurance requirements continue to change. Life changes, such as divorce, will also affect life insurance needs.

8-3 How Much Life Insurance Is Right for You?

LG3 After confirming your need for life insurance, you must determine the appropriate amount of life insurance coverage to buy. You can use one of two methods to estimate how much insurance is needed: the *multiple-of-earnings method* and the *needs analysis method*.

The **multiple-of-earnings method** takes your gross annual earnings and multiplies it by some selected (often arbitrary) number to arrive at an estimate of adequate life insurance coverage. A rule of thumb used by many insurance agents is that your insurance coverage should equal 5 to 10 times your current income. For example, if you currently earn $70,000 a year then, according to the multiple-of-earnings method, you'd need between $350,000 and $700,000 of life insurance. Because the multiple-of-earnings method fails to consider your financial obligations and resources, it should be considered only a rough approximation of life insurance needs.

The second, more detailed, approach is the **needs analysis method**. This method considers both the financial obligations and resources of the insured and involves the three steps shown in Exhibit 8.1 and described in what follows.

8-3a Step 1: Assess Your Family's Total Economic Needs

The first step in needs analysis asks: *What financial resources will my survivors need should I die tomorrow?* The following five items can guide you in answering this question:

1. **Income needed to maintain an adequate lifestyle**. If you died, how much money would your dependents need monthly in order to live a comfortable life? Estimate this amount by reviewing your family's current monthly budget, including expenses for housing costs, utilities, food, clothing, and medical and dental needs. Also consider other expenses such as property taxes, insurance, recreation and travel, and savings. Recognize that the amount needed may change over time.

2. **Extra expenses if the income producer dies**. These expenses include funeral costs and any expenses, such as child care and housekeeping, that might be incurred to replace services currently provided by the insured or surviving spouse, who must give up those responsibilities and find a job.

multiple-of-earnings method A method of determining the amount of life insurance coverage needed by multiplying gross annual earnings by some selected number.

needs analysis method A method of determining the amount of life insurance coverage needed by considering a person's financial obligations and available financial resources *in addition to life insurance*.

Exhibit 8.1   How Much Life Insurance Do You Need?

The needs analysis method uses three steps to estimate life insurance needs.

Step 1:
Assess your family's total economic needs

Income needed to maintain an adequate lifestyle

Extra expenses if the income producer dies

Special needs of dependents

Debt liquidation

Liquidity

— minus —

Step 2:
Determine what financial resources will be available after death

Savings and investments

Income from Social Security survivor's benefits; surviving spouse's annual income; other annual pensions and profit-sharing programs

Other life insurance

Other resources

— equals —

Step 3:

Amount of additional life insurance required to protect your family

3. **Special needs of dependents**. In addition to daily economic needs, you may want to provide for special needs of your dependents, such as long-term nursing care for a disabled or chronically ill child, an emergency fund for unexpected financial burdens, or a college education fund for your children.
4. **Debt liquidation**. To leave the insured's family relatively debt free, it's necessary to determine the average amount needed to pay off outstanding bills and other similar obligations, possibly including the home mortgage.
5. **Liquidity**. If a high percentage of your wealth is in illiquid assets, the cash proceeds from life insurance can be used to pay bills and maintain assets until they can be sold at a fair market value.

8-3b Step 2: Determine What Financial Resources Will Be Available after Death

The second step is to list all current resources that will be available for meeting economic needs. The resources typically include money from savings, investments, Social Security survivor's benefits, proceeds from employer-sponsored group life insurance policies, death benefits payable from accumulated pension plans and profit-sharing programs, as well as proceeds from selling a home and other real estate, jewelry, stocks, bonds, and other assets that can be liquidated. Another important resource is income that can be earned by the surviving spouse or children. After

isolating these resources, reasonable estimates of their value should be made and totaled.

8-3c Step 3: Subtract Resources from Needs to Calculate How Much Life Insurance You Require

Finally, subtract the total available resources (from Step 2) from the total economic needs (from Step 1). If available resources are greater than anticipated needs, then no additional life insurance is required. If the resources are less than the needs—as is the case in most families with children—then the difference is the amount of life insurance necessary to protect the family.

 Go to Smart Sites

Estimate the amount of life insurance your family needs for financial security with SmartMoney's Life Insurance Calculator. For more online resources, whenever you see *"Go to Smart Sites"* in this chapter, visit CourseMate for PFIN 3. Log in at **www.cengagebrain.com.** ●

The needs analysis method may seem complex, but insurance companies and Internet sites have software that can be used to quickly determine the insurance needs of individuals and families. Because *life insurance needs are not static*, you should review and adjust life insurance programs (as necessary) at least every 5 years or after any major family changes occur, such as the birth of a child, the purchase of a home, or a job change.

Financial Planning Tips: Buying the Right Life Insurance for You

The following tips will help you get the right insurance policy at the right price.

- **Don't let an insurance agent tell you how much insurance you need.** Use the methods in this chapter to determine the right amount of insurance for you. Agents are trained and often have a strong motivation to sell large policies—the larger, the better.
- **Consult an independent insurance broker.** Independent brokers have access to more products than the representative of any single company.
- **Just say no to one-meeting recommendations.** A broker who makes a recommendation in the first meeting is moving too fast and probably is not considering all of your best options.
- **Know how your agent is compensated.** Is he or she compensated by a commission-alone, fee-plus-commission, or fee-only structure? If you don't know how your broker is paid, you cannot recognize possible conflicts of interest.
- **Keep your insurance and investment decisions separate.** Term insurance provides protection against premature death alone, without a savings element. Whole life and universal life policies provide

both insurance and savings; consequently, they cost much more. If you combine insurance and investing, make sure you understand why and the costs of doing so. Most people buy separate insurance and investment products.

- **Always do some comparison shopping.** There are lots of alternatives, with major price differences for essentially the same product.
- **Avoid replacing old whole-life insurance policies.** After holding a whole-life policy for years, you may lose the premiums that you've paid and pay more administration fees if you replace it. Just buy more insurance if your circumstances warrant doing so.
- **Avoid buying expensive riders.** Insurance agents are trained to sell riders that provide special extra coverage. Make sure that you need any riders that you buy.
- **Consider your budget when buying insurance.** Make sure you understand and can afford new insurance before you buy it.

Source: Adapted from J. D. Roth, "14 Tips for Purchasing Life Insurance," http://www.getrichslowly.org/blog/2009/04/28/14-tips-for-purchasing-life-insurance/, accessed June 2012.

Needs Analysis in Action: The Meese Family

We can demonstrate the needs analysis method by considering the hypothetical case of Ben and Adele Meese. Ben Meese is 37 and the primary breadwinner in the family; he currently earns $85,000 per year. Ben and his wife, Adele, use Worksheet 8.1. to estimate the amount of life insurance needed to provide for Adele and their two children, ages 6 and 8, if he should die.

Financial Resources *Needed* after Death (Step 1)

Ben and Adele Meese review their budget and decide that monthly living expenses for Adele and the two children would be about $3,500 in current dollars while the children are still living at home, or $42,000 annually. After both children leave home, Adele, now 35, will need a monthly income of $3,000—or $36,000 a year—until she retires at age 65. At that point, the Meese family estimates that Adele's living expenses would fall to $2,750 a month, or $33,000 annually. The life expectancy of a woman Adele's age is 87 years, so the Meese family calculates that Adele will spend about 22 years in retirement. Therefore, as shown in the first section of the worksheet, the total income necessary for the Meese family's living expenses over the next 52 years is $1,878,000.

Although Adele previously worked as a stockbroker, they are concerned that her previous education may be somewhat outdated at that point, so they include $25,000 for Adele to update her education and skills. Ben and Adele also want to fund their children's college educations and decide to establish a college fund of $75,000 for this purpose. Last, they estimate final expenses (i.e., funeral costs and estate taxes) of $15,000.

The Meese family uses credit sparingly, so their outstanding debts total $155,000 (a current mortgage balance of $150,000, an automobile loan of $4,000, and miscellaneous charge account balances of $1,000).

All these estimates are shown in the top half of Ben and Adele's insurance calculations in Worksheet 8.1. Note that $2,148,000 is the total amount of financial resources needed to meet their financial goals if Ben were to die.

Financial Resources *Available* after Death (Step 2)

If Ben died, Adele would be eligible to receive **Social Security survivor's benefits** for both her children and herself. Social Security survivor's benefits, discussed

Social Security survivor's benefits Benefits under Social Security intended to provide basic, minimum support to families faced with the loss of a principal wage earner.

LIFE INSURANCE NEEDS ANALYSIS METHOD

Insured's Name Ben and Adele Meese   **Date** April 12, 2015

Step 1: Financial resources needed after death

1. Annual living expenses and other needs:

		Period 1	Period 2	Period 3	
a.	Monthly living expenses	$ 3,500	$ 3,000	$ 2,750	
b.	Net yearly income needed (a × 12)	$ 42,000	$ 36,000	$ 33,000	
c.	Number of years in time period	12	18	22	
d.	Total living need per time period (b × c)	$ 504,000	$ 648,000	$ 726,000	

TOTAL LIVING EXPENSES (add line d for each period): $ 1,878,000

2. Special needs

a.	Spouse education fund				$ 25,000
b.	Children's college fund				$ 75,000
c.	Other needs				0

3. Final expenses (funeral, estate costs, etc.) $ 15,000

4. Debt liquidation

a.	House mortgage	$ 150,000			
b.	Other loans	5,000			
c.	Total debt (4a + 4b)				$ 155,000

5. Other financial needs 0

TOTAL FINANCIAL RESOURCES NEEDED (add right column) $ 2,148,000

Step 2: Financial resources available after death

1. Income

		Period 1	Period 2	Period 3	
a.	Annual Social Security survivor's benefits	$ 38,400	0	0	
b.	Surviving spouse's annual income	0	$ 35,000	0	
c.	Other annual pensions and Social Security benefits	0	0	$ 27,000	
d.	Annual income	$ 38,400	$ 35,000	$ 27,000	
e.	Number of years in time period	12	18	22	
f.	Total period income (d × e)	$ 460,800	$ 630,000	$ 594,000	

g. TOTAL INCOME $ 1,684,800

2.	Savings and investments	$ 65,000
3.	Other life insurance	$ 100,000
4.	Other resources	0

TOTAL FINANCIAL RESOURCES AVAILABLE (1g + 2 + 3 + 4) $ 1,849,800

Step 3: Additional Life Insurance needed

Step 1: Total financial resources needed $ 2,148,000

Step 2: Total financial resources available $ 1,849,800

ADDITIONAL LIFE INSURANCE NEEDED $ 298,200

© Cengage Learning

in more detail in Chapter 14, are intended to provide basic, minimum support to families faced with the loss of the principal wage earner. Adele and Ben visit the Social Security Administration's Web site and estimate that Adele will receive approximately $3,200 a month, or $38,400 a year, in Social Security survivor's benefits for herself and the children until the youngest child graduates from high school in 12 years.

In the 18 years between the time the children leave home and Adele retires, the Meese family expects that Adele will be employed full-time and earn about $35,000 after taxes. After Adele turns 65, she'd receive approximately $2,250 a month ($27,000 a year) from Ben's survivor's benefits, her own Social Security benefits, and her own retirement benefits. However, Adele will have some other resources available if Ben should die. The couple has saved $65,000 in a mutual fund, and Ben's employer provides a $100,000 life insurance policy for him. Adding these amounts to Adele's expected income means that she'd have $1,849,800 in total resources available.

Additional Life Insurance Needed (Step 3)

To determine the amount of life insurance that the Meese family should buy for Ben, they subtract the total financial resources available ($1,849,800) from the total financial resources needed ($2,148,000) and get $298,200; hence Ben should buy an additional $300,000 of life insurance to protect his family. Now the Meese family can begin to consider which type of policy is best.

 Go to Smart Sites

What is your life worth? There are interactive apps for both Android and iOS devices that allow you to determine how much life insurance coverage you need based on your situation. ●

8-3d Life Insurance Underwriting Considerations

Insurance companies use *underwriting* to determine whom they will insure and what they will charge for the coverage. It begins by asking potential insureds to complete an application designed to gather information for use in estimating the likelihood that the insured will die while the life insurance policy is in effect. Underwriters use life expectancy figures to look at overall longevity for various age groups and also consider specific factors related to the applicant's health, habits, and experiences. This information is used to determine whether to accept you and what premium to charge. For example, someone in excellent health is usually considered "preferred" and pays

the lowest premium. Clearly, if you have any of the risks commonly considered in life insurance underwriting—such as obesity, heart disease, or a high-risk hobby or job—then it's important to shop carefully and compare the cost implications of different types of insurance policies and the underwriting standards used by different companies. For example, an overweight hanggliding enthusiast with a history of heart disease who walks tightropes for a living should expect to pay more for life insurance.

term life insurance Insurance that provides only death benefits, for a specified period, and does not provide for the accumulation of cash value.

straight term policy A term insurance policy written for a given number of years, with coverage remaining unchanged throughout the effective period.

8-4 What Kind of Policy Is Right for You?

LG4 After determining the amount of life insurance that you need, your next step is to choose the correct type of insurance policy. Three major types of policies account for 90 percent to 95 percent of life insurance sales: term life, whole life, and universal life.

8-4a Term Life Insurance

Term life insurance, which provides a specified amount of insurance protection for a set period, is the simplest type of insurance policy. If you die while the policy is in force, your beneficiaries will receive the full amount specified in your policy. Term insurance can be bought for many different time increments, such as 5 years, 10 years, or even 30 years. Premiums typically can be paid annually, semiannually, or quarterly.

Types of Term Insurance

The most common types of term insurance are *straight (or level) term* and *decreasing term*.

STRAIGHT TERM. A straight term life insurance policy is written for a set number of years during which the amount of coverage remains unchanged. The *annual premium* on a **straight term policy** can increase each year on an *annual renewable term policy* or remain level throughout the policy period on a *level premium term policy*. Exhibits 8.2 and 8.3 list representative annual premiums for annual renewable term and level premium term life policies, respectively. (*Note:* The premiums are for nonsmokers; clearly, rates for similar smoker policies would be higher in view of the greater risk and generally shorter life expectancies of smokers.) Annual renewable term policies aren't popular today. Because people now live longer, the rates for level premium term are now well below those on annual renewable term from the first year on, so they're a better value.

Exhibit 8.2 — Representative Annual Renewable Term Life Insurance Premiums: $100,000 Policy, Preferred Nonsmoker Rates

When you buy term life insurance, you're buying a product that provides life insurance coverage and nothing more. This table shows representative rates for several age categories and selected policy years; actual premiums increase every year. As you can see, females pay less than males for coverage, and premiums increase sharply with age.

Policy Year	Age 25		Age 40		Age 60	
	Male	Female	Male	Female	Male	Female
1	$ 95	$ 49	$145	$117	$ 429	$ 366
5	$ 97	$ 63	$177	$151	$ 732	$ 570
10	$107	$ 88	$237	$194	$1,278	$ 864
15	$145	$117	$299	$236	$2,307	$1,620
20	$177	$151	$429	$366	$3,988	$2,902

© Cengage Learning

Exhibit 8.3 — Representative Level Premium Term Life Rates: $100,000 Preferred Nonsmoker Policy

This table shows representative annual premiums for $100,000 of level premium term life insurance. Although level premium costs less than annual renewable term for the same period, you must requalify at the end of each term to retain the low premium.

Age	10 Year	15 Year	20 Year	30 Year
	Male/Female	Male/Female	Male/Female	Male/Female
25	$106/$102	$116/$110	$128/$116	$161/$143
35	$108/$102	$117/$112	$134/$125	$175/$152
40	$122/$115	$135/$129	$157/$145	$222/$185
50	$203/$171	$250/$199	$298/$233	$475/$341
60	$403/$300	$539/$373	$669/$502	Not Available

© Cengage Learning

decreasing term policy A term insurance policy that *maintains a level premium* throughout all periods of coverage while *the amount of protection decreases.*

DECREASING TERM. Because the death rate increases with each year of life, the premiums on annual renewable straight term policies for each successive period of coverage will also increase. As a result, some term policies *maintain a level premium* throughout all periods of coverage, while *the amount of protection decreases.* Such a policy is called a **decreasing term policy** because the amount of protection decreases over its life. Decreasing term is used when the amount of needed coverage declines over time. For example, a homeowner can match her life insurance coverage with the declining balance on her home mortgage. And families with young children can match coverage with the declining level of family income needed as their kids grow up and become independent.

The type and length of term policy that you choose affects the amount of premiums that you'll pay over time. The annual premium for a specified initial amount of coverage, say $250,000, would be lowest for straight term, higher for decreasing term, and highest for annual renewable term. The premium on decreasing term is higher than the premium on straight term because most major insurance companies don't offer decreasing term policies, so there is less competition between companies offering decreasing term policies and they can therefore charge high premiums.

Advantages and Disadvantages of Term Life

One of the biggest advantages of term life is that its initial premiums are lower than other types of insurance, especially for younger people. Term life is an economical way to buy a large amount of life insurance protection over a relatively short period to cover needs that will disappear over time.

The main disadvantage, however, is that term insurance offers only temporary coverage. If you need more coverage when the policy expires, renewal can be a problem if you then have factors that make it difficult to qualify for insurance. Term policies that offer a **renewability** provision give you the option to renew your policy at its expiration, even if you have become uninsurable due to an accident or other illness during the original policy period. Of course, the premium will increase to reflect the greater chance of death at older ages. Renewable term policies are renewable at the end of each term until the insured reaches age 65 or 70.

Another option that overcomes some of the limitations of term insurance is a **convertibility** provision, which at stated times allows you to convert your term policy into a comparable whole life policy. A whole life policy, as we'll discuss next, provides lifelong protection, eliminating the need to continually renew your life insurance. Convertibility, which is standard on most term policies, is particularly useful if you need a large amount of relatively low-cost, short-term protection immediately but in the future, you expect to have greater income that will allow you to purchase permanent insurance.

One way to overcome the drawback of having to pay increased premiums at the end of each term is to purchase a longer term policy. The insurance industry has begun to offer 30-year straight term policies that lock in a set premium. For example, a 35-year-old man who qualifies for preferred rates could lock in a $250,000 death benefit for 30 years in a row and pay only a set premium of $360 a year. As with all insurance policies, however, make sure before signing up that the rate is fully locked in for the duration of the policy.

Who Should Buy Term Insurance?

Because most young families on limited budgets have a high need for death protection, they should focus on guaranteed renewable and convertible term insurance. This will preserve financial resources for meeting immediate and future consumption and savings goals. Healthy older people with adequate financial resources may tend to use term policies to meet specific coverage needs.

8-4b Whole Life Insurance

Unlike term insurance, **whole life insurance** provides permanent insurance coverage during an individual's entire life. In addition to death protection, whole life insurance has a *savings* feature, called **cash value**, that results from the investment earnings on paid-in insurance premiums. Thus, *whole life provides not only insurance coverage, but also a modest return on your investment.* The savings rates on whole life policies are normally *fixed* and *guaranteed* to be more than a certain rate (say, 4 percent to 6 percent). Exhibit 8.4 illustrates how the cash value in a whole life policy builds up over time. Obviously, the longer the insured keeps the policy in force, the greater the cash value. Whole life can be purchased through several different payment plans, all providing for accumulation of cash values.

If a policyholder cancels his contract prior to death, then that portion of the assets set aside to provide payment for the death claim is available to him. This right to a cash value is termed the policyholder's

renewability A term life policy provision allowing the insured to renew the policy at the end of its term without having to show evidence of insurability.

convertibility A term life policy provision allowing the insured to convert the policy to a comparable whole life policy.

whole life insurance Life insurance designed to offer ongoing insurance coverage over the course of an insured's entire life.

cash value The accumulated refundable value of an insurance policy; results from the investment earnings on paid-in insurance premiums.

Exhibit 8.4 **Illustration of the Cash Value and Pure Death Protection in a Whole Life Policy**

Here is an example of the projected cash value for an actual $200,000 whole life policy issued by a major life insurer to a male, age 30. For *each year* of the illustration, the difference between the $200,000 death benefit and the projected cash value represents the *death protection* offered by the insurer.

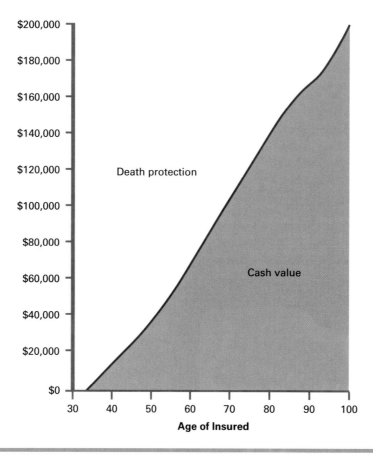

© Cengage Learning

nonforfeiture right A life insurance feature giving the whole life policyholder, upon policy cancellation, the portion of those assets that were set aside to provide payment for the future death claim.

nonforfeiture right. By terminating their insurance contracts, policyholders forfeit their rights to death benefits.

Types of Whole Life Policies
Three major types of whole life policies are available: continuous premium, limited payment, and single premium. To develop a sense of the costs of these policies, look at the representative rates shown in Exhibit 8.5.

CONTINUOUS PREMIUM. Under a *continuous premium whole life* policy—or *straight life,* as it's more commonly called—individuals pay a level premium each year until they either die or exercise a nonforfeiture right. The earlier in life the coverage is purchased, the lower the annual premium. Whole life

should seldom be purchased by anyone simply because the annual premium will be lower now than if it's purchased later. Of the various whole life policies available, continuous premium/straight life offers the greatest amount of permanent death protection and the least amount of savings per premium dollar.

LIMITED PAYMENT. A *limited payment whole life* policy covers your entire life but the premium payment is based on a specified period—for example, 20 or 30 years—during which you pay a level premium. For stipulated age policies, such as those paid up at age 55 or 65, you pay premiums until you reach the stated age. In all cases, on completion of the scheduled payments, *the insurance remains in force, at its face value, for the rest of the insured's life.*

If lifelong death protection is the primary aim of the life insurance policy, then the insured should purchase continuous premium whole life instead of

Exhibit 8.5 Representative Whole Life Insurance Annual Premiums: $100,000 Policy, Preferred Nonsmoker Rates

Like any life insurance product, whole life is more expensive the older you are. Also, whole life is more costly than term because you're getting an investment/savings account, represented by the "total cash value" column, in addition to life insurance coverage.

Age	Annual Premium		Premiums Paid through Year 20		Total Cash Value at Year 20*	Paid-Up Insurance at Year 20	
	Male	Female	Male	Female	Male/Female	Male	Female
25	$ 603	$ 525	$12,060	$10,580	$10,670	$55,700	$56,200
30	$ 727	$ 683	$14,540	$12,760	$13,518	$57,500	$58,600
35	$ 891	$ 775	$17,820	$15,500	$16,908	$58,900	$60,600
40	$1,078	$ 931	$21,560	$18,620	$20,518	$60,000	$62,300
50	$1,590	$1,367	$31,800	$27,340	$29,796	$62,300	$65,300
60	$2,418	$2,050	$48,360	$41,000	$41,796	$66,260	$68,800

*The whole life policy in this example does not pay dividends, so the cash value and guaranteed paid-up insurance amounts are fixed (guaranteed).

© Cengage Learning

© KAREN HERMANN/iSTOCKPHOTO

a limited payment policy. Because more continuous premium whole life insurance can be purchased with the same number of dollars as limited payment whole life, people who need whole life insurance are probably better off using straight life insurance to get the most for their life insurance dollars. Then, once their insurance needs are reduced, they can convert the policy to a smaller amount of paid-up life insurance. On the other hand, if people have life insurance already in force that is sufficient to protect against income loss, then they can use limited payment policies as part of their savings or retirement plans.

SINGLE PREMIUM. *Single premium whole life insurance* is purchased with one cash premium payment at the inception of the contract, thus buying life insurance coverage for the rest of your life. Because of its investment attributes, single premium life insurance, or *SPLI* for short, has limited usefulness for most families but appeals to those looking for a *tax-sheltered investment vehicle*. Like any whole life insurance policy, interest/investment earnings within the policy are tax-deferred; however, any cash withdrawals or loans taken against the SPLI cash value before age 59½ are taxed as capital gains and subject to the 10 percent penalty for early withdrawal.

Advantages and Disadvantages of Whole Life

The most noteworthy advantage of whole life insurance is that premium payments contribute toward building an estate, regardless of how long the insured lives. And the insured can borrow against the policy or withdraw cash value when the need for insurance protection has expired. Another benefit (except for SPLI) is that individuals who need coverage can budget

their premium payments over a relatively long period, thereby avoiding affordability and uninsurability problems. Also, earnings build up on a tax-sheltered basis, which means that the underlying cash value of the policy increases at a much faster rate than it otherwise would. Other valuable options include the ability to continue coverage after the policy lapses because premiums were not paid (nonforfeiture option) and the ability to revive an older, favorably priced policy that has lapsed (policy reinstatement).

Another benefit of whole life policies is shown in the "Paid-Up Insurance at Year 20" column of Exhibit 8.5. This indicates how much insurance coverage the policyholder can retain if the policy premiums are no longer paid beyond that point and the total cash value at that time is exchanged for the indicated amount of coverage. For example, Exhibit 8.5 shows that a male buying insurance at the age of 40 would pay a premium of $1,078 a year. After 20 years, the cash value of the policy would be $20,518. If he decided to quit paying the premiums from then on, he could sacrifice the $20,518 cash value in return for life insurance coverage of $60,000 up to a maximum age specified in the policy, which is often 65. This flexibility of whole life policies is viewed as a benefit by some insurance buyers.

One disadvantage of whole life insurance is its cost. It provides less death protection per premium dollar than does term insurance. Compare the premiums paid for various whole life products with those of term insurance by inspecting Exhibits 8.2, 8.3, and 8.5; you can readily see how much more expensive whole life is than term life. Another frequently cited disadvantage of whole life is that its investment feature provides lower yields than many otherwise comparable vehicles. *A whole life policy should not be used to*

SVETLANA BRAUN/GOLDFAERY/ISTOCKPHOTO.COM

obtain maximum return on investment. However, if a person wishes to combine a given amount of death protection for the entire life of the insured (or until the policy is terminated) with a savings plan that provides a *moderate* tax-sheltered rate of return, then whole life insurance may be a wise purchase.

One way to keep the cost of whole life down is to purchase *low-load whole life insurance.* This is sold directly by insurers to consumers, sometimes via a toll-free number or over the Internet, thereby eliminating sales agents and large commissions from the trans-action. As a result, cash values of low-load policies grow much more quickly than traditional policies sold by agents.

Who Should Buy Whole Life Insurance?

Some financial advisors recommend that you use cash-value insurance to cover your *permanent need for insurance*—the amount that your dependents will need regardless of the age at which you die. Such needs may include final expenses and either the sur-vivor's retirement need (Period 3 in Worksheet 8.1) or additional insurance coverage, whichever is less. This amount is different for every person. Using these guidelines, the Meese family in our earlier exam-ple would need about $147,000 in whole life insurance

BEHAVIOR MATTERS

Whole Life vs. Term Life Insurance and Behavioral Biases

Term life insurance is "pure" insurance, which means that if you don't die during the term, the policy pays nothing. In contrast, a whole (permanent) life insurance policy insures against death in general. The insurance company knows it will eventually pay out on the policy but does not know exactly when. A whole life insurance policy also accumulates cash value over time based on the difference in the premiums on whole life and term life policies for a given individual. A whole life policy may be viewed as life insurance with an internal investment feature. Whole life policies are consequently more expensive than term life. Let's consider how whole life insurance policies can be marketed to exploit behavioral biases.

Whole life insurance can be presented to appeal to the mental accounting behavioral bias. Many people will think of life insurance and saving for retirement as sepa-rate though related "mental accounts," both of which have merit. Yet it's easy to confound the investment and life insurance components of a whole life policy when an agent pitches it as a mandated savings plan. Thus, the pol-icy is marketed as offering both protection for your family in the event of premature death as well as providing a mandatory savings plan that will help you consistently

pursue retirement savings goals. Some agents will even argue that the whole life policy will eventually be "free" when the cash value has grown large enough to cover the insurance premium. Many cannot resist the appar-ent appeal of protecting the family today in the event of premature death combined with a disciplined savings plan that helps you save for retirement and will provide "free" insurance in the future.

A rational decision maker knows that there is no such thing as "free" insurance. And such a person would sepa-rate the need to have a savings plan from the need to have adequate life insurance coverage. So what causes people to confound these decisions? The concept of pre-mature death, protecting one's family, and planning for retirement are emotional issues. An emotionally aware person would likely commit to a savings plan, buy term life insurance, and invest the difference between the whole life and term life premiums. Saving and investing for retire-ment are separate issues that need not be combined in a whole life insurance policy. This is not to say that there are no people for whom whole life insurance is appropriate. However, life insurance and investing for retirement should not be considered without separate analyses.

Source: Adapted from Justin Reckers and Robert Simon, "Behavioral Finance and Life Insurance," MorningstarAdvisor.com, February 17, 2011, accessed May 2012.

(in Worksheet 8.1: $15,000 final expenses [Step 1, line 3] plus about $132,000 of Period 3 living expenses [Step 1, line 1d for Period 3 minus Step 2, line 1f for Period 3—$726,000 – $594,000]) and about another $151,000 in term life (in Worksheet 8.1: about $298,000 [Step 3] minus about $147,000 in permanent insurance just calculated). Limited payment whole life and single premium whole life policies should be purchased only when the primary goal is savings or additional tax-deferred investments and not protection against financial loss resulting from death.

8-4c Universal Life Insurance

Universal life insurance is permanent cash-value insurance that combines term insurance, which provides death benefits, with a tax-sheltered savings/investment account that pays interest, usually at competitive money market rates. The death protection (or pure insurance) portion and the savings portion are identified separately in its premium. This is referred to as *unbundling*. Exhibit 8.6 shows representative annual outlays, premiums, and cash values for a $100,000 universal life policy.

With universal life, part of your premium pays administrative fees, and the remainder is put into the cash-value (savings) portion of the policy, where it earns a certain rate of return. This rate of earnings varies with market yields but is guaranteed to be more than some stipulated minimum rate (say, 4 percent). Then, each month, the cost of one month's term insurance is withdrawn from the cash value to purchase the required death protection. So long as there's enough in the savings portion to buy death protection, the policy

will stay in force. Should the cash value grow to an unusually large amount, the amount of insurance coverage must be increased in order for the policy to retain its favorable tax treatment (tax laws require that the death benefits in a universal life policy *must always exceed the cash value* by a stipulated amount).

Universal life policies enjoy the same favorable tax treatment as do other forms of whole life insurance: death benefits are tax free and, prior to the insured's death, amounts credited to the cash value (including investment earnings) accumulate on a tax-deferred basis. The insurance company sends the insured an annual statement summarizing the monthly credits of interest and deductions of expenses.

Advantages and Disadvantages of Universal Life
As with any insurance policy, universal life has its pros and cons. There are two principal advantages:

- **Flexibility**. The annual premium that you pay can be increased or decreased from year to year because the cost of the death protection *may be covered from either the annual premium or the accumulation account* (i.e., the cash value). If the accumulation account is adequate, you can use it to pay the annual premium. The death benefit also can be increased (subject to evidence of insurability) or decreased, and you can change from the level benefit type of policy to the cash value plus a stated amount of insurance.

universal life insurance Permanent cash-value insurance that combines term insurance (death benefits) with a tax-sheltered savings/investment account that pays interest, usually at competitive money market rates.

© KAREN HERMANN/ISTOCKPHOTO

Exhibit 8.6	Representative Universal Life Insurance Annual Outlays: $100,000 Policy, Preferred Nonsmoker Rates

Universal life premiums are lower than whole life and can vary over the policy's life. After deducting the cost of the death benefit and any administrative fees from your annual contribution, the rest goes into an accumulation account and builds at a variable rate—in this example, the current rate is 3.5 percent. However, the guaranteed rate is only 3 percent, so your actual cash value may be less.

Age	Annual Outlay Male	Annual Outlay Female	Premiums Paid through Year 20 Male	Premiums Paid through Year 20 Female	Cash Surrender Value at Year 20* Male	Cash Surrender Value at Year 20* Female
25	$ 701	$ 628	$14,027	$12,574	$16,206	$14,495
30	$ 830	$ 742	$16,590	$14,833	$19,480	$17,302
35	$ 995	$ 885	$19,896	$17,702	$23,169	$20,481
40	$1,205	$1,067	$24,108	$21,340	$27,366	$24,234
50	$1,806	$1,579	$36,127	$31,573	$38,468	$34,368
60	$2,808	$2,402	$56,155	$48,034	$56,365	$47,912

*Based on an assumed annual rate of 3.5 percent.

© Cengage Learning

variable life insurance Life insurance in which the benefits are a function of the returns being generated on the investments selected by the policyholder.

- **Savings feature.** A universal life insurance policy credits cash value at the "current" rate of interest, and this *current* rate of interest may well be higher than the *guaranteed* minimum rate.

Universal life's flexibility in making premium payments, although an attractive feature, is also one of its two major drawbacks:

- **Changing premiums and protection levels.** A policyholder who economizes on premium payments in early years may find that premiums must be higher than originally planned in later policy years to keep the policy in force. Indeed, some policyholders expect their premiums to vanish once cash value builds to a certain level, but often the premiums never disappear, or they reappear when interest rates fall.

- **Charges or fees.** Universal life carries heavy fees compared to other policy types. Most states require the insurance company to issue an annual disclosure statement spelling out premiums paid, all expenses and mortality costs, interest earned, and beginning and ending cash values.

Go to Smart Sites

For lovely and varied discussion, YouTube features a host of videos by industry groups and popular financial advisors.

Who Should Buy Universal Life Insurance?

Universal life is a suitable choice if you're looking for a savings vehicle with greater potential returns than offered by a whole life policy. Its flexible nature makes it particularly useful for people anticipating changes, such as birth of a child, that require changes in death protection.

8-4d Other Types of Life Insurance

Besides term, whole life, and universal life, you can buy several other types of life insurance products, including variable life insurance, group life, and other special-purpose life policies such as credit life, mortgage life, and industrial life insurance. These insurance products serve diverse needs.

Variable Life Insurance

A **variable life insurance** policy goes further than whole and universal life policies in combining death benefits and savings. The policyholder decides how to invest the money in the savings (cash-value) component. The investment accounts are set up just like *mutual funds*, and most firms that offer variable life policies let you choose from a full menu of different types of funds. Variable life insurance does not guarantee a *minimum return*. And as the name implies, the amount of insurance coverage provided varies with the profits (and losses) generated in the investment account. Exhibit 8.7 demonstrates how two possible investment return scenarios would affect the cash value and death benefits of a variable life insurance policy for a 45-year-old, nonsmoking male over a 20-year period.

© KAREN HERMANN/ISTOCKPHOTO

Exhibit 8.7	**Representative Variable Life Insurance Values: $100,000 Policy, Preferred Nonsmoker, Male, Age 45**

Variable life insurance pays a death benefit whose amount is tied to the policy's investment returns. The cash value created over the life of the policy is also related to investment returns. This table shows the effects of 6 percent and 12 percent annual returns over a 20-year period. Lower returns result in lower cash value and death benefits; higher returns result in higher cash value and death benefits.

| Policy Year | Total Premiums Paid | 6% Return | | 12% Return | |
		Cash Value	Death Benefit	Cash Value	Death Benefit
1	$ 1,575	$ 995	$100,995	$ 1,064	$101,064
5	$ 8,705	$ 5,244	$105,244	$ 5,705	$105,705
10	$19,810	$10,592	$110,592	$15,365	$115,365
15	$33,986	$15,093	$115,093	$27,688	$127,688
20	$52,079	$17,080	$117,080	$43,912	$143,912

© Cengage Learning

Variable life is more of an investment vehicle than a life insurance policy. If you want the benefits of higher investment returns, then you must also be willing to assume the risks of reduced insurance coverage. Therefore, *you should use extreme care when buying variable life insurance.*

Group Life Insurance

Under **group life insurance**, one master policy is issued, and each eligible group member receives a certificate of insurance. Group life is nearly always term insurance, and the premium is based on the group's characteristics as a whole rather than the characteristics of any specific individual. Employers often provide group life insurance as a fringe benefit for their employees. However, just about any type of group (e.g., a labor union, a professional association, or an alumni organization) can secure a group life policy, so long as the insurance is only incidental to the reason for the group's existence.

Accounting for about one-third of all life insurance in the United States, group life insurance is one of the fastest-growing areas of insurance. Group life policies generally provide that individual members who leave the group may continue the coverage by converting their protection to individually issued whole life policies. It is important to note that conversion normally doesn't require evidence of insurability, so long as it occurs within a specified period. Of course, after conversion, the individual pays all premiums. The availability of group coverage through employee benefit programs should be considered when developing a life insurance program. Because of its potentially temporary nature and relatively low benefit amount (often equal to about one year's salary), only in rare cases should a family rely solely on group life insurance to fulfill its primary income-protection requirements.

Other Special-Purpose Life Policies

Use caution before buying any of the following types of life insurance:

- **Credit life insurance.** Banks, finance companies, and other lenders generally sell **credit life insurance** in conjunction with installment loans. Usually credit life is a term policy of less than five years and with a face value corresponding to the outstanding balance on the loan. Although liquidating debts on the death of a family breadwinner is often desirable, it's usually preferable to do so with term or whole life insurance because credit life is an expensive form of life insurance.

- **Mortgage life insurance.** Mortgage life insurance is a term policy designed to pay off the mortgage balance on a home in the event of the borrower's death. As in the case of credit life, this need can usually be met less expensively by shopping the market for a suitable decreasing term policy.

- **Industrial life insurance.** Sometimes called **home service life insurance**, this whole life insurance is issued in policies with small face amounts, often $1,000 or less. Agents call on policyholders weekly or monthly to collect the premiums. Industrial life insurance costs much more per $1,000 of coverage than regular whole life policies, primarily because of its high marketing costs. Even so, some insurance authorities believe that industrial life insurance offers the only practical way to deliver coverage to low-income families.

8-5 Buying Life Insurance

LG5 Once you have evaluated your personal financial needs and have become familiar with the basic life insurance options, you're ready to begin shopping for a life insurance policy. Exhibit 8.8 summarizes the major advantages and disadvantages of the most popular types of life insurance we've discussed in this chapter. The key activities involved in shopping for life insurance include: (1) comparing costs and features of competitive policies, (2) selecting a financially healthy insurance company, and (3) choosing a good agent.

8-5a Compare Costs and Features

The costs of similar life insurance policies can vary considerably from company to company. Comparison shopping can save thousands of dollars over the life of a policy. For example, the total cost for a 10-year, $250,000, term life policy at preferred rates for a 25-year-old can range from $1,170 to more than $2,000. The Bonus Exhibit, "Major Insurance Rating Agencies," summarizes differences in the key features of various types of life insurance. (Visit CourseMate for PFIN 3. Log in at www.cengagebrain.com.) If you have an unusual health problem or some other type of complication, then spending time checking out several companies can really pay off.

group life insurance Life insurance that provides a master policy for a group; each eligible group member receives a certificate of insurance.

credit life insurance Life insurance sold in conjunction with installment loans.

mortgage life insurance A term policy designed to pay off the mortgage balance in the event of the borrower's death.

industrial life insurance (home service life insurance) Whole life insurance issued in policies with relatively small face amounts, often $1,000 or less.

Exhibit 8.8 Major Advantages and Disadvantages of the Most Popular Types of Life Insurance

Major advantages and disadvantages of the most popular types of life insurance are summarized here. They should be considered when shopping for life insurance.

Type of Policy	Advantages	Disadvantages
Term	Low initial premiums Simple, easy to buy	Provides only temporary coverage for a set period May have to pay higher premiums when policy is renewed
Whole life	Permanent coverage Savings vehicle: cash value builds as premiums are paid Some tax advantages on accumulated earnings	Cost: provides less death protection per premium dollar than term Often provides lower yields than other investment vehicles Sales commissions and marketing expenses can increase costs of fully loaded policy
Universal life	Permanent coverage Flexible: lets insured adapt level of protection and cost of premiums Savings vehicle: cash value builds at current rate of interest Savings and death protection identified separately	Can be difficult to evaluate true cost at time of purchase; insurance carrier may levy costly fees and charges
Variable life	Investment vehicle: insured decides how cash value will be invested	Higher risk

© Cengage Learning

Decide how much and what kind of policy you want, and then compare costs.

It is not enough, however, to look only at current rates. You'll also need to ask how long the rates are locked in and to find out about guaranteed rates—the maximum you can be charged when you renew. A guaranteed policy may cost another $20 a year, but you won't be hit with unexpected, larger rate increases later. Establish for how long you'll need the coverage, and then find the best rates for the total period; low premiums for a five-year policy may jump when you renew for additional coverage. Also be sure that you're getting the features you need, such as convertibility of term policies.

Finally, be sure the policies that you are comparing *have similar provisions and amounts*. In other words, don't compare a $100,000 term life policy from one company with a $150,000 universal life policy from another. Instead, *first decide how much and what kind of policy you want, and then compare costs*. For similar cash-value policies, you may find it useful to compare interest-adjusted cost indexes that are often shown on policy illustrations.

It's easy to gather information that allows you to compare costs and features. Term life quote services, available over the phone or on the Internet, can streamline the selection process by providing you, free of charge, with the names of several companies offering the lowest-cost policies based on your specifications. Probably the fastest-growing source of life insurance quotes and policies in recent years is the Internet. You not only can obtain quick, real-time quotes but also can buy insurance electronically. Buying on the Internet allows you to avoid dealing with insurance salespeople, and you can purchase the policies (usually term insurance only) on cost-effective terms. For example, one major life insurer offers discounts of up to 20 percent for term life policies purchased online. Of course, you'll still need a physical exam, but often the insurance company will send a qualified technician/nurse to your home or office to take a blood sample and other basic readings. Efinancial (**http://www.efinancial.com**), Select Quote Insurance Services (**http://www.selectquote.com**), Insure.com (**http://www.insure.com**), and Matrix Direct Insurance Services (**http://matrixdirect.com**) maintain databases of life insurance policy costs for various companies and will also act as your agent to buy the policy if you wish. Insure.com and Matrix Direct provide quotes for both term insurance and whole life. Also, don't overlook companies that sell directly to the public or offer low-load policies, such as Ameritas, Lincoln Benefit, and USAA (for the military and their families).

8-5b Select an Insurance Company

Selecting a life insurance company is an important part of shopping for life insurance. You want to be sure that the company will be around and have the assets to pay your beneficiaries. Factors to consider before making the final choice include the firm's reputation, its financial history, commissions and other fees, and the specifics of their policy provisions. If you're choosing a company for a cash-value life insurance policy, the company's investment performance and dividend history are also important considerations. Unless there's a good reason to do otherwise, you should probably limit the companies that you consider to those that have been doing business for 25 years or more and that have annual premium volume of more than $100 million. These criteria will rule out a lot of smaller firms, but there are still plenty of companies left to choose from. You may also find that one company is preferable for your term protection and another for your whole life needs.

Private rating agencies—A.M. Best, Fitch, Moody's, Standard & Poor's, and Weiss—have done much of the work for you. These agencies use publicly available financial data to evaluate the insurance company's ability to pay future claims made by policyholders, known as their *claims paying ability*. The Bonus Exhibit entitled "Key Features of Various Types of Life Insurance" provides detailed contact information for each of these agencies. (To view this exhibit, go to CourseMate for PFIN 3. Log in at www.cengagebrain.com.) The ratings agencies then give each insurance firm a "grade" based on their analysis of the firm's financial data. Most experts agree that it's wise to purchase life insurance only from insurance companies that are assigned ratings by at least two of the major rating agencies and are consistently rated in the top two or three categories (e.g., rated Aaa, Aa1, or Aa2 by Moody's) by each of the major agencies from which they received ratings. Most public libraries and insurance agents have these ratings, and each of the agencies mentioned previously have an Internet presence where some insurance company ratings may be found.

8-5c Choose an Agent

There's an old axiom in the life insurance business that life insurance is sold, not bought. Life insurance agents play a major role in most people's decision to buy life insurance. Unless you plan to buy all your life insurance via the Internet, selecting a good life insurance agent is important because you'll be relying on him or her for guidance in making some important financial decisions.

When seeking a good life insurance agent, try to obtain recommendations from other professionals who work with agents. Bankers in trust departments, attorneys, and accountants who are specialists in estate planning are usually good sources. In contrast, be a bit wary of selecting an agent simply because of the agent's aggressiveness in soliciting your patronage.

Don't assume that just because agents are licensed, they are competent and will serve your best interests. Consider an agent's formal and professional level of educational attainment. Does the agent have a college degree with a major in business or insurance? Does the agent have a professional designation, such as Chartered Life Underwriter (CLU), Chartered Financial Consultant (ChFC), or Certified Financial Planner® (CFP®)? These designations are awarded only to those who meet certain experience requirements and pass comprehensive examinations in such fields as life and health insurance, estate and pension planning, investments, and federal income tax law.

Observe how an agent reacts to your questions. Does the agent use fancy buzzwords and generic answers, or does she really listen attentively and, after some thought, logically answer your questions? These and other personal characteristics should be considered. In most cases, you should talk with several agents and discuss the pros and cons of each agent with your spouse or other trusted person before committing yourself. Then, when you've decided, call the agent again and finish your business.

Go to Smart Sites

Looking for an insurance agent? Link to the Web site sponsored by the Independent Insurance Agents and Brokers of America, Inc. ●

8-6 Key Features of Life Insurance Policies

LG6 A life insurance policy is a contract that spells out the policyholder's and the insurer's rights and obligations and policy features. There's no such thing as a standard life insurance policy, and policies can vary from state to state. Even so, certain elements are common in most life insurance contracts.

8-6a Life Insurance Contract Features

Key features found in most life insurance contracts are the beneficiary clause, settlement options, policy loans, premium payments, grace period, nonforfeiture options, policy reinstatement, and change of policy.

Financial Planning Tips: Potential Conflicts of Interest in Dealing with Insurance Agents

Most insurance agents are ethical and professional. However, in order to help you identify the others and protect yourself from the few who are not, it's important to keep in mind some potential conflicts of interest between you and insurance agents and brokers. Most have to do with sales commission incentives that can conflict with you getting the best advice.

- Agents only rarely disclose their commissions—and likely will do so only if you ask. Ask agents about the commissions that they receive on competing insurance products. If they balk at the request, it's time to find another agent.
- Agents often avoid bringing up the negative aspects of a policy to make the sale. This also tempts some agents to oversimplify policy features. You need to ask the hard questions.
- While some existing policies should be kept and some replaced, agents only get paid for giving advice when it leads to commissions. So agents can be unreliable sources of advice about the performance of an existing policy. Getting a second opinion from

an agent with another firm is always a good idea.
- Watch out when agents present company illustrations and projections of future policy performance. It's hard to make good decisions solely on be basis of comparing one policy's illustration with another. Don't accept the projections and assumptions uncritically.
- Be aware that some lawyers, accountants, and financial planners don't ask hard questions about life insurance proposals because they depend on life insurance agents for business referrals. Thus, it can be hard to find objective sources of advice concerning life insurance proposals. Consider using a fee-only insurance advisor.

Notwithstanding these potential conflicts of interest, you can accomplish a lot by doing your own homework and by relying on recommended advisors who are true fiduciaries who put their clients first.

Source: Life Insurance Advisors, Inc., "Conflicts and Limitations of Life Insurance Agents," http://www.lifeinsuranceadvisorsinc.com/conflicts.html, accessed June 2012.

Beneficiary Clause

The **beneficiary** is the person who will receive the death benefits of the policy on the insured's death. All life insurance policies should have one or more beneficiaries. An insured should name both a *primary beneficiary* and various *contingent beneficiaries*. The primary beneficiary receives the entire death benefit if he or she is surviving when the insured dies. If the primary beneficiary does not survive the insured, the insurer will distribute the death benefits to the contingent beneficiaries. If neither primary nor contingent beneficiaries are living at the death of the insured, then the death benefits pass to the insured's estate and are distributed by the probate court according to the insured's will or, if no will exists, according to state law.

The identification of named beneficiaries should be clear. For example, if a man designating his beneficiary as "my wife," later divorces and remarries, there could be a controversy as to which "wife" is entitled to the benefits. Obviously, you change your named beneficiary if circumstances, such as marital status, change. The person you name as a beneficiary can be changed at any time by notifying the insurance company, so long as you didn't indicate an *irrevocable beneficiary* when you took out the policy.

Settlement Options

Insurance companies generally offer several ways of paying life insurance policy death proceeds. The distribution method can either be permanently established by the policyholder before death or left up to the beneficiary when the policy proceeds are paid out.

- **Lump sum.** This is the most common settlement option, chosen by more than 95 percent of policyholders. The entire death benefit is paid in a single amount, allowing beneficiaries to use or invest the proceeds soon after death occurs.

- **Interest only.** The insurance company keeps policy proceeds for a specified time; the beneficiary receives interest payments, usually at some guaranteed below-market rate. This option is used when there's no current need for the principal—for example, proceeds could be left on deposit until children go to college, with interest supplementing family income.

- **Fixed period.** The face amount of the policy, along with interest earned, is paid to the beneficiary over a fixed

time period. For example, a 55-year-old beneficiary may need additional income until Social Security benefits start.

- **Fixed amount.** The beneficiary receives policy proceeds in regular payments of a fixed amount until the proceeds run out.

- **Life income.** The insurer guarantees to pay the beneficiary a certain amount for the rest of his or her life, based on the beneficiary's sex, age when benefits start, life expectancy, policy face value, and interest rate assumptions. This option appeals to beneficiaries who don't want to outlive the income from policy proceeds and then become dependent on others for support. An interesting variation of this settlement option is the *life-income-with-period-certain option,* which guarantees a specified number of payments that would pass to a secondary beneficiary if the original beneficiary dies before the period ends.

Policy Loans

An advance made by a life insurance company to a policyholder against a whole life policy is called a **policy loan.** These loans are secured by the cash value of the life insurance policy. Although these loans do *not* have to be repaid, any balance plus interest on the loan remaining at the insured's death is *subtracted from the proceeds of the policy.* Typically, policies offer either a fixed-rate loan or a rate that varies with market interest rates on high-quality bonds. Policy loans should be used only if the insured's estate is large enough to cover the accompanying loss of death proceeds when the loan is not repaid. A word of caution: *Be careful with these loans; unless certain conditions are met, the IRS may treat them as withdrawals, meaning that they could be subject to tax penalties.*

Premium Payments

All life insurance contracts specify when premiums, which are normally paid in advance, are due. Most insurers allow the policyholder to elect to pay premiums annually, semi-annually, quarterly, or monthly, but they typically charge a fee to those paying more often than annually.

Grace Period

The *grace period* permits the policyholder to retain full death protection for a short period (usually 31 days) after

beneficiary A person who receives the death benefits of a life insurance policy after the insured's death.

policy loan An advance, secured by the cash value of a whole life insurance policy, made by an insurer to the policyholder.

© HJALMEDIA/DREAMSTIME.COM

missing a premium payment date. In other words, you won't lose your insurance protection just because you're a little late in making the premium payment.

Nonforfeiture Options
As noted earlier, a *nonforfeiture option* pays a cash value life insurance policyholder the policy's cash value when a policy is terminated before its maturity. State laws require that all permanent whole, universal, or variable life policies contain a nonforfeiture provision. Rather than receiving the policy's cash value, insurance companies usually offer the following two options—*paid-up insurance* and *extended term insurance*.

- **Paid-up insurance.** The policyholder uses the cash value to buy a new, single premium policy with a lower face value. For example, a policy canceled after 10 years might have a cash value of $90.84 per $1,000 of face value, which will buy $236 of paid-up whole life insurance. This paid-up insurance is useful because the cash value would continue to grow from future interest earnings, even though the policyholder makes no further premium payments. This option is useful when a person's income and need for death protection decline, but she still wants some coverage.

- **Extended term insurance.** The insured uses the accumulated cash value to buy a term life policy for the same face value as the lapsed policy and a coverage period determined by the amount of term protection that the single premium payment buys at the insured's present age. This option usually goes into effect automatically if the policyholder quits paying premiums and gives no instructions to the insurer.

Policy Reinstatement
So long as a whole life policy is under the reduced paid-up insurance option or the extended term insurance option, the policyholder may reinstate the original policy, usually within three to five years of its lapsing, by paying all back premiums, plus interest at a stated rate, and by providing evidence that he or she can pass a physical examination and meet any other insurability requirements. *Reinstatement* revives the original contractual relationship between the company and the policyholder. Before exercising a reinstatement option, a policyholder should determine whether buying a new policy would be less costly.

Change of Policy
Many life insurance contracts contain a provision that permits the insured to switch from one policy form to another. For instance, a policyholder may decide that he'd rather have a policy that is paid up at age 65 rather than his current continuous premium whole life policy. A change-of-policy provision allows this change without penalty. When policyholders change from high- to lower-premium policies, they may need to prove insurability.

8-6b Other Policy Features
Along with the key contractual features described earlier, here are some other policy features to consider:

- **Multiple indemnity clause. Multiple indemnity clauses** increase the face amount of the policy, most often doubling or tripling it, if the insured dies in an accident. This benefit is usually offered to the policyholder at a small additional cost. This coverage should be ignored as a source of funds when determining insurance needs because it offers no protection if the insured's death is due to illness.

- **Disability clause.** A **disability clause** may contain a waiver-of-premium benefit alone or coupled with disability income. A *waiver-of-premium benefit* excuses the payment of premiums on the life

ALEKSANDR MARKIN/SHUTTERSTOCK.COM

insurance policy if the insured becomes totally and permanently disabled prior to age 60 (or sometimes age 65). Under the *disability income portion,* the insured not only is granted a waiver of premium, but also receives a monthly income equal to $5 or $10 per $1,000 of policy face value. Some insurers will continue these payments for the life of the insured; others terminate them at age 65. Disability riders for a waiver of premium and disability income protection are relatively inexpensive and can be added to most whole life policies but generally not to term policies.

- **Guaranteed purchase option.** The policyholder who has a **guaranteed purchase option** may purchase additional coverage at stipulated intervals without providing evidence of insurability. This option is frequently offered to buyers of a whole life policy who are under age 40. Increases in coverage usually can be purchased every three, four, or five years in sums equal to the amount of the original policy or $10,000, whichever is lower. This option should be attractive to individuals whose life insurance needs and ability to pay are expected to increase over a 5- to 15-year period.

- **Suicide clause.** Nearly all life insurance policies have a *suicide clause* that voids the contract if an insured commits suicide within a certain period, normally two years after the policy's inception. In these cases, the company simply returns the premiums that have been paid. If an insured commits suicide after this initial period has elapsed, the policy proceeds are paid regardless.

- **Exclusions.** Although all private insurance policies exclude some types of losses, life policies offer broad protection. Other than the suicide clause, the only common exclusions are aviation, war, and hazardous occupation or hobby. However, a company would rarely be able to modify the premium charged or coverage offered should the insured take up, say, Formula One racing or hang gliding *after* a policy is issued.

- **Participation.** In a **participating policy**, the policyholder is entitled to receive *policy dividends* reflecting the difference between the premiums that are charged and the amount of premium necessary to fund the actual mortality experience of the company. When the base premium schedule for participating policies is established, a company estimates what it believes its mortality and investment experience will be and then adds a generous margin of safety to these figures. The premiums charged the policyholder are based on these conservative estimates.

- **Living benefits.** Also called *accelerated benefits*, this feature allows the insured to receive

a percentage of the death benefits from a whole or universal life policy prior to death. Some insurers offer this option at no charge to established policyholders if the insured suffers a terminal illness that is expected to result in death within a specified period (such as 6 months to a year) or needs an expensive treatment (such as an organ transplant) to survive. These benefits can also be added as a *living benefit rider* that pays a portion of a policy's death benefit in advance, usually about 2 percent per month, for long-term health care such as nursing home expenses. This rider can add an extra 5 percent to 15 percent to the normal life insurance premium, and benefits are capped at some fixed percentage of the death benefit.

- **Viatical settlement.** Like a living benefits feature, this option allows a terminally ill insurance holder to receive a percentage of the insurance policy's death benefit for immediate use. But unlike the living benefits feature, this isn't handled through the insurance company but rather through a third-party investor. The insured sells an interest in the life insurance policy to the investor, who then becomes the policy's beneficiary, and then receives a cash amount from that investor—most commonly 60 percent of the policy value. After the insured dies, the investor receives the balance from the policy. Approach viatical settlements carefully because they mean giving up all future claims on the life insurance policy and can also affect a patient's Medicare eligibility in some cases. Note also that some viatical settlement companies—the firms that arrange the transfer between insureds and investors—have been scrutinized by government agencies for unethical practices.

8-6c Understanding Life Insurance Policy Illustrations

A **life insurance policy illustration** is a hypothetical representation of a policy's performance that reflects the most important assumptions that the company relies on when presenting the policy results to a prospective client. Insurance illustrations are complicated and often contain more than 20 pages of numbers and legal disclaimers. The insurance illustration specifies the inflows from premiums paid and interest credits, both of which increase the cash value of the policy.

guaranteed purchase option An option in a life insurance contract giving the policyholder the right to purchase additional coverage at stipulated intervals without providing evidence of insurability.

participating policy A life insurance policy that pays *policy dividends* reflecting the difference between the premiums that are charged and the amount of premium necessary to fund the actual mortality experience of the company.

The illustration also states mortality charges and expenses, both of which decrease the cash value. An illustration typically consists of two main parts:

- **Guaranteed illustration.** The insurance company is required by law to disclose the worst-case scenario, which shows the effects of the insurer crediting the minimum interest and charging the maximum amount based on standard mortality tables. It's safe to assume that the benefits, cash surrender value, and accumulated values will never be lower than what this scenario presents.

- **Current illustration.** This is the insurance company's representation of policy performance based on the credit rates and mortality charges *currently* in effect.

When you look at an insurance illustration, focus first on the basic assumptions that the company used to compute it, including your age, sex, and underwriting health status. As noted above, the illustration will indicate the premiums, cash surrender value, and death benefits. Double-check all of the information. Ask the insurance agent to provide an *inforce reprojection that* shows any changes in credits or charges that the insurance company has declared for the next policy year. These changes in credits and charges will affect premiums or benefits. Most agents will not provide this unless you ask them. Watch for any unanticipated premium increases.

Check to make sure that all of the following sections are present in the narrative summary of the illustration and that no pages are missing:

- **Policy description, terms, and features.** This section overviews the main components of the policy. Double-check that the policy's premiums and benefit projections match your needs.

- **Underwriting discussion.** This provides a detailed description of the policy's benefits, premiums and tax information.

- **Column definitions and key terms.** This defines the terms used in the illustration. Make sure that you understand all the definitions and terms.

- **Disclaimer.** This section informs the prospective client that the illustration's portrayal of future values could vary from actual results.

- **Signature page.** This section provides a numerical summary of the illustration in 5- and 10-year increments. The insurance agent's signature here acknowledges that he or she has explained that the nonguaranteed elements are subject to change, and your signature acknowledges that you understand this.

Planning Over a Lifetime: Life Insurance

Here are some key considerations for life insurance use in each stage of the life cycle.

Pre-family Independence: 20s	Family Formation/Career Development: 30–45	Pre-Retirement: 45–65	Retirement: 65 and Beyond
✓ Term life insurance is needed only if you have dependents relying on you financially.	✓ If you marry, add life insurance to cover the financial needs of your spouse and other dependents.	✓ Re-evaluate insurance coverage if you change jobs or move to a higher-paying job.	✓ Assure the adequate financial protection of your surviving spouse.
	✓ Consider increasing insurance coverage as additional children are born.	✓ Consider reducing insurance coverage as children leave home and graduate from college. More insurance coverage may be needed if you are supporting aging parents. Consider possible use of life insurance in estate planning, which is covered in detail in Chapter 15.	✓ Consider possible use of life insurance in estate planning, which is covered in detail in Chapter 15.
		✓ Evaluate the magnitude of your accumulated assets relative to needs of dependents. Insurance may no longer be needed or could be dramatically decreased.	✓ It may be possible to discontinue coverage for grown dependents. May need to maintain some life insurance to help dependents with special needs.

FINANCIAL PLANNING EXERCISES

LG2, 3, 4

1. *Use Worksheet 8.1.* Adam Modine, 41, is a recently divorced father of two children, ages 8 and 5. He currently earns $95,000 a year as an operations manager for a utility company. The divorce settlement requires him to pay $1,500 a month in child support and $400 a month in alimony to his ex-wife. She currently earns $35,000 a year as a schoolteacher. Adam is now renting an apartment, and the divorce settlement left him with about $100,000 in savings and retirement benefits. His employer provides a $75,000 life insurance policy. Adam's ex-wife is currently the beneficiary listed on the policy. What advice would you give to Adam? What factors should he consider in deciding whether to buy additional life insurance at this point in his life? If he does need additional life insurance, what type of policy or policies should he buy? Use Worksheet 8.1 to help answer these questions for Adam.

LG2, 3, 4

2. *Use Worksheet 8.1.* Rachel Ehrlich is a 72-year-old widow who has recently been diagnosed with Alzheimer's disease. She has limited financial assets of her own and has been living with her daughter Stephanie for two years. Her only income is $850 a month in Social Security survivor's benefits. Stephanie wants to make sure that her mother will be taken care of if Stephanie should die. Stephanie, 40, is single and earns $55,000 a year as a human resources manager for a small manufacturing firm. She owns a condo with a current market value of $100,000 and has a $70,000 mortgage. Other debts include a $5,000 auto loan and $500 in various credit card balances. Her 401(k) plan has a current balance of $24,500, and she keeps $7,500 in a money market account for emergencies. After talking with her mother's doctor, Stephanie believes that her mother will be able to continue living independently for another two to three years. She estimates that her mother would need about $2,000 a month to cover her living expenses and medical costs during this time. After that, Stephanie's mother will probably need nursing home care. Stephanie calls several local nursing homes and finds that it will cost about $5,000 a month when her mother enters a nursing home. Her mother's doctor says it is difficult to estimate her mother's life expectancy but indicates that with proper care, some Alzheimer's patients can live 10 or more years after diagnosis. Stephanie also estimates that her personal final expenses would be around $5,000, and she'd like to provide a $25,000 contingency fund that would be used to pay a trusted friend to supervise her mother's care if Stephanie were no longer alive. Use Worksheet 8.1 to calculate Stephanie's total life insurance requirements and recommend the type of policy that she should buy.

LG4

3. Using the premium schedules provided in Exhibits 8.2, 8.3, and 8.5, how much in *annual* premiums would a 25-year-old male have to pay for $100,000 of annual renewable term, level premium term, and whole life insurance? (Assume a five-year term or period of coverage.) How much would a 25-year-old woman have to pay for the same coverage? Consider a 40-year-old male (or female): Using annual premiums, compare the cost of 10 years of coverage under annual renewable and level premium term options and whole life insurance coverage. Relate the advantages and disadvantages of each policy type to their price differences.

LG6

4. Describe the key elements of an insurance policy illustration and explain what a prospective client should focus on in evaluating an illustration.

PFIN Student Study Tools—Visit CourseMate for PFIN 3. Log in at **www.cengagebrain.com**. Check out the bonus exercises and exhibits, interactive worksheets, Cool Apps, Smart Sites, Critical Thinking Cases, Money Online, Kiplinger videos, quizzing, and more.

9

INSURING YOUR HEALTH

LEARNING GOALS

LG1 Discuss why having adequate health insurance is important, and identify the factors contributing to the growing cost of health insurance.

LG2 Differentiate among the major types of health insurance plans, and identify major private and public health insurance providers and their programs.

LG3 Analyze your own health insurance needs and explain how to shop for appropriate coverage.

LG4 Explain the basic types of medical expenses covered by the policy provisions of health insurance plans.

LG5 Assess the need for and features of long-term-care insurance.

LG6 Discuss the features of disability income insurance and how to determine your need for it.

How Will This Affect Me? Having adequate health insurance is critically important to your financial plan. Health care costs have grown dramatically in recent years, and a major illness or accident could wipe you out financially if you are uninsured. Yet health insurance policies are complicated to price and to compare. This chapter explains the importance of health insurance and the key determinants of its costs. The various types of public and private health insurance are described and a framework for decision making is provided. This includes discussions of how to analyze your health insurance needs, how to make sense of common policy features, and policy buying tips. The implications of the ACA on your decisions are considered. This chapter also discusses how to determine whether you need long-term-care insurance or disability income insurance. After reading this chapter, you should understand how to insure your health most effectively and economically.

9-1 The Importance of Health Insurance Coverage

LG1 The next best thing to good health is a good health insurance plan. In recent years, the price of medical treatment has risen dramatically. The cost of a major illness can easily total tens (or even hundreds) of thousands of dollars in expense due to hospital, medical care, and loss of income. Health insurance helps you pay both routine and major medical care costs. Indeed, in 2012, about 62 percent of all U.S. personal bankruptcies were attributable to medical costs.

> ## In recent years, the price of medical treatment has risen dramatically.

After you read the chapter, explore the STUDY TOOLS listed on page 226.

Despite the financial importance of health insurance, nearly 16 percent of the population under the age of 65—about 50 million people—don't have health insurance. And about 9.8 percent (7.3 million) of children were without health insurance.

Exhibit 9.1 helps to explain why so many are uninsured; from 1999 to 2012, the average annual premium for families increased by about 260 percent! In 2011, the average annual premium was $5,429 for single coverage and $15,073 for family coverage. During 2011, the average percentage of health care premiums paid by covered workers was 28 percent for family plans.

Go to Smart Sites

Healthcare.gov has a state-specific interactive guide to help walk you through you choices in health care plans and providers. For online resources, whenever you see "*Go to Smart Sites*" in this chapter, visit CourseMate for PFIN 3. Log in at **www.cengagebrain.com**. ●

Costly advances in medical technology, an aging U.S. population, and a poor demand-and-supply distribution of health care facilities and services have fueled rapidly rising health care costs. In addition, administrative costs, excessive paperwork, increased regulation, and insurance fraud are also contributing to rising health care costs.

It can be risky to go without adequate health insurance coverage. Concern over health care costs and the number of uninsured Americans has made health care reform a major priority of Congress and the administration. Policy solutions concerning the proper mix between government-run and privately run health insurance programs continue to prompt vigorous debate even after the passage of the Patient Protection and Affordable Care Act and the Reconciliation Act of 2010 (ACA), which is discussed in detail next. Clearly, becoming familiar with current health insurance options and issues should help you make better decisions as well as provide a useful perspective on the health care reform debate.

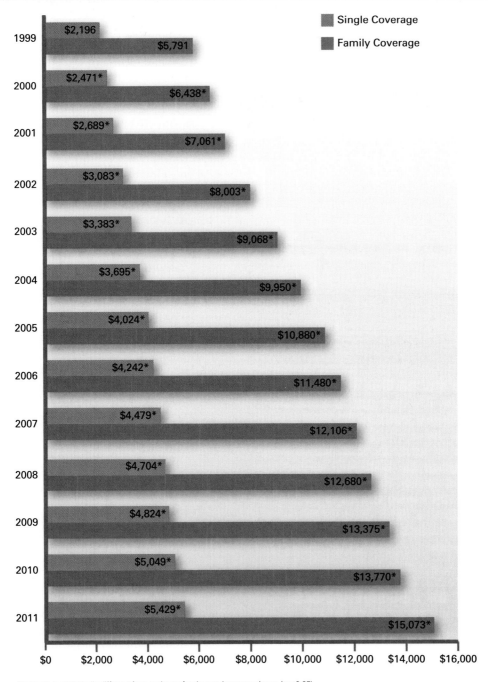

Single Coverage
Family Coverage

Year	Single	Family
1999	$2,196	$5,791
2000	$2,471*	$6,438*
2001	$2,689*	$7,061*
2002	$3,083*	$8,003*
2003	$3,383*	$9,068*
2004	$3,695*	$9,950*
2005	$4,024*	$10,880*
2006	$4,242*	$11,480*
2007	$4,479*	$12,106*
2008	$4,704*	$12,680*
2009	$4,824*	$13,375*
2010	$5,049*	$13,770*
2011	$5,429*	$15,073*

*Estimate is statistically different from estimate for the previous year shown ($p < 0.05$).

Source: Kaiser/HRET Survey of Employer-Sponsored Health Benefits, 1999–2011.

9-2 Health Insurance Plans

LG2 Health insurance coverage can be obtained from private sources and government-sponsored programs. In recent years, 28 percent of national health care expenditures were paid for by households, private businesses paid 21 percent, state and local governments paid 16 percent, and the federal government paid 27 percent.

9-2a Private Health Insurance Plans

Private companies sell a variety of health insurance plans to both groups and individuals. **Group health insurance** is a contract written between a group (such as an employer, union, credit union, or other organization) and the health care provider: a private insurance company, Blue Cross/Blue Shield plan, or managed care organization. Typically, group plans provide comprehensive medical expense coverage and may also offer prescription drug, dental, and vision care services.

If your employer has more than just a few employees, you'll probably have access to some type of group health plan. Due to today's high cost of health care, most employers require employees to pay part of the cost. Some groups self-insure, which means that they take responsibility for the full or partial payment of claims. Health insurance coverage can also be purchased on an individual basis directly from providers. To control rising costs, many employers underwrite employee health care coverage much the way insurers do. In addition, many employers are shifting a larger percentage of health care costs to employees. So be sure to compare group and individual policies before deciding which coverage to buy.

Most private health insurance plans fall into one of two categories: traditional *indemnity (fee-for-service) plans* and *managed care plans*, which include health maintenance organizations (HMOs), preferred provider organizations (PPOs), and similar plans. Both categories of plans cover, in somewhat different ways, the medical care costs arising from illness or accidents. Exhibit 9.2 compares the key differences among the three most common types of health plans.

Traditional Indemnity (Fee-for-Service) Plans

With a traditional **indemnity (fee-for-service) plan**, the health care provider is separate from your insurer.

Your insurer either pays the provider directly or reimburses your expenses when you submit claims for medical treatment. Typically, indemnity plans pay 80 percent of the eligible health care expenses, and the insured pays the other 20 percent. The health insurance company will begin paying its share after you pay a deductible amount of expenses, which typically ranges from $100 to over $2,000. The lower your deductible, the higher your premium.

The amount the insurance company pays is commonly based on the usual, customary, and reasonable (UCR) charges—what the insurer considers to be the prevailing fees within your area, not what your doctor or hospital actually charges. If your doctor charges more than the UCR, you may be responsible for the full amount of the excess. UCR charges vary significantly among insurers, so you should compare your doctor's fees with what a plan pays. Under many indemnity plans, physicians who accept the insurance agree to accept the UCR payments set by the insurer. It should be noted that there are very few indemnity plans left in the United States.

Managed Care Plans

Today, employers are moving toward **managed care plans** under which subscribers/users contract with and make monthly payments directly to the organization that provides the health care service. Most major

group health insurance Health insurance consisting of contracts written between a group, (employer, union, etc.) and the health care provider.

indemnity (fee-for-service) plan Health insurance plan in which the health care provider is separate from the insurer, who pays the provider or reimburses you for a specified percentage of expenses after a deductible amount has been met.

managed care plan A health care plan in which subscribers/users contract with the provider organization, which uses a designated group of providers meeting specific selection standards to furnish health care services for a monthly fee.

Exhibit 9.2	How the Most Common Types of Health Plans Compare

This table highlights some of the key differences among the three most common types of health plans.

Type	Choice of Service Providers	Premium Cost	Out-of-Pocket Costs	Annual Deductible
Indemnity	Yes	Low if high-deductible plan, high if low-deductible plan	Usually 20 percent of medical expenses plus deductible	Yes
HMO	No	Low	Low co-pay	No
PPO	Some	Higher than HMO	Low if using network providers, higher if provider is outside the network	No

© Cengage Learning

DBLIGHT/ISTOCKPHOTO.COM

health maintenance organization (HMO) An organization of hospitals, physicians, and other health care providers who have joined to provide comprehensive health care services to its members, who pay a monthly fee.

group HMO An HMO that provides health care services *from a central facility;* most prevalent in larger cities.

health insurance companies offer both indemnity and managed care plans. Managed care plan members receive comprehensive health care services from a designated group of doctors, hospitals, and other providers.

Under a managed care plan, the insured pays no deductibles and only a small fee, or co-payment, for office visits and medications. Most medical services—including preventive and routine care that indemnity plans may not cover—are fully covered when obtained from plan providers. Managed care plans include health maintenance organizations (HMOs), preferred provider organizations (PPOs), exclusive provider organizations (EPOs), and point-of-service (POS) plans.

HEALTH MAINTENANCE ORGANIZATIONS. A **health maintenance organization (HMO)** is an organization of hospitals, physicians, and other health care providers that provides comprehensive health care services to its members. HMO members pay

a monthly fee that varies according to the number of people in their family. A co-payment of $5 to $30 is charged each time services are provided by the HMO or a prescription is filled. The services provided to HMO members include doctors' office visits, imaging and laboratory services, preventive care, health screenings, hospital inpatient care and surgery, maternity care, mental health care, and drug prescriptions. The advantages of HMO membership include a lack of deductibles, few or no exclusions, and not having to file insurance claims. In the past, the primary disadvantage was that HMO members couldn't always choose their physicians and might face limitations if they needed care outside of the geographic area of their HMO. However, in recent years, many HMOs don't require members to pick one primary care physician, some don't require referrals, and almost all offer some flexibility to get coverage out of network.

There are two main types of HMOs: group and individual practice associations. A **group HMO** employs a group of doctors to provide health care services to members *from a central facility*. Often, the group HMO's hospital facilities are located in the same facility. Group HMOs are most prevalent in larger cities.

An **individual practice association (IPA)** is the most popular type of HMO. IPA members receive medical care from individual physicians practicing *from their own offices and from community hospitals* that are affiliated with the IPA. As a member of an IPA, you have some choice of which doctors and hospitals to use.

PREFERRED PROVIDER ORGANIZATIONS. A **preferred provider organization (PPO)** is a managed care plan that has the characteristics of both an IPA and an indemnity plan. An insurance company or provider group contracts with a network of physicians and hospitals that agree to accept a negotiated fee for medical services provided to the PPO members. Unlike the HMO, however, a PPO also provides insurance coverage for medical services not provided by the PPO network, so you can choose to go to other doctors or hospitals. However, you will pay a higher price for medical services provided by network doctors and hospitals.

OTHER MANAGED CARE PLANS. You may encounter two other forms of managed care plans. An **exclusive provider organization (EPO)** contracts with medical providers to offer services to members at reduced costs, but it reimburses members only when affiliated providers are used. Plan members who use a nonaffiliated provider must bear the entire cost. The **point-of-service (POS) plan** is a hybrid form of HMO that allows members to go outside of the HMO network for care. Payment for nonaffiliated physician services is similar to indemnity plan payments: the plan pays a specified percentage of the cost after your medical costs reach an annual deductible.

Blue Cross/Blue Shield Plans

In a technical sense, **Blue Cross/Blue Shield plans** are not insurance policies but rather prepaid hospital and medical expense plans. Today, there are about 38 independent local Blue Cross/Blue Shield

organizations, all of them for-profit corporations, which cover around 100 million people.

Blue Cross contracts with hospitals that agree to provide specified hospital services to members of subscriber groups in exchange for a specified fee or payment. Blue Cross also contracts for surgical and medical services. Blue Cross serves as the intermediary between the groups that want these services and the physicians who contractually agree to provide them. Today, many Blue Cross and Blue Shield plans have combined to form one provider, and they compete for business with other private insurance companies. Blue Cross/Blue Shield payments for health care services are seldom made to the subscriber but rather directly to the participating hospital or physician.

9-2b Government Health Insurance Plans

In addition to health insurance coverage provided by private sources, federal and state agencies provide health care coverage to eligible individuals. About 31 percent of the U.S. population is covered by some form of government health insurance program. For example, prior to the implementation of the ACA, the government offered the Pre-Existing Condition Insurance Plan (PCIP), which provided health coverage to U.S. citizens or others residing in the United States legally who have been denied health insurance because of a pre-existing condition, so long as the person had been uninsured for at least six months. The program was administered by both the states and by the federal government. In addition, some states provide health insurance for children who do not qualify for Medicaid (discussed next), but whose family still has very low income.

Medicare

Medicare is a health insurance program administered by the Social Security Administration. It's primarily designed to help persons 65 and over meet their

individual practice association (IPA) A form of HMO in which subscribers receive services from physicians practicing *from their own offices and from community hospitals* affiliated with the IPA.

preferred provider organization (PPO) A health provider that combines the characteristics of the IPA form of HMO with an indemnity plan to provide comprehensive health care services to its subscribers within a network of physicians and hospitals.

exclusive provider organization (EPO) A managed care plan that is similar to a PPO but reimburses members only when affiliated providers are used.

point-of-service (POS) plan A hybrid form of HMO that allows members to go outside the HMO network for care and reimburses them at a specified percentage of the cost.

Blue Cross/Blue Shield plans Prepaid hospital and medical expense plans under which health care services are provided to plan participants by member hospitals and physicians.

Medicare A health insurance plan administered by the federal government to help persons age 65 and over, and others receiving monthly Social Security disability benefits, to meet their health care costs.

supplementary medical insurance (SMI) A voluntary program under Medicare (commonly called *Part B*) that provides payments for services not covered under basic hospital insurance (*Part A*).

Medicare Advantage plans Commonly called *Plan C*, these plans provide Medicare benefits to eligible people, but they differ in that they are administered by private providers rather than by the government. Common supplemental benefits include vision, hearing, dental, general checkups, and health and wellness programs.

prescription drug coverage A voluntary program under Medicare (commonly called *Part D*), insurance that covers both brand-name and generic prescription drugs at participating pharmacies. Participants pay a monthly fee and a yearly deductible and must also pay part of the cost of prescriptions, including a co-payment or co-insurance.

health care costs, but it also covers many people under 65 who receive monthly Social Security disability benefits. Funds for Medicare benefits come from Social Security taxes paid by covered workers and their employers. Medicare provides basic hospital insurance, supplementary medical insurance, and prescription drug coverage.

- **Basic hospital insurance.** This coverage (commonly called *Part A*) provides inpatient hospital services such as room, board, and other customary inpatient service for the first 90 days of illness. A deductible is applied during the first 60 days of illness. Co-insurance provisions, applicable to days 61–90 of the hospital stay, can further reduce benefits. Medicare also covers all or part of the cost of up to 100 days in posthospital extended-care facilities that provide skilled care, such as nursing homes. However, it doesn't cover the most common types of nursing home care—intermediate and custodial care. Medicare basic hospital insurance also covers some posthospital medical services such as intermittent nursing care, therapy, rehabilitation, and home health care. Medicare deductibles and co-insurance amounts are revised annually to reflect changing medical costs.

- **Supplementary medical insurance.** The **supplementary medical insurance (SMI)** program (commonly called *Part B*) covers the services of physicians and surgeons in addition to the costs of medical and health services such as imaging, laboratory tests, prosthetic devices, rental of medical equipment, and ambulance transportation. It also covers some home health services (such as in-home visits by a registered nurse) and limited psychiatric care. Unlike Medicare's basic hospital insurance, SMI is a *voluntary program* for which participants pay premiums, which are then matched with government funds. Anyone age 65 or over can enroll in SMI.

- **Medicare Advantage plans.** Medicare Advantage (commonly called *Plan C*) plans provide Medicare benefits to eligible people, but they differ in that they are administered by private providers rather than by the government. Common supplemental benefits include vision, hearing, dental, general checkups, and health and wellness programs. These supplemental benefits are a major reason for interest in these plans. Medicare pays the private health plan a fixed amount every month for each member. The members may pay a monthly premium in addition to the Medicare Part B premium. However, many of the private providers don't charge a premium beyond the Medicare Part B premium, which the member pays directly to Medicare. Members usually pay a fixed amount (for example, a co-payment of $30), every time they visit a doctor, rather than pay a deductible and buy co-insurance (typically 20 percent) under original Medicare. Private plans may use some of the excess payments that they receive from the government to offer supplemental benefits. Most of the plans also include Medicare prescription drug coverage, discussed next. Because Medicare Advantage plans cost the federal government more than standard Medicare, the subsidies paid to these plans will start to decline under the ACA, which may lead to higher premiums or reduced benefits. However, the benefits cannot be reduced if they could normally be received from standard Medicare.

- **Prescription drug coverage.** The **prescription drug coverage** program (commonly called *Part D*) is insurance covering both brand-name and generic prescription drugs at participating pharmacies. It's intended to provide protection for people who have very high drug costs. All Medicare recipients are eligible for this coverage, regardless of their income and resources, health status, or existing prescription expenses. There are several ways to obtain this coverage. Participants in this *voluntary program* pay a monthly fee and a yearly deductible, which was $320 in 2012. They also pay part of the cost of prescriptions, including a co-payment or co-insurance. The plan provides extra help—paying almost all prescription drug costs—for the 1 in 3 Medicare recipients who have limited income and resources.

Although Medicare pays for many health care expenses for the disabled and those over 65, there are still gaps in its coverage. Many Medicare enrollees buy private insurance policies to fill in these gaps.

Medicaid

Medicaid is a state-run public assistance program that provides health insurance benefits only to those who are unable to pay for health care. Each state has its own Medicaid regulations, eligibility requirements, and covered medical services. Although Medicaid is primarily funded by each state, the federal government also contributes funds. More than 58 million people are covered by Medicaid. Depending on how individual states respond to the flexibility in handling Medicaid granted by the 2012 Supreme Court decision on the ACA, millions more could qualify for Medicaid by 2014.

Workers' Compensation Insurance

Workers' compensation insurance is designed to compensate workers who are injured on the job or become ill through work-related causes. Although mandated by the federal government, each state is responsible for workers' compensation legislation and regulation. Specifics vary from state to state, but typical workers' compensation benefits include medical and rehabilitation expenses, disability income, and scheduled lump-sum amounts for death and certain injuries, such as dismemberment. Employers bear nearly the entire cost of workers' compensation insurance in most states. Premiums are based on historical usage; employers who file the most claims pay the highest rates. Self-employed people are required to contribute to workers' compensation for themselves and their employees.

Affordable Health Care Act of 2010

The Patient Protection and Affordable Care Act and the Reconciliation Act of 2010 (usually just called the Affordable Health Care Act, or ACA) is extensive and remains controversial. Its legality was contested, and the U.S. Supreme Court affirmed its constitutionality in June 2012. In making health care insurance decisions, it's important to understand the broad strokes of the new law.

The Supreme Court left most of the provisions of the ACA in place. Some of the key elements of the law are described here.

- **Individual mandate.** All Americans are required to have or buy health insurance beginning in 2014 or pay a penalty. The penalty starts at the greater of $285 per family or 1 percent of income and increases to $2,085 per family or 2.5 percent of income by 2016.

- **Coverage of young adults.** Insurers are required under the law to cover the children of those they insure up to the age of 26. It's estimated that the law allows about 2.5 million children of the insured between the ages of 19 and 25 to remain covered by their parents' health insurance.

- **Pre-existing health conditions.** Insurers are required to cover people with pre-existing medical conditions without limiting or setting unrealistically high insurance rates. Similarly, children younger than the age of 19 cannot be denied benefits or have their benefits limited due to a pre-existing medical condition.

- **Health care insurance exchanges.** Health insurance exchanges will operate in each state. They will provide a marketplace where individuals and small businesses can compare policy features and premiums and buy health insurance. Government subsidies will be available under some circumstances. Exchanges will not consist of insurance companies, but they will determine which insurers are allowed to offer policies on them. Consequently, they are designed to promote health insurance policy transparency and accountability, help broaden the number of insured people, help distribute subsidies, and help facilitate the risk-spreading that will keep insurance premiums reasonable.

Medicaid A state-run public assistance program that provides health insurance benefits only to those who are unable to pay for health care.

workers' compensation insurance Health insurance required by state and federal governments and paid nearly in full by employers in most states; it compensates workers for job-related illness or injury.

© ANDI BERGER/SHUTTERSTOCK.COM

- **Small-firm coverage of employees**. The law requires small firms with more than 50 full-time employees to provide health insurance coverage or pay expensive fines.

The Supreme Court ruled that the part of the law related to Medicaid must change. The law requires expanded eligibility for Medicaid benefits, which would be paid for by both the federal government and the states. Specifically, the law threatened to remove federal funding from states that did not provide this expanded Medicaid eligibility. The Court decided that this threat must be removed. Thus, as noted above, the states have some flexibility in how they deal with Medicaid under the ACA.

The ACA's expenditures are to be financed by several sources of revenue. These include higher Medicare taxes, fees on insurers, and an excise tax on "Cadillac" insurance policies. It is hoped that changes in the Medicare program will provide some offsetting cost savings. The long-term net effect of the ACA on the federal budget deficit remains a hotly debated topic. However, the above key provisions of the law will influence the coverage and cost of your health insurance. Therefore, it's important to understand how health insurance policies are currently structured so that you'll be in a good position to appreciate the significance of the changes that will be brought by the law as it is phased in.

9-3 Health Insurance Decisions

LG3 How can you systematically plan your health insurance purchases? As with other insurance decisions, you'll need to consider potential areas of loss, types of coverage and other resources available to you and your family, and any gaps in protection. Then you can choose a health insurance plan that's best for you.

9-3a Evaluate Your Health Care Cost Risk

Most people need protection against two costs resulting from illness or accidents: (1) expenses for medical care and rehabilitation and (2) loss of income or household services. The cost of medical care can't be estimated easily; but in cases of long-term, serious illness, medical bills and related expenses can easily run into hundreds of thousands of dollars. An adequate amount of protection against these costs for most people would be at least $300,000 and, with a protracted illness or disability, as much as $1 million. In contrast, lost income is typically calculated as a percentage of your (or your spouse's) current monthly earnings, generally 60 percent to 75 percent.

A good health insurance plan embodies more than financing medical expenses, lost income,

and replacement services. It should incorporate other means of risk reduction such as risk avoidance, loss prevention and control, and risk assumption.

- **Risk avoidance**. Look for ways to avoid exposure to health care loss before it occurs. For example, people who don't take illegal drugs never have to worry about disability from overdose, people who refuse to ride on motorcycles avoid the high risk of injury, and people who don't smoke in bed are a lot less likely to doze off and start a fire in their house.

- **Loss prevention and control**. Accept responsibility for your own well-being and live a healthier lifestyle to prevent illness and reduce high medical costs. Smoking, alcohol and drug dependency, improper diet, inadequate sleep, and lack of regular exercise contribute to more than 60 percent of all diagnosed illnesses. Eliminating some or all of these factors from your lifestyle can reduce your chances of becoming ill. Similarly, following highway safety laws, not driving while intoxicated, and wearing a seat belt help prevent injury from car accidents.

- **Risk assumption**. Consider the health risks that you're willing to retain. Some risks pose relatively small loss potential and you can budget for them rather than insure against them. For example, choosing insurance plans with deductibles and waiting periods is a form of risk assumption because it's more economical to pay small amounts from savings than to pay higher premiums to cover them.

9-3b Determine Available Coverage and Resources

Some employers providing health insurance as an employee benefit offer only one plan and pay either all or part of the premiums. If you work for an employer who provides health insurance this way, you should evaluate the plan's benefits and costs to determine if additional coverage—either for yourself or your dependents—is necessary. Other employers offer their employees a choice among several types of health insurance plans during an open enrollment period each year.

Some employers offer employees a *flexible-benefit ("cafeteria") plan* that allows employees to choose fringe benefits. Typically, the menu of benefits includes more than one health insurance option, as well as life insurance, disability income insurance, and other benefits. The employer specifies a set dollar amount that it will provide, and employees choose a combination of benefits. If the employee wants or needs additional insurance benefits, most employers will deduct the additional cost of providing them from the employee's paycheck.

Some employers offer consumer-directed health plans that go one step beyond a flexible-benefit plan. These plans combine a high-deductible health insurance policy with a tax-free **health reimbursement account (HRA)**, a plan funded by employers for each participating employee. When the account balance is used up, you must pay the remaining deductible of the health insurance policy before insurance begins to pay. You can "roll over" the amount of unused money annually.

Another similar type of account is the **health savings account (HSA)**. The HSA is also a tax-free account, but the money is contributed by employees or employers (or both) for use in paying routine medical costs. An HSA is also combined with a high-deductible insurance policy to pay for catastrophic care in case of major accident or illness, and—as with an HRA—any unused money can be rolled over each year. If you change jobs, the money in your HSA belongs only to you and is yours to keep. In addition to the HSA and HRA, there are many other consumer-directed health plans.

If you are married and your spouse is employed, you should evaluate his or her benefit package before making any decisions. You may, for example, already be covered under your spouse's group health insurance plan or be able to purchase coverage for yourself and family members at a cheaper rate than through your own employer's plan.

Another important area of group coverage to consider is retiree benefits. Some companies provide health insurance to retirees, but most don't, so you probably shouldn't count on receiving employer-paid benefits once you retire. Know what your options are to ensure continued coverage for both you and your family after you retire. Medicare will cover basic medical expenses, but you'll probably need to supplement this coverage with one of the 12 standard Medigap plans, which are termed plans "A" through "L."

There are several other possible sources of health care coverage. Homeowner's and automobile insurance policies often contain limited amounts of medical expense protection. For example, your automobile policy may cover your medical expenses if you're involved in an auto accident regardless of whether you're in a car, on foot, or on a bicycle when the accident occurs. In addition to Social Security's Medicare program, various other government programs help pay medical expenses. For instance, medical care is provided for people who've served in the armed services and were honorably discharged. Public health programs exist to treat communicable diseases, handicapped children, and mental health disorders.

If you need or want to purchase additional medical insurance coverage on an individual basis, you can purchase a variety of policies from a private insurance company such as Aetna, CIGNA, and United Healthcare. You should buy health care plans from an insurance agent who will listen to your needs and provide well-thought-out responses to your questions. You should also research carriers and choose one that is rated highly by at least two of the major ratings agencies and that has a reputation for settling claims

fairly and promptly. The National Committee for Quality Assurance (NCQA) is a non-profit, unbiased organization that issues annual "report cards" that rate the service quality of various health plans.

9-3c Choose a Health Insurance Plan

After familiarizing yourself with the different health insurance plans and providers and reviewing your needs, you must choose one or more plans to provide coverage. If you're employed, first review the various health insurance plans that your company offers. If you can't get coverage from an employer, get plan descriptions and policy costs from several providers—including a group plan from a professional or trade organization, if available—for both indemnity and managed care plans. Then take your time and carefully read the plan materials to understand exactly what is covered and at what cost. Next, review your past medical costs, estimate your future costs, and use them to see what your costs would be under various plans.

You'll have to ask yourself some difficult questions to decide whether you want an indemnity or a managed care plan and then to choose the particular plan.

Go to Smart Sites

What grade did your health plan get on its quality "report card" this year? The National Committee for Quality Assurance (NCQA) can tell you. ●

● **How important is cost compared with having freedom of choice?** You may have to pay more to stay with your current doctor if he or she is not part of a managed care plan that you're considering. Also, you have to decide if you can tolerate the managed care plan's approach to health care.

Some states have experimented in recent years with the **community rating approach to health insurance premium pricing**, which prohibits insurance companies from varying rates based on health status or claims history. The community is defined as the area in which the insurance is offered. In the "pure" approach, all policyholders in an area pay the same premium without regard to their personal health, age, gender, or other factors. Under the adjusted (modified) community rating approach insurers can adjust premiums based only on your family size,

health reimbursement account (HRA) An account into which employers place contributions that employees can use to pay for medical expenses. Usually combined with a high-deductible health insurance policy.

health savings account (HSA) A tax-free savings account—funded by employees, employer, or both—to spend on routine medical costs. Usually combined with a high deductible policy to pay for catastrophic care.

community rating approach to health insurance premium pricing Policyholders in a community (area) pay the same premium without regard to their personal health, age, gender, or other factors.

GUNNAR PIPPEL/SHUTTERSTOCK.COM

Financial Road Sign

Choosing a Health Insurance Plan

Ask the following questions when choosing among health care insurance plans:

- Can I choose to use any doctor, hospital, clinic, or pharmacy?
- What coverage, if any, is provided for seeing specialists like eye doctors and dentists?
- Does the plan cover special conditions or treatments like psychiatric care, pregnancy, and physical therapy?
- Does the plan cover home care or nursing home care?
- What kind of limitations are there on the coverage of prescribed medications?
- What are the deductible and any co-payment amounts?
- What is the maximum that I would have to pay out of health care expenses, either in a calendar year or during my lifetime?
- How are billing or service disputes handled under the plan?

Source: Adapted from "Choosing a Health Insurance Plan," http://www.usa.gov/topics/health/health-insurance/choosing.shtml, accessed September 2012.

where you live, whether you use tobacco, and your age. Starting in 2014, the ACA requires insurance companies to adhere to the adjusted community rating approach for individuals and small businesses.

- **Will you be reimbursed if you choose a managed care plan and want to see an out-of-network provider?** For most people, the managed care route is cheaper—even if you visit a doctor only once a year—because of indemnity plans' "reasonable charge" provisions.

- **What types of coverage do you need?** Everyone has different needs; one person may want a plan with good maternity and pediatric care whereas another may want outpatient mental health benefits. Make sure the plans that you consider offer what you want.

- **How good is the managed care network?** Look at the participating doctors and hospitals to see how many of your providers are part of the plan. Check out the credentials of participating providers; a good sign is accreditation from the NCQA. Are the providers' locations convenient for you? What preventive medical programs does it provide? Has membership grown? Talk to friends and associates to see what their experiences have been with the plan.

- **How old are you, and how is your health?** Many financial advisors recommend buying the lowest-cost plan—which may be an indemnity plan with a high deductible—if you're young and healthy.

After considering all of the coverages and resources available to you, isolate gaps in your health insurance coverage and determine how best to fill them. Doing this requires an understanding of the features, policy provisions, and coverage provided by various insurance carriers and policies. We'll discuss these in detail in the next section.

9-4 Medical Expense Coverage and Policy Provisions

LG4 To evaluate different insurance plan options, you should compare and contrast what they cover and how each plan's policy provisions may affect you and your family. By doing so, you can decide which health plan offers the best protection at the most reasonable cost. Worksheet 9.1 provides a convenient checklist for comparing the costs and benefits of competing health insurance plans.

9-4a Types of Medical Expense Coverage

The medical services covered vary among health plans. You can purchase narrowly defined plans that cover only what you consider to be the most important medical services or, if you want the comfort of broader coverage and can afford it, you can purchase insurance that covers most or all of your health care needs. Here, we describe the medical expenses most commonly covered by health insurance.

 After considering all of the coverages and resources available to you, isolate gaps in your health insurance coverage and determine how best to fill them.

Hospitalization

A *hospitalization insurance policy* reimburses you for the cost of your hospital stay. Hospitalization policies usually pay for a portion of (1) the hospital's daily semiprivate room rate, which typically includes meals,

Here is a convenient checklist that you can use to compare the costs and benefits of competing health care plans.

Check those services listed in the first column that are most important to you, determine how these services are handled in each policy, and then write in the co-insurance or co-payment rate and any limits on service under each of the different policy columns. The most important covered service is hospitalization.

Service	Policy #1	Policy #2	Policy #3
Hospital care			
Surgery (inpatient and outpatient)			
Office visits to your doctor			
Maternity care			
Well-baby care			
Immunizations			
Mammograms			
Medical tests, x-rays			
Mental health care			
Dental care, braces and cleaning			
Vision care, eyeglasses and exams			
Prescription drugs			
Home health care			
Nursing home care			
Services you need that are excluded			
Choice of doctors			
Location of doctors and hospitals			
Ease of getting an appointment			
Minimal paperwork			
Waiting period for coverage			

Source: Information provided by ShapeFit.com

© Cengage Learning

nursing care, and other routine services, and (2) the cost of ancillary services such as laboratory tests, imaging, and medications you receive while hospitalized. Many hospitalization plans also cover some outpatient and out-of-hospital services once you're discharged, such as in-home rehabilitation, diagnostic treatment, and preadmission testing. Some hospitalization plans merely pay a flat daily amount for each day the insured is in the hospital, regardless of actual charges. Most policies limit the number of days of hospitalization and a maximum dollar amount on ancillary services that they will pay for.

Surgical Expenses

Surgical expense insurance covers the cost of surgery in or out of the hospital. Usually, surgical expense coverage is provided as part of a hospitalization insurance policy or as a rider to such a policy. Most plans reimburse you for *reasonable and customary* surgical expenses based on a survey of surgical costs during the previous year. They may also cover anesthesia, non-emergency treatment using imaging, and a limited allowance for diagnostic tests. Some plans still pay according to a *schedule of benefits*, reimbursing up to a fixed maximum for a particular surgical procedure. For example, the policy might state that you would receive no more than $1,500 for an appendectomy or $1,200 for diagnostic arthroscopic surgery on a knee. Scheduled benefits are often inadequate when compared with typical surgical costs. Most elective cosmetic surgeries, such as a "nose job" or "tummy tuck," are typically excluded from reimbursement unless they are deemed a medical necessity.

Physician Expenses

Physicians expense insurance, also called *regular medical expense insurance*, covers the cost of visits to a doctor's office or for a doctor's hospital visits, including consultation with a specialist. Also covered are imaging and laboratory tests performed outside of a hospital. Plans are offered on either a *reasonable and customary* or *scheduled benefit* basis. Sometimes, the first few visits with the physician for any single cause are excluded. This exclusion serves the same purpose as the deductible and waiting period features found in other types of insurance. Often, these plans specify a maximum payment per visit, as well as a maximum number of visits per injury or illness.

Major Medical Insurance

Major medical plans provide broad coverage for nearly all types of medical expenses resulting from either illnesses or accidents. In the past, it was common to have lifetime limits of $500,000 or $1,000,000. However, the ACA eliminates lifetime limits on total health care insurance payments by insurers. Because hospitalization, surgical, and physicians expense coverage meets the smaller medical costs, major medical is used to finance more catastrophic medical costs. Many people buy major medical with a high deductible to protect against a catastrophic illness.

Comprehensive Major Medical Insurance

A **comprehensive major medical insurance** plan combines basic hospitalization, surgical, and physicians expense coverage with major medical protection into a single policy, usually with a low deductible. Comprehensive major medical insurance is often written under a group contract, although efforts have been taken to make this type of coverage available to individuals.

Dental Services

Dental insurance covers necessary dental care and some dental injuries sustained through accidents. (Expenses for accidental damage to natural teeth are normally covered under standard surgical expense and major medical policies.) Covered services may include examinations, X-rays, dental cleanings, fillings, extractions, dentures, root canal therapy, orthodontics, and oral surgery. The maximum coverage under most dental policies is often low—$1,000 to $2,500 per patient—so these plans don't fully protect against high dental work costs.

The types of health plans discussed so far are sufficient to meet the protection needs of most individuals and families. But insurance companies offer other options that provide limited protection against certain types of perils:

- *Accident policies* that pay a specified sum to an insured injured in a certain type of accident
- *Sickness policies*, sometimes called *dread disease policies*, that pay a specified sum for a named disease, such as cancer
- *Hospital income policies* that guarantee a specific daily, weekly, or monthly amount so long as the insured is hospitalized

Remember that sound insurance planning seldom dictates the purchase of such policies. The cost of purchasing these insurance options typically outweighs the limited coverage they provide. Accident and sickness policies, for example, usually cover only one type of accident or illness, and hospital income policies generally exclude illnesses that could result in extended hospitalization and health conditions existing at the time of purchase.

© KONSTATIN SUTYAGIN/SHUTTERSTOCK.COM

The problem with buying policies that cover only a certain type of accident, illness, or financial need is that major gaps in coverage will often occur. Financial loss can be just as great if the insured falls down a flight of stairs or if she contracts cancer, lung disease, or heart disease. Most limited-peril policies should be used only to supplement a comprehensive insurance program if the coverage is not overlapping.

9-4b Policy Provisions of Medical Expense Plans

To compare the health insurance plans offered by different insurers, evaluate whether they contain liberal or restrictive provisions. Generally, policy provisions can be divided into two groups: terms of payment and terms of coverage.

Terms of Payment

Four provisions govern how much your health insurance plan will pay: (1) deductibles, (2) participation (co-insurance), (3) internal limits, and (4) coordination of benefits.

DEDUCTIBLES. Because major medical insurance plans are designed to supplement basic hospitalization, surgical, and physicians expense plans, those offered under an indemnity (fee-for-service) plan often have a relatively large *deductible*, typically $500 or $1,000. The **deductible** represents the initial amount that's *not* covered by the policy and thus must be paid by the insured. Comprehensive major medical plans tend to offer lower deductibles, sometimes $100 or less. Most plans offer a calendar-year, all-inclusive deductible, which allows the insured to accumulate the deductible from more than one incident of use. Some plans also include a *carryover provision*, whereby any part of the deductible that occurs during the final three months of the year (October, November, and December) can be applied to the current year's deductible and can *also* be applied to the following calendar year's deductible. In a few plans, the deductible is on a per-illness or per-accident basis. For example, if you were covered by this type of policy with a $1,000 deductible and suffered three separate accidents in one year, each requiring $1,000 of medical expenses, you wouldn't be eligible to collect any benefits from the major medical plan.

PARTICIPATION (CO-INSURANCE). A **participation**, or **co-insurance**, **clause** stipulates that the company will pay some portion—say, 80 percent or 90 percent—of the amount of the covered loss in excess of the deductible rather than the entire amount. Co-insurance helps reduce the possibility that policyholders will fake illness and discourages them from incurring unnecessary medical expenses. Many major medical plans also have a *stop-loss provision* that places a cap on the amount of participation required. Without a stop-loss

provision, a $1 million medical bill could leave the insured responsible for, say, $200,000 of costs. Often such provisions limit the insured's participation to less than $10,000 and sometimes to as little as $2,000.

INTERNAL LIMITS. Most major medical policies are written with **internal limits** that control the amounts paid for certain specified expenses—even if the claim *doesn't* exceed overall policy limits. Charges commonly subject to internal limits are hospital room and board, surgical fees, mental and nervous conditions, and nursing services. If an insured chooses an expensive physician or medical facility, then he or she is responsible for paying the portion of the charges that are above a "reasonable and customary" level or beyond a specified maximum amount. The following example shows how deductibles, co-insurance, and internal limits constrain the amount a company is obligated to pay under a major medical plan.

MAJOR MEDICAL POLICY: AN EXAMPLE. Assume that Roger Kane, a graduate student, has coverage under a major medical insurance policy that specifies a $500,000 lifetime limit of protection, a $1,000 deductible, an 80 percent co-insurance clause, internal limits of $350 per day on hospital room and board, and $6,000 as the maximum payable surgical fee. When Roger was hospitalized for three days to remove a small tumor, he incurred these costs:

Hospitalization: 3 days at $500 a day	$ 1,500
Surgical expense	5,800
Other covered medical expenses	3,800
Total medical expenses	$11,100

By the terms of the policy's co-insurance clause, the maximum the company must pay is 80 percent of the covered loss in excess of the deductible. Without internal limits, the company would pay $8,080 (0.80 × [$11,100 − $1,000]). The internal limits further restrict the payment. Even though 80 percent of the $500-per-day hospitalization charge is $400, the most the company would have to pay is $350 per day. Thus Roger, the insured, becomes liable for $50 per day for three days, or $150. The surgical expense is below the $6,000 internal limit,

deductible The initial amount *not* covered by an insurance policy and thus the insured's responsibility; it's usually determined on a calendar-year basis or on a per-illness or per-accident basis.

participation (co-insurance) clause A provision in many health insurance policies stipulating that the insurer will pay some portion—say, 80 percent or 90 percent—of the amount of the covered loss in excess of the deductible.

internal limits A feature commonly found in health insurance policies that limits the amounts that will be paid for certain specified expenses, even if the claim does *not* exceed overall policy limits.

coordination of benefits provision A provision often included in health insurance policies to prevent the insured from collecting more than 100 percent of covered charges; it requires that benefit payments be coordinated if the insured is eligible for benefits under more than one policy.

preexisting condition clause A clause included in most individual health insurance policies permitting permanent or temporary exclusion of coverage for any physical or mental problems the insured had at the time the policy was purchased. The Patient Protection and Affordable Care Act of 2010 outlawed such exclusions.

Health Insurance Portability and Accountability Act (HIPAA) Federal law that protects people's ability to obtain continued health insurance after they leave a job or retire, even if they have a serious health problem.

so the 80 percent co-insurance clause applies, and the insurer will pay $4,640 (0.80 × $5,800). The company's total obligation is reduced to $7,930 ($8,080 − $150), and Tom must pay a total of $3,170 ($1,000 deductible + 0.20 × [$11,100 − $1,000] co-insurance + $150 excess hospital room and board charges). This example shows that, even though major medical insurance can offer large amounts of reimbursement, the insured may still be responsible for substantial payments.

COORDINATION OF BENEFITS. Health insurance policies are not contracts of *indemnity*. This means that the insured party can collect multiple payments for the same illness or accident unless health insurance policies include a **coordination of benefits provision.** This clause prevents you from collecting more than 100 percent of covered charges by collecting benefits from more than one policy. For example, many private health insurance policies coordinate benefit provisions with medical benefits paid under workers' compensation. Others widely advertise that their policies will pay claims regardless of the policyholder's other coverage and, of course, often charge more per dollar of protection. Using policies with coordination of benefits clauses can help you prevent coverage overlaps and, ideally, reduce your premiums.

Considering the complexity of medical expense contracts, the various clauses limiting payments, and coordination of benefits with other policies, one might expect that insurers often pay only partial claims and sometimes completely deny claims. However, if you make a claim and don't receive satisfactory payment, don't give up. The Bonus Exhibit, "How to Get Paid on a Health Insurance Claim," provides some guidelines on how you might go about getting your health insurance claims paid. (Visit CourseMate for PFIN 3. Log in at **www.cengagebrain.com.**)

Terms of Coverage

Several contract provisions affect a health insurance plan's value to you. Some important provisions address (1) the persons and places covered, (2) cancellation, (3) preexisting conditions, (4) pregnancy and abortion, (5) mental illness, (6) rehabilitation coverage, and (7) continuation of group coverage.

PERSONS AND PLACES COVERED. Some health insurance policies cover only the named insured; others offer protection to all family members. Historically, of those that offer family coverage, some have terminated benefits payable on behalf of children at age 18 and others continued them to age 24 as long as the child remains in school or is single. *The health reform bill allows young adults to remain on their parents' insurance until they turn 26 years old.* Some policies protect you only while you're in the United States or Canada; others offer worldwide coverage but exclude certain specified countries.

CANCELLATION. Many health insurance policies are written to permit *cancellation* at the insurer's option at any time. Some policies explicitly state this; others don't. To protect yourself against premature cancellation, buy policies that specifically state that the insurer won't cancel coverage so long as premiums are paid.

PREEXISTING CONDITIONS. In the past, most health insurance policies sold to individuals (as opposed to group/employer-sponsored plans) contained a **preexisting condition clause.** This means the policy might exclude coverage for any physical or mental problems you had at the time you bought it. In some policies, the exclusion was permanent; in others, it lasted only for the first year or two that the coverage was in force. Some group insurance plans have also historically had preexisting condition clauses, but they tended to be less restrictive than those in individually written policies. The ACA has changed this. The new legislation prohibits insurers from denying coverage due to the presence of pre-existing conditions.

Employees who have recently left a job or retired are covered by the **Health Insurance Portability and Accountability Act,** or **HIPAA.** This federal law, implemented in 1996, is designed to protect people's ability to obtain continued health insurance after they leave a job or retire, even if they have a serious health problem. Under HIPAA, if you've already been covered by a health plan without a break in coverage of more than 63 days and you apply for new insurance, insurers cannot turn you down, charge you higher premiums, or enforce an exclusionary period because of your health status. HIPAA doesn't guarantee you group coverage, but it does protect your ability to buy individual health insurance. While HIPAA will provide protection until the ACA is fully implemented, under that legislation, insurers are not able to deny coverage for pre-existing conditions.

PREGNANCY AND ABORTION. Many individual and group health insurance plans include special clauses for medical expenses incurred through pregnancy or abortion. Some liberal policies pay for all related expenses, including sick-leave pay during the final months of pregnancy, whereas others pay for medical expenses that result from pregnancy or abortion complications, but not for routine procedure expenses. In the most restrictive cases, policies offer no coverage for any costs of pregnancy or abortion.

MENTAL ILLNESS. Many health insurance plans omit or offer only reduced benefits for treatment of mental disorders. For example, a health insurance policy may offer hospitalization benefits that continue to pay so long as you remain hospitalized—except for mental illness. It may restrict payment for mental illness to one-half the normally provided payment amounts and for a period not to exceed 30 days. Unfortunately, mental illness is the number one sickness requiring long-term hospital care. Because coverage for mental illness is an important insurance protection, check your policies to learn how liberal—or how restrictive—they are regarding this feature.

NENAD ALSIC/ISTOCKPHOTO.COM

REHABILITATION COVERAGE. Health insurance plans focus primarily on meeting reasonable and necessary medical expenses. But many policies also include *rehabilitation coverage* for counseling, occupational therapy, and even some educational or job training programs for insureds who are partially or totally disabled because of an illness or accident. This is a good feature to look for in major medical and disability income policies.

CONTINUATION OF GROUP COVERAGE. Under the *Consolidated Omnibus Budget Reconciliation Act (COBRA)*, passed by Congress in 1986, an employee who leaves the insured group voluntarily or involuntarily (except in the case of "gross misconduct") may elect to continue coverage for up to 18 months by paying premiums to his or her former employer on time (up to 102 percent of the company cost). The employee retains all benefits previously available, except for disability income coverage.

Similar continuation coverage is available for retirees and their families for up to 18 months or until they become eligible for Medicare, whichever occurs first. An employee's dependents may be covered for up to 36 months under COBRA under special circumstances, such as divorce or death of the employee. After COBRA coverage expires, most states provide for conversion of the group coverage to an individual policy regardless of the insured's current health and without evidence of insurability.

9-4c Cost Containment Provisions for Medical Expense Plans

In response to the ongoing inflation in medical costs, insurers and employers that sponsor medical expense plans try to control their costs. Cost containment provisions are included in almost all medical expense plans and include the following:

- **Preadmission certification.** This requires you to receive approval from your insurer before entering the hospital for a scheduled stay. Such approval is not normally required for emergency stays.

- **Continued stay review.** To receive normal reimbursement, the insured must secure approval from the insurer for any stay that exceeds the originally approved limits.

- **Second surgical opinions.** Many plans require second opinions on specific nonemergency procedures and, in their absence, may reduce the surgical benefits paid. Most surgical expense plans now fully reimburse the cost of second opinions.

- **Waiver of co-insurance.** Because insurers can save money on hospital room-and-board charges by encouraging outpatient surgery, many now agree to waive the co-insurance clause and pay 100 percent of surgical costs for outpatient procedures. A similar waiver is sometimes applied to generic pharmaceuticals. For example, the patient may choose between an 80 percent payment for a brand-name pharmaceutical costing $35 or 100 percent reimbursement for its $15 generic equivalent.

- **Limitation of insurer's responsibility.** Many policies also have provisions limiting the insurer's financial responsibility to reimbursing only for costs that are considered "reasonable and customary." This provision can sometimes place limitations on the type and place of medical care for which the insurer will pay.

9-5 Long-Term-Care Insurance

LG5 **Long-term care** involves the delivery of medical and personal care, other than hospitalization, to persons with chronic medical conditions in a nursing home, in an assisted living community, or in the patient's home. Long-term care is expensive; for example, a year's stay in a private nursing home averages over $81,000 according to a 2012 cost-of-care survey by Genworth Financial. About two-thirds of people reaching the age of 65 are expected to need long-term care at some time, and the average long-term stay is about 2½ years.

Consumers directly pay about 25 percent of long-term care costs, and government programs such as Medicare and Medicaid cover less than half of the total cost for those meeting their strict eligibility requirements. Major medical insurance plans also exclude most of the costs related to long-term care. Fortunately, long-term-care insurance policies are available that are indemnity policies paying a fixed dollar amount for each day you receive specified care either in a nursing home or at home. The decision to buy long-term-care insurance is an important part of health insurance and retirement financial planning.

The ACA has provisions that relate to long-term care. It includes the Community Living Assistance Services and Support Program (CLASS), which is a voluntary, consumer-financed insurance plan designed to cover long-term care expenses. This is similar to long-term-care programs currently available in the private market. However, it differs in that the program will be administered by the government. Further, any working adult who is 18 or older will be able to enroll, regardless of any pre-existing medical condition.

And the benefits will be good for as long as someone needs long-term care. However, the fate of the long-term-care parts of the ACA are currently unclear. The U.S. Department of Health and Human Services has questioned the financial viability of implementing the long-term-care program presented in the ACA.

Most individual long-term-care products are purchased either through organizations like the American Association of Retired Persons (AARP) or directly from the more than 100 insurance companies that offer them. Employer-sponsored long-term-care insurance is also growing in popularity. Usually, however, employees pay the full cost of premiums, although employer-sponsored plans can often cost less than purchasing long-term care on an individual basis. Whether you purchase long-term-care insurance as an individual or through an employer-sponsored plan, however, it's important to evaluate policy provisions and costs.

9-5a Do You Need Long-Term-Care Insurance?

The odds of needing more than a year of nursing home care before you reach age 65 are 1 in 33, and the expense of a prolonged nursing home stay can cause severe financial hardship. Answer the following questions to decide if you need long-term-care insurance:

- **Do you have many assets to preserve for your dependents?** Because you must deplete most of your assets before Medicaid will pay for nursing home care, some financial advisors recommend that people over 65 whose net worth is more than $100,000 and income exceeds $50,000 a year consider long-term-care insurance—*if* they can afford the premiums. The very wealthy, however, may prefer to self-insure.

- **Can you afford the premiums?** Premiums of many good-quality policies can be 5 percent to 7 percent of annual income or even more. Such high premiums may cause more financial hardship than the cost of a potential nursing home stay. You may be better off investing the amount you'd spend in premiums; it would then be available for *any* future need, including long-term health care.

- **Is there a family history of disabling disease?** This factor increases your odds of needing long-term care. If there's a history of Alzheimer's, neurological disorders, or other potentially debilitating diseases, the need for long-term-care insurance may increase.

 The odds of needing more than a year of nursing home care before you reach age 65 are 1 in 33, and the expense of a prolonged nursing home stay can cause severe financial hardship.

Behavioral Biases in Making Health Insurance Decisions

Research in behavioral economics indicates that individuals have difficulty making decisions involving uncertainty, trade-offs between current and future benefits and costs, or significant complexity are particularly challenging. Economic theory suggests that individuals will determine the expected satisfaction associated with each health insurance plan, compare that with the satisfaction associated with not buying insurance, and then choose the most comprehensively satisfying option. However, this analysis requires estimating the probabilities, financial costs, and levels of happiness associated with possible future health events such as having cancer or a heart attack. People find it hard to do this well.

Research shows that individuals tend to make systematic mistakes in estimating probabilities. For example, they are inclined to overestimate the likelihood of low-probability events, such as dying in a plane crash. And it's almost impossible for most people to estimate the financial costs associated with various health conditions. This is because, for the most part, there is no place to look up health service prices. Similarly, it's hard to predict your level of happiness under different health conditions. People tend to overestimate how much their happiness will decline if they become sick.

Health care choices often require absorbing costs today in the hope of future benefits. This is as much the case for preventative care as it is for more costly and invasive procedures designed to reduce the probability of cancer among high-risk patients. Yet research shows that people tend to invest too little in such activities because they put too much weight on current costs and too little weight on future benefits.

Health care insurance decisions can also be quite complex. Insurance policies include many facets such as deductibles, co-payments, and different levels of coverage for different providers. And health insurance includes trade-offs that many people don't seem to understand. For example, employees may not fully appreciate that they are giving up sacrificing some wages in return for employer health care insurance premium payments.

What are the implications of the above biases?

- It's important to be aware of common behavioral biases when making health insurance decisions. For example, realize that most people don't pay sufficient attention to the importance of preventive health care measures.
- Most of us would be better off if our health insurance plans were mediated by some entity that would screen and restrict health insurance choices down to a manageable number. Research suggests that employers would perform this role better than the government or private insurance agents, which is a provocative finding in light of the ACA.
- Co-payment amounts should be determined using cost-effectiveness analysis.

Source: "Lessons for Health Care from Behavioral Economics," http://www.nber.org/bah/2008no4/w14330.html (see referenced study by Jeffrey Liebman and Richard Zeckhauser, "Simple Humans, Complex Insurance, Subtle Subsidies," Working Paper 14330, http://www.nber.org/papers/w14330, 2008), accessed September 2012.

- **What is your gender?** Women tend to live longer and are more likely to require long-term care. They're also the primary caregivers for other family members, which may mean that when they need care, help won't be available.

- **Do you have family who can care for you?** The availability of relatives or home health services to provide care can reduce the cost of long-term care.

9-5b Long-Term-Care Insurance Provisions and Costs

When purchasing long-term-care insurance, it is important to evaluate and compare policy provisions, which are important factors in determining the premium for each policy. Exhibit 9.3 summarizes the typical provisions of policies offered by leading insurers. Let's take a closer look at the most important policy provisions to consider when purchasing long-term-care insurance.

- **Type of care.** Some long-term-care policies offer benefits only for nursing home care, whereas others pay only for services in the insured's home, such as skilled or unskilled nursing care, physical therapy, homemakers, and home health aides. Because it's hard to predict whether a person might need to be in a nursing home, most financial planners recommend policies covering both. Many of these policies focus on nursing home care, and any expenses for health care in the insured's home are covered in a rider to the basic policy. Many policies also cover assisted living, adult day care and other community care programs, alternative care, and respite care for the caregiver.

- **Eligibility requirements.** Some important *gatekeeper provisions* determine whether the insured will receive payment for claims. The most liberal policies state that the insured will qualify for benefits so long as his or her physician orders the care. A popular and much more restrictive provision pays only for long-term care that's medically necessary because of sickness or injury. One common gatekeeper provision requires the insured's inability to perform a given number of *activities of daily living (ADLs)* such as bathing, dressing, or eating. Some policies also provide care for cognitive impairment or when

Exhibit 9.3 Typical Provisions in Long-Term-Care Insurance Policies

Long-term-care insurers offer a wide range of provisions in their policies. A typical policy includes the following.

Services covered	Skilled, intermediate, and custodial care; home health care; adult day care (often)
Benefit eligibility	Physician certification and/or medically necessary
Daily benefit	$100–$450/day, nursing home; $50–$150/day, home health care
Benefit period	3–4 years
Maximum benefit period	5 years; unlimited
Waiting period	0–100 days
Renewability	Guaranteed
Preexisting conditions	Conditions existing 6–12 months prior to policy coverage
Inflation protection	Yes, for an additional premium
Deductibility periods	0, 20, 30, 90, 100 days
Alzheimer's disease coverage	Yes
Age limits for purchasing	40–84

© Cengage Learning

waiting period (elimination period) The period, after an insured meets the policy's eligibility requirements, during which he or she must pay expenses out-of-pocket; when the waiting period expires, the insured begins to receive benefits.

guaranteed renewability Policy provision ensuring continued insurance coverage for the insured's lifetime as long as the premiums continue to be paid.

medically necessary and prescribed by the patient's physician. In the case of an Alzheimer's patient who remains physically healthy, inclusion of cognitive abilities as ADLs would be extremely important.

- **Services covered.** Most policies today cover several levels of service in state-licensed nursing homes: skilled, intermediate, and custodial care. *Skilled care* is needed when a patient requires constant attention from a medical professional, such as a physician or registered nurse. *Intermediate care* is provided when the patient needs medical attention or supervision but not the constant attention of a medical professional. *Custodial care* provides assistance in the normal activities of daily living but no medical attention or supervision; a physician or nurse may be on call, however. Most long-term-care policies also cover home care services, such as skilled or unskilled nursing care, physical therapy, homemakers, and home health aides provided by state-licensed or Medicare-certified home health agencies.

- **Daily benefits.** Long-term-care policies reimburse the insured for the cost of services incurred up to a daily maximum. For nursing home care policies, the daily maximums generally range from $100 to $500, depending on the amount of premium that the insured is willing to pay. For combination

nursing home and home care policies, the maximum home care benefit is normally half the nursing home maximum.

- **Benefit duration.** The maximum duration of benefits ranges from one year to the insured's lifetime. Lifetime coverage is expensive, however. Most financial planners recommend the purchase of a policy with a duration of three to six years to give the insured protection for a longer-than-average period of care.

- **Waiting period.** Even if the policy's eligibility requirements are met, the insured must pay long-term care expenses during the **waiting**, or **elimination, period.** Typical waiting periods are 90 to 100 days. Although premiums are much lower for policies with longer waiting periods, the insured must have liquid assets to cover his or her expenses during that period. An insured who still requires care after the waiting period expires will begin to receive benefits for the duration of the policy, so long as its eligibility requirements continue to be met.

© GEOPAUL/ISTOCKPHOTO

Go to Smart Sites

Want to learn more about disability income insurance? America's Health Insurance Plans offers a Guide to Disability Income Insurance. ●

- **Renewability.** Most long-term-care insurance policies now include a **guaranteed renewability** provision to ensure continued coverage for your lifetime as long as you continue to pay the premiums. This clause does not ensure a level premium over time, however. Nearly all policies allow the insurer to raise premiums if the claims experience for your peer group of policyholders is unfavorable. Watch out for policies with an **optional renewability** clause because they are renewable *only at the insurer's option.*

- **Preexisting conditions.** Some policies once included a preexisting conditions clause, similar to those described previously. If someone has already been diagnosed with Parkinson's or Alzheimer's disease, takes memory drugs, needs any type of assistance in walking, has had a stroke, or has osteoporosis, an insurance company may not be willing to sell that person a long-term insurance policy.

- **Inflation protection.** Many policies offer inflation protection riders that, for an additional premium, let you increase benefits by a flat amount, often 5 percent, per year. Others offer benefits linked to the rise in the consumer price index (CPI). Most policies discontinue inflation adjustments after either 10 or 20 years. Inflation protection riders can add between 25 percent and 40 percent to the basic premium for a long-term-care insurance policy.

- **Premium levels.** Long-term-care insurance is rather expensive, and premiums vary widely among insurance companies. For example, an average healthy 65-year-old male may pay about $2,800 per year for a policy that pays for three years' care at $150 per day for nursing home care with a 90-day waiting period and a 5 percent inflation rider. The same coverage may cost a 55-year-old male $1,800 per year and a 80-year-old around $7,100 per year. Given the significant rise in premium with age, some financial planners recommend buying long-term-care insurance when you are fairly young. But keep in mind that, although the annual premiums are lower, you'll be paying for a lot longer time before you would likely need the benefits.

9-5c How to Buy Long-Term-Care Insurance

optional renewability
Contractual clause allowing the insured to continue insurance *only at the insurer's option.*

When buying long-term-care insurance, make sure the insurer is a financially sound company (based on ratings from the major ratings agencies) with a proven track record in this market segment. Here are some additional guidelines to help you choose the right policy:

- **Buy the policy when you're healthy.** Once you have a disease, such as Alzheimer's or multiple sclerosis, or have a stroke, you become uninsurable. So the best time to buy is when you're in your mid-50s or 60s.

- **Buy the right types of coverage—but don't buy more coverage than you need.** Your policy should cover skilled, intermediate, and custodial care as well as adult day care centers and assisted living facilities. If you have access to family caregivers or home health services, opt for only nursing home coverage; if not, select a policy with generous home health care benefits. To reduce costs, increase the waiting period before benefits begin; the longer you can cover the costs yourself, the lower your premiums. You may also choose a shorter benefit payment period; three years is a popular choice, but the average nursing home stay is about 2½ years. Lifetime coverage increases the premium for a 65-year-old by as much as 40 percent.

- **Understand what the policy covers and when it pays benefits.** The amounts paid, benefit periods, and services covered vary among insurers. One rule of thumb is to buy a policy covering 80 percent to 100 percent of current nursing home costs in your area. Some policies pay only for licensed health care providers, whereas others include assistance with household chores. Know how the policy defines benefit eligibility.

9-6 Disability Income Insurance

LG6 When a family member becomes sick for an extended period, the effect on the family goes beyond medical bills. About one-third of people between the ages of 35 and 65 will be disabled for 90 days or longer before age 65, and about one in seven people between the ages of 35 and 65 will become disabled for five years or more. During the working years, becoming disabled is more likely than death. For a 35-year-old male, the odds are nearly 2 to 1, and for a 35-year-old female, the odds are nearly 3 to 1. Although most Americans have life insurance, few have taken steps to protect their family should a serious illness or accident prevent them from working for an extended period.

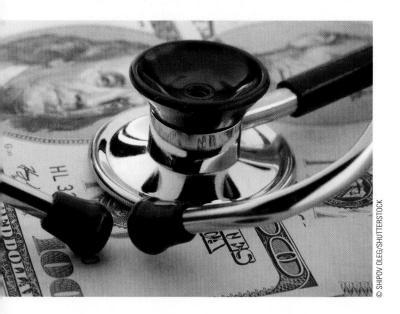

© SHIPOV OLEG/SHUTTERSTOCK

disability income insurance Insurance that provides families with weekly or monthly payments to replace income when the insured is unable to work because of a covered illness, injury, or disease.

The best way to protect against the potentially devastating financial consequences of a health-related disability is with disability income insurance. **Disability income insurance** provides families with weekly or monthly payments to replace income when the insured is unable to work because of a covered illness, injury, or disease. Some companies also offer disability income protection for a spousal homemaker; such coverage helps pay for the services that the spouse would normally provide.

Almost all employers offer disability income insurance at attractive rates, but it is often voluntary, and you may have to pay the entire premium yourself. Group coverage is usually a good buy because the premiums average $200 to $400 a year—about one-third less than the cost of comparable private coverage. Of course, if you change jobs then you may lose the coverage. The benefits received from a group plan for which you pay the premiums are tax free (unless paid through a flexible spending account).

Social Security offers disability income benefits, but you must be unable to do *any* job whatsoever to receive benefits. Benefits are payable only if your disability is expected to last at least one year (or to be fatal), and they don't begin until you've been disabled for at least five months. The actual amount paid is a percentage of your previous monthly earnings, with some statistical adjustments. The percentage is higher for people with low earnings. For example, a 35-year-old who was earning $20,000 annually and has dependents would receive about $1,300 per month (about 78 percent of earnings); if he or she had earned $50,000, the amount would rise to about $2,250 per month (but would fall to 54 percent of earnings).

The need for disability income coverage is great. Although most workers receive some disability insurance benefits from their employer, in many cases the group plan falls short and pays only about 60 percent of salary for a limited period. The first step in considering disability income insurance is to determine the dollar amount that your family would need (typically monthly) if an earner becomes disabled. Then you can buy the coverage that you need or supplement existing coverage if necessary.

9-6a Estimating Your Disability Insurance Needs

The main purpose of disability income insurance is to replace all (or most) of the income—that is, earnings—that would be lost if you became disabled and physically unable to hold a job. In essence, it should enable you to maintain a standard of living at or near your present level. To help decide how much disability income insurance is right for you, use Worksheet 9.2 to estimate your monthly disability benefit needs. Here is all you have to do.

1. **Calculate take-home pay.** Disability benefits are generally (but not always) tax free, so you typically need to replace only your *take-home (after-tax) pay*. Benefits from employer-paid policies are fully or partially taxable. To estimate take-home pay, subtract income and Social Security taxes paid from your gross earned income (salary only). Divide this total by 12 to get your monthly take-home pay.

2. **Estimate the monthly amounts of disability benefits from government or employer programs.**
   a. *Social Security disability benefits.* Obtain an estimate of your benefits by using the online calculators provided by the Social Security Administration at http://www.ssa.gov/planners/benefitcalculators.htm. The average Social Security disability benefit is about $1,700 per month for a wage earner with dependents.
   b. *Other government program disability benefits* for which you qualify (armed services, Veterans Administration, civil service, the Federal Employees Compensation Act, state workers' compensation systems). There are also special programs for railroad workers, longshoremen, and people with black-lung disease.
   c. *Company disability benefits.* Ask your company benefits supervisor to help you calculate company-provided benefits, including sick pay or wage continuation plans (these are essentially short-term disability income insurance) and plans formally designated as disability insurance. For each benefit that your employer offers, check on its tax treatment.
   d. *Group disability policy benefits.* A private insurer provides the coverage and you pay for it, often through payroll deduction.

3. **Add up your existing monthly disability benefits.**

GOODLUZ/PHOTOS.COM

Using a worksheet like this makes the job of estimating disability benefit insurance needs a lot easier.

DISABILITY BENEFIT NEEDS

Name(s) _____ Date _____

1. Estimate current monthly *take-home* pay $ _____
2. Estimate existing monthly benefits
   a. Social Security benefits $ _____
   b. Other government program benefits   _____
   c. Company disability benefits   _____
   d. Group disability policy benefits   _____
3. Total existing monthly disability benefits (2a + 2b + 2c + 2d) $ _____
4. **Estimated monthly disability benefits needed ([1] – [3])** $ _____

© Cengage Learning

4. **Subtract your existing monthly disability benefits from your current monthly take-home pay.** The result shows the estimated monthly disability benefits that you'll need in order to maintain your present after-tax income. Note that investment income and spousal income (if the spouse is presently employed) are ignored because it's assumed that this income will continue and is necessary to maintain your current standard of living. If your spouse is now unemployed but would enter the workforce if you ever became disabled, then his or her estimated monthly income (take-home pay) could be subtracted from Item 4 of Worksheet 9.2 to determine your net monthly disability benefit needs.

9-6b Disability Income Insurance Provisions and Costs

The scope and cost of your disability income coverage depend on its contractual provisions. Although disability income insurance policies can be complex, certain features are important: (1) definition of disability, (2) benefit amount and duration, (3) probationary period, (4) waiting period, (5) renewability, and (6) other provisions.

Definition of Disability

Disability policies vary in the standards that you must meet to receive benefits. Some pay benefits if you're unable to perform the duties of your customary occupation—the *own occupation* (or "Own Occ") definition—whereas others pay only if you can engage in no gainful employment at all—the *any occupation*

(or "Any Occ") definition. Under the "Own Occ" definition, a professor who lost his voice—yet could still be paid to write or do research—would receive full benefits because he couldn't lecture, a primary function of his occupation. With a *residual benefit option*, you would be paid partial benefits if you can work only part-time or at a lower salary. The "Any Occ" definition is considerably less expensive because it gives the insurer more leeway in determining whether the insured should receive benefits.

Benefit Amount and Duration

Most individual disability income policies pay a flat monthly benefit, which is stated in the policy, whereas group plans pay a fixed percentage of gross income. In either case, insurers normally won't agree to amounts of more than 60 percent to 70 percent of the insured's gross income. Insurers won't issue policies for the full amount of gross income because this would give some people an incentive to fake a disability (for example, "bad back") and collect more in insurance benefits than they normally would receive as take-home pay.

Monthly benefits can be paid for a few months or a lifetime. If you're ensured a substantial pension, Social Security, or other benefits at retirement, then a policy that pays benefits until age 65 is adequate. Most people, however, will need to continue their occupations for many more years and should consider a policy offering lifetime benefits. Many policies offer benefits for periods as short as two or five years. Although these policies may be better than nothing, they don't protect against the major financial losses associated with long-term disabilities.

Financial Planning Tips: Buying Disability Income Insurance

Consider the following tips in evaluating disability income insurance policies:

- **Know what the government can do for you.** Social Security disability benefits are available only to those with a condition that makes them unable to work for at least a year or that is terminal. The average benefit payout is only about 40 percent of pre-disability income. Qualified applicants should expect to wait between three and five months to get Social Security disability benefits. Only a few states provide additional benefits, although it's worth checking that. If you buy a private disability income insurance policy, be aware that most require you to apply for Social Security benefits, which will be subtracted from the benefit that you receive from the insurer.

- **Buying a policy at work is usually cheapest.** Many employers provide disability income insurance and pay part of the premiums. If you go this route, make sure that you have both short- and long-term coverage. Short-term coverage usually lasts for a few months and long-term coverage often starts paying after 90 to 180 days. Make sure that you're not exposed to a significant gap between the two. If you buy a policy through your employer, you may be able to pay the premiums directly out of your paycheck on a pretax basis. However, this means that your benefits would be taxable.

- **Determine if a policy purchased through your employer is portable.** It's good to know if you can keep the policy if you leave your current company.

- **Understand the circumstances in which the disability insurance benefit will be paid.** The best trigger is when you cannot do your current job. However, some policies pay only if you cannot do any comparable job, which is a much more complicated constraint.

- **Read the fine print.** It's important to know what percentage of pre-disability income is paid out by the policy. And does it include just base salary or additional compensation like commissions or bonuses? Are there limits on benefit payouts for certain conditions like mental illness? You'll want to know the ins and outs of each policy that you consider.

Source: Anna Wilde Matthews, "Just in Case: The Skinny on Buying Disability Insurance," http://professional.wsj.com/article/SB100014240527487045610045750130731003107 94.html?mg=reno-wsj, accessed September 2012.

Probationary Period

Both group and individual disability income policies are likely to include a probationary period, usually 7 to 30 days, which is a time delay from the date the policy is issued until benefit privileges are available. Any disability stemming from an illness, injury, or disease that occurs during the probationary period is *not* covered—even if it continues beyond this period. This feature keeps costs down.

Waiting Period

The waiting period (elimination period) provisions in a disability income policy are similar to those discussed for long-term-care insurance. Typical waiting periods range from 30 days to a year. If you have an adequate emergency fund to provide family income during the early months of disability then you can choose a longer waiting period and substantially reduce your premiums, as shown in Exhibit 9.4.

Exhibit 9.4 Representative Disability Income Insurance Premium Costs

The cost of disability income insurance varies with the terms of payment, as well as the length of the waiting period. Women pay substantially higher rates than men do. This table shows premiums for basic disability income coverage for a 35-year-old that pays $2,000 per month in benefits and has guaranteed premiums to age 65. The policy also includes a 3 percent inflation rider.

Benefit Period:	2 Years		5 Years		10 Years		To Age 65	
Waiting Period	Male	Female	Male	Female	Male	Female	Male	Female
60 days	$378	$486	$546	$740	$731	$1,122	$974	$1,575
90 days	294	357	412	532	552	828	747	1,189
6 months	269	317	393	487	519	758	713	1,136
One year	N/A	N/A	361	441	488	720	689	1,084

With most insurers, you can trade an increase in the waiting period—say, from 60 days to 90 days—for an increase in the duration of benefits from five years to age 65. In fact, as Exhibit 9.5 shows, the premium charged by this insurer for a policy covering a 35-year-old male with a 60-day waiting period and two-year benefit period ($378) is about the same as one charged for a five-year benefit period with a six-month waiting period ($393). Accepting this type of trade-off usually makes sense because the primary purpose of insurance is to protect the insured from a catastrophic loss, not from smaller losses that are better handled through proper budgeting and saving.

Renewability

Most individual disability income insurance is either *guaranteed renewable* or *noncancelable*. As with long-term-care policies, guaranteed renewability ensures that you can renew the policy until you reach the age stated in the clause, usually age 65. Premiums can be raised over time if justified by the loss experience of all those in the same class (usually based on age, sex, and occupational category). Noncancelable policies offer guaranteed renewability, but they also guarantee that future premiums will remain the same as those stated in the policy at issuance. Because of this stable premium guarantee, noncancelable policies generally are more expensive than those with only a guaranteed renewability provision.

Other Provisions

The purchasing power of income from a long-term disability policy that pays, say, $2,000 per month could be severely affected by inflation. In fact, a 3 percent inflation rate would reduce the purchasing power of this $2,000 benefit to less than $1,500 in 10 years. To counteract such a reduction, many insurers offer a *cost-of-living adjustment (COLA)*. With a COLA provision, the monthly benefit is adjusted upward each year, often in line with the CPI, although these annual adjustments are often capped at a given rate (say, 8 percent). Although some financial advisors suggest buying COLA riders, others believe that the 10 percent to 25 percent additional premium is too much to pay for this protection.

Although the COLA provision applies only once the insured is disabled, the *guaranteed insurability option (GIO)* can allow you to purchase additional disability income insurance in line with inflation increases while you're still healthy. Under the GIO, the price of this additional insurance is fixed at the contract's inception, and you don't have to prove insurability.

A *waiver of premium* is standard in disability income policies. If you're disabled for a minimum period, normally 60 or 90 days, then the insurer will waive any future premiums that come due while you remain disabled. In essence, the waiver of premium gives you additional disability income insurance in the amount of your regular premium payment.

Remember that disability income insurance is just one part of your overall personal financial plan. You'll need to find your own balance between cost and coverage.

Planning Over a Lifetime: Insuring Your Health

Here are some key ideas concerning how insuring your health changes over the stages in the life cycle.

Independent Lifestyle (20s)	Family and Career Development (30s–40s)	Mature Lifestyle (50s–60s)	Retirement (65+)
✓ Assess your health and take steps to stay healthy: exercise, eat well, and avoid smoking and too much alcohol.	✓ Consider HMOs and PPOs to lower deductibles and to maximize flexibility of choices.	✓ Evaluate the need for long-term-care insurance.	✓ Consider the best way to get prescription benefits in light of Medicare options.
✓ While in school or unemployed, take advantage of your opportunity to stay on your parents' health insurance until the age of 26.	✓ Re-evaluate the need for disability income insurance.	✓ Re-evaluate the need for long-term-care insurance.	✓ Re-evaluate the need for long-term-care insurance.
✓ When employed, take out health care insurance coverage with your employer.		✓ Familiarize yourself with Medicare benefits.	
✓ Evaluate the appropriateness of disability income insurance.			
✓ Consider pre-tax accounts like flexibility spending to save money.			

FINANCIAL PLANNING EXERCISES

LG2, 3, 4

1. *Use Worksheet 9.1.* Emily Walsh, a recent college graduate, has decided to accept a job offer from a nonprofit organization. She'll earn $34,000 a year but will receive no employee health benefits. Emily estimates that her monthly living expenses will be about $2,000 a month, including rent, food, transportation, and clothing. She has no health problems and expects to remain in good health in the near future. Using the Internet or other resources, gather information about three health insurance policies that Emily could purchase on her own. Include at least one HMO. Use Worksheet 9.1 to compare the policies' features. Should Emily buy health insurance? Why or why not? Assuming that she does decide to purchase health insurance, which of the three policies would you recommend and why?

LG6

2. *Use Worksheet 9.2.* Bruce Kaplan, a 35-year-old computer programmer, earns $72,000 a year. His monthly take-home pay is $3,750. His wife, Barbara, works part-time at their children's elementary school but receives no benefits. Under state law, Bruce's employer contributes to a workers' compensation insurance fund that would provide $2,250 per month for six months if Bruce were disabled and unable to work.
   a. Use Worksheet 9.2 to calculate Bruce's disability insurance needs assuming that he won't qualify for Medicare under his Social Security benefits.
   b. Based on your answer in part a, what would you advise Bruce about his need for additional disability income insurance? Discuss the type and size of disability income insurance coverage that he should consider, including possible provisions that he might want to include. What other factors should he take into account if he decides to purchase a policy?

LG5

3. Discuss the pros and cons of long-term-care insurance. Does it make sense for anyone in your family right now? Why or why not? What factors might change this assessment in the future?

LG6

4. *Use Worksheet 9.2.* Do you need disability income insurance? Calculate your need using Worksheet 9.2. Discuss how you'd go about purchasing this coverage.

LG1, 2, 3, 4

5. Assess your current health insurance situation. Do you have any health insurance now? What does your policy cover? What is excluded? Are there any gaps that you think need to be filled? Are there any risks in your current lifestyle or situation that might make additional coverage necessary? If you were to purchase health insurance for yourself in the near future, what type of plan would you select, and why? What steps can you take to keep your health costs down?

PFIN Student Study Tools—Visit CourseMate for PFIN 3. Log in at **www.cengagebrain.com**. Check out the bonus exercises and exhibits, interactive worksheets, Smart Sites, Critical Thinking Cases, Money Online, Kiplinger videos, quizzing, and more.

Cool Apps—Look for this new feature on CourseMate for PFIN 3. Cool Apps navigates the growing world of apps that are available for personal financial planning and tracking.

© PALI RAO/ISTOCKPHOTO

10

PROTECTING YOUR PROPERTY

LEARNING GOALS

LG1 Discuss the importance and basic principles of property insurance, including types of exposure, indemnity, and co-insurance.

LG2 Identify the types of coverage provided by homeowner's insurance.

LG3 Select the right homeowner's insurance policy for your needs.

LG4 Analyze the coverage in a personal automobile policy (PAP) and choose the most cost-effective policy.

LG5 Describe other types of property and liability insurance.

LG6 Choose a property and liability insurance agent and company, and settle claims.

How Will This Affect Me? The chapter explains the key property insurance concepts of indemnity, subrogation, and co-insurance. It then describes the common sources of property and liability risk exposures and the insurance coverage available to address them. The main characteristics of homeowner's and auto insurance are covered, as well as how to choose the version of each policy type that's best for you. Supplemental insurance to protect against floods and earthquakes and personal liability umbrella policies are also described. Especially practical tips can be found in the discussions of how to choose an insurance agent and how to settle property and liability insurance claims. When you finish this chapter you should understand the best and most cost-effective ways to use insurance to protect your property and associated liability exposures.

10-1 Basic Principles of Property Insurance

LG1 Suppose that a severe storm destroyed your home. Could you afford to replace it? Most people couldn't. To protect yourself from this and other similar types of property loss, you need property insurance. What's more, every day you face some type of risk of negligence. For example, you might be distraught over a personal problem and unintentionally run a red light, seriously injuring a pedestrian. Could you pay for the medical and other costs? Because consequences like this and other potentially negligent acts could cause financial ruin, having appropriate liability insurance is essential.

Property and liability insurance should be as much a part of your personal financial plans as life and health insurance. Such coverage protects the assets that you've already acquired and safeguards your progress toward financial goals. **Property insurance** guards against catastrophic losses of real and personal property caused by such perils as fire, theft, vandalism, windstorms, and other calamities. **Liability insurance** offers protection

against the financial consequences that may arise from the insured's responsibility for property loss or personal injuries to others.

Inefficient or inadequate insurance protection is at odds with the objectives of personal financial planning. It is consequently important to become familiar with the principles of property and liability insurance. Here, we begin with a discussion of the basic principles of property and liability insurance.

10-1a Types of Exposure

Most individuals face two basic types of exposure: physical loss of property and loss through liability.

Exposure to Property Loss

Most property insurance contracts define the property covered and name the **perils**—the causes of loss—for which the insured will be compensated in case of a claim against their policy. As a rule, most property insurance contracts impose two obligations on the property owner: (1) developing a complete inventory of the property being insured and (2) identifying the perils against which protection is desired. Some property contracts limit coverage by excluding certain types of property and perils, while others offer more comprehensive protection.

PROPERTY INVENTORY. Inventorying property is part of the financial planning process. It is especially important in the case of a total loss—if your home is destroyed by fire, for example. Because all property insurance companies require you to show *proof of loss* when making a claim, your personal property inventory, along with corresponding values, can provide this information. A comprehensive property inventory not only helps you settle a claim when a loss occurs

ROBERT KNESCHKE/SHUTTERSTOCK.COM

> ❝ **Inefficient or inadequate insurance protection is at odds with the objectives of personal financial planning.** ❞

After you read the chapter, explore the STUDY TOOLS listed on page 248.

but also serves as a useful guide for selecting the most appropriate coverage for your particular needs.

Most families have a home, household furnishings, clothing and personal belongings, lawn and garden equipment, and motor vehicles, all of which need to be insured. Fortunately, most homeowner's and automobile insurance policies provide coverage for these types of belongings. But many families also own such items as motorboats and trailers, various types of off-road vehicles, business property and inventories, jewelry, stamp or coin collections, guns, musical instruments, antiques, paintings, bonds, securities, and other items of special value, such as cameras, golf clubs, electronic equipment, and personal computers. Coverage for these belongings (and those that accompany you when you travel) often require special types of insurance.

Many insurance companies have easy-to-complete personal property inventory forms available to help policyholders prepare inventories. A partial sample of one such form is shown in Exhibit 10.1. These inventory forms can be supplemented with photographs or videos of household contents and belongings. *Every*

Exhibit 10.1 A Personal Property Inventory Form

Using a form like this will help you keep track of your personal property, including its date of purchase, original purchase price, and replacement cost.

Living Room

Stereo System

Brand	
Model	
Serial #	Date purchased
Purchase price $	Replacement cost $

Large-Screen TV

Brand	
Model	
Serial #	Date purchased
Purchase price $	Replacement cost $

Compact Disc Player/MP3 Player

Brand	
Model	
Serial #	Date purchased
Purchase price $	Replacement cost $

Home Theater System

Brand	
Model	
Serial #	Date purchased
Purchase price $	Replacement cost $

DVD Player

Brand	
Model	
Serial #	Date purchased
Purchase price $	Replacement cost $

Living Room

Article	Qty.	Date Purchased	Purchase Price	Replacement Cost
Air conditioners (window)				
Blinds/shades				
Bookcases				
Books				
Cabinets				
Carpets/rugs				
Chairs				
Chests				
Clocks				
Couches/sofas				
Curtains/draperies				
Fireplace fixtures				
Lamps/lighting fixtures				
Mirrors				
Pictures/paintings				
CDs				
Planters				
Stereo equipment				
Tables				
Television sets				
Other				
Other				

effort should be made to keep these documents in a safe place, where they can't be destroyed—such as a bank safe-deposit box. You might also consider keeping a *duplicate copy* with a parent or trusted relative. Remember that you may need inventories and photographs to authenticate any property losses that may occur.

IDENTIFYING PERILS. Many people feel a false sense of security after buying insurance because they believe that they're safeguarded against all contingencies. The fact is, however, that certain *perils* cannot be reasonably insured. For example, most homeowner's or automobile insurance policies limit or exclude damage or loss caused by flood (remember Hurricane Katrina in New Orleans in 2005), earthquake, backing up of sewers and drains, mudslides, mysterious disappearance, war, nuclear radiation, and ordinary wear and tear. In addition, property insurance contracts routinely limit coverage based on the location of the property, time of loss, persons involved, and types of hazards to which the property is exposed.

Liability Exposures

We all encounter a variety of liability exposures daily. Driving a car, entertaining guests at home, volunteer activities, or being careless in performing professional duties are some common liability risks. Loss exposures result from **negligence**, which is failing to act in a reasonable manner or take necessary steps to protect others from harm. Even if you're never negligent and always prudent, someone might *believe* that you are the cause of a loss and bring a costly lawsuit against you. Losing the judgment could cost you thousands—or even millions—of dollars, and it could result in bankruptcy or financial ruin.

Fortunately, *liability insurance* protects you against losses resulting from these risks, *including the high legal fees* required to defend yourself against lawsuits. It's important to obtain adequate liability insurance through your homeowner's and automobile policies or through a separate umbrella policy.

10-1b Principle of Indemnity

The **principle of indemnity** states that the insured may not be compensated by the insurance company in an amount exceeding the insured's economic loss. Most property and liability insurance contracts are based on this principle—although this *principle does not apply to life and health insurance.* Several important concepts relate to the principle of indemnity.

Actual Cash Value versus Replacement Cost
The principle of indemnity limits the amount that an insured may collect to the **actual cash value** of the property: the replacement cost minus the value of physical depreciation. Some insurers pay replacement cost without taking depreciation into account—for example, most homeowner's policies cover building losses on a replacement cost basis if the proper type and amount of insurance is purchased. If an insured property is damaged and there is no replacement cost provision, then the insurer is obligated to pay no more than the property would cost new today (its replacement cost) less the amount of depreciation from wear and tear.

For example, assume that fire destroys two rooms of furniture that were 6 years old and had an estimated useful life of 10 years. The replacement cost is $5,000. Therefore, at the time of loss, the furniture was subject to an assumed physical depreciation of 60 percent (6 years/10 years)—in this case, $3,000. Because the actual cash value is estimated at $2,000 ($5,000 replacement cost minus $3,000 of depreciation), the maximum that the insurer would have to pay is $2,000. Note that the original cost of the property has no bearing on the settlement.

negligence Failing to act in a reasonable manner or to take necessary steps to protect others from harm.

principle of indemnity An insurance principle stating that an insured may not be compensated by the insurance company in an amount exceeding the insured's economic loss.

actual cash value A value assigned to an insured property that is determined by subtracting the amount of physical depreciation from its replacement cost.

© CHRISTINA RICHARDS/SHUTTERSTOCK

right of subrogation
The right of an insurer, who has paid an insured's claim, to request reimbursement from either the person who caused the loss or that person's insurer.

co-insurance In property insurance, a provision requiring a policyholder to buy insurance in an amount equal to a specified percentage of the replacement value of their property.

comprehensive policy Property and liability insurance policy covering all perils unless they are specifically excluded.

named peril policy Property and liability insurance policy that individually names the perils covered.

Subrogation

After an insurance company pays a claim, its **right of subrogation** allows it to request reimbursement from either the person who caused the loss or that person's insurance company. For example, if you're in an automobile accident in which the other party damages your car, you may collect the amount of the loss from your insurer, or from the at-fault party's insurer, but not from both. Clearly, collecting the full amount of the loss from both parties would violate the principle of indemnity by leaving you better off after the loss than before it. So if your insurer pays you and the other party is at fault, your insurance company can go after the responsible party to recover the amount it paid out to you.

Other Insurance

Nearly all property and liability insurance contracts have an *other-insurance clause*, which normally states that if a person has more than one insurance policy on a property, each company is liable for only a prorated amount of the loss based on its proportion of the total insurance covering the property. Without this provision, insured persons could use duplicate property insurance policies to collect from multiple companies and actually profit from their losses.

10-1c Co-insurance

Co-insurance, a provision commonly found in property insurance contracts, requires policyholders to buy insurance in an amount equal to a specified percentage of the replacement value of their property. The provision stipulates that if a property isn't properly covered, the property owner will become the "co-insurer" and bear part of the loss. If the policyholder has the stipulated amount of coverage (usually 80 percent of the value of the property), then the insurance company will reimburse for covered losses, dollar-for-dollar, up to the amount of the policy limits. Assume, for example, that Michael and Valerie have a fire insurance policy on their $300,000 home with an 80 percent co-insurance clause. Further, assume that they ran short of money and decided to save by buying a $180,000 policy instead of $240,000 (80 percent of $300,000) as required by the co-insurance clause. If a loss occurred, then the company would be obligated to pay only 75 percent ($180,000/$240,000) of the loss, up to the amount of the policy limit. Thus, on damages of $40,000, the insurer would pay only

$30,000 (75 percent of $40,000). Clearly, it is important to meet the requirements of the co-insurance clauses of your property insurance policies.

Go to Smart Sites

For basic coverage questions, check out "About Coverage" choices under the Auto and Home/Renter tabs at insurance.com's Web site. For online resources, whenever you see "Go to Smart Sites" in this chapter, visit CourseMate for PFIN 3. Log in at www.cengagebrain.com. ●

10-2 Homeowner's Insurance

LG2, LG3 Homeowners can choose from five different forms (HO-1, HO-2, HO-3, HO-5, and HO-8). Two other forms (HO-4 and HO-6) meet the needs of renters and owners of condominiums (see Exhibit 10.2). An HO-4 renter's policy offers essentially the same broad protection as an HO-2 homeowner's policy, but the coverage doesn't apply to the rented dwelling unit because the tenant usually doesn't own it.

All HO forms are divided into two sections. Section I applies to the dwelling, accompanying structures, and personal property of the insured. Section II deals with comprehensive coverage for personal liability and for medical payments to others. The scope of coverage under Section I is least with an HO-1 policy and greatest with an HO-5 policy. HO-8 is a modified coverage policy for older homes, which is used to insure houses that have market values well below their cost to rebuild. The coverage in Section II is the same for all forms.

In the following paragraphs, we'll explain the important features of homeowner's forms HO-3 and HO-5, the most common policies. (As Exhibit 10.2 shows, HO-1 is a basic, seldom-used policy with relatively narrow coverage.) The key difference in coverage under the HO-3 and HO-5 forms is the number of perils against which protection applies to the personal property coverage.

10-2a Perils Covered

Some property and liability insurance agreements, called **comprehensive policies**, cover all perils except those specifically excluded, whereas **named peril policies** name particular, individual perils covered.

Section I Perils

The perils against which the home and its contents are insured are shown in Exhibit 10.2. Coverage on the dwelling is the same for the HO-3 and HO-5 forms, but coverage on the house itself and other structures (for example, a detached garage) is comprehensive under HO-3 and HO-5 but is a named

Exhibit 10.2 A Guide to Homeowner's Policies

The amount of insurance coverage you receive depends on the type of homeowner's (HO) policy you buy. You can also obtain coverage if you're a renter or a condominium owner.

Form	Coverages*	Covered perils
Basic Form (HO-1)	A—$15,000 minimum; B—10% of A; C—50% of A; D—10% of A; E—$100,000; F—$1,000 per person	Fire, smoke, lightning, windstorm, hail, volcanic eruption, explosion, glass breakage, aircraft, vehicles, riot or civil commotion, theft, vandalism or malicious mischief
Broad Form (HO-2)	Minimum varies; other coverages in same percentages or amounts except D—20% of A	Covers all basic-form risks plus weight of ice, snow, sleet; freezing; accidental discharge of water or steam; falling objects; accidental tearing, cracking, or burning of heating/cooling/sprinkler system or appliance; damage from electrical current
Special Form (HO-3)	Minimum varies; other coverages in same percentages or amounts except D—20% of A	Dwelling and other structures covered against risks of direct physical loss to property except losses specifically excluded; personal property covered by same perils as HO-2 plus damage by glass or safety glazing material that is part of a building, storm door, or storm window
Renter's Form (HO-4)	Coverages A and B—Not applicable C—Minimum varies by company D—20% of C E—$100,000 F—$1,000 per person	Covers same perils covered by HO-2 for personal property
Comprehensive Form (HO-5)	Coverages A and B—Not applicable C—Minimum varies by company D—20% of C E—$100,000 F—$1,000 per person	Covers same perils as HO-4 but covered perils are dwelling, other structures and personal property covered against risks of direct physical loss, except losses as specifically excluded
Condominium Form (HO-6)	Coverage A—Minimum $1,000 B—Not applicable C—Minimum varies by company D—40% of C E—$100,000 F—$1,000 per person	Covers same perils covered by HO-2 for personal property
Modified Coverage Form (HO-8)	Same as HO-1, except losses are paid based on the amount required to repair or replace the property using common construction materials and methods	Same perils as HO-1, except theft coverage applies only to losses on the residence premises up to a maximum of $1,000; certain other coverage restrictions also apply

* Coverages:
A. Dwelling   D. Loss of use
B. Other structures   E. Personal liability
C. Personal property   F. Medical payments to others

© Cengage Learning

peril in HO-2. An HO-5 provides comprehensive coverage on the personal property where the HO-3 provides only named perils. Whether homeowners should buy an HO-5 or an HO-3 form depends primarily on how much they're willing to spend to secure the additional protection. The size of premiums for HO-5 and HO-3 policies can differ substantially among insurance companies and states. Buying an HO-1 or HO-2 policy is not recommended because of its more limited coverage.

STALE EDSTROM/SHUTTERSTOCK.COM

Note in Exhibit 10.2 that the types of Section I perils covered include just about every situation, from fire and explosions to lightning and wind damage to theft and vandalism. Some perils are specifically excluded from most homeowner's contracts—in particular, *most policies (even HO-5 and HO-3 forms) exclude earthquakes and floods*, even if you live in an area where the risk of an earthquake or a flood is relatively high and the catastrophic nature of such events causes widespread and costly damage. Of course, you can obtain coverage for earthquakes and floods under a separate policy or a rider.

Section II Perils

The coverage under Section II of the homeowner's contract is called *comprehensive personal liability coverage* because it offers protection against personal liability (major exclusions are noted later) resulting from *negligence*. It does not insure against other losses for which one may become liable, such as libel, slander, defamation of character, and contractual or intentional wrongdoing. For example, coverage would apply if you carelessly, but unintentionally, knocked someone down your stairs. If you purposely struck and injured another person, however, or harmed someone's

reputation either orally or in writing, then homeowner's liability coverage would not protect you.

Section II also provides a limited amount of medical coverage, irrespective of negligence or fault, for persons other than the homeowner's family in certain types of minor accidents on or off the insured's premises. This coverage helps homeowners to meet their moral obligations and helps deter possible lawsuits.

10-2b Factors Affecting Home Insurance Costs

Several influences affect premiums for home and property insurance.

- **Type of structure.** The construction materials used as well as the style and age of your home affect the cost of insuring it. For example, a home built from brick costs less to insure than a similar home made of wood, yet the reverse is true when it comes to earthquake insurance—brick homes are more expensive to insure.

- **Location of home.** Local crime rates, weather, and proximity to a fire hydrant all affect your home's insurance premium costs. If many claims are filed from your area, insurance premiums for all the homeowners there will be higher.

- **Credit score.** Research shows that people with lower credit scores tend to file more insurance claims. Credit scores affect premiums more than any other factor. If you have a poor credit score, you may pay two or three times more than an otherwise comparable person with an excellent credit score.

- **Other factors.** If you have a swimming pool, trampoline, large dog, or other potentially hazardous risk factors on your property, your homeowner's premiums will be higher. Deductibles and the type and amount of coverage also affect the cost.

10-2c Property Covered

The homeowner's policy offers property protection under Section I for the dwelling unit, accompanying structures, and personal property of homeowners and their families. Coverage for certain types of loss also applies to lawns, trees, plants, and shrubs. However, the policy excludes structures on the premises used for business purposes (except incidentally), animals (pets or otherwise), and motorized vehicles not used in maintaining the premises (such as autos, motorcycles, golf carts, or snowmobiles). *Business inventory* (for example, goods held by an insured who is a traveling salesperson, or other goods held for sale) is not covered. Although the policy doesn't cover business inventory, it does cover *business property* (such as books, computers, copiers, office furniture, and supplies), typically up to a maximum of $2,500, while it is on the insured premises.

10-2d Personal Property Floater

Because your homeowner's policy may not protect your expensive personal property adequately, you can either add the **personal property floater (PPF)** as an endorsement to your homeowner's policy or take out a separate floater policy. *The PPF provides either blanket or scheduled coverage of items that are not covered adequately in a standard homeowner's policy.* A *blanket*, or *unscheduled*, *PPF* provides the maximum protection available for virtually all the insured's personal property. *Scheduled PPFs* list the items to be covered and provide supplemental coverage under a homeowner's contract. This coverage is especially useful for expensive property, such as jewelry, fine art, guns, and collections, that is valued at more than coverage C limits (discussed later), and it includes loss, damage, and theft. For example, you should itemize a diamond ring valued at $7,500 because it's worth more than the standard $1,000 coverage C allowance for all jewelry stolen.

10-2e Renter's Insurance: Don't Move In Without It

If you live in an apartment (or some other type of rental unit), be aware that although the building you live in is likely to be fully insured, *your furnishings and other personal belongings are not*. As a renter (or even the owner of a condominium unit), you need a special type of HO policy to obtain insurance coverage on your personal possessions.

> **personal property floater (PPF)** An insurance endorsement or policy providing either blanket or scheduled coverage of expensive personal property not adequately covered in a standard homeowner's policy.

> ## As a renter (or even the owner of a condominium unit), you need a special type of HO policy to obtain insurance coverage on your personal possessions.

Consider, for example, Joan Snyder's predicament. She never got around to insuring her personal possessions in the apartment that she rented in Baltimore. One wintry night, a water pipe ruptured and the escaping water damaged her furniture, rugs, and other belongings. When the building owner refused to pay for the loss, Joan hauled him into court—and lost. Why did she lose her case? Simple: *Unless a landlord can be proven negligent—and this one wasn't—he or she isn't responsible for a tenant's property.* The moral of this story is clear: once you've accumulated valuable personal belongings (from clothing and home furnishings to stereo equipment, TVs, computers, and DVD players), make sure that they're covered adequately by insurance, even if you're only renting a place to live! Otherwise, you could risk losing everything you own.

Renter's insurance, Form HO-4, is a scaled-down version of homeowner's insurance that is available at reasonable rates. It covers the contents of a house, apartment, or cooperative unit, but not the structure itself, against the same perils as Form HO-2. Owners of condominium units need Form HO-6; it's similar but includes a minimum of $1,000 in protection for any building alterations, additions, and decorations paid for by the policyholder. HO-4 and HO-6 policies include liability coverage and protect you at home and away. For example, if somebody is injured and sues you, the policy would pay for damages up to a specified limit—generally $100,000, although some insurers go as high as $500,000.

A standard renter's insurance policy covers furniture, carpets, appliances, clothing, and most other personal items for their cash value at the time of loss. Expect to pay around $200 to $250 a year for about $15,000 in coverage, depending on where you live. For maximum protection, you can pay about 10 percent more and buy *replacement-cost insurance*, which pays the actual cost of replacing articles with comparable ones. The standard renter's policy provides limited coverage of such valuables as jewelry, furs, and silverware, although some insurers pay up to $1,000 for the loss of watches, gems, and furs and up to $2,500 for silverware.

10-2f Coverage: What Type, Who, and Where?

Homeowner's policies define the types of losses that they cover and the persons and locations covered.

Types of Losses Covered

There are three types of property-related losses when misfortune occurs:

1. Direct loss of property
2. Indirect loss occurring due to loss of damaged property
3. Additional expenses resulting from direct and indirect losses

Homeowner's insurance contracts offer compensation for each type of loss.

SECTION I COVERAGE. When a house is damaged by an insured peril, the insurance company will pay reasonable living expenses, such as the cost of renting alternative accommodations, while the insured's home is being repaired or rebuilt. The insurer will also pay for damages caused by perils other than those mentioned in the policy if a named peril is determined to be the underlying cause of the loss. For example, if lightning (a covered peril) strikes a house while a family is away and knocks out the power, causing $400 worth of food in the freezer and refrigerator to spoil, then the loss will be paid even though temperature change (the direct cause) is not mentioned in the policy.

SECTION II COVERAGE. In addition to paying successfully pursued liability claims against an insured, a homeowner's policy covers (1) the cost of defending the insured, (2) reasonable expenses incurred by an insured in helping the insurance company's defense, and (3) the payment of court costs. This coverage applies even when the liability suit is found to be without merit.

10-2g Persons Covered

A homeowner's policy covers the persons named in the policy and members of their families who are residents of the household. A person, such as a college student, can be a resident of the household even while temporarily living away from home. The parents' homeowner's policy may cover the college student's belongings at school—including such items as stereo equipment, TVs, personal computers, and microwave ovens—but there could be limits and exceptions to the coverage. The standard homeowner's contract also extends limited coverage to guests of the insured.

Locations Covered

Most homeowner's policies offer coverage worldwide when off premises temporarily. For example, an insured's personal property is fully covered when lent to the next-door neighbor or kept in a hotel room in Tibet. The only exception is property left at a second home where coverage is reduced unless the loss occurs while the insured is residing there.

Homeowners and their families have liability protection for their negligent acts wherever they occur. Excluded are negligent acts involving certain types of motorized vehicles (such as large boats and aircraft) and those occurring in the course of employment or professional practice.

10-2h Limitations on Payment

Other factors that influence the amount an insurance company will pay for a loss include replacement-cost provisions, policy limits, and deductibles.

Replacement Cost

The amount necessary to repair, rebuild, or replace an asset at today's prices is the **replacement cost**. When replacement-cost coverage is in effect, a homeowner's reimbursement for damage to a house or accompanying structures is based on the cost of repairing or replacing those structures, without taking any deductions for depreciation. Exhibit 10.3 illustrates a replacement-cost calculation for a 2,400-square-foot home with a two-car garage.

However, for homeowners to be eligible for reimbursement on a full replacement-cost basis, they must keep their homes insured for at least 80 percent of the amount that it would cost to build them today, not including the value of the land. Because inflation could cause coverage to fall below the 80 percent requirement, homeowners can purchase an inflation protection rider that automatically adjusts the amount of coverage based on prevailing inflation rates. Without the rider, maximum compensation for losses would be based on a specified percentage of loss.

Even if a home is in an excellent state of repair, its market value may be lessened by functional obsolescence within the structure—as, for example, when a house that doesn't have enough electrical power

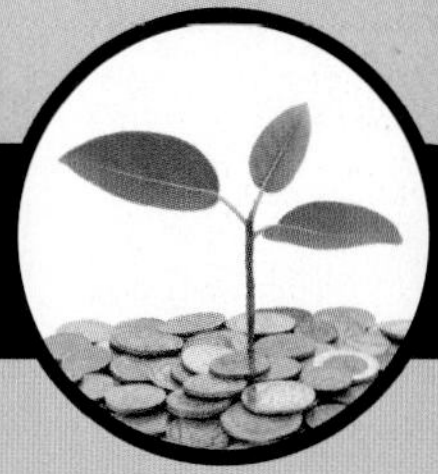

Financial Planning Tips: How to Lower Your Homeowner's Insurance Premiums

Having the right amount of homeowner's insurance is important. But there's no need to overpay. Here are some ways to reduce your insurance premiums:

- **Increase your deductible.** A primary goal of insurance is to protect your family's financial resources from cataclysmic losses, not to totally insulate you from having to pay out much of anything under any circumstances. Think of your insurance as risk sharing, not risk elimination. Increasing your deductible from $500 to $1,000 could reduce your insurance premiums by 25 percent! And if you file a claim, many insurers will increase your premiums so much that it's often not worth filing the claim.
- **Bundle your homeowner's and auto insurance.** Buying your homeowner's and auto insurance from the same insurer can provide a discount of 5 percent to 15 percent. First, get quotes from separate companies for each policy and then compare them with bundled quotes.
- **Check on the discounts that you may get from insurers.** Some relatively minor improvements to your home can earn you discounts. Examples include discount for smoke detectors, deadbolt locks, security and fire alarms, and fire extinguishers. Often, seniors also can get an additional 10 percent discount.
- **Ask your insurance agent what you can do to reduce the risk of your home from the insurer's perspective.** For example, updating an old heating system or replacing old wiring can reduce your insurance premiums.
- **Avoid risks that insurers don't like to insure.** Owning dogs that are known to be more frequently involved in claims (such as pit bulls) can limit or void your policy. Similarly, having a swimming pool or a trampoline can increase your insurance premium. You may have to buy additional coverage to protect yourself against certain risk exposures.
- **Manage your credit score.** Allowing your credit score to get too low can increase your insurance premium.
- **Shop carefully for homeowner's insurance.** While it's worthwhile to shop around from time-to-time, keep in mind that you may be getting a longevity discount if you've been with your insurer for a few years. It's common to get a 5 percent discount if you've been with your company for three to five years and to get a 10 percent discount if you've been with the company for at least six years.

Source: Adapted from Deborah Fowles, "Ten Ways to Cut the Cost of Your Homeowner's Insurance," http://financialplan.about.com/od/homeownersinsurance/a/Homeowners.htm, accessed September 2012.

to run a dishwasher, microwave, and hair dryer at the same time. The HO-8 homeowner's form (for older homes) was adopted as a partial response to this problem. A 2,200-square-foot home in an older neighborhood might have a market value (excluding land) of $195,000, yet the replacement cost might be $260,000. The HO-8 policy solves this problem by covering property in full up to the amount of the loss or up to the property's market value, whichever is less.

Policy Limits

In Section I of the homeowner's policy, the amount of coverage on the dwelling unit (coverage A) establishes the amounts applicable to the accompanying structures (coverage B), the unscheduled personal property (coverage C), and the temporary living expenses (coverage D). Generally, the limits under coverage B, C, and D are 10 percent, 50 percent, and 10 percent to 20 percent, respectively, of the amount of coverage under A.

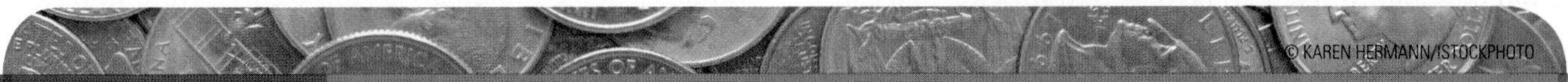

Exhibit 10.3 Calculating Replacement Cost

Here's a typical example of how an insurance company calculates replacement cost. It would take $374,400 to fully replace this home today.

Dwelling cost: 2,400 sq. ft. at $125 per sq. ft.	$300,000
Extra features: built-in appliances, mahogany cabinets, 3 ceiling fans	15,000
Porches, patios: screened and trellised patio	3,700
Two-car garage: 900 sq. ft. at $55 per sq. ft.	49,500
Other site improvements: driveway, storage, landscaping	6,200
Total replacement cost	$374,400

For example, if a house is insured for $150,000, then the respective limits for coverage B, C, and D would be $15,000, $75,000, and $30,000 (that is, 10 percent of $150,000, 50 percent of $150,000, and 20 percent of $150,000). Each of these limits can be increased if it's considered insufficient to cover the exposure. Also, for a small reduction in premium, some companies will permit a homeowner to reduce coverage on unscheduled personal property to 40 percent of the amount on the dwelling unit.

Remember that homeowner's policies usually specify limits for certain types of personal property included under the coverage C category. These coverage limits are *within the total dollar amount* of coverage C and in no way act to increase that total. For example, the dollar limit for losses of money, bank notes, bullion, and related items is $200; securities, accounts, deeds, evidences of debt, manuscripts, passports, tickets, and stamps have a $1,000 limit. Loss from jewelry theft is limited to $1,000, and payment for theft of silverware, goldware, and pewterware has a $2,500 limit. Some policies also offer $5,000 coverage for home computer equipment. You can increase these limits by increasing coverage C.

In Section II, the personal liability coverage (coverage E) often starts out at $100,000, and the medical payments portion (coverage F) normally has a limit of $1,000 per person. Additional coverage included in Section II consists of claim expenses, such as court costs and attorney fees; first aid and medical expenses, including ambulance costs; and damage to others' property of up to $500 per occurrence.

Although these are the most common limits, most homeowners need additional protection, especially liability coverage. In these days of high damage awards by juries, a $100,000 liability limit may not be adequate. The cost to increase the liability limit with most companies is small. For example, the annual premium difference between a $100,000 personal liability limit and a $300,000 limit is likely to be only $20 to $30. You can also increase personal liability coverage by purchasing a personal liability umbrella policy.

Deductibles

Each of the preceding limits on recovery constrains the maximum amount an insurance company must pay under the policy. *Deductibles*, which limit what a company must pay for small losses, help reduce insurance premiums by doing away with the frequent small loss claims that are proportionately more expensive to administer. The standard deductible in most states is $250 on the physical damage protection covered in Section I. However, choosing higher deductible amounts of $500 or $1,000 results in considerable

premium savings—as much as 10 percent to 20 percent in some states. Deductibles don't apply to liability and medical payments coverage because insurers want to be notified of all claims in order to investigate properly and prepare adequate defenses for resulting lawsuits.

10-2i Homeowner's Insurance Premiums

As you might expect, the size of insurance premiums vary widely depending on the insurance provider (company) and the location of the property (neighborhood/city/state). It pays to shop around! When you're shopping, be sure to state clearly the type of insurance you're looking for and to obtain and compare the cost, net of any discounts, offered by a number of agents or insurance companies. Remember that each type of property damage coverage is subject to a deductible of $250 or more.

Most people need to modify the basic package of coverage by adding an inflation rider and increasing the coverage on their homes to 100 percent of the replacement cost. Changing the contents protection from actual cash value to replacement cost and scheduling some items of expensive personal property may be desirable. Most insurance professionals also advise homeowners to increase their liability and medical payments limits. Each of these changes results in an additional premium charge.

And to reduce your total premium, you can increase the amount of your deductibles. Because it's better to budget for small losses than to insure against them, larger deductibles are a popular strategy. You may also qualify for discounts for deadbolt locks, monitored security systems, and other safety features, such as smoke alarms and sprinkler systems.

10-3 Automobile Insurance

LG4 Automobiles also involve risk because damage to them or negligence in their use can result in significant loss. Fortunately, insurance can protect individuals against a big part of these costs. Automobile insurance includes several types of coverage packaged together. Here, we begin by describing the major features of a private passenger automobile policy. Then, we'll briefly explain no-fault laws, followed by discussions of auto insurance premiums and financial responsibility laws.

10-3a Types of Auto Insurance Coverage

The **personal automobile policy (PAP)** is a comprehensive automobile insurance policy designed to be easily understood by the "typical" insurance purchaser. Made up of six parts, the policy's first four parts identify the coverage provided.

© EDG/SHUTTERSTOCK.COM

- Part A: Liability coverage
- Part B: Medical payments coverage
- Part C: Uninsured motorists coverage
- Part D: Coverage for damage to your vehicle

Part E pertains to your duties and responsibilities if you're involved in an accident, and Part F defines basic provisions of the policy, including the policy coverage period and the right of termination.

You're almost sure to purchase liability, medical payments, and uninsured motorists protection, but you may *not* buy protection against damage to your automobile if it's an older vehicle of relatively little value. On the other hand, if your vehicle is leased or you have a loan against it, then you'll probably be required to have a specified amount of physical damage coverage—part D.

Exhibit 10.4 illustrates how the four basic parts of a PAP might be displayed in a typical automobile insurance policy and shows the premium for a six-month period. Here we will take a closer look at the coverage provided by parts A through D.

Part A: Liability Coverage
Most states require you to buy at least a minimum amount of liability insurance. Under the typical PAP, the insurer agrees to:

1. Pay damages for bodily injury and/or property damage for which you are legally responsible as a result of an automobile accident
2. Settle or defend any claim or suit asking for such damages

The provision for legal defense is important and could save thousands of dollars, even if you're not at fault in an automobile accident. The policy does *not* cover defense of criminal charges against the insured due to an accident (such as a drunk driver who's involved in

an accident). Part A also provides for certain supplemental payments (not restricted by the applicable policy limits) for expenses incurred in settling the claim, reimbursement of premiums for appeal bonds, bonds to release attachments of the insured's property, and bail bonds required as a result of an accident.

POLICY LIMITS. Although the insurance company provides both bodily injury and property damage liability insurance under part A, it typically sets *a dollar limit up to which it will pay for damages from any one accident*. Typical limits are $50,000, $100,000, $300,000, and $500,000. You'd be well advised to consider no less than $300,000 coverage in today's legal liability environment. Damage awards are increasing, and the insurer's duty to defend you *ends when the coverage limit has been exhausted*. It's easy to "exhaust" $50,000 or $100,000, leaving you to pay any additional costs above the policy limit. So be sure to purchase adequate coverage—*regardless of the minimum requirements in your state*. Otherwise, you place your personal assets at risk. As Exhibit 10.4 shows, the Johnson family obtained fairly high coverage limits.

Some insurers make so-called *split limits* of liability coverage available, with the first amount in each combination the per-individual limit and the second, the per-accident limit. Some policy limit combinations for protecting individuals against claims made for **bodily injury liability losses** are $25,000/$50,000, $50,000/$100,000, $100,000/$300,000, $250,000/$500,000, and $500,000/$1,000,000. Because the Johnsons purchased the $250,000/$500,000 policy limits, the maximum amount that any one person negligently injured in an accident could receive from the insurance company would be $250,000. Further, the total amount that the insurer would pay to all injured victims in one accident would not exceed $500,000. If a jury awarded a claimant $80,000, the defendant whose insurance policy limits were $50,000/$100,000 could be required to pay $30,000 out of his or her pocket ($80,000 award minus $50,000 paid by insurance). For the defendant, this could mean loss of home, cars, bank accounts, and other assets. In many states, if the value of these assets is too little to satisfy a claim, then defendant's wages may be garnished (taken by the court and used to satisfy the outstanding debt).

The policy limits available to cover **property damage liability losses** are typically $10,000, $25,000, $50,000, and $100,000. In contrast to bodily injury liability limits, property damage limits are stated as a per-accident limit, without specifying limits applicable on a per-item or per-person basis.

bodily injury liability losses A PAP provision that protects the insured against claims made for bodily injury.

property damage liability losses A PAP provision that protects the insured against claims made for damage to property.

Exhibit 10.4 The Four Parts of a Personal Automobile Policy (PAP)

This automobile insurance statement for six months of coverage shows how the four major parts of a PAP might be incorporated. Notice that the premium for collision/comprehensive damage is relatively low because of the age and type of car (a 2010 Honda CRV); these drivers also enjoyed a premium reduction of more than $130 for the six months due to having other insurance with the same provider, a car alarm system, and a good driving record.

ANYSTATE INSURANCE COMPANIES   **AUTO RENEWAL**

Anystate Automobile Insurance Company
1665 West Anywhere Drive
Yourtown, CO 80209   2010 Honda CRV

POLICY NUMBER	PERIOD COVERED	DATE DUE	PLEASE PAY THIS AMOUNT
ABC-123-XYZ-456	MAY 26 2015 to NOV 26 2015	MAY 26 2015	$505

1 H -1582   A

Johnson, Stephen R. & Anne S.
1643 Thunder Rd. #32
Yourtown, CO 80209

Coverages and Limits | | | **Premiums**
Part A	A	Liability	
		Bodily Injury 250,000/500,000	$219
		Property Damage 100,000	
Part B	M	Medical 5,000	19
Part C	U	Uninsured Motor Vehicle	
		Bodily Injury 100,000/300,000	71
Part D	G	500 Deductible Collision	140
	D-WG	500 Deductible Comprehensive	50
	H	Emergency Road Service	6

Amount Due $505

Your premium has already been adjusted by the following:

Premium Reductions
Multiple Line	22
Antitheft devices	40
Good driver	70

Your premium is based on the following …
If not correct, contact your agent.

2010 Honda CRV
Serial number: 4 ABCD12M3NP456789

Drivers of vehicle in your household …
There are no male or unmarried female drivers under age 25.
Younger drivers included if rated on another car insured with us.

Ordinary use of vehicle …
To and from work or school, more than 100 miles weekly.
Driven more than 7,500 miles annually.
(National average is 10,000 miles annually.)

Source: Adapted from a major automobile insurance company quote.

PERSONS INSURED. Two basic definitions in the PAP determine who is covered under part A: insured person and covered auto. Essentially, an *insured person* includes you (the named insured) and any family member, any person using a covered auto, and any person or organization that may be held responsible for your actions. The *named insured* is the person named in the declarations page of the policy. The spouse of the person named is considered a named insured if he or she resides in the same household. Family members are persons related by blood, marriage, or adoption and residing in the same household. An unmarried college student living away from home usually is considered a family member. *Covered autos* are the vehicles shown in the declarations page of your PAP, autos acquired during the policy period, any trailer owned, and any auto or trailer used as a temporary substitute while your auto or trailer is being repaired or serviced. An automobile that you lease for an extended time can be included as a covered automobile.

The named insured and family members have part A liability coverage regardless of the automobile they are driving. However, for persons other than the named insured and family members to have liability coverage, they must be driving a covered auto.

Part B: Medical Payments Coverage

Medical payments coverage insures a covered individual for reasonable and necessary medical expenses incurred within three years of an automobile accident in an amount not to exceed the policy limits. It provides for reimbursement even if other sources of recovery, such as health or accident insurance, also make payments. What's more, in most states, the insurer reimburses the insured for medical payments even if the insured proves that another person was negligent in the accident and receives compensation from that party's liability insurer.

A person need not be occupying an automobile when the accidental injury occurs to be eligible for benefits. Injuries sustained as a pedestrian, or on a bicycle in a traffic accident, are also covered. (Motorcycle accidents are normally not covered.) Part B insurance also pays on an excess basis. For instance, if you're a passenger in a friend's automobile during an accident and suffer $8,000 in medical expenses, you can collect under his medical payments insurance up to his policy limits. Further, you can collect (up to the amount of your policy limits) from your insurer the amount exceeding what the other medical payments provide.

POLICY LIMITS. Medical payments insurance usually has per-person limits of $1,000, $2,000, $3,000, $5,000, or $10,000. Thus, an insurer could conceivably pay $60,000 or more in medical payments benefits for one accident involving a named insured and five passengers. Most families are advised to buy the $5,000 or $10,000 limit because, even though they may have other health insurance available, they can't be sure that their passengers are as well protected.

PERSONS INSURED. Coverage under an automobile medical payments insurance policy applies to the named insured and to family members who are injured while occupying an automobile (whether owned by the named insured or not) or when struck by an automobile or trailer of any type. Part B also applies to any other person occupying a covered automobile.

Part C: Uninsured Motorists Coverage

Uninsured motorists coverage is available to meet the needs of "innocent" victims of accidents who are negligently injured by uninsured, underinsured, or hit-and-run motorists. Nearly all states require uninsured motorists insurance to be included in each liability insurance policy issued, but the coverage can be rejected in most of these states. Rejecting uninsured motorists coverage is not a good idea. Under uninsured motorists coverage, an insured is legally entitled to collect an amount equal to the sum that could have been collected from the negligent motorist's liability insurance, had such coverage been available, up to a maximum amount equal to the policy's stated *uninsured motorists limit*.

Three points must be proven to receive payment through uninsured motorists insurance: (1) another motorist must be at fault, (2) the motorist has no available insurance or is underinsured, and (3) damages were incurred. With uninsured motorists coverage, you generally can collect only for losses arising from bodily injury.

POLICY LIMITS. Because uninsured motorists insurance is fairly low in cost (usually around $50 to $75 per year), drivers should purchase at least its minimum available limits. The Johnsons purchased $100,000/$300,000 coverage for just $71 per year.

PERSONS INSURED. Uninsured motorists protection covers the named insured, family members, and any other person occupying a covered auto.

UNDERINSURED MOTORISTS COVERAGE. In addition to *uninsured motorists*, in some states, for a small premium, you can obtain **underinsured motorists coverage**, which protects against damages caused by being in an accident with an underinsured motorist who is found liable. Underinsured motorists insurance

SVLUMA/SHUTTERSTOCK

collision insurance Automobile insurance that pays for collision damage to an insured automobile *regardless of who is at fault.*

comprehensive automobile insurance Coverage that protects against loss to an insured automobile caused by any peril (with a few exceptions) *other than collision.*

no-fault automobile insurance Automobile insurance that reimburses the parties involved in an accident without regard to negligence.

has become increasingly popular and *can be purchased for both bodily injury and property damage.* If an at-fault driver causes more damage to you than the limit of her liability, your insurance company makes up the difference (up to the limits of your coverage) and then goes after the negligent driver for the deficiency. Clearly, if it's available in your state, you should consider purchasing this optional coverage.

Part D: Coverage for Physical Damage to a Vehicle

This part of the PAP provides coverage for damage to your auto. The two basic types of coverage are collision and comprehensive (or "other than collision").

COLLISION INSURANCE. Collision insurance is automobile insurance that pays for collision damage to an insured automobile *regardless of who is at fault.* The amount of insurance payable is the actual cash value of the loss in excess of your deductible. Remember that *actual cash value is defined as replacement cost minus depreciation.* So, if a car is demolished, the insured is paid an amount equal to the car's depreciated value minus any deductible. Deductibles typically range between $50 and $1,000, and selecting a higher deductible, as did the Johnsons, will reduce your premium.

Lenders and lessors typically require collision insurance on cars they finance. In some cases, especially when the auto dealer is handling the financing, it will try to sell you this insurance. *Avoid buying automobile insurance from car dealers or finance companies.* It is best to buy such insurance from your regular insurance agent and include collision insurance as part of your full auto insurance policy (i.e., the PAP). A full-time insurance agent is better able to assess and meet your insurance needs. The collision provision of your insurance policy often fully protects you in a rental car, so be sure to check before purchasing supplemental collision insurance when renting a car.

Go to Smart Sites

Is there ever a time to drop comprehensive coverage? eHow's site helps you decide. ●

COMPREHENSIVE AUTOMOBILE INSURANCE. Comprehensive automobile insurance protects against loss to an insured automobile caused by any peril (with a few exceptions) *other than collision.*

The maximum compensation provided under this coverage is the actual cash value of the automobile. Coverage includes, but is not limited to, damage caused by fire, theft, glass breakage, falling objects, malicious mischief, vandalism, riot, and earthquake. The automobile insurance policy normally does *not* cover the theft of personal property left in the insured vehicle; instead, this may be covered by the off-premises coverage of the homeowner's policy if the auto was locked when the theft occurred.

10-3b No-Fault Automobile Insurance

No-fault automobile insurance is a system under which each insured party is compensated by his or her own company, regardless of which party caused the accident. In return, legal remedies and payments for pain and suffering are restricted. Under the concept of *pure* no-fault insurance, the driver, passengers, and injured pedestrians are reimbursed by the insurer of the car for economic losses stemming from bodily injury. The insurer doesn't have to cover claims for losses to other motorists who are covered by their own policies.

Unfortunately, advocates of no-fault forget that the sole purpose of liability insurance is to protect the assets of the insured—not to pay losses, *per se.* State laws governing no-fault insurance vary widely, but most states provide from $2,000 to $10,000 in personal injury protection and restrict legal recovery for pain and suffering to cases where medical or economic losses exceed some threshold level, such as $500 or $1,000. In all states, recovery based on negligence is permitted for economic loss exceeding the amount payable by no-fault insurance.

10-3c Automobile Insurance Premiums

The cost of car insurance depends on many things, including your age, where you live, the car you drive, your driving record, the coverage you have, and the amount of your deductible. Consequently, car insurance premiums—even for the same coverage—vary all over the map.

Factors Affecting Premiums

Factors that influence how auto insurance premiums are set include (1) rating territory, (2) amount of use the automobile receives, (3) personal characteristics of the driver, (4) type of automobile, and (5) insured's driving record.

● **Rating territory.** Rates are higher in geographic areas where accident rates, number of claims filed, and average cost of claims paid are higher. Rates reflect auto repair costs, hospital and medical expenses, jury awards, and theft and vandalism in the area. Even someone with a perfect driving record will be charged the going rate for the area where the automobile is garaged. Exhibit 10.5 gives some helpful tips for protecting your vehicle wherever you live. Some jurisdictions prohibit the use of rating territories, age, and gender factors because they believe these factors unfairly discriminate against the urban, the young, and the male.

- **Use of the automobile.** Rates are also lower if the insured automobile isn't usually driven to work or is driven less than 3 miles one way. Premiums rise slightly if you drive more than 3 but fewer than 15 miles to work and increase if your commute exceeds 15 miles each way.

- **Drivers' personal characteristics.** The insured's age, sex, and marital status can also affect automobile insurance premiums. Insurance companies base their premium differentials on the number of accidents involving certain age groups. For example, drivers aged 25 and under make up only about 15 percent of the total driving population, but they are involved in nearly 30 percent of auto accidents and in 26 percent of all fatal accidents. Male drivers are involved in a larger percentage of fatal crashes, so unmarried males under age 30 (and married males under age 25) pay higher premiums than do older individuals. Females over age 24, as well as married females of any age, are exempt from the youthful operator classification and pay lower premiums.

- **Type of automobile.** Insurance companies charge higher rates for automobiles classified as intermediate-performance, high-performance, and sports vehicles and also for rear-engine models. Some states even rate four-door cars differently from two-door models. If you're thinking of buying, say, a Corvette or a Porsche, be prepared for some hefty insurance rates.

- **Driving record.** The driving records—traffic violations and accidents—of those insured and the people who live with them affect premium levels. More severe traffic convictions—driving under the influence of alcohol or drugs, leaving the scene of an accident, homicide or assault arising from the operation of a motor vehicle, and driving with a revoked or suspended driver's license—result in higher insurance premiums. Any conviction for a moving traffic violation that results in the accumulation of points under a state point system also may incur a premium surcharge. In most states, accidents determined to be the insured's fault also incur points and a premium surcharge.

Go to Smart Sites

Can you save money on your insurance by using a direct underwriter? Get a quote from GEICO Direct and compare it with your current policies and premiums.

Driving Down the Cost of Auto Insurance
One of the best ways to reduce the cost of auto insurance is to take advantage of the insurer's discounts, which can knock from 5 percent to 50 percent off your annual premium. Some give overall *safe-driving (accident-free) discounts*, and most give youthful operators lower rates if they've had *driver's training*.

Exhibit 10.5 | Prevent Auto Theft

You can help prevent your car from being stolen by taking the following precautions:

- Close the windows and lock your doors.
- Don't leave your vehicle registration and proof of insurance in your car. No personal identifying information should be left in your car.
- Park in well-lit, heavily traveled areas.
- Take any packages that are in plain sight with you.
- Invest in and install a good anti-theft device like a burglar alarm or a steering wheel lock.
- Never leave your car unattended with the motor running.
- When parking your car, turn the wheels sharply toward or away from the curb and set the emergency brake.
- Don't leave a spare key in the car. Thieves always know where to look.
- Etch the VIN (vehicle identification number) in the windows and on other major parts of your car, which makes it harder to resell the car or its major components.

Sources: Adapted from "Prevent Your Car from Being Stolen," http://www.insurance.com/auto-insurance/claims/prevent-your-car-from-being-stolen.aspx, accessed September 2012; "Protect Yourself from Auto Theft," accessed September 2012.

High school and college students may also receive *good-student discounts* for maintaining a B average or making the dean's list at their school.

Nearly all insurance companies give discounts to families with two or more automobiles insured by the same company (the *multicar discount*). Most insurers also offer discounts to owners who install *antitheft devices* in their cars. Likewise, some insurers offer *nonsmoker* and *nondrinker discounts*. Some insurers accept only persons who are educators or executives;

> **Nearly all insurance companies give discounts to families with two or more automobiles insured by the same company (the *multicar discount*).**

others accept only government employees. Through more selective underwriting, these companies are able to reduce losses and operating expenses, which results in lower premiums.

Clearly, it's to your advantage to look for and use as many of these discounts as you can. Take another look at the auto insurance statement in Exhibit 10.4, and you'll see that the insured reduced his overall cost of coverage by 25 percent by qualifying for just three of the discounts (labeled "Premium Reductions"). Another effective way to drive down the cost of car insurance is to *raise your deductibles* (as discussed earlier in this chapter). For example, the premium difference between a $100 deductible and a $500 deductible may be as much as 25 percent on collision coverage and 30 percent on comprehensive coverage; and a $1,000 deductible may save you as much as 50 percent on both collision and comprehensive coverage.

10-3d Financial Responsibility Laws

Most states have **financial responsibility laws**, whereby motorists *must buy a specified minimum amount of automobile liability insurance* or provide other proof of comparable financial responsibility. The required limits are low in most states—well below what you should carry. Financial responsibility laws

fall into two categories. *Compulsory auto insurance laws* require motorists to show evidence of insurance coverage *before* receiving their license plates. Penalties for not having liability insurance include fines and suspension of your driver's license. The second category requires motorists to show evidence of their insurance coverage only *after* being involved in an accident. If they then fail to demonstrate compliance with the law, their registrations and driver's licenses are suspended.

10-4 Other Property and Liability Insurance

LG5 Homeowner's and automobile insurance policies provide the basic protection needed by most families, but some need other more specialized types of insurance. Popular forms of other insurance include supplemental property insurance—earthquake, flood, and other forms of transportation—as well as the personal liability umbrella policy.

10-4a Supplemental Property Insurance Coverage

Because homeowner's policies exclude certain types of damage, you may want to consider some of the following types of supplemental coverage.

- **Earthquake insurance.** In addition to California, areas in other states are also subject to this type of loss. Very few homeowners buy this coverage because these policies typically carry a 15 percent deductible on the replacement cost of a home damaged or destroyed by earthquake.

- **Flood insurance.** In 1968, the federal government established a subsidized flood insurance program in cooperation with private insurance agents, who can now sell this low-cost coverage to homeowners and tenants living in designated communities. The flood insurance program also encourages communities to initiate land-use controls to reduce future flood losses.

- **Other forms of transportation insurance.** In addition to automobiles, you can buy policies to insure other types of vehicles, such as mobile homes, recreational vehicles, or boats.

10-4b Personal Liability Umbrella Policy

Persons with moderate to high levels of income and net worth may want to purchase a **personal liability umbrella policy**, which provides added liability coverage for homeowner's and automobile insurance. Umbrella policies often include limits of $1 million or more. Some also provide added amounts of coverage for a family's major medical insurance. The premiums are usually quite reasonable for the broad coverage offered—$150 to $300 a year for as much as $1 million in coverage. The insured party must already have relatively high liability limits ($100,000 to $300,000) on their homeowner's and auto coverage in order to purchase a personal liability umbrella policy.

10-5 Buying Insurance and Settling Claims

LG6 The first step when buying property and liability insurance is to develop an inventory of exposures to loss and then arrange them from highest to lowest priority. Losses that lend themselves to insurance protection are those that seldom occur but are potentially substantial—for example, damage to a home and its contents or liability arising from a negligence claim. Somewhat less important, but still desirable, is insurance to cover losses that could disrupt a family's financial plans, even if the losses might not result in insolvency. Such risks include physical damage to automobiles, boats, and other personal property of moderate value. Lowest-priority exposures can be covered by savings or from current income.

10-5a Property and Liability Insurance Agents

A good property insurance agent can make the purchase process much easier. Most property insurance agents fall into either the captive or independent category. A **captive agent** represents only one insurance company and is more or less an employee of that company. Allstate, Nationwide, and State Farm are major insurance companies that market their products through captive agents. In contrast, **independent agents** typically represent from 2 to 10 different insurance companies. These agents may place your coverage with any of the companies with whom they have an agency relationship. Some well-known companies that operate through independent agents include The Hartford, Unitrin Kemper, Chubb, and Travelers. Either type of agent can serve your needs well and should take the time to do the following:

- Review your total property and liability insurance exposures
- Inventory property and identify exposures
- Determine appropriate covered perils, limits, deductibles, and floater policies

Because of large variations in premiums and services, it pays to comparison shop.

Property insurance agents who meet various experiential and educational requirements, including passing a series of written examinations, qualify for the *Chartered Property and Casualty Underwriter (CPCU)* or *Certified Insurance Counselor (CIC)* designation. Another alternative to consider is companies that sell directly to the consumer through an 800 number or online. Generally, their premiums are lower. Examples of direct sellers are Amica, Erie, GEICO, and USAA.

10-5b Property and Liability Insurance Companies

When selecting an agent, you should ask questions about the company, including its financial soundness, its claims-settlement practices, and the geographic range of its operations (this could be important if you're involved in an accident 1,000 miles from home). As with any form of insurance, you should check the company's ratings (see Chapter 8) and stick with those rated in the top categories. Friends and acquaintances often can provide insight into its claims settlement policy. Many insurance companies now have elaborate home pages on the Web containing basic information about the provider and its products, directions to local agents, or calculators to crunch the numbers and generate sample premiums.

10-5c Settling Property and Liability Claims

Insurance companies typically settle claims promptly and fairly—especially life and health care claims. But in settling property and liability claims, there is often some claimant–insurer disagreement. Here, we'll review the claims settlement process, beginning with consideration of what you should do immediately following an accident.

First Steps Following an Accident
After an accident, record the names, addresses, and phone numbers of all witnesses, drivers, occupants, and injured parties, along with the license numbers of the automobiles involved. Never leave the scene of an accident, even if the other party says it's all right. Immediately notify law enforcement officers and your insurance agent of the accident. Never discuss liability at the scene of an accident, or with anyone other than the police and your insurer. It's the duty of the police to assess the probability of a law violation and maintain order at the scene of an accident—not to make judgments about liability.

captive agent An insurance agent who represents only one insurance company and who is, in effect, an employee of that company.

independent agent An insurance agent who may place coverage with any company with which he or she has an agency relationship, as long as the insured meets that company's underwriting standards.

claims adjustor An insurance specialist who works for the insurance company, as an independent adjustor, or for an adjustment bureau to investigate claims.

Steps in Claims Settlement

If you're involved in an accident, one of the first things to decide is whether you want to file a claim. Most experts agree that unless it's a very minor or insignificant accident, the best course of action is to file a claim. Be aware, though, that if you've made several claims then your insurance company may decide to drop you after settling the current one. The claims settlement process typically involves these steps:

1. **Notice to your insurance company.** You must notify your insurance company that a loss (or potential for loss) has occurred. Timely notice is extremely important.

2. **Investigation.** Insurance company personnel may talk to witnesses or law enforcement officers and gather physical evidence to determine whether the claimed loss is covered by the policy, and they'll check to make sure that the date of the loss falls within the policy period. If you delay filing your claim, you hinder the insurer's ability to check the facts. All policies specify the period within which you must give notice. Failure to report can result in losing your right to collect.

3. **Proof of loss.** This proof requires you to give a sworn statement. You may have to show medical bills, submit an inventory, and certify the value of lost property (for example, a written inventory, photographs, and purchase receipts). You may also have to submit an employer statement of lost wages and, if possible, physical evidence of

damage (e.g., X-rays if you claim a back injury; a broken window or pried door if you claim a break-in and theft at your home). After reviewing your proof of loss, the insurer may (1) pay you the amount you asked for, (2) offer you a lesser amount, or (3) deny that the company has any legal responsibility under the terms of your policy.

If the amount is disputed, most policies provide for some form of claims arbitration. You hire a third party, the company hires a third party, and these two arbitrators jointly select one more person. When any two of the three arbitrators reach agreement, their decision binds you and the company to their solution. When a company denies responsibility, you do not get the right of arbitration. In such cases, the company is saying the loss does not fall under the policy coverage. You must then either forget the claim or bring in an attorney or, perhaps, a public adjustor (discussed next).

Claims Adjustment

Usually the first person to call when you need to file a claim is your insurance agent. If your loss is relatively minor, the agent can process it quickly and, in fact, often gives you a check right on the spot. If your loss is more complex, your company probably will assign a claims adjustor to the case. A **claims adjustor** is an insurance specialist who works for the insurance company either as an independent adjustor or for an adjustment bureau. The adjustor investigates claims, looking out for the company's interests—which might very well be to keep you, its

Financial Planning Tips: How to Handle a Denied Claim

If your homeowner's or automobile insurance company refuses to pay all or part of your claim, that can be an upsetting or even infuriating experience. Here are some key steps to take if you decide to fight back:

- **Understand the claim and the insurer's stated reason for denying it.** Determine whether there is a discrepancy between the terms stated in your policy and the rationale provided in the denial. Make sure that you know your policy maximums. You can't fight the denial effectively if you can't point out the discrepancy to your insurance company.
- **Document every step.** Obtain written copies of police or fire department reports and outside appraisals, and take photos.
- **Request a review of the claim denial.** Complain to your insurance company and ask for a review of your case. Do this as soon as possible, because some

companies require you to file an appeal within one year of the date of the first decision.

- **If the insurance company does not honor your claim or takes weeks to respond, then go to your state's insurance department.** In most states, insurers have about six weeks to resolve a dispute.
- **Weigh the costs and the benefits carefully before you file a lawsuit.** The legal fees and hassle might be worth it if you have a homeowner's claim for $25,000 or $50,000. But a denied auto claim for a few thousand dollars may not be worth pursuing in light of the legal costs.

Source: Adapted from "What To Do If Your Homeowners Insurance Claim is Denied," http://www.2mrealty.com/blog/homeowners-insurance-claim-is-denied.html, accessed September 2012; and Kalen Smith, "What to Do If Your Homeowners Insurance Claim Is Denied," http://www.moneycrashers.com/homeowners-insurance-claim-denied/, accessed September 2012.

customer, satisfied. However, many claimants are out to collect all they can from insurance companies, which they think have "deep pockets." Thus adjustors walk a fine line: they must diligently question and investigate while at the same time offering service to minimize settlement delays and financial hardship. To promote your own interest in the claim, cooperate with your adjustor and answer inquiries honestly—keeping in mind that the insurance company signs the adjustor's paycheck.

Planning Over a Lifetime: Protecting Your Property

Here are some suggestions on how to insure your property and protect against liability exposures over the different stages of your life.

Independent Lifestyle (20s)	Family and Career Development (30s–40s)	Mature Lifestyle (50s–60s)	Retirement (65+)
✓ Evaluate renter's insurance to protect your personal property and to limit liability exposure.	✓ Buy homeowner's insurance with appropriate property and liability coverage.	✓ Review homeowner's insurance coverage. Keep in mind the possible need for riders on expensive, otherwise insufficiently uncovered personal items.	✓ Revise homeowner's and liability coverage in light of retirement situation.
✓ Make sure to get adequate auto insurance. Don't try to save by buying too little liability coverage.	✓ Document your personal items with photos and purchase receipts.	✓ Consider bundling your homeowner's and auto policies with the same insurer for a discount.	✓ Revise auto insurance in light of your retirement situation.
	✓ Re-evaluate auto insurance coverage.	✓ Consider getting policy discounts by buying a security system for your home and/or car.	

FINANCIAL PLANNING EXERCISES

LG1

1. Assume that Mary Boyle had a homeowner's insurance policy with $150,000 of coverage on the dwelling. Would a 90 percent co-insurance clause be better than an 80 percent clause in such a policy? Give reasons to support your answer.

LG2

2. Last year, Paul and Joanna Stillman bought a home with a dwelling replacement value of $250,000 and insured it (via an HO-5 policy) for $210,000. The policy reimburses for actual cash value and has a $500 deductible, standard limits for coverage C items, and no scheduled property. Recently, burglars broke into the house and stole a two-year-old television set with a current replacement value of $600 and an estimated useful life of eight years. They also took jewelry valued at $1,850 and silver flatware valued at $3,000.
   a. If the Stillmans's policy has an 80 percent co-insurance clause, do they have enough insurance?
   b. Assuming a 50 percent coverage C limit, calculate how much the Stillmans would receive if they filed a claim for the stolen items.
   c. What advice would you give the Stillmans about their homeowner's coverage?

LG3

3. Fred and Sasha Seidel, both graduate students, moved into an apartment near the university. Sasha wants to buy renter's insurance, but Fred thinks they don't need it because their furniture isn't worth much. Sasha points out that, among other things, they have some expensive computer and stereo equipment. To help the Seidels resolve their dilemma, suggest a plan for deciding how much insurance to buy, and give them some ideas for finding a policy.

LG3

4. Sarah Kavenna's luxurious home in in Washington, D.C., was recently gutted in a fire. Her living and dining rooms were completely destroyed, and the damaged personal property had a replacement value of $27,000. The average age of the damaged personal property was 5 years, and its useful life was estimated to be 15 years. What is the maximum amount the insurance company would pay Sarah, assuming that it reimburses losses on an actual cash-value basis?

LG4

5. David Salter has a personal automobile policy (PAP) with coverage of $25,000/$50,000 for bodily injury liability, $25,000 for property damage liability, $5,000 for medical payments, and a $500 deductible for collision insurance. How much will his insurance cover in each of the following situations? Will he have any out-of-pocket costs?
   a. David loses control and skids on ice, running into a parked car and causing $3,785 damage to the unoccupied vehicle and $2,350 damage to his own car.
   b. David runs a stop sign and causes a serious auto accident, badly injuring two people. The injured parties win lawsuits against him for $30,000 each.
   c. David's 18-year-old son borrows his car. He backs into a telephone pole and causes $450 damage to the car.

PFIN Student Study Tools—Visit CourseMate for PFIN 3. Log in at **www.cengagebrain.com**. Check out the bonus exercises and exhibits, interactive worksheets, Smart Sites, Critical Thinking Cases, Money Online, Kiplinger videos, quizzing, and more.

Cool Apps—Look for this new feature on CourseMate for PFIN 3. Cool Apps navigates the growing world of apps that are available for personal financial planning and tracking.

PART 5

MANAGING INVESTMENTS

THORSTEN RUST/SHUTTERSTOCK.COM

Shares 40%

Asset Allocat

Cash

Fixed

11

INVESTMENT PLANNING

LEARNING GOALS

LG1 Discuss the role that investing plays in the personal financial planning process and identify several different investment objectives.

LG2 Distinguish between primary and secondary markets as well as between broker and dealer markets.

LG3 Explain the process of buying and selling securities and recognize the different types of orders.

LG4 Develop an appreciation of how various forms of investment information can lead to better investing skills and returns.

LG5 Gain a basic understanding of the growing impact of the computer and the Internet on the field of investments.

LG6 Describe an investment portfolio and how you'd go about developing, monitoring, and managing a portfolio of securities.

How Will This Affect Me? Investing is the means by which many important financial goals in life are achieved. This chapter discusses how to determine how much investment capital is needed to reach common financial goals and shows how to invest for retirement, to fund major expenditures, to earn needed income, and to establish tax shelters. The market context in which investing occurs is described, and how to buy and sell investments is explained. A framework for evaluating investments is also presented, which includes how to describe, monitor, and manage a portfolio. Sources of investment information are discussed, as well as some of the useful investing tools available online. After reading this chapter, you should be able to plan your investments to better meet your financial goals.

11-1 The Objectives and Rewards of Investing

LG1 People invest their money for all sorts of reasons. Some do it as a way to accumulate the down payment on a new home; others do it as a way to supplement their income; still others invest to build up a nest egg for retirement. Actually, the term *investment* means different things to different people; that is, while millions

If you're like most investors, at first you'll probably keep your funds in some type of savings vehicle (as described in Chapter 4). Once you have *sufficient savings*—for emergencies and other purposes—you can start building up a *pool of investable capital.* This often means making sacrifices and doing what you can to *live within your budget.* Granted, it's far easier to spend money than to save it, but if you're really serious about getting into investments, you'll have to accumulate the necessary capital! In addition to a savings and capital accumulation program, it's also important to have adequate *insurance coverage* to provide protection against the unexpected. For our purposes here, we'll assume that you're adequately insured and that the cost of insurance coverage is built into your family's monthly cash budget. Ample insurance and liquidity (cash and savings) with which to meet life's emergencies are two *investment prerequisites* that are absolutely essential to developing a successful investment program. Once these conditions are met, you're ready to start investing.

investing The process of placing money in some medium such as stocks or bonds in the expectation of receiving some future benefit.

speculating A form of investing in which future value and expected returns are highly uncertain.

> ## "Ample insurance and liquidity are two *investment prerequisites* that are absolutely essential to developing a successful investment program."

of people *invest* regularly in securities like stocks, bonds, and mutual funds, others *speculate* in commodities or options. **Investing** is generally considered to take a long-term perspective and is viewed as a process of purchasing securities wherein stability of value and level of return are somewhat predictable. **Speculating**, on the other hand, is viewed as a short-term activity that involves the buying and selling of securities in which future value and expected return are highly uncertain. Think of an investor as someone who wears both a belt *and* suspenders and a speculator as one who wears neither.

 Go to Smart Sites

Investopedia has a series of videos that will help you navigate the Byzantine world of investing. For more online resources, whenever you see "*Go to Smart Sites*" in this chapter, visit CourseMate for PFIN 3. Log in at **www.cengagebrain.com.** ●

11-1a How Do I Get Started?

Contrary to what you may believe, there's really nothing magical about the topic of investments. The terminology may seem baffling at times, and some of the procedures and techniques may

After you read the chapter, explore the STUDY TOOLS listed on page 278.

seem quite complicated. But don't let that mislead you into thinking there's no room for the small, individual investor. Nothing could be farther from the truth! As we'll see in this and the next two chapters, individual investors can choose from a wide array of securities and investment vehicles.

How, then, do you get started? First, you need some money—not a lot; $500 to $1,000 will do, although $4,000 or $5,000 would be better (and remember, this is *investment capital* we're talking about here—money you've accumulated above and beyond basic emergency savings). Besides the money, you need knowledge and know-how. Never invest in something you don't understand—that's the quickest way to lose money. Instead, learn as much as you can about the market, different types of securities, and various trading strategies. Also try to stay current with major developments as they occur in the market; start following the stock market, interest rates, and developments in the bond market.

We strongly suggest that, after you've learned a few things about stocks and bonds, you set up a portfolio of securities on paper and make *paper trades* in and out of your portfolio, for six months to a year, to get a feel for what it's like to make (and lose) money in the market. Start out with an imaginary sum of, say, $50,000 (if you're going to dream, you might as well dream big). Then keep track of the stocks, bonds, and mutual funds you hold, record the number of shares bought and sold, dividends received, and so on. Throughout this exercise, be sure to use actual prices (as obtained from *The Wall Street Journal,* CNN.com, or your local newspaper) and keep it as realistic as possible. You might even want to use one of the *portfolio tracking* programs offered at such sites as **www.quicken.com** or **moneycentral. msn.com.** Eventually, you'll become familiar with the market and be comfortable with how things are done there. When that happens, you'll be ready to take the plunge.

As a beginning investor with limited funds, it's probably best to confine your investment activity to the basics. Stick to stocks, bonds, and mutual funds. Avoid getting fancy, and certainly don't try to make a killing every time you invest—that will only lead to frustration, disappointment, and possibly heavy losses. Further, *be patient!* Don't expect the price of the stock to double overnight, and don't panic when things don't work out as expected in the short run (after all, security prices do occasionally go down). Finally, remember that you don't need spectacular returns in order to make a significant amount in the market. Instead, be consistent and let the concept of compound interest work for you. While the type of security you invest in is a highly personal decision, you might want to seriously consider a mutual fund as your first investment (see Chapter 13). These funds

provide professional management and diversification that individual investors—especially those with limited resources—can rarely obtain on their own.

11-1b The Role of Investing in Personal Financial Planning

Buy a car, build a house, enjoy a comfortable retirement—these are goals we'd all like to attain some day, and in many cases, they're the centerpieces of well-developed financial plans. As a rule, a financial goal such as building a house is not something we pay for out of our cash reserves. Instead, we must accumulate the funds over time, which is where investment planning and the act of investing enters into the personal financial planning process.

It all starts with an objective: a particular financial goal you'd like to achieve within a certain period of time. Take the case of the Maxwells. Shortly after the birth of their first child, they decided to start a college education fund. After doing some rough calculations, they concluded they'd need to accumulate about $160,000 over the next 18 years to have enough money for their daughter's education. Simply by setting that objective, the Maxwells created a well-defined, specific financial goal. The purpose is to meet their child's educational needs, and the amount of money involved is $160,000 to be earned over 18 years.

Coming Up with the Capital

So far, the Maxwells know how much money they want to accumulate ($160,000) and how long they have to accumulate it (18 years). The only other thing they need to determine at this point is the *rate of return* that they think they can earn on their money. The Maxwells know that the amount of money they'll have to put into their investment program largely depends on *how much they can earn from their investments:* the higher their rate of return, the less they'll have to put up. Let's say they feel comfortable using a 6 percent rate of return. That's a fairly conservative number—one that won't require them to put all or most of their money into high-risk investments—and they're reasonably certain they can reach that level of return, *on average,* over the long haul. It's important to use some care in coming up with a projected rate of return. Don't saddle yourself with an unreasonably high rate because that will simply reduce the chance of reaching your targeted financial goal.

Now, there are two ways of coming up with the capital needed to reach a targeted sum of money: (1) you can make a lump-sum investment right up front and let that amount grow over time; or (2) you can set up a systematic savings plan and put away a certain amount of money each year. Worksheet 11.1 is designed to help you find the amount of investment

You can use a worksheet like this one to find out how much money you must come up with to reach a given financial goal. This worksheet is based on the same future value concepts introduced in Chapter 2.

DETERMINING AMOUNT OF INVESTMENT CAPITAL

Financial goal: *To accumulate $160,000 in 18 years for the purpose of meeting the cost of daughter's college education.*

1. Targeted Financial Goal (see Note 1)	$ 160,000
2. Projected Average Return on Investments	6%
A. Finding a Lump-Sum Investment:	
3. Future Value Factor, from Appendix A ■ based on _____ years to target date and a projected average return on investment of ___%___	0.000
4. Required Lump-Sum Investment ■ line 1 ÷ line 3	$ 0
B. Making a Series of Investments over Time:	
5. Amount of Initial Investment, if any (see Note 2)	$ 7,500
6. Future Value Factor, from Appendix A ■ based on __18__ years of target date and a projected average return on investment of __6%__	2.854
7. Terminal Value of Initial Investment ■ line 5 × line 6	$ 21,408
8. Balance to Come from Savings Plan ■ line 1 − line 7	$ 138,592
9. Future Value Annuity Factor, from Appendix B ■ based on __18__ years to target date and a projected average return on investment of __6%__	30.906
10. Series of Annual Investments Required over Time ■ line 8 ÷ line 9	4,484.00

Note 1: The "targeted financial goal" is the amount of money you want to accumulate by some target date in the future.

Note 2: If you're starting from scratch—i.e., there is *no* initial investment—enter zero on line 5, *skip* lines 6 and 7, and then use the total targeted financial goal (from line 1) as the amount to be funded from a savings plan; now proceed with the rest of the worksheet.

investment plan A statement— preferably written— that specifies how investment capital will be invested to achieve a specified goal.

capital that you'll need to reach a given financial goal. It employs the *compound value* concept discussed in Chapter 2 and is based on a given financial target (of $160,000, line 1) and a projected average rate of return on your investments (of 6 percent, line 2). You can use this worksheet to find either a required lump-sum investment (Part A of the worksheet) or an amount that will have to be put away each year in a savings plan (Part B). For our purposes here, we'll assume that the Maxwells have $7,500 to start with (this comes mostly from gifts their daughter received from her grandparents). Because they know they'll need a lot more than that to reach their target, the Maxwells decide to use Part B of the worksheet to find out how much they'll have to save annually.

The first thing to do is find the future value of the $7,500 initial investment. The question here is: How much will that initial lump-sum investment grow to over an 18-year period? Using the compound value concept and the appropriate "future value factor" (from Appendix A), we see in line 7 that this deposit will grow to some $21,408. But that's only about 13 percent of the target amount of $160,000. Indeed, by subtracting the terminal value of the initial investment (line 7) from our target (line 1), we find the amount that must be generated from some sort of annual savings plan—see line 8. Again, using the appropriate future value factor (this time from Appendix B), we find that the Maxwells will have to put away about $4,484 a year in order to reach their target of $160,000 in 18 years. That is, the $4,484 a year will grow to $138,592, and this amount plus $21,408 (the amount to which the initial $7,500 will grow) equals the Maxwells' targeted financial goal of $160,000. As you might have suspected, the last few steps in the worksheet can just as easily be done on

CALCULATOR	
Inputs	**Functions**
18	N
6	I/Y
−138,592	FV
	CPT
	PMT
	Solution
	4484.40

SEE APPENDIX E FOR DETAILS.

a good handheld calculator. That is, after determining the size of the nest egg (as in Step 8), you can use a financial calculator to find the amount of money that must be put away each year to fund the nest egg.

An Investment Plan Provides Direction

Now that the Maxwells know how much they have to save each year, their next step is deciding how they'll save it. It's probably best to follow some type of *systematic savings plan*—for example, build a set amount of savings each month or quarter into the household

Calculator Keystrokes

You can use a financial calculator to *find the annual payments necessary to fund a target amount* by first putting the calculator in the *annual compounding* mode. Then, to determine the amount of money that must be put away each year (at a 6 percent rate of return) to accumulate $138,592 in 18 years, use the keystrokes shown here, where:

N = number of *years* in investment horizon

I/Y = expected average *annual* rate of return on investments

FV = the targeted amount of money you want to accumulate, entered as a *negative* number

The calculator should then display a value of $4,484.36, which is the amount of money that must be put away each year to reach the targeted amount of $138,592 in 18 years. (*Note:* The calculator keystrokes take you from Steps 8 to 10 in Worksheet 11.1. You can also do Steps 5 to 7 on the calculator by letting $N = 18$, $I/Y = 6.0$, and $PV = -7,500$; then solve for (CPT)FV. Try it—you should come up with a number fairly close to the amount shown on line 7 of Worksheet 11.1.)

budget and then stick with it. But whatever procedure is followed, keep in mind that all we're doing here is *accumulating the required investment capital*. That money still has to be put to work in some kind of investment program, and that's where an investment plan enters the picture. An **investment plan** is a simple and preferably written statement explaining how the accumulated investment capital will be invested in order to reach the targeted goal. In the Maxwells' case, their capital accumulation plan calls for a

6 percent rate of return as a target they feel they can achieve. Now they need to find a way to obtain that 6 percent return on their money—meaning that they must specify, in general terms at least, the kinds of investment vehicles that they intend to use.

11-1c What Are Your Investment Objectives?

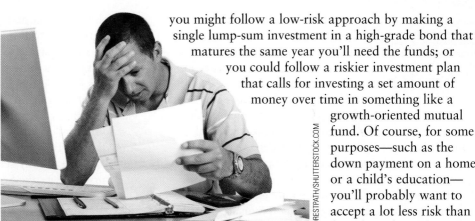

Some people buy securities for the protection they provide from taxes. Others put money aside for that proverbial rainy day or, perhaps, to build up a nice retirement nest egg. *Your goals tend to set the tone for your investment program, and they play a major role in determining how conservative (or aggressive) you're likely to be in making investment decisions.* These goals define the purpose for your investments. The most frequent investment objectives are to (1) enhance current income, (2) save for a major purchase, (3) accumulate funds for retirement, and (4) seek shelter from taxes.

Current Income

The idea with current income is to put your money into investments that will enable you to supplement your income. In other words, it's for people who want to live off their investment income. A secure source of high current income, from dividends or interest, is the primary concern of such investors. Retired people, for example, often choose investments offering high current income at low risk.

Major Expenditures

People often put money aside, sometimes for years, to save up enough to make just one major expenditure. Here are the most common ones:

- The down payment on a home
- Money for a child's college education
- Some capital for going into business
- An expensive (perhaps once-in-a-lifetime) vacation
- The purchase of a special, expensive item
- Funds for retirement (discussed in the next section)

Whatever your goal, the idea is to set your sights on something and then go about building your capital with that objective in mind. It certainly makes the act of investing more pleasurable. Once you know about how much money you'll need to attain one of these goals (following a procedure like the one illustrated in Worksheet 11.1), you can specify the types of investment vehicles that you intend to use. For example,

you might follow a low-risk approach by making a single lump-sum investment in a high-grade bond that matures the same year you'll need the funds; or you could follow a riskier investment plan that calls for investing a set amount of money over time in something like a growth-oriented mutual fund. Of course, for some purposes—such as the down payment on a home or a child's education—you'll probably want to accept a lot less risk than for others, because attaining these goals should not be jeopardized by the types of investment vehicles that you choose to employ.

Retirement

Accumulating funds for retirement is *the single most important reason for investing.* Too often, though, retirement planning occupies only a small amount of our time because we tend to rely too heavily on employers and Social Security for our retirement needs. As many people learn too late in life, that can be a serious mistake. A much better approach is to review the amounts of income that you can realistically expect to receive from Social Security and your employee pension plan, and then to decide, based on your retirement goals, *whether they'll be adequate to meet your needs.* You'll probably find that you'll have to supplement them through personal investing. (Retirement plans are discussed in Chapter 14.)

Shelter from Taxes

As explained in Chapter 3, federal income taxes do not treat all sources of income equally. For example, if you own real estate, then you may be able to take depreciation deductions against certain other sources of income, thereby reducing the amount of your final taxable income. This tax write-off feature can make real estate an attractive investment vehicle for some investors, even though its pre-tax rate of return may not appear very high. The goal of sheltering income from taxes is a legitimate one that, for some investors, often goes hand in hand with the goals of saving for a major outlay or for retirement. Clearly, if you can avoid paying taxes on the income from an investment, then all other things considered, you will have more funds available for reinvestment during the period.

11-1d Different Ways to Invest

After establishing your investment objectives, you can use a variety of investment vehicles to fulfill those goals. In this section, we'll briefly describe various types of investmentss that are popular with (and widely used by) individual investors.

Common Stock

Common stocks are a form of *equity*—each share of stock represents a fractional ownership position in a corporation.

A share of stock entitles the holder to equal participation in the corporation's earnings and dividends, an equal vote, and an equal voice in management. From the investor's perspective, the return to stockholders comes from dividends and/or appreciation in share price. Common stock has no maturity date and, as a result, remains outstanding indefinitely (common stocks are discussed in Chapter 12).

Bonds

In contrast to stocks, *bonds* are *liabilities*—they're IOUs of the issuer. Governments and corporations issue bonds that pay a stated return, called *interest*. An individual who invests in a bond receives a stipulated interest income, typically paid every six months, plus the return of the principal (face) value of the bond at maturity. For example, if you purchased a $1,000 bond that paid 10 percent interest in semiannual installments, then you could expect to receive $50 every six months (that is, 10 percent × 0.5 years × $1,000) and at maturity recover the $1,000 face value of the bond. Of course, a bond can be bought or sold prior to maturity at a price that may differ from its face value because bond prices, like common stock prices, fluctuate in the marketplace (see Chapter 12).

Preferreds and Convertibles

These are *hybrid securities* in that each has the characteristics of both stocks and bonds. *Preferred securities* are issued as stock and, as such, represent an equity position in a corporation. But unlike common stock, preferreds have a stated (fixed) dividend rate that is paid before the dividends to holders of common stock are paid. Like bonds, preferred stocks are usually purchased for the current income (dividends) that they pay. A *convertible security*, in contrast, is a special type of fixed-income obligation (usually a bond) that carries a conversion feature permitting the investor to convert it into a specified number of shares of common stock. Thus, convertible securities provide the fixed-income benefits (interest) of a bond while offering the price appreciation (capital gains) potential of common stock. (Convertibles are briefly discussed in Chapter 12.)

Mutual Funds, Exchange Traded Funds, and Exchange Traded Notes

An organization that invests in and professionally manages a diversified portfolio of securities is called a *mutual fund*. A mutual fund sells shares to investors, who then become part owners of the fund's securities portfolio. Most mutual funds issue and repurchase shares at a price that reflects the underlying value of the portfolio at the time the transaction is made. Mutual funds have become popular with individual investors because they offer not only a wide variety of investment opportunities, but also a full array of services that many investors find particularly appealing. *Exchange traded funds (ETFs)* are similar to mutual funds in that they, too, represent portfolios of securities. They are usually set up to track a basket or index of securities (e.g., the S&P 500) or a particular sector, such as telecommunications or utility stocks. They also can include other types of investments, including bonds and real estate. Whereas mutual funds can be bought or sold only at the end of the day, investors can trade ETFs throughout the trading day, just like individual shares of stock. Further, ETFs provide more favorable tax treatment than mutual funds.

Exchange traded notes (ETNs) are more similar to ETFs than to mutual funds. They are senior, unsecured, unsubordinated debt securities issued by an underwriting bank. As such, ETNs are debt securities that have a maturity date and are backed only by the credit of the issuer. Like ETFs, most ETNs are designed to reproduce the returns on a market benchmark, net of investment management fees. Thus, the underwriting bank promises to pay an amount based on the value of the index, net of fees, upon maturity. It's important to realize that an ETN bears a different risk than an ETF. If the bank underwriting the ETN goes bankrupt, the ETN might lose value just as a senior debt security would. Consequently, ETFs only face the risk of market fluctuations, while ETNs face both market risk and the risk that the issuing bank will default. Unfortunately, this credit risk is hard for investors to evaluate. Like ETFs, ETNs are traded on an exchange and can be sold short. Also like ETFs, ETNs provide tax advantages over mutual funds. (More information on these advantages and disadvantages will be given in Chapter 13.)

Real Estate

Investments in *real estate* can take many forms, ranging from speculating in raw land to limited-partnership shares in commercial property; there are even mutual funds that specialize in real estate. The returns on real estate come from rents, capital gains, and certain tax benefits. (Various types of real estate investments are discussed in Chapter 13.)

11-2 Securities Markets

LG2 The term **securities markets** generally describes the arena where stocks, bonds, and other financial instruments are traded. Such markets can be physical places, but they can just as easily be *electronic* *networks* that allow buyers and sellers to come together to execute trades. Securities markets can be broken into two parts: capital markets and money markets. The *capital market* is where long-term securities like stocks and bonds are traded. The *money market* is the marketplace for short-term, low-risk credit instruments with maturities of one year or less; these include U.S. Treasury bills, commercial paper, and so on. Each market provides a mechanism for bringing the buyers and sellers of securities together. Some of the more popular money market securities were discussed in Chapter 4; in this chapter, we'll concentrate on the capital markets.

11-2a Primary and Secondary Markets

In the *primary market*, new securities are sold to the public and one party to the transaction is always the issuer. In contrast, old (outstanding) securities are bought and sold in the *secondary market*, where the securities are "traded" between investors. A security is sold in the primary market just once, when it's originally issued by a corporation or a governmental body (e.g., a state or municipality). Subsequent transactions, in which securities are sold by one investor to another, take place in the secondary market.

Primary Markets

When a corporation sells a new issue to the public, several financial institutions will participate in the transaction. To begin with, the corporation will probably use an *investment banking firm*, which specializes in *underwriting* (selling) new security issues. The investment banker will give the corporation advice on pricing and other aspects of the issue and will either sell the new security itself or arrange for a *selling*

group to do so. The selling group is normally made up of several brokerage firms, each responsible for selling a certain portion of the new issue. On large issues, the originating investment banker will bring in other underwriting firms and form an *underwriting syndicate* in order to spread the risks associated with underwriting and selling the new securities. A potential investor in a new issue must be given a **prospectus**, which is a document describing the firm and the issue. Certain federal agencies are responsible for ensuring that all the information included in a prospectus accurately represents the facts.

prospectus A document made available to prospective security buyers that describes the firm and a new security issue.

Secondary Markets

The secondary markets permit investors to execute transactions among themselves; it's the marketplace where an investor can easily sell his or her holdings to someone else. Unlike primary market transactions, the secondary market does not generate cash for the underlying company (issuer). Included among the secondary markets are the various *securities exchanges*, in which the buyers and sellers of securities are brought together for the purpose of executing trades. Another major segment of the market is made up of those securities that are listed and traded on the *NASDAQ market*, which employs an all-electronic trading platform to execute trades. Finally, the *over-the-counter (OTC)* market deals in smaller, unlisted securities.

11-2b Broker Markets and Dealer Markets

By far, the vast majority of trades made by small individual investors take place in the secondary market, so we'll focus on that for the rest of this chapter. When you look at the secondary market *on the basis of how securities are traded,* you'll find that you can essentially divide the market into two segments: broker markets and dealer markets. Exhibit 11.1 shows the structure of the secondary market in terms of broker or dealer markets. As you can see, the *broker market* consists of national and regional "securities exchanges," while the *dealer market* is made up of both the NASDAQ market and the OTC market.

Probably *the biggest difference in these two markets is a technical point about how the trades are executed.* That is, when a trade occurs in a *broker market* (on one of the so-called securities exchanges), then the two sides to the transaction—the buyer and the seller—are brought together and the trade takes place at that point: Party A sells his securities directly to the buyer, Party B. In a sense, with the help of a *broker*, the securities change hands right there on the floor of the exchange. In contrast, when trades are

Exhibit 11.1 **Broker and Dealer Markets**

On a typical trading day, the secondary market is a beehive of activity where literally billions of shares change hands daily. This market consists of two parts, the broker market and the dealer market. As can be seen, each of these markets is made up of various exchanges and trading venues.

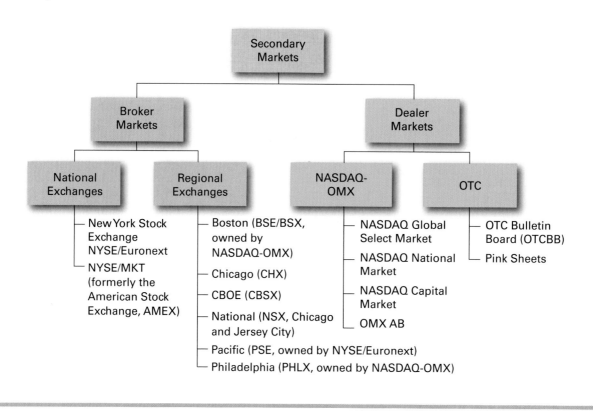

made in one of the *dealer markets*, the buyer and seller are never brought together directly; instead, their buy/ sell orders are executed separately through *securities dealers*, who act as *market makers*. Essentially, two separate trades are made: Party A sells his securities (in, say, the XYZ Corp.) to one dealer, and Party B buys her securities (in the same XYZ Corp.) from the same or another dealer. Thus, there is always a dealer (market maker) on one side of the transaction.

Broker Markets

When you think of the stock market, if you're like most individual investors then the first name to come to mind is the New York Stock Exchange (NYSE), which is the largest stock exchange in the United States. In 2007, the NYSE merged with Euronext, a combination of stock exchanges in Amsterdam, Brussels, Lisbon, and Paris. The combined entity, *NYSE Euronext*, operates six securities exchanges in seven countries. In June 2012, it had about 8,000 listed issues with a market capitalization in excess of *$13 trillion*. It includes about 90 percent of the firms in the Dow Jones Industrial Average (DJIA) and 80 percent of the firms in the S&P 500 index.

In 2008, the NYSE Euronext also acquired the American Stock Exchange (AMEX), which was formerly the second-largest U.S. exchange. The AMEX has less restrictive listing requirements than the NYSE, so the acquisition allowed the NYSE to broaden the types of companies falling under its umbrella. The organization is also referred to as NYSE MKT. NYSE Euronext also owns about 5 percent of India's National Stock and Exchange and has a cooperative agreement with the Tokyo Stock Exchange. The NYSE Euronext entity is a part of the broker market— indeed, it's their biggest player! Trading on NYSE Euronext takes place on centralized trading floors. It accounts for nearly 40 percent of world equity trading.

In early 2011, Deutsche Boerse offered to buy NYSE Euronext for $10 billion. If it had gone through, this merger would have created the largest stock exchange in the world. However, soon after that offer, NASDAQ OMX Group, Inc., and Intercontinental Exchange (ICE) launched a counterbid for NYSE Euronext that totaled $11.3 billion. Yet U.S. regulators blocked this counteroffer. These merger efforts reflect a consolidation wave as exchanges seek new sources of growth.

Besides the NYSE Euronext, a handful of *regional exchanges* are also part of the broker market. The number of securities listed on each of these exchanges typically ranges from about 100 to 500 companies. The best-known of these are the Boston, National, Pacific, and Philadelphia exchanges. These exchanges deal primarily in securities with local and regional appeal. To enhance their trading activity, regional exchanges often list securities that are also listed on the NYSE.

Dealer Markets

A key feature of the dealer market is that, unlike the NYSE, it doesn't have centralized trading floors. Instead, it's made up of many market makers who are linked via a mass telecommunications network. Each market maker is actually a securities dealer who makes a market in one or more securities by offering to either buy or sell them at stated bid/ask prices. (The **bid price** and **ask price** represent, respectively, the highest price offered to purchase a given security and the lowest price at which the security is offered for sale; in effect, an investor pays the ask price when *buying* securities and receives the bid price when *selling* them.) Consisting of both the NASDAQ and OTC markets, dealer markets account for about 40 percent of all shares traded in the U.S. market—with NASDAQ accounting for the overwhelming majority of those trades.

The biggest dealer market, hands down, is made up of a select list of stocks that are listed and traded on the *National Association of Securities Dealers Automated Quotation System*, or *NASDAQ* for short. Founded in 1971, NASDAQ had its origins in the OTC market but today it is considered *a totally separate entity that's no longer a part of the OTC market.*

In fact, in 2006, the SEC formally recognized NASDAQ as a "listed exchange," giving it much the same stature and prestige as the NYSE. To be traded on NASDAQ, all stocks must have at least two market makers—although the bigger, more actively traded stocks (such as Apple) will have many more than that. These dealers electronically post all their bid/ask prices so that, when investors place (market) orders, they're immediately filled at the best available price. In 2008, NASDAQ combined its business with OMX AB, which owned and operated the largest securities market in northern Europe. It also acquired the Philadelphia and Boston stock exchanges. Across its markets, NASDAQ listed more than 2,700 companies from all over the world in mid-2012.

NASDAQ sets various listing standards, the most comprehensive of which are for the 2,000 or so stocks traded on the *NASDAQ National Market (NNM)* and the roughly 1,000 stocks traded on the *NASDAQ Global Select Market* (created in 2006, this market is reserved for the biggest and bluest NASDAQ stocks). Stocks included on these two markets are all actively traded and, in general, have a *national following*. These securities are widely quoted, and the trades, all executed electronically, are just as efficient as they are on the floor of the NYSE. Indeed, just as the NYSE has its list of big-name players (e.g., ExxonMobil, Wal-Mart, Pfizer, IBM, Coca-Cola, Home Depot, and UPS), so too does NASDAQ—including names like Apple, Microsoft, Intel, Cisco Systems, Dell, eBay, and Google. (The *NASDAQ Capital Market* is yet another NASDAQ market; it includes about

bid price The price at which one can sell a security.

ask price The price at which one can purchase a security.

Financial Planning Tips: "Dark Pools": Trading off of the Exchanges

In public equity markets like the NYSE and NASDAQ, the prices at which brokers buy and sell equities and the identities of the transacting parties are publicly available. But some large institutional investors like pension and hedge funds prefer to transact privately with other institutions without revealing their identities or the prices at which they trade. As much as 40 percent of all trades now occur off of the exchanges. A "dark pool" is an arena in which institutions execute these larger trades without displaying their identities or the details of the trades to the public. There are independent dark pools like Pipeline and Liquidnet and broker-operated dark pools like Goldman Sachs' Sigma X.

The benefits of dark pools include the ability to set up and trade large blocks of stocks without letting the whole market know what an institutional investor is doing.

Institutions prefer to trade big blocks of stocks off of an organized exchange because they know that big trades can move prices against them. On the other hand, a cost of dark pools is that some market participants are disadvantaged because they cannot see the trades before they are executed. Consequently, pricing is not transparent. Some argue that this harms price discovery, which is the ability to find the best price for a security. Needless to say, the exchanges don't like dark pools because they deprive them of business.

Sources: Adapted from Christopher Matthews, "Do 'Dark Pools' Threaten the Health of America's Financial Markets?" http://business.time.com/2012/06/22/do-dark-pools-threaten-the-health-of-americas-financial-markets/, accessed August 2012; and John Grgurich, "'Dark Pools': Are Hidden Trades Undermining the Stock Market?" http://www.dailyfinance.com/2012/07/09/dark-pools-hidden-trades-undermining-stock-market/, accessed August 2012.

600 or 700 stocks that, for various reasons, aren't eligible for the NNM.)

The other part of the dealer market is made up of securities that trade in the *over-the-counter (OTC) market*. This market is separate from NASDAQ and includes mostly small companies that either can't or don't wish to comply with NASDAQ listing requirements. They trade on either the *OTC Bulletin Board (OTCBB)* or in the so-called *Pink Sheets*. The OTCBB is an electronic quotation system that links the market makers who trade the shares of small companies. The OTCBB is regulated by the Securities and Exchange Commission (SEC), which requires (among other things) that all companies traded on this market file audited financial statements and comply with federal securities law. In sharp contrast, the OTC Pink Sheets represent the *unregulated* segment of the market, where the companies aren't even required to file with the SEC.

11-2c Foreign Securities Markets

In addition to those in the United States, more than 100 other countries worldwide have organized securities exchanges. Indeed, actively traded markets can be found not only in such major industrialized nations as Japan, Great Britain, Germany, and Canada, but also in emerging economies. In terms of market capitalization (total market value of all shares traded), the NYSE Euronext is the biggest stock market in the world, followed by the Tokyo stock market and then the NASDAQ market. Other major exchanges are located in Sydney, Zurich, Hong Kong, Singapore, Rome, and Amsterdam. Besides these markets, you'll find developing markets all over the globe—from Argentina and Armenia to Egypt and Fiji; from Iceland, Israel, and Malaysia to New Zealand, Russia, and Zimbabwe.

11-2d Regulating the Securities Markets

Several laws have been enacted to regulate the activities of various participants in the securities markets and to provide for adequate and accurate disclosure of information to potential and existing investors. State laws, regulating the sale of securities within state borders, typically establish procedures that apply to the sellers of securities doing business within the state. However, the most important and far-reaching securities laws are those enacted by the federal government.

- **Securities Act of 1933.** This act was passed by Congress to ensure full disclosure of information with respect to new security issues and to prevent a stock market collapse similar to the one that occurred during 1929–1932. The Act requires the issuer of a new security to file a registration statement containing information about the new issue with the **Securities and Exchange Commission (SEC)**, an agency of the U.S. government established to enforce federal securities laws.

- **Securities Exchange Act of 1934.** This act expanded the scope of federal regulation and formally established the SEC as the agency in charge of the administration of federal securities laws. The act gives the SEC power to regulate organized securities exchanges and the OTC market by extending disclosure requirements to outstanding securities.

- **Investment Company Act of 1940.** This act protects those purchasing investment company (mutual fund) shares. It established rules and regulations for investment companies and formally authorized the SEC to regulate the companies' practices and procedures. It also prohibits investment companies from paying excessive fees to their advisors and from charging excessive commissions to purchasers of company shares.

- **The Sarbanes-Oxley Act of 2002.** The purpose of this act (known as "SOX" for short) is to eliminate corporate fraud as related to accounting practices and other information released to investors. Among other things, SOX requires an annual evaluation of internal controls and procedures for financial reporting; it also requires the top executives of the corporation, as well as its auditors, to certify the accuracy of its financial statements and disclosures.

- **The Dodd–Frank Wall Street Reform and Consumer Protection Act of 2010.** Prompted by the financial crisis of 2007–2009, this legislation is designed primarily to improve accountability and transparency in the U.S. financial system, to discontinue the "too big to fail" regulatory approach, to protect American taxpayers from costly government bailouts, and to protect consumers from exploitative financial services practices. The Act is the most significant change in financial regulation since the Great Depression. The legislation contains the so-called Volcker Rule, which prohibits depository banks from proprietary trading. However, they can still invest up to 3 percent of some capital in private equity and hedge funds and they can trade for hedging purposes. Finally, the Act created new federal agencies, which include the Financial Stability Oversight Council, the Office of Financial Research, and the Bureau of Consumer Financial Protection.

- **Other significant federal legislation.** The *Maloney Act of 1938* provided for the establishment of trade associations for the purpose of self-regulation within the securities industry. This act led to the creation of the **National Association of Securities Dealers (NASD)**, which is made up of all brokers and dealers who participate in the OTC market. The NASD is a self-regulatory organization that polices the activities of brokers and dealers to ensure that its standards are upheld. *The Securities Investor Protection Act of 1970* created the Securities Investor Protection Corp. (SIPC), an organization that protects investors against the financial failure of brokerage firms—much as the Federal Deposit Insurance Corporation (FDIC) protects depositors against bank failures (we'll examine the SIPC later in this chapter).

11-2e Bull Market or Bear?

The general condition of the market is termed as either *bullish* or *bearish*, depending on whether securities prices are rising or falling over extended periods. Changing market conditions generally stem from changing investor attitudes, changes in economic activity, and certain governmental actions aimed at stimulating or slowing down the economy. Prices go *up* in **bull markets**; these favorable markets are normally associated with investor optimism, economic recovery, and growth. In contrast, prices go *down* in **bear markets**, which are normally associated with investor pessimism and economic slowdowns. These terms are used to describe conditions in the bond and other securities markets as well as the stock market. As a rule, investors can earn attractive rates of return during bull markets and only low (or negative) returns during bear markets. Exhibit 11.2 shows historical U.S. stock market performance going all the way back to 1825.

Look closely at the exhibit and you'll notice that, over the past 50 years or so, stock market behavior has been generally bullish, reflecting the growth and prosperity of the economy (the market was up in three-quarters of the last 50 years). Since World War II, the longest bull market lasted 125 months—from November 1990 through March 2000. This bull market is probably as well known for *how it ended* as it is for the returns it generated. That record-breaking bull market ended abruptly in the spring of 2000, when a nasty bear market took over. After recovering in October 2002, the market generally advanced until about October 2007, when the full effects of the financial crisis started to become apparent. The losses continued through 2008, as the S&P 500 lost about 37 percent, but rose by about 40 percent between March and May of 2009. The S&P 500 produced annual returns of 25.94 percent, 14.82 percent, and 2.07 percent in 2009, 2010, and 2011, respectively.

11-3 Making Transactions in the Securities Markets

LG3 In many respects, dealing in the securities markets almost seems like operating in another world, one with all kinds of unusual orders and strange-sounding transactions. Actually, making securities transactions is relatively simple once you understand the basics—in fact, you'll probably find that it's no harder than using a checking account!

11-3a Stockbrokers

Stockbrokers (or **account executives**, as they're also called) buy and sell securities for their customers. Although deeply ingrained in our language, the term *stockbroker* is really a bit of a misnomer because they help investors to buy and sell not only stocks but also bonds, convertibles, mutual funds, options, and many other types of securities. Brokers must be licensed by the exchanges and must abide by the strict ethical guidelines of the exchanges and the SEC. They work for brokerage firms and in essence are there to execute the orders placed. As we saw earlier, procedures for executing orders in broker markets differ a bit from those in dealer markets; but you as an investor would never know the difference because you'd place your order in exactly the same way.

National Association of Securities Dealers (NASD) An agency made up of brokers and dealers in over-the-counter securities that regulates OTC market operations.

bull market A market condition normally associated with investor optimism, economic recovery, and expansion; characterized by generally rising securities prices.

bear market A condition of the market typically associated with investor pessimism and economic slowdown; characterized by generally falling securities prices.

stockbroker (account executive, financial consultant) A person who buys and sells securities on behalf of clients and gives them investment advice and information.

MONKEY BUSINESS IMAGES/SHUTTERSTOCK.COM

Exhibit 11.2

Historical Performance of U.S. Stocks as Measured by NYSE Returns

© KAREN HERMANN/ISTOCKPHOTO

This graphical portrayal of U.S. stock market performance since 1825 shows that the high returns in recent years are quite uncommon. Fortunately, the recent low returns have also been rare in the historical record.

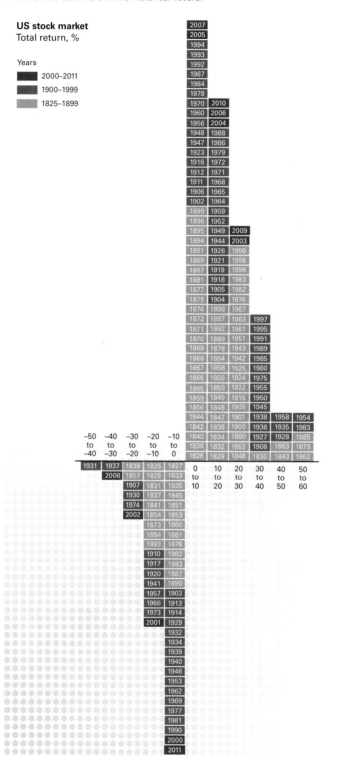

Sources: Adapted from "U.S. Stockmarket Returns: Booms and Busts," http://www.economist.com/daily/chartgallery/displaystory.cfm?story_id-12811306, January 6, 2012. Based in part on data from Value Square Asset Management, "A New Historical Database of the NYSE 1815 to 1925: Performance and Predictability," Yale School of Management Working Paper, July 2000; data updated by authors.

Selecting a Broker

If you decide to start investing with a *full-service broker*, it's important to select someone *who understands your investment objectives and who can effectively help you pursue them*. If you choose a broker whose own disposition toward investing is similar to yours, then you should be able to avoid conflict and establish a solid working relationship. A good place to start the search is to ask friends, relatives, or business associates to recommend a broker. It's not important to know your stockbroker socially because most, if not all, of your transactions/orders will probably be placed by phone or online. But a broker should be far more than just a salesperson; *a good broker is someone who's more interested in your investments than in his or her own commissions*. Should you find that you're dealing with someone who's always trying to get you to trade your stocks or who's pushing new investments on you, then by all means dump that broker and find a new one!

Full-Service, Discount, and Online Brokers

Just a few years ago, there were three distinct types of brokers—full-service, discount, and online—and each occupied a well-defined market niche. Today, the lines between these three types of brokers are blurred. Most brokerage firms, even the more traditional ones, now offer online services to compete with the increasingly popular online firms. And many discount brokers now offer services, such as research reports for clients, that once were available only from a full-service broker.

The traditional **full-service broker** offers investors a wide array of brokerage services, including investment advice and information, trade executions, holding securities for safekeeping, online brokerage services, and margin loans. Such services are fine for investors who want such help—and are willing to pay for it. In contrast, investors who simply want to execute trades and aren't interested in obtaining all those brokerage services should consider either a *discount broker* or an *online broker*. **Discount brokers** tend to have low-overhead operations and offer fewer customer services than do full-service brokers. Transactions are initiated by calling a toll-free number—or visiting the broker's Web site—and placing the desired buy or sell order. The brokerage firm then executes the order at the best possible price and confirms the transaction details by phone, e-mail, or regular mail. Depending on the transaction size, *discount brokers can save investors from 30 percent to 80 percent of the commissions charged by full-service brokers*.

With the technology that's available to almost everyone today, it's not surprising that investors can just as easily trade securities online as on the phone. All you need is an **online broker** (also called an *Internet* or *electronic broker*) and you, too, can execute trades electronically. The investor merely accesses the online broker's Web site to open an account, review the commission schedule, or see a demonstration of available transaction services and procedures. Confirmation of electronic trades can take as little as a few seconds, and most occur within a minute. Online investing is increasingly popular, particularly among young investors who enjoy surfing the Web—so popular, in fact, that it has prompted virtually every traditional full-service broker (and many discount brokers) to offer online trading to their clients. Some of the major full-service, discount, and online brokers are listed here:

Type of Broker		
Full-Service	**Discount**	**Online**
Raymond James	Bank of America	AccuTrade
Edward Jones	Charles Schwab	TD Ameritrade
Morgan Stanley	J.D. Seibert	E*Trade
Merrill Lynch	Muriel Siebert	Fidelity Brokerage Services
Wachovia/Wells Fargo	Vanguard Brokerage Services	Scottrade
UBS	York Securities	TD Waterhouse

Go to Smart Sites

Confused about which broker is right for you? Use The Motley Fool's checklist, "10 Ways to Size Up a Broker," at the Fool's Broker Center. ●

Brokerage Fees

Brokerage firms receive commissions for executing buy and sell orders for their clients. These commissions are said to be *negotiated*, meaning they're not fixed. In practice, however, most firms have *established fee schedules* that they use with small transactions. Fees definitely do differ from one brokerage firm to another, and so it pays to shop around. If you're an "active trader" who generates a couple thousand dollars (or more) in annual commissions, then by all means try to negotiate a reduced commission schedule with your broker. Chances are, they'll probably agree to a deal with you: brokers much prefer active traders to buy-and-hold investors because traders generate a lot more commissions. Generally speaking, brokerage

---

full-service broker A broker who, in addition to executing clients' transactions, offers a full array of brokerage services.

discount broker A broker with low overhead who charges low commissions and offers little or no services to investors.

online broker Typically a discount broker through which investors can execute trades electronically/online through a commercial service or on the Internet; also called *Internet broker* or *electronic broker*.

odd lot A quantity of fewer than 100 shares of a stock.

round lot A quantity of 100 shares of stock or multiples thereof.

fees on a round lot of common stock will amount to roughly 1 percent to 2 percent of the transaction value.

Because there are so many discount brokers today, there is greater variation in the fees charged and services offered. The way commissions are calculated also varies; some firms base them on the dollar value of the transaction, some on the number of shares, and some use both.

Exhibit 11.3 ranks the best brokerage firms using criteria that include commissions. The firms with higher commissions generally offer more services; similarly, many discounters charge clients extra for their research services.

Security transactions can be made in either odd or round lots. An **odd lot** consists of fewer than 100 shares of stock, while a **round lot** represents a 100-share unit or multiples thereof. The sale of 400 shares of stock would be considered a round-lot transaction, but the purchase of 75 shares would be

---

Exhibit 11.3 — SmartMoney's 2012 Broker Rankings (Rated on a Scale of 5 Stars)

They say it pays to shop around, and that advice certainly applies when it comes to selecting a broker. Just look at the different commissions these brokers charge to execute essentially the same trade.

RANK[1]	BROKER	COMMENT	COMMISSION ON STOCK PER TRADE[2]	SCORES					
				COMMISSIONS AND FEES[3]	MUTUAL FUNDS & INVESTMENT PRODUCTS	BANKING SERVICES	TRADING TOOLS[4]	RESEARCH[5]	CUSTOMER SERVICE
4	**E-Trade** Etrade.com	Its 24-7 online chat feature is a nice touch, but its fees are above those at rival firms.	9.99	★★	★★★★	★★★★	★★★★★	★★★★★	★★★★
1	**Fidelity** Fidelity.com	Top spot for third year running. Offers the biggest selection of funds and the most comprehensive website.	7.95	★★★	★★★★★	★★★★★	★★★★★	★★★★★	★★★
5	**Charles Schwab** Schwab.com	Offers a wide assortment of investment and banking options. Its fees on some services aren't cheap.	8.95	★★★	★★★★	★★★★★	★★★★	★★★★★	★★★
6	**TradeKing** Tradeking.com	Has strong customer service, but customers can't get stocks listed on foreign exchanges.	4.95	★★★	★★★	★	★★★	★★	★★★★★
3	**TD Ameritrade** TDameritrade.com	Want to trade? Its website and mobile apps are top-notch, but slow e-mail and phone response times hurt.	9.99	★★	★★★★	★★★★★	★★★★★	★★★★★	★★★
2	**Scottrade** Scottrade.com	Doesn't have the cheapest stock trades but compensates for that with few fees on nearly everything else.	7.00	★★★★★	★★★★★	★★★★★	★★★	★★★★	★★★★
8	**Merrill Edge** MerrillEdge.com	It can be your bank and your broker, but high fees and slow-to-execute trades keep it from ranking higher.	6.95	★★	★★★★	★★★★★	★★★	★★★	★
10	**WellsTrade** WellsFargo.com	Online trades were slow to execute. Got low marks for its website, trading tools and research offerings.	8.95	★	★★★	★★★★	★	★	★
9	**ShareBuilder** Sharebuilder.com	Offers low fees, but its customers can't buy individual corporate or government bonds.	9.95	★★★★★	★	★★★	★★★	★★	★
7	**Zecco** Zecco.com	Doesn't have risk-assessment or automated asset-allocation tools. Lacks many banking services.	4.95	★★★	★★★	★	★★★	★★★	★★★★

[1]Criteria are not equally weighted.
[2]Commission on a 200-share trade at $20 a share.
[3]For clients with a brokerage balance of $50,000 who make as many as five trades a month.
[4]Includes data from Gomez.
[5]Includes data from Corporate Insight.

Source: J. Alex Tarquinio, "Best and Worst Brokers of 2012," in *SmartMoney*, http://www.smartmoney.com/invest/markets/smartmoneys-annual-broker-survey-23119/, May 16, 2012, accessed July 2012. SmartMoney Content © 2012 SmartMoney. Licensed for use by Cengage Learning. SmartMoney is a registered trademark of SmartMoney, a Joint Venture of Dow Jones & Company, Inc. & Hearst SM Partnership.

© KAREN HERMANN/ISTOCKPHOTO

an odd-lot transaction; trading 250 shares of stock would involve two round lots and an odd lot. Because the purchase or sale of odd lots requires additional processing, an added fee—known as an *odd-lot differential*—is often tacked on to the normal commission charge, driving up the costs of these small trades. Indeed, the relatively high cost of an odd-lot trade is why it's best to deal in round lots whenever possible.

Investor Protection

As a client, you're protected against the loss of securities or cash held by your broker by the **Securities Investor Protection Corporation (SIPC)**, a nonprofit corporation authorized by the Securities Investor Protection Act of 1970 to protect customer accounts against the financial failure of a brokerage firm. Although subject to SEC and congressional oversight, the SIPC is *not* an agency of the U.S. government.

SIPC insurance covers each account for up to $500,000 (of which up to $250,000 may be in cash balances held by the firm). Note, however, that SIPC insurance does not guarantee that the dollar value of the securities will be recovered. It ensures only that *the securities themselves will be returned*. So what happens if your broker gives you bad advice and you lose a lot of money on an investment? SIPC won't help you because it's not intended to insure you against bad investment advice, stock market risk, or broker fraud. If you do have a dispute with your broker, first discuss the situation with the managing officer at the branch where you do your business. If that doesn't help, then write or talk to the firm's compliance officer and contact the securities office in your home state. If you still aren't satisfied, you may have to take the case to **arbitration**, a process whereby you and your broker present the two sides of the argument before an arbitration panel, which then decides how the case will be resolved. If it's *binding* arbitration, and it usually is, then you have no choice but to accept the decision—you cannot go to court to appeal your case.

11-3b Executing Trades

For most individual investors, a securities transaction involves placing a buy or sell order, usually by phone or on the Internet, and later receiving confirmation that the order has been completed. These investors have no idea what happens to their orders. In fact, a lot goes on—and very quickly—once the order is placed. It has to, because on a typical day, the NYSE alone executes *millions* of trades, and many more occur on the NASDAQ and the rest of the market. In most cases, if the investor places a market order (which we will explain later), then it should take *less than two minutes* to place, execute, and confirm a trade.

The process starts with a phone call to the broker, who then transmits the order via sophisticated telecommunications equipment to the stock exchange floor, the NASDAQ market, or the OTCBB, where it's promptly executed. Confirmation that the order has been executed is transmitted to the originating broker and then to the customer. Once the trade takes place, the investor has three (business) days to "settle" his or her account with the broker— that is, to pay for the securities. Investors can also use their computers to execute online securities trades. In an online trade, your order goes from your computer to the broker's computer, which checks the type of order and confirms that it's in compliance with regulations. It is then transmitted to the exchange floor or to a NASDAQ (or OTC) dealer for execution. The time for the whole process, including a confirmation that's sent back to your computer, is usually less than a minute.

11-3c Types of Orders

Investors may choose from several different kinds of orders when buying or selling securities. The type of order chosen normally depends on the investor's goals and expectations regarding the given transaction. The three basic types of orders are the market order, limit order, and stop-loss order.

Market Order

An order to buy or sell a security at the best price available at the time it's placed is a **market order**. It's usually the quickest way to have orders filled because market orders are executed as soon as they reach the trading floor. In fact, on small trades of less than a few thousand shares, it takes less than 10 seconds to fill a market order once it hits the trading floor. These orders are executed through a process that attempts to allow *buy orders* to be filled at the lowest price and *sell orders* at the highest, thereby providing the best possible deal to both the buyers and sellers of a security.

Limit Order

An order to buy at a specified price (or lower) or to sell at a specified price (or higher) is known as a **limit order**. The broker transmits a limit order to a *specialist* dealing in the given security on the floor of the exchange. The order is executed as soon as the specified market price is reached and all other such orders with precedence have been filled. For example, assume

Securities Investor Protection Corporation (SIPC) A nonprofit corporation, created by Congress and subject to SEC and congressional oversight, that insures customer accounts against the financial failure of a brokerage firm.

arbitration A procedure used to settle disputes between a brokerage firm and its clients; both sides present their positions to a board of arbitration, which makes a final and usually binding decision on the matter.

market order An order to buy or sell a security at the best price available at the time it is placed.

limit order An order to either buy a security at a specified or lower price or to sell a security at or above a specified price.

that you place a limit order to buy 100 shares of a stock at a price of $20, even though the stock is currently selling at $20.50. Once the stock hits $20 and the specialist has cleared all similar orders received before yours, the specialist will execute the order. Although a limit order can be quite effective, it can also cost you money. If, for instance, you want to buy at $20 or less and the stock price moves from its current $20.50 to $32 while you're waiting, your limit order will have caused you to forgo an opportunity to make a profit of $11.50 per share. Had you placed a market order, this profit would have been yours.

Stop-Loss Order

An order to *sell a stock* when the market price reaches or drops below a specified level is called a **stop-loss**, or **stop order**. Used to protect the investor against rapid declines in stock prices, the stop order is placed on the specialist's book and activated when the stop price is reached. At that point, the stop order becomes a *market order* to sell. This means that the stock is offered for sale at the prevailing market price, which could be less than the price at which the order was initiated by the stop. For example, imagine that you own 100 shares of DEF, which is currently selling for $25. Because of the high uncertainty associated with the price movements of the stock, you decide to place a stop order to sell at $21. If the stock price drops to $21, your stop order is activated and the specialist will sell all your DEF stock at the best price available, which may be $18 or $19 a share. Of course, if the market price increases, or stays at or about $25 a share, then nothing will have been lost by placing the stop-loss order.

Types of Limit Orders

With a limit order, you set not only the price you want, but also the time period that you want the order to remain outstanding. Here are some choices:

- **Fill-or-kill order.** An order that is executed immediately (at the specified price or better), or else it is cancelled.
- **Day order.** An order that expires at the end of the day, even if it hasn't been executed.
- **Good-till-canceled (GTC) order.** An order that will remain open indefinitely until it's either executed or canceled.
- **All-or-none order.** An order to buy or sell a *specified quantity* of stocks (at a given price, or better), which remains open until executed or canceled.

11-4 Becoming an Informed Investor

LG4 Face it: Some people know more about investing than others. As a result, they may use certain investment vehicles or tactics that aren't even in another investors' vocabulary. Investor know-how, in short, defines the playing field. It helps determine how well you'll meet your investment objectives. While being an informed investor can't guarantee you success, it can help you avoid unnecessary losses—as happens all too often when people put their money into investment vehicles that they don't fully understand. Thus, before making any major investment decision, thoroughly investigate the security and its merits. Formulate some basic expectations about its future performance and gain an understanding of the sources of risk and return. This can usually be done by reading the popular financial press and referring to other print or Internet sources of investment information.

> **While being an informed investor can't guarantee you success, it can help you avoid unnecessary losses.**

11-4a Annual Stockholders' Reports

Every publicly traded corporation is required to provide its stockholders and other interested parties with **annual stockholders' reports**. These documents contain a wealth of information about the companies, including balance sheets, income statements, and other financial reports. They usually describe the firm's business activities, recent developments, and future plans and outlook. Financial ratios describing past performance are also included, along with other relevant statistics. In fact, annual reports offer a great deal of insight into the company's past, present, and future operations. You can obtain them for free directly from the companies, through a brokerage firm, or at most large libraries; and with today's technology, most companies are also posting their annual reports on the Internet, so now you can obtain them online.

Here are some suggestions to help you get the most information when reading an annual report.

- **Start with the highlights or selected financial data sections.** These provide a quick overview of performance by summarizing key information, such as the past two years' revenues, net income, assets, earnings per share (EPS), and dividends.

- **Read the chief executive's letter.** But read it with a careful eye, looking for euphemisms like "a slowing of growth" to describe a drop in earnings.

- **Move on to the discussion of operations in management's discussion and analysis.** This section provides information on sales, earnings, debt, ongoing litigation, and so on.

- **Review the financial statements, including the notes.** These will tell you about the company's financial condition and performance.

- **Read the auditor's report.** Look for phrases like "except for" or "subject to," as they mean just one thing: *there may be problems that you need to understand.*

11-4b The Financial Press

The most common source of financial news is the local newspaper. The newspapers in many larger cities often devote several pages to business news and information. Of course, big-city papers, like *The New York Times*, provide even more information. Other, more specific sources of financial news include *The Wall Street Journal, Barron's, Investor's Business Daily*, and the "Money" section of *USA Today*. These are all national publications that include articles on the behavior of the economy, the market, various industries, and individual companies. The most comprehensive and up-to-date coverage of financial news is provided Monday through Saturday by *The Wall Street Journal*. Other excellent sources of investment information include magazines, such as *Money, Forbes, Fortune, Business Week*, and *Kiplinger's Personal Finance*. The Internet has also become a major source of information for investors.

Market Data

Usually presented in the form of averages, or indexes, *market data* describe the general behavior of the securities markets. The averages and indexes are based on the price movements of a select group of securities over an extended period. They're used to capture the overall performance of the market as a whole. You would want to follow one or more of these measures to get *a feel for how the market is doing over time* and, perhaps, an indication of what lies ahead. The absolute level of the index at a specific time (or on a given day) is far less important than *what's been happening to that index over a given period*. The most commonly cited market measures are those calculated by Dow Jones, Standard & Poor's, the NYSE, and NASDAQ. These measures are all intended to track the behavior of the stock market, particularly NYSE stocks the (Dow, S&P, and NYSE averages all follow stocks on the "big board," which is the NYSE).

DOW JONES INDUSTRIAL AVERAGES. The granddaddy of them all, and probably the most widely followed measure of stock market performance, is the **Dow Jones Industrial Average (DJIA)**. Actually, the Dow Jones averages, which began in 1896, are made up of four parts: (1) an industrial average, the DJIA, which is based on 30 stocks; (2) a transportation average based on 20 stocks; (3) a utility average based on 15 stocks; and (4) a composite average based on all 65 industrial, transportation, and utility stocks. Most of the stocks in the DJIA are picked from the NYSE; but a few NASDAQ stocks, such as Intel and Microsoft, are included as well. Although these stocks are intended to represent a cross section of companies, there's a strong bias toward blue chips, which is a major criticism of the DJIA. The Bonus Exhibit entitled "The Dow Jones Industrial Average" lists the 30 stocks currently in the DJIA. (Visit CourseMate for PFIN 3. Log in at **www.cengagebrain.com**.)

STANDARD & POOR'S INDEXES. The **Standard & Poor's (S&P) indexes** are similar to the Dow Jones averages in that both are used to capture the overall

annual stockholders' report A report made available to stockholders and other interested parties that includes a variety of financial and descriptive information about a firm's operations in the recent past.

Dow Jones Industrial Average (DJIA) The most widely followed measure of stock market performance; consists of 30 blue-chip stocks listed mostly on the NYSE.

Standard & Poor's (S&P) indexes Indexes compiled by Standard & Poor's that are similar to the DJIA but employ different computational methods and consist of far more stocks.

performance of the market. However, some important differences exist between the two measures. For one thing, the S&P uses a lot more stocks; the popular S&P 500 composite index is based on 500 different stocks, whereas the DJIA uses only 30. What's more, the S&P index is made up of all large NYSE stocks in addition to some major AMEX and NASDAQ stocks, so there are not only more issues in the S&P sample, but also a greater breadth of representation. Finally, there are some technical differences in the mathematical procedures used to compute the two measures; the Dow Jones is an *average*, whereas the S&P is an *index*. Despite the technical differences, movements in these two measures are, in fact, *highly correlated*. Even so, the S&P has a much lower value than the DJIA—for example in July 2012, the Dow stood at over 13,000, whereas the S&P index of 500 stocks was just over 1,385. Now this doesn't mean that the S&P consists of less valuable stocks; rather, the disparity is due solely to the different methods used to compute the measures. In addition to the S&P 500, two other widely followed S&P indexes are the *MidCap 400* (made up of 400 medium-sized companies with market values ranging from about $1 billion to $4.4 billion) and the *SmallCap 600* (consisting of companies with market caps of around $300 million to $1.4 billion).

THE NYSE, NASDAQ, AND OTHER MARKET INDEXES. The most widely followed exchange-based indexes are those of the New York Stock Exchange (NYSE) and NASDAQ. The **NYSE index** includes all the stocks listed on the "big board" and provides a measure of performance in that market. Behavior in the NASDAQ market is measured by several indexes, the most comprehensive of which is the *NASDAQ Composite index*, which is calculated using virtually all the stocks traded on NASDAQ. In addition, there's the *NASDAQ 100 index*, which tracks the price behavior of the biggest 100 (non-financial) firms traded on NASDAQ—companies like Apple, Microsoft, Intel, Oracle, Cisco, Staples, and Dell. The NASDAQ Composite is often used as a benchmark in assessing the price behavior of *high-tech* stocks.

Besides these major indexes, there are a couple of other measures of market performance, one of which is the **Dow Jones Wilshire 5000 index**. It's estimated that the Wilshire index reflects the *total market value of 98 percent to 99 percent of all publicly traded stocks in the United States*. In essence, it shows what's happening in the stock market as a whole—the dollar amount of market value added or lost as the market moves up and down. Another widely followed measure is the *Russell 2000*, which tracks the behavior of 2,000 relatively small companies and is widely considered to be a fairly accurate measure of the small-cap segment of the market.

Industry Data

Local newspapers, *The Wall Street Journal*, *Barron's*, and various financial publications regularly contain articles and data about different industries. For example, Standard & Poor's *Industry Surveys* provides detailed descriptions and statistics for all the major industries; on a smaller scale, *Business Week* and other magazines regularly include indexes of industry performance and price levels.

Stock Quotes

Stock price quotes appear daily on many sites, which include Yahoo! Finance (**http://finance.yahoo.com**), the *Wall Street Journal* (**http://wsj.com**), and CNN (**www.cnn.com**). Most online quotations provide not only current prices but a great deal of additional information as well.

Consider representative information available on numerous Internet sites. Exhibit 11.5 shows that Apple's stock price was at $590.91 on the morning of November 2, 2012, which was a decrease of $5.63 from the prior day's closing price of $596.54. Over the year to date, Apple shares have generated a return of 45.89%. The shares are shown as listed on the NASDAQ market. We see that Apple's trading symbol is AAPL. Its annual cash dividend yield is 1.79 percent, which is found by dividing the annual dividend by the indicated market price. The firm's recent P/E ratio is also shown, which is the current market price divided by the per-share earnings for the most recent 12-month period; as can be seen, Apple is trading at a P/E of 13.9 times earnings—a nice solid multiple. The median analyst's target forecast for Apple's stock price in one year is $770.00. And the exhibit shows that Apple's overall market capitalization (stock price times the number of shares) is $561.2 billion. This makes it the largest company in the world, as measured by market capitalization.

11-4c Advisory Services

Subscription advisory services provide information and recommendations on various industries and specific securities. The services normally cost from fifty to several hundred dollars a year, although you can usually review such material (for free) at your broker's office, at university and public libraries, or online. Probably the best-known investment advisory services are those provided by Standard & Poor's, Moody's Investors Service, and Value Line. An example of

Exhibit 11.4 Listed Stock Quote for Apple

This exhibit provides information on one day's trading activity and the price quote for Apple, which is traded on NASDAQ. Note that, in addition to the latest stock prices, a typical stock quote conveys an array of other information.

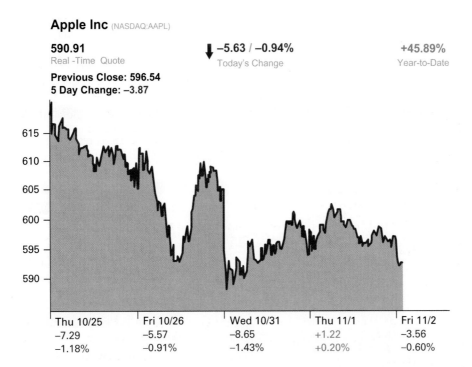

Apple Inc (NASDAQ:AAPL)

590.91
Real -Time Quote

⬇ **−5.63 / −0.94%**
Today's Change

+45.89%
Year-to-Date

Previous Close: 596.54
5 Day Change: −3.87

Thu 10/25	Fri 10/26	Wed 10/31	Thu 11/1	Fri 11/2
−7.29	−5.57	−8.65	+1.22	−3.56
−1.18%	−0.91%	−1.43%	+0.20%	−0.60%

Today's Trading

Previous close	596.54
Today's open	595.89
Day's range	591.30 - 596.95
Volume	1,547,711
Average volume (3 months)	16,931,607
Market cap	$561.2B
Dividend yield	1.79%

Data as of 9:49am ET, 11/02/2012

Growth & Valuation

Earnings growth (last year)	+82.71%
Earnings growth (this year)	--
Earnings growth (next 5 years)	+21.45%
Revenue growth (last year)	+66.90%
P/E ratio	13.9
Price/Sales	3.44
Price/Book	7.24

Financials

Next reporting date	--
EPS forecast (this quarter)	--
Annual revenue (last year)	$108.6B
Annual profit (last year)	$25.9B
Net profit margin	23.87%

Forecasts

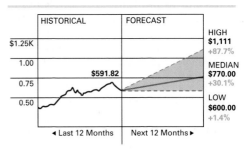

Source: From *The Wall Street Journal*, July 27, 2012; quotes for July 27, 2012, http://finance.yahoo.com/q/ks?s=AAPL.

Exhibit 11.5 An S&P Stock Report

© KAREN HERMANN/ISTOCKPHOTO

An S&P report like this one provides a wealth of information about the operating results and financial condition of the company and is an invaluable source of information to investors.

Stock Report | July 27, 2012 | NNM Symbol: **AAPL** | **AAPL** is in the S&P 500

STANDARD &POOR'S

Apple Inc

S&P Recommendation	BUY ★★★★☆	Price $585.16 (as of Jul 27, 2012)	12-Mo. Target Price $800.00	Investment Style Large-Cap Growth

GICS Sector Information Technology
Sub-Industry Computer Hardware

Summary This company is a prominent provider of hardware and software, including Mac computers, the iPod digital media player, the iPhone smartphone, and the iPad tablet.

Key Stock Statistics (Source S&P, Vickers, company reports)

52-Wk Range	$644.00– 353.02	S&P Oper. EPS 2012**E**	43.80	Market Capitalization(B)	$548.533	Beta	1.23
Trailing 12-Month EPS	$42.55	S&P Oper. EPS 2013**E**	52.25	Yield (%)	1.81	S&P 3-Yr. Proj. EPS CAGR(%)	31
Trailing 12-Month P/E	13.8	P/E on S&P Oper. EPS 2012**E**	13.4	Dividend Rate/Share	$10.60	S&P Credit Rating	NR
$10K Invested 5 Yrs Ago	$40,678	Common Shares Outstg. (M)	937.4	Institutional Ownership (%)	67		

Price Performance

30-Week Mov. Avg. ··· 10-Week Mov. Avg.– – **GAAP Earnings vs. Previous Year**   Volume Above Avg.▟ STARS
12-Mo. Target Price — Relative Strength ▲ Up ▼ Down ▶ No Change   Below Avg.▟ ★

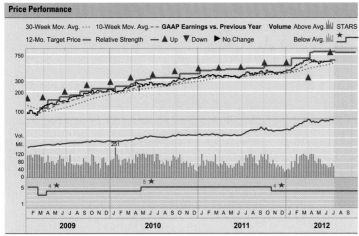

Options: ASE, CBOE, P, Ph

Qualitative Risk Assessment

LOW	MEDIUM	HIGH

Our risk assessment reflects our view of a seemingly ever-evolving market for consumer-oriented technology products, potential challenges associated with the company's growing size and offerings, and possible changes to the pace or success of product innovations following recent management changes.

Quantitative Evaluations

S&P Quality Ranking   **B**

D	C	B-	**B**	B+	A-	A	A+

Relative Strength Rank   **MODERATE**

53

LOWEST = 1   HIGHEST = 99

Revenue/Earnings Data

Revenue (Million U.S. $)

	1Q	2Q	3Q	4Q	Year
2012	46,333	39,186	35,023	--	--
2011	26,741	24,667	28,571	28,270	108,249
2010	15,683	13,499	15,700	20,343	65,225
2009	11,880	9,084	9,734	12,207	42,905
2008	9,608	7,512	7,464	7,895	32,479
2007	7,115	5,264	5,410	6,217	24,006

Earnings Per Share (U.S. $)

2012	13.87	12.30	9.32	E8.33	E43.80
2011	6.43	6.40	7.79	7.05	27.68
2010	3.67	3.33	3.51	4.64	15.15
2009	2.50	1.79	2.01	2.77	9.08
2008	1.76	1.16	1.19	1.26	5.36
2007	1.14	0.87	0.92	1.01	3.93

Fiscal year ended Sep. 30. Next earnings report expected: NA. EPS Estimates based on S&P Operating Earnings; historical GAAP earnings are as reported.

Dividend Data (Dates: mm/dd Payment Date: mm/dd/yy)

Amount ($)	Date Decl.	Ex-Div. Date	Stk. of Record	Payment Date
2.650	07/24	08/09	08/13	08/16/12

Dividends have been paid since 2012. Source: Company reports.

Highlights

▶ The 12-month target price for AAPL has recently been changed to $800.00 from $825.00. The Highlights section of this Stock Report will be updated accordingly.

Investment Rationale/Risk

▶ The Investment Rationale/Risk section of this Stock Report will be updated shortly. For the latest News story on AAPL from MarketScope, see below.

▶ 07/27/12 10:03 am ET ... S&P REITERATES BUY OPINION ON SHARES OF APPLE (AAPL 573.29****): Mobile and network security company AuthenTec (AUTH 8, NR) announces its pending acquisition by AAPL, in a transaction worth around $355 million in cash. AuthenTec's technology enables users to easily access secure mobile devices and computers via fingerprints. With mobile security becoming an increasing concern and priority for users and businesses, we think this planned move by AAPL makes strong sense. Interestingly, less than 2 weeks ago AUTH announced it would provide network security technology integrated into smartphones and tablets from Samsung, a large AAPL competitor. /S. Kessler

The McGraw-Hill Companies

Exhibit 11.5   An S&P Stock Report (*continued*)

© KAREN HERMANN/ISTOCKPHOTO

Stock Report | July 27, 2012 | NNM Symbol: **AAPL**

Apple Inc

STANDARD & POOR'S

Quantitative Evaluations

S&P Fair Value Rank   **5**

1	2	3	4	**5**

LOWEST   HIGHEST

Based on S&P's proprietary quantitative model, stocks are ranked from most overvalued (1) to most undervalued (5).

Fair Value Calculation   **$799.30**

Analysis of the stock's current worth, based on S&P's proprietary quantitative model suggests that AAPL is Undervalued by $214.14 or 36.6%.

Investability Quotient Percentile   **96**

LOWEST = 1   HIGHEST = 100

AAPL scored higher than 96% of all companies for which an S&P Report is available.

Volatility

LOW	**AVERAGE**	HIGH

Technical Evaluation   **BULLISH**

Since July, 2012, the technical indicators for AAPL have been BULLISH.

Insider Activity

UNFAVORABLE	NEUTRAL	FAVORABLE

Expanded Ratio Analysis

	2011	2010	2009	2008
Price/Sales	3.50	4.57	4.45	2.37
Price/EBITDA	10.65	15.37	15.32	11.41
Price/Pretax Income	11.09	16.09	15.84	11.17
P/E Ratio	14.63	21.29	23.21	15.93
Avg. Diluted Shares Outstg (M)	936.6	924.7	907.0	902.1

Figures based on calendar year-end price

Key Growth Rates and Averages

Past Growth Rate (%)	1 Year	3 Years	5 Years	9 Years
Sales	65.96	49.64	40.47	38.62
Net Income	84.99	74.54	65.04	97.86
Ratio Analysis (Annual Avg.)				
Net Margin (%)	23.95	21.54	18.81	13.15
Return on Equity (%)	41.67	36.41	32.98	24.07

Company Financials Fiscal Year Ended Sep. 30

Per Share Data (U.S. $)	2011	2010	2009	2008	2007	2006	2005	2004	2003	2002
Tangible Book Value	77.68	50.99	34.66	23.04	16.27	11.47	8.83	6.36	5.61	5.54
Cash Flow	29.61	16.26	9.89	5.88	4.29	2.52	1.77	0.55	0.50	0.25
Earnings	27.68	15.15	9.08	5.36	3.93	2.27	1.56	0.36	0.10	0.09
S&P Core Earnings	27.60	15.15	9.08	5.36	3.93	2.27	1.47	0.22	-0.17	-0.19
Dividends	NA	Nil	Nil	Nil	Nil	Nil	Nil	Nil	Nil	Nil
Payout Ratio	Nil	Nil	Nil	Nil	Nil	Nil	Nil	Nil	Nil	Nil
Prices:High	426.70	326.66	213.95	200.26	202.96	93.16	75.46	34.79	12.51	13.09
Prices:Low	310.50	190.25	78.20	79.14	81.90	50.16	31.30	10.59	6.36	6.68
P/E Ratio:High	15	22	24	37	52	41	48	98	NM	NM
P/E Ratio:Low	11	13	9	15	21	22	20	30	NM	NM

Income Statement Analysis (Million U.S. $)										
Revenue	108,249	65,225	42,905	32,479	24,006	19,315	13,931	8,279	6,207	5,742
Operating Income	35,604	19,412	12,474	6,748	4,726	2,645	1,829	499	138	164
Depreciation	1,814	1,027	734	473	317	225	179	150	113	118
Interest Expense	NA	NA	Nil	Nil	Nil	Nil	Nil	3.00	8.00	11.0
Pretax Income	34,205	18,540	12,066	6,895	5,008	2,818	1,815	383	92.0	87.0
Effective Tax Rate	24.2%	24.4%	31.8%	29.9%	30.2%	29.4%	26.4%	27.9%	26.1%	25.3%
Net Income	25,922	14,013	8,235	4,834	3,496	1,989	1,335	276	68.0	65.0
S&P Core Earnings	25,851	14,013	8,235	4,834	3,496	1,989	1,259	164	-119	-137

Balance Sheet & Other Financial Data (Million U.S. $)										
Cash	25,952	25,620	23,464	24,490	9,352	6,392	3,491	2,969	3,396	2,252
Current Assets	44,988	41,678	31,555	34,690	21,956	14,509	10,300	7,055	5,887	5,388
Total Assets	116,371	75,183	47,501	39,572	25,347	17,205	11,551	8,050	6,815	6,298
Current Liabilities	27,970	20,722	11,506	14,092	9,299	6,471	3,484	2,680	2,357	1,658
Long Term Debt	NA	NA	Nil	Nil	Nil	Nil	Nil	Nil	Nil	316
Common Equity	76,615	47,791	31,640	21,030	14,532	9,984	7,466	5,076	4,223	4,095
Total Capital	76,615	47,791	31,640	21,705	15,151	10,365	7,466	5,076	4,223	4,640
Capital Expenditures	4,260	2,005	1,144	1,091	735	657	260	176	164	174
Cash Flow	27,736	15,040	8,969	5,307	3,813	2,214	1,514	426	181	183
Current Ratio	1.6	2.0	2.7	2.5	2.4	2.2	3.0	2.6	2.5	3.2
% Long Term Debt of Capitalization	Nil	Nil	Nil	Nil	Nil	Nil	Nil	Nil	Nil	6.8
% Net Income of Revenue	24.0	21.5	19.2	14.9	14.6	10.3	9.6	3.3	1.1	1.1
% Return on Assets	27.1	21.7	19.7	14.9	16.4	13.9	13.6	3.7	1.0	1.1
% Return on Equity	41.7	37.1	30.5	27.2	28.5	22.8	21.3	5.9	1.6	1.6

Data as orig reptd.; bef. results of disc opers/spec. items. Per share data adj. for stk. divs.; EPS diluted. 2009 data as amended from SEC Form 10-K/A to reflect application of new accounting principles. E-Estimated. NA-Not Available. NM-Not Meaningful. NR-Not Ranked. UR-Under Review.

The McGraw·Hill Companies

Source: Reprinted by permission of Standard & Poor's Financial Services LLC, a division of the McGraw-Hill Companies © 2012.

one of these reports is given in Exhibit 11.5. This two-page report, prepared by Standard & Poor's, presents a concise summary of a company's financial history, current finances, and future prospects; similar stock reports are also available from Value Line and Morningstar.

11-5 Online Investing

LG5 The Internet today is a major force in the investing environment. It has opened the world of investing to individual investors, leveling the playing field and providing access to tools and market information formerly restricted to professionals. Not only can you trade all types of securities online, you can also find a wealth of information, from real-time stock quotes to securities analysts' research reports. So instead of weeding through mounds of paper, investors can sort quickly through vast databases to find appropriate investments, monitor their current investments, and make securities transactions—all without leaving their computers. However, online investing also carries risks. The Internet requires investors to exercise the same—and possibly more—caution as they would if they were getting information from and placing orders with a human broker. You don't have the safety net of a live broker suggesting that you rethink your trade. Online or off, the basic rules for smart investing are still the same: *Know what you're buying, from whom, and at what level of risk*.

11-5a Online Investor Services

The Internet offers a full array of online investor services, from up-to-the-minute stock quotes and research reports to charting services and portfolio tracking. When it comes to investing, you name it and you can probably find it online! Unfortunately, although many of these are truly high-quality sites offering valuable information, many others are pure garbage, so be careful when entering the world of online investing. Let's now review the kinds of investor services you can find online, starting with investor education sites.

Investor Education

The Internet offers a wide array of tutorials, online classes, and articles to educate the novice investor. Even experienced investors will find sites that expand their investing knowledge. Although most good investment-oriented Web sites include many educational resources, here are a few good sites featuring *investment fundamentals*.

- *The Motley Fool* (**http://www.fool.com**) *Fool's School* has sections on fundamentals of investing,

mutual fund investing, choosing a broker, investment strategies and styles, lively discussion boards, and more.

- Morningstar (**http://www.morningstar.com**) provides comprehensive information on stocks mutual funds, ETFs, and more.

- Zacks Investment Research (**http://www.zacks.com**) is an excellent starting place to learn what the Internet can offer investors.

- NASDAQ (**http://www.nasdaq.com**) has Investing and Personal Finance sections with financial planning and choosing a broker.

Investment Tools

Once you're familiar with the basics of investing, you can use the Internet to develop financial plans and set investment goals, find securities that meet your investment objectives, analyze potential investments, and organize your portfolio. Many of these tools, once used only by professional money managers, are free to anyone who wants to go online.

Financial Planning Tips

Starting Online Investing

- **Set aside some money to get started and choose a broker.** You don't need much—your initial deposit can be as little as $50. Choose an online broker with no minimum deposit. Consider the results of the SmartMoney broker rankings provided in Exhibit 11.3 earlier in this chapter.
- **Learn the key investing jargon.** Some useful sources are Investopedia (http://www.investopedia.com) and InvestorWords (http://www.investorwords.com).
- **Practice with a paper account before investing real money.** Try out the Investing Simulator Center (http://www.investingonline.org/isc/index.html) and then practice with different investment strategies using online trading simulators like Icarra (http://www.icarra.com) or paperTrade (http://www.trademonster.com).
- **Gradually add more money to your brokerage account.** Add amounts regularly that are consistent with your investment goals.
- **Monitor your portfolio's performance.** Data can be obtained easily using Yahoo! Finance (http://finance.yahoo.com/) or GoogleFinance (http://www.google.com/finance).
- **Keep up with financial news.** In addition, read as much as you can on how to invest.

Source: Adapted from Matt Krantz, "How to Get Started Investing Online," http://www.dummies.com/how-to/content/investing-online-for-dummies-cheat-sheet.html, accessed August 2012.

DBLIGHT/ISTOCKPHOTO.COM

INVESTMENT PLANNING. Online calculators and worksheets can help you find answers to your financial planning and investing questions. With them, you can figure out how much to save each month for a particular goal, such as the down payment for your first home, a college education for your children, or to be able to retire by the time you reach 55. For example, Fidelity (**http://www.fidelity.com**) has a wide selection of planning tools that deal with such topics as investment growth, college planning, and retirement planning. One of the best sites for financial calculators is *Kiplinger* (**http://www.kiplinger.com**). Go to their personal finance page, click on "TOOLS" and you'll find calculators dealing with everything from stocks, bonds, and mutual funds to retirement planning, home buying, and taxes.

INVESTMENT RESEARCH AND SCREENING. One of the best investor services offered online is the ability to conduct high-quality, in-depth research on stocks, bonds, mutual funds, and other types of investment vehicles. Go to a site like **http://www.kiplinger.com**, click on "Investing," and you can obtain literally dozens of pages of financial and market information about a specific stock or mutual fund. Many of these sites have links back to the company itself, so with a few mouse clicks, you can obtain the company's annual report, detailed financial statements, and historical summaries of a full array of financial and market ratios. In addition, you'll also find various *online screening tools* that can be used to identify attractive and potentially rewarding investment vehicles. These tools, available at sites like Quicken, Morningstar, or MSN Money Central, enable you to sort quickly through huge databases of stocks and mutual funds to find those that meet specific characteristics, such as stocks with low or high P/E multiples, small market capitalizations, high dividend yields, specific revenue growth, and low debt-to-equity ratios. You answer a series of questions to specify the type of stock or fund you're looking for, performance criteria you desire, cost parameters, and so on. The screen then provides a list of stocks (or funds) that meet the standards that you've set.

Go to Smart Sites

Tune your investment portfolio for retirement with etrade's Easy Retirement Calculator. ●

PORTFOLIO TRACKING. Almost every investment-oriented Web site includes *portfolio tracking tools*. Simply enter the number of shares held, the purchase price, and the symbol for the stocks or mutual funds that you want to follow; the tracker then automatically updates the value of your portfolio in real time. What's more, you can usually click on one of the provided links and quickly obtain detailed information about each stock or mutual fund in your portfolio. Quicken.com, MSN MoneyCentral (**http:// moneycentral.msn.com/investor**), and E*Trade (**http://www. etrade.com**) all have portfolio trackers that are easy to set up and use. For example, Quicken's tracker alerts you whenever an analyst changes the rating on one of your stocks or funds and tells you how well you're diversified among the major asset classes or sectors you hold.

11-6 Managing Your Investment Holdings

LG6 Buying and selling securities is not difficult; the hard part is finding securities that will provide the kind of return you're looking for. Like most individual investors, you too will be buying, selling, and trading securities with ease in time. Eventually, your investment holdings will increase to the point where you're managing a whole portfolio of securities. In essence, a **portfolio** is a collection of investment vehicles assembled to meet a common investment goal. But a portfolio is far more than a collection of investments. It breathes life into your investment program, as it combines your personal and financial traits with your investment objectives to give some structure to your investments.

Seasoned investors often devote lots of attention to constructing diversified portfolios of securities. Such portfolios consist of stocks and bonds selected not only for their returns, but also for their combined risk–return behavior. The idea behind **diversification** is that by combining securities with dissimilar risk–return characteristics, you can produce a portfolio of reduced risk and more predictable levels of return. In recent years, investment researchers have shown that you can achieve a noticeable reduction in risk simply by diversifying your investment holdings. For the small investor with a moderate amount of money to invest, this means that *investing in several securities rather than a single one should be beneficial.* The payoff from diversification comes in the form of reduced risk without a significant impact on return.

portfolio A collection of securities assembled for the purpose of meeting common investment goals.

diversification The process of choosing securities with dissimilar risk–return characteristics in order to create a portfolio that provides an acceptable level of return and an acceptable exposure to risk.

11-6a Building a Portfolio of Securities

In developing a portfolio of investment holdings, it's assumed that diversification is a desirable investment attribute that leads to improved returns and/or reduced risk. Again, as emphasized previously, holding a variety of investments is far more desirable than concentrating all your investments in a single security or industry. When you first start investing, you probably won't be able to do much, if any, diversifying because of insufficient investment capital. However, as you build up your investment funds, your opportunities for diversification will increase dramatically. Certainly, by the time you have $10,000 to $15,000 to invest, you should start to diversify your holdings. To get an idea of the kind of portfolio diversification employed by investors, look at the following numbers, which shows the types of investments held by *average individual investors*:

Type of Investment Product	Percentage of Portfolio (July 2012)
Stocks and stock mutual funds	59%
Bonds and bond mutual funds	21%
Short-term investments (CDs, money market deposit accounts, etc.)	19%
Total	100%

This portfolio reflects the results of monthly asset allocation surveys conducted by the *American Association of Individual Investors*; whether this is what your portfolio should look like depends on a number of factors, including your own needs and objectives. (Note that the numbers given do not add up to 100 percent due to rounding.)

Investor Characteristics

To formulate an effective portfolio strategy, begin with an honest evaluation of your own financial condition and family situation. Pay particular attention to variables like these:

- Level and stability of income
- Family factors
- Investment horizon
- Net worth
- Investment experience and age
- Disposition toward risk

These variables set the tone for your investments. They determine the kinds of investments you should consider and how long you can tie up your money. For your portfolio to work, it must be tailored to meet your personal financial needs. For example, the size and predictability of an investor's employment income has a significant bearing on portfolio strategy. An investor with a secure job is more likely to embark on a more aggressive investment program than is an investor with a less secure position. Income taxes also bear on the investment decision. The higher an investor's income, the more important the tax ramifications of an investment program become.

In addition, an individual's investment experience will influence the type of investment strategy employed. It's best to "get your feet wet" in the investment market by slipping into it slowly, rather than leaping in head first. Investors who make risky initial investments often suffer heavy losses, damaging the long-run potential of their entire investment program. A cautiously developed investment program will likely provide far more favorable long-run results than an impulsive, risky one. Finally, investors should consider risk carefully. High-risk investments have not only high return potential but also high risk of loss. A good rule to remember is that *an investor's exposure to risk should never exceed his ability to bear that risk*.

Investor Objectives

After developing a personal financial profile, the investor's next question is: "What do I want from my portfolio?" This seems like an easy question to answer. Ideally, we would all like to double our money every year by making low-risk investments. However, the realities of the highly competitive investment environment make this outcome unlikely, so the question must be answered more realistically. There's generally a trade-off between earning a high current income from an investment and obtaining significant capital appreciation from it. An investor must choose one or the other; it's hard to obtain both from a single investment vehicle. Of course, it's possible to have a *balance* of both income and growth (capital gains) in a portfolio; but most often, that involves "tilting" the portfolio in one direction (e.g., toward income) or the other (toward growth).

An investor's needs should determine which avenue to choose. For instance, a retired investor whose income depends partly on her portfolio will probably choose a lower-risk, current-income-oriented approach for financial survival. In contrast, a high-income, financially secure investor may be much more willing to take on risky investments in hopes of improving her net worth. Likewise, a young investor with a secure job may be less concerned about current income and more able to bear risk. This type of investor will likely be more capital gains–oriented and may choose speculative investments.

11-6b Asset Allocation and Portfolio Management

A portfolio must be built around an individual's needs, which in turn depend on income, family responsibilities, financial resources, age, retirement plans, and ability to bear risk. These needs shape one's financial goals. But to create a portfolio geared to those goals, you need to develop an **asset allocation** strategy. Asset allocation centers on the question of *how to divide your portfolio among different types of securities*. For example, what portion of your portfolio will be devoted to short-term securities, to longer bonds and bond funds, and to common stocks and equity funds? The idea is to position your assets in such a way that you can protect your portfolio from negative developments in the market while still taking advantage of potential positive developments. There's substantial evidence that over the long run, *the total return on a portfolio is influenced far more by its asset allocation plan than by specific security selections.* Asset allocation deals in broad categories and *does not tell you which individual securities to buy or sell*. It might look something like this:

Type of Investment	Asset Mix
Short-term securities	5%
Longer bonds (7- to 10-year maturities)	20%
Equity funds	75%
Total portfolio	100%

- The proportion of an asset rises or falls considerably and thereby changes your target allocation for that class by more than, say, 5 percent.
- You're close to reaching a certain goal (such as saving for your child's college education).

asset allocation A plan for dividing a portfolio among different classes of securities in order to preserve capital by protecting the portfolio against negative market developments.

Periodically, you may find it necessary to *rebalance* your portfolio—that is, to reallocate the assets in your portfolio. For example, suppose that your asset allocation plan calls for 75 percent equities but then the stock market falls, so stocks represent only 65 percent of your total portfolio value. If you're still bullish on the (long-term) market and if stocks are still appropriate for your portfolio, then you may view this as a good time to buy stocks and, in so doing, bring your portfolio back up to 75 percent in equities. But don't be too quick to rebalance every time your portfolio gets a little out of whack; you should allow for some variation in the percentages because market fluctuations will make it impossible to maintain exact percentages constantly. And don't forget to consider tax implications and the costs from commissions or sales charges.

Portfolio management involves the buying, selling, and holding of various securities in order to meet a set of predetermined investment needs and objectives. To give you an idea of portfolio management in action, Exhibit 11.6 provides examples of four

> ## *Over the long run,* the total return on a portfolio is influenced far more by its asset allocation plan than by specific security selections.

As you can see, all you're really doing here is deciding how to cut up the pie. You still have to decide which particular securities to invest in. Once you've decided that you want to put, say, 20 percent of your money into intermediate-term (7- to 10-year) bonds, your next step is to select those specific securities.

After establishing your asset allocation strategy, you should check it regularly to make sure that your portfolio is still in line with your desired asset mix and to see if that mix is still appropriate for your investment objectives. Here are some reasons to reevaluate your asset allocations:

- A major change in personal circumstances—marriage, birth of a child, loss of job, or family illness—that changes your investment goals.

portfolios, each developed with a particular financial situation in mind. Notice that in each case, the asset allocation strategies and portfolio structures change with the different financial objectives. The first one is the *newlywed couple*; in their late 20s, they earn $58,000 a year and spend just about every cent. Next is the *two-income couple*; in their early 40s, they earn $115,000 a year and are concerned about college costs for their children, ages 17 and 12. Then there is the *single parent*; she is 34, has custody of her children, ages 7 and 4, and receives $40,000 a year in salary and child support. Finally, we have the *older couple*; in their mid-50s, they're planning for retirement in 10 years, when the husband will retire from his $95,000-a-year job.

Exhibit 11.6 **Four Model Portfolios**

The type of portfolio you put together will depend on your financial and family situation as well as on your investment objectives. Clearly, what is right for one family may be totally inappropriate for another.

Family Situation	Portfolio
Newlywed couple	80 percent to 90 percent in common stocks, with three-quarters of that in mutual funds aiming for maximum capital gains and the rest in growth-and-income or equity-income funds
	10 percent to 20 percent in a money market fund or other short-term money market securities
Two-income couple	60 percent to 70 percent in common stocks, with three-quarters of that in blue chips or growth mutual funds and the rest in more aggressive issues or mutual funds aiming for maximum capital gains
	25 percent to 30 percent in discount Treasury notes whose maturities correspond with the bills for college tuition
	5 percent to 10 percent in money market funds or other short-term money market securities
Single parent	50 percent to 60 percent in growth and income mutual funds
	40 percent to 50 percent in money market funds or other short-term money market securities
Older couple	60 percent to 70 percent in blue-chip common stocks, growth funds, or value funds
	25 percent to 30 percent in municipal bonds or short- and intermediate-term discount bonds that will mature as the couple starts needing the money to live on
	5 percent to 10 percent in CDs and money market funds

© Cengage Learning

11-6c Keeping Track of Your Investments

Just as you need investment objectives to provide direction for your portfolio, so too do you need to *monitor* it by keeping track of what your investment holdings consist of, how they've performed over time, and whether they've lived up to your expectations. Sometimes investments fail to perform the way that you thought they would. Their return may be well below what you'd like, or you may even have suffered a loss. In either case, it may be time to sell the investments and put the money elsewhere. A monitoring system should allow you to identify such securities in your portfolio. It should also enable you to stay on top of the holdings that are performing to your satisfaction. Knowing when to sell and when to hold can significantly affect the amount of return you're able to generate from your investments.

You can use a tool like Worksheet 11.2 to keep an inventory of your investment holdings. All types of investments can be included on this worksheet—from stocks, bonds, and mutual funds to real estate and savings accounts. To see how it works, consider the investment portfolio that has been built up since 2000 by Neal and Mary Carter, a two-income couple in their early 40s. Worksheet 11.2 shows that, as of July 2012, Neal and Mary hold common stock in three companies, two mutual funds, some real estate, and a savings account. Using a worksheet like this in conjunction with an *online portfolio tracker* would give an investor plenty of information about the performance of his or her portfolio—the *worksheet* providing long-term information from the date of purchase of an asset, and the *online portfolio tracker* providing year-to-date or annual returns. Note that the Carters earned about $28,000 in dividends and interest on their investments and that—thanks largely to their investments in a couple of stocks and stock funds—their holdings have grown from around $170,200 to more than $267,500. The cumulative earnings indicate that the Carters have made a good amount of income from their investments, and the latest market values show that their investments have appreciated nicely. A report like this should be prepared at least once a year; when completed, it provides a quick overview of your investment holdings and lets you know where you stand at a given point in time.

A worksheet like this one will enable you to keep track of your investment holdings and to identify investments that aren't performing up to expectations.

AN INVENTORY OF INVESTMENT HOLDINGS

Name(s): Neal and Mary Carter

Date: July 30, 2012

Type of Investment	Description of Investment Vehicle	Date Purchased	Amount of Investment (Quote - $ Amount)	Cumulative Amount of Income from Dividends, Interest, etc.	Latest Market Value (Quote - $ Amount)
Common stock	250 shares - McDonalds	12/7/2005	$35.26 - $8,815.00	$3,091.25	$89.30 - $22,325.00
Common stock	300 shares - Disney	10/19/2007	$33.81 - $10,143.00	$615.00	$49.80 - $14,940.00
Common stock	150 shares - Intel	8/11/2010	$19.43 - $2,914.50	$204.00	$25.76 - $3,864.00
Corporate bond	$5,000 Wal-Mart 6.5 - 37	8/24/2007	100 - $5,000	$1,462.50	124.39 - $6,219.50
Mutual fund	200 shares - Vanguard Health Care	6/16/2004	$125.71 - $25,142.00	$11,954.40	$141.29 - $28,258.00
Mutual fund	725 shares - Fidelity Contrafund	6/16/2004	$51.24 - $37,149.00	$10,638.65	$75.78 - $54,940.50
Real estate	house at 1700 West Market Street	9/16/2000	$280,000 - $56,000	N/A	(est) $400,000 - $112,000
Savings	1.05% savings account at First National Bank	7/30/2011	N/A - $25,000	$262.50	N/A $25,000
	Totals		$170,163.50	$28,228.30	$267,547.00

© Cengage Learning

Planning Over a Lifetime: Investing

Here are some key considerations for investment planning in each stage of the life cycle.

Pre-family Independence: 20s	Family Formation/Career Development: 30–45	Pre-Retirement: 45–65	Retirement: 65 and Beyond
✓ Describe specific, tangible investments goals concerning retirement, major purchases, ways to enhance current income, and tax shelters.	✓ Revise investment plan to focus more on retirement and funding children's education, if applicable.	✓ Revise investment plan in light of recent developments.	✓ Revise investment plan to include more conservative assets.
✓ Align your investment goals with an amount regularly set aside from your income.	✓ Consider rebalancing investment portfolio consistent with long-term strategy.	✓ Monitor portfolio performance and consider rebalancing asset exposures.	✓ Monitor portfolio performance and match current income to expenditures.
✓ Establish an emergency fund equal to six months of income.	✓ Gradually increase the amount set aside for investments and savings.	✓ Continue to gradually increase the amount you invest and save.	✓ Integrate investment strategy with estate planning.
✓ Make paying off college loans a priority. They often have high rates and will limit your financial flexibility.			

FINANCIAL PLANNING EXERCISES

LG1

1. *Use Worksheet 11.1.* Linda Scales is now employed as the managing editor of a well-known business journal. Although she thoroughly enjoys her job and the people she works with, what she would really like to do is open a bookstore of her own. She would like to open her store in about eight years and figures she'll need about $50,000 in capital to do so. Given that she thinks she can make about 10 percent on her money, use Worksheet 11.1 to answer the following questions.
    a. How much would Linda have to invest today, in one lump sum, to end up with $50,000 in eight years?
    b. If she's starting from scratch, how much would she have to put away annually to accumulate the needed capital in eight years?
    c. If she already has $10,000 socked away, how much would she have to put away annually to accumulate the required capital in eight years?
    d. Given that Linda has an idea of how much she needs to save, briefly explain how she could use an *investment plan* to help reach her objective.

LG2

2. Why do you suppose that well-known companies such as Apple and Facebook prefer to have their shares traded on the NASDAQ rather than on one of the major listed exchanges, such as the NYSE (for which they'd easily meet all listing requirements)? What's in it for them? What would they gain by switching over to the NYSE?

LG3

3. Suppose that Leonard Krauss places an order to buy 100 shares of Google. Explain how the order will be processed if it's a market order. Would it make any difference if it had been a limit order? Explain.

LG4

4. Using a resource like *The Wall Street Journal* or *Barron's* (either in print or online), find the latest values for each of the following market averages and indexes, and indicate how each has performed over the past six months:
    a. DJIA
    b. S&P 500
    c. NASDAQ Composite
    d. S&P MidCap 400
    e. Dow Jones Wilshire 5000
    f. Russell 2000

LG4

5. Using the Web site for Yahoo! Finance *(http://finance.yahoo.com)*, find the 52-week high and low for Google's common stock (symbol GOOG). What is the stock's latest dividend yield? What was Google's most recent closing price, and at what P/E ratio was the stock trading?

LG4

6. Using the S&P report in Exhibit 11.5, find the following information for Apple.
    a. What was the amount of revenues (i.e., sales) generated by the company in 2011?
    b. What were the latest annual dividends per share and dividend yield?
    c. What were the earnings per share (EPS) projections for 2012?
    d. How many common shareholders were there?
    e. What were the book value per share and EPS in 2011?
    f. How much long-term debt did the company have in 2011?

PFIN Student Study Tools—Visit CourseMate for PFIN 3. Log in at **www.cengagebrain.com**. Check out the bonus exercises and exhibits, interactive worksheets, Smart Sites, Critical Thinking Cases, Money Online, Kiplinger videos, quizzing, and more.

Cool Apps—Look for this new feature on CourseMate for PFIN 3. Cool Apps navigates the growing world of apps that are available for personal financial planning and tracking.

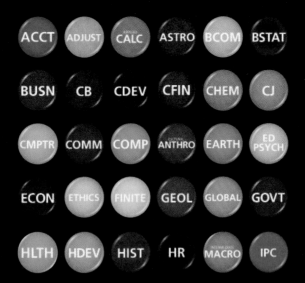

ONE APPROACH.
70 UNIQUE SOLUTIONS.

www.cengage.com/4ltrpress

12

INVESTING IN STOCKS AND BONDS

LEARNING GOALS

LG1 Describe the various types of risks to which investors are exposed as well as the sources of return.

LG2 Know how to search for an acceptable investment on the basis of risk, total return, and yield.

LG3 Discuss the merits of investing in common stock and be able to distinguish among the different types of stocks.

LG4 Become familiar with the various measures of performance and how to use them in placing a value on stocks.

LG5 Describe the basic issue characteristics of bonds as well as how these securities are used as investment vehicles.

LG6 Distinguish between the different types of bonds, gain an understanding of how bond prices behave, and know how to compute different measures of yield.

How Will This Affect Me? Once you've figured out how much you need to invest to meet important financial goals, it's time to decide which specific investments to buy. This chapter describes the basic characteristics of stocks and bonds, explains their potential returns and risks, and provides a framework for choosing among stocks and bonds to meet your financial objectives. Care is taken to explore how stock and bond prices behave and how to evaluate their performance over time. After reading this chapter, you should be able to choose the most appropriate stocks and bonds for your portfolio in light of your objectives and constraints.

12-1 The Risks and Rewards of Investing

LG1, LG2 Most rational investors are motivated to buy or sell a security based on its expected (or anticipated) return: buy if the return looks good, sell if it doesn't. But a security's return is just part of the story; you can't consider the return on an investment without also looking at its *risk*—the chance that the actual return from an investment may differ from (that is, fall short—you wouldn't mind if it exceeded expectations, after all) what was expected. Generally speaking, you expect riskier investments to provide higher levels of return. Otherwise, what incentive is there for an investor to risk his or her capital? These two concepts (risk and return) are of vital concern to investors. So, before taking up the issue of investing in stocks and bonds, let's look more closely at the risks of investing and the various components of return.

> ## A security's return is just part of the story; you can't consider the return on an investment without also looking at its risk.

WATCHARAKUN/SHUTTERSTOCK.COM

After you read the chapter, explore the STUDY TOOLS listed on page 307.

Equally important, we'll see how these two components can be used together to find potentially attractive investment vehicles.

12-1a The Risks of Investing

Just about any type of investment is subject to some risk—some more than others. The basic types of investment risk are business risk, financial risk, market risk, purchasing power risk, interest rate risk, liquidity risk, and event risk. Other things being equal, you'd like to reduce your exposure to these risks as much as possible.

Go to Smart Sites

What's your investment risk tolerance? Take a quiz at the Smarter About Money site, and find out more about your risk profile and investing style. For more online resources, whenever you see "*Go to Smart Sites*" in this chapter, visit CourseMate for PFIN 3. Log in at **www.cengagebrain.com**. ●

© GEOPAUL/ISTOCKPHOTO

Business Risk

When investing in a company, you may have to accept the possibility that the firm will fail to maintain sales and profits or even to stay in business. Such failure is due either to economic or industry factors or, as is more often the case, to poor management decisions. **Business risk**, in essence, represents the degree of uncertainty surrounding the firm's cash flows and its ability to meet operating expenses in a timely fashion.

Financial Risk

Financial risk concerns the amount of debt used to finance the firm as well as the possibility that the firm will not have sufficient cash flows to meet these obligations on time. Look to the company's balance sheet in order to get a handle on a firm's financial risk. As a rule, companies that have little or no long-term debt are fairly low in financial risk. This is the case particularly if the company also has a healthy earnings picture. The problem with debt financing is that it creates principal and interest obligations that must be met regardless of how much profit the company is generating.

> **business risk** The degree of uncertainty associated with a firm's cash flows and with its subsequent ability to meet its operating expenses.

> **financial risk** A type of risk associated with the mix of debt and equity financing used by the issuing firm and its ability to meet its financial obligations.

281

Market Risk

Market risk results from the behavior of investors in the securities markets that can lead to swings in security prices. These price changes can be due to underlying intrinsic factors, as well as to changes in political and economic conditions or in investor tastes and preferences. Essentially, market risk is reflected in the *price volatility* of a security: the more volatile the price of a security, the greater its market risk.

Purchasing Power Risk

Changes in the general level of prices within an economy produce **purchasing power risk**. In periods of rising prices (inflation), the purchasing power of the dollar declines. This means that a smaller quantity of goods and services can be purchased with a given number of dollars. In general, investments (like stocks or real estate) whose values tend to move with general price levels are most profitable during periods of rising prices, whereas investments (such as bonds) that provide fixed returns are preferred during periods of low or declining price levels.

Interest Rate Risk

Fixed-income securities—which include notes, bonds, and preferred stocks—offer investors a fixed periodic return and, as such, are most affected by **interest rate risk**. As interest rates change, the prices of these securities fluctuate, decreasing with rising interest rates and increasing with falling rates. For example, the prices of fixed-income securities drop when interest rates increase, giving investors rates of return that are competitive with securities offering higher levels of interest income. Changes in interest rates are due to fluctuations in the supply of or demand for money.

Liquidity Risk

The risk of not being able to liquidate (i.e., sell) an investment conveniently and at a reasonable price is called **liquidity (or marketability) risk**. In general, investment vehicles traded in *thin markets*, where supply and demand are small, tend to be less liquid than those traded in *broad markets*. However, to be liquid, an investment not only must be easy to sell, but also must be so *at a reasonable price*. Vehicles such as mutual funds, common stocks, and U.S. Treasury securities are generally highly liquid; others, such as raw land, are not.

Event Risk

Event risk occurs when something substantial happens to a company and that event, in itself, has a sudden impact on the company's financial condition. It involves a largely (or totally) unexpected event that has a significant and usually immediate effect on the underlying value of an investment. A good example of event risk was the action by the Food and Drug Administration (FDA) years ago to halt the use of silicone breast implants. The share price of Dow Corning—the dominant producer of this product—was quickly affected (negatively) by this single event! Another comparable example is the controversy over Vioxx, a drug produced by Merck, which was eventually withdrawn from the market and brought civil and criminal litigation that ultimately cost the company at least $5.8 billion. Fortunately, event risk tends to be confined to specific companies, securities, or market segments.

12-1b The Returns from Investing

Any investment vehicle—whether it's a share of stock, a bond, a piece of real estate, or a mutual fund—has just two basic sources of return: *current income* and *capital gains*. Some investments offer only one source of return (for example, non–dividend-paying stocks provide only capital gains), but many others offer both income and capital gains, which together make up what's known as the *total return* from an investment. Of course, when both elements of return are present, the relative importance of each will vary among investments. For example, whereas current income is more important with bonds, capital gains are usually a larger portion of the total return from common stocks.

Current Income

Current income is generally received with some degree of regularity over the course of the year. It may take the form of dividends on stock, interest from bonds, or rents from real estate. People who invest to obtain income look for investment vehicles that will provide regular and predictable patterns of income. Preferred stocks and bonds, which are expected to pay known amounts at specified times (for example, quarterly or semiannually), are usually viewed as good income investments.

Capital Gains

The other type of return available from investments is capital appreciation (or growth), which is reflected as an increase in the market value of an investment vehicle. Capital gains occur when you're able to sell

© GEORGE ALLEN PENTON/SHUTTERSTOCK.COM

a security for more than you paid for it or when your security holdings go up in value. Investments that provide greater growth potential through capital appreciation normally have lower levels of current income because the firm achieves its growth by reinvesting its earnings instead of paying dividends to the owners. Many common stocks, for example, are acquired for their capital gains potential.

Earning Interest on Interest: Another Source of Return

When does a 4 percent investment end up yielding only 3 percent? Probably more often than you think! Obviously, it can happen when investment performance fails to live up to expectations. But it can also happen even when everything goes right. That is, so long as at least part of the return from an investment involves the periodic receipt of current income (such as dividends or interest payments), then that income must be *reinvested* at a given rate of return in order to achieve the yield you thought you had going into the investment. Consider an investor who buys a 4 percent U.S. Treasury bond and holds it to maturity, a period of 20 years. Each year the bondholder

---

Financial Planning Tips: Keys Concepts in Successful Stock and Bond Investing

Asset Allocation, Diversification, and Rebalancing

Here are some key concepts that will help you successfully manage your portfolio:

- **Asset allocation.** This is the decision on how to divide your investments among the different major asset classes, which include stocks, bonds, and cash. The best mix depends on your *tolerance for risk* and on your *time horizon*. Longer-term investors, like someone in her 20s saving for retirement, are often more comfortable investing in riskier assets like stocks. In contrast, shorter-term investors, like someone saving for a house down payment or a child's education, often will be comfortable with less risk. This often implies that such a person will invest less in stocks and more in bonds. Most investors change their asset allocation as their time horizon changes—for instance, as they approach retirement. Thus, most investors tend to hold fewer stocks and more bonds and cash as they get older. Take a look at the Cool Apps feature later in this chapter, about an asset allocation calculator.

- **Diversification.** This is the strategy of spreading your money among different investments so that losses on some investments will be offset, at least somewhat, by gains on other investments in your portfolio. Your portfolio should be diversified both *among* and *within*

asset classes. This means that your asset allocation strategy should spread out your money among stocks, bonds, and cash and that your money should be spread out *among* different securities *within* each asset class. For example, within the equity asset class it's important to identify stocks that perform differently in different equity market conditions. This often involves investing in stocks in different sectors and industries.

- **Rebalancing.** Over time, changes in market values could make your portfolio inconsistent with your financial goals. For example, what if you have decided that your portfolio should consist of 70 percent stocks, but a market turndown has reduced the value of your stock holdings to only 60 percent of your portfolio? In order to rebalance your holdings, you'll need to buy more equities outright or sell some bonds and/or use some cash to fund the additional exposure to stocks. But before you rebalance, you should consider carefully the transaction costs and any possible tax consequences. Many financial advisors suggest that you consider rebalancing your portfolio every 6 to 12 months, and whenever the asset allocation gets out of kilter by a given percentage, like 5 percent or 10 percent.

Source: "Beginners' Guide to Asset Allocation, Diversification, and Rebalancing," http://www.sec.gov/investor/pubs/assetallocation.htm, accessed August 2012.

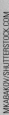

MKABAKOV/SHUTTERSTOCK.COM

receives $40 in interest, and at maturity, the $1,000 in principal is repaid. There's no loss in capital, no default; everything is paid right on time. Yet this sure-fire investment ends up yielding only 3 percent. Why? Because the investor failed to reinvest the semiannual interest payments he was receiving at the original interest rate of 4 percent. By not plowing back all the investment earnings, the bondholder failed to earn any *interest on interest*.

Take a look at Exhibit 12.1. It shows the three elements of return for a 4 percent, 20-year bond: (1) the recovery of principal; (2) periodic interest income; and (3) the interest on interest earned from reinvesting the semiannual interest payments. Note that because the bond was originally bought at par ($1,000), you start off with a 4 percent invest-ment. *Where you end up depends, in large part, on what you do with the interest earnings from this*

investment. If you don't reinvest the interest income at the original 4 percent, then you'll end up on the 3 percent line—or even lower.

You have to earn interest on interest from your investments in order to move to the 4 percent line. Specifically, because you started out with a 4 percent investment, *that's the rate of return that you need to earn when reinvesting your income.* And keep in mind that even though we used a bond in our illustration, *this same concept applies to any type of long-term investment vehicle*, so long as current income is part of an investment's return. This notion of earning interest on interest is what the market refers to as a *fully compounded rate of return.* The amount of interest on interest embedded in a security's return depends in large part on the length of your investment horizon. That is, *long-term investments* (e.g., 20-year bonds) are subject to a lot more interest on interest

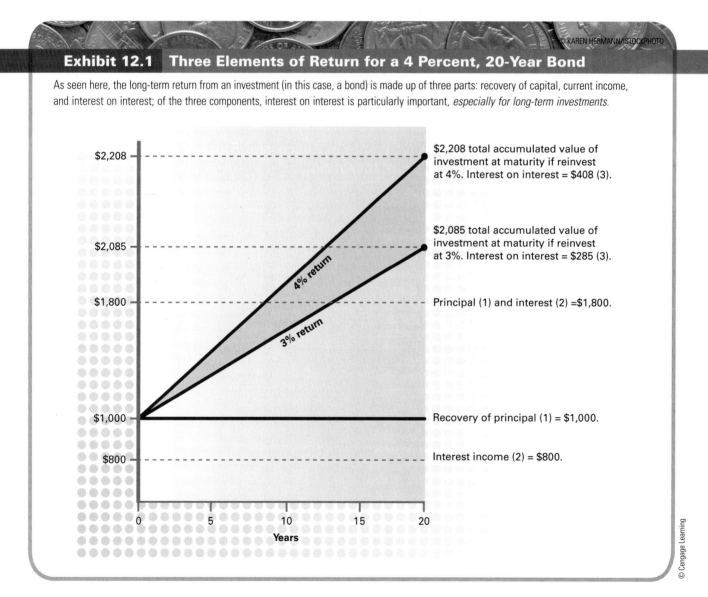

Exhibit 12.1   Three Elements of Return for a 4 Percent, 20-Year Bond

As seen here, the long-term return from an investment (in this case, a bond) is made up of three parts: recovery of capital, current income, and interest on interest; of the three components, interest on interest is particularly important, *especially for long-term investments.*

© KAREN HERMANN/ISTOCKPHOTO

© Cengage Learning

than are short-term investments (e.g., six-month T-bills or dividend-paying stocks that you hold for only 2 or 3 years).

12-1c The Risk-Return Trade-off

The amount of risk associated with a given investment vehicle is directly related to its expected return. This universal rule of investing means that if you want a higher level of return, you'll probably have to accept greater exposure to risk. While higher risk generally is associated with higher levels of return, this relationship doesn't necessarily work in the opposite direction. That is, you can't invest in a high-risk security and expect to earn a high rate of return automatically. Unfortunately, it doesn't work that way—risk isn't, by definition, that predictable!

Exhibit 12.2 portrays the risk-return trade-off for some popular investment vehicles. Note that it's possible to receive a positive return for zero risk, such as at point A. This is referred to as the **risk-free rate of return**, which is often measured by the return on a short-term government security, such as a 90-day Treasury bill (T-bill).

12-1d What Makes a Good Investment?

In keeping with the preceding risk-return discussion, it follows that the value of any investment depends on the amount of return that it's expected to provide relative to the amount of perceived risk involved. And this applies to all types of investment vehicles, including stocks, bonds, or real estate and commodities. In this respect, they should all be treated the same.

Future Return

In investments, it's the *expected future return on a security* that matters. Aside from the help that they can provide in getting a handle on future income, *past returns are of little value to investors*—after all, it's not what the security did last year that matters but rather what it's expected to do next year. To get an idea of the future return on an investment, we must *formulate expectations of its future current income and future capital appreciation*. As an illustration, assume you're thinking of buying some stock in Robotic Solutions

risk-free rate of return The rate of return on short-term government securities, such as Treasury bills, that is free from default risk.

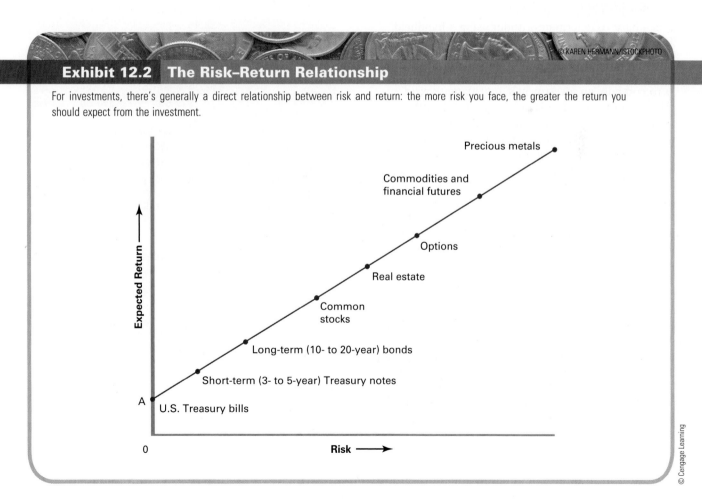

© KAREN HERMANN/ISTOCKPHOTO

Exhibit 12.2   The Risk–Return Relationship

For investments, there's generally a direct relationship between risk and return: the more risk you face, the greater the return you should expect from the investment.

- Precious metals
- Commodities and financial futures
- Options
- Real estate
- Common stocks
- Long-term (10- to 20-year) bonds
- Short-term (3- to 5-year) Treasury notes
- A U.S. Treasury bills

Expected Return

Risk ⟶

0

© Cengage Learning

desired rate of return The minimum rate of return an investor feels should be earned in compensation for the amount of risk assumed.

Company, Inc. (RSC) at the beginning of 2015. After reviewing several financial reports, you've estimated the future dividends and price behavior of RSC as follows:

Expected average annual dividends, 2015–2017 $2.15 a share

Expected market price of the stock, 2017 $95.00 a share

Because the stock is now selling for $60 a share, the difference between its current and expected future market price ($95 – $60) represents the amount of *capital gains* you expect to receive over the next three years—in this case, $35 a share. The projected future price, along with expected average annual dividends, gives you an estimate of the stock's *future income stream*; what you need now is a way to measure the *expected return*.

Approximate Yield

Finding the exact rate of return on an investment involves a complex mathematical procedure—one that's hard to determine without using a handheld financial calculator (which we'll demonstrate shortly). There is, however, a fairly easy way to obtain a reasonably close estimation of expected return, and that is to compute an investment's *approximate yield*. Although this measure is only an approximation, it's useful when dealing with forecasted numbers (that are subject to some degree of uncertainty anyway). The measure considers not only current income and capital gains but interest on interest as well. Hence, *approximate yield provides a measure of the fully compounded rate of return* from an investment. Finding the approximate yield on an investment is shown in the equation below. If you briefly study the formula, you will see it's really not as formidable as it may appear at first. All it does is relate (1) average current income and (2) average capital gains to the (3) average amount of the investment.

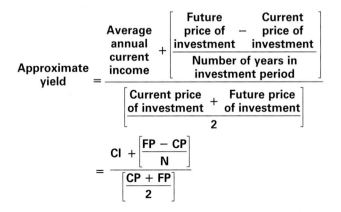

where
CI = average annual current income (amount that you expect to receive annually from dividends, interest, or rent)
FP = expected future price of investment
CP = current market price of investment
N = investment period (length of time, in years, that you expect to hold the investment)

Crunching the Numbers

To illustrate, let's use the RSC example again. Given the average current income (CI) from annual dividends of $2.15, current stock price (CP) of $60, future stock price (FP) of $95, and an investment period (N) of three years (you expect to hold the stock from the beginning of 2015 through the end of 2017), you can use this equation to find the expected approximate yield on RSC as follows:

$$\text{Approximate yield} = \frac{\$2.15 + \left[\dfrac{\$95 - \$60}{3}\right]}{\left[\dfrac{\$60 + \$95}{2}\right]}$$

$$= \frac{\$2.15 + \left[\dfrac{\$35}{3}\right]}{\left[\dfrac{\$155}{2}\right]}$$

$$= \frac{\$2.15 + \$11.67}{\$77.50} = \frac{\$13.82}{\$77.50}$$

$$= 17.83\%$$

In this case, if your forecasts of annual dividends and capital gains hold up, an investment in RSC should provide a return of around 17.83 percent per year.

Whether you should consider RSC a viable investment candidate depends on how this expected return stacks up to the amount of risk you must assume. Suppose that you've decided the stock is moderately risky. To determine whether the expected rate of return on this investment will be satisfactory, you can compare it to some benchmark. One of the best is the rate of return you can expect from a *risk-free* security, such as a *U.S. T-bill*. The idea is that the return on a *risky* security should be greater than that available on a risk-free security. If, for example, U.S. T-bills are yielding 4 percent or 5 percent, then you'd want to receive considerably more—perhaps 10 percent to 12 percent—to justify your investment in a moderately risky security like RSC. In essence, the 10 percent to 12 percent is your **desired rate of return**: the minimum rate of return that you believe

286   Part 5 • Managing Investments

CALCULATOR

Inputs	Functions
3	N
−60	PV
2.15	PMT
95.00	FV
	CPT
	I/Y
	Solution
	19.66

SEE APPENDIX E FOR DETAILS.

you should receive in compensation for the amount of risk that you must assume. *An investment should be considered acceptable only if it's expected to generate a rate of return that meets (or exceeds) your desired rate of return.* In the case of RSC, the stock should be considered a viable investment candidate because it provides more than the minimum or desired rate of return.

Calculator Keystrokes

You can easily find the *exact* return on this investment by using a handheld financial calculator. Here's what you do. First, put the calculator in the *annual compounding* mode. Then—to find the expected return on a stock that you buy at $60 a share, hold for three years (during which time you receive average annual dividends of $2.15 a share), and then sell at $95—use the keystrokes shown above, where:

N   = number of *years* that you hold the stock
PV = the price that you pay for the stock (entered as a *negative* value)
PMT = *average* amount of dividends received each year
FV = the price that you expect to receive when you *sell* the stock (in three years)

You'll notice there is a difference in the computed yield measures (17.83% with the approximate procedure versus 19.66% here). That's to be expected because the former is only an approximate measure of performance whereas this is exact measure.

12-2 Investing in Common Stock

LG3, LG4 Common stocks appeal to investors for a variety of reasons. To some, investing in stocks is a way to hit it big if the issue shoots up in price; to others, it's the level of current income that they offer. The basic investment attribute of a share of common stock is that it enables the investor to participate in the profits of the firm. Every shareholder is, in effect, a part owner of the firm and, as such, is entitled to a

piece of its profit. But this claim on income has limitations, for common stockholders are really the **residual owners** of the company, meaning that they're entitled to dividend income and a prorated share of the company's earnings, but only after all the firm's other obligations have been met.

residual owners
Shareholders of the company; they are entitled to dividend income and a share of the company's profits only after all of the firm's other obligations have been met.

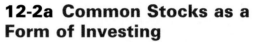

> **Every shareholder is, in effect, a part owner of the firm and, as such, is entitled to a piece of its profit.**

12-2a Common Stocks as a Form of Investing

Given the nature of common stocks, if the market is strong, then investors can generally expect to benefit from steady price appreciation. A good example is the performance in 1995, when the market, as measured by the Dow Jones Industrial Average (DJIA), went up more than 33 percent. Unfortunately, when markets falter, so do investor returns. Look at what happened over the three-year period from early 2000 through late 2002, when the market (again, as measured by the DJIA) fell some 38 percent. Excluding dividends, a $100,000 investment would have declined in value to a little over $60,000. And in 2008, the Dow fell yet again, this time by almost 34 percent, while the S&P 500 Composite Index (S&P 500) fell by about 38 percent.

Make no mistake, the market does have its bad days, and sometimes those bad days seem to go on for months. It may not always appear that way, but those bad days *really are the exception, not the rule.* That was certainly the case over the 83-year period from 1929 through 2011, when the Dow went down (for the year) just 21 times. That's only about 25 percent of the time; the other 75 percent, the market was up—anywhere from around 2 percent on the year to nearly 40 percent! True, there's some risk and price volatility (even in good markets), but that's the price that you have to pay for all the upside potential. Consider, for example, the behavior of the market from 1982 through early 2000. Starting in August 1982, when the Dow stood at 777, this market saw the DJIA climb nearly 11,000 points to reach a high of 11,723 in January 2000. Unfortunately, that all came to a screeching halt in early 2000, when each of the three major market measures peaked. Over the course of the next 32 months, through September 2002, these market measures fell flat on their collective faces. Although the Dow recovered from 2003 through mid-2007, it fell big time in 2008 as well. In fact, it fell from about 14,000 in July 2007 to around 6,500 in March 2009, with most of that loss occurring in 2008, when the Dow dropped by nearly 34 percent.

Take a look at Exhibit 12.3, which tracks the behavior of the DJIA and the NASDAQ Composite from 2002 to July 2012, and you'll quickly get a feel for just how volatile this market was! As the exhibit shows, despite all those market gyrations, both the Dow and the NASDAQ—which track two totally different segments of the market—ended up with relatively modest returns (2.5 percent and 3.95 percent, respectively), largely because of the bear markets of 2000–2002, 2008, and the low returns in 2010. Specifically, a $10,000 investment in the DJIA in January of 2002 would have grown to about $12,981 by July of 2012, while $10,000 invested in the NASDAQ would have grown to about $15,071.

Issuers of Common Stock

Shares of common stock can be issued by any corporation in any line of business. All corporations have stockholders, but not all of them have publicly traded shares. The stocks of interest to us in this book are the so-called *publicly traded issues*—the shares that are readily available to the general public and that are bought and sold in the open market. Aside from the initial distribution of common stock when the corporation is formed, subsequent sales of additional shares may be made through a procedure known as a *public offering*. In a public offering, the corporation, working with its underwriter, simply offers the investing public a certain number of shares of its stock at a certain price.

Voting Rights

The holders of common stock normally receive *voting rights*, which means that for each share of stock held, they receive one vote. In some cases, common stock may be designated as nonvoting at the time of issue,

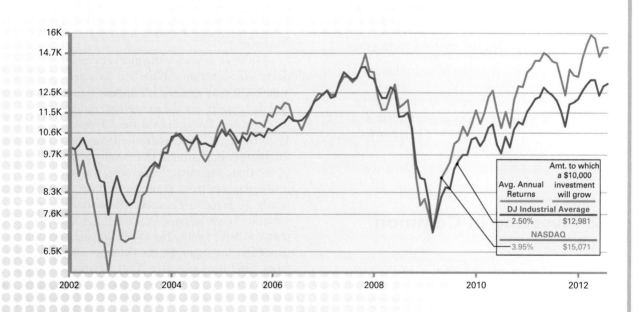

© KAREN HERMANN/ISTOCKPHOTO

| Exhibit 12.3 | Performance of Dow Jones Industrial Average and NASDAQ Composite, 2002 through mid-2012 |

One of the greatest bull markets in history began on August 12, 1982, with the Dow at 777. It continued through the 1980s and into the 1990s, but it all ended in early 2000. The market went from a rip-snorting bull to a full-fledged bear in 2000, which lasted until 2002. After recovering, the market entered one of the worst bear markets in history during 2007 and 2008, as the markets experienced the impact of the global financial crisis. This graph shows how the value of a $10,000 investment changed between 2002 and mid-2012.

	Avg. Annual Returns	Amt. to which a $10,000 investment will grow
DJ Industrial Average	2.50%	$12,981
NASDAQ	3.95%	$15,071

but this is the exception rather than the rule. Although different voting systems exist, small stockholders need not concern themselves with them because, regardless of the system used, their chances of affecting corporate control with their votes are quite slim.

Corporations have annual stockholders' meetings, at which time new directors are elected and special issues are voted on. Because most small stockholders can't attend these meetings, they can use a proxy to assign their votes to another person, who will vote for them. A **proxy** is a written statement assigning voting rights to another party.

Basic Tax Considerations

Common stocks provide income in the form of dividends, usually paid quarterly, and/or capital gains, which occur when the price of the stock goes up over time. From a tax *rate* perspective, it really makes no difference whether the investment return comes in the form of dividends or long-term capital gains—in late 2012, they're both taxed at the same rate of 15 percent or less (it's 0 percent for those filers in the 10 percent and 15 percent tax brackets). There's one slight difference between the taxes due on dividends and those due on capital gains: namely, there is no tax liability on any capital gains until the stock is actually sold (*paper gains*—that is, any price appreciation occurring on stock that you still own—accumulate tax free). *Bottom line: taxes are due on any dividends and capital gains in the year in which the dividends are received or the stock is actually sold.*

Here's how it works. Assume that you just sold 100 shares of common stock for $50 per share. Also assume that the stock was originally purchased two years ago for $20 per share and that, during each of the past two years, you received $1.25 per share in cash dividends. Thus, for tax purposes, you would have received cash dividends of $125 (i.e., $1.25/share × 100 shares) *both* this year and last, plus you would have generated a capital gain, which is taxable this year, of $3,000 ($50/share − $20/share × 100 shares). Suppose that you are in the 33 percent tax bracket. Even though you're in one of the higher brackets, both the dividends and capital gains earned on this investment qualify for the lower 15 percent tax rate. Therefore, on the dividends, you'll pay taxes of $125 × 0.15 = $18.75 (for each of the past two years), and on the capital gains, you'll owe $3,000 × 0.15 = $450 (for this year only). Therefore, last year, your tax liability would have been $18.75 (for the dividends), and this year, it will be $468.75 (for the dividends and capital gains). Bottom line: out of the $3,250 that you earned on this investment over the past two years, you keep $2,762.50 after taxes.

proxy A written statement used to assign a stockholder's voting rights to another person, typically one of the directors.

dividend yield The percentage return provided by the dividends paid on common stock.

12-2b Dividends

Corporations pay dividends to their common stockholders in the form of cash and/or additional stock. *Cash dividends* are the most common. Cash dividends are normally distributed quarterly in an amount determined by the firm's board of directors. For example, if the directors declared a quarterly cash dividend of 50 cents a share, and if you owned 200 shares of stock, then you'd receive a check for $100.

A popular way of assessing the amount of dividends received is to measure the stock's dividend yield. **Dividend yield** is a measure of common stock dividends on a relative (percentage) basis—that is, the dollar amount of dividends received is compared to the market price of the stock. Dividend yield is an indication of the rate of current income being earned on the investment. It's computed as follows:

$$\text{Dividend yield} = \frac{\text{Annual dividend received per share}}{\text{Market price per share of stock}}$$

Financial Planning Tips

Don't Be Taken in by Common Investing Myths

Here are some myths that you should be aware of when investing:

- **During volatile markets it makes sense to sell your stocks and wait for calmer conditions.** While it sounds so reasonable, investors who remain in the market outperform those who move in and out to manage their market exposure. When trading in and out, you pay more commissions and, more important, you tend to miss the upturns in the market that can make you whole—or even more than whole—again.

- **Gold is a good addition to any portfolio.** It's true that gold can be a good asset to add because its returns tend to move opposite those of stocks, which is good for diversification. However, few advisors would recommend allocating more than 5 or 10 percent of a portfolio to gold in most cases. There have been long periods when gold has had poor returns. For example, between 1948 and 1992, gold earned only about 4.8 percent. This was about the return on T-bills, but with much more risk.

- **The S&P 500 is the best place for long-term stock investors.** The large stocks in the S&P 500 do not always pay the best returns. Small capitalization and value stocks tend to outperform the S&P 500 over the long haul.

Source: Adapted from Daniel Solin, "5 Investment Myths That Can Cost You," http://money.usnews.com/money/blogs/on-retirement/2011/03/17/5-investment-myths-that-can-cost-you, accessed August 2012.

MKABAKOV/SHUTTERSTOCK.COM

For example, a company that pays $2 per share in annual dividends and whose stock is trading at $50 a share will have a dividend yield of 4 percent ($2/$50 = 0.04). Dividend yield is widely used by income-oriented investors looking for (reasonably priced) stocks with a long and sustained record of regularly paying higher-than-average dividends.

Occasionally, the directors may declare a stock dividend as a supplement to or in place of cash dividends. **Stock dividends** are paid in the form of additional shares of stock. That is, rather than receiving cash, shareholders receive additional shares of the company's stock—say, 1/10 of a share of new stock for each share owned (as in a *10 percent stock dividend*). Although they often satisfy the needs of some investors, stock dividends really have no value because they represent the receipt of something already owned. For example, if you owned 100 shares of stock in a company that declared a 10 percent stock dividend, you'd receive 10 new shares of stock. Unfortunately, you'll be no better off after the stock dividend than you were before. That's because the total market value of the shares owned would be roughly the same after the stock dividend as before.

12-2c Some Key Measures of Performance

Seasoned investors use a variety of financial ratios and measures when making common stock investment decisions. They look at such things as dividend yield (just described), book value, return on equity, and earnings per share (EPS) to get a feel for the investment merits of a particular stock. Fortunately, most of the widely followed ratios can be found in published reports—like those produced by *Value Line* or Standard & Poor's (see Exhibit 11.5 in Chapter 11 for an example of an S&P stock report)—so you don't have to compute them yourself. Even so, if you're thinking about buying a stock or already have some stocks, there are a few measures of performance that you'll want to keep track of, such as book value (or book value per share), net profit margin, and the like.

Book Value

The amount of stockholders' equity in a firm is measured by **book value**. This accounting measure is found by subtracting the firm's liabilities and preferred stocks from the value of its assets. Book value indicates the amount of stockholder funds used to finance the firm. For instance, assume that our example company (RSC) had assets of $8 million, liabilities of $2 million, and preferred stock valued at $1 million. The book value of the firm's common stock would be $5 million ($8 million − $2 million − $1 million). When the book value is divided by the number of shares outstanding, the result is *book value per share*. So if RSC had 100,000 shares of common stock outstanding, its book value per share would be $50 ($5,000,000/100,000 shares). Because of the impact that it can have on the firm's growth, you'd like to see book value per share steadily increasing over time. Also look for stocks whose market prices are comfortably above their book values.

Net Profit Margin

As a yardstick of profitability, **net profit margin** is one of the most widely followed measures of corporate performance. This ratio relates the firm's net profits to its sales, providing an indication of how well the company is controlling its cost structure. The higher the net profit margin, the more money the company earns. Look for a relatively stable—or even better, an increasing—net profit margin.

Return on Equity

Another important and widely followed measure, **return on equity (ROE)** reflects the firm's overall profitability from the equityholders' perspective. It captures, in a single ratio, the amount of success the firm is having in managing its assets, operations, and capital structure. ROE is important because it is significantly related to the profits, growth, and dividends of the firm. So long as a firm is not borrowing too much money, the better the ROE and the better the company's financial condition and competitive position. Look for a stable or increasing ROE; watch out for a falling ROE because that could spell trouble.

Earnings per Share

With stocks, the firm's annual earnings are usually measured and reported in terms of **earnings per share (EPS)**. This metric translates total corporate profits into profits on a per-share basis and provides a convenient measure of the amount of earnings available to stockholders. EPS is found by using this simple formula:

$$EPS = \frac{\text{Net profit after taxes } - \text{ Preferred dividends paid}}{\text{Number of shares of common stock outstanding}}$$

For example, if RSC reported a net profit of $600,000, paid $100,000 in dividends to preferred stockholders, and had 100,000 shares of common stock outstanding, then it would have an EPS of $5.00 [($600,000 − $100,000)/100,000]. Note that preferred dividends are *subtracted* from profits because they must be paid before any monies can be made available to common stockholders. Stockholders follow EPS closely because it represents the amount the firm has earned on behalf of each outstanding share of common stock. Look for steady growth in EPS, too.

Price/Earnings Ratio

When the prevailing market price of a share of common stock is divided by the annual earnings per share, the result is the **price/earnings (P/E) ratio**, a measure that's viewed as an indication of investor confidence and expectations. The higher the P/E multiple, the more confidence that investors are presumed to have in a given security. In the case of RSC, whose shares are currently selling for $60, the price/earnings ratio is 12 ($60 per share/$5.00 per share). In other words, RSC stock is selling for 12 times its earnings. P/E ratios are important to investors because they reveal how aggressively the stock is being priced in the market. Watch out for very high P/Es—that is, P/Es that are way out of line with the market—because that could indicate the stock is overpriced (and thus might be headed for a big drop in price). P/E ratios tend to move with the market. So when the market is soft, a stock's P/E will be low; when the market heats up, the stock's P/E will rise.

Beta

A stock's **beta** is an indication of its *price volatility;* it shows how responsive the stock is to changes in the overall stock market. In recent years, using betas to measure the *market risk* of common stock has become widely accepted. As a result, published betas are now available from most brokerage firms and investment services. The beta for a given stock is determined by a statistical technique that relates the stock's historical returns to the market. The market (as measured by something like the S&P index of 500 stocks) is used as a benchmark of performance and always has a beta of 1.0. From there, everything is relative: low-beta stocks—those with betas of less than 1.0—have low price volatility, whereas high-beta stocks—those with betas of more than 1.0—are considered to be volatile. In short, the higher a stock's beta, the riskier it's considered to be. Beta is thus an *index* of relative

 Go to Smart Sites

Enter a stock's ticker symbol at Yahoo! Finance's Stock Research Center and you see a complete page of stock data: price, news, financial blogs, charts, and fundamentals. ●

price performance. So if RSC has a beta of, say, 0.8, then it should rise (or fall) only 80 percent as fast as the market. In contrast, if the stock had a beta of 1.8, then it would go up or down 1.8 times as fast—the price of the stock would rise higher and fall harder than the general market. Other things being equal, if you're looking for a relatively conservative investment, then you should stick with low-beta stocks; on the other hand, if it's potentially high capital gains and price volatility you're after, go with high-beta securities.

12-2d Types of Common Stock

Common stocks are often classified on the basis of their dividends or their rate of growth in EPS. Some popular types of common stock are blue-chip, growth, tech stocks, income, speculative, cyclical, defensive, large-cap, mid-cap, and small-cap stocks.

Blue-Chip Stocks

Blue-chip stocks are the cream of the common stock crop; these stocks are unsurpassed in quality and have a long and stable record of earnings and dividends. They're issued by large, well-established firms that have impeccable financial credentials—firms like Apple, Wal-Mart, IBM, Microsoft, and ExxonMobil. These companies hold important if not leading positions in their industries, and they often determine the standards by which other firms are measured. Blue chips are particularly attractive to investors who seek high-quality investment outlets offering decent dividend yields and respectable growth potential.

Growth Stocks

Stocks that have experienced—and are expected to continue experiencing—consistently high rates of growth in operations and earnings are known as **growth stocks**. A good growth stock might exhibit a *sustained* rate of growth in earnings of 15 percent to 20 percent over a period when common stocks are averaging only 6 percent to 8 percent. In mid-2012, prime examples of large capitalization stocks expected to exhibit great growth included Alexion Pharmaceuticals, Lululemon Athletica, Union Pacific, and F5 Networks. These stocks often pay little or nothing in dividends because these firms tend to plow back all or most of their earnings. Because of their potential for dramatic price appreciation, they appeal mostly to investors who are seeking capital gains rather than dividend income.

© GEOPAUL/ISTOCKPHOTO

tech stock A stock that represents the technology sector of the market.

income stock A stock whose appeal is the dividends it pays out; offers dividend payments that can be expected to increase over time.

speculative stock Stock that is purchased on little more than the hope that its price per share will increase.

cyclical stock A stock whose price movements tend to parallel the various stages of the business cycle.

defensive stock A stock whose price movements are usually contrary to movements in the business cycle.

Tech Stocks

Tech stocks represent the technology sector of the market and include all those companies that produce or provide technology-based products and services such as computers, semiconductors, computer software and hardware, peripherals, Internet services, and wireless communications. There are literally thousands of companies that fall into the tech stock category, including everything from very small firms providing some service on the Internet to huge multinational companies. Tech stocks may offer the potential for attractive, even phenomenal returns, but they also involve considerable risk and so are probably most suitable for investors with high tolerance for such risk. Included in the tech stock category are some big names—Microsoft, Cisco Systems, Google, and Dell—as well as many not-so-big -names, such as Qihoo 360 Technology, OYO Geospace, Neonode, and Glu Mobile.

FRANK LEONHARD/EPA/NEWSCOM

Income Stocks versus Speculative Stocks

Stocks whose appeal is based primarily on the dividends they pay are known as **income stocks**. They have a fairly stable stream of earnings, a large portion of which is distributed in the form of dividends. Income shares have relatively high dividend yields and thus are ideally suited for investors seeking a relatively safe and high level of current income from their investment capital. An added (and often overlooked) feature of these stocks is that, unlike bonds and preferred stock, holders of income stock can expect *the amount of dividends paid to increase over time*. Examples of income stocks include Johnson & Johnson, PepsiCo, and Procter & Gamble.

Rather than basing their investment decisions on a proven record of earnings, investors in **speculative stocks** gamble that some new information, discovery, or production technique will favorably affect the firm's growth and inflate its stock price. The value of speculative stocks and their P/E ratios tend to fluctuate widely as additional information about the firm's future is received. Investors in speculative stocks should be prepared to experience losses as well as gains because *these are high-risk securities*. In early 2011, they included companies like Billabong International, Integra Mining, Sirtex Medical, Cedar Fair, Synergy Pharmaceuticals, and Vaalco Energy.

Financial Road Sign

The Biggest of the Big in the Market

The total market value of a company, defined as the price of the stock multiplied by the number of shares outstanding, is a measure of what investors think a company is worth. In October 2012, Apple topped the list of U.S.-based firms with a market value of about $573.52 billion, followed by ExxonMobil at $421.70 billion, Walmart at $242.95 billion, PetroChina at $252.36 billion, Microsoft at $235.13 billion, General Electric at $224.69 billion, Google at $222.49 billion, China Mobile at $219.67 billion, IBM at $218.56 billion, and Royal Dutch Shell at $217.68 billion. It's interesting to notice the Chinese firms on this list of largest firms, which reflects the growing economic importance of the country. These weren't necessarily the companies with the most assets or profits. Rather, what made these companies special–as far as investors are concerned–was their promise for the future!

Cyclical Stocks or Defensive Stocks

Stocks whose price movements tend to follow the business cycle are called **cyclical stocks**. This means that when the economy is in an expansionary stage, the prices of cyclical stocks tend to increase; during a contractionary stage (recession), they decline. Most cyclical stocks are found in the basic industries—automobiles, steel, and lumber, for example—which are generally sensitive to changes in economic activity. Alcoa, eBay, Time Warner, Kohl's, Goodyear Tire & Rubber, Dow Chemical, and Ford Motor Company are all examples of cyclical stocks.

The prices and returns from **defensive stocks**, unlike those of cyclical stocks, are expected to remain stable during periods of contraction in business

Gunnar Pippel/Shutterstock.com

activity. For this reason, they're often called *counter-cyclical*. The shares of consumer goods companies, certain public utilities, and gold mining companies are good examples of defensive stocks. Because they're basically income stocks, their earnings and dividends tend to keep their market prices up during periods of economic decline. Coca-Cola, McDonald's, Procter & Gamble, and Merck are all examples of defensive stocks.

Large-Caps, Mid-Caps, and Small-Caps

In the stock market, a stock's size is based on its market value—or, more commonly, on what's known as its *market capitalization* or *market cap*. A stock's market cap is found by multiplying its market price by the number of shares outstanding. The market can generally be broken into three major segments, as measured by a stock's market "cap":

Large-cap—Market caps of more than $10 billion

Mid-cap—Market caps of $2 to $10 billion

Small-cap—Stocks with market caps of less than $2 billion

Of the three major categories, the **large-cap stocks** are the real biggies—the Apples, Wal-Marts, GEs, and Microsofts of the world. Just because they're big, however, doesn't mean they're better. Indeed, both the small- and mid-cap segments of the market tend to hold their own with, or even outperform, large stocks over time.

Mid-cap stocks offer investors some attractive return opportunities as they provide much of the sizzle of small-stock returns but without all the price volatility. At the same time, because these are fairly good-sized companies and many of them have been around for a long time, they offer some of the safety of the big, established stocks. Among the ranks of the mid-caps are Allegiant Travel, Dillards, Verisign, Primerica, and H&R Block. These securities offer a nice alternative to large stocks without all the drawbacks and uncertainties of small-caps, although they're probably most appropriate for investors who are willing to tolerate a bit more risk and price volatility.

Some investors consider small companies to be in a class by themselves. They believe these firms hold especially attractive return opportunities, and in many cases this has turned out to be true. Known as **small-cap stocks**, these companies often have annual revenues of less than $250 million; because of their size, spurts of growth can dramatically affect their earnings and stock prices. Wendy's, Hecla Mining, Caribou Coffee, Domino's Pizza, and RTI Biologics are just a few of the interesting small-cap stocks out there. Although some small-caps are solid companies with equally solid financials, that's definitely not the case with most of them! Because many of these companies are so small, they don't have a lot of stock outstanding and their shares aren't widely traded. These stocks may hold the potential for high returns, but investors should also be aware of the high-risk exposure associated with them.

large-cap stock A stock with a total market value of more than $10 billion.

mid-cap stock A stock whose total market value falls somewhere between $2 billion and $10 billion.

small-cap stock A stock with a total market value of less than $2 billion.

12-2e Market Globalization and Foreign Stocks

Besides investing in many of the different types of stocks already mentioned, a growing number of American investors are turning to foreign markets as a way to earn attractive returns. Ironically, as our world is becoming smaller, our universe of investment opportunities is growing by leaps and bounds! Consider, for example, that in 1970, the U.S. stock market accounted for fully *two-thirds of the world market*. In essence, our stock market was twice as big as the rest of the world's stock markets *combined*. That's no longer true. The U.S. share of the world equity market is now more like 32 percent. Among the various ways of investing in foreign shares, two stand out: mutual funds and American Depositary Receipts (ADRs). Without a doubt, the best and easiest way to invest in foreign markets is through *international mutual funds* (we'll discuss such funds in Chapter 13). An alternative to mutual funds is to buy ADRs, which are *denominated in dollars and are traded directly on U.S. markets* (such as the NYSE). They're just like common stock, except that each ADR represents a specific number of shares in a specific foreign company. The shares of more than 1,000 companies from some 50 foreign countries are traded on U.S. exchanges as ADRs; these companies include Honda Motor Co., Nestlé, Nokia, Ericsson, Tata Motors, and Vodafone. ADRs are a great way to invest in foreign stocks because their prices are quoted in dollars—not in British pounds, Swiss francs, or euros. What's more, all dividends are paid in dollars.

12-2f Investing in Common Stock

There are three basic reasons for investing in common stock: (1) to use the stock as a warehouse of value, (2) to accumulate capital, and (3) to provide a source of income. Storage of value is important to all investors because nobody likes to lose money. However, some investors are more concerned about it than others, and they put safety of principal first in their stock selection process. These investors are more quality conscious and tend to gravitate toward blue chips and other low-risk securities. Accumulation of capital generally is an important goal to individuals with long-term investment horizons. These investors use the capital gains and dividends that stocks provide to build up their wealth. Some use growth stocks for such purposes; others do it with income shares; still others use a little of both. Finally, some people use stocks as a source of income; to them, a dependable flow of dividends is essential. High-yielding, good-quality income shares are usually their preferred investment vehicle.

Advantages and Disadvantages of Stock Ownership

Ownership of common stock has both advantages and disadvantages. Its advantages are threefold. First, the potential returns, in the form of both dividend income and price appreciation, can be substantial. Second, many stocks are actively traded and so are a highly liquid form of investment. Finally, market and company information about literally thousands of common stocks is widely published and readily available.

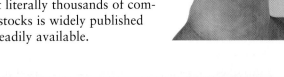

ZEKAG/ISTOCKPHOTO.COM

The disadvantages of owning common stock include risk, the problem of timing purchases and sales, and the uncertainty of dividends. Although potential common stock returns may be high, the risk and uncertainty associated with the actual receipt of that return is also great. Even though the careful selection of stocks may reduce the amount of risk to which the investor is exposed, a significant risk-return trade-off still exists. When it comes to common stock, not even dividends are guaranteed. If things turn bad, the company can always shut off the stream of dividends and suffer no legal ramifications. Finally, there's the timing of purchases and sales; human nature being what it is, we don't always do it right. Take a common stock that's loaded with uncertainty, add in our lack of accurate foresight, and you have the perfect recipe for making mistakes.

12-2g Making the Investment Decision

The first step in investing is to know *where* to put your money; the second is to know *when* to make your moves. The first question basically involves matching your risk and return objectives with the available

BEHAVIOR MATTERS

Investor Overreaction and Investment Returns

Research shows that the average investor consistently earns below-average returns. For example, between about 1990 and 2010, the S&P 500 index earned an average return of about 9.14 percent a year, while the average equity fund investor earned a paltry return of just 3.83 percent. One likely explanation is that the average equity investor is just too emotional and tends to overreact to financial market developments.

Consider how investors tend to overreact. It's well known that when the stock market advances, many investors chase performance by moving money into equity mutual funds. Similarly, they tend to take their money out when the stock market is declining. This often leads to buying high and selling low—a recipe for disaster in terms of rate of return. There's a natural behavioral tendency for investors to overreact to both good and bad news.

What can you do to take into account the tendency to overreact to investment news? Consider the following guidelines and investment truths.

- **Constructively decide to do nothing.** The evidence is that a long-term, buy-and-hold strategy is an effective, deliberate approach to investing. Take into account

the tendency to overreact and purposely decide to do nothing in response to news in most cases. Doing nothing is an action.

- **Money is like soap.** The famous financial economist at the University of Chicago, Eugene Fama, Jr., argues that "Your money is like soap. The more you handle it, the less you'll have." Handling your money too often brings high transaction costs and frequently results from overreacting to financial news.
- **Resist the urge to sell stocks in a declining market.** Patiently reevaluate your asset allocation and wait out the decline. Consider the analogy of putting your house up for sale when housing prices drop. Most people would not decide to put their house up for sale as soon as the market drops. They would be more likely to wait it out. Why should managing your stocks be any different?
- **Discipline works.** The evidence supports the value of a consistent, unemotional, and disciplined approach to investing. Simply put, your risk-adjusted returns are likely to be higher over the long term if you don't overreact to financial news.

Source: Adapted from Dana Anspach, "Why Average Investors Earn Below-Average Market Returns," http://moneyover55.about.com/od/howtoinvest/a/averageinvestor.htm, accessed August 2012.

investment vehicles. *A stock (or any other investment vehicle) should be considered a viable investment candidate as long as it looks likely to generate a sufficiently attractive rate of return* and, in particular, one that fully compensates you for any risks that you must take. Indeed, if you can't get enough return from the security to offset the risk, then you shouldn't invest in the stock!

Putting a Value on Stock

No matter what kind of investor you are or what your investment objectives happen to be, sooner or later you'll have to face one of the most difficult questions in the field of investments: *How much are you willing to pay for a stock?* To answer this question, you must place a value on the stock. As noted earlier, we know that the value of a stock depends on its expected stream of future earnings. Once you have a handle on the expected stream of future earnings, you can use that information to find the *expected rate of return on the investment*. If the expected return from the investment exceeds your desired or minimum rate of return, then you should make the investment. If the expected return is less than your desired rate of return, then you should not buy the stock now because it's currently "overpriced," and you won't be able to earn your desired rate of return.

How do you go about finding a stock that's right for you? The answer is by doing a little digging and crunching a few numbers. Here's what you'd want to do. First, find a company you like and then take a look at how it has performed *over the past three to five years*. Find out what kind of growth rate (in sales) it has experienced, if it has a strong ROE and has been able to maintain or improve its profit margin, how much it has been paying out to stockholders in the form of dividends, and so forth. This kind of information is readily available in publications like *Value Line* and *S&P Stock Reports* or from a number of Web sites. The idea is to find stocks that are financially strong, have done well in the past, and continue to hold prominent positions in a given industry or market segment. But looking at the past is only the beginning; what's really important to stock valuation is the *future!*

Therefore, let's turn our attention to the expected future performance of a stock. Of particular concern are future dividends and share price behavior. As a rule, it doesn't make much sense to go out more than two or three years (five at the most) because the accuracy of most forecasts begins to deteriorate rapidly after that. Thus, using a three-year investment horizon, you'd want to forecast annual dividends per share for each of the next three years *plus* the future price of the stock at the end of the three-year holding period. You can try to generate these forecasts yourself or you can check such publications as *Value Line* to obtain projections (*Value Line* projects dividends and share prices three to five years into the future).

After projecting dividends and share price, you can use the approximate yield equation or a handheld calculator to determine the expected return from the investment.

Thus, if Apple's stocks performs as expected, it should give us a return of around 26 percent to 31 percent.

Crunching the Numbers

Consider the common shares of Apple, Inc., which provides hardware and software that includes Mac computers, iPod digital media players, iPhone smartphones, and iPad tablets. According to several financial reporting services, the company has strong financials; its sales have been growing at a bit more than 40 percent per year for the past five years, its recent net profit margin is almost 24 percent, and its ROE is around 42 percent. Thus, historically, the company has performed astoundingly well and is definitely a market leader in its field. Indeed, it's currently the largest company in the world! In late July 2012, the stock was trading at around $585 a share and was starting to pay annual dividends again at the initial rate of about $2.65 a share in 2012. *Value Line* was projecting dividends to grow to $10.60 a share in 2013, and to an average of about $16 a share between 2015 and 2017. It was also estimating that the price of the stock could rise to an average of $1,280 a share over that period. For simplicity, we'll look at these forecasts as applying to a planned holding period of about three years and average the data accordingly.

Because the below approximate yield equation uses "average annual current income" as one of the inputs, let's use a rough average of our projected dividends ($9.75 a share) as a proxy for average annual dividends. Because this stock is currently trading at $585 a share and has a projected average future price of $1,280 a share, we can find the expected return (for our three-year investment horizon) as follows:

$$\text{Approximate yield (Expected return)} = \frac{\$9.75 + \left[\dfrac{\$1,280 - \$585}{3}\right]}{\left[\dfrac{\$1,280 + \$585}{2}\right]}$$

$$= \frac{\$9.75 + \$231.67}{\$952.50}$$

$$= 25.89\%$$

Calculator Keystrokes

You can use a handheld financial calculator—set in the *annual compounding mode*—to find the expected return on a stock that you purchase at $585 a share, hold for three years (during which time you receive average annual dividends of $9.75 a share), and then sell at $1,280 per share. Simply use the keystrokes shown in the margin, where

N   = number of *years* you hold the stock
PV   = the price you pay for the stock (entered as a *negative* value)
PMT = average amount of dividends received each *year*
FV   = the price you expect to receive when you *sell* the stock (in three years)

The expected return (of 31.14%) is a bit higher here, but even so, it's still reasonably close to the return (of 25.89%) that we computed using the approximate yield method.

dividend reinvestment plan (DRP) A program whereby stockholders can choose to take their cash dividends in the form of more shares of the company's stock.

In today's market, that would be a very attractive return and one that likely will be close to our required rate of return (which probably should be around 12 percent to 14 percent in normal market conditions). If that's the case, then this stock *should* be considered a possible investment candidate.

CALCULATOR

Inputs	Functions
3	N
−585	PV
9.75	PMT
1,280.00	FV
	CPT
	I/Y
	Solution
	31.14

SEE APPENDIX E FOR DETAILS.

Timing Your Investments

Once you find a stock that you think will give you the kind of return that you're looking for, then you're ready to deal with the matter of timing your investment. So long as the prospects for the market and the economy are positive, the time may be right to invest in stocks. Sometimes, however, investing in stocks makes no sense—in particular, *don't* invest in stocks under the following conditions.

- You believe *strongly* that the market is headed down in the short run. If you're absolutely certain the market's in for a big fall (or will continue to fall, if it's already doing so), then wait until the market drops and buy the stock when it's cheaper.

- You feel uncomfortable with the general tone of the market—it lacks direction, or there's way too much price volatility to suit you. Once again, wait for the market to settle down before buying stocks.

Be Sure to Plow Back Your Earnings

Unless you're living off the income, the basic investment objective with stocks is the same as it is with any other security: to earn an attractive, fully compounded rate of return. This requires regular reinvestment of dividend income. And there's no better way to accomplish such reinvestment than through a **dividend reinvestment plan (DRP)**. In a DRP, shareholders can sign up to have their cash dividends automatically reinvested in additional shares of the company's common stock—in essence, it's like taking your cash dividends in the form of more shares of common stock. Such an approach can have a tremendous impact on your investment position over time, as seen in Exhibit 12.4.

Today, over 1,000 companies have DRPs, and each one gives investors a convenient and inexpensive way to accumulate capital. Stocks in most DRPs are acquired free of any brokerage commissions, and most plans allow *partial participation*. That is, rather than committing all their cash dividends to these plans, participants may specify a portion of their shares for dividend reinvestment and receive cash dividends on the rest. Some plans even sell their shares in their DRP programs at discounts of 3 percent to 5 percent. Most plans also credit fractional shares to the investors' accounts. There is a catch, however: even though these dividends take the form of additional shares of stock, *reinvested dividends are taxable, in the year they're received, just as if they had been received in cash.*

12-3 Investing in Bonds

LG5, LG6 In contrast to stocks, *bonds are liabilities*—they're publicly traded IOUs where the bondholders are actually *lending money* to the issuer. Bonds are often referred to as *fixed-income securities* because the debt service obligations of the issuer are fixed—that is, the issuing organization agrees to pay a *fixed amount of interest periodically and to repay a fixed amount of principal at or before maturity.* Bonds normally have face values of $1,000 or $5,000 and have maturities of 10 to 30 years or more.

12-3a Why Invest in Bonds?

Bonds provide investors with two kinds of income: (1) they provide a generous amount of current income, and (2) they can often be used to generate substantial amounts of capital gains. The current income, of course, is derived from the interest payments received

Exhibit 12.4   **Cash or Reinvested Dividends**

© KAREN HERMANN/ISTOCKPHOTO

Participating in a dividend reinvestment plan is a simple yet highly effective way of building up capital over time. Over the long haul, it can prove to be a great way of earning a fully compounded rate of return on your money.

Situation: Buy 100 shares of stock at $25 a share (total investment $2,500); stock currently pays $1 a share in annual dividends. Price of the stock increases at 8 percent per year; dividends grow at 5 percent per year.

Investment Period	Number of Shares Held	Market Value of Stock Holdings	Total Cash Dividends Received
Take Dividends in Cash			
5 years	100	$ 3,672	$ 552
10 years	100	$ 5,397	$1,258
15 years	100	$ 7,930	$2,158
20 years	100	$11,652	$3,307
Participate in a DRP			
5 years	115.59	$ 4,245	$0
10 years	135.66	$ 7,322	$0
15 years	155.92	$12,364	$0
20 years	176.00	$20,508	$0

© Cengage Learning

periodically over the life of the issue. Indeed, this regular and highly predictable source of income is a key factor that draws investors to bonds. But these securities can also produce capital gains, which occurs whenever market interest rates fall. A basic trading rule in the bond market is that *interest rates and bond prices move in opposite directions:* when interest rates rise, bond prices fall; conversely, when interest rates fall, bond prices rise. Thus, it's possible to buy bonds at one price and, if interest rate conditions are right, to sell them sometime later at a higher price. Taken together, the current income and capital gains earned from bonds can lead to highly competitive investor returns. In addition, because of the general high quality of many bonds, they can also be used for the preservation and long-term accumulation of capital. In fact, some individuals commit all or a good deal of their investment funds to bonds because of this single attribute.

12-3b Bonds versus Stocks

Although bonds definitely do have their good points—low risk and high levels of current income, along with *desirable diversification properties*—they also have a significant downside: their *comparative* returns. The fact is, *relative to stocks*, there's usually a big sacrifice in returns when investing in bonds—which, of course, is the price you pay for the even bigger reduction in risk! But just because there's a deficit in long-term returns, it doesn't mean that bonds are always the underachievers. Consider, for example, what's happened over the past

COMSTOCK IMAGES/GETTY IMAGES

coupon A bond feature that defines the annual interest income that the issuer will pay the bondholder.

20 years or so. Starting in the 1980s, fixed-income securities held their own and continued to do so through the mid-1990s, only to fall far behind for the rest of the decade. But then along came a couple of nasty bear markets in stocks (2000–2002 and 2007–2008). The net results of all this can be seen in Exhibit 12.5, which tracks the comparative returns of stocks (via the S&P 500) and bonds (using the Bank of America U.S. Treasuries 15+ year maturity total return index) from 1992 through July 2012.

As can be seen in the exhibit, the bear markets of 2000–2002 and 2007–2008 had devastating effects on stocks. However, over the roughly 20-year period from 1992 to mid-2012, the S&P 500 underperformed long-term Treasury bonds by 0.63 percentage points (8.21 percent versus 8.84 percent). The net result was that a $10,000 investment in 1992 would have generated a terminal value in mid-2012 of about $50,877 for stocks, compared with about $57,281 for bonds. Although the long-term performance of stocks typically outstrips that of bonds, there have been times when that just wasn't so. And the margin was

particularly small over this time period owing to the effects of the financial crisis. And recent market history certainly dramatizes this.

12-3c Basic Issue Characteristics

A bond is a negotiable, long-term debt instrument that carries certain obligations on the part of the issuer. Unlike the holders of common stock, bondholders have no ownership or equity position in the issuing firm or organization. This is so because bonds are debt and thus the bondholders, in a roundabout way, are only lending money to the issuer.

As a rule, bonds pay interest every six months. The amount of interest paid depends on the **coupon**, which defines the annual interest that the issuer will pay to the bondholder. For instance, a $1,000 bond with an 8 percent coupon would pay $80 in interest every year ($1,000 × 0.08 = $80), generally in the form of two $40 semiannual payments. The principal amount of a bond, also known as its *par value*, specifies the amount of capital that must be repaid at maturity—there's $1,000 of principal in a $1,000 bond.

© KAREN HERMANN/ISTOCKPHOTO

| Exhibit 12.5 | Comparative Performance of Stocks and Bonds: 1992 to Mid-2012 |

This graph shows what happened to $10,000 invested in bonds over the (roughly) 20-year period from January 1992 through mid-2012, versus the same amount invested in stocks. It is clear that, although stocks held a commanding lead through early 2000 and then again in 2003–2006, the bear markets of 2000–2002 and 2008 largely erased all of that. As a result, bonds actually finished the period with a higher ending (or "terminal") value than stocks. So bonds actually performed better than stocks!

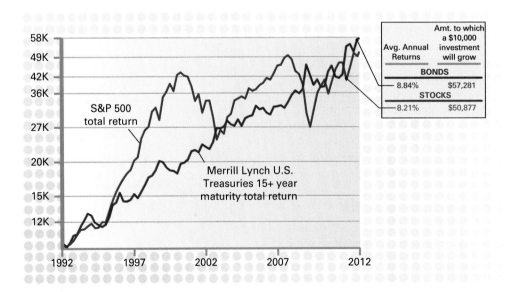

	Avg. Annual Returns	Amt. to which a $10,000 investment will grow
BONDS		
	8.84%	$57,281
STOCKS		
	8.21%	$50,877

Of course, debt securities regularly trade at market prices that differ from their principal (or par) values. This occurs whenever an issue's coupon differs from the prevailing market rate of interest; in essence, the price of an issue will change until its yield is compatible with prevailing market yields. Such behavior explains why a 7 percent issue will carry a market price of only $825 when the market yield is 9 percent; the drop in price is necessary to raise the yield on this bond from 7 percent to 9 percent. Issues with market values lower than par are known as *discount bonds* and carry coupons that are less than those on new issues. In contrast, issues with market values above par are called *premium bonds* and have coupons greater than those currently being offered on new issues.

Types of Issues

In addition to their coupons and maturities, bonds can be differentiated from one another by the type of collateral behind them. In this regard, the issues can be viewed as having either junior or senior standing. *Senior bonds are secured obligations* because they're backed by a legal claim on some specific property of the issuer that acts as *collateral* for the bonds. Such issues include **mortgage bonds**, which are secured by real estate, and **equipment trust certificates**, which are backed by certain types of equipment and are popular with railroads and airlines. *Junior bonds,* on the other hand, are backed only with a promise by the issuer to pay interest and principal on a timely basis. There are several classes of *unsecured* bonds, the most popular of which is known as a **debenture**. Issued as either notes (with maturities of 2 to 10 years) or bonds (maturities of more than 10 years), debentures are totally unsecured in the sense that there's no collateral backing them up—other than the issuer's good name.

Sinking Fund

Another provision that's important to investors is the **sinking fund**, which describes how a bond will be paid off over time. Not all bonds have these requirements; but for those that do, a sinking fund specifies the annual repayment schedule to be used in paying off the issue and indicates how much principal will be retired each year. Sinking fund requirements generally begin one to five years after the date of issue and continue annually thereafter until all or most of the issue has been paid off. Any amount not repaid by maturity is then retired with a single balloon payment.

Call Feature

Every bond has a **call feature**, which stipulates whether a bond can be called (that is, retired) before its regularly scheduled maturity date and, if so, under what conditions. Basically, there are three types of call features.

- A bond can be *freely callable*, which means the issuer can retire the bond prematurely at any time.

- A bond can be *noncallable*, which means the issuer is prohibited from retiring the bond prior to maturity.

- The issue could carry a *deferred call*, which means the issue cannot be called until after a certain length of time has passed from the date of issue. In essence, the issue is noncallable during the deferment period and then becomes freely callable thereafter.

Call features are normally used to retire a bond prematurely and replace it with one that carries a lower coupon; in this way, the issuer benefits from being able to realize a reduction in annual interest cost. In an attempt to compensate investors who have their bonds called out from under them, a *call premium* (usually equal to about six months to 1 year of interest) is tacked onto the par value of the bond and paid to investors, along with the issue's par value, at the time the bond is called. For example, if a company decides to call its 7 percent bonds some 15 years before they mature, then it might have to pay $1,052.50 for every $1,000 bond outstanding (in this case, a call premium equal to nine months' interest—$70 × 0.75 = $52.50—would be added to the par value of $1,000). Although this might sound like a good deal, it's really not for the investor. The bondholder may indeed get a few extra bucks when the bond is called; but in turn, she loses a source of

mortgage bond A bond secured by a claim on real assets, such as a manufacturing plant.

equipment trust certificate A bond secured by certain types of equipment, such as railroad cars and airplanes.

debenture An unsecured bond issued on the general credit of the firm.

sinking fund A bond provision specifying the annual repayment schedule to be used in paying off the issue.

call feature A bond feature that allows the issuer to retire the security prior to maturity.

URBANMYTH/ALAMY

Treasury bond A bond issued by and backed by the full faith and credit of the U.S. government.

Treasury inflation-indexed bond (TIPS) A bond issued by the U.S. government that has principal payments that are adjusted to provide protection again inflation, as measured by the Consumer Price Index (CPI).

agency bond An obligation of a political subdivision of the U.S. government.

mortgage-backed securities Securities that are a claim on the cash flows generated by mortgage loans; bonds backed by mortgages as collateral.

municipal bond A bond issued by state or local governments; interest income is usually exempt from federal taxes.

high current income. For example, the investor may have a 7 percent bond called away at a time when the best she can do in the market may be 4 percent or 5 percent.

12-3d The Bond Market

One thing that really stands out about the bond market is its size—the U.S. bond market is huge and getting bigger almost daily. Indeed, in 2011, the dollar value of bonds outstanding in this country was about $36 trillion! Given such size, it's not surprising that today's bond market offers securities to meet just about any type of investment objective and suit virtually any type of investor, no matter how conservative or aggressive.

Treasury Bonds

Treasury bonds (sometimes called *Treasuries* or *governments*) are a dominant force in the bond market and, if not the

securities—which are issued with maturities of 5, 10, or 20 years—give investors the opportunity to keep up with inflation by periodically adjusting their returns for any inflation that has occurred. For instance, if inflation is running at an annual rate of 3 percent then, at the end of the year, the par (or maturity) value of your bond will increase by 3 percent. Unfortunately, the coupons on these securities are set very low because they're meant to provide investors with *real (inflation-adjusted) returns*. So one of these bonds might carry a coupon of only 1.5 percent (when regular T-bonds are paying, say, 3.5 percent or 4 percent). But there's an upside even to this: The actual *size of the coupon payment will increase over time as the par value on the bond increases.*

Agency and Mortgage-Backed Bonds

Agency bonds are an important segment of the U.S. bond market. Although issued by political subdivisions of the U.S. government, *these securities are not obligations of the U.S. Treasury*. An important feature of these securities is that they customarily provide yields that are comfortably above the market rates for Treasuries and thus offer investors a way to increase returns with little or no real difference in risk. Some actively traded and widely quoted agency issues include those sold by the Federal Farm Credit Bank, the Federal National Mortgage Association

 The U.S. bond market is huge ($36 trillion) and getting bigger almost daily.

most popular, are certainly the best known. The U.S. Treasury issues bonds, notes, and other types of debt securities (such as the T-bills discussed in Chapter 4) as a means of meeting the federal government's ever-increasing needs. All Treasury obligations are of the highest quality (backed by the full faith and credit of the U.S. government), a feature that—along with their liquidity—makes them extremely popular with individual and institutional investors both domestically and abroad.

Treasury notes are issued with maturities of 2, 3, 5, and 10 years, whereas *Treasury bonds* carry 20- and 30-year maturities. The Treasury issues its securities at regularly scheduled auctions, and it's through this process that the Treasury establishes the initial yields and coupons on the securities it issues. All Treasury notes and bonds are sold in minimum denominations of $1,000. Although interest income is subject to normal federal income tax, *it is exempt from state and local taxes.*

The newest type of Treasury issue is the **Treasury inflation-indexed bond**, or **TIPS** (which stands for "Treasury Inflation-Protected Securities"). These

(or Fannie Mae), the Student Loan Marketing Association, and the Federal Home Loan Mortgage Corporation (FHLMC, or Freddie Mac). Although the various agencies issue traditional unsecured notes and bonds, they are perhaps best known for their **mortgage-backed securities**. Two of the biggest issuers of such securities are Fannie Mae and Freddie Mac, who package and issue bonds backed by mortgages that have no government guarantee. The Government National Mortgage Association (or Ginnie Mae) is also active in the mortgage market. Owned by the U.S. government, it insures bonds that are backed by Veterans Administration (VA) and Federal Housing Administration (FHA) home loans.

Municipal Bonds

Municipal bonds are the issues of states, counties, cities, and other political subdivisions, such as school districts and water and sewer districts. They're unlike other bonds in that their interest income is usually free from federal income tax (which is why they're known as *tax-free bonds*). Note, however, that this tax-free status does not apply to any capital gains that may be earned on these securities; such gains are subject to the usual federal taxes. A tax-free yield is probably the most important feature of municipal bonds and is certainly a major reason why individuals invest in them.

As a rule, the yields on municipal bonds are (usually, but not always) lower than the returns available from fully taxable issues. So unless the tax effect is sufficient to raise the yield on a municipal to a level that equals or exceeds the yields on taxable issues, it obviously doesn't make sense to buy municipal bonds. You can determine the return that a fully taxable bond must provide in order to match the after-tax return on a lower-yielding tax-free issue by computing the *fully taxable equivalent yield*:

$$\text{Fully taxable equivalent yield} = \frac{\text{Yield on municipal bond}}{1 - \text{Tax rate}}$$

For example, if a certain municipal bond offered a yield of 6 percent, then an individual in the 35 percent federal tax bracket would have to find a fully taxable bond with a yield of more than 9 percent to reap the same after-tax return—that is: 6 percent/(1 − 0.35) = 6 percent/0.65 = 9.23 percent. The Bonus Exhibit, "Table of Taxable Equivalent Yields" shows what a taxable bond (such as a corporate issue) would have to yield to equal the take-home yield of a tax-free municipal bond. (Visit CourseMate for PFIN 3. Log in at **www.cengagebrain.com**.) It demonstrates how the yield attractiveness of municipal bonds varies with an investor's income level; clearly, the higher the individual's tax bracket, the more attractive municipal bonds become.

Municipal bonds are generally issued as **serial obligations**; this means that the issue is broken into a series of smaller bonds, each with its own maturity date and coupon rate. Thus, instead of the bond having just one maturity date 20 years from now, it will have a series of (say) 20 maturity dates over the 20-year time frame. Although it may not seem that municipal issuers would default on either interest or principal payments, it does occur! Investors should be especially cautious when investing in **revenue bonds**, which are municipal bonds serviced from the income generated by specific income-producing projects, such as toll roads. Unlike issuers of so-called **general obligation bonds**—which are backed by the full faith and credit of the municipality—the issuer of a revenue bond is obligated to pay principal and interest *only if a sufficient level of revenue* is generated. General obligation municipal bonds, in contrast, are required to be serviced in a prompt and timely fashion regardless of the level of tax income generated by the municipality.

Corporate Bonds

The major nongovernmental issuers of bonds are corporations. The market for **corporate bonds** is customarily subdivided into several segments, which include *industrials* (the most diverse of the group), *public utilities* (the dominant group in terms of volume of new issues), *rail and transportation bonds*, and *financial issues* (banks, finance companies, etc.). In this market, you'll find the widest range of different types of issues, from first mortgage and convertible bonds (discussed next) to debentures, subordinated debentures, and income bonds. Interest on corporate bonds is paid semiannually, and sinking funds are common. The bonds usually come in $1,000 denominations, and maturities usually range from 5 to 10 years but can be up to 30 years or more. Many of the issues carry call provisions that prohibit prepayment of the issue during the first 5 to 10 years. Corporate issues are popular with individuals because of their relatively high yields.

Convertible Bonds

Another popular type of specialty issue, convertible bonds are found only in the corporate market. They are a type of *hybrid security* because they possess the features of both corporate bonds and common stocks. That is, although they are initially issued as debentures (unsecured debt), they carry a provision that enables them to be converted into a certain number of shares of the issuing company's common stock.

The key element of any convertible issue is its **conversion privilege**, which stipulates the conditions and specific nature of the conversion feature. First, it states exactly when the bond can be converted. Sometimes there'll be an initial waiting period of six months to perhaps two years after the date of issue, during which time the issue cannot be converted. The *conversion period* then begins, after which the issue can be converted at any time. From the investor's point of view, the most important item of information is the **conversion ratio**, which specifies the number of shares of common stock into which the bond can be converted. For example, one of these bonds might carry a conversion ratio of 20, meaning you can "cash in" one convertible bond for 20 shares of stock.

Given the significance of the price behavior of the underlying common stock to the value of a convertible

serial obligation An issue that is broken down into a series of smaller bonds, each with its own maturity date and coupon rate.

revenue bond A municipal bond serviced from the income generated by a specific project.

general obligation bond A municipal bond backed by the full faith and credit of the issuing municipality.

corporate bond A bond issued by a corporation.

conversion privilege The provision in a convertible issue that stipulates the conditions of the conversion feature, such as the conversion period and conversion ratio.

conversion ratio A ratio specifying the number of shares of common stock into which a convertible bond can be converted.

conversion value A measure of what a convertible issue would trade for if it were priced to sell based on its stock value.

conversion premium The difference between a convertible security's market price and its conversion value.

junk bond Also known as *high-yield bonds*, these are highly speculative securities that have received low ratings from Moody's or Standard & Poor's.

security, one of the most important measures to a convertible bond investor is conversion value. In essence, **conversion value** is an indication of what a convertible issue would trade for *if it were priced to sell based on its stock value*. Conversion value is easy to find: simply multiply the conversion ratio of the issue by the current market price of the underlying common stock. For example, a convertible that carried a conversion ratio of 20 would have a conversion value of $1,200 if the firm's stock traded at $60 per share (20 × $60 = $1,200). But convertibles seldom trade precisely at their conversion value; instead, they usually trade at **conversion premiums**, which means the convertibles are priced in the market at more than their conversion values. For example, a convertible that traded at $1,400 and had a conversion value of $1,200 would have a conversion premium of $200 (i.e., $1,400 − $1,200 = $200). Convertible securities appeal to investors who want *the price potential of a common stock along with the downside risk protection of a corporate bond.*

12-3e Bond Ratings

Bond ratings are like grades: a letter grade is assigned to each bond that designates its investment quality. Ratings are widely used and are an important part of the municipal and corporate bond markets. The two largest and best-known rating agencies are Moody's and Standard & Poor's. Every time a large, new corporate or municipal issue comes to the market, a staff of professional bond analysts determine its default risk exposure and investment quality. The financial records of the issuing organization are thoroughly examined and its future prospects assessed. The result of all this is the assignment of a bond rating at the time of issue that indicates *the ability of the issuing organization to service its debt in a prompt and timely manner*. Exhibit 12.6 lists the various ratings assigned to bonds by each of the two major agencies. Note that the top four ratings (Aaa through Baa; or AAA through BBB) designate *investment-grade bonds*—such ratings are highly coveted by issuers because they indicate financially strong, well-run companies or municipalities. The next two ratings (Ba/B; or BB/B) are where you'll find most **junk bonds**; these ratings indicate that, although the principal and interest payments on the bonds are still being met, the risk of default is relatively high because the issuers lack the financial strength found with investment-grade issues.

© KAREN HERMANN/ISTOCKPHOTO

Exhibit 12.6   Moody's and Standard & Poor's Bond Ratings

Agencies like Moody's and Standard & Poor's rate corporate and municipal bonds; these ratings provide an indication of the bonds' investment quality (particularly regarding an issue's default risk exposure).

Bond Ratings*		
Moody's	S&P	Description
Aaa	AAA	*Prime-Quality Investment Bonds*—This is the highest rating assigned, denoting extremely strong capacity to pay.
Aa A	AA A	*High-Grade Investment Bonds*—These are also considered very safe bonds, though they're not quite as safe as Aaa/AAA issues; double A–rated bonds (Aa/AA) are safer (have less risk of default) than single A–rated issues.
Baa	BBB	*Medium-Grade Investment Bonds*—These are the lowest of the investment-grade issues; they're felt to lack certain protective elements against adverse economic conditions.
Ba B	BB B	*Junk Bonds*—With little protection against default, these are viewed as highly speculative securities.
Caa Ca C D	CCC CC C D	*Poor-Quality Bonds*—These are either in default or very close to it; they're often referred to as "zombie bonds."

*Some ratings may be modified to show relative standing within a major rating category; for example, Moody's uses numerical modifiers (1, 2, 3), whereas S&P uses plus (+) or minus (−) signs.

© Cengage Learning

Go to Smart Sites

If bonds are still a mystery to you, Investopedia's "Bond Basics" section site has an eight-part series that covers all the basics. ●

Once a new issue is rated, the process doesn't stop there. Older, outstanding bonds are also regularly reviewed to ensure that their assigned ratings are still valid. Most issues will carry a single rating to maturity, but ratings can change over time as new information becomes available. Finally, although it may appear that the issuing firm or municipality is receiving the rating, it's actually the individual issue that is being rated. As a result, a firm (or municipality) can have different ratings assigned to its issues. Most investors pay careful attention to ratings because they affect comparative market yields: other things being equal, *the higher the rating, the lower the yield of an obligation.* Thus, whereas an A-rated bond might offer a 5 percent yield, a comparable AAA-rated issue would probably yield something like 4.25 percent or 4.50 percent.

12-3f Pricing a Bond

Unlike stocks, bonds aren't widely quoted in the financial press, not even in *The Wall Street*

Why Would You Buy Junk?

Junk bonds are low-rated debt securities that carry a relatively high risk of default. You'd expect to find a bunch of no-name companies residing in this neighborhood, but that's not always the case. Here's a list of some companies whose bonds were rated as junk in mid-2012:

- Albertsons (Caa1–)*
- Alliance Healthcare Services (B3)
- Bon Ton Department Stores (Caa3)
- Claire's Stores(Caa3)
- Clear Channel Communications (Ca)
- Colt Defense (Caa1)
- Harrah's Operations (Caa3)
- Supervalu (Caa1)

These companies were slapped with low ratings because their operating earnings lack the quality and consistency of high-grade bonds. So why invest in them? For their high returns! For example, in the summer of 2012, the average yield on junk bonds was 7.4 percent, when the yield on 10-year U.S. Treasury bonds was 1.839 percent and the yield on 30-year U.S. Treasury bonds was 2.954 percent. So the attraction of junk bonds is clear–but they're not for everyone.

*The rating is by Moody's.

Journal. So, rather than looking at how bonds are quoted, let's look at how they're priced in the marketplace. Regardless of the type, *all bonds are priced as a percentage of par*; this means that a quote of, say, 85 translates into a price of 85 percent of the bond's par value. In the bond market, 1 point = $10; hence a quote of 85 does not mean $85 but rather $850. This is so because market convention assumes that bonds carry par values of $1,000. Also keep in mind that the price of any bond is always related to the issue's coupon and maturity—those two features are always a part of any listed price because of their effect on the price of a bond. (We'll talk more about the impact of coupons and maturities on bond price behavior in the section entitled "Bond Prices and Yields," later in this chapter.)

In the corporate and municipal markets, bonds are priced in decimals, using three places to the right of the decimal point. Thus a quote of 87.562, as a percentage of a $1,000 par bond, converts to a price of $875.62; similarly, a quote of 121.683 translates into a price of $1.21683 \times \$1,000 = \$1,216.83$. In contrast, U.S. Treasury and agency bond quotes are stated in *32s of a point* (where, again, 1 point = $10). For example, you might see the price of a T-bond listed at, "94:16." Translated, this means that the bond is being priced at $94^{16}/_{32}$, or 94.5 percent of par—in other words, it's being priced at $945.00. With government bonds, the figures to the right of the colon (:) show the number of 32s embedded in the price.

Bond Prices and Accrued Interest

The price of a bond quoted on your favorite financial Web site is unlikely to be the price that you would actually pay as a buyer. This is because such quoted prices usually do not include the interest that accrues between the coupon payment dates of the bond. **Accrued interest** is the amount of interest that's been earned since the last coupon payment date by the bond holder/seller, but which will be received by the new owner/buyer of the bond at the next regularly scheduled coupon payment date. When a bond is sold between coupon payment dates, the buyer pays the seller for the accrued interest, which is the prorated share of the upcoming coupon payment.

Consider a specific example of how accrued interest affects the price paid for a bond between coupon payments. Assume that you're selling a corporate bond with $1,000 par value and paying a 4 percent coupon semiannually, which is $20 every six months. The bond is quoted on the Web at $1,000, and it's three months after the last coupon payment. Because the bond is half-way between coupon payments,

accrued interest The amount of interest that's been earned since the last coupon payment date by the bond holder/seller, but which will be received by the new owner/buyer of the bond at the next regularly scheduled coupon payment date.

clean price The quoted price of a bond plus accrued interest, the total of which is the relevant price to be paid by a bond buyer.

dirty (full) price The quoted price of a bond plus accrued interest, the total of which is the relevant price to be paid by a bond buyer.

accrued interest is $20 × 3/6 = $10. Thus, the buyer's actual price paid to the seller will be the $1,000 quoted price plus the accrued interest of $10, for a total of $1,010.

In market jargon, how accrued interest is treated in bond pricing is the basis for the distinction between **clean prices** and **dirty (full) prices**. This can be concisely summarized as:

Dirty (full) price = quoted price + accrued interest

Clean price = quoted price − accrued interest

So what's the significance of the distinction between dirty and clean prices for bond investors? It's important to realize that the commonly cited prices in the financial press and on the Web are most likely net of

accrued interest and are so-called clean bond prices. The relevant sale or invoice price of a bond to the buyer is the dirty price, which adds the accrued interest to the quoted price. In terms of this example, the buyer of the 4 percent coupon bond would pay the dirty price of $1,010, not the clean price of $1,000. In summary, the quoted clean price *understates* the true (dirty) price that must be paid to actually purchase the bond in the open market.

12-3g Bond Prices and Yields

The price of a bond depends on its coupon, maturity, and the movement of market interest rates. *When interest rates go down, bond prices go up,* and vice versa. The relationship of bond prices to market rates is captured in Exhibit 12.7. The graph serves to reinforce the *inverse* relationship between bond prices and market interest rates; note that *lower* rates lead to *higher* bond prices. The exhibit also shows the difference between

© KAREN HERMANN/ISTOCKPHOTO

Exhibit 12.7 | **Price Behavior of a Bond with a 4 Percent Coupon**

A bond sells at its par value so long as the prevailing market interest rate remains the same as the bond's coupon (for example, when both coupon and market rates equal 4 percent). But if market rates drop, then bond prices rise, and vice versa; moreover, as a bond approaches its maturity, the issue price always moves toward its par value no matter what happens to interest rates.

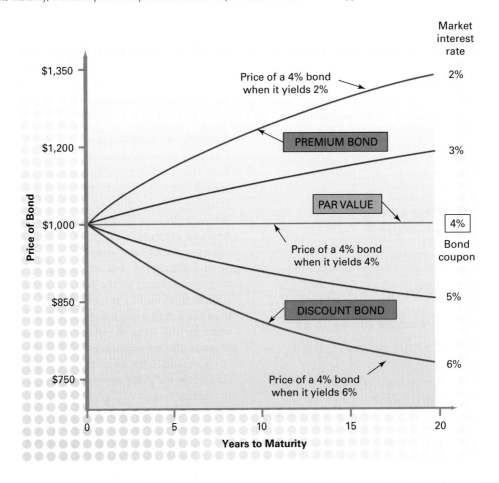

© Cengage Learning

premium and discount bonds. A **premium bond** is one that sells for more than its par value, which occurs whenever market interest rates drop below the coupon rate on the bond; a **discount bond**, in contrast, sells for less than par and is the result of market rates being greater than the issue's coupon rate. Thus the 4 percent bond in our illustration traded as a premium bond when market rates were at 2 percent but as a discount bond when rates stood at 6 percent.

What happens to the price of the bond over time is of considerable interest to most bond investors. We know that how much bond prices move depends not only on the *direction* of interest rates changes but also on the *magnitude* of such changes; the greater the moves in interest rates, the greater the swings in bond prices. But there's more, because bond prices will also vary according to the coupon and maturity of the issue—that is, bonds with *lower coupons* and/or *longer maturities* will respond more vigorously to changes in market rates and undergo *greater price swings*. Thus, if interest rates are moving up, then the investor should seek high coupon bonds with short maturities because this will cause minimal price variation and *preserve as much capital as possible*. In contrast, if rates are heading down, that's the time to be in long-term bonds: if you're a speculator looking for a lot of capital gains, then go with long-term, *low coupon bonds*; but if you're trying to lock in a high level of coupon (interest) income, then stick with long-term, *high coupon* bonds that offer plenty of call protection.

Current Yield and Yield to Maturity

The two most commonly cited bond yields are current yield and yield to maturity. **Current yield** reflects the amount of annual interest income the bond provides relative to its current market price. Here's the formula for current yield:

$$\text{Current yield} = \frac{\text{Annual interest income}}{\text{Market price of bond}}$$

As you can see, the current yield on a bond is basically the same as the dividend yield on a stock. Assume, for example, that a 6 percent bond with a $1,000 par value is currently selling for $910. Because annual interest income would amount to $60 and because the current market price of the bond is $910, its current yield would be 6.59 percent ($60/$910). This measure would be of interest to *investors seeking current income*; other things being equal, the higher the current yield, the more attractive the bond would be.

The annual rate of return a bondholder would receive *if she held the issue to its maturity* is captured by the bond's **yield to maturity**. This measure captures both the annual interest income and the recovery of principal at maturity; it also includes the impact of interest on interest and therefore provides a fully compounded rate of return. If a bond is purchased at its face value, then its yield to maturity will equal the

coupon, or stated, rate of interest. On the other hand, if the bond is purchased at a discount or premium, then its yield to maturity will vary according to the prevailing level of market yields.

You can find the yield to maturity on discount or premium bonds by using the *approximate yield* formula introduced earlier in this chapter. Or you can use a hand-held financial calculator (which we'll demonstrate soon) to obtain a yield to maturity that's a bit more accurate and is, in fact, very close to the measure used in the market; the only difference is that market participants normally use semi-annual compounding in their calculations whereas we use annual compounding.

By setting the future price (FP) of the investment equal to the bond's face value ($1,000), you can use the following version of the equation to find the *approximate yield to maturity on a bond:*

$$\text{Approximate yield to maturity} = \frac{\text{CI} + \left[\dfrac{\$1,000 - \text{CP}}{\text{N}}\right]}{\left[\dfrac{\text{CP} + \$1,000}{2}\right]}$$

Recall that CI equals annual current income (or in this case, annual interest income), CP is the current price of the bond, and N is the investment period (number of years to maturity).

Crunching the Numbers

Now assume that you're contemplating the purchase of a $1,000, 6 percent bond with 15 years remaining to maturity and that the bond is trading at a price of $910. Given CI = $60, CP = $910, and N = 15, the approximate yield to maturity on this bond will be:

$$\text{Approximate yield to maturity} = \frac{\$60 + \left[\dfrac{\$1,000 - \$910}{15}\right]}{\left[\dfrac{\$910 + \$1,000}{2}\right]}$$

$$= \frac{\$60 + \left[\dfrac{\$90}{15}\right]}{\left[\dfrac{\$1,910}{2}\right]} = 6.91\%$$

Note that, because this bond was purchased at a discount, its computed yield to maturity is above both the 6 percent stated coupon rate and the 6.59 percent current yield.

Calculator Keystrokes

You can also *find the yield to maturity on a bond* by using a financial calculator; here's what you'd do. With the calculator in the *annual mode*, to find the yield to maturity on our 6 percent (annual pay), 15-year bond that's currently trading at $910, use the keystrokes shown below, where:

N   = number of *years* to maturity
PV   = the current market price of the bond (entered as a *negative* value)
PMT   = the size of the annual coupon payments (in *dollars*)
FV   = the par value of the bond

A value of 6.99 should appear in the calculator display, which is the bond's yield to maturity using annual compounding: note that it's very close to the approximate yield of 6.91 percent that we just computed.

Measures of yield to maturity are used by investors to assess the attractiveness of a bond investment. The higher the yield to maturity, the more attractive the investment, other things being equal. *If a bond provided a yield to maturity that equaled or exceeded an investor's desired rate of return, then it would be considered a worthwhile investment candidate* because it would promise a yield that should compensate the investor adequately for the perceived amount of risk involved.

CALCULATOR

Inputs	Functions
15	N
−910	PV
60	PMT
1,000	FV
	CPT
	I/Y
	Solution
	6.99

SEE APPENDIX E FOR DETAILS.

Planning Over a Lifetime: Investing in Stocks and Bonds

Here are some key considerations for investment planning in each stage of the life cycle.

Pre-family Independence: 20s	Family Formation/ Career Development: 30–45	Pre-Retirement: 45–65	Retirement: 65 and Beyond
✓ Determine major investment goals and how much money needs to be invested each month to achieve them.	✓ Revise investment plan to focus more on retirement and funding children's education, if applicable.	✓ Revise investment plan in light of recent developments.	✓ Revise investment plan to lean more toward debt and cash instruments than to stocks.
✓ Determine your asset allocation among stocks, bonds, and cash based on your time horizon and attitude toward risk.	✓ Review your asset allocation and rebalance if it is inconsistent with your goals.	✓ Review your asset allocation and rebalance if it is inconsistent with your goals.	✓ Review your asset allocation and rebalance if it is inconsistent with your goals.
✓ Make sure to participate in any employer-sponsored 401(k) retirement plan and match your asset allocation plan.	✓ Gradually increase the amount invested in any employer-sponsored 401(k) retirement plan and re-evaluate how it relates to your asset allocation plan.	✓ Continue to gradually increase the amount you invest in any employer-sponsored 401(k) retirement plan and re-evaluate how it relates to your asset allocation plan.	✓ Integrate investment asset allocation strategy with estate planning.
✓ Consider opening traditional and/or a Roth IRAs.	✓ Consider increasing your contribution to traditional and/or a Roth IRAs.	✓ Consider increasing your contribution to traditional and/or a Roth IRAs.	✓ Carefully plan for mandatory withdrawals from tax shelter accounts and associated tax consequences.

FINANCIAL PLANNING EXERCISES

LG1, 2

1. **What makes for a good investment? Use the approximate yield formula or a financial calculator to rank the following investments according to their expected returns.**
   a. Buy a stock for $30 a share, hold it for three years, and then sell it for $60 a share (the stock pays annual dividends of $2 a share).
   b. Buy a security for $40, hold it for two years, and then sell it for $100 (current income on this security is zero).
   c. Buy a one-year, 5 percent note for $1,000 (assume that the note has a $1,000 par value and that it will be held to maturity).

LG3, 4

2. **An investor is thinking about buying some shares of Razortronics, Inc., at $75 a share. She expects the price of the stock to rise to $115 a share over the next three years. During that time, she also expects to receive annual dividends of $4 per share. Assuming that the investor's expectations (about the future price of the stock and the dividends that it pays) hold up, what rate of return can the investor expect to earn on this investment? (*Hint:* Use either the approximate yield formula or a financial calculator to solve this problem.)**

LG3, 4

3. **The price of Garden Designs, Inc. is now $85. The company pays no dividends. Sean Perth expects the price four years from now to be $125 a share. Should Sean buy Garden Designs if he wants a 15 percent rate of return? Explain.**

LG3, 4

4. **The Clarkson Company recently reported net profits after taxes of $15.8 million. It has 2.5 million shares of common stock outstanding and pays preferred dividends of $1 million a year. The company's stock currently trades at $60 per share.**
   a. Compute the stock's earnings per share (EPS).
   b. What is the stock's P/E ratio?
   c. Determine what the stock's dividend yield would be if it paid $1.75 per share to common stockholders.

LG5, 6

5. **An investor in the 28 percent tax bracket is trying to decide which of two bonds to select: one is a 5.5 percent U.S. Treasury bond selling at par; the other is a municipal bond with a 4.25 percent coupon, which is also selling at par. Which of these two bonds should the investor select? Why?**

LG5, 6

6. **Describe and differentiate between a bond's (a) current yield and (b) yield to maturity. Why are these yield measures important to the bond investor? Find the yield to maturity of a 20-year, 9 percent, $1,000 par value bond trading at a price of $850. What's the current yield on this bond?**

LG5, 6

7. **Which of these two bonds offers the highest current yield? Which one has the highest yield to maturity?**
   a. A 6.55 percent, 22-year bond quoted at 52.000
   b. A 10.25 percent, 27-year bond quoted at 103.625

LG5, 6

8. **Go to the asset allocation tool discussed in the chapter's Cool Apps feature, which is at http://www.ipers.org/calcs/AssetAllocator.html. Enter assumptions that fit your current and anticipated situation and produce an asset allocation recommendation. Then add 20 years to your age and redo the calculations. Finally, redo the calculations assuming that you have minimal risk tolerance. Explain the results of changing these key assumptions.**

PFIN Student Study Tools—Visit CourseMate for PFIN 3. Log in at **www.cengagebrain.com**. Check out the bonus exercises and exhibits, interactive worksheets, Smart Sites, Critical Thinking Cases, Money Online, Kiplinger videos, quizzing, and more.

Cool Apps—Look for this new feature on CourseMate for PFIN 3. Cool Apps navigates the growing world of apps that are available for personal financial planning and tracking.

© PALI RAO/ISTOCKPHOTO

13

INVESTING IN MUTUAL FUNDS, ETFs, AND REAL ESTATE

LEARNING GOALS

LG1 Describe the basic features and operating characteristics of mutual funds and exchange traded funds.

LG2 Differentiate between open- and closed-end mutual funds as well as exchange traded funds, and discuss the various types of fund loads and charges.

LG3 Discuss the types of funds available to investors and the different kinds of investor services offered by mutual funds and exchange traded funds.

LG4 Gain an understanding of the variables that should be considered when selecting funds for investment purposes.

LG5 Identify the sources of return and calculate the rate of return earned on an investment in a mutual fund as well as evaluate the performance of an exchange traded fund.

LG6 Understand the role that real estate plays in a diversified investment portfolio along with the basics of investing in real estate, either directly or indirectly.

How Will This Affect Me? Having a financial plan and being aware that diversification is crucial is a great start to the task of investment planning. The next step is figuring out how to implement your plan by deciding what to invest in. For most people, diversification is best achieved using mutual funds and exchange traded funds (ETFs). This chapter describes the key characteristics of each type of fund, sorts through the various options you have, shows how to calculate rates of return and evaluate performance, and explains how to choose among funds. The essential elements of investing in real estate and its role in diversifying your overall investment portfolio are also covered. After reading this chapter, you should be in a good position to invest in mutual funds, ETFs, and real estate in a way that will help you achieve your financial objectives.

13-1 Mutual Funds and Exchange Traded Funds: Some Basics

LG1, LG2 Sound investment planning involves finding investment vehicles with risk-return characteristics that are compatible with your financial objectives. In this chapter, we'll look beyond stocks and bonds and consider other types of investment products that enjoy widespread use among individual investors: mutual funds, exchange traded funds (ETFs), and real estate. These investment outlets offer risk-return opportunities that you may not be able to obtain from stocks or bonds. For example, investors interested in receiving the benefits of professional portfolio management, but who don't have the funds to purchase a diversified portfolio of securities, may find mutual fund shares attractive. Let's now take a closer look at each of these investments, starting with mutual funds. Keep in mind that many of the issues in analyzing and choosing mutual funds are essentially the same for ETFs.

A **mutual fund** is a financial services organization that receives money from its shareholders and invests those funds on their behalf in a diversified portfolio of securities. An **exchange traded fund (ETF)** is an investment company whose shares trade on stock exchanges. Unlike mutual funds, ETF shares can be bought or sold (or sold short) throughout the day. ETFs are usually structured as an index fund that's set up to match the performance of a certain market segment. Thus, when investors buy shares in a mutual fund, or an ETF they usually become *part owners of a widely diversified portfolio of securities*.

A mutual fund or an ETF share can be thought of as the *financial product* that's sold to the public by an investment company. That is, the investment company builds and manages a portfolio of securities and sells ownership interests—shares of stock—in that portfolio through a vehicle known as a mutual fund. This concept underlies the whole mutual fund structure and is depicted in Exhibit 13.1. For individual investors today, mutual funds are the investment vehicle of choice. They're popular because they offer not only a variety of interesting investment opportunities, but also a wide array of services that many investors find appealing. They're an easy and convenient way to invest—one that's especially suited to beginning investors.

13-1a The Mutual Fund Concept

The first mutual fund in this country was started in Boston in 1924, and by 1980, there were some 564 mutual funds in operation. But that was only the beginning, as assets under management in the United States grew to $11.6 trillion by 2011. Indeed, by 2011, *investors could choose from nearly 7,700 publicly traded mutual funds.* (Actually, counting duplicate or multiple fund offerings from the same portfolio, there were closer to *27,000 funds* available; such duplication occurs because sometimes two or three versions of the same fund are offered, with each "fund" having a different type of load charge or fee structure.) Clearly, mutual funds appeal to a lot of investors, who all share one view: they've decided, for one reason or another, to turn the problems of security selection and portfolio management over to professional money managers.

mutual fund A financial services organization that receives money from its shareholders and invests those funds on their behalf in a diversified portfolio of securities.

exchange traded fund (ETF) An investment company whose shares trade on stock exchanges; unlike mutual funds, ETF shares can be bought or sold (or sold short) throughout the day.

After you read the chapter, explore the STUDY TOOLS listed on page 332.

Exhibit 13.1 Basic Mutual Fund Structure

A mutual fund brings together the funds from many individual investors and uses this pool of money to acquire a diversified portfolio of stocks, bonds, and other securities.

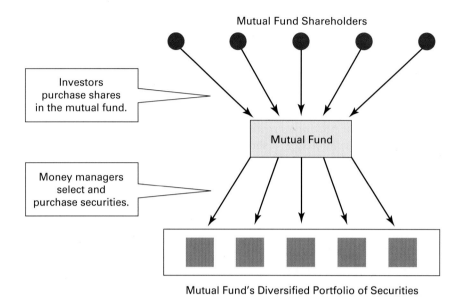

Mutual Fund Shareholders

Investors purchase shares in the mutual fund.

Mutual Fund

Money managers select and purchase securities.

Mutual Fund's Diversified Portfolio of Securities

Go to Smart Sites

What is your fund's sector allocation, and past performance? The Street's Web site has detailed fund breakdowns. For more online resources, whenever you see "*Go to Smart Sites*" in this chapter, visit CourseMate for PFIN 3. Log in at **www.cengagebrain.com**. ●

Pooled Diversification

A mutual fund combines the investment capital of many people with similar investment goals and invests those funds in a wide variety of securities. Investors receive shares of stock in the mutual fund and, through the fund, enjoy much wider investment diversification than they could otherwise achieve. Indeed, a single mutual fund commonly holds literally hundreds of different stocks or bonds—some funds, in fact, have hundreds of different holdings! For example, in early 2012, Fidelity Contrafund held about 350 different securities while the Dreyfus GNMA bond fund had over 925 holdings. Clearly, for all but the super-rich, that's far more diversification than most investors could ever hope to attain. Yet each investor who owns shares in a fund is, in effect, a part owner of that fund's diversified portfolio of securities. Regardless of the fund size, as the securities held by it move up and down in price,

the market value of the mutual fund shares moves accordingly. And when the fund receives dividend and interest payments, they too are passed on to the mutual fund shareholders and distributed on the basis of prorated ownership.

> " **A mutual fund is a financial services organization that receives money from its shareholders and invests those funds on their behalf in a diversified portfolio of securities.** "

13-1b Why Invest in Mutual Funds or ETFs?

Mutual funds and ETFs can be used by individual investors in various ways. One investor may buy a fund because of the substantial capital gains opportunities that it provides; another may buy a totally different fund not for its capital gains, but instead for its current income. Whatever kind of income a fund provides, individuals tend to use these investment vehicles for one or more of the following reasons: (1) to achieve diversification in their investment holdings, (2) to obtain the services of professional money managers, (3) to generate an attractive rate of return on their investment capital, and (4) for the convenience that they offer.

Diversification

As we just saw, diversification is a primary motive for investing in mutual funds and ETFs. This ability to diversify allows investors to reduce their exposure to risk sharply by indirectly investing in several types of securities and companies rather than just one or two. If you have only $500 or $1,000 to invest, you obviously won't achieve much diversification on your own. But if you invest that money in a mutual fund or an ETF, you'll end up owning part of a well-diversified portfolio of securities.

Professional Management

Another major appeal of a mutual fund is the professional management that it offers. Though management is paid a fee for its services, the contributions of a full-time expert manager should be well worth the fee. These professionals know where to look for return and how to avoid unnecessary risk; at the minimum, their decisions should result in better long-run returns than the average individual investor can achieve. The mutual fund concept rests on the concept of **pooled diversification** and works much like insurance.

Financial Returns

Although professional managers *may* be able to achieve better returns than small investors can generate, the relatively high purchase fees, coupled with the management and operating costs, tend to reduce the returns actually earned on mutual fund investments. But the mutual fund industry hasn't attracted millions of investors by generating substandard returns. Quite the contrary; over the long haul, mutual funds have provided relatively attractive returns.

Convenience

Mutual funds make it easy to invest, and most don't require much capital to get started. They handle all the paperwork and recordkeeping, their prices are widely quoted, and it's usually possible to deal in fractional shares. What's more, opening a mutual fund account is about as easy as opening a checking account. Just fill in a few blank spaces, send in the minimum amount of money, and you're in business!

13-1c How Mutual Funds Are Organized and Run

Although it's tempting to think of a mutual fund as a monolithic entity, that's really not the case. Various functions—investing, recordkeeping, safekeeping, and others—are split among two or more companies. Besides the fund itself, which *is owned by the shareholders*, there are several other major players:

- The *management company* runs the fund's daily operations.
- The *investment advisor* buys and sells the stocks or bonds and otherwise oversees the portfolio.
- The *distributor* sells the fund shares, either directly to the public or through certain authorized dealers.
- The *custodian* (such as a bank) physically safeguards the securities and other assets of a fund.
- The *transfer agent* executes transactions, keeps track of shareholder trades, and maintains other records.

pooled diversification A process whereby investors buy into a diversified portfolio of securities for the collective benefit of individual investors.

open-end investment company A firm that can issue an unlimited number of shares that it buys and sells at a price based on the current market value of the securities it owns; also called a *mutual fund*.

All this separation of duties is designed for just one thing—to protect the mutual fund investor/shareholder. Obviously, you can always lose money if your fund's stock or bond holdings go down in value. But that's really the only risk of loss that you face because the chance of ever losing money from fraud or a mutual fund collapse is almost nonexistent.

13-1d Open-End versus Closed-End Funds

It may seem that all mutual funds are organized in roughly the same way, but that's certainly not the case. One way that funds differ is in how they are structured. That is, funds can be set up either as *open-end companies*, which can sell an unlimited number of ownership shares, or as *closed-end companies*, which can issue only a limited number of shares.

Open-End Investment Companies

The term *mutual fund* commonly denotes an **open-end investment company**. Such organizations are the dominant type of investment company and account for well over 95 percent of assets under management. In an open-end investment company, investors actually buy their shares from, and sell them back to, the mutual fund itself. When they buy shares in the fund, the fund issues new shares of stock and fills the purchase order with these new shares. There's no limit, other than investor demand, to the number of shares the fund can issue. Further, all open-end mutual funds stand behind their shares and buy them back when investors decide to sell. So there's never any trading among individuals.

Buy and sell transactions in an open-end mutual fund are carried out at prices based on the current value of all the securities held in the fund's portfolio.

net asset value (NAV) The current market value of all the securities the fund owns, less any liabilities, on a per-share basis.

closed-end investment company An investment company that issues a fixed number of shares, which are themselves listed and traded like any other share of stock.

This is known as the fund's **net asset value (NAV)**, which is found by taking the total market value of all securities held by the fund, subtracting any liabilities, and dividing the result by the number of shares outstanding.

Closed-End Investment Companies

The term *mutual fund* is supposed to be used only with open-end funds, but as a practical matter, it's regularly used with closed-end investment companies as well. Basically, **closed-end investment companies** operate with a fixed number of shares outstanding and do *not* regularly issue new shares of stock. In effect, they are like any other corporation, except that the corporation's business happens to be investing in marketable securities. Like open-end funds, closed-end investment companies have enjoyed remarkable growth in the past decade or so. Only 34 of these funds existed in 1980; by the end of 2011, there were about 634 closed-end funds with total net assets of nearly $239 billion—although this is just a fraction of the $11.6 trillion invested in the mutual fund industry. Shares in closed-end investment companies are actively traded in the secondary market, just like any other common stock; but unlike open-end funds, *all trading is done between investors in the open market.* The fund itself plays no role in either buy or sell transactions; once the shares are issued, the fund is out of the picture.

While open- and closed-end funds may appear to be pretty much the same, there really are some major differences that exist between them. To begin with, closed-end funds don't have to worry about stock redemptions or new money coming into the fund; hence, they don't have to be concerned about keeping cash on hand to meet redemptions. Equally important, because closed-end funds don't have new money flowing in all the time, they don't have to worry about finding new investments for that money. Instead, they can concentrate on a set portfolio of securities and do the best job they can in managing it. But this puts added pressures on the money managers because their investment results are closely monitored and judged by the market. That is, the share prices of closed-end companies are determined not only by their NAVs, but also by general supply and demand conditions in the market. Depending on the market outlook and investor expectations, closed-end companies generally trade at a *discount* or *premium* to their NAVs.

13-1e ETFs

Combine some of the operating characteristics of an open-end fund with some of the trading characteristics of a closed-end fund, and you'll end up with something called an ETF. As defined above, an ETF is an investment company whose shares trade on one of the stock exchanges. They have been around only since 1993, but ETFs are growing in popularity and offer a competitive alternative to comparable mutual funds in many cases. Most ETFs are structured as *index funds*, set up to match the performance of a certain market segment; they do this by owning all or a representative sample of the stocks (or bonds) in a targeted market segment or index. ETFs offer the professional money management of traditional mutual funds and the liquidity of an exchange traded stock. In 2011, there were about 1,100 ETFs managing over $1 trillion in assets. About 34 actively managed ETFs had over $5 billion in assets under management.

Even though ETFs are like closed-end funds (they're traded on listed exchanges), *they are actually open-end mutual funds* whose number of shares outstanding can be increased or decreased in response to market demand. That is, ETFs can be bought or sold like any other stock, and *the ETF distributor can also create new shares or redeem old shares.* This is done to prevent the fund from trading at (much of) a premium or discount to the underlying value of its holdings, thereby avoiding a major pitfall of closed-end funds. These funds cover a wide array of domestic and international stock indexes and submarkets, as well as just about any type of U.S. Treasury, corporate, or municipal bond index. The biggest and oldest ETFs (dating back to 1993) are based on the S&P 500 and are known as *Spiders* (SPDRs). In addition, there are *Qubes* (based on the NASDAQ 100), Diamonds (based on the DJIA), and ETFs based on dozens of international markets (from Australia and Canada to Germany, Japan, and the United Kingdom). Just about every major U.S. index, in fact, has its own ETF, along with a lot of minor indexes covering specialized market segments. The NAVs of ETFs are set at a fraction of the underlying index value at any given time. For example, in September 2012, when the S&P 500 index was 1,465.76, the ETF on that index traded at $146.90 (or about 1/10 of the index); likewise, the ETF on the Dow is set at about 1/100 of the DJIA (so when the Dow closed at 13,593.37 at this time, the ETF closed at $135.62).

ETFs combine many advantages of closed-end funds with those of traditional (open-end) index funds. That is, like closed-end funds, ETFs can be bought and sold at *any time of the day;* you can place an order through your broker (and pay a standard commission just as you would with any other stock). In contrast, you *cannot* trade a traditional open-end fund on an intraday basis because all buy and sell orders for these funds are filled, at the closing prices, at the end of the trading day. What's more, because most ETFs are passively managed, they offer all the advantages of any index fund: low costs, low portfolio turnover, and low taxes. Yet because ETFs trade as securities, their prices can sometimes differ by a modest amount from their

NAVs, which can dilute the cost advantage of ETFs over mutual funds. And whereas ETFs are traded for a fee using a broker, no-load mutual funds involve no trading costs. The fund's tax liability is kept low because ETFs rarely distribute any capital gains to shareholders; you could hold one of these things for decades and never pay a dime in capital gains taxes (at least not until you sell the shares).

Actively managed ETFs could have higher costs, portfolio turnover, and taxes than passively managed ETFs. As the name suggests, an actively managed ETF tries to outperform rather than to just track a given index. Leveraged ETFs seek to outperform a benchmark, which is usually achieved by using derivatives like options, futures, and swaps. If you're thinking that this can be extremely risky, you're right. Innovation continues in the ETF market to provide investors with more choices, so they can either moderate or enhance their risk exposure. Exhibit 13.2 lists examples of available ETF investments.

© KAREN HERMANN/ISTOCKPHOTO

Exhibit 13.2 Examples of Available ETFs

The ETF market remains dominated by products that seek to track various domestic and international indexes. However, actively managed ETFs that focus on selecting and trading a dynamic mix of securities are growing. Below are representative examples of available ETFs.

Type of ETF	Ticker	Tracking Goal
U.S. Equity Indexes		
Spiders	SPY	S&P 500 index
Cubes	QQQ	Nasdaq-100 index
Diamonds	DIA	Dow Jones Industrial Average index
iShares Russell 2000	IWM	Russell 2000 index
VIPERs	VTI	Wilshire 5000 broad market index
U.S. Equity Sector Indexes		
U.S. Energy Sector SPDR*	XLE	S&P 500 energy sector
U.S. Financial Sector SPDR	XLF	S&P 500 financial sector
U.S. Technology Sector SPDR	XLK	Technology Select Sector Index
U.S. Bond Market		
iShares Barclays Aggregate Bond ETF	AGG	Total U.S. investment grade bond market
Vanguard Short-Term Bond ETF	BSV	Market-weighted bond index with short-term dollar-weighted average maturity
iShares 10+ Government/Credit Bond Fund	GLJ	Long-term, investment-grade U.S. corporate and government bond markets
International Markets		
MSCI EAFE Index Fund	EFA	MSCI European, Australasian, and Far Eastern "EAFE" index
MSCI Emerging Markets Index Fund	EEM	MSCI emerging markets index
Actively Managed Funds		*Goal*
PIMCO Enhanced Short Term Maturity Strategy	MINT	Seek greater income and total return than money market funds
PowerShares Active U.S. Real Estate Fund	PSR	Selects securities in the FTSE NAREIT Equity REIT index
Dent Tactical ETF	DENT	Long-term capital growth using proprietary analysis

*SPDRS are available on all of the S&P 500 sectors as well as on variously defined industries.
Sources: Adapted from "Popular ETFs," Yahoo! Finance, http://finance.yahoo.com/etf/education/04, accessed September 2012; "Broad U.S. Bond ETFs," http://seekingalpha.com/article/30351-broad-u-s-market-etfs, accessed September 2012; Ron Rowland, "Complete List of 27 Actively Managed ETFs," http://seekingalpha.com/article/ 194752-complete-list-of-27-actively-managed-etfs, accessed September 2012.

13-1f Choosing Between ETFs and Mutual Funds

The preceding discussion identifies the relative advantages and disadvantages of mutual fund and ETF investing. Yet this begs the question of how you choose between ETFs and mutual funds. The answer depends on what you want to invest in and how sensitive you are to taxes and costs. Consider the following three criteria suggested by Morningstar:

- *Broad or narrow focus?* ETFs have been developed to accommodate investors pursuing narrow market segments. If you want to focus on a single market sector, industry, or geographic region, there's likely an ETF for you. Furthermore, there are far more ETFs that track single foreign countries than mutual funds that do. The downside is that narrowly focused ETFs are not as well diversified as are many mutual funds. So consider mutual funds for broad index investing and ETFs for more narrow, targeted investing.

- *Tax management.* ETFs are set up to protect investors from capital gains taxes better than most mutual funds can. Most ETFs are index funds that trade less than the average actively managed mutual fund, which means that they should generate fewer taxable gains.

- *Costs.* ETFs have lower overhead expenses than most mutual funds because they don't have to manage customer accounts or staff call centers. This means that ETFs tend to have lower expense ratios than mutual funds. ETFs are often the most cost-effective choice for investors using discount brokers, for those investing a large lump sum of money, and for those with a long-term horizon.

13-1g Some Important Cost Considerations

When you buy or sell shares in a *closed-end* investment company, or in an ETF for that matter, you pay a commission just as you would with any other type of listed or over-the-counter (OTC) common stock transaction. This isn't so with *open-end* funds, however. In particular, the cost of investing in an open-end mutual fund depends on the types of fees and load charges that the fund levies on its investors.

Load Funds

Most open-end mutual funds are so-called **load funds** because they charge a commission *when the shares are purchased* (such charges are often referred to as *front-end loads*). Front-end loads can be fairly substantial and amount to as much as 8½ percent of the *purchase price* of the shares. However, very few funds today charge the maximum; instead, many funds charge commissions of only 2 percent or 3 percent—such funds are known as **low-load funds**. The good news on front-end load funds is that there's normally no charge or commission to pay when you *sell* your shares! Occasionally, however, you'll run into funds that charge a commission—or a so-called *redemption fee*—when you sell your shares. Known as **back-end load funds**, they may charge as much as 7¼ percent of the value of the shares sold, although back-end loads tend to decline over time and usually disappear altogether after five or six years.

No-Load Funds

Some open-end investment companies charge you nothing at all to buy their funds; these are known as **no-load funds**. Less than half of the funds sold today are true no-loads; all the rest charge some type of load or fee. Even funds that don't have front-end loads (and may be categorized as no-loads) can have back-end load charges—or something called a 12(b)-1 fee, which you'd pay for so long as you hold your shares.

12(b)-1 Fees

Also known as *hidden loads*, **12(b)-1 fees** have been allowed by the Securities and Exchange Commission (SEC) since 1980 and were originally designed to help no-load funds cover their distribution and marketing expenses. Not surprisingly, the popularity of these fees spread rapidly among fund distributors, so they're now used by most open-end mutual funds. The fees are assessed annually and can amount to as much as 1 percent of assets under management. In good markets and bad, they're paid right off the top—and that can take its toll. Consider, for instance, $10,000 in a fund that charges a 1 percent 12(b)-1 fee. That translates into an annual charge of *$100 a year*, certainly a significant amount of money.

Management Fees

The **management fee** is the cost that you incur to hire the professional money managers to run the fund's portfolio of investments. These fees are also assessed annually and usually range from less than 0.5 percent to as much as 3 percent or 4 percent of assets under management. All funds—whether they're load or no-load, open- or closed-end—have these fees; and, like 12(b)-1 fees, they bear watching because high management fees will take their toll on performance. As a rule, the size of the management fee is totally unrelated to the fund's performance—you'll pay the same amount whether it has been a winning year or a real loser. In addition to these management fees, some funds may charge an *annual maintenance fee* to help defer the costs of providing service to low-balance accounts.

Keeping Track of Fund Fees and Loads

Critics of the mutual fund industry have come down hard on the proliferation of fund fees and charges. Fortunately, steps have been taken to bring fund fees and loads out into the open. For one thing, fund charges are more widely reported now than they were in the past. Most notably, today you can find detailed information about the types and amounts of fees and charges on just about any mutual fund by going to one of the dozens of Web sites that report on mutual funds, including Quicken.com, Kiplinger.com, Morningstar.com, and a host of others. Or you could use the mutual fund quotes that appear daily in (most) major newspapers and in *The Wall Street Journal*. For example, take a look at the online quotations in Exhibit 13.3; right after the (abbreviated) name of the fund, you'll often find the letters *r*, *p*, or *t*. If you see an *r* after a fund's name, it means

that the fund charges some type of redemption fee, or back-end load, when you sell your shares. The use of a *p* means that the fund levies a 12(b)-1 fee. Finally, a *t* indicates funds that charge redemption fees *and* 12(b)-1 fees. The quotations, of course, tell you only what kinds of fees are charged by the funds; they don't tell you how much is charged. What's more, these quotes *tell you nothing about the front-end loads*, if any, charged by the funds. You can access Web (or other) sources to find out whether a particular fund charges a front-end load or to obtain specifics on any amounts charged.

Mutual funds are required by the SEC to *disclose fully* all their fees and expenses in a standardized, easy-to-understand format. Every fund prospectus must contain, right up front, a fairly detailed *fee table*, which breaks total fund fees into three parts. The first specifies all *shareholder transaction costs*. This section tells you what it's going to cost to buy and sell shares in the mutual fund. The next section lists all *annual operating expenses* of the fund. Showing these expenses as a percentage of average net assets, the fund must break out management fees, those elusive 12(b)-1 fees, and any other expenses. The third section gives the *total cost over time* of buying, selling, and

BEHAVIOR MATTERS

Behavioral Biases in Mutual Fund Investing

In theory, rational investors should pursue a simple investment strategy that involves well-diversified, low-expense mutual funds, accompanied by only minimal portfolio rebalancing. The time-tested approach is to choose index mutual funds with low fees and low portfolio turnover. In contrast, current research indicates that many individual investors exhibit the following puzzling behaviors:

- Investors tend to sell winners too quickly and hold losers too long.
- Investors often buy mutual funds with high fees in general and even pay high fees for index funds that passively hold the components of indexes like the S&P 500.
- Individual investors often chase funds with high past returns.

What does behavioral finance research have to say about the above biased behavior?

- **Disposition effect.** People dislike taking losses much more than they enjoy realizing gains. Consequently, they tend to hold assets that have lost value too long and tend to take gains too soon. In mutual fund investing, this bias may encourage some investors to overestimate their expected holding periods and mistakenly select high-expense (front-end load) funds, the effect of which declines with the expected holding period. This often leads to too-frequent trading.

- **Narrow framing.** It's possible that investors buy and sell mutual funds without adequately considering the effects of the costs on their *total* portfolio. Similarly, if investors tend to view mutual funds as much safer than buying individual stocks, they may spend less time than they should evaluating mutual fund performance and costs.

- **Representativeness.** There is evidence that investors view recent performance as overly representative of a mutual fund's future performance (despite those warning statements we've probably all seen if we've read a prospectus). This could cause them to buy mutual funds inappropriately, just because of their past records. This bias may be partially explained by Morningstar's rating of funds based on past returns.

So what's the remedy for the above behavioral biases? The answer is clear: education! There is evidence that sophisticated investors are far less likely to fall into these behavioral traps. "Sophisticated" investors are better informed about key investment principles, understand these behavioral tendencies, are more experienced, and have higher incomes. They use mutual funds effectively, which means that the hold most funds for long periods, avoid high expense funds, and consequently enjoy relatively good performance. And based on what you now know, this could be you.

Source: Adapted from Warren Bailey, Alok Kumar, and David Ng, 2011, "Behavioral Biases of Mutual Fund Investors," *Journal of Financial Economics*, v. 102, pp.1–27.

Exhibit 13.3 **Mutual Fund Quotes**

Open-end mutual funds are listed separately from other securities and have their own quotation system; an example is shown here in online quotes from *The Wall Street Journal*. Note that these securities are also quoted in dollars and cents and that the quotes include not only the fund's NAV but also year-to-date (YTD) returns. Also included as part of the quotes is an indication of whether the fund charges redemption and/or 12(b)-1 fees.

Family/Fund	Symbol	NAV	Chg	YTD % return	3-year % chg	
Artio Global Funds						
GlbEqA *t*	BJGQX	36.35	0.42	10.9	3.9	← *Artio Select Opportunities Fund*, class A shares; a fund with both a 12(b)-1 fee (*p*) and a redemption fee (*r*).
GlbEql	JGEIX	36.73	0.43	11.1	4.2	← *Artio Select Opportunities Fund*; a true no-load fund (no front-end, back-end, or 12b-1 fees)
GblHilncl *r*	JHYIX	9.9	0.04	12.1	10.9	
IntlEqll I *r*	JETIX	10.78	0.16	12.9	−0.6	← *Artio International Equity Fund II*; a fund with a redemption fee (*r*).
USSmCpA *p*	JSCAX	10.58	0.16	11.6	9.5	← *Artio U.S. Small Cap Fund*; a fund with a 12(b)-1 fee (*p*).
Artisan Funds						
EmgMktsAdv	ARTZX	12.91	0.24	11.8	1.6	
EmgMktsInst	APHEX	12.9	0.24	12	1.9	
IntlVal Inv	ARTKX	29.53	0.21	17.7	10.4	
MidCapInv	ARTMX	40.3	0.49	22.4	19.1	
MidCapVal Inv	ARTQX	21.91	0.22	11.2	13.2	
SmCapVal Inv	ARTVX	16.12	0.16	8	9.3	
ValueInv	ARTLX	11.66	0.08	16.7	13.8	

p—Distribution costs apply, 12b-1.
r—Redemption charge may apply.
t—Footnotes p and r apply.

Source: *The Wall Street Journal*, http://online.wsj.com/mdc/public/page/2_3048-usmfunds_A-usmfunds.html?mod=mdc_h_mfhl, accessed September 14, 2012; NAV-net asset value. Chg—change in NAV from previous trading day; 3-year % chg—is trailing three-year annualized.

owning the fund. This part of the table contains both transaction and operating expenses and shows what the total costs would be over hypothetical 1-, 3-, 5-, and 10-year holding periods.

13-1h Buying and Selling Funds

Buying and selling shares of closed-end investment companies or ETFs is no different from buying shares of common stock. The transactions are executed through brokers or dealers who handle the orders in the usual way. They're subject to the normal transaction costs and, because they're treated like any other listed or OTC stock, their shares can even be margined or sold short, which are discussed in Chapter 11.

The situation is considerably different, however, with *open-end mutual funds*. Such funds can be bought through a discount or full-service broker, or directly from the mutual fund company itself. Most mutual funds allow you to open an account online, and once your account is open and the company has your initial deposit, you are ready to buy and sell shares. Selling shares in a fund is a do-it-yourself affair that simply requires using an online account or an 800 telephone number. When selling, it is wise to see whether your company offers the ability to switch funds. A common feature is the ability to go online (or simply pick up the phone) to move money from one fund to another—the only constraint is that the funds must be managed by the same "family" of funds. Most companies charge little or nothing for these shifts, although funds that offer free exchange privileges often limit the number of times you can switch each year.

13-2 Types of Funds and Fund Services

LG3 Categorizing mutual funds and EFTs according to their investment policies and objectives is widely practiced in the investment industry. This is because it tends to reflect similarities not only in how the funds manage their money but also in their risk and return characteristics. Every fund has a particular stated investment objective, of which the most common are capital appreciation, income, tax-exempt income, preserving investment capital, or some combination thereof. Some popular types of mutual funds include growth, aggressive growth, value, equity-income, balanced, growth-and-income, bond, money market, index, sector, socially responsible, international, and asset allocation funds. Let's now look at these funds to see what they are and what they have to offer investors. After that, we'll look at the kinds of investor services these funds offer.

13-2a Types of Funds

Growth Funds

The objective of a *growth fund* is simple—capital appreciation. As a result, they invest principally in common stocks with above-average growth potential. Because of the uncertain nature of their investment income, growth funds involve a fair amount of risk exposure. They're usually viewed as long-term investment vehicles that are most suitable for the aggressive investor who wants to build capital and has little interest in current income.

Aggressive Growth Funds

Aggressive growth funds are highly speculative investment vehicles that seek large profits from capital gains; in many ways, they're really an extension of the growth fund concept. Many are fairly small (with average assets under management of less than $300 million), and their portfolios consist mainly of high-flying common stocks. They often buy stocks of small, unseasoned companies, stocks with relatively high price/earnings multiples, and stocks whose prices are highly volatile. All this is designed, of course, to yield big returns. However, aggressive growth funds are perhaps the most volatile of all the fund types.

Value Funds

Value funds confine their investing to stocks considered to be *undervalued* by the market; that is, the funds look for stocks that are fundamentally sound but have yet to be discovered and as such remain undervalued by the market. In stark contrast to growth funds, value funds look for stocks with relatively low price/earnings (P/E) ratios, high dividend yields, and moderate amounts of financial leverage. They prefer undiscovered companies that offer the potential for growth. Value investing involves extensive evaluation of corporate financial statements and any other documents that will help fund managers *uncover value before the rest of the market does*—that's the key to getting low P/Es. And the approach seems to work: Even though value investing is generally regarded as being *less risky* than growth investing, the long-term returns to investors in value funds are quite competitive with those earned from growth or even aggressive growth funds. Thus, value funds are often viewed as a viable alternative for relatively conservative investors who are looking for the attractive returns that common stocks have to offer but want to keep share price volatility and investment risk in check.

Equity-Income Funds

Equity-income funds emphasize current income, which they provide by investing primarily in high-yielding common stocks. Preserving capital is also a goal of these funds; so is increasing capital gains, although it's not their primary objective. These funds invest heavily in high-grade common stocks, some convertible securities and preferred stocks, and occasionally even junk bonds. Because of their emphasis on dividends and current income, these funds tend to hold higher-quality securities that are subject to less price volatility than seen in the market as a whole. They're generally viewed as a fairly low-risk way of investing in stocks.

Balanced Funds

Balanced funds are so named because they tend to hold a balanced portfolio of both stocks and bonds, and they do so to generate a well-balanced return of current income and long-term capital gains. In many ways, they're like equity-income funds, except that balanced funds usually put much more into fixed-income securities: generally they keep 30 percent to 40 percent (and sometimes more) of their portfolios in bonds. The bonds are used primarily to provide current income, and stocks are selected mainly for their long-term growth potential. Balanced funds tend to confine their investing to high-grade securities and therefore are usually considered a relatively safe form of investing—one that can earn you a competitive rate of return without a lot of price volatility.

Growth-and-Income Funds

Like balanced funds, *growth-and-income funds* seek a balanced return made up of current income and long-term capital gains, but they put greater emphasis on growth of capital. Moreover, unlike balanced funds, growth-and-income funds put most of their money into equities. They tend to confine their investing to high-quality issues, so you can expect to find a lot of growth-oriented blue-chip stocks in their portfolios

along with a fair number of high-quality income stocks. These funds do involve a fair amount of risk if for no other reason than their emphasis on stocks and capital gains.

Bond Funds

As their name implies, *bond funds* invest in various kinds of fixed-income securities. Income is their primary investment objective, although they don't ignore capital gains. There are three important advantages to buying shares in bond funds rather than investing directly in bonds. First, bond funds generally are more liquid; second, they offer a cost-effective way of achieving a high degree of diversification in an otherwise expensive investment vehicle (most bonds carry minimum denominations of $1,000 to $5,000 or more); and third, bond funds automatically reinvest interest and other income, thereby allowing the investor to earn fully compounded rates of return. Bond funds are considered to be fairly conservative, but they're not totally without risk because the prices of the bonds held in their portfolios will fluctuate with changing interest rates. At the end of 2011, bond mutual funds had $2.9 trillion under management, while bond ETFs had about $184.2 million under management. Listed below are some of the different types of bond funds currently available in the market.

- **Government bond funds,** which invest in U.S. Treasury and agency securities.
- **Mortgage-backed bond funds,** which put their money into various types of mortgage-backed securities.
- **High-grade corporate bond funds,** which invest chiefly in high-grade securities rated triple-B or better.
- **High-yield corporate bond funds,** which are risky investments that buy *junk bonds* for the yields that they offer, which can be higher than standard bonds.
- **Convertible bond funds,** which invest in securities that can be converted or exchanged into common stocks.
- **Municipal bond funds,** which invest in tax-exempt securities.
- **Intermediate-term bond funds,** which invest in bonds with maturities of 7 to 10 years or less.

Money Market Mutual Funds

Money market mutual funds invest in a widely diversified portfolio of short-term money market instruments. These funds are very popular with investors, and for good reason: They give investors with modest amounts of capital access to the higher-yielding end of the money market, where many instruments require minimum investments of $100,000 or more. Today, there are more than 630 money market mutual funds that, together, hold nearly $2.7 *trillion* in assets.

There are several different kinds of money market mutual funds. **General-purpose money funds** essentially invest in any and all types of money market investment vehicles, from Treasury bills to corporate commercial paper and bank certificates of deposit. They invest their money wherever they can find attractive short-term returns. Most money funds are of this type. The **tax-exempt money fund** limits its investments to tax-exempt municipal securities with very short (30- to 90-day) maturities. Because their income is free from federal income tax, they appeal predominantly to investors in high tax brackets. **Government securities money funds** eliminate any risk of default by confining their investments to Treasury bills (T-bills) and other short-term securities of the U.S. government or its agencies (such as the Government National Mortgage Association/GNMA). Money funds are highly liquid investment vehicles that are very low in risk because they're virtually immune to capital loss. However, the interest income that they produce will follow interest rate conditions, so the returns to shareholders are subject to the ups and downs of market interest rates.

Index Funds

"If you can't beat 'em, join 'em." That's the idea behind the *index fund,* which is a type of fund that buys and holds a portfolio of stocks (or bonds) equivalent to those in a market index such as the S&P 500. An index fund that's trying to match the S&P 500, for example, would hold the same 500 stocks that are held in that index and in the same proportion. Rather than trying to beat the market, *index funds simply try to match the market*—that is, to match the performance of the index on which the fund is based. They do this through low-cost investment management; in fact, in most cases, the whole portfolio is run almost entirely by a computer that matches the fund's holdings with those of the targeted index. Besides the S&P 500, a number of other market indexes are used, including the S&P MidCap 400, Russell 2000, and Wilshire 5000, as well as value stock indexes, growth stock indexes, international stock indexes, and even bond indexes. Index funds form a part of the overall mutual fund market, but they comprise the vast majority of ETFs.

The investment approach of index funds is strictly buy and hold. In fact, about the only time there's a change to the portfolio of an index fund is when the targeted market index alters its "market basket" of securities. A pleasant by-product of this buy-and-hold approach is that the funds have extremely low portfolio turnover rates and therefore very little in *realized* capital gains. As a result, aside from a modest amount of dividend income, these funds produce very

little taxable income from year to year, which leads many high-income investors to view them as a type of tax-sheltered investment. But these funds provide something else—namely they produce *highly competitive returns* for investors! It's tough to outperform the market consistently, so these don't even try. The net result is that, on average, index funds tend to produce better returns than do most other types of stock funds.

Sector Funds

As the name implies, a *sector fund* restricts its investments to a particular sector of the market. These funds concentrate their investment holdings in the one or more industries that make up the targeted sector. For example, a *health care* sector fund would confine its investments to those industries that make up this segment of the market: drug companies, hospital management firms, medical suppliers, and biotech concerns. The underlying investment objective of sector funds is *capital gains*. The idea behind sector funds is that the really attractive returns come from small segments of the market. So, rather than diversifying a portfolio across wide segments of the market, put your money where the action is. Some popular sector funds are those in real estate (real estate investment trusts, or REITs), technology, financial services, natural resources, electronics, and telecommunications.

Socially Responsible Funds

For some investors, the security selection process doesn't end with bottom lines, P/E ratios, and growth rates; rather, it also includes the *active, explicit consideration of moral, ethical, and environmental issues.* The idea is that social concerns should play just as big a role in the investment decision as profits and other financial matters. **Socially responsible funds (SRFs)** actively and directly incorporate morality and ethics into the investment decision. These funds consider only what they view as socially responsible companies for inclusion in their portfolios—if a company doesn't meet certain moral, ethical, or environmental tests, they simply won't consider buying the stock, no matter how good the bottom line looks. Generally speaking, these funds abstain from investing in companies that derive revenues from tobacco, alcohol, or gambling; that are weapons contractors; or that operate nuclear power plants. They also tend to favor firms that produce "responsible" products and services, have

general-purpose money fund A money fund that invests in virtually any type of short-term investment vehicle.

tax-exempt money fund A money fund that limits its investments to short-term, tax-exempt municipal securities.

government securities money fund A money fund that limits its investments to short-term securities of the U.S. government and its agencies.

socially responsible fund (SRF) A fund that invests only in companies meeting certain moral, ethical, and/or environmental criteria.

international fund A mutual fund that does all or most of its investing in foreign securities.

automatic investment plan An automatic savings program that enables an investor to channel a set amount of money systematically into a given mutual fund.

positive environmental records, and are socially responsive to the communities in which they operate.

International Funds

In searching for higher returns and better diversification, American investors have shown increased interest in foreign securities. The mutual fund industry has responded with a wide array of **international funds**. In 1985, there were only about 40 of these funds; by 2012, that number had grown to several thousand. Technically, the term *international fund* is used to describe a type of fund that *invests exclusively in foreign securities*, often confining the fund's activities to specific geographical regions (such as Mexico, Australia, Europe, or the Pacific Rim). In contrast, there's another class of international funds, known as *global funds*, that invest not only in foreign securities *but also in U.S. companies*—usually multinational firms. As a rule, global funds provide more diversity and, with access to both foreign and domestic markets, can go wherever the action is.

YURI ARCURS/SHUTTERSTOCK.COM

Asset Allocation Funds

The most important decision an investor can make is where to allocate his or her investment assets. This is known as *asset allocation*, and it involves deciding how you're going to divide your investments among different types of securities. Because a lot of individual investors have a tough time making asset allocation decisions, the mutual fund industry has created a product to do the job for them. Known as *asset allocation funds*, these funds spread investors' money across all different types of markets. That is, whereas most mutual funds concentrate on one type of investment—whether it be stocks, bonds, or money market securities—asset allocation funds put money into all these markets. They're for people who want to hire fund managers not only to select individual securities for them, but also to make the strategic decision of how to allocate money among the various markets. Here's how many asset allocation funds work. The money manager will establish a desired allocation mix, which might look something like this: 50 percent of the portfolio goes to U.S. stocks, 10 percent to foreign securities, 30 percent to bonds, and 10 percent to money market securities. Securities are then purchased for the fund in this proportion, and the overall portfolio maintains the desired mix. *As market conditions change over time, the asset allocation mix also changes.* Of course, there's no assurance that the money manager will make the right moves at the right time, but that's the idea behind these funds.

13-2b Services Offered by Mutual Funds

Ask most investors why they buy a particular mutual fund, and they'll probably tell you that the fund offers the kind of income and return they're looking for. Now, no one would question the importance of return in the investment decision, but there are other reasons for investing in mutual funds, not the least of which are the valuable services that they provide. Some of the most sought-after *mutual fund services* are automatic investment and reinvestment plans, regular income programs, conversion privileges, and retirement programs.

Automatic Investment Plans

It takes money to make money, and for an investor that means being able to accumulate the capital to put into the market. Not to worry—most mutual funds provide a program that makes savings and capital accumulation as painless as possible. The **automatic investment plan** allows fund shareholders to funnel fixed amounts of money *from their paychecks or bank accounts* automatically into a mutual fund. It's very much like a payroll deduction plan that treats savings a lot like insurance coverage—that is, just as insurance premiums are deducted automatically from your paycheck (or bank account), so too are investments

320   **Part 5 • Managing Investments**

to your mutual fund. Just about every major fund group offers some kind of automatic investment plan. To enroll, you simply fill out a form authorizing the fund to transfer a set amount (usually it has to be a minimum of $25 to $100 per period) from your bank account or paycheck at regular intervals—typically monthly or quarterly. Once enrolled, you'll be buying shares in the funds of your choice every month or quarter (most funds deal in fractional shares). Of course, if it's a load fund, you'll still have to pay normal sales charges on your periodic investments.

Automatic Reinvestment Plans

Automatic reinvestment is one of the real draws of mutual funds, and it's offered by just about every open-ended mutual fund. Whereas automatic investment plans deal with money shareholders put into a fund, **automatic reinvestment plans** deal with the dividends and other distributions that the funds pay to their shareholders. Much like the dividend reinvestment plans we looked at with stocks, the automatic reinvestment plans of mutual funds enable you to keep all your capital fully employed. Through this service, dividend and capital gains income is *used to buy additional shares in the fund automatically*, which enables the investor to earn a fully compounded rate of return. Keep in mind, however, that even though you reinvest your dividends and capital gains, the Internal Revenue Service (IRS) still treats them as cash receipts and taxes them in the year that they're paid.

The important point is that, by plowing earnings (reinvested dividends and capital gains distributions) back into a fund, investors can put this money to work generating even more earnings. Indeed, the effects of these plans on total accumulated capital over the long haul can be substantial. Exhibit 13.4 shows the

> **automatic reinvestment plan** A plan that gives shareholders the option of electing to have dividends and capital gains distributions reinvested in additional fund shares.

Exhibit 13.4 Effects of Reinvesting Income

Reinvesting dividends and/or capital gains can have tremendous effects on your investment position. This graph shows the results of a hypothetical investor who initially invested $10,000 and reinvested all dividends and capital gains distributions in additional fund shares. No adjustment has been made for any income taxes payable by the shareholder, which would be appropriate provided that the fund was held in a tax-deferred account like an individual retirement account (IRA) or a 401(k) account. This example is for the Fidelity Contrafund.

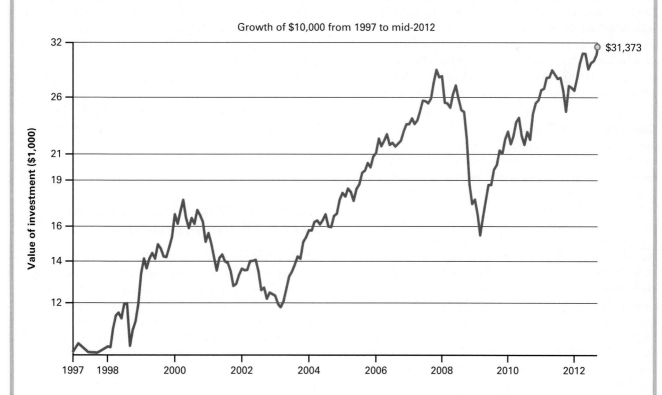

Growth of $10,000 from 1997 to mid-2012

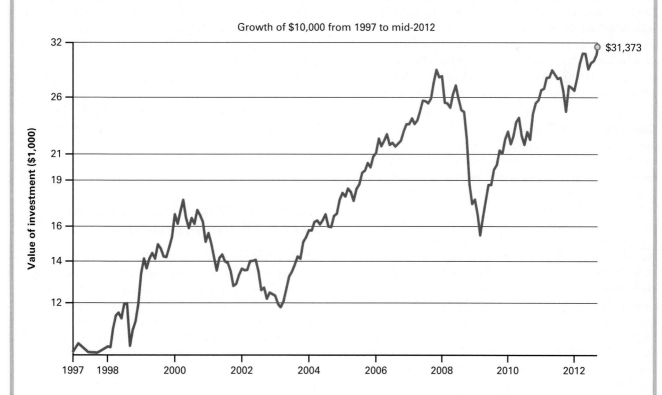$31,373

Source: MorningstarDirect, September 2012. © 2012 Morningstar, Inc. All rights reserved. The Morningstar data contained herein (1) is proprietary to Morningstar; (2) may not be copied or distributed without written permission; and (3) is not warranted to be accurate, complete, or timely. Morningstar is not responsible for any damages or losses arising from any use of this information and has not granted its consent to be considered or deemed an "expert" under the Securities Act of 1933.

systematic withdrawal plan A plan offered by mutual funds that allows shareholders to be paid specified amounts of money each period.

conversion (exchange) privileges A feature that allows investors to switch from one mutual fund to another within a family of funds.

long-term impact of one such plan. (These are the actual performance numbers for a real mutual fund—Fidelity Contrafund, in this case.) In the illustration, we assume that the investor starts with $10,000 and, except for reinvesting dividends and capital gains distributions, *adds no new capital over time*. Even so, the initial investment of $10,000 grew to some $31,373 over the roughly 15-year period from 1997 to August 2012 (which, by the way, amounts to a compounded rate of return of 8 percent). Clearly, so long as care is taken in selecting the fund, *attractive benefits can be derived from the systematic accumulation of capital offered by automatic reinvestment plans.*

Regular Income

Automatic reinvestment plans are great for the long-term investor, but how about the investor who's looking for a steady stream of income? Mutual funds also have a service to meet this need. It's called a **systematic withdrawal plan**, and it's offered by most open-ended funds. Once enrolled in one of these plans, you'll automatically receive a predetermined amount of money every month or quarter. Depending on how well the fund is doing, the annual return generated by the fund may actually be greater than the withdrawals, thus allowing the investor not only to receive regular income but also to enjoy an automatic accumulation of *additional* shares in the plan. On the other hand, if the fund isn't performing well, then the withdrawals could eventually deplete the original investment.

Conversion Privileges

Sometimes investors find it necessary to switch out of one fund and into another; for example, their investment objectives may change or the investment environment itself may have changed. **Conversion (or exchange) privileges** conveniently and economically meet the needs of these investors. Investment companies that offer a number of different funds to the investing public—known as *fund families*—usually provide conversion privileges that enable shareholders to move easily from one fund to another; this can be done either by phone or online. The only limitation is that the investor must confine the switches to the same *family* of funds. For example, an investor can switch from a Fidelity growth fund to a Fidelity money fund, or to its income fund, or to any other fund managed by Fidelity. Conversion privileges are attractive because they permit investors to manage their holdings more aggressively by allowing them to move in and out of funds as the investment environment changes. There's one major drawback; although you never see

BLEND IMAGES/ARIEL SKELLEY/JUPITER IMAGES

the cash, the exchange of shares from one fund to another is regarded as a sale followed by the purchase of a new security. As a result, if any capital gains exist at the time of the exchange, the investor is liable for the taxes on that profit.

Retirement Plans

Government legislation permits self-employed individuals to divert part of their income into self-directed *retirement plans*. And all working Americans, whether they're self-employed or not, are allowed to establish individual retirement accounts—in the form of either a standard tax-deductible IRA or the newest type of retirement account, the Roth IRA (all of which we'll look at in the next chapter). Today, all mutual funds provide a special service that allows individuals to set up tax-deferred retirement programs quickly and easily as either IRA or Keogh accounts—or, through their place of employment, to participate in a qualified tax-sheltered retirement plan such as a 401(k). The funds set up the plans and handle all the administrative details so that the shareholders can take full advantage of available tax savings.

13-3 Making Mutual Fund and ETF Investments

LG4, LG5 Suppose that you have money to invest and are trying to select the right place to put it. You obviously want to pick an investment that not only meets your idea of an acceptable risk, but also generates an attractive rate of return. The problem is that you have to choose from literally thousands of investments. Sound like a "mission impossible"? Well, that's what a typical investor is up against when trying to select a suitable mutual fund. But perhaps if you approach the problem systematically, it may not be so formidable. For as we'll see, it is possible to whittle down the list of alternatives by matching your investment needs with the investment objectives of the funds.

13-3a The Selection Process

When it comes to mutual funds and ETFs, one question that every investor must answer is: Why invest in a mutual fund or an ETF to begin with; why not just go it alone (that is, buy individual stocks and bonds directly)? For beginning investors, or investors with limited capital, the answer is pretty simple—mutual funds and ETFs provide far more diversification than these investors could ever achieve on their own, plus they get the help of professional money managers, and at a reasonable cost to boot.

> **Mutual funds provide far more diversification than investors could ever achieve on their own, plus they get the help of professional money managers and at a reasonable cost to boot.**

For more seasoned, better-heeled investors, the answers are probably a bit more involved. Certainly, the diversification and professional money management come into play, but there are other reasons. The competitive returns offered by mutual funds and ETFs have to be a factor with many investors, and so do the services they provide. Many of these investors will use part of their capital to buy and sell individual securities on their own, and they'll use the rest *to buy mutual funds or ETFs that invest in areas they don't fully understand or aren't well informed about*—for example, they'll use mutual funds or ETFs to get into foreign markets or as a way to buy mortgage-backed securities.

After deciding to use mutual funds or ETFs, the investor then must decide which funds to buy. The selection process itself obviously plays an important role in defining the amount of success you'll have with mutual funds or ETFs. Given that you have an asset allocation strategy in place and that you're trying to select funds compatible with your targeted mix, the selection process begins with an assessment of your own investment needs; this sets the tone for your investment program. Many of these same principles also apply when choosing mutual funds and ETFs to include in a 401(k) retirement plan.

Objectives and Motives for Using Funds

Selecting the right investment means finding those funds that are most suitable to your investment needs. *The place to start is with your own investment objectives.* In other words, why do you want to invest in a mutual fund or an ETF, and what are you looking for in a fund? Obviously, an attractive rate of return would be desirable, but there's also the matter of ensuring a tolerable amount of risk exposure. More than likely, when looking at your own risk temperament in relation to the various types of mutual funds and ETFs available, you'll discover that certain types of funds are more appealing to you than others.

Another important factor is the intended use of the mutual fund or ETF. That is, do you want to invest in mutual funds or ETFs as a way of *accumulating capital* over an extended time, to *speculate* with your money in the hopes of generating high rates of return, or to *conserve your capital* by investing in low-risk securities where preservation of capital is no less important than return on capital. Finally, there's the matter of the services provided. If you're particularly interested in some services, be sure to look for them in the funds that you select. Having assessed what you're looking for in a fund, now you can look at what the funds have to offer.

What Funds Have to Offer

The ideal mutual fund or ETF would achieve maximum capital growth when security prices rise, provide complete protection against capital loss when prices decline, and achieve high levels of current income at all times. Unfortunately, such funds don't exist. Instead, just as each individual has a set of investment needs, each fund has its own *investment objective*, its own *manner or style of operation*, and its own *range of services*. These three factors are useful in helping you assess investment alternatives. But where does the investor look for such information? One obvious place is the fund's *profile* (or its prospectus), where information on investment objectives, portfolio composition, management, and past performance can be obtained. In addition, there's a wealth of useful information in Morningstar's online (http://morningstar.com) and software-based products, *The Value Line Fund Advisor,* and *The Value Line ETF Survey* (these reports are similar to its stock reports, but they apply to both mutual funds and ETFs). These sources publish a wealth of operating and performance statistics in a convenient, easy-to-read format. Services are also available that provide background information and assessments on a wide variety of funds. And, of course, all sorts of performance statistics are available on the Internet. The Bonus Exhibit, "Mutual Fund Information," provides an example of the type of in-depth information available to mutual fund investors. (Visit CourseMate for PFIN 3. Log in at **www.cengagebrain.com.**)

Whittling Down the Alternatives

At this point, fund selection becomes a process of elimination as you weigh your investment needs against the types of funds available. Many funds can be eliminated from consideration simply because they don't meet these needs. Some may be too risky; others may be unsuitable as a storehouse of value. So, rather than trying to evaluate thousands of different funds, you can use a process of elimination to narrow the list down to two or three *types* of funds that best match your investment (and asset allocation) needs. From here, you can whittle the list down a bit more by introducing other constraints. For example, you may want to deal only in no-load or low-load funds, or you may be seeking certain fund services that are important to your investment goals.

Now we're ready to introduce the final (but certainly not the least important) element in the selection process: *the fund's investment performance.* Useful information includes (1) how the fund has performed over the past five to seven years; (2) the type of return that it has generated in good markets as well as bad; (3) the level of dividend and capital gains distributions, which is an important indication not only of how much current income the fund distributes annually, but also of the fund's *tax efficiency* (as a rule, funds with low dividends and low asset turnovers expose their shareholders to lower taxes and consequently have higher tax-efficiency ratings); and (4) the level of investment stability that the fund has enjoyed over time (or, put another way, the amount of volatility/risk in the fund's return). By evaluating such information, you can identify some of the more successful mutual funds—those that not only offer the investment objectives and services you seek, but also provide the best payoffs.

Go to Smart Sites

Before investing in ETFs, visit Morningstar to learn more about index funds, get price quotes, and find the right ETF for your portfolio. ●

Stick with No-Load or Low-Load Mutual Funds

There's a longstanding "debate" in the mutual fund industry regarding load funds and no-load funds. The question is, do load funds add enough value to overcome the load fees? And if not, why pay the load charges? The evidence indicates that load fund returns generally aren't, on a risk-adjusted basis, any better than the returns from no-load funds. In fact,

the funds with abnormally high loads and 12(b)-1 fees often produce returns that are far *less* than what you can get from no-loads after taking risk into account! That shouldn't be surprising, though, because big load charges and/or 12(b)-1 fees do nothing more than *reduce your investable capital*, thus reducing the amount of money you have working for you. In fact, the only way that a load fund can overcome this handicap is to *produce superior returns*—which is not easy to do, year in and year out. Granted, a handful of load funds have produced attractive returns over extended periods, but they're the exception rather than the rule.

Obviously, it's in your best interest to pay close attention to load charges (and other fees) whenever you're considering an investment in a mutual fund. As a rule, to maximize returns, *you should seriously consider sticking to no-load funds, or low-loads* (funds with total load charges, including 12(b)-1 fees, of 3 percent or less). At the very least, you should consider a more expensive load fund *only* if it has a much better performance record (and offers more return potential) than a less expensive fund.

13-3b Getting a Handle on Mutual Fund Performance

If you were to believe all the sales literature, you'd think there was no way you could go wrong by investing in mutual funds. Just put your money into one of these funds and let the good times roll! Unfortunately, the hard facts of life are that *when it comes to investing, performance is never guaranteed.* And that applies just as much to mutual funds as it does to any other form of investing—perhaps even more so because, with mutual funds, the single variable driving a fund's market price and return behavior is the performance of its securities portfolio.

Measuring Fund Performance

Any mutual fund (open- or closed-end) or any ETF has three potential sources of return: (1) dividend income, (2) capital gains distribution, and (3) change in the fund's share price. Depending on the type of fund, some will derive more income from one source than another. For example, we'd normally expect income-oriented funds to generate higher dividend income than capital gains–oriented funds do. Mutual funds regularly publish reports that recap investment performance. One such report is *The Summary of Income and Capital Changes;* an example of which is provided in Exhibit 13.5. Of interest to us in this discussion is the top part of the report (from "Net asset value, beginning of period" through "Net asset value, end of period"—lines 1 to 10). This part shows

Exhibit 13.5   A Summary of Income and Capital Changes

The return on a mutual fund is made up of (1) the (net) investment income the fund earns from dividends and interest and (2) the realized and unrealized capital gains the fund earns on its security transactions. Mutual funds provide such information to their shareholders in a standardized format (like the statement here) that highlights, among other things, the amount of income, expenses, and capital gains generated by the fund.

	2015	2014	2013
1. **Net asset value, beginning of period:**	$24.47	$27.03	$24.26
2. **Income from investment operations:**			
3. Net investment income	$ .60	$ .66	$ .50
4. Net gains on securities (realized and unrealized)	6.37	(1.74)	3.79
5. Total from investment operations	6.97	(1.08)	4.29
6. **Less distributions:**			
7. Dividends from net investment income	($ .55)	($ .64)	($ .50)
8. Distributions from realized gains	(1.75)	(.84)	(1.02)
9. Total distributions	(2.30)	(1.48)	(1.52)
10. **Net asset value, end of period:**	$29.14	$24.47	$27.03
11. **Total return:**	28.48%	(4.00%)	17.68%
12. **Ratios/supplemental data:**			
13. Net assets, end of period ($000)	$307,951	$153,378	$108,904
14. Ratio of expenses to average net assets	1.04%	0.85%	0.94%
15. Ratio of net investment income to average net assets	1.47%	2.56%	2.39%
16. Portfolio turnover rate*	85%	144%	74%

* *Portfolio turnover rate* measures the number of shares bought and sold by the fund against the total number of shares held in the fund's portfolio; a high turnover rate (e.g., one exceeding 100%) would mean the fund has been doing a lot of trading.

© Cengage Learning

© KAREN HERMANN/ISTOCKPHOTO

the amount of dividend income and capital gains distributed to the shareholders, along with any change in NAV.

Dividend income (see line 7 of Exhibit 13.5) is the amount derived from the dividend and interest income earned on the security holdings of the mutual fund. When the fund receives dividends or interest payments, it passes these on to shareholders in the form of dividend payments. Because the mutual fund itself is tax exempt, any taxes due on dividend earnings are payable by the individual investor. For funds that are not held in tax-deferred accounts [e.g., IRAs and 401(k)s], the amount of taxes due on dividends will depend on the source of such dividends. That is, *if these distributions are derived from dividends earned on the fund's common stock holdings, then they're subject to the preferential tax rate of 15 percent or less*. But if these distributions are derived from

interest earnings on bonds, dividends from REITs, or dividends from most types of preferred stocks, then such dividends *do not qualify for preferential tax treatment* and instead are taxed as ordinary income (see Chapter 4 for details).

Capital gains distributions (see line 8) work on the same principle as dividends, except that they're derived from the *capital gains actually earned* by the fund. Note that these distributions apply only to *realized* capital gains—that is, where the securities holdings were actually sold and capital gains actually earned. *Unrealized* capital gains (or "paper profits") make up the third and final element in a mutual fund's return. This change (or movement) in the NAV is what makes up the unrealized capital gains of the fund. It represents the profit that shareholders would receive (and are entitled to) if the fund were to sell its holdings.

Crunching the Numbers

A simple but effective way of measuring performance is to describe mutual fund returns based on the three major sources of return noted previously—dividends earned, capital gains distributions received, and change in share price. These payoffs can be converted to a convenient return figure by using the standard *approximate yield* formula that was first introduced in Chapter 12. The calculations necessary for finding such a return measure can be shown using the 2015 figures from Exhibit 13.5. Referring to the exhibit, we can see that this hypothetical no-load fund paid $0.55 per share in dividends and another $1.75 in capital gains distributions; also, its price (NAV) at the beginning of the year (that is, at the end of 2014) of $24.47 rose to $29.14 by the end of the year (see lines 1 and 10, respectively). Putting this data into the familiar approximate yield formula, we see that the hypothetical mutual fund provided an annual rate of return of 26 percent.

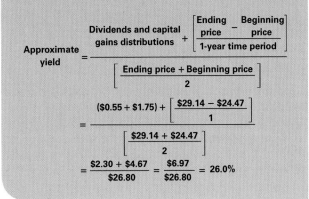

Calculator Keystrokes

You can just as easily find the *exact return* on this investment with a handheld financial calculator. Here's what you'd do: Using *annual compounding*, to find the return on this mutual fund in 2015, we use the same input data as given before. Namely, we start with a price at the beginning of the year of $24.47; add in total dividends and capital gains distributions of $2.30 a share (i.e., $0.55 + $1.75); and then, using a year-end price of $29.14, we enter the keystrokes shown below, where:

N = number of *years* you hold the fund
PV = the *initial* price of the fund (entered as a *negative number*)

PMT = *total* amount of dividends and capital gains distributions received
FV = the *ending* price of the fund

Note that our computed return (of 28.48 percent) is exactly the same as the "Total Return" shown on line 11 of Exhibit 13.5—that's because this is basically the same procedure that the mutual funds must use to report their return performance. The approximate yield measure (26 percent) may be close to the actual return, but clearly it's not close enough for fund-reporting purposes.

Evaluating ETF Performance

ETFs and mutual funds are similar in that their prices depend on the value of the funds' underlying investments. Both have NAVs and depend on dividends and capital gains to generate returns. So let's focus on the aspects that are particularly important in ETF performance evaluation. As discussed previously, while there are some actively managed ETFs, the vast majority are designed to replicate an index. So now we'll consider the issues associated with evaluating the index-based form of ETF.

The primary reason for investing in an index-based ETF, of course, is to replicate the performance of the index. It follows that an important aspect of ETF performance is how well it tracks the performance of the underlying index. You can determine this by checking the so-called R-Squared (R^2) statistical measure, which shows how much of the variability in an ETF's total returns is explained by the variability in the total returns of the underlying index. The R^2 varies between 0 percent and a maximum of 100 percent. Obviously, the higher the R^2, the closer is the relationship between the ETF and the associated target index. It's also wise to check how the ETF's expense ratio compares with reasonable benchmarks.

Consider the example of the PowerShares QQQ ETF (QQQ). This ETF is designed to replicate the performance of the NASDAQ 100 index, which includes the 100 largest domestic and international non-financial firms trading on the NASDAQ stock exchange. In September 2012, Morningstar reported that the R^2 of the QQQ ETF relative to the NASDAQ 100 index was 97.09 percent. This is a very tight fit. And Morningstar indicated that the expense ratio for the QQQ ETF was only 0.20 percent and that the investment style category average was 0.40 percent. Thus, an investor wanting consistent exposure to the large non-financial growth stocks that characterize the NASDAQ 100 index could rest assured that the QQQ ETF replicates the performance of that index well, with relatively low expenses.

What About Future Performance?

There's no question that approximate yield and return on investment are simple yet highly effective measures that capture all the important elements of mutual fund and ETF returns. Looking at past performance is one thing, but what about the future? Ideally, we'd want to evaluate the same three elements of return over the future much as we did for the past. The trouble is, when it comes to the future performance of a mutual fund or an ETF, it's difficult—if not impossible—to get a handle on what the future holds for dividends, capital gains, and NAV. The reason is that a mutual fund's or an ETF's future investment performance is directly linked to the future makeup of its securities portfolio, which is impossible to predict.

So where do you look for insight into the future? The key factors apply to the evaluation of both mutual funds and ETFs. First, carefully consider the *future direction of the market as a whole*. This is important because the behavior of a well-diversified mutual fund or ETF tends to reflect the general tone of the market. Thus, if the feeling is that the market is going to be generally drifting up, that should bode well for the investment performance of mutual funds and ETFs. Second, take a hard look at the past performance of the mutual fund itself; it's a good way to see how successful the fund's investment managers have been. The success of a mutual fund or an ETF rests largely *on the investment skills of the fund managers*. So, when investing in a fund, look for consistently good performance in up as well as down markets, as well as over extended periods (of five to seven years or more). Most important, check to see whether the same key people are still running the fund. Although past success is certainly no guarantee of future performance, a strong, consistent team of money managers can have a significant bearing on the level of fund returns. Put another way: when you buy a mutual fund, you're buying a formula (investment policy + money management team), which has worked in the past, in the expectation that it will work again in the future.

13-4 Investing in Real Estate

LG6 For many years, investing in real estate was quite lucrative. Real estate, it seemed, was one of the few investment vehicles that just couldn't go wrong. When the economy is growing and inflation is relatively high, as it was in the 1970s and early 1980s, real estate

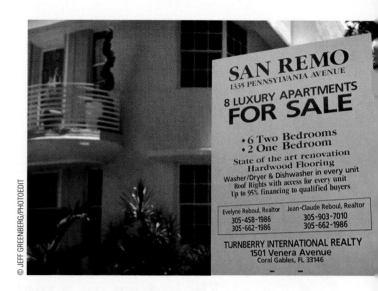

prices are also strong. In the early 1990s, however, the market weakened and prices started to level off. That didn't last long, though, as real estate values began to climb again in the latter part of the 1990s. One example of this behavior was housing prices, which rose rapidly—indeed, shot almost straight up—from 2001 through 2006. But then, from a market peak in 2006, housing prices fell almost as quickly as they had risen, with the average price of a home plummeting nearly 26 percent by late 2010. This is a bit greater than the drop in housing values experienced during the Great Depression between 1928 and 1933. And as of mid-2012, housing prices had not shown a significant, consistent upward trend that would indicate a recovery from the housing debacle of 2007–2009.

Real estate includes everything from homes and raw land to different types of income-producing properties such as warehouses, commercial and retail space, office and apartment buildings, and condominiums. Investments in real estate can take several forms. For example, investors can buy land or property directly, or they may prefer to invest in various types of real estate securities, such as real estate mutual funds (discussed earlier in this chapter), REITs, mortgages, stocks of real-estate–related companies, or real estate limited partnerships. A key reason for including real estate in your investment portfolio is that it *provides greater diversification than does holding just stocks or bonds.* That's because *real estate typically doesn't move in tandem with stocks.* Before deciding to buy real estate for your portfolio, however, it's essential for you to evaluate such issues as the outlook for the national economy, interest rate levels, supply and demand for space, and regional considerations.

13-4a Some Basic Considerations

The attractiveness of a real estate investment depends on the expected cash flows over the planned holding period and the riskiness of those cash flows. The expected ongoing cash flows are determined by rent, depreciation, and taxes—and, of course, the all-important expected future sales price. The return on a real estate investment is determined by the relationship between the expected future cash flows relative to the initial investment, which is typically reduced by using a significant amount of borrowed funds. The value of the investment is assessed in light of the returns available on alternative investments of comparable risk (such as stocks, bonds, and mutual funds). Far more than with most other types of investment vehicles, financial leverage (borrowing) is a key determinant of real estate investment returns. We'll now briefly describe the basic factors affecting the value of real estate investments, including after-tax cash flows, appreciation in value, and the use of leverage.

$5,000 of net rental income. The other $10,000 could be charged directly against your ordinary income, thereby reducing your taxable income and your taxes. Because of its effect on taxes, *depreciation is considered an important component of real estate investments.*

Appreciation in Value

An investment evaluation of a proposed piece of real estate should include not only the recurring cash flows from the property, but also expected changes in property values. In most cases, such appreciation has a much greater impact on rate of return than does the net annual cash flow from the property. Hence, if the market price of the real estate is expected to increase

 The return on a real estate investment is determined by the relationship between the expected future cash flows relative to the initial investment, which is typically reduced by using a significant amount of borrowed funds.

Cash Flow and Taxes

The after-tax *cash flow* on a real estate investment depends on the revenues generated by the property, on any operating expenses, and on depreciation and taxes. Real estate typically provides large depreciation write-offs that tend to lower the taxable income of certain (*qualified*) investors. Depreciation gives the property owner an allowance for the decline in the physical condition of real estate over time. Although it's a bookkeeping entry that's considered an expense for tax purposes, it involves no actual outflow of cash. Depreciation can result in lower taxes; for this reason, it's viewed as a *tax shelter.* For tax purposes, real estate is considered a *passive* investment. Therefore, the amount of expenses, *including depreciation,* that can be written off is generally limited to the amount of income generated by this and any other passive investments owned by the investor. For example, if you owned some apartments that generated $25,000 a year in rental income and if you had mortgage interest and other operating expenses of $20,000 annually, then you might be able to write off up to $5,000 in depreciation ($25,000 income minus $20,000 other expenses). However, if your *adjusted gross income (AGI)* is less than $100,000 a year, then you might be able to write off even more depreciation—specifically, as much as $25,000 in losses on *rented real estate* can be used to offset the ordinary income of people who "actively participate" in the rental activity of the buildings *and* whose AGI is less than $100,000. In this example, if you had $90,000 in adjusted gross income and $15,000 in depreciation expense, then $5,000 of it could be written off as before against the remaining

by $100,000, then that price appreciation should be treated as capital gains and included as part of the return from the investment (minus, of course, the capital gains taxes paid).

Use of Leverage

A big attraction for investing in real estate is the high degree of financial leverage that it permits. Leverage involves using borrowed money to magnify returns. Because real estate is a tangible asset, investors can borrow as much as 75 percent to 90 percent of its cost. As a result, if the profit rate on the investment is greater than the cost of borrowing, then the return on a leveraged investment will be *proportionally greater* than the return generated from an unleveraged investment. For example, imagine that you're considering a real estate investment costing $100,000. Let's assume that you can purchase the property in one of two ways: you can either pay cash for it or you can put up $10,000 of your own money and borrow the remaining $90,000 at, say, 10 percent annual interest. If the property earns $13,000 per year after expenses, then the leveraged investment will provide a much better rate of return than the cash deal.

13-4b Speculating in Raw Land

Investing in real estate can take several forms. One approach that's popular with many investors is to *speculate in raw land.* In this approach, *which is often viewed as highly risky,* investors seek to generate high rates of return by investing in property that they *hope* will undergo dramatic increases in value. The key to such speculation is to isolate areas of potential population growth and/or real estate demand (ideally, before anyone else does) and purchase property in these areas in anticipation of their eventual development.

13-4c Investing in Income Property

One of the most popular forms of real estate investing is the purchase of **income (or income-producing) property**, including both commercial and residential properties. Investments in income properties offer both attractive returns and tax advantages for investors. The purchased real estate is leased to tenants to generate income from rent. And although the primary purpose of investing in income property is to produce an attractive annual cash flow, certain types of strategically located income properties also offer attractive opportunities for appreciation in value. Before buying income property, be sure you know what you're getting into. The owner of income property is responsible for leasing the units and maintaining the property.

Calculating the value of income-producing property requires estimating the annual net operating income (NOI), *which equals gross rental income (less an allowance for vacancies and bad debts) minus all operating expenses, such as property (but not income) taxes, insurance, maintenance, and so on.* Once you have a property's NOI, you can apply a *cap rate* (the expected annual rate of return on the property) to arrive at an estimated value for the property. A typical cap rate for income property is around 9 percent or 10 percent. For example, assume that you're thinking about buying an office building that generates an estimated $50,000 per year in NOI. With a 9 percent cap rate, that property would have an estimated value of some $555,000 (i.e., $50,000/0.09 = $555,556).

Commercial Properties

Commercial income properties consists of everything from office buildings, industrial space, and warehouses to retail space and hotels. The risks and returns on commercial real estate investments are tied to business conditions and location. The value of commercial property, especially retail businesses, is enhanced by a location in a high-traffic area. Because commercial properties call for professional management and involve significant expenses, investing in this category of income property is generally the domain of more seasoned real estate investors.

Residential Properties

First-time investors often choose income-producing *residential properties*, such as homes, apartments, and smaller multifamily buildings. This category of income property is available in various sizes, prices, and types ranging from single family homes, duplexes and triplexes to large apartment buildings. Aside from the considerations of purchase and financing costs, major factors influencing the profitability of these investments are the occupancy rates—the percentage of available space rented over the year—and maintenance and management costs. Other factors to consider are the neighborhood where the units are located, local regulations regarding tenants, and supply and demand trends for the type of property.

income (income-producing) property Real estate purchased for leasing or renting to tenants in order to generate ongoing monthly/annual income in the form of rent receipts.

real estate investment trust (REIT) An investment company that accumulates money, by selling shares to investors, in order to invest it in various forms of real estate including mortgages; similar to a mutual fund, but REITs invest only in specific types of real estate or real estate–related products.

Go to Smart Sites

Need investing ideas for which ETFs to add to your portfolio? Read the Blog at iShare's site, or follow them on Twitter: @iSharesETFs. ●

13-4d Other Ways to Invest in Real Estate

Another way to own real estate is by purchasing specialized securities. For example, you can buy shares in a *real estate mutual fund* (discussed earlier in this chapter). Or you can buy stock in *publicly traded real estate–related companies*. These include residential homebuilders, construction companies, mortgage lenders, home improvement retailers, and real estate brokerage firms. Let's now look at two of these investment vehicles: *real estate investment trusts (REITs)* and *real estate limited partnerships* (LPs; otherwise known as *limited liability companies*, or *LLCs*).

Real Estate Investment Trusts

Arguably the best way for most individuals to invest in real estate is through a **real estate investment trust (REIT)**, which is a type of closed-end investment company that invests money in various types of real estate and real estate mortgages. REITs are like mutual funds in that they sell shares of stock to the investing public and use the proceeds, along with borrowed funds, to invest in a portfolio of real estate investments. The investor therefore owns part of the real estate portfolio held by the REIT. REITs appeal to investors because they offer the benefits of real estate ownership without the headaches of property management. REITs are popular with investors because they have relatively low correlations with other market sectors, such as common stocks and bonds. In addition, they provide attractive dividend yields—well above the yields on common stocks. And they produce competitive returns. In fact, the compound annual return from equity REITs for the last 30 years was 11.71 percent, compared to 10.71 percent for the S&P 500. The performance of REITs over this period is significantly influenced by the real estate losses resulting from the financial crisis of 2007–2009. However, the one-year return from mid-2011 to mid-2012 on equity REITs was 15.85 percent and the three-year return was 23.64 percent, which suggests that the REIT market has recovered somewhat. REITs can be particularly attractive investments during periods of high inflation, which is projected to result from the large deficit spending induced by the financial crisis of 2007–2009.

Like any investment fund, each REIT has certain stated investment objectives, which should be considered carefully before acquiring shares. There are three basic types of REITs:

- **Equity REITs.** They own and operate income-producing real estate such as office buildings and hotels.
- **Mortgage REITs.** These make both construction and mortgage loans to real estate investors.
- **Hybrid REITs.** They invest in both income-producing properties and mortgage loans.

Equity REITs produce both attractive current yields and the potential to earn excellent capital gains as their properties appreciate in value. In contrast, mortgage REITs tend to be more income oriented; they emphasize the high current yields they generate by investing in debt. Equity REITs are the dominant investment vehicle, accounting for 90 percent of the market, followed by mortgage REITs. The income earned by a REIT isn't taxed, but *the income distributed to owners is designated and taxed as ordinary income*. Whereas dividends on common stocks normally are taxed at preferential rates (of 15 percent or less), this is not the case with REITs, whose cash dividends are treated as ordinary income and taxed accordingly.

Real Estate Limited Partnerships or Limited Liability Companies

Special-purpose syndicates organized to invest in real estate are another type of real estate investment. These can be structured as limited partnerships (LPs) or limited liability companies (LLCs). With LPs, the managers assume the role of *general partner,* which means their liability is unlimited and that the other investors are *limited partners* who are legally liable only for the amount of their initial investment. In recent years, the LLC has become a more popular way to form these entities. Rather than general and limited partners, the LLC has a managing member and other members—none of whom have any liability. Investors buy *units* in an LP or LLC; a unit represents an ownership position that is similar to a share of stock. Real estate LPs and LLCs are highly illiquid and are felt to be far riskier investments than REITs. As a rule, they tend to appeal to more affluent investors, who can afford the typical cost of $100,000 per unit or more.

Financial Planning Tips: How to Choose the Best REIT for Your Portfolio

REITs can provide diversification benefits for your portfolio because they often perform differently than the major equity market indexes. Here are some important factors to consider in choosing the best REIT for your portfolio:

- **Adjusted funds from operations (AFFO).** This is earnings plus depreciation minus capital expenditures. It measures the cash flow generated by a REIT after netting the investment required to be productive. AFFO consequently is the source of REIT distributions to investors and its level and variability provides insight into the sustainability of those distributions. Other factors being constant, an increasing trend with limited variability is attractive.
- **NAV.** The NAV of a REIT is the appraised value of the real estate portfolio minus the borrowings of the REIT. It is helpful to compare a REIT's NAV to industry averages. If a REIT is trading at several times the normal industry NAV, then it's quite possibly overvalued. Similarly, if the NAV is trading at a big discount, it is either undervalued or in trouble. And you're way ahead in the game if you can figure out which is which.
- **Loan-to-value ratios.** Other things being equal, the lower the ratio, the safer is the REIT.
- **Property holdings.** If you're interested in investing in a REIT, find out what properties they own, where they're located, and consider even visiting them. Determine if they are well maintained and occupied and if the associated businesses are occupied. Actually visiting the properties is seldom done by most investors, but doing that could provide you with some real insights.

Source: Adapted from "How to Invest in REITs," http://www.thickenmywallet.com/blog/wp/2009/07/13/how-to-invest-in-reits/, accessed September 2012.

Planning Over a Lifetime: Investing in Mutual Funds, ETFs, and Real Estate

Here are some key considerations for investment planning in each stage of the life cycle.

Pre-family Independence: 20s	Family Formation/Career Development: 30–45	Pre-Retirement: 45–65	Retirement: 65 and Beyond
✓ Determine your major investment goals and how much money needs to be invested each month to achieve them.	✓ Revise investments in mutual funds, ETFs, and real estate to focus more on retirement and funding children's education, if applicable.	✓ Revise your investment plan in light of recent developments.	✓ Revise your investment plan to lean more toward debt and cash instruments than to stocks in your mutual funds and ETFs.
✓ Determine your asset allocation among stocks, bonds, real estate, and cash based on your time horizon and attitude toward risk. Choose mutual funds and ETFs accordingly.	✓ Review your asset allocation and rebalance it to be more consistent with your goals.	✓ Review your asset allocation and rebalance investments among mutual funds, ETFs, and real estate if it is inconsistent with your goals.	✓ Review your asset allocation, and rebalance it if it is inconsistent with your goals.
✓ Match your investments in any employer-sponsored 401(k) retirement plan with your overall asset allocation plan.	✓ Gradually increase the amount invested in any employer-sponsored 401(k) retirement plan and re-evaluate how it relates to your asset allocation plan.	✓ Continue to gradually increase the amount you invest in any employer-sponsored 401(k) retirement plan and re-evaluate how it relates to your asset allocation plan.	✓ Integrate investment asset allocation strategy with estate planning.
✓ Consider investing in mutual funds and ETFs under a traditional IRA, a Roth IRA, or both.	✓ Consider increasing your contribution to traditional IRA, a Roth IRA, or both.	✓ Consider increasing your contribution to traditional and/or Roth IRAs using mutual funds and ETFs.	✓ Plan carefully for mandatory withdrawals from tax-sheltered accounts and associated tax consequences.

FINANCIAL PLANNING EXERCISES

LG1, 2

1. Kate Wittman is considering whether she should invest some extra money in a mutual fund or an ETF. Explain the key factors that should influence her decision.

LG4

2. For *each pair* of funds listed below, select the fund that would be the *least* risky and briefly explain your answer.
   a. Growth versus growth-and-income
   b. Equity-income versus high-grade corporate bonds
   c. Intermediate-term bonds versus high-yield municipals
   d. International versus balanced

LG5

3. About a year ago, Nigel Palmer bought some shares in the Equity Partners Fund. He bought the stock at $24.50 a share, and it now trades at $26.00. Last year, the fund paid dividends of 40 cents a share and had capital gains distributions of $1.83 a share. Using the approximate yield formula, what rate of return did Nigel earn on his investment? Repeat the calculation using a handheld financial calculator. Would he have made a 20 percent rate of return if the stock had risen to $30 a share?

LG2, 3

4. Describe an ETF and explain how these funds combine the characteristics of open- and closed-end funds. In the Vanguard family of funds, which would most closely resemble a "Spider" (SPDR)? In what respects are the Vanguard fund (that you selected) and SPDRs the same and how are they different? If you could invest in only one of them, which would it be? Explain.

LG4, 5

5. Do an online search and see what information you can find on the PowerShares QQQ ETF. Discuss what information you need to evaluate the performance of the ETF, and use what you find to evaluate the QQQ ETF. What kind of investor should invest in this ETF?

LG5

6. A year ago, the Alpine Growth Fund was being quoted at an NAV of $21.50 and an offer price of $23.35; today, it's being quoted at $23.04 (NAV) and $25.04 (offer). Use the approximate yield formula or a handheld financial calculator to find the rate of return on this load fund; it was purchased a year ago, and its dividends and capital gains distributions over the year totaled $1.05 a share. (*Hint:* As an investor, you buy fund shares at the offer price and sell at the NAV.)

LG6

7. Lilia Castillo is thinking about investing in some residential income-producing property that she can purchase for $200,000. Lilia can either pay cash for the full amount of the property or put up $50,000 of her own money and borrow the remaining $150,000 at 8 percent interest. The property is expected to generate $30,000 per year after all expenses but *before* interest and income taxes. Assume that Lilia is in the 28 percent tax bracket. Calculate her annual profit and return on investment assuming that she (a) pays the full $200,000 from her own funds or (b) borrows $150,000 at 8 percent. Then discuss the effect, if any, of leverage on her rate of return. (*Hint:* Earnings Before Interest & Taxes *minus* Interest Expenses (if any) *equals* Earnings Before Taxes *minus* Income Taxes (@28 percent) *equals* Profit After Taxes.)

PFIN Student Study Tools—Visit CourseMate for PFIN 3. Log in at **www.cengagebrain.com**. Check out the bonus exercises and exhibits, interactive worksheets, Smart Sites, Critical Thinking Cases, Money Online, Kiplinger videos, quizzing, and more.

Cool Apps—Look for this new feature on CourseMate for PFIN 3. Cool Apps navigates the growing world of apps that are available for personal financial planning and tracking.

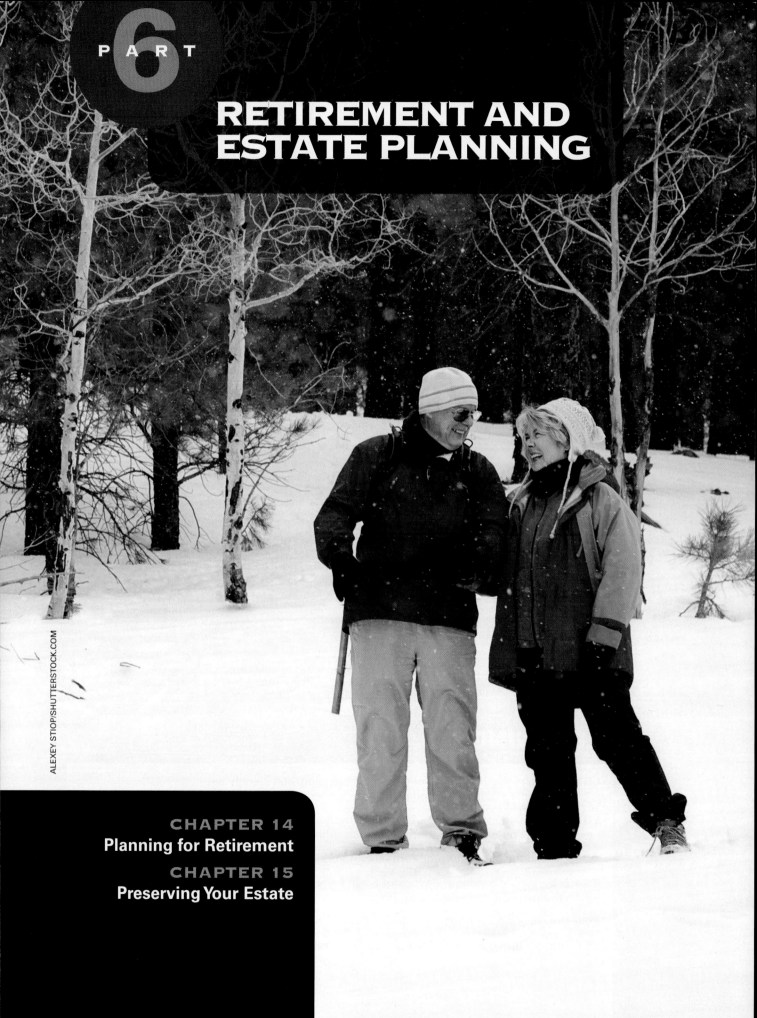

PART 6

RETIREMENT AND ESTATE PLANNING

14

PLANNING FOR RETIREMENT

LEARNING GOALS

LG1 Recognize the importance of retirement planning, and identify the three biggest pitfalls to good planning.

LG2 Estimate your income needs in retirement and the level of retirement income you've estimated from various sources.

LG3 Explain the eligibility requirements and benefits of the Social Security program.

LG4 Differentiate among the types of basic and supplemental employer-sponsored pension plans.

LG5 Describe the various types of self-directed retirement plans.

LG6 Choose the right type of annuity for your retirement plan.

How Will This Affect Me? While almost everyone understands that planning for retirement is important, far too few people actually implement a comprehensive plan, much less set aside enough savings to fund their retirement adequately. This chapter discusses the importance of retirement planning and encourages action by identifying the major pitfalls that you must overcome. In order to make the process more concrete and accessible, the steps for estimating your retirement income needs and the income that your investments will support are explained. Eligibility requirements to receive Social Security benefits and their amounts are detailed, as well as the key aspects of supplemental employer-sponsored pension plans and the potential benefits of self-directed retirement programs like traditional and Roth individual retirement accounts (IRAs). In addition, the usefulness of various annuity products in retirement planning is evaluated. After reading this chapter, you should understand how to develop and implement a financial plan that will help you achieve your long-term retirement objectives.

14-1 An Overview of Retirement Planning

LG1, LG2 Retiring is easy. What's difficult is retiring in style, and that's where retirement planning comes into play! But to enjoy a comfortable retirement, you must *start now*—for one of the biggest mistakes people make in retirement planning is waiting too long to begin. Accumulating adequate retirement funds is a daunting task that takes careful planning. Like budgets, taxes, and investments, retirement planning is vital to your financial well-being and is a critical link in your personal financial plans.

ZULUFOTO/SHUTTERSTOCK.COM

14-1a Role of Retirement Planning in Personal Financial Planning

The financial planning process would be incomplete without retirement planning. Certainly no financial goal is more important than achieving a comfortable standard of living in retirement. In many respects, retirement planning captures the very essence of financial planning. It is forward-looking, affects both your current and future standard of living, and can be highly rewarding and contribute significantly to your net worth.

The first step in retirement planning is to set *retirement goals* for yourself. Take some time to describe the things you want to do in retirement, the standard of living you hope to maintain, the level of income you'd like to receive, and any special retirement goals you may have (like buying a retirement home in Florida). Such goals are important because *they give direction to your retirement planning*. Of course, like all goals, they're subject to change over time as the situations and conditions in your life change.

Once you know what you want out of retirement, the next step is to establish the *size of the nest egg* that you're going to need to achieve your retirement goals. And while you're at it, you'll also want to formulate an *investment program* that'll enable you to build up your required nest egg. This usually involves (1) creating some type of systematic savings plan in which you put away a certain amount of money each year and (2) identifying the types of investment vehicles that will best meet your retirement needs.

Investments and investment planning are the vehicles for building up your retirement funds. They're the active, ongoing part of retirement planning in which you invest and manage the funds you've set aside for retirement. It's no

> ## Like budgets, taxes, and investments, retirement planning is vital to your financial well-being and is a critical link in your personal financial plans.

coincidence that a major portion of most individual investor portfolios is devoted to building up a pool of funds for retirement. Tax planning is also important because a major objective of sound retirement planning is to shield as much income as possible from taxes legitimately and, in so doing, maximize the accumulation of retirement funds.

After you read the chapter, explore the STUDY TOOLS listed on page 356.

14-1b The Three Biggest Pitfalls to Sound Retirement Planning

Human nature being what it is, people often get a little carried away with the amount of money they want to build up for retirement. Having a nest egg of $4 million or $5 million would be great, but it's beyond the reach of most people. Besides, you don't need that much to live comfortably in retirement. So set a more realistic goal. But when you set that goal, remember: it's not going to happen by itself; you'll have to do something to bring it about. And this is precisely where things start to fall apart. Why? Because when it comes to retirement planning, people tend to make three big mistakes:

● Starting too late.

● Putting away too little.

● Investing too conservatively.

Many people in their 20s, or even 30s, find it hard to put money away for retirement. Most often that's because they have other, more pressing financial concerns—such as buying a house, paying off a student loan, or paying for child care. The net result is that they *put off retirement planning until later in life*— in many cases, until they're in their late 30s or 40s. Unfortunately, the longer people put it off, the less they're going to have in retirement. Or they won't to be able to retire as early as they'd hoped. Even worse, once people start a retirement program, *they tend to put away too little*. Although this may also be due to pressing financial needs, all too often it boils down to lifestyle choices. They'd rather spend today than save for tomorrow.

On top of all this, many *people tend to be far too conservative* in the way that they invest their retirement money. The fact is, they place way too much of their retirement money into *low-yielding*, fixed-income securities such as CDs and Treasury notes. Although you should *never speculate* with something as important as your retirement plan, there's no need to avoid risk totally. There's nothing wrong with following an investment program that involves a reasonable amount of risk, provided that it results in a correspondingly higher level of expected return. Being overly cautious can be costly in the long run. Indeed, a low rate of return can have an enormous impact on the long-term accumulation of capital and, in many cases, may mean the difference between just getting by or enjoying a comfortable retirement.

Compounding the Errors

All three of these pitfalls become even more important when we introduce *compound interest*. That's because *compounding essentially magnifies the impact of these mistakes*. As an illustration, consider the first variable—starting too late. If you were to start a retirement program at age 35 by putting away $2,000 a year, it would grow to almost $160,000 by the time you're 65 if invested at an average rate of return of 6 percent. Not a bad deal. But look at what you end up with if you start this investment program just 10 years earlier, at age 25: that same $2,000 a year will grow to over $309,000 by the time you're 65. Think of it—for another $20,000 ($2,000 a year for an extra 10 years), you can nearly double the terminal value of your investment! Of course, it's not the extra $20,000 that's doubling your money; rather, it's *compound interest* that's doing most of the work.

The same holds true for the rate of return that you earn on the investments in your retirement account. Take the second situation just described—starting a retirement program at age 25. Earning 6 percent yields a retirement nest egg of over $309,000; increase that rate of return to 8 percent and your retirement nest egg will be worth just over $518,000! *You're still putting in the same amount of money*, but because your money is working harder, you end up with a much bigger nest egg. Of course, when you seek higher returns, that generally means you also have to take on more risks. But not everyone can tolerate higher levels of risk. And if that applies to you, then simply stay away from the higher-risk investments. Instead, stick to safer, lower-yielding securities and find some other way to build up your nest egg. For instance, contribute more each year to your plan or extend the length of your investment period. The only other option—and not a particularly appealing one—is to accept the possibility that you won't be able to build up as big a nest egg as you had thought and therefore will have to accept a lower standard of living in retirement.

14-1c Estimating Income Needs

Retirement planning would be much simpler if we lived in a static economy. Unfortunately (or perhaps fortunately), we don't, so you'll have to live with the fact that both your personal budget and the general state of the economy will change over time. This makes accurate forecasting of retirement needs difficult at best. Even so, you'll have to live with the fact that it's a necessary task, and you can handle it in one of two ways. One strategy is to plan for retirement over *a series of short-run time frames*. A good way to do this is to state your retirement income objectives as a percentage of your present earnings. Then, every 3 to 5 years, you can revise and update your plan.

Alternatively, you can follow *a long-term approach* in which you formulate the level of income that you'd like to receive in retirement, along with the amount of funds that you must amass to achieve that desired standard of living. Rather than addressing the problem in a series of short-run plans, this approach goes 20 or 30 years into the future—to the time when you'll retire—in determining how much saving and investing you must do today in order to achieve your long-run retirement goals. Of course, if conditions or expectations should happen to change dramatically in the future, then it may be necessary to make corresponding alterations to your long-run retirement goals and strategies.

Determining Future Retirement Needs

To illustrate how future retirement needs and income requirements can be formulated, let's consider the case of Jared and Trish Roberts. In their mid-30s, they have two children and an annual income of about $80,000 before taxes. Even though it's still some 30 years away, Jared and Trish recognize it's now time to seriously consider their situation to see if they'll be able to pursue the kind of retirement lifestyle that appeals to them. Worksheet 14.1 provides the basic steps to follow in determining retirement needs. It shows how the Robertses have estimated their retirement income and determined the amount of investment assets they must accumulate to meet their retirement objectives.

Jared and Trish began by determining what their *household expenditures* will likely be in retirement. A simple way to derive an estimate of expected household expenditures is to base it on the current level of such expenses. Assume that the Robertses' annual household expenditures (*excluding savings*) currently run about $56,000 a year (this information can be readily obtained by referring to their most recent income and expenditures statement). After making some obvious adjustments for the different lifestyle they'll have in retirement—e.g., their children will no longer be living at home, their home will be paid for, and so on—the Robertses estimate that they should be able to achieve the standard of living they'd like in retirement at an annual level of household expenses equal to about 70 percent of the current amount. Thus, *based on today's dollars*, their estimated household expenditures in retirement will be $56,000 × 0.70 = $39,200. (This process is summarized in steps A through D in Worksheet 14.1.)

Estimating Retirement Income

The next question is: Where will the Robertses get the money to meet their projected household expenses of $39,200 a year? They've addressed this problem by estimating what their *income* will be in retirement—again *based on today's dollars*. Their two basic sources of retirement income are Social Security and employer-sponsored pension plans. They estimate that they'll receive about $24,000 a year from Social Security and another $9,000 from their employer pension plans, for a total projected annual income of $33,000. When comparing this figure to their projected household expenditures, it's clear that the Robertses will be facing an annual shortfall of $6,200 (see steps E through I in Worksheet 14.1). This is the amount of

additional retirement income they must come up with; otherwise, they'll have to reduce their standard of living they hope to enjoy in retirement.

At this point, we need to introduce the *inflation factor* to our projections in order to put the annual shortfall of $6,200 in terms of retirement dollars. Here we assume that both income and expenditures will undergo approximately the same average annual rate of inflation, which will cause the shortfall to grow by that rate over time. In essence, 30 years from now, the annual shortfall is going to amount to a lot more than $6,200. How large this number becomes will, of course, depend on what happens to inflation. Assume that the Robertses expect inflation over the next 30 years to average 5 percent; that's a bit on the high side by today's standards, but the Robertses are concerned that the ballooning federal deficit will cause inflation to rise. Using the compound value table from Appendix A, we find that the *inflation factor* for 5 percent and 30 years is 4.322; multiplying this inflation factor by the annual shortfall of $6,200 gives the Roberts an idea of what that figure will be by the time they retire: $6,200 × 4.322 = $26,796 (see steps J to L in Worksheet 14.1). Thus, based on their projections, the shortfall should amount to about $26,796 a year when they retire 30 years from now. *This is the annual shortfall they'll have to cover using their own supplemental retirement program.*

Funding the Shortfall

The final two steps in the Robertses' estimation process are to determine (1) *how big the retirement nest egg must be* to cover the projected annual income shortfall

A worksheet like this one will help you define your income requirements in retirement, the size of your retirement nest egg, and the amount you must save annually to achieve your retirement goals.

PROJECTING RETIREMENT INCOME AND INVESTMENT NEEDS

Name(s) _Jared and Trish Roberts_ Date _8/31/2015_

I. Estimated Household Expenditures in Retirement:

A. Approximate number of years to retirement _____ 30

B. Current level of annual household expenditures, excluding savings $ _56,000_

C. Estimated household expenses in retirement as a *percent* of current *expenses* _____ 70 %

D. Estimated annual household expenditures in retirement (B × C) $ _39,200_

II. Estimated Income in Retirement:

E. Social Security, annual income $ _24,000_

F. Company/employer pension plans, annual amounts $ _9,000_

G. Other sources, annual amounts $ _0_

H. Total annual income (E + F + G) $ _33,000_

I. Additional required income, or annual shortfall (D − H) $ _6,200_

III. Inflation Factor:

J. Expected average annual rate of inflation over the period to retirement _____ 5 %

K. Inflation factor (in Appendix A):   Based on _30_ years to retirement (A) and an expected average annual rate of inflation (J) of _5 %_ _____ 4.322

L. Size of inflation-adjusted annual shortfall (I × K) $ _26,796_

IV. Funding the Shortfall:

M. Anticipated return on assets held *after* retirement _____ 8 %

N. Amount of retirement funds required—size of nest egg (L ÷ M) $ _334,950_

O. Expected rate of return on investments *prior* to retirement _____ 6 %

P. Compound interest factor (in Appendix B):
   Based on _30_ years to retirement (A) and an expected rate of return on investments of _6 %_ _____ 79.058

Q. Annual savings required to fund retirement nest egg (N ÷ P) $ _4,237_

Note: Parts I and II are prepared in terms of current (today's) dollars. Parts III and IV can be computed with a handheld calculator that has a time value function.

© Cengage Learning

and (2) *how much to save each year* to accumulate the required amount by the time they retire. To find out how much money they need to accumulate by retirement, they must estimate the rate of return they think they'll be able to earn on their investments *after* they retire. This will tell them how big their nest egg will have to be by retirement in order to eliminate the expected annual shortfall of $26,796. Let's assume that this rate of return is estimated at 8 percent, in which case the Robertses must accumulate $334,950 by retirement. This figure is found by *capitalizing* the estimated shortfall of $26,796 at an 8 percent rate of return: $26,796/0.08 = $334,950 (see steps M and N). Given an 8 percent rate of return, such a nest egg will yield $26,796 a year:

$334,950 × 0.08 = $26,796. So long as the capital ($334,950) remains untouched, it will generate the same amount of annual income for as long as the Robertses live and can eventually become a part of their estate.

Go to Smart Sites

E*TRADE's Retirement Planning Calculator can walk you through any number of hypothetical savings and retirement scenarios. For more online resources, whenever you see "*Go to Smart Sites*" in this chapter, visit CourseMate for PFIN 3. Log in at **www.cengagebrain.com**. ●

BEHAVIOR MATTERS

Behavioral Biases in Retirement Planning

Theory argues that the rational investor is good at forecasting retirement needs by considering expected future lifetime earnings, investment returns, tax rates, family and health situation, and expected longevity. However, research indicates that most people save too little, make questionable investment decisions, and tend to spend their accumulated assets too quickly in retirement. Alarmingly, surveys indicate that people are not particularly good at planning and saving for retirement. About 40 percent of people have not calculated how much they need to retire, 30 percent haven't saved a significant amount, and only 20 percent feel confident that they can live comfortably in retirement.

There are some behavioral biases that explain this disturbing lack of preparation for retirement. Recognizing them is more than half of the battle:

- **Self-control.** Most people *intend* to save and plan, but they do not actually get around to doing so. Commitment approaches like "pay yourself first" and automatic 401(k) deductions are helpful ways to modify behavior to encourage saving and planning follow-through.
- **Choice overload.** Faced with complex retirement investment choices, many people just give up and choose a default or even decide not to participate in an employer-offered plan. Making the decision to ask for help can make all the difference.
- **Inertia in managing retirement investments.** Many people tend to "anchor" on their *initial* retirement account investment mix and don't revise it enough over their lives. Recognizing this tendency and scheduling periodic investment reviews with an advisor can limit any resulting damage to your retirement accounts.
- **Representativeness and availability biases.** People tend to view recent investment returns as overly representative of returns in general and are inclined to overweight them in their decision making. For example, just because a mutual fund was a top performer last year does not mean that it will be next year. Similarly, many people tend to rely on the most readily available information in making investment decisions. Just because data are easy to get does not mean they are sufficient to the task.
- **Overconfidence.** Many retirement investors are overconfident in their choices and consequently do not diversify their investments enough.

Source: Adapted from Olivia S. Mitchell and Stephen P. Utkus, "How Behavior Can Inform Retirement Plan Design," *Journal of Applied Corporate Finance,* Winter 2006, pp. 82–94.

Calculator Keystrokes

As you might have suspected, the last few steps in the worksheet can just as easily be done on a handheld financial calculator. For example, consider Part III, *the inflation-adjusted annual shortfall.* With the calculator in the *annual mode,* you can determine how big the current annual shortfall of $6,200 will grow to in 30 years (given an average annual inflation rate of 5 percent) by using these keystrokes, where:

N = number of *years* to retirement
I/Y = *expected* annual rate of inflation
PV = additional required annual income (line I in Worksheet 14.1), entered as a *negative number*

Hit CPT (FV) and you should end up with an answer (FV) that is close to $26,796 (see step L in Worksheet 14.1); in this case, it's $26,796.04.

Now take a look at Part IV, *funding the shortfall* (step Q in Worksheet 14.1). Again, with the calculator in the *annual mode,* to find the amount that must be put away annually to fund a $334,950 retirement nest egg in 30 years (given an expected return of 6 percent), use the keystrokes shown here, where:

N = number of *years* over which the retirement nest egg is to be accumulated
I/Y = *expected* annual return on invested capital
FV = the size of the targeted nest egg, entered as a *negative number*

Hit CPT (PMT) and a value of 4,236.75 should appear in the display, indicating the amount you must put away annually to reach a target of $334,950 in 30 years.

Now that the Robertses know how big their nest egg must be, the final question is: How are they going to accumulate such an amount by the time they retire? For most people, that means setting up a *systematic savings plan* and putting away a certain amount *each* year. To find out how much must be saved each year to achieve a targeted sum in the future, we can use the table of annuity factors in Appendix B. The appropriate interest factor depends on of the rate of return one can or expects to generate and the length of the investment period. In the Robertses' case, there are

CALCULATOR

Inputs	Functions
30	N
5.0	I/Y
–6,200	PV
	CPT
	FV
	Solution
	26,796.04

SEE APPENDIX E FOR DETAILS.

CALCULATOR

Inputs	Functions
30	N
6.0	I/Y
–334,950	FV
	CPT
	PMT
	Solution
	4,236.75

SEE APPENDIX E FOR DETAILS.

30 years to go until retirement, meaning that the length of their investment period is 30 years. Suppose that they believe they can earn a 6 percent average rate of return on their investments over this 30-year period. From Appendix B, we see that the 6 percent, 30-year interest factor is 79.058. Because the Robertses must accumulate $334,950 by the time they retire, *the amount they'll* *have to save each year* (over the next 30 years) can be found by *dividing* the amount they need to accumulate by the appropriate interest factor; that is, $334,950 / 79.058 = $4,237 (see steps O to Q in Worksheet 14.1).

The Robertses now know what they must do to achieve the kind of retirement they want: *Put away $4,237 a year and invest it at an average annual rate of 6 percent over the next 30 years.* If they can do that, then they'll have their $334,950 retirement nest egg in 30 years. How they actually invest their money so as to achieve the desired 6 percent rate of return will, of course, depend on the investment vehicles and strategies they use. All the worksheet tells them is how much money they'll need, not how they will get there; it's at this point that investment management enters the picture.

14-1d Sources of Retirement Income

As seen in Exhibit 14.1, the principal sources of income for retired people are Social Security, earnings from income-producing assets (such as savings, stocks, and

© KAREN HERMANN/ISTOCKPHOTO

Exhibit 14.1   Sources of Income for the Average Retiree

Social Security is the single largest source of income for the average U.S. retiree. This source alone is larger than the amount the average retiree receives from pension plans and personal wealth/investment assets *combined*.

Percentage distribution of sources of income for married couples and nonmarried people who are age 65 and over, 1962–2010

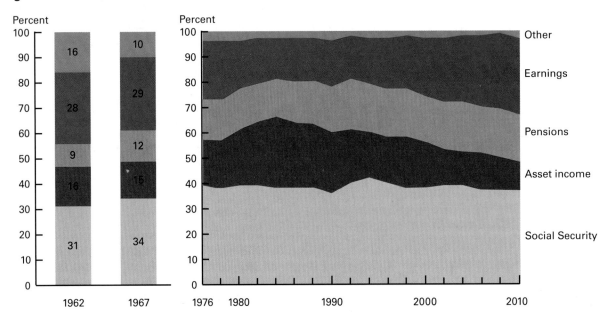

Note: A married couple is age 65 and over if the husband is age 65 and over or the husband is younger than age 55 and the wife is age 65 and over. The definition of "other" includes, but is not limited to, public assistance, unemployment compensation, worker's compensation, alimony, child support, and personal contributions. Reference population: These data refer to the civilian noninstitutionalized population.

Source: Federal Interagency Forum on Aging-Related Statistics, *Older Americans 2012: Key Indicators of Well-Being*, Indicator 9, June 2012, p. 14, http://www.aoa.gov/Agingstatsdotnet/Main_Site/Default.aspx, accessed September 2012.

bonds), earnings generated from full- or part-time jobs, and pension plans. As of 2010, the largest source of income was Social Security, which represented about 37 percent of total retiree income. In recent years, earned income has accounted for a growing amount of total retirement income, as more and more people continue to work in retirement as a way to supplement their other sources of income. Keep in mind that these are percentage *sources* of retirement income and not dollar amounts. The *amount* of income retired individuals will receive, of course, will vary from amounts that are barely above the poverty line to six-figure incomes. Obviously, the more that individuals make before they retire, the more that they'll receive in Social Security benefits (up to a point) and from company-sponsored pension plans—and, very likely, the greater the amount of income-producing assets that they'll hold.

14-2 Social Security

LG3 The Social Security Act of 1935 was landmark legislation. It created a basic retirement program for working Americans at all income levels, and it established several other social programs, all administered under the auspices of the *Old Age, Survivor's, Disability, and Health Insurance (OASDHI) program*. Some of the other services include supplementary security income (SSI), Medicare, unemployment insurance, public assistance, welfare services, and provision for black lung benefits. In this section, we give primary attention to the old age and survivor's portions of the act because they bear directly on retirement planning. We discussed the disability and health/Medicare benefits of Social Security in Chapter 9.

14-2a Coverage

Social Security coverage today extends to nearly all gainfully employed workers. Only two major classes of employees are exempt from *mandatory* participation in the Social Security system: (1) federal *civilian* employees who were hired before 1984 and are covered under the Civil Service Retirement System, and (2) employees of state and local governments who have chosen not to be covered (although most of these employees are covered through *voluntary participation* in Social Security). Certain marginal employment positions, such as newspaper carriers under age 18 and full-time college students working in fraternity and sorority houses, are also exempt.

To obtain Social Security benefits, an application must be filed with the Social Security Administration, which then determines the applicant's eligibility for benefits based on whether he or she has had enough quarters (three-month periods) of participation in the system. To qualify for full retirement benefits, workers must be employed in a job covered by Social Security

for at least 40 quarters, or 10 years. These quarters need not be consecutive. The surviving spouse and dependent children of a *deceased worker* are also eligible for monthly benefits if the worker was fully insured at the time of death.

14-2b Social Security Payroll Taxes

The cash benefits provided by Social Security are derived from the payroll (FICA) taxes paid by covered employees and their employers. The tax rate in 2012 was 4.2 percent for Social Security and 1.45 percent for Medicare, or a total of 5.65 percent. The Social Security rate is scheduled to rise to 6.2 percent in 2013. The reduction to 4.2 percent was brought by the Tax Relief Act of 2010 in response to the financial crisis. Employers paid a Social Security rate of 6.2 percent and a Medicare rate of 1.45 percent in 2012. Self-employed people are also covered by Social Security; in 2012, they had to pay a Social Security rate of 10.4 percent and a Medicare rate of 2.9 percent.

Whether the individual is an employee or self-employed, the indicated tax rate stays in effect only until the employee reaches a maximum *wage base*, which usually increases each year. For 2012, basic Social Security taxes were paid on the first $110,100 of wages earned or self-employed income. Thus, the maximum Social Security tax paid by an employee in 2012 was about $6,221 ($110,100 × 0.0565) and by the *self-employed* was about $14,643 ($110,100 × 0.1330). Note that, starting in 1991, a second tax was added to cover the rising costs of Medicare. Now, once the Social Security wage base is passed, the new, higher Medicare wage base kicks in, and employees become subject to a tax rate of 1.45 percent *on all earnings* over $110,100, whereas the added earnings of the self-employed are taxed at the rate of 2.9 percent.

14-2c Social Security Retirement Benefits

Basic Social Security benefits that are important to retired people and their dependents include (1) old-age benefits and (2) survivor's benefits. Both programs provide extended benefits to covered workers and their spouses.

Old-Age Benefits
Workers who are fully covered (that is, who have worked the required 40 quarters) may receive old-age benefits for life once they reach full retirement age. For anyone born in 1960 or later, the Social Security Administration defines "full retirement age" as age 67. (If you were born before 1960, your full retirement age is between 65 and 67; it can be calculated at **http://www.ssa.gov**. For our discussions here, we'll use 67 as the full retirement age.) Workers who elect to retire early—at age 62—will receive reduced benefits,

currently 70 percent to 80 percent of the full amount (again, depending on when they were born). If the retiree has a spouse age 67 or older, the spouse may be entitled to benefits equal to one-half of the amount received by the retired worker. For retirement planning purposes, it seems reasonable to expect Social Security to provide the average retired wage earner (who is married) with perhaps 40 percent to 60 percent of the wages that he or she was earning in the year before retirement. Clearly, by itself, Social Security is *insufficient to enable a worker and spouse to maintain their preretirement standard of living!*

In two-income families, both the husband and wife may be eligible for full Social Security benefits. When they retire, they can choose to receive their benefits in one of two ways: each can (1) take the full benefits to which each is entitled from his or her account or (2) take the husband and wife benefits of the higher-paid spouse. If each takes his or her own full share, there are no spousal benefits.

Survivor's Benefits

If a covered worker dies, the spouse can receive survivor's benefits from Social Security. These benefits include a small lump-sum payment of several hundred dollars, followed by monthly benefit checks. To be eligible for monthly payments, the surviving spouse generally must be at least 60 years of age or have a dependent and unmarried child of the deceased worker in his or her care. (To qualify for *full* benefits, the surviving spouse must be at least 67 years of age; reduced benefits are payable between ages 60 and 67.) If the children of a deceased worker reach age 16 before the spouse reaches age 60, the monthly benefits cease and do not resume until the spouse turns 60.

14-2d How Much Are Monthly Social Security Benefits?

The amount of Social Security benefits to which an eligible person is entitled is set by law and defined according to a fairly complex formula. But you don't need to worry about doing the math yourself; the Social Security Administration has a computerized service that does the benefits estimating for you. Indeed, the government is required by law to provide all covered workers with a *Social Security Statement.* You can request a statement

by going to the Social Security Administration Web site: **http://www.ssa.gov.** This statement lists the year-by-year Social Security earnings you've been credited with and shows (in today's dollars) what benefits you can expect under three scenarios: (1) if you retire at age 62 and receive 70 percent to 80 percent of the full benefit, (2) the full benefit at age 65 to 67, and (3) the increased benefit that's available if you delay retirement until age 70. The statement also estimates what your children and surviving spouse would get if you die and how much you'd receive monthly if you became disabled.

Range of Benefits

Using information provided by the Social Security Administration, we show the average *current average level of benefits* paid in mid-2012 in Exhibit 14.2. The benefits shown here are for retired workers, spouses, and children. Bear in mind that these amounts will be adjusted upward each year with subsequent increases in the cost of living.

Note that Social Security *may be reduced* if the recipient is *under age 67 and still gainfully employed*—perhaps in a part-time job. In particular, given that full retirement age is now 67, retirees aged 62 through 66 are subject to an earnings test that effectively limits the amount of income they can earn before they start losing some (or all) of their Social Security benefits. In 2012, that limit was $14,640 per year. The rule states that if you're a Social Security recipient aged 62 through 66, you will lose $1 in benefits for every $2 you earn above the earnings test amount. So if you earned, say, $18,000 a year at a part-time job, you'd lose $1,680 in annual Social Security benefits—that is, $18,000 − $14,640 = $3,360, which is divided in two to yield $1,680. *Once you reach "full retirement age," the earnings test no longer applies, so you can earn any amount without penalty*. In contrast to earned income, there never have been any limits on so-called unearned income derived from such sources as interest, dividends, rents, or profits on securities transactions—a retiree can receive an unlimited amount of such income with no reduction in benefits.

Taxes on Benefits

Even though Social Security "contributions" are made in after-tax dollars, you may actually have to pay taxes (again) on at least some of your Social Security benefits. Specifically, in 2012, *Social Security retirement benefits are subject to federal income taxes if the beneficiary's annual income exceeds one of the following base amounts: $25,000 for a single*

Exhibit 14.2 **Average Monthly Social Security Benefits Paid in Mid-2012**

© KAREN HERMANN/ISTOCKPHOTO

The Social Security benefits listed here are averages that include a variety of ages at which beneficiaries retired. As time passes, the beneficiary will receive correspondingly higher benefits as the cost of living goes up. However, these average benefits dramatize that you should not rely on such benefits too heavily in your retirement planning.

Type of Beneficiary	Average Monthly Benefit
Retired worker	$1,229
Retired couple	$1,994
Disabled worker	$1,111
Disabled worker with a spouse and child	$1,892
Widow or widower	$1,184
Young widow or widower with two children	$2,543

Source: "Understanding the Benefits," SSA Publication No. 05-10024, ICN 454930, http://www.socialsecurity.gov/pubs/10024.html#a0=8, accessed September 2012.

taxpayer, $32,000 for married taxpayers filing jointly, and zero for married taxpayers filing separately. In determining the amount of income that must be counted, the taxpayer starts with his or her *adjusted gross income (AGI)* as defined by current tax law (see Chapter 3) and then adds all nontaxable interest income (such as income from municipal bonds) plus a stipulated portion of the Social Security benefits received. For single taxpayers, if the resulting amount is between $25,000 and $34,000, 50 percent of Social Security benefits are taxable. If income exceeds $34,000, 85 percent of Social Security benefits are subject to income tax for a single taxpayer. If the combined income of married taxpayers filing joint returns is between $32,000 and $44,000, then 50 percent of the Social Security benefits are taxable; the percentage of benefits taxed increases to 85 percent when their combined income exceeds $44,000.

14-3 Pension Plans and Retirement Programs

LG4, LG5 Accompanying the expansion of the Social Security system has been a corresponding growth in employer-sponsored pension and retirement plans. In 1940, when the Social Security program was in its infancy, fewer than 25 percent of the workforce had the benefit of an employer-sponsored plan. Today, around 65 percent of all wage earners and salaried workers (in both the private and public sectors) are covered by some type of employer-sponsored retirement or profit-sharing plan.

In 1948, the National Labor Relations Board (NLRB) ruled that pensions and other types of insurance programs are legitimate subjects for collective bargaining. In response, many employers established new pension plans or liberalized the provisions of existing ones to meet or anticipate union demands.

Qualified pension plans (discussed later in this section) allow firms to deduct for tax purposes their contributions to employee retirement programs. Even better, the employees can also deduct these contributions from their taxable income and can thus build up their own retirement funds on a tax-deferred basis.

Government red tape, however, has taken a toll on pension plans. In particular, the **Employee Retirement Income Security Act of 1974** (sometimes referred to as **ERISA** or the *Pension Reform Act*), which was established to protect employees participating in private employer retirement plans, has actually led to a reduction in the number of new retirement plans started among firms, especially the smaller ones. Indeed, the percentage of workers covered by company-sponsored plans has fallen dramatically since the late 1970s. It's estimated that today, *in the private sector, only about 40 percent of all full-time workers are covered by company-financed plans*—even worse, only about one-third (or less) of the part-time labor force is covered. In contrast, *there has been a significant increase in salary-reduction forms of retirement plans* (discussed later in this chapter). In addition to ERISA, the widespread availability of Keogh plans, Roth, traditional, and SEP IRAs, and other programs have lessened the urgency for small firms (and bigger ones as well) to offer their own company-financed pension plans.

14-3a Employer-Sponsored Programs: Basic Plans

Employers can sponsor two types of retirement programs—*basic plans*, in which employees automatically participate after a certain period of employment, and

Employee Retirement Income Security Act (ERISA) A law passed in 1974 to ensure that workers eligible for pensions actually receive such benefits; also permits uncovered workers to establish individual tax-sheltered retirement plans.

vested rights Employees' nonforfeitable rights to receive benefits in a pension plan based on their own and their employer's contributions.

noncontributory pension plan A pension plan in which the employer pays the total cost of the benefits.

contributory pension plan A pension plan in which the employee bears part of the cost of the benefits.

defined contribution plan A pension plan specifying the contributions that both employer and employee must make; *it makes no promises concerning the size of the benefits at retirement.*

supplemental plans, which are mostly voluntary programs that enable employees to increase the amount of funds being set aside for retirement.

Participation Requirements

The vast majority of pension plans require that employees meet certain criteria before becoming eligible for participation. Most common are requirements relating to years of service, minimum age, level of earnings, and employment classification. Years of service and minimum age requirements are often incorporated into retirement plans in the belief that a much higher labor turnover rate applies to both newly hired and younger employees. Therefore, to reduce the administrative costs of the plans, employees in these categories are often excluded—at least initially—from participation. Once these (or any other) participation requirements are met, the employee automatically becomes eligible to participate in the program.

However, not everyone who participates in a pension plan will earn *the right to receive retirement benefits.* Pension plans impose certain criteria that must be met before the employee can obtain a nonforfeitable right to a pension, known as **vested rights.** As the law now stands, *full vesting* rights are required after only three to six years of employment. More specifically, companies must now choose between two vesting schedules. One, the so-called *cliff vesting,* requires full vesting after no more than three years of service—but you obtain no vesting privileges until then. Once vested, you're entitled to everything that's been paid in so far (your contributions *plus* your employer's) and everything that will be contributed in the future. Under the alternate procedure, the so-called *graded schedule,* vesting takes place gradually over the first six years of employment. At the minimum, after two years, you'd have a nonforfeiture right to at least 20 percent of the benefits, with an additional 20 percent each year thereafter until you're 100 percent vested after six years.

What happens if you quit your job and move to another employer? If you're not vested, you normally have no choice but to take out your money; but if you are vested, you can usually do one of two things: either take your money out or leave it in your current employer's retirement program. However, because of inflation, the value of the benefit for a worker who leaves the firm long before retirement age is typically

very small. Consequently, the employee might be better off simply withdrawing his or her own contributions (which always vest immediately) and terminating participation in the plan at the same time he or she leaves the employer. Of course, any worker who leaves the firm before accumulating the required years of service would be entitled only to a return of his or her own contributions to the plan (plus nominal investment earnings). But keep in mind: whenever you terminate employment, *resist the urge to spend the money you have built up in your retirement account! Over time, that can have a devastating effect on your ability to accumulate retirement capital. Instead, when you take money out of one retirement account, roll it over into another one.*

 When you take money out of one retirement account, roll it over into another one.

What's Your Contribution?

Whether you, as an employee, must make payments toward your own pension depends on the type of plan you're in. If you belong to a **noncontributory pension plan,** the employer pays the total cost of the benefits—you don't have to pay a thing. Under a **contributory pension plan,** the employer and the employee share the cost. Today, the trend is toward contributory plans. In addition, nearly all plans for employees of federal, state, and local governments require a contribution from the employee. In contributory plans, the employee's share of the costs is often between 3 percent and 10 percent of annual wages and is typically paid through a payroll deduction. Probably the most common arrangement is for the employer to match the employee's contribution—the employee puts up half the annual contribution and the employer puts up the other half.

Defined Contributions or Defined Benefits

The two most commonly used methods to compute benefits at retirement are the defined contribution plan and the defined benefit plan. A **defined contribution plan** specifies the amount of contribution that both the employer and employee must make. At retirement, the worker is awarded whatever level of monthly benefits those contributions will purchase. Although such factors as age, income level, and the amount of contributions made to the plan have a great deal to do with the amount of monthly benefits received at retirement, probably no variable is more important than the level of *investment performance*

COURTNEY KEATING/ISTOCKPHOTO.COM

generated on the contributed funds. A defined contribution plan promises nothing at retirement except the returns the fund managers have been able to obtain. The only thing that's defined is the amount of contribution that the employee and/or employer must make. The benefits at retirement depend totally on investment results.

Under a **defined benefit plan**, the formula for computing benefits, not contributions, is stipulated in the plan provisions. These benefits are paid out regardless of how well (or poorly) the retirement funds are invested. If investment performance falls short, the employer must make up the difference in order to fund the benefits agreed to in the plan. This type of plan allows employees to calculate before retirement how much their monthly retirement income will be. Often the number of years of service and amount of earnings are prime factors in the formula. For example, workers might be paid 2.5 percent of their final 3-year average annual salary for each year of service. Thus, the *annual* benefit to an employee whose final 3-year average

annual salary was $85,000 and who was with the company for 20 years would be $42,500 (2.5 percent × $85,000 × 20 years).

Many defined benefit plans also increase retirement benefits periodically to help retirees keep up with the cost of living. In periods of high inflation, these increases are essential to maintain retirees' standards of living. While the number of *people* covered by such plans continues to rise, especially in the ranks of government employees, the number of (private-sector) defined benefit *plans* in existence has steadily declined. In fact, there are now *more assets* held in defined contribution plans than there are in traditional (defined benefit) pension plans. And it's very likely that this shift to defined contribution plans will only accelerate in the coming years.

Regardless of the method used to calculate benefits, the employee's basic concern should be with the percentage of final take-home pay that the plan is likely to produce at retirement. A pension is usually thought to be good if, when combined with Social Security, it will result in a monthly income equal to about 70 percent to 80 percent of preretirement net earnings. To reach this goal, however, today's employees must take some responsibility because *there's a growing trend for companies to switch from defined benefit plans to defined contribution programs*. Companies don't like the idea of being faced with uncertain future pension liabilities. Now, more and more of them are avoiding these problems altogether by changing to defined contribution plans. As a result, *the employee is being forced to assume more responsibility for ensuring the desired level of postretirement income*.

> **defined benefit plan** A pension plan in which the formula for computing benefits is stipulated in its provisions.

Financial Road Sign

GUNNAR PIPPEL/SHUTTERSTOCK.COM

Protecting Private Sector Defined Benefit Retirement Plans: The Pension Benefit Guaranty Corporation

The Pension Benefit Guaranty Corporation (PBGC) is a federal agency created by ERISA to protect defined-benefit (DB) retirement plans in the private sector. A DB plan is typically structured to pay a defined monthly monetary benefit when an employee retires. If a DB plan ends without sufficient resources to pay all benefits, the PBGC insurance program will pay the employees of covered companies the promised benefits to the limits set by law. The insurance pays benefits from the insurance premiums paid by companies with protected plans, from the agency's investments, from the assets of pension plans taken over by the PBGC as trustee, and from whatever can be recovered from the companies formerly responsible for the terminated DB plans. It's important to note that benefits are not paid from taxes. The PBGC does not usually insure plans offered by professional service providers like doctors and lawyers, church groups, and federal, state, and local governments, nor does it insure defined contribution plans, such as 401(k) plans.

In 2012, by law, the maximum guaranteed monthly pension amount was about $55,841 per year for workers who begin receiving payments at age 65. The maximum amount payable is lower for those who begin receiving payments before the age of 65 or if the pension covers a surviving spouse of other beneficiary. There is no cost-of-living adjustment under the law.

Source: Adapted from http://www.pbgc.gov/about/faq.html, accessed September 2012.

qualified pension plan A pension plan that meets specified criteria established by the Internal Revenue Code.

profit-sharing plan An arrangement in which the employees of a firm participate in the company's earnings.

thrift and savings plan A plan to supplement pension and other fringe benefits; the firm contributes an amount equal to a set proportion of the employee's contribution.

This means that where you end up in retirement will depend, more than ever, on what *you've* done, rather than on what your employers have done. *Very likely, you're the one who is going to control not only how much goes into the company's retirement programs, but also where it goes.*

Qualified Pension Plans

The Internal Revenue Code permits a corporate employer making contributions to a **qualified pension plan** to deduct from taxable income its contributions to the plan. As a result, the employees on whose behalf the contributions are made don't have to include these payments as part of their taxable income until the benefits are actually received. Further, in contributory plans, *employees can also shelter their contributions from taxes*. In other words, such contributions aren't counted as part of taxable income in the year that they're made; hence they act to reduce the amount of taxable income reported to the Internal Revenue Service (IRS) and therefore lead to lower taxes for the employee. Still another tax advantage of these plans is that any and all investment income is allowed to accumulate tax free; as a result, investment capital can build up more quickly.

 Very likely, you're the one who is going to control not only how much goes into the company's retirement programs, but also where it goes.

14-3b Employer-Sponsored Programs: Supplemental Plans

In addition to basic retirement programs, many employers offer supplemental plans. These plans are often *voluntary* and enable employees not only to increase the amount of funds being held for retirement but also to enjoy attractive tax benefits. There are three types of supplemental plans: profit-sharing, thrift and savings, and salary reduction plans.

Profit-Sharing Plans

Profit-sharing plans enable employees to participate in the earnings of their employer. A **profit-sharing plan** may be qualified under IRS rules and become eligible

for essentially the same tax treatment as other types of pension plans. The major argument supporting the use of profit-sharing plans is that they encourage employees to work harder because the employees benefit when the firm prospers. Contributions to these plans are invested in different types of fixed-interest products, stocks and bonds, and, in many cases, securities issued by the employing firm itself. Employees who receive the firm's securities may actually benefit twice. When profits are good, larger contributions are made to the profit-sharing plan, and the price of the shares already owned is likely to increase as well.

Some big companies offer *voluntary profit-sharing plans* that invest heavily (almost exclusively) in their own stock. It's common in many of these cases for long-term career employees to accumulate several hundred thousand dollars worth of the company's stock. And we're not talking about highly paid corporate executives here; rather, these are just average employees who had the discipline to divert a portion of their salary consistently to the company's profit-sharing plan. However, *there is a real and significant downside to this practice*: if the company should hit hard times, then not only could you face salary cuts (or even worse, the loss of your job) but the value of your profit-sharing account will likely tumble as well. Just look at what happened to employees in the technology sector during the 2000–2002 bear market.

Thrift and Savings Plans

Thrift and savings plans were established to supplement pension and other fringe benefits. Most plans require the employer to make contributions to the savings plan in an amount equal to a set proportion of the amount contributed by the employee. For example, an employer might match an employee's contributions at the rate of 50 cents on the dollar up to, say, 6 percent of salary. These contributions are then deposited with a trustee, who invests the money in various types of securities, including stocks and bonds of the employing firm. With IRS-qualified thrift and savings plans, the *employer's* contributions and earnings on the savings aren't included in the *employee's* taxable income until he or she withdraws the money. Unfortunately, this attractive tax feature doesn't extend to the *employee's contributions*, so any money put into one of these savings plans is still considered part of the employee's taxable income and subject to regular income taxes. An employee who has the option should seriously consider participating in a thrift plan. The returns are

 © GEOPAUL/ISTOCKPHOTO

🌐 *Go to Smart Sites*

Is the future of Social Security secure? The nonpartisan Congressional Budget Office has forecasts under various policies. ●

SANDRA GLIGORIJEVIC/SHUTTERSTOCK.COM

usually pretty favorable, especially when you factor in the employer's contributions.

Salary Reduction Plans

Another type of supplemental retirement program—and certainly the most popular, judging by employee response—is the **salary reduction plan**, or the **401(k) plan** as it's more commonly known. Our discussion here centers on 401(k) plans, but similar programs are available for employees of public, nonprofit organizations, including public schools, colleges, hospitals, and state and local governments. Known as *403(b) plans* or *457 plans*, they offer many of the same features and tax shelter provisions as 401(k) plans.

Today, more and more companies are cutting back on their contributions to traditional (defined benefit) retirement plans. They're turning instead to 401(k) plans, a type of defined contribution plan. A 401(k) plan basically gives employees the option to divert part of their salary to a company-sponsored, tax-sheltered savings account. In this way, the earnings diverted to the savings plan accumulate tax free. Taxes must be paid eventually, but not until the employee starts drawing down the

> **salary reduction, or 401(k), plan** An agreement by which part of a covered employee's pay is withheld and invested; taxes on the contributions and the account earnings are deferred until the funds are withdrawn.

Financial Planning Tips: Managing Your 401(K) Retirement Account

A few basic ideas on managing your 401(k) account can take you a long way:

- **A reasonable asset allocation is more important than choosing the "right" funds for your 401(k) account money**. Research shows that over 90 percent of your investment performance will be determined by how much you allocate to cash, bonds, and equity funds. So less than 10 percent of performance is determined by choosing the right funds and by trying to time the market (which is never a good idea anyway). Remember that the conventional wisdom as a starting place: put 100—your age as the percentage in equities and the residual in bonds and cash. For example, if you're 30, start out with a plan to put 70 percent in equities and 30 percent in bonds and cash. Then adjust the mix to match your risk tolerance. Take a look at an asset allocation calculator like that offered by *SmartMoney* (see http://www.smartmoney.com/calculator/investing/managing-asset-allocation-1304479164310/).
- **Invest enough in your 401(k) account**. Invest at least up to your company's matching amount, if you can possibly afford it. For example, if your company matches the first 6 percent of your annual contribution, then you should contribute at least that much or you're just throwing away money. A reasonable overall goal is to contribute at least 10 percent of your annual income to retirement investment accounts, which include 401(k)s, IRAs, and other investment vehicles.
- **Invest in your 401(k) consistently regardless of its performance.** Some investors panic when their 401(k) accounts lose money and *reduce or even stop* making contributions in an effort to protect themselves from further losses. This is the opposite of what you should do. When you're losing money, it's time to grit your teeth and contribute more to your account, not less! This is because you've got to make up for your losses. If you stop or reduce your contributions, you'll be even less likely to achieve your retirement goal. And keep in mind that when investment values fall, you're buying more shares at lower prices (a principle known as "dollar-cost averaging"). In the long term, this should contribute positively to performance.

Source: Adapted from Tatiana Morales, "How to Manage Your 401K Wisely," http://www.cbsnews.com/2100-500200_162-640129.html, accessed September 2012.

MKABAKOV/SHUTTERSTOCK.COM

account at retirement. In 2012, an individual employee could put as much as $17,000 into a tax-deferred 401(k) plan. (Contribution limits for 403(b) and 457 plans are the same as those for 401(k) plans.) And for those over 50 years old, there is a "catch-up" provision that allows them to contribute up to $22,500 in 2012.

To see how such tax-deferred plans work, consider an individual who is under 50 years old with taxable income of $75,000 in 2012 who would like to contribute the maximum allowable—$17,000—to the 401(k) plan where she works. Doing so will reduce her taxable income to $58,000 and, assuming that she's in the 25 percent tax bracket, will lower her federal tax bill by some $4,250 (i.e., $17,000 × 0.25). Such tax savings will offset a big chunk of her 401(k) contribution, as she'll add $17,000 to her retirement program with only $12,750 of her own money; the rest will come from the IRS via a reduced tax bill.

These plans are generally viewed as attractive *tax shelters* that offer not only substantial tax savings, but also a way to save for retirement. So long as you can afford to put the money aside, *you should seriously consider joining a 401(k)/403(b)/457 plan if one is offered at your place of employment.* This is especially true when one considers the matching features offered by many of these plans. Most companies that offer 401(k) plans have some type of matching contributions program, often putting up 50 cents (or more) for every dollar contributed by the employee. Such matching plans give both tax and savings incentives to individuals and clearly enhance the appeal of 401(k) plans.

Today, another kind of 401(k) plan is being offered by a growing number of firms. This new retirement savings option, which first became available in January 2006, is the so-called *Roth 401(k)*. It's just like a traditional 401(k) except for one important difference: *All contributions to Roth 401(k) plans are made in after-tax dollars.* That means there are no tax savings to be derived from the annual employee contributions; if you earn, say, $75,000 a year and want to put $15,000 into your Roth 401(k), you'll end up paying taxes on the full $75,000. That's the bad news; now the good news. Because all contributions are made in after-tax dollars, *there are no taxes to be paid on plan withdrawals (in other words, they're tax free)*, provided you're at least 59½ and have held the account for five years or more. Like traditional 401(k) plans, Roth 401(k)s also have a contribution cap of $17,000 (in 2012, for those under 50). And that limit applies to *total contributions to both types of 401(k) plans combined*, so you can't put $15,000 into a traditional 401(k) plan and then put another $15,000 into a Roth 401(k). You can also have employer matches with the Roth plans, although technically those matches will accumulate in a separate account that will be taxed as ordinary income at withdrawal. Essentially, *employer* contributions represent tax-free

income to employees, so they'll pay taxes on that income (and on any account earnings) when the funds are withdrawn—as is done with a traditional 401(k).

Both Roth and traditional 401(k) plans typically offer their participants various investment options, including equity and fixed-income mutual funds, company stock, and a variety of interest-bearing vehicles such as bank CDs. Indeed, the typical 401(k) has about 10 choices, and some plans have as many as 20, or even more. Today, the trend is toward giving plan participants more options and providing seminars and other educational tools to help employees make informed retirement plan decisions.

14-3c Evaluating Employer-Sponsored Pension Plans

When participating in a company-sponsored pension plan, you're entitled to certain benefits in return for meeting certain conditions of membership—which may or may not include making contributions to the plan. Whether your participation is limited to the firm's basic plan or includes one or more of the supplemental programs, *it's vital that you take the time to acquaint yourself with the various benefits and provisions* of these plans. And be sure to familiarize yourself not only with the basic plans, but also with any (voluntary) supplemental plans that you may be eligible to join.

So, how should you evaluate these plans? Most experts agree that you can get a pretty good handle on essential plan provisions and retirement benefits by taking a close look at the following features.

- **Eligibility requirements.** Precisely what are they?

- **Defined benefits or contributions.** Which one is defined? If it's the benefits, exactly what formula is used to define them? Pay particular attention to how Social Security benefits are treated in the formula. If it's a defined contribution program, do you have any control over how the money is invested? If so, what are your options?

- **Vesting procedures.** Does the company use a cliff or graded procedure?

- **Contributory or noncontributory.** If the plan is contributory, how much comes from you and how much from the company? If it's noncontributory, what is the company's contribution as a percentage of your salary?

- **Retirement age.** What's the normal retirement age, and what provisions are there for *early retirement?* Are the pension benefits *portable*—that is, can you take them with you if you change jobs?

- **Voluntary supplemental programs.** How much of your salary can you put into one or more of these plans, and what—if anything—is matched by the company?

Finding answers to these questions will help you determine where you stand and what improvements are needed to be made in your retirement plans. As part of this evaluation process, try to determine, as best as you can, *what your benefits are likely to be at retirement*. Before you start cranking out the numbers, check with the people who handle employee benefits at your workplace; they'll usually give you the help you need. Then, using a procedure similar to that followed in Worksheet 14.1, you can estimate what portion of your retirement needs will be met from your company's basic pension plan. If there's a shortfall—*and it's likely there will be*—it will indicate the extent to which you need to participate in some type of company-sponsored supplemental program, such as a 401(k) plan, or (alternatively) how much you'll need to rely on your own savings and investments to reach the standard of living you're looking for in retirement.

14-3d Self-Directed Retirement Programs

In addition to participating in company-sponsored retirement programs, individuals can set up their own tax-sheltered retirement plans. There are two basic types of self-directed retirement programs: *Keogh and SEP plans*, which are for self-employed individuals, and *individual retirement arrangements (IRAs)*, which can be set up by almost anyone.

Keogh and SEP Plans

Keogh plans were introduced in 1962 as part of the Self-Employed Individuals Retirement Act, or simply the Keogh Act. Keogh plans allow self-employed individuals to set up tax-deferred retirement plans for themselves and their employees. Like contributions to 401(k) plans, payments to Keogh accounts may be taken as deductions from taxable income. As a result, they reduce the tax bills of self-employed individuals. The maximum contribution to this tax-deferred retirement plan in 2012 was $50,000 or 25 percent of earned income for sole proprietors (20 percent for unincorporated businesses), whichever is less. If an employee is 50 or older, an additional "catch-up" contribution of $5,500 is allowed in 2012. Any individual who is self-employed, either full- or part-time, is eligible to set up a Keogh account. These accounts can also be used by individuals who hold full-time jobs and moonlight part-time—for instance, the accountant who does tax returns on a freelance basis at night and on weekends. And note that even though he has a Keogh account, this individual is still eligible to receive full retirement benefits from his full-time job and to have his own IRA. (SEP plans are just like Keogh plans except that they're aimed at small business owners, particularly those with no employees,

who want a plan that's simple and easy to administer. Except for some administrative details, they have the same features and limitations as standard Keogh accounts.)

Keogh accounts can be opened at banks, mutual funds, and other financial institutions. Annual contributions must be made at the time the respective tax return is filed or usually by April 15 of the following calendar year (for example, you have until the filing due date of April 15, 2013, to contribute to your Keogh for 2012). Although a designated financial institution acts as custodian of all the funds held in a Keogh account, *actual investments held in the account are directed completely by the individual contributor*. These are self-directed retirement programs; the *individual* decides which investments to buy and sell.

Income earned from the investments must be reinvested in the account. This income also accrues tax free. All Keogh contributions and investment earnings must remain in the account until the individual turns 59½ unless he or she becomes seriously ill or disabled; early withdrawals for any other reason are subject to 10 percent tax penalties. However, the individual is not *required* to start withdrawing the funds at age 59½; the funds can stay in the account (and continue earning tax-free income) until the individual is 70½. Then the individual *must* begin withdrawing funds from the account—unless he or she continues to be gainfully employed past the age of 70½. Of course, once an individual starts withdrawing funds (upon or after turning 59½), all such withdrawals are treated as ordinary income and are subject to normal income taxes.

Individual Retirement Accounts (IRAs)

Some people mistakenly believe that an IRA is a specialized type of investment. It's not. An **individual retirement account (IRA)**, or individual retirement *account*, as it's more commonly known, is virtually the same as any other investment account you open with a bank, stockbroker, or mutual fund *except* that it's clearly designated as an IRA. That is, you make out a form that designates the account as an IRA and makes the institution its trustee. That's all there is to it. Any gainfully employed person (and spouse) can have an IRA account, although the type of accounts that a person can have and the tax status of those accounts depend on several variables. All IRAs, however, have one thing in common: they're designed to encourage retirement savings

Keogh plan An account to which self-employed persons may make specified payments that may be deducted from taxable income; earnings also accrue on a tax-deferred basis.

individual retirement account (IRA) A retirement plan, open to any working American, to which a person may contribute a specified amount each year.

for individuals. Today, an individual has three IRA types to choose from, as follows.

- **Traditional (deductible) IRAs,** which can be opened by anyone without a retirement plan at his or her place of employment, *regardless of income level,* or by couples filing jointly who—even if they are covered by retirement plans at their places of employment—have adjusted gross incomes of less than $92,000 (or single tax payers with AGIs of less than $58,000). In 2012, individuals who qualify may make tax-deductible contributions of up to $5,000 a year to their accounts (an equal tax-deductible amount can be contributed by a nonworking spouse). All account earnings grow tax free until withdrawn, when ordinary tax rates apply (though a 10 percent penalty normally applies to withdrawals made before age 59½).

- **Nondeductible (after-tax) IRA,** which is open to anyone regardless of their income level or whether they're covered by a retirement plan at their workplace. In 2012, contributions of up to $5,000 a year can be made to this account, but they're *made with after-tax dollars* (that is, the contributions are not tax deductible). However, *the earnings do accrue tax free and are not subject to tax until they are withdrawn* after the individual reaches age 59½ (funds withdrawn before age 59½ may be subject to the 10% penalty).

- **Roth IRAs** are the newest kid on the block (available only since 1998); they can be opened by couples filing jointly with adjusted gross incomes of up to $173,000 (singles up to $110,000), whether or not they have other retirement or pension plans. But the best part of the Roth IRA is its tax features—although the annual contributions of up to $6,000 a person in 2012 are made with nondeductible/after-tax dollars, all earnings in the account grow tax free. And *all withdrawals from the account are also tax free* provided that the account has been open for at least five years and the individual is past the age of 59½. In other words, so long as these conditions are met, you won't have to pay taxes on any withdrawals you make from your Roth IRA!

It is possible to convert a traditional IRA to a Roth IRA. If you convert, you will have to pay taxes on any earnings and pretax contributions. So why would you want to do that? It may make sense to convert if you expect your tax rate to remain the same or go up after retirement. Thus, converting to a Roth IRA could allow you to pay a lower amount of taxes on your IRA investments in the long run. However, it's important to be able to pay the taxes using money that doesn't come out of your IRA account. If you make a withdrawal from an IRA account before age 59 ½, you generally owe a 10 percent penalty on that amount. And you

would give up the opportunity for tax-free Roth IRA compounding on that amount—permanently. It usually makes less sense to convert a traditional IRA to a Roth IRA the older you are. This is because the older you are, the less time you have to make up for what you paid in taxes on the conversion. However, it can still be wise for an older person to convert a traditional to a Roth IRA for estate tax planning purposes. Conversions can be complicated, and it's best to consult a tax advisor. However, you can get a good idea of whether conversion looks like a reasonable possible move using an online conversion calculator like that offered by *SmartMoney* (see http//smartmoney.com and look for the retirement calculator on Roth IRA conversions). Key features and provisions of all three of these IRAs are outlined in the Bonus Exhibit, "Qualifying for an IRA." (Visit CourseMate for PFIN 3. Log in at **www.cengagebrain.com**.)

Regardless of the type and notwithstanding the conditions just described, penalty-free withdrawals are generally allowed from an IRA so long as the funds are being used for first-time home purchases (up to $10,000), qualifying educational costs, certain major medical expenses, or other qualified emergencies. Also, with both the traditional/deductible and nondeductible IRAs, you must start making withdrawals from your account once you reach age 70½—although *this requirement does not apply to Roth IRAs.*

Self-Directed Accounts and Their Investment Vehicles

IRAs are like Keogh and SEP plans; they're *self-directed accounts,* which means that you are free to make almost any kind of investment decision you want. An individual can be conservative or aggressive in choosing securities for an IRA (or Keogh), though conventional wisdom favors funding your IRA (and Keogh) with *income-producing assets.* This would also suggest that if you're looking for capital gains, it's best to do so *outside* your retirement account. This doesn't mean, however, that it would be totally inappropriate to place a good-quality growth stock or mutual fund in a Keogh or IRA. In fact, many advisors contend that growth investments should always have a place in your retirement account because of their often impressive performance and ability to protect against inflation. Such investments may pay off handsomely because they appreciate totally free of taxes. And in the end, *it's how much you have in your retirement account that matters, not how your earnings were made along the way.*

No matter what type of investment vehicle you use, keep in mind that once you place money in an IRA, it's meant to stay there for the long haul. Like most tax-sheltered retirement programs, there are restrictions on when you can withdraw the funds from an IRA. And when you move your IRA account to a new firm (this is known as a *rollover*), the transfer will be subject to a *20 percent withholding tax* if the proceeds from the transfer are paid to you directly. The rule is very clear on this: if you take possession of the funds (even for just a few days), you'll be hit with the withholding tax. So, the best way to handle IRA rollovers is to *arrange for the transfer of funds from one firm to another*.

So, should you contribute to an IRA or not? Obviously, as long as you qualify for either a traditional IRA or a Roth IRA, you should seriously consider making the maximum payments allowable. There are no special record-keeping requirements or forms to file, and the IRA is an excellent vehicle for sheltering income from taxes. Probably the biggest decision you'll have to make is which IRA is right for you—the traditional or the Roth? (*Hint:* The Roth is probably most appropriate for people in their 30s or 40s.)

14-4 Annuities

LG6 An annuity is just the opposite of life insurance. As pointed out in Chapter 8, life insurance is the systematic accumulation of an estate that is used for protection against financial loss resulting from premature death. In contrast, an **annuity** is the systematic *liquidation* of an estate in such a way that it provides protection against the economic difficulties that could result from outliving personal financial resources. The period during which premiums are paid toward the purchase of an annuity is called the **accumulation period**; correspondingly, the period during which annuity payments are made is called the **distribution period**.

Under a pure life annuity contract, a life insurance company will guarantee regular monthly payments to an individual for as long as he or she lives. These benefits are composed of three parts: principal, interest, and survivorship benefits. The *principal* consists of the premium amounts paid in by the *annuitant* (person buying the annuity) during the accumulation period. *Interest* is the amount earned on these funds between the time they're paid and distributed. The interest earnings on an annuity accrue (that is, accumulate) tax free—but note that, whereas the earnings in an annuity accumulate on a tax-sheltered basis, the amounts paid into an annuity are all made with *after-tax dollars* (that is, no special tax treatment is given to the capital contributions). The portion of the principal and interest that has not been returned to the annuitant before death is the **survivorship benefit**. These funds are available to those members of the annuity group who survive in each subsequent period.

14-4a Classification of Annuities

As seen in Exhibit 14.3, annuities may be classified according to several key characteristics, including payment of premiums, disposition of proceeds, inception date of benefits, and method used in calculating benefits.

Single Premium or Installments There are two ways to pay the premiums when you purchase an annuity contract: you can make one large (lump-sum) payment up front, or pay the premium in installments. The **single premium annuity contract** usually requires a *minimum investment* of anywhere from $2,500 to $10,000, with $5,000 the most common figure. These annuities have become popular primarily because of their attractive tax features. They're often purchased just before retirement as a way of creating a future stream of income. In these circumstances, the individual normally purchases an **immediate annuity**, in which case the stream of monthly benefits begins immediately—the first check arrives a month or so after purchase.

Although most *group* annuity policies are funded with single premiums, many *individuals* still buy annuities by paying for them in installments. With these **installment premium annuity contracts**, the set payments, which can start as low as $100, are made at regular intervals (monthly, quarterly, or annually) over an extended period of time. Sometimes these annuities are set up with a fairly large initial payment (of perhaps several thousand dollars) followed by a series

annuity An investment product created by life insurance companies that provides a series of payments over time.

accumulation period The period during which premiums are paid for the purchase of an annuity.

distribution period The period during which annuity payments are made to an annuitant.

survivorship benefit On an annuity, the portion of premiums and interest that has not been returned to the annuitant before his or her death.

single premium annuity contract An annuity contract purchased with a lump-sum payment.

immediate annuity An annuity in which the annuitant begins receiving monthly benefits immediately.

installment premium annuity contract An annuity contract purchased through periodic payments made over time.

© PHOTOGOLFER/SHUTTERSTOCK.COM

Exhibit 14.3 **Types of Annuity Contracts**

Annuity contracts vary according to how you pay for the annuity, how the proceeds are disbursed, how earnings accrue, and when you receive the benefits.

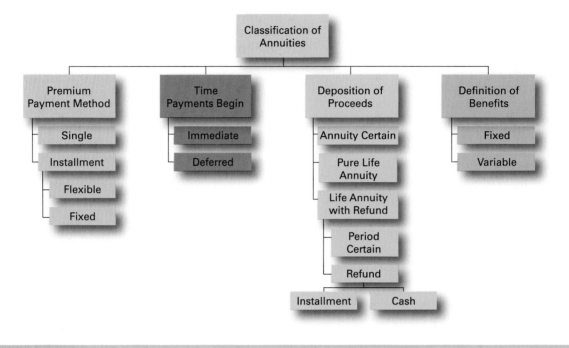

© Cengage Learning

deferred annuity An annuity in which benefit payments are postponed for a certain number of years.

life annuity with no refund (pure life) An option under which an annuitant receives a specified amount of income for life, regardless of the length of the distribution period.

guaranteed-minimum annuity (life annuity with refund) An annuity that provides a guaranteed minimum distribution of benefits.

life annuity, period certain A type of guaranteed-minimum annuity that guarantees the annuitant a stated amount of monthly income for life; the insurer agrees to pay for a minimum number of years.

of much smaller installment payments (of, say, $250 a quarter). This approach would be used to purchase a **deferred annuity**, a type of contract in which cash benefits are deferred for several years (note that single premiums can also be used to purchase deferred annuities). A big advantage of *installment premium deferred annuities* is that your savings can build up over time *free of taxes*. With no taxes to pay, you have more money working for you and can build up a bigger retirement nest egg. You'll have to pay taxes on your earnings eventually, of course, but not until you start receiving benefit payments from your annuity.

Disposition of Proceeds

All annuities revolve around the basic concept of "pay now, receive later," so they allow individuals to prepare for future cash needs, such as planning for retirement,

while obtaining significant tax benefits. When the annuity is distributed, you can take a lump-sum payment or, as is more often the case, you can *annuitize* the distribution by systematically parceling out the money into regular payments over a defined or open-ended period. Because most people choose to annuitize their proceeds (which is how an annuity is intended to be used), let's look at the most common annuity disbursement options.

- **Life annuity with no refund (pure life).** The annuitant receives a specified amount of income for life, whether the disbursement period turns out to be 1 year or 50 years. The estate or family receives no refunds when the annuitant dies. This results in the largest monthly payments of any of the distribution methods.

- **Guaranteed-minimum annuity (life annuity, period certain).** In this type of contract, the benefits (future cash flows) aren't limited to the annuitant only and may extend to named beneficiaries. With a life annuity, period certain, the annuitant gets a guaranteed monthly income for life with the added provision that the insurance company will pay the monthly benefits for a minimum number of years (5 or 10, for example). If the annuitant dies soon after the distribution begins, then his or her beneficiaries receive the monthly benefits for the balance of the "period certain."

- **Annuity certain.** This type of annuity pays a set amount of monthly income for a specified number of years, thereby filling a need for monthly income that will expire after a certain length of time. An annuitant selecting a 10-year annuity certain receives payments for 10 years, regardless of whether he or she lives for 2 or 20 more years.

Fixed versus Variable Annuity

When you put your money into an annuity, the premium is invested on your behalf by the insurance company, much as a mutual fund invests the money you put into it. From the time you pay the first (or only) annuity premium until it's paid back to you as a lump sum or as an annuitized monthly benefit, you'll earn a rate of return on your investment. How that rate of return is figured determines whether you own a fixed or variable annuity. In a **fixed-rate annuity**, the insurance company safeguards your principal and agrees to pay a guaranteed minimum rate of interest over the life of the contract. These are conservative, very low-risk annuity products that essentially promise to return *the original investment plus interest* when the money is paid out to the annuitant (or any designated beneficiaries). Unlike bond mutual funds, fixed annuities don't fluctuate in value when interest rates rise or fall; so your principal is always secure.

Imagine an investment vehicle that lets you move between stocks, bonds, and money funds and, at the same time, accumulate profits tax free. That, in a nutshell, is a variable annuity. With a **variable annuity**, the amount that's ultimately paid out to the annuitant varies with the investment results obtained by the insurance company—*nothing is guaranteed, not even the principal!* When you buy a variable annuity, *you decide* where your money will be invested based on your investment objectives and tolerance for risk; you can usually choose from stocks, bonds, money market securities, real estate, alternative investments, or some combination thereof. As an annuity holder, you can stay put with a single investment for the long haul; or, as with most variable annuities, you can more aggressively play the market by switching from one fund to another. Obviously, when the market goes up, investors in variable annuities do well; but when the market falters, the returns on these policies will likewise be reduced.

Go to Smart Sites

For tips on investing and saving strategies for retirement, Investopedia's retirement section has answers. ●

14-4b Sources and Costs of Annuities

Annuities are administered by life insurance companies, so it's no surprise that they're also the leading sellers of these financial products. Annuities can also be purchased from stock brokers, mutual fund organizations, banks, and financial planners. When you buy an annuity, the cost will vary with the annuitant's age at issue, the annuitant's age when payments begin, the method used to distribute benefits, the number of lives covered, and the annuitant's gender.

As with mutual funds, there are some annual fees that you should be aware of. In particular, be prepared to pay insurance fees of 1 percent or more—in addition to the annual management fees of perhaps 1 percent to 2 percent paid on variable annuities. That's a total of 2 percent to 3 percent or more taken right off the top, year after year. There is also a *contract charge* (or maintenance fee) that's deducted annually to cover various contract-related expenses; these fees usually run from about $30 to $60 per year. Obviously, these fees can drag down returns and reduce the advantage of tax-deferred income. Finally, most annuities charge hefty *penalties for early withdrawal*. This means that, in order to get out of a poorly performing annuity, you'll have to forfeit a chunk of your money.

14-4c Investment and Income Properties of Annuities

A major attribute of most types of annuities is that they're a source of income that can't be outlived. Although individuals might be able to create a similar arrangement by simply living off the interest or dividends from their investments, they'd find it difficult to liquidate their principal systematically so that the last payment would coincide closely (or exactly) with their death. Another advantage is that the income earned in an annuity is allowed to accumulate tax free, so it's a form of *tax-sheltered investment*. Actually, the income from an annuity is *tax deferred*, meaning that taxes on the earnings will have to be paid when the annuity is liquidated.

Shelter from taxes is an attractive investment attribute, but there's a hitch. You may be faced with a big tax penalty if you close out or withdraw money from an annuity before it's time. Specifically, the IRS treats annuity withdrawals like withdrawals from an IRA: that is, except in cases of serious illness, *anyone who takes money out before reaching age 59½ will incur a 10 percent tax penalty*. All of which only

annuity certain An annuity that provides a specified monthly income for a stated number of years without consideration of any life contingency.

fixed-rate annuity An annuity in which the insurance company agrees to pay a guaranteed rate of interest on your money.

variable annuity An annuity in which the monthly income provided by the policy varies as a function of the insurer's actual investment experience.

Financial Planning Tips: Is an Annuity Right for You?

Most of us don't have a traditional defined benefit pension and have to manage with a 401(k) plan along with careful investing to fund our retirement. But we still long for the steady income that defined benefit plans provide. Annuities are designed to provide a monthly income for the rest of your life. You enter into an agreement with an insurer that provides that benefit for a predefined time period after you pay in advance for this service. Annuities are designed to assure that you do not outlive your money.

So when does it make sense to buy an annuity? If you have guaranteed income from several different sources, you may not need an annuity. However, if you don't have a traditional pension plan and want the security of a fixed monthly payment in retirement, you may want to consider using some of your savings to purchase an annuity. Here is some more specific guidance.

A *deferred annuity* is worth considering when:

- You are making the maximum contribution to your employer-sponsored retirement plan and to your IRA (or if you're not eligible for an IRA).
- You don't expect to need the annuity funds until you are at least 59½ years old.
- You have an emergency fund that covers at least six months of living expenses.
  An *immediate annuity* may be a good choice when:
- You want to convert part of your retirement savings into income now.
- You are in good health and expect to live at least another 20 years.
- You have sufficient assets to cover large expenses like medical bills.

Source: Adapted in part from Phil Taylor, "Do You Need an Annuity?" http://money .usnews.com/money/blogs/On-Retirement/2012/01/06/do-you-need-an-annuity, accessed September 2012.

MKABAKOV/SHUTTERSTOCK.COM

reinforces the notion that *an annuity should always be considered a long-term investment.* Assume that it's a part of your retirement program (after all, that's the way the IRS looks at it) and that you're getting in for the long haul.

From an investment perspective, the returns generated from an annuity can be, in some cases, a bit disappointing. For instance, as we discussed earlier, the returns on *variable annuities* are tied to returns in the money and capital markets; even so, they're still no better than what you can get from other investment vehicles—indeed, they're often lower, in part because of higher annuity fees. Keep in mind that these differential returns aren't due to tax features because, in both cases, returns are measured on a before-tax basis. But *returns from annuities are tax sheltered,* so that makes those lower returns a lot more attractive.

If you're considering a variable annuity, go over it much as you would a traditional mutual fund: look for superior past performance, proven management talent/track record, and the availability of attractive investment alternatives that you can switch in and out of. And *pay particular attention to an annuity's total expense rate.* These products

have a reputation of being heavily loaded with fees and charges, but it's possible to find annuities with both above-average performance and relatively low fee structures. That's the combination you're looking for.

One final point: If you're seriously considering buying an annuity, be sure to read the contract carefully and see what the guaranteed rates are, how long the initial rate applies, and if there's a bailout provision. (A *bailout provision* allows you to withdraw your money, free of any surrender fees, if the rate of return on your annuity falls below a specified minimum level. Of course, even if you exercise a bailout provision, you may still have to face a tax penalty for early withdrawal—unless you transfer the funds to another annuity through what's known as a *1035 exchange.*) Just as important, because *the annuity is only as good as the insurance company that stands behind it,* check to see how the company is rated by Best's, Standard & Poor's, or Moody's. It's important to make sure that the insurance company itself is financially sound before buying one of its annuity products. See Chapter 8 for more discussion on these insurance ratings and how they work.

Planning Over a Lifetime: Retirement Planning

Here are some key considerations for retirement planning in each stage of the life cycle.

Pre-family Independence: 20s	Family Formation/Career Development: 30–45	Pre-Retirement: 45–65	Retirement: 65 and Beyond
✓ Estimate how much you will need to retire comfortably while taking inflation into account.	✓ Aim to invest between 10 percent and 15 percent of your income for retirement. The more you invest early on, the better off you'll be at retirement.	✓ Revise your retirement plan in light of recent developments. Try to save even more.	✓ Revise your retirement plan to weight your investments more toward debt and liquid instruments than stocks.
✓ Determine your asset allocation among stocks, bonds, real estate, and cash based on your time horizon and attitude toward risk. Most people are comfortable taking more risk earlier in life.	✓ Review your asset allocation and rebalance it to be more consistent with your goals. Most people are more comfortable reducing the risk of their investments a bit.	✓ Review your asset allocation and rebalance investments within and beyond your employer's retirement plan. Most people reduce the risk of their investments.	✓ Compare your spending rate to your assets and reassess how long your spending rate can be maintained. Consider how the current income produced by your portfolio relates to your day-to-day spending needs.
✓ Match your investments in any employer-sponsored 401(k) retirement plan with your overall asset allocation plan.	✓ Gradually increase the amount invested in any employer-sponsored 401(k) retirement plan and re-evaluate how it relates to your asset allocation plan.	✓ Continue to increase the amount you invest in any employer-sponsored 401(k) retirement plan gradually, and re-evaluate it periodically to see how it fits into your asset allocation plan.	✓ Integrate your investment asset allocation strategy with estate planning. Keep in mind that the equity in your home can be borrowed against if needed.
✓ Start setting aside money for investment outside your employer's retirement plan. Consider investing in mutual funds and exchange-traded funds (ETFs) under a traditional IRA, a Roth IRA, or both.	✓ Consider increasing your contribution to traditional IRA, a Roth IRA, or both.	✓ Consider increasing your contribution to traditional and Roth IRAs using mutual funds and exchange traded funds (ETFs). Consider purchasing an annuity to supplement retirement income.	✓ Plan for mandatory withdrawals from tax-sheltered accounts and the associated tax consequences.

FINANCIAL PLANNING EXERCISES

LG2 1. Jacqueline Strauss, a 25-year-old personal loan officer at Second National Bank, understands the importance of starting early when it comes to saving for retirement. She has committed $3,000 per year for her retirement fund and assumes that she'll retire at age 65.
   a. How much will she have accumulated when she turns 65 if she invests in equities and earns 8 percent on average?
   b. Jacqueline is urging her friend, Mike Goodman, to start his plan right away, too, because he's 35. What would his nest egg amount to if he invested in the same manner as Jacqueline and he, too, retires at age 65? Comment on your findings.

LG4 2. Kristin Caldwell has just graduated from college and is considering job offers from two companies. Although the salary and insurance benefits are similar, the retirement programs are not. One firm offers a 401(k) plan that matches employee contributions with 25 cents for every dollar contributed by the employee, up to a $10,000 limit. The other has a contributory plan that allows employees to contribute up to 10% of their annual salary through payroll deduction and matches it dollar for dollar; this plan vests fully after five years. Because Kristin is unfamiliar with these plans, she turns to you for help. Explain the features of each plan so that she can make an informed decision.

LG4, 5 3. Ralph Porter is in his early 30s and is thinking about opening an IRA. He can't decide whether to open a traditional/deductible IRA or a Roth IRA, so he turns to you for help.
   a. To support your explanation, you decide to *run some comparative numbers on the two types of accounts;* for starters, use a 25-year period to show Ralph what contributions of $5,000 per year will amount to (after 25 years) if he can earn, say, 10 percent on his money. Will the type of account he opens have any impact on this amount? Explain.
   b. Assuming that Ralph is in the 30 percent tax bracket (and will remain there for the next 25 years), determine the annual and total (over 25 years) tax savings he'll enjoy from the $5,000-a-year contributions to his IRA. Contrast the (annual and total) tax savings he'd generate from a traditional IRA with those from a Roth IRA.
   c. Now, fast-forward 25 years. Given the size Ralph's account in 25 years (as computed in part a), assume that he takes it all out in one lump sum. If he's still in the 30 percent tax bracket, how much will he have, *after taxes,* with a traditional IRA as compared with a Roth IRA? How do the taxes computed here compare with those computed in part b? Comment on your findings.
   d. Based on the numbers you have computed as well as any other factors, what kind of IRA would you recommend to Ralph? Explain. Would knowing that maximum contributions are scheduled to increase to $7,000 per year make any difference in your analysis? Explain.

LG5 4. Explain the circumstances in which it make sense to convert a traditional IRA to a Roth IRA.

LG6 5. Explain how buying a variable annuity is much like investing in a mutual fund. Do you, as a buyer, have any control over the amount of investment risk to which you're exposed in a variable annuity contract? Explain.

PFIN Student Study Tools—Visit CourseMate for PFIN 3. Log in at **www.cengagebrain.com**. Check out the bonus exercises and exhibits, interactive worksheets, Smart Sites, Critical Thinking Cases, Money Online, Kiplinger videos, quizzing, and more.

Cool Apps—Look for this new feature on CourseMate for PFIN 3. Cool Apps navigates the growing world of apps that are available for personal financial planning and tracking.

4LTR Press solutions are designed for today's learners through the continuous feedback of students like you. Tell us what you think about **PFIN** and help us improve the learning experience for future students.

YOUR FEEDBACK MATTERS.

Complete the Speak Up survey in CourseMate at www.cengagebrain.com

 Follow us at www.facebook.com/4ltrpress

15

PRESERVING YOUR ESTATE

LEARNING GOALS

LG1 Describe the role of estate planning in personal financial planning, and identify the seven steps involved in the process.

LG2 Recognize the importance of preparing a will and other documents to protect you and your estate.

LG3 Explain how trusts are used in estate planning.

LG4 Determine whether a gift will be taxable and use planned gifts to reduce estate taxes.

LG5 Calculate federal taxes due on an estate.

LG6 Use effective estate planning techniques to minimize estate taxes.

How Will This Affect Me? No, you can't take it with you. But there's a next best thing: A carefully designed estate plan will allow your loved ones and family to keep as much of your accumulated wealth as possible. This chapter explains the role of estate planning and the need for a will. It discusses the use and design of living wills, advance medical directives, and trusts. It also explains how federal estate taxes are calculated. After reading this chapter you should understand the key elements in handling and preserving your estate for your loved ones.

15-1 Principles of Estate Planning

LG1 In the previous chapters, we have discussed how to build your wealth. Like it or not, no one lives forever. And you really cannot take it with you. So what happens to your wealth when you die? It will be transferred either to your beneficiaries—your family, friends, charities, and those you love—or, unless you do some planning, to the government through either transfer taxes or the process of escheat. This process, called *estate planning*, requires knowledge of wills, trusts, and taxes.

Estate planning is the process of developing a plan to administer and distribute your assets after death, in a manner consistent with your wishes and the needs of your survivors, while minimizing taxes. It includes plans to manage your affairs if you become disabled and a statement of your personal wishes for medical care should you become unable to clearly state them. A key focus of estate planning is to eliminate or minimize taxes and thereby maximize the amount of your estate that ultimately passes to your heirs and beneficiaries. Estate planning also includes steps that you take to ensure that your estate is properly administered if you are unable to manage your assets because of illness or other incapacity. The plans you make are a form of insurance to protect your assets when you are not able to take care of them. These plans include directions about your medical care, whom to rely on for financial or legal advice, and other special instructions you want to give to your family when you are unable to do so personally.

ESBIN-ANDERSON/AGE FOTOSTOCK

If an individual fails to plan, then state and federal laws will control the disposition of that person's assets at death and determine who bears the burden of expenses and taxes, which may be higher because of the lack of planning. People who wish to plan their estates must systematically uncover problems in several important areas and solve them. Exhibit 15.1 lists the major types of problems and their associated causes or indicators.

Frequently, one of the major concerns of estate planning is to minimize the amount of transfer taxes that your estate must pay. Three kinds of taxes are of particular concern:

- Transfer taxes on gifts, referred to as the "gift tax"
- Transfer taxes on your estate, referred to as the "estate tax"
- Income taxes to be paid by your beneficiaries because of the property that they receive from your estate

Some have said that transfer taxes are elective. In other words, you elect to pay these taxes when you do no planning to avoid them. With planning and the discipline to follow through on the plan, most people will incur no transfer taxes and will minimize the related income taxes. Thus, you decide whether your property is transferred to the government or to your loved ones.

> **estate planning** The process of developing a plan to administer and distribute your assets after death, in a manner consistent with your wishes and the needs of your survivors, while minimizing taxes.

> ❝ **A key focus of estate planning is to eliminate or minimize taxes and thereby maximize the amount of your estate that ultimately passes to your heirs and beneficiaries.** ❞

After you read the chapter, explore the STUDY TOOLS listed on page 381.

© KAREN HERMANN/ISTOCKPHOTO

Careful estate planning can prevent many problems that arise when settling an estate. The first step toward preventing problems is an awareness and understanding of their major causes or indicators.

Problem	Major Cause or Indicator
Excessive transfer costs	Taxes and estate administrative expenses higher than necessary.
Lack of liquidity	Insufficient cash; not enough assets that are quickly and inexpensively convertible to cash within a short period of time to meet tax demands and other costs.
Improper disposition of assets	Beneficiaries receive the wrong asset, or the proper asset in the wrong manner or at the wrong time.
Inadequate income at retirement	Capital insufficient or not readily convertible to income-producing status.
Inadequate income, if disabled	High medical costs; capital insufficient or not readily convertible to income-producing status; difficulty in reducing living standards.
Inadequate income for family at estate owner's death	Any of the above causes.
Insufficient capital	Excessive taxes, inflation, improper investment planning.
Special problems	A family member with a serious illness or physical or emotional problem; children of a prior marriage; beneficiaries who have extraordinary medical or financial needs; beneficiaries who can't agree on how to handle various estate matters, business problems, or opportunities.

© Cengage Learning

15-1a Who Needs Estate Planning?

Estate planning should be part of your financial plan, whether you're married or single and have five children or none. For example, married couples who own many assets jointly and have designated beneficiaries for them need to name an executor to administer the estate, specify a guardian for children, clarify how estate taxes will be paid, and direct the distribution of property that doesn't go directly to a joint owner. Unmarried partners and single persons also need estate planning, particularly if they own

BEHAVIOR MATTERS

Recognizing and Overcoming Aversion to Ambiguity in Estate Planning

While many people recognize the need for an estate plan, they often have too little understanding of the process. Thus, too few of us take action at the right time. Why? Estate planning forces us to face and confirm our own mortality, which is hard to do. All too often, therefore, it takes a dramatic and serious health change to push the average American to plan for the worst. There's nothing like a heart attack or a cancer diagnosis to motivate estate planning. But this may well be too late. Consider how to overcome the *aversion to ambiguity* behavioral barrier so you can establish a timely and effective estate plan.

Estate planning can appear ambiguous to those who do not understand it. And most people dislike this ambiguity but fail to confront it. Two conflicting thoughts create this perceived ambiguity. First, we acknowledge that estate planning is important both for the planner and for the planner's family. Second, we often focus on living long

and productive lives—a practice that is wrongly taken to imply that there is no hurry to start the estate planning process. The resulting conflicted feelings draw into question the importance of estate planning. Many, consequently, are paralyzed and do no planning.

So how do we move beyond the aversion to ambiguity and get the estate planning process going? We have to admit that life is short (even though we want it to be as long as possible) and that we need to plan for the inevitable. In other words, life won't just end for others; it will for us, too. After admitting this, the aversion to ambiguity barrier can be overcome by becoming more familiar with the basics of estate planning. This chapter should go a long way in addressing that issue. In summary, we must face our mortality, familiarize ourselves with the estate planning process, and decisively contact a professional to get the process moving forward.

Source: Adapted from Justin A. Reckers and Robert A. Simon, "Resolving the Aversion to Estate Planning," originally published by MorningstarAdvisor.com on April 21, 2011, http://behavioralfinances.com/category/estate-planning/, accessed July 2012.

a home or other assets that they want to leave to a partner, a specific individual, or to a charity. Estate planning involves both *people planning* and *asset planning*.

People Planning

People planning means anticipating the psychological and financial needs of those you love and providing adequate resources to ensure continuation of their way of life. It involves keeping Mother's cameo brooch in the family or preserving the business that Granddad started 75 years ago. People planning is especially important for individuals with children who are minors; children who are exceptionally artistic or intellectually gifted; children or other dependents who are emotionally, mentally, or physically handicapped; and spouses who can't or don't want to handle money, securities, or a business.

 Go to Smart Sites

What should you do first when someone close to you dies? The National Institutes of Health (NIH) has a publication to help you through difficult end-of-life issues. For more online resources, whenever you see *"Go to Smart Sites"* in this chapter, visit CourseMate for PFIN 3. Log in at **www.cengagebrain.com**. ●

How many of us have handled hundreds of thousands of dollars? Clearly, minor children can't legally handle large sums of money or deal directly with real estate or securities. Think of the burden that we place on others when we expect people who can't—or don't want to—handle such large sums of money or securities to do so. Engaging in people planning demonstrates a high degree of caring. People planning also involves talking about estate planning with your loved ones.

Asset Planning

Because you care about the people in your life, you need to plan who will receive your assets upon your death or incapacity. Under the 2012 transfer tax law, estates of less than $5,120,000 will not be subject to taxes on their transfer either by gift or by estate. For a married couple, that number is doubled to $10,240,000. So it is not just about taxes. Your estate plan should match your assets with the people you wish to receive them. When an estate involves a closely held business, planning is essential to stabilize and maximize value not only during the owner's lifetime, but also upon the owner's death or disability. Likewise, estate planning is essential to avoid the special problems that occur when an estate owner holds title to property in more than one state. How you own your property (i.e., who is on the deed or title for the property) will affect your ability to plan

for its transfer. The nature of the asset—whether it is cash, real property, cars, collectibles, stocks, or bonds—will also affect your ability to match your assets with the people you want to have them. The estate planning process is complicated for blended families and for those with special needs due to mental or physical disabilities. Careful planning is needed to make sure that your assets will go to the desired beneficiaries.

15-1b Why Does an Estate Break Up?

Quite often, when people die, their estates die with them—not because they've done anything wrong, but because they haven't done anything. There are numerous forces that, if unchecked, tend to shrink an estate, reduce the usefulness of its assets, and frustrate the objectives of the person who built it. These include death-related costs, inflation, lack of liquidity, improper use of vehicles of transfer, and disabilities.

1. **Death-related costs.** When someone dies, their estate incurs certain types of death-related costs. For example, medical bills for a final illness and funeral expenses are good examples of *first-level death-related costs. Second-level death-related costs* consist of fees for attorneys, appraisers, and accountants, along with probate expenses—so-called administrative costs, federal estate taxes, and state death taxes. Most people also die with some current bills unpaid, outstanding long-term obligations (such as mortgages, business loans, and installment contracts), and unpaid income taxes and property taxes.

2. **Inflation.** Failure to reappraise and rearrange an estate plan continuously to counter the effects of inflation can impair the ability of assets—personal property and investments—to provide steady and adequate levels of financial security for your survivors.

3. **Lack of liquidity.** Insufficient cash to cover death costs and other estate obligations has always been a major factor in estate impairment. Sale of the choicest parcel of farmland or a business that's been in the family for generations, for instance, often has undesirable financial and psychological effects on the heirs.

4. **Improper use of vehicles of transfer.** Improper use of vehicles of transfer may pass property to unintended beneficiaries or to the proper beneficiaries in an improper manner or at an incorrect time. For example, spendthrift spouses or minors may be left large sums of money outright in the form of life insurance, through joint ownership of a savings account, or as the beneficiaries of an employee fringe benefit plan.

5. **Disabilities**. A prolonged and expensive disability of a family wage earner that results in loss of income is often called a *living death*. This financial situation is further complicated by inadequate management of currently owned assets. These circumstances can not only threaten a family's financial security, but can also quickly diminish the value of the estate.

15-1c What Is Your Estate?

Your **probate estate** consists of the real and personal property you own in your own name that can be transferred at death according to the terms of a will or, if you have no valid will, under *intestate* laws. The probate estate is distinct from the **gross estate**, which includes all the property—both probate and nonprobate—that might be subject to federal estate taxes at your death. Life insurance, jointly held property with rights of survivorship, and property passing under certain employee benefit plans are common examples of nonprobate assets that might be subject to federal (and state) estate taxes.

You also can provide for property that's not probate property and won't be part of your estate for federal estate tax purposes yet will pass to your family and form part of their financial security program. Upon your death, all of the property that you own goes into your gross estate. This includes cash, personal property, real property, insurance policies, investments—everything. Some of this property will be transferred by operation of property law—that is, because the owners are listed on the deed, the property is transferred to your co-owners. The rest of your property will be in your probate estate and be transferred according to your will or, if there is no valid will, under the intestate laws of your state. Life insurance, jointly held property with rights of survivorship, and property passing under certain employee benefits are common examples of property that are in your gross estate but not the probate estate. All property in your gross estate may be subject to the estate tax.

The key point is that your gross estate includes all property that you own at the time of your death. Suppose, for example, you give your daughter cash that she uses to purchase a life insurance policy on your life. Later, upon your death, the proceeds from that policy are not in your gross estate because you do not own the policy. Similarly, proceeds from Social Security received by a surviving spouse were never yours, and so are not part of your gross estate. Property that you have previously given to others is not part of your gross estate, either. In short, planning what property you will continue to own until your death is an essential part of estate planning.

15-1d The Estate Planning Process

The estate planning process consists of seven important steps, as summarized in Exhibit 15.2. First, you must assess your family situation, evaluate its

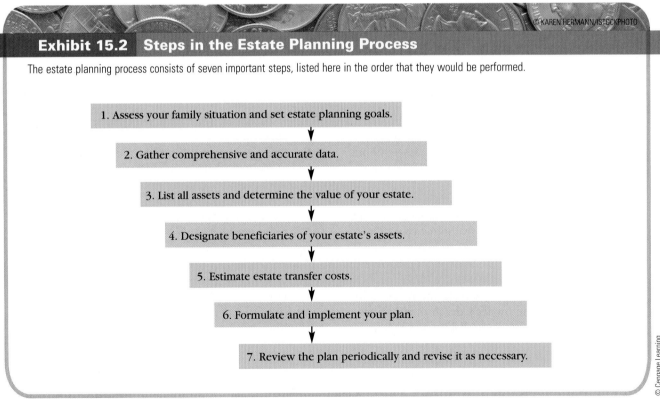

Exhibit 15.2   Steps in the Estate Planning Process

The estate planning process consists of seven important steps, listed here in the order that they would be performed.

1. Assess your family situation and set estate planning goals.

2. Gather comprehensive and accurate data.

3. List all assets and determine the value of your estate.

4. Designate beneficiaries of your estate's assets.

5. Estimate estate transfer costs.

6. Formulate and implement your plan.

7. Review the plan periodically and revise it as necessary.

© Cengage Learning

strengths and weaknesses, and set estate planning goals. Next, gather comprehensive and accurate data on all aspects of the family. The Bonus Exhibit, "Data Needed for Estate Planning," summarizes the data that professionals require to prepare detailed estate plans. (Visit CourseMate for PFIN 3. Log in at **www.cengagebrain.com.**) Then, you should take inventory and determine the value of your estate. Next, you must designate beneficiaries of your estate's assets, estimate estate transfer costs, and formulate and implement your plan. The final step is ongoing: review your estate plan periodically—at least every three to five years—and revise it as circumstances dictate.

The objective of estate plans, of course, is to maximize the usefulness of people's assets during their lives and to achieve their personal objectives after their deaths. As the needs, desires, and circumstances of the parties involved change, you must modify your estate plan. Key events that should trigger an estate plan review include the death or disability of a spouse or other family member, moving to another state, changing jobs, getting married or divorced, having children, acquiring new assets, and substantial changes in income, health, or living standards. Because of the general complexity of the laws relating to estate transfer, obtaining professional assistance from an attorney, accountant, and/or financial planner is often necessary to develop an effective estate plan.

15-2 Thy Will Be Done...

LG2 A **will** is a written, legally enforceable expression or declaration of a person's wishes concerning the disposition of his or her property upon death. Unfortunately, about 70 percent of all Americans do not have valid wills. The importance of a valid will is apparent when you consider what happens when someone dies without one.

15-2a Absence of a Valid Will: Intestacy

Suppose that Jason Harless died without a valid will, a situation called **intestacy**. State intestacy laws "draw the will that the decedent failed to make" in order to determine the disposition of the probate property of those who have died intestate. Generally, under these statutes, the decedent's spouse is favored, followed by the children and then other offspring. If the spouse and children or other offspring (e.g., grandchildren or great-grandchildren) survive, then they will divide the estate, and other relatives will receive nothing. If no spouse, children, or other offspring survive, then the deceased's parents, brothers, and sisters will receive a share of the estate.

The Bonus Exhibit, "Distribution of a Typical Intestate Estate," gives an example of how a typical intestate estate is distributed. (View this exhibit at CourseMate for PFIN 3. Log in at **www.cengagebrain.com.**) After paying debts and taxes and deducting state-defined family exemptions, that individual's separately owned property would be distributed as shown. When property goes to the state due to the absence of a will, the property is said to *escheat* to the state.

In addition to not controlling the disposition of their property, a person who dies intestate also forfeits the privilege of naming a personal representative to guide the disposition of the estate, naming a guardian for persons and property, and specifying which beneficiaries would bear certain tax burdens. Estate planning and a valid will may also minimize the amount of estate shrinkage through transfer taxes. Clearly, it's important to have a valid will—regardless of the estate size.

will A written and legally enforceable document expressing how a person's property should be distributed upon his or her death.

intestacy The situation that exists when a person dies without a valid will.

Financial Planning Tips

Write a Will—No Excuses

Two out of three people don't have a will! Consider the following common excuses, and why they fall apart.

- **I'm too young to need a will.** There's a chance you won't live as long as you hope. Without a will, your heirs will have to figure it all out. Youth is no excuse—you need a will at all ages.
- **My family knows how to distribute my assets.** That may be true, but without a will it's the state that decides who gets what. For example, even if you want your spouse to inherit your assets, your children will still be given a piece of your estate.
- **I don't have enough assets to need a will.** It's not just how much you have, it's who gets whatever you own.
- **My mother would take care of the kids.** Perhaps she would, but what if your mother-in-law decides *she* wants the kids? If there is no will, then a judge will decide who gets your children.
- **Writing a will is too expensive.** It doesn't cost much to write a will. Many state bar associations make available forms for a simple will. There's even software to do it.
- **I have no kids and I'm single, so there is no one to protect.** Single or married, if you have no will then the state will leave everything to your relatives. And if you have no relatives, the state gets it all.

Source: Adapted from Finances for Women Expert, February 18, 2003, http://www.ivillage.com/wills-and-estates-write-your-will-today/7-a-219552, accessed July 2012.

MKABAKOV/SHUTTERSTOCK.COM

15-2b Preparing the Will

A will allows a person, called a **testator**, to direct the disposition of property at his or her death. The testator can change or revoke a will at any time; on the death of the testator, the will becomes operative.

Will preparation (or drafting) varies in difficulty and cost, depending on individual circumstances. In some cases, a two-page will costing $150 may be adequate; in others, a complex document costing $1,500 or more may be necessary. A will must effectively accomplish the objectives specified for distributing assets, while also taking into consideration income, gift, and estate tax laws. Will preparation also requires a knowledge of corporate, trust, real estate, and securities laws.

wills and *codicils*—legally binding modifications of an existing will.

- **Direction of payments.** This clause directs the estate to make certain payments of expenses. As a general rule, however, the rights of creditors are protected by law, so this clause might be left out of a professionally drafted will.

- **Disposition of property.** Colin's will has three examples of clauses dealing with disposition of property:

  1. *Disposition of personal effects:* A testator may also make a separate detailed and specific list of personal property and carefully identify each item, and to whom it is given, as an informal guide to help the executor divide the property. (This list generally should not

"Will drafting, no matter how modest the estate size, should not be attempted by a layperson."

A properly prepared will should meet these three important requirements:

- Provide a plan for distributing the testator's assets according to his or her wishes, the beneficiaries' needs, and federal and state dispositive and tax laws

- Consider the changes in family circumstances that might occur after its execution

- Be concise and complete in describing the testator's desires

Will drafting, no matter how modest the estate size, should not be attempted by a layperson. The complexity and interrelationships of tax, property, domestic relations, and other laws make the homemade will a potentially dangerous document. Few things may turn out to be more disastrous in the long run than the do-it-yourself will.

15-2c Common Features of the Will

There's no absolute format that must be followed when preparing a will, but most wills contain similar distinct sections. Exhibit 15.3, which presents the will of Colin Scott Burke, includes generalized examples of each of these clauses. Refer to the exhibit as you read these descriptions of the clauses.

- **Introductory clause.** An introductory clause, or preamble, normally states the testator's name and residence; this determines the county that will have legal jurisdiction and be considered the testator's domicile for tax purposes. The evocation statement nullifies old and forgotten

appear in the will itself because it's likely to be changed frequently.)

  2. *Giving money to a specifically named party:* Be sure to use the correct legal title of a charity.

  3. *Distribution of residual assets after specific gifts have been made:* Bequests to close relatives (as defined in the statute) who die before the testator will go to the relative's heirs unless the will directs otherwise. Bequests to nonrelatives who predecease the testator will go to the other residual beneficiaries.

- **Appointment clause.** Appointment clauses name the *executors* (the decedent's personal representatives who administer the estate), guardians for minor children, and trustees and their successors.

- **Tax clause.** In the absence of a specified provision in the will, the *apportionment statutes* of the testator's state will allocate the burden of taxes among the beneficiaries. The result may be an inappropriate and unintended reduction of certain beneficiaries' shares or adverse estate tax effects. Because the spouse's share and the portion going to a charity are deducted from the gross estate before arriving at the taxable estate, neither is charged with taxes.

- **Simultaneous death clause.** The assumption that the spouse survives in the event of simultaneous death is used mainly to permit the marital deduction, which offers a tax advantage. Other types of clauses are similarly designed to avoid double probate of the same assets—duplication of administrative and probate costs. Such clauses require that the survivor live for a certain period, such as 30 or 60 days, to be a beneficiary under the will.

Exhibit 15.3 **A Representative Will for Colin Scott Burke**

© KAREN HERMANN/ISTOCKPHOTO

Colin Scott Burke's will illustrates the eight distinct sections of most wills.

The Last Will and Testament of Colin Scott Burke

Section 1 — Introductory Clause

I, Colin Scott Burke, of the city of Chicago, state of Illinois, do, hereby make my last will and revoke all wills and codicils made prior to this will.

Section 2 — Direction of Payments

Article 1: Payment of Debts and Expenses

I direct payment out of my estate of all just debts and the expenses of my last illness and funeral.

Section 3 — Disposition of Property

Article 2: Disposition of Property

I give and bequeath to my wife, Rebecca Olsen Burke, all my jewelry, automobiles, books, and photography equipment, as well as all other articles of personal and household use.

I give to the Chicago Historical Society the sum of $100,000.

All the rest, residue, and remainder of my estate, real and personal, wherever located, I give in equal one-half shares to my children, Sean Bruce and Deborah Jane, their heirs and assigns forever.

Section 4 — Appointment Clause

Article 3: Nomination of Executor and Guardian

I hereby nominate as the Executor of this Will my beloved wife, Rebecca Olsen Burke, but if she is unable or unwilling to serve then I nominate my brother, John David Burke. In the event both persons named predecease me, or shall cease or fail to act, then I nominate as Executor in the place of said persons, the Midwestern Trust Bank of Chicago, Illinois.

If my wife does not survive me, I appoint my brother, James Franklin Burke, Guardian of the person and property of my son, Sean Bruce, during his minority.

Section 5 — Tax Clause

Article 4: Payment of Taxes

I direct that there shall be paid out of my residuary estate (from that portion which does not qualify for the marital deduction) all estate, inheritance, and similar taxes imposed by a government in respect to property includable in my estate for tax purposes, whether the property passes under this will or otherwise.

Section 6 — Simultaneous Death Clause

Article 5: Simultaneous Death

If my wife and I shall die under such circumstances that there is not sufficient evidence to determine the order of our deaths, then it shall be presumed that she survived me. My estate shall be administered and distributed in all respects in accordance with such assumption.

Section 7 — Execution and Attestation Clause

In witness thereof, I have affixed my signature to this, my last will and testament, which consists of five (5) pages, each of which I have initialed, this 15th day of September, 2015.

Colin Scott Burke
_____

Section 8 — Witness Clause

Signed, sealed, and published by Colin Scott Burke, the testator, as his last will, in the presence of us, who, at his request, and in the presence of each other, all being present at the same time, have written our names as witnesses.

(Note: Normally the witness signatures and addresses would follow this clause.)

© Cengage Learning

- **Execution and attestation clause.** Every will should be in writing and signed by the testator at its end as a precaution against fraud. Many attorneys suggest that the testator also initial each page after the last line or sign in a corner of each page.

- **Witness clause.** The final clause helps to affirm that the will in question is really that of the deceased. All states require two witnesses to the testator's signing of the will. Most states require witnesses to sign in the presence of one another after they witness the signing by the testator. Their addresses should be noted on the will. If the testator is unable to sign his or her name for any reason, most states allow the testator to make a mark and to have another person (properly witnessed) sign for him or her.

15-2d Requirements of a Valid Will

To be valid, a will must be the product of a person with a sound mind, there must have been no *undue influence* (influence that would remove the testator's freedom of choice), the will itself must have been properly executed, and its execution must be free from fraud.

1. **Mental capacity.** You must be of "sound mind" to make a valid will. This means that you:

   a. Know what a will is and are aware that you are making and signing one

   b. Understand your relationship with persons for whom you would normally provide, such as a spouse or children, and who would generally be expected to receive your estate (even though you might not be required to leave anything to them)

   c. Understand what you own

   d. Are able to decide how to distribute your property

   Generally, mental capacity is presumed. Setting aside a will requires clear and convincing proof of mental incapacity, and the burden of proof is on the person contesting the will.

2. **Freedom of choice.** When you prepare and execute your will, you must not be under the undue influence of another person. Threats, misrepresentations, inordinate flattery, or some physical or mental coercion employed to destroy the testator's freedom of choice are all types of undue influence.

3. **Proper execution.** To be considered properly executed, a will must meet the requirements of the state's wills act or its equivalent. It must also be demonstrable that it is, in fact, the will of the testator. Most states have statutes that spell out who may make a will (generally any person of sound mind, age 18 or older but 14 in Georgia and 16 in Louisiana), the form and execution the will must have (most states require a will to be in writing and to be signed by the testator at the logical end), and requirements for witnesses. Generally, a beneficiary should not serve as a witness.

15-2e Changing or Revoking the Will: Codicils

Because a will is inoperative until the testator's death, the testator (only) can change it at any time, so long as he or she has the mental capacity. In fact, periodic revisions should occur, especially upon these events:

- His or her (or the beneficiaries') health or financial circumstances change significantly.

- Births, deaths, marriages, or divorces alter the operative circumstances.

Financial Planning Tips: Tips on Writing a Will

Here's a scary statistic: At the end of 2010, a survey by FindLaw.com found that about 55 percent of Americans didn't have a will! That means that they will have no opportunity to guide who will get their assets when they die. This leaves the family with a lot of legal uncertainty and some may inherit absolutely nothing. Here are some tips on how to write an effective will:

- **Be clear and precise: leave no room for interpretation.** Your will should state your name and address, assert that you are of sound mind, and explicitly note that you are not writing under any kind of duress. State exactly how you want your estate distributed. Using percentages helps to adapt to the situation when asset values go up or down significantly after the will is written.
- **Nullify the past.** If you wrote a will, clearly indicate as much and formally revoke all previous wills and codicils.
- **Manage expectations.** It's best to explain your will to all affected parties. Surprises upon your death should be minimized.
- **Don't leave any loose ends.** Use a "residual clause" to distribute any assets that you forgot to mention in the will. Bequeath any residue in whole or in part to specific individuals or charities.

- **Pick your executor carefully.** The executor is the person you choose to carry out the wishes described in your will. So this should be someone you know and trust. Always choose a backup person in case your first choice is unable to perform the function.
- **Handle your last bills.** Grant your executor the ability to pay all the taxes and funeral costs out of your estate.
- **Make sure your will is available.** A common place to store your will is in a safe-deposit box. Just make sure that your executor has access to it and that family members and your lawyer have a copy.
- **Use a lawyer.** So what if there are forms and guidance available online? Use a lawyer. Your will is important, and a lawyer will assure that you don't miss anything.

Source: "How to Write a Will," http://www.smartmoney.com/taxes/estate/how-to-write-a-will-1304667127685/, accessed July 2012.

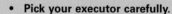

- The testator moves to a state other than where the will was executed.
- An executor, trustee, or guardian can no longer serve.
- Substantial changes occur in the tax law.

Changing the Will

A **codicil** is a simple, often single-page document that provides a convenient legal means of making minor changes in a will. It reaffirms all the existing provisions in the will except the one to be changed, and it should be executed and witnessed in the same formal manner as a will.

When a will requires substantial changes, a new will is usually preferable to a codicil. In addition, if a gift in the original will is removed, it may be best to make a new will and destroy the old in order to avoid offending the omitted beneficiary. Sometimes, however, the prior will should not be destroyed even after the new will has been made and signed. If the new will fails for some reason (because of the testator's mental incapacity, for example), then the prior will may qualify. Also, a prior will could help to prove a "continuity of testamentary purpose"—in other words, that the latest will (which may have provided a substantial gift to charity) continued an

earlier intent and wasn't an after-thought or the result of an unduly influenced mind.

Revoking the Will

A will may be revoked either by the testator or automatically by the law. A testator can revoke a will in one of four ways:

1. Making a later will that expressly revokes prior wills
2. Making a codicil that expressly revokes all wills before the one being modified
3. Making a later will that is inconsistent with a former will
4. Physically mutilating, burning, tearing, or defacing the will with the intention of revoking it

The law automatically modifies a will under certain circumstances, which vary from state to state but generally center on divorce, marriage, birth or adoption, and murder. In many states, if a testator becomes divorced after making a will, all provisions in the will relating to the spouse become ineffective. If a testator marries after making a will, the spouse receives that portion of the estate that would have been received had the testator died without a valid will. If a testator did not provide for a child born or adopted after the will was made (unless it appears that such lack of provision was intentional), the child receives that share of the estate not passing to the testator's spouse that would have been given to him or her had the deceased not had a will. Finally, almost all states have some type of slayer's statute that forbids a person who commits murder from acquiring property as the result of the deed.

15-2f Safeguarding the Will

In most cases, you should keep your original will in a safe-deposit box, with copies in a safe and accessible place at home and with the attorney who drafted it. Worksheet 15.1 contains an executor's checklist of documents and information that should be kept in a safe-deposit box. If each spouse has a separate safe-deposit box, then the couple may want to keep their wills in each other's boxes. Some states provide for *lodging* of the will, a mechanism for filing and safekeeping it in the office of the probate court (also called *orphan's* or *surrogate's court*), which satisfies the need to safeguard the will.

15-2g Letter of Last Instructions

A **letter of last instructions** is the best way to communicate to others your thoughts and instructions that aren't appropriate to include in a will. It's typically an informal memorandum separate from the will. (The letter of last instructions should contain no bequests because it has no legal standing.) It's best to make several copies of the letter, keeping one at home and the

codicil A document that legally modifies a will without revoking it.

letter of last instructions An informal memo-randum that is separate from a will and contains suggestions or recommendations for carrying out a decedent's wishes.

COMSTOCK IMAGES/GETTY IMAGES

This checklist itemizes the various documents and information that the executor may need to carry out the terms of the will effectively. These items should be kept in a safe-deposit box.

CHECKLIST FOR EXECUTORS

Name (Testator) _____ Date _____

_____ 1. Marriage certificates (including prior marriages)
_____ 2. Your will and trust agreements
_____ 3. Life insurance policies or certificates
_____ 4. Your Social Security number
_____ 5. Military discharge papers

_____ 6. Bonds, stocks, and securities
_____ 7. Real estate deeds
_____ 8. Business agreements
_____ 9. Automobile titles and insurance policies
_____ 10. Property insurance policies
_____ 11. Tax information
_____ 12. Letter of last instructions

List all checking and savings account numbers, bank addresses, and locations of safe-deposit boxes:

_____ _____ _____

_____ _____ _____

List names, addresses, and phone numbers of property and life insurance agents:

_____ _____ _____

_____ _____ _____

List names, addresses, and phone numbers of attorney and accountant:

_____ _____ _____

_____ _____ _____

List names, addresses, and phone numbers of (current or last) employer. State retirement date, if applicable. Include employee benefits booklets:

_____ _____ _____

_____ _____ _____

List all debts owed to *and* by you, including names and account numbers:

_____ _____ _____

_____ _____ _____

List the names, addresses, telephone numbers, and birth dates of your children and other beneficiaries (including charities):

_____ _____ _____

_____ _____ _____

Sources: Based on Stephan R. Leimberg, Stephen N. Kandell, Ralph Gano Miller, Morey S. Rosenbloom, and Timothy C. Polacek, The Tools & Techniques of Estate Planning, 14th ed. (Upper Saddle River, NJ: Prentice Hall, 2006); http://www.enotes.com/everyday-law-encyclopedia/wills, accessed July 2012; Metropolitan Life Insurance Company, Executor's Checklist, http://www.metlife.com/assets/cao/mmi/life-advice/finances/taking-legal-action/executors-check-list.pdf, accessed July 2012.

others with the estate's executor or attorney, who can deliver it to beneficiaries at the appropriate time.

A letter of last instructions might provide directions regarding such items as:

1. Location of the will and other documents
2. Funeral and burial instructions (often a will is not opened until after the funeral)

3. Suggestions or recommendations as to the continuation, sale, or liquidation of a business
4. Personal matters that the testator might prefer not be made public in the will, such as statements (e.g., comments about a spendthrift spouse or a reckless son) that might sound unkind or inconsiderate but would be valuable to the executor

5. Recommended legal and accounting services
6. An explanation of the actions taken in the will, which may help avoid litigation (for instance, "I left only $5,000 to my son, Michael, because ..." or "I made no provisions for my oldest daughter, Victoria, because ...")
7. Suggestions on how to divide the personal property

15-2h Administration of an Estate

When people die, they usually own property and owe debts and may be owed money by other persons. The **probate process**, similar to that used in liquidating a business, is often required to settle an estate. A local court generally supervises the probate process through the *decedent's personal representative*—either an **executor** named in the decedent's will or, if the decedent died without a valid will, through a court-appointed **administrator**. The executor or administrator becomes the decedent's legal representative, taking care of such matters as collecting bank accounts and money owed the decedent, paying off debts, creating clear title to make real estate marketable, and distributing what's left to those entitled to it by will or the state's intestate laws. Clearly, an executor should not only be familiar with the testator's affairs but also be able to effectively handle the responsibilities of being an executor.

15-2i Other Important Estate Planning Documents

Several other documents that are useful in protecting your family and you include a durable power of attorney for financial matters, a living will, a durable power of attorney for health care, and an ethical will.

Power of Attorney

A **durable power of attorney for financial matters** allows you to name the person (perhaps a spouse or other relative) that you want to take over your financial affairs in the event of a serious illness. Because this simple document transfers enormous power to your designated appointee, it is important to name a qualified, trustworthy person. To make it durable—that is, effective even when you are incapacitated—the document must clearly state that your agent's authority to act on your behalf will continue during your incapacity. It is also a good idea to clear your power of attorney with all brokerage firms and mutual funds where you have accounts.

Living Will and Durable Power of Attorney for Health Care

Suppose a person falls into a coma with little or no hope of recovery. Without a *living will* or *durable power of attorney for health care* to guide them, his family could face difficult decisions regarding his medical care. These documents specify the medical care a person wants to receive, or *not* receive, if he or she becomes seriously ill and unable to give informed consent. The **living will** states, precisely, the desired treatments and the degree to which they are to be continued. The document must specifically state your wishes; otherwise, it might be put aside because it is too vague.

Many experts recommend a **durable power of attorney for health care**, often called *advanced directives for health care,* instead of a living will. The durable power of attorney for health care authorizes an individual (your *agent*) to make health care decisions for you if you're unable to do so either temporarily or permanently. Unlike a living will, it applies in any case where you cannot communicate your wishes, not just when you're terminally ill. You should spend some time specifying the scope of the power and instructions for medical treatment; then review your thinking with your family and the person you designate as your agent. These documents, held by your designated agent and your doctor, should make it easier for your family to deal with these difficult issues.

Ethical Wills

In addition to a traditional will, many people today also prepare an **ethical will**, sometimes called a *legacy statement.* They are informal documents that are usually added to formal wills and read at the same time, that allow the deceased to share their morals, business ethics, life experiences, family stories and history, and more with future generations. They can be in the form of handwritten letters or essays, computer files, or electronic media. It's a good idea to have your lawyer review your ethical will because its interpretation could lead to a challenge of your formal will.

probate process The court-supervised disposition of a decedent's estate.

executor The personal representative of an estate designated in the decedent's will.

administrator The personal representative of the estate appointed by the court if the decedent died intestate.

durable power of attorney for financial matters A legal document that authorizes another person to take over someone's financial affairs and act on his or her behalf.

living will A document that precisely states the treatments a person wants if he or she becomes terminally ill.

durable power of attorney for health care A written power of attorney authorizing an individual to make health care decisions on behalf of the principal when the principal is unable to make such decisions. Also called *advanced directive for health care.*

ethical will A personal statement left for family, friends, and community that shares your values, blessings, life's lessons, and hopes and dreams for the future. Also called *legacy statement.*

15-2j What About Joint Ownership?

The two forms of joint ownership—*joint tenancy* or *tenants by the entirety*—share the following characteristics:

1. Under the **right of survivorship**, the interest of a decedent passes directly to the surviving joint tenant(s)—that is, to the other joint owner(s)—by operation of the law and is free from the claims of the decedent's creditors, heirs, or personal representatives.
2. A **joint tenancy** may consist of any number of persons, who don't have to be related. A **tenancy by the entirety** can exist only between husband and wife.
3. In a *joint tenancy*, each joint tenant can unilaterally sever the tenancy, whereas a *tenancy by the entirety* can be severed only by mutual agreement, divorce, or conveyance by both spouses to a third party.
4. The co-owners must have equal interests.

Joint tenancy, the more common form of joint ownership, offers a sense of family security, quick and easy transfer to the spouse at death, exemption of jointly owned property from the claims of the deceased's creditors, and avoidance of delays and publicity in the estate settlement process. The key disadvantage of joint tenancy is the inability to control jointly owned property by a will, so that the first joint owner to die cannot control the property's disposition and management on his or her death.

For example, a father who has two unmarried children—a daughter with whom he has a good relationship and an estranged son—purchases property and places it in his own and his daughter's name as joint tenants. The father has a will that leaves everything he has to his daughter and specifically disinherits his son. The daughter has no estate planning documents. While traveling together, the father is killed outright in a car accident and the daughter is severely injured; indeed, she never fully recovers, and she dies two months later. At her death, intestate, her estate will likely pass to her brother. Had her father held the property in his name only, then he could have stipulated in his will a longer survivorship requirement (say, six months) with a provision that,

in the event his daughter did not survive that period, there would be an alternative disposition (e.g., to a charity or to friends).

You should also be familiar with two other forms of ownership: *tenancy in common* and *community property*.

Tenancy in Common

Under a **tenancy in common**, there is *no right of survivorship*, and each co-owner can leave his or her share to whomever he or she desires. Thus, the decedent owner's will controls the disposition of the decedent's partial interest in the asset. Unlike joint tenancy, where all interests must be equal, tenancy in common interests can be unequal; hence, a property owned by three co-owners could be apportioned such that their respective shares are 50 percent, 30 percent, and 20 percent of the property.

Community Property

Community property, a form of marital ownership found primarily in Southwestern states, is all property acquired by the effort of either or both spouses during marriage while they reside in a community property state. For example, wages and commissions earned and property acquired by either spouse while living in a community property state are automatically owned equally by both spouses, even if only one was directly involved in acquiring the additional wealth. Property acquired before marriage or by gift or inheritance can be maintained as the acquiring spouse's separate property. Each spouse can leave his or her half of the community property to whomever he or she chooses, so there's *no right of survivorship* inherent in this form of ownership.

15-3 Trusts

LG3 Trusts, which are another important estate planning tool, facilitate the transfer of property and the income from that property to another party. A **trust** is a legal relationship created when one party, the **grantor** (also called the *settlor, trustor,* or *creator*), transfers property to a second party, the **trustee** (an organization or individual), for the benefit of third parties, the **beneficiaries**, who may or may not include the grantor. The property placed in the trust is called *trust principal* or *res* (pronounced "race"). The trustee holds the legal title to the property in the trust and must use the property and any income that it produces solely for the benefit of trust beneficiaries as specified by the grantor.

A trust may be *living* (funded during the grantor's life) or *testamentary* (created in a will and funded by the probate process). It may be *revocable* or *irrevocable*. The grantor can regain property placed into a revocable trust and alter or amend the terms of the trust. The grantor cannot recover property placed into an irrevocable trust during its term.

15-3a Why Use a Trust?

Trusts are designed for various purposes. The most common motives are to attain income and estate tax savings and to manage and conserve property over a long period.

Income and Estate Tax Savings
Under certain circumstances, a grantor who is a high-bracket tax-payer can shift the burden of paying taxes on the income produced by securities, real estate, and other investments to a trust itself or to its beneficiary, both of whom are typically subject to lower income tax rates than the grantor. Impressive *estate tax* savings are possible because the appreciation in the value of property placed into such a trust can be entirely removed from the grantor's estate and possibly benefit several generations of family members without incurring adverse federal estate tax consequences.

Managing and Conserving Property
The trustee assumes the responsibility for managing and conserving the property on behalf of the beneficiaries. Management by the trustee is sometimes held in reserve in case a healthy and vigorous individual is unexpectedly incapacitated and becomes unable or unwilling to manage his or her assets.

trust A legal relationship created when one party transfers property to a second party for the benefit of third parties.

grantor A person who creates a trust and whose property is transferred into it. Also called *settlor, trustor, or creator*.

trustee An organization or individual selected by a *grantor* to manage and conserve property placed in trust for the benefit of the *beneficiaries*.

beneficiaries Those who receive benefits—property or income—from a trust or from the estate of a decedent. A grantor can be a beneficiary of his own trust.

Financial Planning Tips: Reasons to Use a Trust

Trusts can be used to achieve various financial objectives. Consider the key reasons they are so commonly used.

- **Avoid probate.** A trust may be used to avoid the probate process, which can be expensive. However, the costs of setting up a trust should be compared with the expected cost of probate. Notwithstanding the outcome of the cost comparison, it's important to keep in mind that a probated will is a public document and trusts offer increased privacy.
- **Protection in old age and disability.** You can set up a trust, name yourself as beneficiary, and then name yourself and another person as trustees. If you become gravely ill or mentally incapacitated, the other trustee can manage your assets and distribute them as you direct in the trust arrangement.
- **Provide for minors and young adults.** You can use a trust to leave assets to minors and young adults. The trustee will manage the trust until the beneficiary reaches the age that you designate is old enough to handle the assets responsibly.

- **Avoid estate taxes.** You can set up a trust to transfer assets to an irrevocable trust to avoid estate taxes. These assets are not included in your gross estate. However, it's important that the grantor trust is not also a beneficiary or there will be limits on distributions to shield from taxation. The possibility of gift taxes must be considered. And planning must recognize that if a grantor transfers a life insurance policy to an irrevocable trust within three years before the grantor's death, the policy may well be included in the estate.
- **Reduce income taxes.** Certain types of trusts may be used to transfer income to heirs in a lower income tax bracket, which can reduce overall taxes.
- **Benefit charity.** You can transfer assets to a trust, receive income from the trust, and distribute the assets to a charity upon death. Thus, trusts may be used to provide income and estate tax benefits to support your favorite charity.

Source: Adapted from Joseph Nicholson, "How to Use a Trust to Avoid Income Taxes," http://www.ehow.com/how_5002770_use-trust-avoid-income-taxes.html, accessed July 2012.

MKABAKOV/SHUTTERSTOCK.COM

15-3b Selecting a Trustee

Five qualities are essential in a trustee. He or she must

1. Possess sound business knowledge and judgment
2. Have an intimate knowledge of the beneficiary's needs and financial situation
3. Be skilled in investment and trust management
4. Be available to beneficiaries (specifically, the trustee should be young enough to survive the trust term)
5. Be able to make decisions impartially

A corporate trustee, such as a trust company or bank that has been authorized to perform trust duties, may be best able to meet these requirements. On the other hand, a corporate trustee may charge high fees or be overly conservative in investments, be impersonal, or lack familiarity with and understanding of family problems and needs. Often a compromise involves appointing one or more individuals and a corporate trustee as co-trustees.

15-3c Common Types and Characteristics of Trusts

Although there are various types of trusts, the most common ones are the *living trust*, the *testamentary trust*, and the *irrevocable life insurance trust*, each of which is described in the following sections. Exhibit 15.4 describes seven other popular trusts.

Living Trusts

A **living (inter vivos) trust** is one created and funded during the grantor's lifetime. It can be either revocable or irrevocable and can last for a limited period or continue long after the grantor's death.

© KAREN HERMANN/ISTOCKPHOTO

Exhibit 15.4 Seven Popular Trusts

Trusts shift assets (and thus appreciation) out of one's estate while retaining some say in the future use of the assets. The drawback is that trusts can be cumbersome and expensive to arrange and administer. Here are brief descriptions of seven popular trusts:

- **Credit shelter trust.** The most common tax-saving trust for estate planning; couples with combined assets worth more than the applicable exclusion amount (AEA) can gain full use of each partner's exclusion by having that amount placed in a bypass trust—that is, one that bypasses the surviving spouse's taxable estate. It's called a *credit shelter trust* because, when one spouse dies, the trust receives assets from the decedent's estate equal in value to the estate AEA. So if the first death occurred in the year 2012, then the trust would be funded with assets worth exactly $5,120,000. This trust does not qualify for the marital deduction, but no tax is due because the tentative tax is equal to the available *unified credit*. The surviving spouse is usually given the right to all the trust income and, in an emergency, even has access to the principal. When the surviving spouse dies, the credit shelter trust is not included in his or her estate regardless of the trust's value, so it avoids having to pay a tax at both deaths.

- **Qualified terminable interest property (QTIP) trust.** Usually set up in addition to a *credit shelter trust* to ensure that money stays in the family; it receives some or all of the estate assets over the applicable exclusion amount ($5,120,000 in 2012). Assets left outright to a spouse who remarries could be claimed by the new spouse. The survivor receives all income from the property until death, when the assets go to the persons chosen by the first spouse to die. Estate taxes on QTIP trust assets can be delayed until the second spouse dies. It is also useful for couples with children from prior marriages because the QTIP property can be distributed to the children of the grantor spouse only after the death of the surviving spouse; hence, the survivor benefits from the trust's income, and the deceased spouse's children are assured that they will receive the remainder of the QTIP trust eventually.

- **Special needs trust.** An irrevocable trust established for the benefit of a person with disabilities; it is designed to provide extra help and life enrichment without reducing state and federal government help to the beneficiary.

- **Minor's section 2503(c) trust.** Set up for a minor, often to receive tax-free gifts; however, assets must be distributed to the minor before he or she turns 21.

- **Crummey trust.** Named after the first person to successfully use this trust structure, this is used to make tax-free gifts up to the annual exclusion amounts to children; unlike a *minor's section 2503(c) trust*, these funds need not be distributed before age 21. However, the beneficiary can withdraw the funds placed into the trust for a limited time (e.g., for up to 30 days), after which the right to make a withdrawal ceases.

- **Charitable lead (or income) trust.** Pays some or all of its income to a charity for a period of time, after which the property is distributed to noncharitable beneficiaries; the grantor receives an immediate income tax deduction based on expected future payout to charity. If the grantor's children are the so-called remaindermen of the trust, then the value of the gift for gift or estate tax purposes is greatly reduced because their possession and enjoyment of the trust assets is delayed until the charitable interest terminates.

- **Charitable remainder trust.** Similar to a *charitable lead trust*, except that income goes to taxable beneficiaries (e.g., the grantor or the grantor's children) and the principal goes to a charity when the trust ends; the grantor gets an immediate income tax deduction based upon the value of the remainder interest that is promised to the charity.

© Cengage Learning

REVOCABLE LIVING TRUST. The grantor reserves the right to revoke the trust and regain trust property in a **revocable living trust**. For federal income tax purposes, grantors of these trusts are treated as owners of the property in the trust and are therefore taxed on any income produced by the trust.

Revocable living trusts have three basic advantages.

1. Management continuity and income flow are ensured even after the grantor's death. No probate is necessary because the trust continues to operate after the death of the grantor just as it did while he or she was alive.

2. The trustee assumes the burdens of investment decisions and management responsibility. For example, an individual may want to control investment decisions and management policy as long as he or she is alive and healthy but sets up a trust to provide backup help in case he or she becomes unable or unwilling to continue managing the assets.

3. The details of the estate plan and the value of assets placed into the trust do not become public knowledge, as they would during the probate process.

The principal disadvantages of these trusts include the fees charged by the trustee for managing the property placed into the trust and the legal fees charged for drafting the trust instruments.

IRREVOCABLE LIVING TRUST. Grantors who establish an **irrevocable living trust** relinquish title to the property that they place in it and give up the right to revoke or terminate the trust. Such trusts have all the advantages of revocable trusts plus the potential for reducing taxes. Disadvantages of such a trust relate to the fees charged by trustees for managing assets placed into it, possible gift taxes on assets placed into it, and the grantor's forfeiture of the right to alter the terms of the trust as circumstances change.

LIVING TRUSTS AND POUR-OVER WILLS. A will can be written so that it "pours over" designated assets into a previously established revocable or irrevocable living trust. The trust may also be named the beneficiary of the grantor's insurance policies. The **pour-over will** generally contains a provision passing the estate—after debts, expenses, taxes, and specific bequests—to an existing living trust, ensuring that property left out of the living trust will make its way into the trust (that is, "pour over" into it). Such an arrangement provides for easily coordinated and well-administered management of estate assets.

Testamentary Trust
A trust created by a decedent's will is called a **testamentary trust**. Such a trust comes into existence only after the will is probated and a court order directs the executor to transfer the property to the trustee in order to fund the trust. The revocable living trust and the testamentary trust can have pretty much the same terms and long-range functions—for example, providing for asset management for the trustor's family long after the trustor has died. Indeed, the two main differences are: (1) only the living trust provides for management when and if the trustor becomes incapacitated; and (2) the living trust is funded by transfers to the trustee by assignment or deed during the trustor's life, whereas the funding mechanism for the testamentary trust is a court order distributing the property to the trustee at the end of the probate process.

Irrevocable Life Insurance Trust
A wealthy individual might want to establish an **irrevocable life insurance trust** in which the major asset of the trust is life insurance on the grantor's life. To avoid having the proceeds of the policy included in the grantor's estate, the independent trustee usually acquires the policy on the life of the wealthy person and names the trustee as the beneficiary. The terms of the trust enable the trustee to use the proceeds to pay the grantor's estate taxes, to take care of the grantor's spouse and children, and probably eventually to distribute the remainder of the proceeds to the children or other beneficiaries as specified in the trust document.

15-4 Federal Unified Transfer Taxes

LG4 The federal unified transfer tax is a tax on the right to transfer property from one individual to another. The tax affects two types of transfers: transfer by gift, referred to as the **gift tax**; and transfers through the estate, referred to as the **estate tax**. The tax base for both transfers is the fair market value of the property that is transferred. Beginning in 2012, both transfer taxes are reduced by a credit of $1,772,800, which is based upon the **applicable exclusion amount (AEA)** of $5,120,000. In addition, taxable gifts are reduced by an annual exclusion of $13,000 (adjusted for inflation)

irrevocable living trust A trust in which the grantor gives up the right to revoke or terminate the trust.

pour-over will A provision in a will that provides for the passing of the estate—after debts, expenses, taxes, and specific bequests—to an existing living trust.

testamentary trust A trust created by a decedent's will and funded through the probate process.

irrevocable life insurance trust An irrevocable trust in which the major asset is life insurance on the grantor's life.

gift tax A tax levied on the value of certain gifts made during the giver's lifetime.

estate tax A tax levied on the value of property transferred at the owner's death.

applicable exclusion amount (AEA) Credit given to each person that can be applied to the amount of federal estate tax owed by that person at death. In 2011, the AEA was $5,000,000 per spouse.

unified rate
schedule A
graduated table of
rates applied to all
taxable transfers;
used for *both* federal
gift and estate tax
purposes.

per donee. Thus, combined transfers of $5,120,000 plus the annual gift tax exclusion are not subject to the federal transfer tax. If the taxpayer is married, then the two married taxpayers each have an AEA of $5,120,000, or a total of $10,240,000, before any tax applies. The tax rate for gifts and estates is specified by the **unified rate schedule** (see the graduated table of rates in Exhibit 15.5). Also, for 2011 and 2012, if one of the spouses dies then any unused applicable exclusion amount will carry over to the other spouse; this is referred to as the *portability* of the unified transfer tax credit.

The applicable exclusion amount is high enough to remove transfer taxes from the concerns of estate planning for the middle-income taxpayer. For the upper-income taxpayer, however, the transfer tax is a major concern. For example, if a couple has a taxable estate of $20,000,000, then the transfer tax due is $3,519,200. That is a significant concern. The remainder of this section addresses these issues.

15-4a Gifts and Taxes

The transfer tax applies to the fair market value of property transferred to a donee *less* the amount of compensation given to the donor. To determine the taxable gift, this amount is reduced by the annual exclusion ($13,000 in 2011). The annual exclusion applies to each donee who is given gifts. Thus, if the taxpayer gave three people $10,000 each, none of the

Exhibit 15.5   Federal Unified Transfer Tax Rates

This *unified rate schedule* defines the amount of federal gift and estate taxes that estates of various sizes would have to pay; it incorporates the rates passed in the *Economic Growth and Tax Relief Reconciliation Act of 2001* and the *2010 Tax Relief Act*. Estates and gifts under the exclusion amount pay no federal tax. The estate exclusion amount increased annually from $2,000,000 in 2006 to $5,000,000 in 2012 (see Exhibit 15.8). From 2009 to 2012, the top tax rates for estates worth more than $2,000,000 decreased from 45 percent to 35 percent.

Taxable Estate Value		Tentative Tax		
More Than	But Not More Than	Base Amount	+Percent	On Excess Over
$ 0	$ 10,000	$ 0		
10,000	20,000	1,800	20%	$ 10,000
20,000	40,000	3,800	22	20,000
40,000	60,000	8,200	24	40,000
60,000	80,000	13,000	26	60,000
80,000	100,000	18,200	28	80,000
100,000	150,000	23,800	30	100,000
150,000	250,000	38,800	32	150,000
250,000	500,000	70,800	34	250,000
500,000	750,000	155,800	37	500,000
750,000	1,000,000	248,300	39	750,000
1,000,000	1,250,000	345,800	41	1,000,000
1,250,000	1,500,000	448,300	43	1,250,000
1,500,000	2,000,000	555,800	45	1,500,000
Top rate, 2009				
2,000,000		780,800	45	2,000,000
2010	Repealed for estates. The maximum rate for gifts is 35 percent starting at $500,000.			
2011 and 2012	The maximum rate is 35 percent starting at $500,000 for both gifts and estates.			
2013 and beyond	Returns to pre-2001 tax law levels unless otherwise modified by Congress. Most observers believe that the top rate will be 45 percent for 2013 and beyond.			

Source: Internal Revenue Code, Section 2001.

transfers would be subject to the gift tax because the annual exclusion reduces each taxable gift to $0. The one requirement is that the transfer be a gift of *present interest*, not of a future interest. A typical example of the latter is the transfer of money to a trust with the provision that the trust's beneficiary must be 30 before withdrawing funds from the trust. This beneficiary has only a future interest, not a present interest.

There are two major exceptions to the present interest rule. Transfers to a minor trust—that is, a trust that allows no withdrawals until the minor is 18—qualify for the annual exclusions. A second exception is the Crummey provision, which provides for withdrawal rights to the beneficiary for a specified period (e.g., 30 days). If the beneficiary does not ask for a withdrawal in that time period, the property must remain in the trust until it can be distributed according to the trust terms. Thus, with the Crummey withdrawal rights, transfers to the trust are considered a present and will qualify for the annual exclusion interest to the extent of the withdrawal right.

An essential first step to estate planning is making annual gifts to your potential heirs. Giving gifts reduce the taxable estate in two ways. First, any future appreciation of the gifted property is excluded from the estate because the decedent does not own the property on the date of death. Second, if the gift is so large that taxes are due, the money used to pay the tax is also removed from the estate. (There is an exception for gift taxes paid within three years of death.)

Exhibit 15.6 — Unified Credits and Applicable Exclusion Amounts for Estates and Gifts

On December 17, 2010, the Tax Relief, Unemployment Insurance Reauthorization and Job Creation Act of 2010 was signed into law. The major features of the transfer tax provisions were to reinstate the transfer tax on estates, change the applicable exclusion amount to $5 million for both gift transfers and estate transfers, and add the portability of the unified transfer tax credit. This table shows the recent history of the applicable exclusion amounts.

Year	Unified Tax Credit—Estates	Applicable Exclusion Amount—Estates	Unified Tax Credit—Gifts	Applicable Exclusion Amount—Gifts
2006	$780,800	$2,000,000	$345,800	$1,000,000
2007	$780,800	$2,000,000	$345,800	$1,000,000
2008	$780,800	$2,000,000	$345,800	$1,000,000
2009	$1,455,800	$3,500,000	$345,800	$1,000,000
2010	Estate tax repealed for 2010		$330,800	$1,000,000
2012	$1,772,800	$5,120,000	$1,772,800	$5,120,000
2013	$ 345,800	$1,000,000	$ 345,800	$1,000,000

Source: Internal Revenue Service.

Another consideration when making gifts is their impact on the income taxes of the donee. If the gifted property is to be sold by the donee for a gain, it should be noted that property received by gift has a tax basis equal to its basis in the hands of the donor (i.e., a carryover basis). Property that is inherited has a basis equal to the fair market value at the date of death. For example, assume that a taxpayer owns a beach house that was purchased for $100,000 in 1960 and now has a value of $600,000. If the beach house is gifted, the basis to the donee will be $100,000; if passed through the estate, its basis to the heir will be $600,000. So long as the property is not sold or depreciated, the basis really does not matter. However, if it is sold, then there is a difference in income tax of $75,000 (15 percent capital gains rate multiplied by the difference in basis or $500,000) between receiving the property by gift rather than through the estate.

15-4b Is It Taxable?

Not everything that's transferred by an individual is subject to a gift tax. **Annual exclusions, gift splitting,** charitable deductions, and marital deductions are all means of reducing the total amount for tax purposes.

- **Marital deduction.** Transfers between spouses, either by gift or through the estate, are generally not subject to tax because of the marital deduction. The marital deduction is the fair market value of property transferred between a married couple minus the annual exclusion. The one potential issue is that the receiving spouse must have a terminable interest in the property. This means that, upon her (or his, the second to die) death, the property must be in her estate and subject to tax—although it may not be taxed because of the transfer tax credit or other deductions.

- **The Qualified Terminable Interest Trust (QTIP).** This is an exception to the prohibition against a nonterminable interest. In this case, property transferred to a QTIP will qualify for the marital deduction even though the surviving spouse's interest terminates at death. The essential requirements are that the receiving spouse have a life estate (i.e., an interest for the reminder of her or his life) in the income from the property and that the income be paid to the spouse during her or his life. Upon the death of the surviving spouse, the property is distributed as provided by the first-to-die spouse in the trust agreement. This type of trust is most useful when there are two sets of

children (his and hers) and the first to die wants to insure that (say) his children and his surviving spouse are provided for in the estate plan.

- **Gift splitting.** Recall that donors may make gifts up to the annual exclusion ($13,000 in 2011) with no tax impact. Thus, a husband and wife may give a total of $26,000 to a single donee and incur no tax. Sometimes it is convenient for only one of the spouses to transfer property to a single donee. If the amount is over the annual exclusion, it may be taxable. In such cases, the donor's spouse may elect to split the donation of a gift. Thus, two annual exclusions apply and each spouse's unified transfer tax credit will apply to the transfer. Because this election by the spouse must be reported, gift tax returns must be filed.

- **Charitable contributions.** Many estate plans include a provision for charitable contributions. Transfers to charities are not subject to tax because of the deduction for charitable contributions. Once the decision has been made to make charitable contributions, the issue becomes whether to give now (during life) or later (at death) through bequests from the estate. There are many advantages to giving now rather than later. A lifetime gift results in an income tax deduction (namely, a tax savings of 35 percent at the top 2011 rate). In addition, such gifts are removed from the estate and so there is an estate tax saving (35 percent top 2011 rate). Finally, a lifetime gift allows the donor to observe the effect of the gift on the charitable organization and to receive psychic income in the form of gratitude or other recognition. Another consideration is the need of funds for living. Obviously, you cannot give so much of your wealth to charity that you no longer have enough to live on. You must provide for yourself and your family before charity. However, most large estates are able and desire to give charitable gifts.

15-4c Gifts and the Estate Plan

Gift giving is the number one component of an estate plan. The reasons for its importance are listed here:

- **Annual exclusion.** As noted earlier, gifts up to the $13,000 (2011) may be transferred with no tax impact.

- **Gift splitting.** This is the case in which gifts may be split between husband and wife. Thus, $26,000 may be transferred to one donee per year.

- The **unified transfer tax credit** ($1,772,800 in 2012), which is based on the applicable exclusion amount ($5,120,000 in 2012), may be used to reduce any gift tax. Of course, the more credit is used for gifts, the less credit is available to reduce the estate tax.

- The **marital deduction** exempts from taxation any property that is transferred between spouses.

- **Charitable contributions** given during life provide an income tax deduction and remove property from the estate.

- If **property is expected to appreciate in value**, transferring now, before that appreciation is realized, will reduce the amount of transfer tax assessed on the property.

- If a gift tax is paid, then the amount of that tax goes out of the estate. However, that portion of the gift in excess of the annual exclusion (the adjusted taxable gift) is added to the gross estate to determine the tax on the estate.

- Finally, the joy of seeing others enjoy your wealth creates psychic income that will brighten your days.

15-5 Calculating Estate Taxes

LG5 Federal estate taxes are levied on the transfer of property at death, so one goal of effective estate planning is to minimize the amount of estate taxes paid. The tax is based on the value of the property that the deceased transfers (or is deemed to transfer) to others. The phrase "is deemed to transfer" is important because the estate tax applies not only to transfers that a deceased actually makes at death, but also to certain transfers made during the person's lifetime—called *lifetime gifts*. For example, if the owner-insured gives away his or her life insurance policy within three years of his or her death, the proceeds will be included in the insured's gross estate.

> **unified tax credit** The credit that can be applied against the tentative tax on the estate tax base.

15-5a Computing the Federal Estate Tax

The computation of federal estate taxes involves six steps.

1. Determine the *gross estate*, the fair market value of all property in which the decedent had an interest and that is required to be included in the estate.

2. Find the *adjusted gross estate* by subtracting from the gross estate any allowable funeral and administrative expenses, debts, and other expenses incurred during administration.

3. Calculate the *taxable estate* by subtracting any allowable marital deduction or charitable deduction from the adjusted gross estate.

4. Compute the *estate tax base*. After determining the value of the taxable estate, any "adjusted taxable gifts" (i.e., gifts above the annual exclusion) made after 1976 are added to the taxable estate. The unified tax rate schedule, shown in Exhibit 15.5, is used to determine a *tentative tax* on the estate tax base.

5. After finding the tentative tax, subtract both the gift taxes the decedent paid on the adjusted taxable gifts and the **unified tax credit** (described below). The result is the total death taxes.

6. Determine the *federal estate tax due*. Some estates will qualify for additional credits, which are fairly rare but when available result in a dollar-for-dollar reduction of the tax. After reducing the total death taxes by any eligible credits, the federal estate tax due is payable by the decedent's executor, generally within nine months of the decedent's death.

You can use Worksheet 15.2 to estimate federal estate taxes. The worksheet depicts the computations for a hypothetical situation involving a death in 2012, when the $5,120,000 million estate AEA applies. Note that the AEA is not subtracted from the gross estate. The worksheet is useful in following the flow of dollars from the gross estate to the federal estate tax due. The worksheet factors the unified credit for the year 2011 into the calculation at line 9b. The $1,772,800

This worksheet is useful in determining federal estate tax due. Note that taxes are payable at the marginal tax rate applicable to the estate tax base (line 7), which is the amount that exists before the tax-free exclusion is factored in by application of the unified credit.

COMPUTING FEDERAL ESTATE TAX DUE

Name Trevor Haddon   Date 9/5/2012

Line	Computation	Item	Amount	Total Amount
1		Gross estate		$ 7,850,000
2	Subtract sum of:	(a) Funeral expenses	$ 6,800	
		(b) Administrative expenses	75,000	
		(c) Debts	125,000	
		(d) Other expenses	0	
		Total		(206,800)
3	Result:	Adjusted gross estate		$ 7,643,200
4	Subtract sum of:	(a) Marital deduction	0	
		(b) Charitable deduction	180,000	
		Total		(180,000)
5	Result:	Taxable estate		$ 7,463,200
6	Add:	Adjusted taxable gifts (post-1976)		$ 0
7	Result:	Estate tax base		$ 7,463,200
8	Compute:	Tentative tax on estate tax base[a]		$ 2,592,920
9	Subtract sum of:	(a) Gift tax payable on post-1976 gifts	$ 0	
		(b) Unified tax credit[b]	$ 1,772,800	
		Total		($ 1,772,800)
10	Result:	Total estate taxes[c]		820,120
11	Subtract:	Other credits		($ 0)
12	Result:	Federal estate tax due		$ 820,120

[a]Use Exhibit 15.5 to calculate the tentative tax.

[b]Use Exhibit 15.6 to determine the appropriate unified credit.

[c]Note that the tax amount shown on line 10 is the significant number because most states are "pickup tax" states, meaning that the state simply collects the state death tax credit, a dollar-for-dollar credit.

shown on that line is equal to the tentative tax on an estate tax base of $5 million. If the tentative tax shown on line 8 is less than the unified credit available for the decedent's year of death, then no federal estate tax is due.

15-6 Estate Planning Techniques

LG6 Estate planning is the process of developing a plan to administer and distribute your estate after your death, in a manner consistent with your wishes and the needs of your survivors, while minimizing taxes. The primary taxes to consider are the income tax, the gift tax, and the estate tax. In developing a plan to distribute your estate, these three taxes must be taken into account. For 2012, the applicable exemption amount is $5,120,000, with a portability feature that allows the surviving spouse to use the unified transfer tax credit not used by the deceased spouse. For a married couple, then, there is no transfer tax until $10,240,000 is transferred. In the balance of this section we discuss common estate planning techniques.

> **An estate plan will administer and distribute your estate after your death, in a manner consistent with your wishes and the needs of your survivors, while minimizing taxes.**

15-6a Gift Giving Program

With the annual exclusion of $13,000 and the ability to split gifts, a married couple may transfer $26,000 per year per donee. Giving gifts reduces the transfer tax and gives added joy to the donor. When selecting the property to give, the impact on income tax must be considered. Recall that the basis of gifted property is generally the cost of the property to the donor and that the basis of inherited property is the fair market value reported on the estate tax return. So if the property is expected to be sold, then there will be a higher gain for income tax purposes if the property is gifted (though only at the capital gains tax rate, at 15 percent in and 2012) than if the property is transferred at death through the estate. If the transfer will result in transfer taxes being paid, then the 35 percent transfer tax will probably be greater than the associated income tax relating to the property. In this case, it would be better to gift the property early, when the value is relatively low, even though the donee will have to pay tax on the gain when the property is sold.

15-6b Use of the Unified Transfer Tax Credit

Prior to 2011, the unified transfer tax (UTT) credit was unique to the individual. Thus, if an individual did not use it, then he or she would lose it. For 2011 and 2012, Congress added portability to the credit, which allows the surviving spouse to use the deceased spouse's UTT credit. Because it is not certain that the portability feature will remain in the tax law, it is appropriate to take steps to ensure that the combination of the marital deduction and the UTT credit does not result in losing part of the credit. The common tools used are the "credit shelter trust"

(also referred to as the *bypass trust*) and the QTIP trust, discussed earlier in this chapter. Property equal in value to the unused applicable exemption amount will be transferred at death to the credit shelter trust, resulting in tax for the first to die. The related unused UTT credit will reduce the estate tax to zero. The property in the credit shelter trust will bypass the surviving spouse's estate. The balance of the estate will be transferred either directly to the surviving spouse or to the QTIP and thereby qualify for the marital deduction resulting in no tax. Thus, the full UTT credit has been used by both spouses, and no credit has been lost.

15-6c Charitable Contributions

If the taxpayer desires to make charitable contributions, the question to answer is whether the contribution should be made now (during life) or later (at death). If made now, the taxpayer gets an income tax deduction and the property is out of the estate. The added benefit of the income tax savings tips the charitable contribution timing question in favor of giving during life. Of course, if the funds are needed to live, then no contribution should be made until death. Transfers to charity at death are appropriate in such cases.

15-6d Life Insurance Trust

Many estates have life insurance as one of their major assets. The primary purpose of life insurance is to replace lost income upon the death of the insured or to provide cash to pay a transfer tax at death. To minimize the transfer tax when that is the purpose of the insurance, the taxpayer may transfer the insurance to a life insurance trust in order to get the proceeds out of the estate. The transfer of the policy to the trust must be at least three years before death or it is ignored, in which case the life insurance benefits are included in the taxable estate.

15-6e Trusts

One of the many uses of trusts is to split the income among family members and thereby reduce total income tax paid. However, the trust income tax rates are extremely compressed: in 2010, the top rate of 35 percent applied to income over $11,200. The trust income tax may be avoided by transferring income property to the beneficiaries. If the beneficiary is a minor, however, such income may be taxed at his or her parents' tax rate.

15-6f Valuation Issues

The tax base for the transfer tax is fair market value. When the estate includes closely held stocks, real estate, or large blocks of listed securities, there are discounts that apply to valuation of the property. The following are the most used discounts.

- **Minority interest.** If the ownership of a closely held company is less than 50 percent of the stock, then it is a minority interest. Discounts of 25 percent to 30 percent are common. Thus, if the stock is considered to have a value of $100 per share, then a 30 percent minority interest discount will reduce the fair market value for inclusion in the taxable estate to $70 per share.

- **Marketability discount.** If a large amount of real estate is for sale in one market or area, the value will be reduced solely because of marketability factors. These discounts range from 10 percent to 30 percent.

- **Blockage discounts.** If a large block of stock of a listed company is sold, the market will react to reduce the price of the stock. For a publicly held company, 1 percent of the stock is a large enough block to reduce the value. So if that amount of stock is in the gross estate, then the value subject to the tax will be reduced by the blockage discount. Discounts of 5 percent to 15 percent are common.

15-6g Future of the Transfer Tax

The Congress began discussing changes to the transfer tax in 2009. The changes were enacted in December 2010, and the changes that were enacted (top rate of 35 percent, AEA of $5,000,000, adjusted for inflation, and portability of the UTT credit) only apply to the years 2011 and 2012. What happens in 2013?—that is the question. In April 2011, the best guess (and it is only a guess) is that the top rate will be made equal to the top rate for income tax purposes, which may be as high as 40 percent. The AEA should remain about the same: between $3 and $5 million. The future of the UTT credit's portability is unknown.

The transfer tax is a major concern to taxpayers with wealth over $10,000,000 but much less so for less wealthy taxpayers. However, estate planning is a concern to all, and the issues discussed in this chapter apply to all estates, large and small. With respect to the future of the UTT, bear in mind that the only certainty in life is change. What the tax law is today will not be the law in the future. Keep your estate plan in a word processing file so you can edit it on an annual basis.

Planning Over a Lifetime: Estate Planning

Here are some key considerations for estate planning in each stage of the life cycle.

Pre-family Independence: 20s	Family Formation/Career Development: 30–45	Pre-Retirement: 45–65	Retirement: 65 and Beyond
✓ While it might seem unnecessary when you're getting started, a will should be made.	✓ Update your will as your circumstances change. Specify who will care for your children if you and your spouse die prematurely.	✓ Start estate planning and consider trust arrangements for children.	✓ Establish a well-thought-out estate plan. Update your will to be as specific as possible about the distribution of all property, especially personal property.
✓ A living will is a good idea as well as a durable power of attorney for health care. Make them available to your family and physicians.	✓ Make sure your will is available to family members.	✓ Revise your will as your children become adults and finish school.	✓ Consider explaining to your children what they will inherit and your rationale.
	✓ Prepare a durable power of attorney for financial matters.	✓ Review and revise as needed your durable power of attorney for financial matters and health care at least every few years.	✓ Make sure that a comprehensive list of your financial accounts is available to your spouse and family.
			✓ You and your spouse should make and fund your funeral arrangements to spare your family this burden.

FINANCIAL PLANNING EXERCISES

LG1 1. David and Cheryl Allen are in their mid-30s and have two children, ages 8 and 5. They have combined annual income of $95,000 and own a house in joint tenancy with a market value of $310,000, on which they have a mortgage of $250,000. David has $100,000 in group term life insurance and an individual universal life policy for $150,000. However, the Allens haven't prepared their wills. David plans to do one soon, but they think that Cheryl doesn't need one because the house is jointly owned. As their financial planner, explain why it's important for both David and Cheryl to draft wills as soon as possible.

LG2 2. Your best friend has asked you to be executor of his estate. What qualifications do you need, and would you accept the responsibility?

LG2, 3, 5 3. George Reed, 48 and a widower, and Debbie Moore, 44 and divorced, were married five years ago. They have children from their prior marriages, two children for George and one child for Debbie. The couple's estate is valued at $1.4 million, including a house valued at $475,000, a vacation home in the mountains, investments, antique furniture that has been in Debbie's family for many years, and jewelry belonging to George's first wife. Discuss how they could use trusts as part of their estate planning, and suggest some other ideas for them to consider when preparing their wills and related documents.

LG4, 5 4. *Use Worksheet 15.2.* When Russell Hypes died in 2012, he left an estate valued at $5,850,000. His trust directed distribution as follows: $20,000 to the local hospital, $160,000 to his alma mater, and the remainder to his three adult children. Death-related costs were $6,800 for funeral expenses, $40,000 paid to attorneys, $5,000 paid to accountants, and $30,000 paid to the trustee of his living trust. In addition, there were debts of $125,000. Use Worksheet 15.2 and Exhibits 15.5 and 15.6 to calculate the federal estate tax due on his estate.

LG4, 5 5. Althea has accumulated substantial wealth and plans to gift some of her wealth to her son Jamal. She is considering two assets: a beach house, which cost $150,000 20 years ago and now has a fair market value of $500,000; and stock in Rich Corporation, which cost her $400,000 5 years ago and now has a fair market value of $500,000. Prepare a memo advising Althea which property to give to Jamal. In your memo, consider two scenarios: one where Jamal sells the property and one where he does not.

LG4, 5 6. Michael died in 2012, leaving an estate of $23,000,000. Michael's wife died in 2010. In 2009, Michael gave his son property that resulted in a taxable gift of $3,000,000 and upon which Michael paid $885,000 in transfer taxes. Michael had made no other taxable gifts during his life. Michael's will provided a charitable bequest of $1,000,000 to his church. Determine the federal transfer tax on Michael's estate.

PFIN Student Study Tools—Visit CourseMate for PFIN 3. Log in at **www.cengagebrain.com**. Check out the bonus exercises and exhibits, interactive worksheets, Smart Sites, Critical Thinking Cases, Money Online, Kiplinger videos, quizzing, and more.

Cool Apps—Look for this new feature on CourseMate for PFIN 3. Cool Apps navigates the growing world of apps that are available for personal financial planning and tracking.

THE **CROWD**
IN-

Share your 4LTR Press story on Facebook at
www.facebook.com/4ltrpress for a chance to win.

To learn more about the In-
Crowd opportunity 'like' us
on Facebook.

© Go Media | © Cengage Learning 2011

APPENDIX A
Table of Future Value Factors

Instructions: To use this table, find the future value factor that corresponds to both a given time period (year) and an interest rate. For example, if you want the future value factor for 6 years and 10%, move across from year 6 and down from 10% to the point at which the row and column intersect: 1.772. Other illustrations: for 3 years and 15%, the proper future value factor is 1.521; for 30 years and 8%, it is 10.063.

INTEREST RATE

Period	1%	2%	3%	4%	5%	6%	7%	8%	9%	10%	11%	12%	13%	14%	15%	16%	17%	18%	19%	20%	25%	30%
1	1.010	1.020	1.030	1.040	1.050	1.060	1.070	1.080	1.090	1.100	1.110	1.120	1.130	1.140	1.150	1.160	1.170	1.180	1.190	1.200	1.250	1.300
2	1.020	1.040	1.061	1.082	1.103	1.124	1.145	1.166	1.188	1.210	1.232	1.254	1.277	1.300	1.323	1.346	1.369	1.392	1.416	1.440	1.563	1.690
3	1.030	1.061	1.093	1.125	1.158	1.191	1.225	1.260	1.295	1.331	1.368	1.405	1.443	1.482	1.521	1.561	1.602	1.643	1.685	1.728	1.953	2.197
4	1.041	1.082	1.126	1.170	1.216	1.262	1.311	1.360	1.412	1.464	1.518	1.574	1.630	1.689	1.749	1.811	1.874	1.939	2.005	2.074	2.441	2.856
5	1.051	1.104	1.159	1.217	1.276	1.338	1.403	1.469	1.539	1.611	1.685	1.762	1.842	1.925	2.011	2.100	2.192	2.288	2.386	2.488	3.052	3.713
6	1.062	1.126	1.194	1.265	1.340	1.419	1.501	1.587	1.677	1.772	1.870	1.974	2.082	2.195	2.313	2.436	2.565	2.700	2.840	2.986	3.815	4.827
7	1.072	1.149	1.230	1.316	1.407	1.504	1.606	1.714	1.828	1.949	2.076	2.211	2.353	2.502	2.660	2.826	3.001	3.185	3.379	3.583	4.768	6.275
8	1.083	1.172	1.267	1.369	1.477	1.594	1.718	1.851	1.993	2.144	2.305	2.476	2.658	2.853	3.059	3.278	3.511	3.759	4.021	4.300	5.960	8.157
9	1.094	1.195	1.305	1.423	1.551	1.689	1.838	1.999	2.172	2.358	2.558	2.773	3.004	3.252	3.518	3.803	4.108	4.435	4.785	5.160	7.451	10.604
10	1.105	1.219	1.344	1.480	1.629	1.791	1.967	2.159	2.367	2.594	2.839	3.106	3.395	3.707	4.046	4.411	4.807	5.234	5.695	6.192	9.313	13.786
11	1.116	1.243	1.384	1.539	1.710	1.898	2.105	2.332	2.580	2.853	3.152	3.479	3.836	4.226	4.652	5.117	5.624	6.176	6.777	7.430	11.642	17.922
12	1.127	1.268	1.426	1.601	1.796	2.012	2.252	2.518	2.813	3.138	3.498	3.896	4.335	4.818	5.350	5.936	6.580	7.288	8.064	8.916	14.552	23.298
13	1.138	1.294	1.469	1.665	1.886	2.133	2.410	2.720	3.066	3.452	3.883	4.363	4.898	5.492	6.153	6.886	7.699	8.599	9.596	10.699	18.190	30.288
14	1.149	1.319	1.513	1.732	1.980	2.261	2.579	2.937	3.342	3.797	4.310	4.887	5.535	6.261	7.076	7.988	9.007	10.147	11.420	12.839	22.737	39.374
15	1.161	1.346	1.558	1.801	2.079	2.397	2.759	3.172	3.642	4.177	4.785	5.474	6.254	7.138	8.137	9.266	10.539	11.974	13.590	15.407	28.422	51.186
16	1.173	1.373	1.605	1.873	2.183	2.540	2.952	3.426	3.970	4.595	5.311	6.130	7.067	8.137	9.358	10.748	12.330	14.129	16.172	18.488	35.527	66.542
17	1.184	1.400	1.653	1.948	2.292	2.693	3.159	3.700	4.328	5.054	5.895	6.866	7.986	9.276	10.761	12.468	14.426	16.672	19.244	22.186	44.409	86.504
18	1.196	1.428	1.702	2.026	2.407	2.854	3.380	3.996	4.717	5.560	6.544	7.690	9.024	10.575	12.375	14.463	16.879	19.673	22.901	26.623	55.511	112.455
19	1.208	1.457	1.754	2.107	2.527	3.026	3.617	4.316	5.142	6.116	7.263	8.613	10.197	12.056	14.232	16.777	19.748	23.214	27.252	31.948	69.389	146.192
20	1.220	1.486	1.806	2.191	2.653	3.207	3.870	4.661	5.604	6.727	8.062	9.646	11.523	13.743	16.367	19.461	23.106	27.393	32.429	38.338	86.736	190.050
21	1.232	1.516	1.860	2.279	2.786	3.400	4.141	5.034	6.109	7.400	8.949	10.804	13.021	15.668	18.822	22.574	27.034	32.324	38.591	46.005	108.420	247.065
22	1.245	1.546	1.916	2.370	2.925	3.604	4.430	5.437	6.659	8.140	9.934	12.100	14.714	17.861	21.645	26.186	31.629	38.142	45.923	55.206	135.525	321.184
23	1.257	1.577	1.974	2.465	3.072	3.820	4.741	5.871	7.258	8.954	11.026	13.552	16.627	20.362	24.891	30.376	37.006	45.008	54.649	66.247	169.407	417.539
24	1.270	1.608	2.033	2.563	3.225	4.049	5.072	6.341	7.911	9.850	12.239	15.179	18.788	23.212	28.625	35.236	43.297	53.109	65.032	79.497	211.758	542.801
25	1.282	1.641	2.094	2.666	3.386	4.292	5.427	6.848	8.623	10.835	13.585	17.000	21.231	26.462	32.919	40.874	50.658	62.669	77.388	95.396	264.698	705.641
26	1.295	1.673	2.157	2.772	3.556	4.549	5.807	7.396	9.399	11.918	15.080	19.040	23.991	30.167	37.857	47.414	59.270	73.949	92.092	114.475	330.872	917.333
27	1.308	1.707	2.221	2.883	3.733	4.822	6.214	7.988	10.245	13.110	16.739	21.325	27.109	34.390	43.535	55.000	69.345	87.260	109.589	137.371	413.590	1,192.533
28	1.321	1.741	2.288	2.999	3.920	5.112	6.649	8.627	11.167	14.421	18.580	23.884	30.633	39.204	50.066	63.800	81.134	102.967	130.411	164.845	516.988	1,550.293
29	1.335	1.776	2.357	3.119	4.116	5.418	7.114	9.317	12.172	15.863	20.624	26.750	34.616	44.693	57.575	74.009	94.927	121.501	155.189	197.814	646.235	2,015.381
30	1.348	1.811	2.427	3.243	4.322	5.743	7.612	10.063	13.268	17.449	22.892	29.960	39.116	50.950	66.212	85.850	111.065	143.371	184.675	237.376	807.794	2,619.996
35	1.417	2.000	2.814	3.946	5.516	7.686	10.677	14.785	20.414	28.102	38.575	52.800	72.069	98.100	133.176	180.314	243.503	327.997	440.701	590.668	2,465.190	9,727.860
40	1.489	2.208	3.262	4.801	7.040	10.286	14.974	21.725	31.409	45.259	65.001	93.051	132.782	188.884	267.864	378.721	533.869	750.378	1,051.668	1,469.772	7,523.164	36,118.865

Note: All factors are rounded to the nearest 1/1000 in order to agree with values used in the text.

APPENDIX B

Table of Future Value Annuity Factors

Instructions: To use this table, find the future value of annuity factor that corresponds to both a given time period (year) and an interest rate. For example, if you want the future value of annuity factor for 6 years and 10%, move across from year 6 and down from 10% to the point at which the row and column intersect: 7.716. Other illustrations: for 3 years and 15%, the proper future value of annuity factor is 3.473; for 30 years and 6%, it is 79.058.

INTEREST RATE

Period	1%	2%	3%	4%	5%	6%	7%	8%	9%	10%	11%	12%	13%	14%	15%	16%	17%	18%	19%	20%	25%	30%
1	1.000	1.000	1.000	1.000	1.000	1.000	1.000	1.000	1.000	1.000	1.000	1.000	1.000	1.000	1.000	1.000	1.000	1.000	1.000	1.000	1.000	1.000
2	2.010	2.020	2.030	2.040	2.050	2.060	2.070	2.080	2.090	2.100	2.110	2.120	2.130	2.140	2.150	2.160	2.170	2.180	2.190	2.200	2.250	2.300
3	3.030	3.060	3.091	3.122	3.153	3.184	3.215	3.246	3.278	3.310	3.342	3.374	3.407	3.440	3.473	3.506	3.539	3.572	3.606	3.640	3.813	3.990
4	4.060	4.122	4.184	4.246	4.310	4.375	4.440	4.506	4.573	4.641	4.710	4.779	4.850	4.921	4.993	5.066	5.141	5.215	5.291	5.368	5.766	6.187
5	5.101	5.204	5.309	5.416	5.526	5.637	5.751	5.867	5.985	6.105	6.228	6.353	6.480	6.610	6.742	6.877	7.014	7.154	7.297	7.442	8.207	9.043
6	6.152	6.308	6.468	6.633	6.802	6.975	7.153	7.336	7.523	7.716	7.913	8.115	8.323	8.536	8.754	8.977	9.207	9.442	9.683	9.930	11.259	12.756
7	7.214	7.434	7.662	7.898	8.142	8.394	8.654	8.923	9.200	9.487	9.783	10.089	10.405	10.730	11.067	11.414	11.772	12.142	12.523	12.916	15.073	17.583
8	8.286	8.583	8.892	9.214	9.549	9.897	10.260	10.637	11.028	11.436	11.859	12.300	12.757	13.233	13.727	14.240	14.773	15.327	15.902	16.499	19.842	23.858
9	9.369	9.755	10.159	10.583	11.027	11.491	11.978	12.488	13.021	13.579	14.164	14.776	15.416	16.085	16.786	17.519	18.285	19.086	19.923	20.799	25.802	32.015
10	10.462	10.950	11.464	12.006	12.578	13.181	13.816	14.487	15.193	15.937	16.722	17.549	18.420	19.337	20.304	21.321	22.393	23.521	24.709	25.959	33.253	42.619
11	11.567	12.169	12.808	13.486	14.207	14.972	15.784	16.645	17.560	18.531	19.561	20.655	21.814	23.045	24.349	25.733	27.200	28.755	30.404	32.150	42.566	56.405
12	12.683	13.412	14.192	15.026	15.917	16.870	17.888	18.977	20.141	21.384	22.713	24.133	25.650	27.271	29.002	30.850	32.824	34.931	37.180	39.581	54.208	74.327
13	13.809	14.680	15.618	16.627	17.713	18.882	20.141	21.495	22.953	24.523	26.212	28.029	29.985	32.089	34.352	36.786	39.404	42.219	45.244	48.497	68.760	97.625
14	14.947	15.974	17.086	18.292	19.599	21.015	22.550	24.215	26.019	27.975	30.095	32.393	34.883	37.581	40.505	43.672	47.103	50.818	54.841	59.196	86.949	127.913
15	16.097	17.293	18.599	20.024	21.579	23.276	25.129	27.152	29.361	31.772	34.405	37.280	40.417	43.842	47.580	51.660	56.110	60.965	66.261	72.035	109.687	167.286
16	17.258	18.639	20.157	21.825	23.657	25.673	27.888	30.324	33.003	35.950	39.190	42.753	46.672	50.980	55.717	60.925	66.649	72.939	79.850	87.442	138.109	218.472
17	18.430	20.012	21.762	23.698	25.840	28.213	30.840	33.750	36.974	40.545	44.501	48.884	53.739	59.118	65.075	71.673	78.979	87.068	96.022	105.931	173.636	285.01
18	19.615	21.412	23.414	25.645	28.132	30.906	33.999	37.450	41.301	45.599	50.396	55.750	61.725	68.394	75.836	84.141	93.406	103.74	115.27	128.117	218.045	371.52
19	20.811	22.841	25.117	27.671	30.539	33.760	37.379	41.446	46.018	51.159	56.939	63.440	70.749	78.969	88.212	98.603	110.28	123.41	138.17	154.740	273.556	483.97
20	22.019	24.297	26.870	29.778	33.066	36.786	40.995	45.762	51.160	57.275	64.203	72.052	80.947	91.025	102.444	115.380	130.033	146.628	165.418	186.688	342.945	630.165
21	23.239	25.783	28.676	31.969	35.719	39.993	44.865	50.423	56.765	64.002	72.265	81.699	92.470	104.768	118.810	134.841	153.139	174.021	197.847	225.026	429.681	820.215
22	24.472	27.299	30.537	34.248	38.505	43.392	49.006	55.457	62.873	71.403	81.214	92.503	105.491	120.436	137.632	157.415	180.172	206.345	236.438	271.031	538.101	1,067.280
23	25.716	28.845	32.453	36.618	41.430	46.996	53.436	60.893	69.532	79.543	91.148	104.603	120.205	138.297	159.276	183.601	211.801	244.487	282.362	326.237	673.626	1,388.464
24	26.973	30.422	34.426	39.083	44.502	50.816	58.177	66.765	76.790	88.497	102.174	118.155	136.831	158.659	184.168	213.978	248.808	289.494	337.010	392.484	843.033	1,806.003
25	28.243	32.030	36.459	41.646	47.727	54.865	63.249	73.106	84.701	98.347	114.413	133.334	155.620	181.871	212.793	249.214	292.105	342.603	402.042	471.981	1,054.791	2,348.803
26	29.526	33.671	38.553	44.312	51.113	59.156	68.676	79.954	93.324	109.182	127.999	150.334	176.850	208.333	245.712	290.088	342.763	405.272	479.431	567.377	1,319.489	3,054.444
27	30.821	35.344	40.710	47.084	54.669	63.706	74.484	87.351	102.723	121.100	143.079	169.374	200.841	238.499	283.569	337.502	402.032	479.221	571.522	681.853	1,650.361	3,971.778
28	32.129	37.051	42.931	49.968	58.403	68.528	80.698	95.339	112.968	134.210	159.817	190.699	227.950	272.889	327.104	392.503	471.378	566.481	681.112	819.223	2,063.952	5,164.311
29	33.450	38.792	45.219	52.966	62.323	73.640	87.347	103.966	124.135	148.631	178.397	214.583	258.583	312.094	377.170	456.303	552.512	669.447	811.523	984.068	2,580.939	6,714.604
30	34.785	40.568	47.575	56.085	66.439	79.058	94.461	113.283	136.308	164.494	199.021	241.333	293.199	356.787	434.745	530.312	647.439	790.948	966.712	1,181.882	3,227.174	8,729.985
35	41.660	49.994	60.462	73.652	90.320	111.435	138.237	172.317	215.711	271.024	341.590	431.663	546.681	693.573	881.170	1,120.713	1,426.491	1,816.652	2,314.214	2,948.341	9,856.761	32,422.868
40	48.886	60.402	75.401	95.026	120.800	154.762	199.635	259.057	337.882	442.593	581.826	767.091	1,013.704	1,342.025	1,779.090	2,360.757	3,134.522	4,163.213	5,529.829	7,343.858	30,088.655	120,392.883

Note: All factors are rounded to the nearest 1/1000 in order to agree with values used in the text.

APPENDIX C
Table of Present Value Factors

Instructions: To use this table, find the present value factor that corresponds to both a given time period (year) and an interest rate. For example, if you want the present value factor for 25 years and 7%, move across from year 25 and down from 7% to the point at which the row and column intersect: .184. Other illustrations: for 3 years and 15%, the proper present value factor is .658; for 30 years and 8%, it is .099.

INTEREST RATE

Period	1%	2%	3%	4%	5%	6%	7%	8%	9%	10%	11%	12%	13%	14%	15%	16%	17%	18%	19%	20%	25%	30%
1	0.990	0.980	0.971	0.962	0.952	0.943	0.935	0.926	0.917	0.909	0.901	0.893	0.885	0.877	0.870	0.862	0.855	0.847	0.840	0.833	0.800	0.769
2	0.980	0.961	0.943	0.925	0.907	0.890	0.873	0.857	0.842	0.826	0.812	0.797	0.783	0.769	0.756	0.743	0.731	0.718	0.706	0.694	0.640	0.592
3	0.971	0.942	0.915	0.889	0.864	0.840	0.816	0.794	0.772	0.751	0.731	0.712	0.693	0.675	0.658	0.641	0.624	0.609	0.593	0.579	0.512	0.455
4	0.961	0.924	0.888	0.855	0.823	0.792	0.763	0.735	0.708	0.683	0.659	0.636	0.613	0.592	0.572	0.552	0.534	0.516	0.499	0.482	0.410	0.350
5	0.951	0.906	0.863	0.822	0.784	0.747	0.713	0.681	0.650	0.621	0.593	0.567	0.543	0.519	0.497	0.476	0.456	0.437	0.419	0.402	0.328	0.269
6	0.942	0.888	0.837	0.790	0.746	0.705	0.666	0.630	0.596	0.564	0.535	0.507	0.480	0.456	0.432	0.410	0.390	0.370	0.352	0.335	0.262	0.207
7	0.933	0.871	0.813	0.760	0.711	0.665	0.623	0.583	0.547	0.513	0.482	0.452	0.425	0.400	0.376	0.354	0.333	0.314	0.296	0.279	0.210	0.159
8	0.923	0.853	0.789	0.731	0.677	0.627	0.582	0.540	0.502	0.467	0.434	0.404	0.376	0.351	0.327	0.305	0.285	0.266	0.249	0.233	0.168	0.123
9	0.914	0.837	0.766	0.703	0.645	0.592	0.544	0.500	0.460	0.424	0.391	0.361	0.333	0.308	0.284	0.263	0.243	0.225	0.209	0.194	0.134	0.094
10	0.905	0.820	0.744	0.676	0.614	0.558	0.508	0.463	0.422	0.386	0.352	0.322	0.295	0.270	0.247	0.227	0.208	0.191	0.176	0.162	0.107	0.073
11	0.896	0.804	0.722	0.650	0.585	0.527	0.475	0.429	0.388	0.350	0.317	0.287	0.261	0.237	0.215	0.195	0.178	0.162	0.148	0.135	0.086	0.056
12	0.887	0.788	0.701	0.625	0.557	0.497	0.444	0.397	0.356	0.319	0.286	0.257	0.231	0.208	0.187	0.168	0.152	0.137	0.124	0.112	0.069	0.043
13	0.879	0.773	0.681	0.601	0.530	0.469	0.415	0.368	0.326	0.290	0.258	0.229	0.204	0.182	0.163	0.145	0.130	0.116	0.104	0.093	0.055	0.033
14	0.870	0.758	0.661	0.577	0.505	0.442	0.388	0.340	0.299	0.263	0.232	0.205	0.181	0.160	0.141	0.125	0.111	0.099	0.088	0.078	0.044	0.025
15	0.861	0.743	0.642	0.555	0.481	0.417	0.362	0.315	0.275	0.239	0.209	0.183	0.160	0.140	0.123	0.108	0.095	0.084	0.074	0.065	0.035	0.020
16	0.853	0.728	0.623	0.534	0.458	0.394	0.339	0.292	0.252	0.218	0.188	0.163	0.141	0.123	0.107	0.093	0.081	0.071	0.062	0.054	0.028	0.015
17	0.844	0.714	0.605	0.513	0.436	0.371	0.317	0.270	0.231	0.198	0.170	0.146	0.125	0.108	0.093	0.080	0.069	0.060	0.052	0.045	0.023	0.012
18	0.836	0.700	0.587	0.494	0.416	0.350	0.296	0.250	0.212	0.180	0.153	0.130	0.111	0.095	0.081	0.069	0.059	0.051	0.044	0.038	0.018	0.009
19	0.828	0.686	0.570	0.475	0.396	0.331	0.277	0.232	0.194	0.164	0.138	0.116	0.098	0.083	0.070	0.060	0.051	0.043	0.037	0.031	0.014	0.007
20	0.820	0.673	0.554	0.456	0.377	0.312	0.258	0.215	0.178	0.149	0.124	0.104	0.087	0.073	0.061	0.051	0.043	0.037	0.031	0.026	0.012	0.005
21	0.811	0.660	0.538	0.439	0.359	0.294	0.242	0.199	0.164	0.135	0.112	0.093	0.077	0.064	0.053	0.044	0.037	0.031	0.026	0.022	0.009	0.004
22	0.803	0.647	0.522	0.422	0.342	0.278	0.226	0.184	0.150	0.123	0.101	0.083	0.068	0.056	0.046	0.038	0.032	0.026	0.022	0.018	0.007	0.003
23	0.795	0.634	0.507	0.406	0.326	0.262	0.211	0.170	0.138	0.112	0.091	0.074	0.060	0.049	0.040	0.033	0.027	0.022	0.018	0.015	0.006	0.002
24	0.788	0.622	0.492	0.390	0.310	0.247	0.197	0.158	0.126	0.102	0.082	0.066	0.053	0.043	0.035	0.028	0.023	0.019	0.015	0.013	0.005	0.002
25	0.780	0.610	0.478	0.375	0.295	0.233	0.184	0.146	0.116	0.092	0.074	0.059	0.047	0.038	0.030	0.024	0.020	0.016	0.013	0.010	0.004	0.001
26	0.772	0.598	0.464	0.361	0.281	0.220	0.172	0.135	0.106	0.084	0.066	0.053	0.042	0.033	0.026	0.021	0.017	0.014	0.011	0.009	0.003	0.001
27	0.764	0.586	0.450	0.347	0.268	0.207	0.161	0.125	0.098	0.076	0.060	0.047	0.037	0.029	0.023	0.018	0.014	0.011	0.009	0.007	0.002	0.001
28	0.757	0.574	0.437	0.333	0.255	0.196	0.150	0.116	0.090	0.069	0.054	0.042	0.033	0.026	0.020	0.016	0.012	0.010	0.008	0.006	0.002	0.001
29	0.749	0.563	0.424	0.321	0.243	0.185	0.141	0.107	0.082	0.063	0.048	0.037	0.029	0.022	0.017	0.014	0.011	0.008	0.006	0.005	0.002	*
30	0.742	0.552	0.412	0.308	0.231	0.174	0.131	0.099	0.075	0.057	0.044	0.033	0.026	0.020	0.015	0.012	0.009	0.007	0.005	0.004	0.001	*
35	0.706	0.500	0.355	0.253	0.181	0.130	0.094	0.068	0.049	0.036	0.026	0.019	0.014	0.010	0.008	0.006	0.004	0.003	0.002	0.002	*	*
40	0.672	0.453	0.307	0.208	0.142	0.097	0.067	0.046	0.032	0.022	0.015	0.011	0.008	0.005	0.004	0.003	0.002	0.001	0.001	0.001	*	*

*Present value factor is zero to three decimal places.

Note: All factors are rounded to the nearest 1/1000 in order to agree with values used in the text.

APPENDIX D

Table of Present Value Annuity Factors

Instructions: To use this table, find the present value of annuity factor that corresponds to both a given time period (year) and an interest rate. For example, if you want the present value of annuity factor for 30 years and 7%, move across from year 30 and down from 7% to the point at which the row and column intersect: 12.409. Other illustrations: for 3 years and 15%, the proper present value of annuity factor is 2.283; for 30 years and 8%, it is 11.258.

INTEREST RATE

Period	1%	2%	3%	4%	5%	6%	7%	8%	9%	10%	11%	12%	13%	14%	15%	16%	17%	18%	19%	20%	25%	30%
1	0.990	0.980	0.971	0.962	0.952	0.943	0.935	0.926	0.917	0.909	0.901	0.893	0.885	0.877	0.870	0.862	0.855	0.847	0.840	0.833	0.800	0.769
2	1.970	1.942	1.913	1.886	1.859	1.833	1.808	1.783	1.759	1.736	1.713	1.690	1.668	1.647	1.626	1.605	1.585	1.566	1.547	1.528	1.440	1.361
3	2.941	2.884	2.829	2.775	2.723	2.673	2.624	2.577	2.531	2.487	2.444	2.402	2.361	2.322	2.283	2.246	2.210	2.174	2.140	2.106	1.952	1.816
4	3.902	3.808	3.717	3.630	3.546	3.465	3.387	3.312	3.240	3.170	3.102	3.037	2.974	2.914	2.855	2.798	2.743	2.690	2.639	2.589	2.362	2.166
5	4.853	4.713	4.580	4.452	4.329	4.212	4.100	3.993	3.890	3.791	3.696	3.605	3.517	3.433	3.352	3.274	3.199	3.127	3.058	2.991	2.689	2.436
6	5.795	5.601	5.417	5.242	5.076	4.917	4.767	4.623	4.486	4.355	4.231	4.111	3.998	3.889	3.784	3.685	3.589	3.498	3.410	3.326	2.951	2.643
7	6.728	6.472	6.230	6.002	5.786	5.582	5.389	5.206	5.033	4.868	4.712	4.564	4.423	4.288	4.160	4.039	3.922	3.812	3.706	3.605	3.161	2.802
8	7.652	7.325	7.020	6.733	6.463	6.210	5.971	5.747	5.535	5.335	5.146	4.968	4.799	4.639	4.487	4.344	4.207	4.078	3.954	3.837	3.329	2.925
9	8.566	8.162	7.786	7.435	7.108	6.802	6.515	6.247	5.995	5.759	5.537	5.328	5.132	4.946	4.772	4.607	4.451	4.303	4.163	4.031	3.463	3.019
10	9.471	8.983	8.530	8.111	7.722	7.360	7.024	6.710	6.418	6.145	5.889	5.650	5.426	5.216	5.019	4.833	4.659	4.494	4.339	4.192	3.571	3.092
11	10.368	9.787	9.253	8.760	8.306	7.887	7.499	7.139	6.805	6.495	6.207	5.938	5.687	5.453	5.234	5.029	4.836	4.656	4.486	4.327	3.656	3.147
12	11.255	10.575	9.954	9.385	8.863	8.384	7.943	7.536	7.161	6.814	6.492	6.194	5.918	5.660	5.421	5.197	4.988	4.793	4.611	4.439	3.725	3.190
13	12.134	11.348	10.635	9.986	9.394	8.853	8.358	7.904	7.487	7.103	6.750	6.424	6.122	5.842	5.583	5.342	5.118	4.910	4.715	4.533	3.780	3.223
14	13.004	12.106	11.296	10.563	9.899	9.295	8.745	8.244	7.786	7.367	6.982	6.628	6.302	6.002	5.724	5.468	5.229	5.008	4.802	4.611	3.824	3.249
15	13.865	12.849	11.938	11.118	10.380	9.712	9.108	8.559	8.061	7.606	7.191	6.811	6.462	6.142	5.847	5.575	5.324	5.092	4.876	4.675	3.859	3.268
16	14.718	13.578	12.561	11.652	10.838	10.106	9.447	8.851	8.313	7.824	7.379	6.974	6.604	6.265	5.954	5.668	5.405	5.162	4.938	4.730	3.887	3.283
17	15.562	14.292	13.166	12.166	11.274	10.477	9.763	9.122	8.544	8.022	7.549	7.120	6.729	6.373	6.047	5.749	5.475	5.222	4.990	4.775	3.910	3.295
18	16.398	14.992	13.754	12.659	11.690	10.828	10.059	9.372	8.756	8.201	7.702	7.250	6.840	6.467	6.128	5.818	5.534	5.273	5.033	4.812	3.928	3.304
19	17.226	15.678	14.324	13.134	12.085	11.158	10.336	9.604	8.950	8.365	7.839	7.366	6.938	6.550	6.198	5.877	5.584	5.316	5.070	4.843	3.942	3.311
20	18.046	16.351	14.877	13.590	12.462	11.470	10.594	9.818	9.129	8.514	7.963	7.469	7.025	6.623	6.259	5.929	5.628	5.353	5.101	4.870	3.954	3.316
21	18.857	17.011	15.415	14.029	12.821	11.764	10.836	10.017	9.292	8.649	8.075	7.562	7.102	6.687	6.312	5.973	5.665	5.384	5.127	4.891	3.963	3.320
22	19.660	17.658	15.937	14.451	13.163	12.042	11.061	10.201	9.442	8.772	8.176	7.645	7.170	6.743	6.359	6.011	5.696	5.410	5.149	4.909	3.970	3.323
23	20.456	18.292	16.444	14.857	13.489	12.303	11.272	10.371	9.580	8.883	8.266	7.718	7.230	6.792	6.399	6.044	5.723	5.432	5.167	4.925	3.976	3.325
24	21.243	18.914	16.936	15.247	13.799	12.550	11.469	10.529	9.707	8.985	8.348	7.784	7.283	6.835	6.434	6.073	5.746	5.451	5.182	4.937	3.981	3.327
25	22.023	19.523	17.413	15.622	14.094	12.783	11.654	10.675	9.823	9.077	8.422	7.843	7.330	6.873	6.464	6.097	5.766	5.467	5.195	4.948	3.985	3.329
26	22.795	20.121	17.877	15.983	14.375	13.003	11.826	10.810	9.929	9.161	8.488	7.896	7.372	6.906	6.491	6.118	5.783	5.480	5.206	4.956	3.988	3.330
27	23.560	20.707	18.327	16.330	14.643	13.211	11.987	10.935	10.027	9.237	8.548	7.943	7.409	6.935	6.514	6.136	5.798	5.492	5.215	4.964	3.990	3.331
28	24.316	21.281	18.764	16.663	14.898	13.406	12.137	11.051	10.116	9.307	8.602	7.984	7.441	6.961	6.534	6.152	5.810	5.502	5.223	4.970	3.992	3.331
29	25.066	21.844	19.188	16.984	15.141	13.591	12.278	11.158	10.198	9.370	8.650	8.022	7.470	6.983	6.551	6.166	5.820	5.510	5.229	4.975	3.994	3.332
30	25.808	22.396	19.600	17.292	15.372	13.765	12.409	11.258	10.274	9.427	8.694	8.055	7.496	7.003	6.566	6.177	5.829	5.517	5.235	4.979	3.995	3.332
35	29.409	24.999	21.487	18.665	16.374	14.498	12.948	11.655	10.567	9.644	8.855	8.176	7.586	7.070	6.617	6.215	5.858	5.539	5.251	4.992	3.998	3.333
40	32.835	27.355	23.115	19.793	17.159	15.046	13.332	11.925	10.757	9.779	8.951	8.244	7.634	7.105	6.642	6.233	5.871	5.548	5.258	4.997	3.999	3.333

Note: All factors are rounded to the nearest 1/1000 in order to agree with values used in the text.

APPENDIX E
Using a Financial Calculator

Important Financial Keys on the Typical Financial Calculator

The important financial keys on a typical financial calculator are depicted and defined below. On some calculators, the keys may be labeled using lowercase characters for "N" and "I". Also, "I/Y" may be used in place of the "I" key.

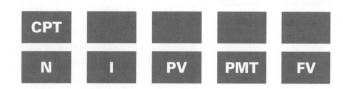

CPT   Compute key; used to initiate financial calculation once all values are input
   N   Number of periods
    I   Interest rate per period
 PV   Present value
PMT   Amount of payment; used only for annuities
 FV   Future value

The handheld financial calculator makes it easy to calculate time value. Once you have mastered the time value of money concepts using tables, we suggest you use such a calculator. For one thing, it becomes cumbersome to use tables when calculating anything other than annual compounding. For another, calculators rather than tables are used almost exclusively in the business of personal financial planning.

You don't want to become overly dependent on calculators, however, because you may not be able to recognize a nonsensical answer in the event that you accidentally push the wrong button. The important calculator keys are shown and labeled above. Before using your calculator to make the financial computations described in this text, be aware of the following points.

1. The keystrokes on some of the more sophisticated and expensive calculators are menu-driven: after you select the appropriate routine, the calculator prompts you to input each value; a compute key (CPT) is not needed to obtain a solution.

2. Many calculators allow the user to set the number of payments per year. Most of these calculators are preset for monthly payments, or 12 payments per year. Because we work primarily with *annual* payments—one payment per year—it is important to make sure that your calculator is set for one payment per year. Although most calculators are preset to recognize that all payments occur at the end of the period, it is also important to make sure your calculator is actually in that so-called END mode. Consult the reference guide that accompanies your calculator for instructions on these settings.

3. To avoid including previous data in current calculations, always clear all registers of your calculator before inputting values and making a new computation.

4. The known values can be punched into the calculator in any order; the order specified here and in the text simply reflects the authors' personal preference.

Calculator Keystrokes

Let's go back to the future value calculation on page 43, where we are trying to calculate the future value of $5,000 at the end of 6 years if invested at 5%. Here are the steps for solving the problem with a calculator:

1. Punch in 5000 and press PV.
2. Punch in 6 and press N.
3. Punch in 5 and press I.
4. To calculate the future value, press CPT and then FV. The future value of 6,700.48 should appear on the calculator display.

On many calculators, this value will be preceded by a minus sign, which is a way of distinguishing between cash inflows and cash outflows. For our purposes, this sign can be ignored.

To calculate the yearly savings (the amount of an annuity), let's continue with the example on page 44. For this example, the interest rate is 5%, the number of periods is 6, and the future value is $38,300. Your task is to solve the equation for the annuity. The steps using the calculator are:

1. Punch in 6 and press N.
2. Punch in 5 and press I.
3. Punch in 38300 and press FV.
4. To calculate the yearly payment or annuity, press CPT and then PMT.

The annuity of 5,630.77 should appear on the calculator display. Again, a negative sign can be ignored.

A similar procedure is used to find present value of a future sum or an annuity, except you would first input the FV or PMT before pressing CPT and then PV to calculate the desired result. To find the equal annual future withdrawals from an initial deposit, the PV would be input first; you solve for the PMT by pressing CPT and then PMT.

CALCULATOR

Inputs	Functions
5000	PV
6	N
5	I
	CPT
	FV
	Solution
	6,700.48

SEE APPENDIX E FOR DETAILS.

CALCULATOR

Inputs	Functions
6	N
5	I
38300	FV
	CPT
	PMT
	Solution
	5,630.77

SEE APPENDIX E FOR DETAILS.

INDEX

automobile insurance coverage
  liability coverage (Part A), 239–241
  medical payments coverage (Part B), 241
  physical damage to a vehicle (Part D), 242
  uninsured motorists coverage (Part C), 241–242
automobile rebate programs, 137
auto theft, prevent, 243
average American, financial snapshot of, 6
average daily balance (ADB) method, 145–146
average propensity to consume, 4
average tax rate, 50–51
aversion to ambiguity behavioral barrier, 360

B

back-end load funds, 314
bailout provision, 354
balanced funds, 318
balance sheet
  assets on, 28–29
  defined, 27
  example, 30, 32
  format and preparation, 31–32
  liabilities on, 29
  net worth on, 30–331
balance sheet equation, 28
balance sheet ratios, 36–37
balance transfer cards, average interest rates for, 148
balancing the checkbook, 87
bank(s)
  brick-and-mortar, 78
  choosing new, 85
  commercial, 77–79
  Internet, 78
  savings, 77–79
  "too big to fail," 76
bank-by-phone accounts, 83
bank credit card
  cash advance, 135–136
  defined, 135
  interest charges, 136–137
  line of credit, 135
  monthly statement, 147

Bank of America, 298
bankruptcy, credit card abuse and, 150
bank statement, 87–88
Barron's, 267, 268
base rate (of interest), 136
basic hospital insurance (Medicare Part A), 208
bear market, 261
behavioral bias
  anchoring, 102
  credit card use and, 137
  health insurance decisions and, 219
  in mutual fund investing, 315
  procrastination, 77
  property insurance and, 235
  real estate bubble and, 107
  in retirement planning, 339
  whole life *vs.* term life insurance and, 190
beneficiaries
  life insurance, 197
  trust, 371
Best's annuity ratings, 354
beta (stock's), 291
Better Business Bureau, 68
bid price, 259
Billabong International, 292
bill payment services, online, 83
biweekly mortgages, 123
blanket PPF, 225
blockage discount, 380
blue-chip stocks, 291
Blue Cross/Blue Shield plan, 205, 207
bodily injury liability losses, 239
bond funds, 318
bonds, 256
  bond ratings, 302–303
  call feature, 299–300
  issue characteristics, 298–300
  market for, 300–302
  prices and yields, 304–306
  pricing, 303–304
  reasons to invest in, 296–297
  sinking fund, 299
  stocks *vs.*, 297–298
  types of issues, 299
book value, 290
bounced check, 86
brick-and-mortar banks, 78
broad markets, 282

broker markets, 257–259
budget. *See also* budgeting
  annual cash (example), 38
  example, 40–41
  realistic plans, 31
budget control schedule, 41–42
budgeting. *See also* budgets
  biggest mistakes, 34
  budgeting process, 37–39
  deficits, 39
  defined, 27
  estimating expenses, 39
  estimating income, 38–39
  pessimistic, 41
  planning over a lifetime, 46
  preparing and using, 37–41
  using, 41
bull market, 261, 292
Bureau of Consumer Financial Protection, 260
business, financial planning and, 17
business cycles, 19
business inventory, 234
business meals, travel, and entertainment, 66
business property, 234
business risk, 281
BusinessWeek magazine, 267
buydowns, 124

C

cafeteria plans, 15
call feature, 299–300
call premium, 299
capital cost reduction, 104
capital gains
  ETFs and, 314
  investing and, 282–283
  mutual funds and, 325
  sector funds and, 319
  taxation of, 54
  tax categories (2011), 54
capitalized cost, 104
capital market, 257
captive agent, 245
captive finance companies, 160
Car and Driver magazine, 99
career
  as income determinant, 22
  planning your, 22–23
  salaries for selected, 22

Caribou Coffee, 293
carryover provision, 215
cash advance, 135–136
cash back cards, average interest rates for, 148
cash basis, 32
cash budget. *See also* budgets
  annual (example), 38
  defined, 37
  example, 40–41
  finalizing, 39
cash deficit, 34
cash dividend, 289
cash flow, after-tax, on real estate investment, 328
cashier's check, 87
cash management
  defined, 75
  low interest rates and, 75–77
  role in financial planning, 75–77
cash management products, 79–84
  asset management accounts, 81–82
  checking accounts, 80–81. *See also* checking accounts
  electronic banking services, 82–84
  interest-paying checking accounts, 81
  safe-deposit boxes, 84
  savings accounts, 81. *See also* savings account; savings program
  trust services, 84
cash surplus, 34
cash value
  actual, property insurance and, 231
  loans against insurance policy, 160
  of whole life insurance, 187–188
casualty and theft losses, 56
CD (certificate of deposit), 90, 92–93
Cedar Fair, 292
central asset account, 81–82
certificate of deposit (CD), 90, 92–93
certified check, 87
Certified Financial Planner (CFP), 196
Certified Insurance Counselor (CIC), 245
certified public accountant (CPA), 64, 67

R

rate of interest, annual, on consumer loans, 162
rate(s) of return
  on investments, 252
  representative, 76
ratio analysis, 36–37
raw land, speculating in, 328–329
real estate, 327–330
  appreciating value of, 328
  cash flow, taxes and, 328
  defined, 327
  financial leverage and, 328
  income property, 329
  investing in, 256
  joint ownership of, 370
  LPs or LLCs and, 330
  raw land speculation, 328–329
  real estate investment trust (REIT), 329–330
real estate investment trust (REIT), 329–330
Real Estate Settlement Procedures Act (RESPA), 119
real estate short sale, 118–119
real estate taxes, as tax deduction, 55–56
real GDP, 19
real property
  as assets, 12
  defined, 29
rebalancing your portfolio, 283
rebate cards, 137
record keeping, 35
redemption fee, 314–315
refinancing mortgages, 124–125
regional exchanges, 259
regular checking account, 80
rehabilitation coverage, 217
renewability provision, 187
rental units, 108
renter's insurance, 235–236
renting *vs.* buying a home, 108–110
rent ratio, 108
replacement cost, 231, 236–237
reported taxable income, 56
residential properties, investing in, 329
residual benefit option, 223

residual owners, 287
residual value, 104
RESPA (Real Estate Settlement Procedures Act), 119
restrictive endorsement, 86
retail charge cards, 138
retail stores
  debit cards and, 82
  open account credit from, 135
retirement, as reason for investing, 255
retirement goals, 335
retirement planning, 5, 9, 14–16
  annuities, 351–354
  behavioral bias in, 339
  biggest pitfalls to, 336
  estimating income needs, 336–340
  estimating retirement needs, 338
  pension plans and, 343–353. *See also* pension plans
  role in personal financial planning, 335
  self-directed plans, 322
  Social Security and, 341–343
  sources of retirement income, 340–341
return on equity (ROE), 290
revenue bonds, 301
revocable living trust, 373
revocable trust, 371
revolving credit lines, 139–141
  home equity credit line, 140–141
  overdraft protection and, 139–140
  unsecured personal credit line, 140
reward (co-branded) credit cards, 137
rewards cards, average interest rates for, 148
right of subrogation, 232
right of survivorship, 370
risk assumption, 180
risk avoidance, 179
risk-free rate of return, 285
risk-return trade-off, 285
risks of investing, 281–282
Road and Track magazine, 99
ROE (return on equity), 290
Roth IRA, 70, 322, 350–351

Roth 401(k), 348
round lot, 264
row houses, 107
R-Squared (R²) statistical measure, 326
RTI Biologics, 293
rule of 78s, 172

S

safe-deposit box, 84
  items to keep in, 368
  personal property inventory form in, 231
  will stored in, 367
safe-driving discounts, 243
salary reduction plan, 347
sales contract, for car, 104
sales finance companies, 160
Sallie Mae, 156
Sarbanes-Oxley Act of 2002 (SOX), 260
savings, life insurance and, 181
savings account, 81, 90
savings and investment planning, 13–14
savings and loan associations (S&Ls), 77–79, 160
savings banks, 77–79
savings program
  earning interest, 91–92
  starting, 90
  systematic, 254
  vehicles for. *See* savings vehicles
savings ratio, 36–37
savings vehicles
  certificates of deposit (CDs), 92–93
  I savings bonds, 94
  Series EE bonds, 93–94
  U.S. Treasury bill (T-bill), 93
scheduled PPF, 225
secondary market, 257
second mortgage, 170
Section I perils, 232–234
Section II perils, 234
sector funds, 319
secured credit cards, 138
securities
  building portfolio of, 274
  fixed-income, 282
  hybrid, 301
  mortgage-backed, 300
Securities Act of 1933, 260
Securities and Exchange Commission (SEC), 260

  mutual fund disclosure and, 315
  12(b)-1 fees and, 314
Securities Exchange Act of 1934, 260
securities exchanges, 257
Securities Investor Protection Act of 1970, 261, 265
Securities Investor Protection Corporation (SIPC), 82, 261
securities markets, 256–261
  broker markets, 257–259
  bull *vs.* bear, 261
  dealer markets, 257–260
  executing trades, 265
  foreign, 260
  primary, 257
  regulating, 260–261
  secondary, 257
  transactions in, 261–272
  types of orders, 265
Select Quote Insurance Services, 194
self-directed accounts, 350
self-directed retirement account, 79
self-directed retirement programs, 349–351
self-employed persons, prepaying taxes, 51
selling group, 257
separate trust account, 79
SEPs (Simplified Employee Pensions), 55, 349
serial obligations, 301
Series EE bonds, 69–70, 93–94
settlement options
  life insurance, 197
settlor, 371
share draft accounts, 78
Shiller, Robert, 107
short-term liabilities, 29
sickness policies (medical expense insurance), 214
simple interest, 91
simple-interest method, 167, 169
Simplified Employee Pensions (SEPs), 55, 349
single-family homes, 107
single-payment loans, 155, 159, 165–169
  finance charges and APR, 167–169
  loan collateral, 165
  loan maturity, 165
  loan repayment, 165–167

STUDENT TESTED, **FACULTY APPROVED**

We would like to thank the following faculty for collaborating with us to create a completely new solution for personal finance.

Reviewers, all editions: Thomas J. Alexander, *Northwood University* • Ania Antus, *Normandale Community College* • Robert J. Bartelli, *Labette Community College* • Patricia Bernson, *County College of Morris* • Anne Berre, *Schreiner University* • Bill Blackerby, *Siena Heights University* • David A. Bodkin, *Cumberland University* • Karin B. Bonding, *University of Virginia* • Kathryn L. Brownell, *Jefferson Community College* • Chuck Gahala, *Benedictine University* • Joseph Cheng, *Ithaca College* • Fernando Conde, *Columbia College* • Dean Danielson, *San Joaquin Delta College* • David Darst, *Central Ohio Technical College* • Pierre A. David, *Baldwin-Wallace College* • Susan Dechand, *Allen County Community College* • Beth Deinert, *Southeast Community College-Milford* • Ginger Dennis, *West Georgia Technical College* • Gregg Dimkoff, *Grand Valley State University* • Shannon Donovan, *Bridgewater State College* • David A. Dumpe, *Kent State University* • Jeannette Eberle, *Webber International University* • Pennie Eddy, *Chattahoochee Technical College* • W. Michael Fagan, *Raritan Valley Community College* • John Farlin, *Ohio Dominican University* • Jacques Federman, *Moorpark College* • John F. Fitzgerald, Jr., *Ball State University* • Joseph L. Flack, Jr., *Washtenaw Community College* • Joseph L. Fowler, Jr., *Florida State College at Jacksonville* • Barry Freeman, *Bergen Community College* • Arthur Friedberg, *Mohawk Valley Community College* • Caren Fullerton, *Lubbock Christian University* • Heriberto Garcia, *Texas A&M International University* • Wayne Gawlik, *Joliet Junior College* • Glenn Gelderloos, *Grand Rapids Community College* • David Globig, *Spring Arbor University* • Bruce K. Grace, *Morehead State University* • Michelle Grant, *Bossier Parish Community College* • Patricia Halliday, *Santa Monica College* • Eric W. Hayden, *UMassBoston* • Sueann Hely, *West Kentucky Community & Technical College* • Samira Hussein, *Johnson County Community College* • Ray Ingram, *South West Georgia Technical College* • Starla Ivey, *University of Missouri* • Jim Keys, *Florida International University* • Sara Kimmel, *Belhaven College* • Pamela Knight, *ColumbusTechnical College* • Robert Koenig, *Santa Ana College* • Thomas Krueger, *University of Wisconsin-LaCrosse* • YingChou Lin, *Missouri University of Science and Technology* • Gary Lunkenheimer, *Cottey College* • Thomas E. Lynch, *Hocking College* • Barbara MacLeod, *Ohio Wesleyan University* •Jennings B. Marshall, *Samford University* • Linda Miller, *Northeast Community College* • Susan Milstein, *McDaniel College* •Eddy P. Miracle, *Southeast Kentucky Community and Technical College* • Robert W. Moreschi, *Virginia Military Institute* • Marcus Morreale, *Passaic County Community College* • Dianne R. Morrison, *UW–La Crosse* • Lorrie Mowry, *McCook Community College* • Bary Mulholland, *University of Wisconsin Oshkosh* • Betty K. Mullins, *Hesser College* • David W. Murphy, *Madisonville Community College* • Jack Muryn, *University of Wisconsin-Washington County* • Susan Moak Nealy, *Baton Rouge Community College* • Urvi Neelakantan, *University of Illinois at Urbana-Champaign* • Carolyn Nelson, *Coffeyville Community College* • Jerome P. Niemiec, *Texas State University* • Terri J. Nix, *Howard College* • Susan Pallas, *Southeast Community College-Lincoln* • Bruce C. Payne, *Barry University* • Lora Reinholz, *Marquette University* • Barbara Rice, *Gateway Community & Technical College* • Sheryl H. Rogers, *Ogeechee Technical College* • Mark Ryan, *Hawkeye Community College* • Abdel Khalik Shabayek, *Lane College* • Lawrence P. Shao, *Marshall University* • Brandi Shay, *Southwestern Community College* • Keith Shishido, *Santa Monica College* • John Slayton, *Elon University* • Kenneth Small, *Coastal Carolina University* • Paul J. Speaker, *West Virginia University* • David B. Stewart, *Winston-Salem State University* • Paul A. Stock, *University of Mary Hardin-Baylor* • Ronald Stunda, *Birmingham Southern College* • Stephen A. Tolbert, Jr., *Montgomery County Community College* • Stephen Trimby, *Worcester State College* • Sam Veraldi, *Duke University* • Ron Vogel, *College of Eastern Utah* • Scott Wallace, *Blue Mountain Community College* • Roger Wallenburg, *Missouri State University* • Ken Ward, *Southeastern University* • Shunda Ware, *Atlanta Technical College* • Wendel Weaver, *Oklahoma Wesleyan University* • Larry Weaver, *Navarro College* • Ira Wilsker, *Lamar Institute of Technology* • Charles Zellerbach, *Orange Coast College* • Kermit C. Zieg, Jr., *Florida Institute of Technology* • Troy Bethards, *Southwest Baptist University* • Connie Barton, *Shasta Bible College and Graduate School* • Albert R. Tetrault, *Flagler College* • Corolyn Clark, *Saint Joseph's University* • Debbie Psihountas, *Webster University* • Melodi Guilbault, *Warner University* • Gary C. Raffaele, *Covenant College* • Gretchen Graham, *Community College of Allegheny County-Boyce Campus* • Shayne Crawshaw, *John A. Logan College* • Ryan Sean Carrigan, *Riverside Community College* • C. Baird, *Tri-State Business Institute* • Donald Bateman, *DePaul University* • Connie Belden, *Butler Community College* • Richard Bodenhamer, *Samford University* • Kevin Bosner, *Medaille College* • John Braden, *University of Illinois* • Harvey Bronstein, *Oakland Community College* • Renee Cabourne, *Chaffey College* • Thomas R Determan, *University of Wisconsin-Parkside* • Lisa Frank, *Central Connecticut State University* • Robert Friederichs, *Alexandria Technical and Community College* • Drew Hensley, *Western Kentucky University* • James V. Isherwood, *Community College of Rhode Island* • Nanette Lareau, *University of Arkansas Community College at Morrilton* • Carole Maske, *Southwestern Community College* • Simon Medcalfe, *Augusta State University* • John Micetich, *University of Illinois* • Tim Muth, *Florida Institute of Technology* • Cathy Nash, *DeKalb Technical College* • Ramona Rucker, *DeKalb Technical College* • Todd Saville, *Kirkwood Community College* • Elizabeth Scull, *University of South Carolina* • Oran Randall Spindle, *Southern Nazarene University* • Mark O. Tengesdal, *Texas Woman's University* • Milos Vulanovic, *Western New England College* • Randall Wade, *Rogue Community College*

We also wish to thank John A. Brozovsky for assistance in the chapter on taxes; Sam A. Hicks for help in revising and updating the estate planning chapter; Thomas C. Via Jr., CLU, for his help in the chapter on life and property insurance, Kent Dodge for his help on updating material on health insurance, Hongbok Lee for helpful observations, and Marlene Bellamy of Writeline Associates for her help with the real estate material.

KEY TERMS

average propensity to consume *The percentage of each dollar of income, on average, that a person spends for current needs rather than savings.* 4

consumer price index (CPI) *A measure of inflation based on changes in the cost of consumer goods and services.* 20

contraction *The phase of the economic cycle when real GDP falls.* 19

expansion *The phase of the economic cycle when real GDP increases until it hits a peak.* 19

financial assets *Intangible assets, such as savings accounts and securities, that are acquired for some promised future return.* 5

financial goals *Results that an individual wants to attain, such as buying a home, building a college fund, or achieving financial independence.* 6

flexible-benefit (cafeteria) plans *The employer allocates a certain amount of money to each employee and then lets the employee "spend" that money for benefits that suit his or her age, marital status, number of dependent children, and level of income.* 15

goal dates *Target dates in the future when certain financial objectives are expected to be completed.* 9

inflation *A state of the economy in which the general price level is increasing.* 20

money *The medium of exchange used as a measure of value in financial transactions.* 7

peak *The phase of the economic cycle when an expansion ends and a contraction begins.* 19

personal financial planning *A systematic process that considers important elements of an individual's financial affairs in order to fulfill financial goals.* 5

purchasing power *The amount of goods and services that each dollar buys at a given time.* 20

standard of living *The necessities, comforts, and luxuries enjoyed or desired by an individual or family.* 3

tangible assets *Physical assets, such as real estate and automobiles, that can be held for either consumption or investment purposes.* 5

LEARNING GOAL SUMMARIES

LG1 **Identify the benefits of using personal financial planning techniques to manage your finances.**

Personal financial planning helps you marshal and control your financial resources. It should allow you to improve your standard of living, get more enjoyment from your money by spending it wisely, and accumulate wealth. By setting short- and long-term financial goals, you'll enhance your quality of life both now and in the future.

LG2 **Describe the personal financial planning process and define your goals.**

Personal financial planning is a six-step process that helps you achieve your financial goals: (1) define financial goals; (2) develop financial plans and strategies to achieve goals; (3) implement financial plans and strategies; (4) periodically develop and implement budgets to monitor and control progress toward goals; (5) use financial statements to evaluate results of plans and budgets, taking corrective action as required; and (6) redefine goals and revise plans and strategies as personal circumstances change. It is critically important to realistically spell out your short-term, intermediate, and long-term financial goals. Your goals, which reflect your values and circumstances, may change due to personal circumstances.

Exhibit 1.3 The Six-Step Financial Planning Process
The financial planning process translates personal financial goals into specific financial plans and strategies, implements them, and then uses budgets and financial statements to monitor, evaluate, and revise plans and strategies as needed. This process typically involves the six steps shown in sequence here.

1. Define financial goals.

2. Develop financial plans and strategies to achieve goals.

3. Implement financial plans and strategies.

4. Periodically develop and implement budgets to monitor and control progress toward goals.

5. Use financial statements to evaluate results of plans and budgets, taking corrective action as required.

6. Redefine goals and revise plans and strategies as personal circumstances change.

© Cengage Learning

LG3 **Explain the life cycle of financial plans, the role they play in achieving your financial goals, how to deal with special planning concerns, and the use of professional financial planners.**

In moving through various life-cycle stages, you must revise your financial plans to include goals and strategies appropriate to each stage. Income and expense patterns change with age. Changes in your life due to marriage, children, divorce, remarriage, and job status also necessitate adapting financial plans to meet current needs. Although these plans change over time, they are the roadmap that you'll follow to achieve your financial goals. After defining your goals, you can develop and implement an appropriate personal financial plan. A complete set of financial plans covers asset acquisition, liability and insurance, savings and investments, employee benefits, taxes, and retirement and estate planning. Review these plans regularly and revise them accordingly. Situations that require special attention include managing two incomes, managing employee benefits, and adapting to changes in

trough *The phase of the economic cycle when a contraction ends and an expansion begins.* 19

utility *The amount of satisfaction received from purchasing certain types or quantities of goods and services.* 8

wealth *The total value of all items owned by an individual, such as savings accounts, stocks, bonds, home, and automobiles.* 5

To access Bonus Exhibits, additional Smart Sites, Concept Checks, and more, please visit CourseMate for PFIN 3. Log in at www.cengagebrain.com.

your personal situation, such as marital status or taking responsibility for elderly relatives' care. Professional financial planners can help you with the planning process.

Exhibit 1.4 The Personal Financial Planning Life Cycle

As you move through life and your income patterns change, you'll typically have to pursue a variety of financial plans. For instance, after graduating from college your focus will likely be on buying a car and a house, and you'll be concerned about health and automobile insurance to protect against loss.

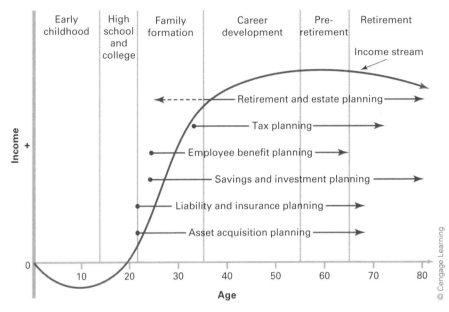

LG4 Examine the economic environment's influence on personal financial planning.

Financial planning occurs in an environment where the government, business, and consumers are all influential participants. Personal financial decisions are affected by economic cycles (expansion, recession, depression, and recovery) and the impact of inflation on prices (purchasing power and personal income).

LG5 Evaluate the impact of age, education, and geographic location on personal income.

Demographics, education, and career are all important factors affecting your income level. As a rule, people between 45 and 64 years old tend to earn more than others, as do those who are married. Equally important, that income generally increases with the level of education. Where you live is an additional consideration—salaries and living costs are higher in some areas than in others. Career choices also affect your level of income—those in professional and managerial positions tend to earn the highest salaries.

LG6 Understand the importance of career choices and their relationship to personal financial planning.

Career planning is a lifetime process that involves goal setting and career development strategies. A career plan should be flexible and able to adapt to new workplace requirements. When making career plans, identify your interests, skills, needs, and values; set specific long- and short-term career goals; develop and use an action plan to achieve your goals; and review and revise your career plans as your situation changes. Coordinate your career plans with your personal financial plans.

To help you succeed, we have designed a review card for each chapter.

KEY TERMS

average propensity to consume *The percentage of each dollar of income, on average, that a person spends for current needs rather than savings.* 4

consumer price index (CPI) *A measure of inflation based on changes in the cost of consumer goods and services.* 20

contraction *The phase of the economic cycle when real GDP falls.* 19

expansion *The phase of the economic cycle when real GDP increases until it hits a peak.* 19

financial assets *Intangible asset* *such as savings accounts and securities, that are acquired for some promised future return.* *b*

financi *ind* *as* *coll* *ind*

Here, you'll find the key terms and definitions in alphabetical order.

flexible-benefit (cafeteria) plans *The employer allocates a certain amount of money to each employee and then lets the employee "spend" that money for benefits that suit his or her age, marital status, number of dependent children, and level of income.* 15

goal dates *Target dates in the future when certain financial objectives are expected to be completed.* 9

inflation *A state of the economy in which the general price level is increasing.* 20

money use fina

peak cyc a c

perso sys imp ind to f

purcha goo buy

standa cor or c fam

tangib as can or i

How to use the card:

1. Look over the card to preview the new concepts you'll be introduced to in the chapter.

2. Read your chapter to fully understand the material.

3. Go to class (and pay attention).

4. Review the card one more time to make sure you've registered the key concepts.

5. Don't forget, this card is only one of many PFIN learning tools available to help you succeed in your personal finance course.

LEARNING GOAL SUMMARIES

LG1 **Identify the benefits of using personal financial planning techniques to manage your finances.**

Personal financial planning helps you marshal and control your financial resources. It should allow you to improve your standard of living, get more enjoyment from your money by spending it wisely, and accumulate wealth. By setting short- and long-term financial goals, you'll enhance your quality of life both now and in the future.

LG2 **Describe the personal financial planning process and define your goals.**

Personal financial planning is a six-step process that (1) define financial goals; (2) develop financial plans (3) implement financial plans and strategies; (4) perio gets to monitor and control progress toward goals; (results of plans and budgets, taking corrective action and revise plans and strategies as personal circumsta tant to realistically spell out your short-term, interm Your goals, which reflect your values and circumstances, may change due to personal circumstances.

In this column, you'll find summary points often supported by key exhibits from the chapters. Exhibits help further cement the concepts in your mind.

Exhibit 1.3 The Six-Step Financial Planning Process
The financial planning process translates personal financial goals into specific financial plans and strategies, implements them, and then uses budgets and financial statements to monitor, evaluate, and revise plans and strategies as needed. This process typically involves the six steps shown in sequence here.

1. Define financial goals.
2. Develop financial plans and strategies to achieve goals.
3. Implement financial plans and strategies.
4. Periodically develop and implement budgets to monitor and control progress toward goals.
5. Use financial statements to evaluate results of plans and budgets, taking corrective action as required.
6. Redefine goals and revise plans and strategies as personal circumstances change.

© Cengage Learning

LG3 **Explain the life cycle of financial plans, the role they play in achieving your financial goals, how to deal with special planning concerns, and the use of professional financial planners.**

In moving through various life-cycle stages, you must revise your financial plans to include goals and strategies appropriate to each stage. Income and expense patterns change with age. Changes in your life due to marriage, children, divorce, remarriage, and job status also necessitate adapting financial plans to meet current needs. Although these plans change over time, they are the roadmap that you'll follow to achieve your financial goals. After defining your goals, you can develop and implement an appropriate personal financial plan. A complete set of financial plans covers asset acquisition, liability and insurance, savings and investments, employee benefits, taxes, and retirement and estate planning. Review these plans regularly and revise them accordingly. Situations that require special attention include managing two incomes, managing employee benefits, and adapting to changes in

When it's time to prepare for exams, use the card and the technique to the left to ensure successful study sessions.

trough *The phase of the economic cycle when a contraction ends and an expansion begins.* 19

utility *The amount of satisfaction received from purchasing certain types or quantities of goods and services.* 8

wealth *The total value of all items owned by an individual, such as savings accounts, stocks, bonds, home, and automobiles.* 5

To access Bonus Exhibits, additional Smart Sites, Concept Checks, and more, please visit CourseMate for PFIN 3. Log in at www.cengagebrain.com.

your personal situation, such as marital status or taking responsibility for elderly relatives' care. Professional financial planners can help you with the planning process.

Exhibit 1.4 The Personal Financial Planning Life Cycle

As you move through life and your income patterns change, you'll typically have to pursue a variety of financial plans. For instance, after graduating from college your focus will likely be on buying a car and a house, and you'll be concerned about health and automobile insurance to protect against loss.

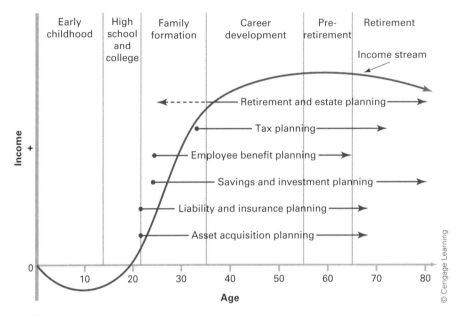

LG4 Examine the economic environment's influence on personal financial planning.

Financial planning occurs in an environment where the government, business, and consumers are all influential participants. Personal financial decisions are affected by economic cycles (expansion, recession, depression, and recovery) and the impact of inflation on prices (purchasing power and personal income).

LG5 Evaluate the impact of age, education, and geographic location on personal income.

Demographics, education, and career are all important factors affecting your income level. As a rule, people between 45 and 64 years old tend to earn more than others, as do those who are married. Equally important, that income generally increases with the level of education. Where you live is an additional consideration—salaries and living costs are higher in some areas than in others. Career choices also affect your level of income—those in professional and managerial positions tend to earn the highest salaries.

LG6 Understand the importance of career choices and their relationship to personal financial planning.

Career planning is a lifetime process that involves goal setting and career development strategies. A career plan should be flexible and able to adapt to new workplace requirements. When making career plans, identify your interests, skills, needs, and values; set specific long- and short-term career goals; develop and use an action plan to achieve your goals; and review and revise your career plans as your situation changes. Coordinate your career plans with your personal financial plans.

KEY TERMS

annuity *A fixed sum of money that occurs annually. 43*

assets *Items that one owns. 28*

balance sheet *A financial statement that describes a person's financial position at a given point in time. 27*

budget *A detailed financial report that looks forward, based on expected income and expenses. 27*

budget control schedule *A summary that shows how actual income and expenses compare with the various budget categories and where variances (surpluses or deficits) exist. 41*

cash basis *A method of preparing financial statements in which only transactions involving actual cash receipts or actual cash outlays are recorded. 32*

cash budget *A budget that takes into account estimated monthly cash receipts and cash expenses for the coming year. 37*

cash deficit *An excess amount of expenses over income, resulting in insufficient funds as well as in decreased net worth. 34*

cash surplus *An excess amount of income over expenses that results in increased net worth. 34*

compounding *When interest earned each year is left in the account and becomes part of the balance (or principal) on which interest is earned in subsequent years. 43*

current (short-term) liability *Any debt due within 1 year of the date of the balance sheet. 29*

debt service ratio *Total monthly loan payments divided by monthly gross (before-tax) income; provides a measure of the ability to pay debts promptly. 37*

discounting *The process of finding present value; the inverse of compounding to find future value. 44*

equity *The actual ownership interest in a specific asset or group of assets. 30*

expenses *Money spent on living expenses and to pay taxes, purchase assets, or repay debt. 32*

fair market value *The actual value of an asset, or the price for which it can reasonably be expected to sell in the open market. 29*

fixed expenses *Contractual, predetermined expenses involving equal payments each period. 34*

LEARNING GOAL SUMMARIES

LG1 **Understand the relationship between financial plans and statements.**

Preparing and using the balance sheet and the income and expense statement are important to personal financial planning. These tools help you to keep track of your current financial position and to monitor progress toward achieving financial goals. A budget allows you to monitor and control your spending in light of your financial plans.

Exhibit 2.1 The Interlocking Network of Financial Plans and Statements
Personal financial planning involves a network of financial reports that link future goals and plans with actual results. Such a network provides direction, control, and feedback.

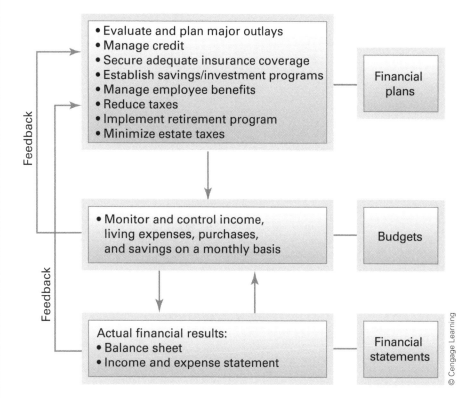

© Cengage Learning

LG2 **Prepare a personal balance sheet.**

A balance sheet reports on your financial position at a specific time. It summarizes the things you own (assets), the money you owe (liabilities), and your financial worth (net worth). Net worth represents your actual wealth and is the difference between your total assets and total liabilities.

LG3 **Generate a personal income and expense statement.**

The income and expense statement summarizes the income you received and the money you spent over a specific period. It's prepared on a cash basis and thus reflects your actual cash flow. Expenses consist of cash outflows to (1) meet living expenses, (2) pay taxes, (3) purchase various kinds of assets, and (4) pay debts. A cash surplus (or deficit) is the difference between income and expenses.

future value *The value to which an amount today will grow if it earns a specific rate of interest over a given period. 42*

income *Earnings received as wages, salaries, bonuses, commissions, interest and dividends, or proceeds from the sale of assets. 32*

income and expense statement *A financial statement that measures financial performance over time. 27*

insolvency *The financial state in which net worth is less than zero. 31*

investments *Assets such as stocks, bonds, mutual funds, and real estate that are acquired in order to earn a return rather than provide a service. 28*

liabilities *Debts, such as credit card charges, loans, and mortgages. 29*

liquid assets *Assets that are held in the form of cash or can readily be converted to cash with little or no loss in value. 28*

liquidity ratio *Total liquid assets divided by total current debts; measures the ability to pay current debts. 36*

long-term liability *Any debt due 1 year or more from the date of the balance sheet. 29*

net worth *An individual's or family's actual wealth; determined by subtracting total liabilities from total assets. 30*

open account credit obligations *Current liabilities that represent the balances outstanding against established credit lines. 29*

personal financial statements *Balance sheets and income and expense statements that serve as planning tools that are essential to developing and monitoring personal financial plans. 27*

personal property *Tangible assets that are movable and used in everyday life. 29*

present value *The value today of an amount to be received in the future; it's the amount that would have to be invested today at a given interest rate over a specified time period to accumulate the future amount. 44*

real property *Tangible assets that are immovable: land and anything fixed to it, such as a house. 29*

savings ratio *Cash surplus divided by net income (after tax); indicates relative amount of cash surplus achieved during a given period. 37*

solvency ratio *Total net worth divided by total assets; measures the degree of exposure to insolvency. 36*

Exhibit 2.3 How We Spend Our Income
Almost three-quarters of expenditures made with pre-tax income fall into one of four categories: food, housing, and transportation.

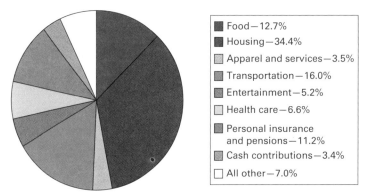

- Food—12.7%
- Housing—34.4%
- Apparel and services—3.5%
- Transportation—16.0%
- Entertainment—5.2%
- Health care—6.6%
- Personal insurance and pensions—11.2%
- Cash contributions—3.4%
- All other—7.0%

Source: "Consumer Expenditures—2010" Washington, D.C.: U.S. Department of Labor, Bureau of Labor Statistics, News Release, USDL-11-1395, Chart 1, "Shares of Average Annual Expenditures Spent on Major Components, 2010," September 27, 2011, p. 2.

LG4 **Develop a good record-keeping system and use ratios to evaluate personal financial statements.**

Good records make it easier to prepare accurate personal financial statements. Ratio analysis allows you to assess how well you are doing relative to your past performance. Four important financial ratios are the solvency, liquidity, savings, and debt service ratios.

LG5 **Construct a cash budget and use it to monitor and control spending.**

A cash budget helps you to carry out a system of disciplined spending. Household budgets identify planned monthly cash income and cash expenses for the coming year. The objective is to take in more money than you spend, so you'll save money and add to your net worth over time.

LG6 **Apply *time value of money* concepts to put a monetary value on financial goals.**

When putting a dollar value on financial goals, be sure to consider the time value of money and, if appropriate, use the notion of future value or present value to prepare your estimates.

time value of money *The concept that a dollar today is worth more than a dollar received in the future. 41*

variable expenses *Expenses involving payment amounts that change from one time period to the next. 34*

To access Bonus Exhibits, additional Smart Sites, Concept Checks, and more, please visit CourseMate for PFIN 3. Log in at www.cengagebrain.com.

KEY TERMS

adjusted gross income (AGI) *The amount of income remaining after subtracting all allowable adjustments to income from gross income. 55*

adjustments to (gross) income *Allowable deductions from gross income, including certain employee, personal retirement, insurance, and support expenses. 54*

amended return *A tax return filed to adjust for information received after the filing date of the taxpayer's original return or to correct errors. 66*

average tax rate *The rate at which each dollar of taxable income is taxed on average; calculated by dividing the tax liability by taxable income. 50*

estimated taxes *Tax payments required on income not subject to withholding that are paid in four installments. 65*

exemptions *Deductions from AGI based on the number of persons supported by the taxpayer's income. 56*

Federal Insurance Contributions Act (FICA) or Social Security tax *The law establishing the combined old-age, survivor's, disability, and hospital insurance tax levied on both employer and employee. 52*

federal withholding taxes *Taxes— based on the level of earnings and the number of withholding allowances claimed—that an employer deducts from the employee's gross earnings each pay period. 52*

filing extension *An extension of time beyond the usual April 15 deadline during which taxpayers, with the approval of the IRS, can file their returns without incurring penalties. 66*

gross income *The total of all of a taxpayer's income (before any adjustments, deductions, or exemptions) subject to federal taxes; it includes active, portfolio, and passive income. 52*

income shifting *A technique used to reduce taxes in which a taxpayer shifts a portion of income to relatives in lower tax brackets. 70*

income taxes *A type of tax levied on taxable income by the federal government and by many state and local governments. 50*

LEARNING GOAL SUMMARIES

LG1 **Discuss the basic principles of income taxes and determine your filing status.**

The dominant tax in our country is the federal income tax, a levy that provides the government with most of the funds it needs to cover its operating costs. Federal income tax rates are progressive, so that your tax rate increases as your income rises. Other types of taxes include state and local income taxes, sales taxes, and property taxes. The administration and enforcement of federal tax laws is the responsibility of the IRS, a part of the U.S. Department of the Treasury. The amount of taxes you owe depends on your filing status—single, married filing jointly, married filing separately, head of house- hold, or qualifying widow(er) with dependent child—and the amount of taxable income you report. Because the government operates on a pay-as-you-go basis, employers are required to withhold taxes from their employees' paychecks.

LG2 **Describe the sources of gross income and adjustments to income, differentiate between standard and itemized deductions and exemptions, and calculate taxable income.**

Gross income includes active income (such as wages, bonuses, pensions, alimony), portfolio income (dividends, interest, and capital gains), and passive income (income derived from real estate, limited partnerships, and other tax shelters). You must decide whether to take the standard deduction or itemize your various deductions. Some allowable deductions for those who itemize include mortgage interest, medical expenses over 7.5% of AGI, and certain job-related expenses. To calculate taxable income, deduct allowable adjustments, such as IRA contributions and alimony paid, from gross income to get AGI; then subtract from AGI the amount of deductions and personal exemptions claimed.

Exhibit 3.1 Calculating Your Taxable Income and Total Tax Liability Owed
To find taxable income, you must first subtract all adjustments to gross income and then subtract deductions and personal exemptions. Your total tax liability owed includes tax on this taxable income amount, less any tax credits, plus other taxes owed.

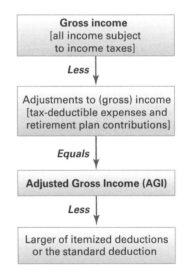

Step A:
Determine Adjusted Gross Income

Gross income
[all income subject to income taxes]

Less

Adjustments to (gross) income
[tax-deductible expenses and retirement plan contributions]

Equals

Adjusted Gross Income (AGI)

Less

Step B:
Calculate Taxable Income

Larger of itemized deductions or the standard deduction

Continued

itemized deductions *Personal expenditures that can be deducted from AGI when determining taxable income. 56*

marginal tax rate *The tax rate you pay on the next dollar of taxable income. 50*

progressive tax structure *A tax structure in which the larger the amount of taxable income, the higher the rate at which it is taxed. 50*

standard deduction *A blanket deduction that depends on the taxpayer's filing status, age, and vision and that can be taken by a taxpayer whose total itemized deductions are too small. 55*

tax audit *An examination by the IRS to validate the accuracy of a given tax return. 66*

tax avoidance *The act of reducing taxes in ways that are legal and compatible with the intent of Congress. 69*

tax credits *Deductions from a taxpayer's tax liability that directly reduce his or her taxes due (rather than reducing taxable income). 59*

tax deferred *Income that is not subject to taxes immediately but that will later be subject to taxes. 70*

tax evasion *The illegal act of failing to accurately report income or deductions and, in extreme cases, failing to pay taxes altogether. 69*

taxable income *The amount of income subject to taxes; it is calculated by subtracting adjustments, the larger of itemized or standard deductions, and exemptions from gross income. 52*

taxes *The dues paid for membership in our society; the cost of living in this country. 49*

To access Bonus Exhibits, additional Smart Sites, Concept Checks, and more, please visit CourseMate for PFIN 3. Log on to www.cengagebrain.com.

Exhibit 3.1 (Continued)

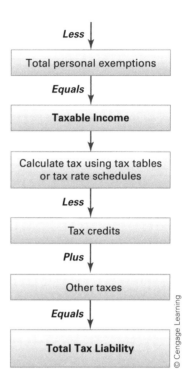

LG3 **Prepare a basic tax return using the appropriate tax forms and rate schedules.**

After determining your taxable income, you can find the amount of taxes owed using either the tax rate tables or, if your taxable income is over $100,000, the tax rate schedules. Tax rates vary with the level of taxable income and filing status. Personal tax returns are filed using one of these forms: 1040EZ, 1040A, or 1040. Certain taxpayers must include schedules with their Form 1040.

LG4 **Explain who needs to pay estimated taxes, when to file or amend your return, and how to handle an audit.**

Persons with income not subject to withholding may need to file a declaration of estimated taxes and make tax payments in four installments. Annual returns must usually be filed usually on or before April 15, unless the taxpayer requests an automatic 6-month filing extension. The IRS audits selected returns to confirm their validity by carefully examining the data reported in them.

LG5 **Know where to get help with your taxes and how software can make tax return preparation easier.**

Assistance in preparing returns is available from the IRS and from private tax preparers such as national and local tax firms, certified public accountants, enrolled agents, and tax attorneys. Computer programs can help do-it-yourselfers with both tax planning and tax preparation.

LG6 **Implement an effective tax-planning strategy.**

Effective tax planning is closely tied to other areas of personal financial planning. The objectives of tax planning are to reduce, shift, or defer taxes so that the taxpayer gets maximum use of and benefits from the money he or she earns. Some of the more popular tax strategies include maximizing deductions, shifting income to relatives in lower tax brackets, investing in tax-exempt municipal bonds, setting up IRAs, and using other types of pension and retirement plans and annuities to generate tax-deferred income.

KEY TERMS

account reconciliation *Verifying the accuracy of your checking account balance in relation to the bank's records as reflected in the bank statement, which is an itemized listing of all transactions in the checking account. 87*

asset management account (AMA) *A comprehensive deposit account; offered primarily by brokerage houses and mutual funds. 81*

automated teller machine (ATM) *A remote computer terminal that customers of depository institutions can use to make basic transactions 24 hours a day, 7 days a week. 82*

cashier's check *A check payable to a third party that is drawn by a bank on itself in exchange for the amount specified plus, in most cases, a service fee (of about $5). 87*

cash management *The routine, day-to-day administration of cash and near-cash resources, also known as liquid assets, by an individual or family. 75*

certificate of deposit (CD) *A type of savings instrument issued by certain financial institutions in exchange for a deposit; typically requires a minimum deposit and has a maturity ranging from 7 days to as long as 7 or more years. 92*

certified check *A personal check that is guaranteed (for a fee of $10 to $15 or more) by the bank on which it is drawn. 87*

checkbook ledger *A booklet, provided with a supply of checks, used to maintain accurate records of all checking account transactions. 86*

compound interest *When interest earned in each subsequent period is determined by applying the nominal (stated) rate of interest to the sum of the initial deposit and the interest earned in each prior period. 91*

debit cards *Specially coded plastic cards used to transfer funds from a customer's bank account to the recipient's account to pay for goods or services. 82*

demand deposit *An account held at a financial institution from which funds can be withdrawn on demand by the account holder; same as a checking account. 80*

LEARNING GOAL SUMMARIES

LG1 Understand the role of cash management in the personal financial planning process.

Cash management plays a vital role in personal financial planning. It involves the administration and control of liquid assets—cash, checking accounts, savings, and other short-term investment vehicles. With good cash management practices, you'll have the necessary funds to cover your expenses and establish a regular savings program.

Exhibit 4.2 Depository Financial Institutions
Depository financial institutions differ from their nonbank counterparts, such as stock brokerages and mutual funds, in their ability to accept deposits. Most consumers use these institutions to meet their checking and savings account needs.

Institution	Description
Commercial bank	Offers checking and savings accounts and a full range of financial products and services; the only institution that can offer *non-interest-paying checking accounts (demand deposits)*. The most popular of the depository financial institutions. Most are traditional *brick-and-mortar banks*, but **Internet banks**—online commercial banks—are growing in popularity because of their convenience, lower service fees, and higher interest paid on account balances.
Savings and loan association (S&L)	Channels the savings of depositors primarily into mortgage loans for purchasing and improving homes. Also offers many of the same checking, saving, and lending products as commercial banks. Often pays slightly higher interest on savings than do commercial banks.
Savings bank	Similar to S&Ls, but located primarily in the New England states. Most are *mutual* associations—their depositors are their owners and thus receive a portion of the profits in the form of interest on their savings.
Credit union	A nonprofit, member-owned financial cooperative that provides a full range of financial products and services to its *members*, who must belong to a common occupation, religious or fraternal order, or residential area. Generally small institutions when compared with commercial banks and S&Ls. Offer interest-paying checking accounts—called **share draft accounts**—and a variety of saving and lending programs. Because they are run to benefit their members, they pay higher interest on savings and charge lower rates on loans than do other depository financial institutions.

© Cengage Learning

LG2 Describe today's financial services marketplace, both depository and nondepository financial institutions.

Today's financial services marketplace is highly competitive and offers consumers expanded product offerings at attractive prices. Individuals and families continue to rely heavily on traditional depository financial institutions for most of their financial services needs. Nondepository financial institutions also offer some banking services such as credit cards and money market fund accounts with check-writing privileges. You should make sure your bank has federal deposit insurance and is financially sound. Most depository institutions are traditionally federally-insured for up to $250,000 per depositor name.

LG3 Select the checking, savings, electronic banking, and other bank services that meet your needs.

Financial institutions provide a variety of accounts to help you manage your cash: regular checking accounts, savings accounts, and interest-paying checking accounts, such as NOW accounts, money market deposit accounts, and money market mutual funds. Asset management accounts offered by brokerage firms and mutual funds combine checking, investment,

deposit insurance *A type of insurance that protects funds on deposit against failure of the institution; can be insured by the FDIC and the NCUA. 79*

effective rate of interest *The annual rate of return that is actually earned (or charged) during the period the funds are held (or borrowed). 91*

electronic funds transfer systems (EFTSs) *Systems using the latest telecommunications and computer technology to electronically transfer funds into and out of customers' accounts. 82*

Internet bank *An online commercial bank. 78*

I Savings bond *A savings bond issued at face value by the U.S. Treasury; its practically fixed rates provides some inflation protection. 94*

money market deposit account (MMDA) *A federally insured savings account, offered by banks and other depository institutions, that competes with money market mutual funds. 81*

money market mutual fund (MMMF) *A mutual fund that pools the funds of many small investors and purchases high-return, short-term marketable securities. 81*

negotiable order of withdrawal (NOW) account *A checking account on which the financial institution pays interest; NOWs have no legal minimum balance. 81*

nominal (stated) rate of interest *The promised rate of interest paid on a savings deposit or charged on a loan. 91*

overdraft *The result of writing a check for an amount greater than the current account balance. 86*

overdraft protection *An arrangement between the account holder and the depository institution wherein the institution automatically pays a check that overdraws the account. 86*

Series EE bond *A savings bond issued in various denominations by the U.S. Treasury. 94*

share draft account *An account offered by credit unions that is similar to interest-paying checking accounts offered by other financial institutions. 78*

simple interest *Interest that is paid only on the initial amount of the deposit. 91*

stop payment *An order made by an account holder instructing the depository institution to refuse payment on an already issued check. 86*

and borrowing activities and pay higher interest on deposits than do other more traditional checking accounts. Other money management services include electronic funds transfer systems (EFTSs) that use telecommunications and computer technology to electronically transfer funds. Popular EFTS services include debit cards, ATMs, preauthorized deposits and payments, bank-by-phone accounts, and online banking and bill-paying services. Many banks also provide safe-deposit boxes, which serve as a storage place for valuables and important documents.

LG4 Open and use a checking account.

A checking account is a convenient way to hold cash and pay for goods and services. The sharp increase in bank service charges makes it important to evaluate different types of checking accounts and their service charges, minimum balance requirements, and other fees. You should understand how to write and endorse checks, make deposits, keep good checking account records, prevent overdrafts, and stop payment on checks. The account reconciliation, or checkbook balancing, process confirms the accuracy of your account records and monthly bank statement. Other special types of checks you may use occasionally include cashier's, traveler's, and certified checks.

LG5 Calculate the interest earned on your money using compound interest and future value techniques.

Once you know the interest rate, frequency of compounding, and how the bank determines the balance on which interest is paid, you can calculate how much interest you'll earn on your money. Use future value and future value of an annuity formulas to find out how your savings will grow. The more often interest is compounded, the greater the effective rate for a given nominal rate of interest. Most banks use the actual balance, or day of deposit to day of withdrawl method to determine which balances qualify to earn interest, which is the fairest method for depositors.

LG6 Develop a cash management strategy that incorporates a variety of savings plans.

Your cash management strategy should include establishing a regular pattern of saving with liquid reserves at least 6 months of after-tax income. The choice of savings products depends on your needs, your risk preference, the length of time you plan to leave money on deposit, and current and expected interest rates. You may wish to put some of your savings into vehicles that pay a higher rate of interest than savings or NOW accounts, such as certificates of deposit, U.S. Treasury bills, Series EE bonds, and I savings bonds.

time deposit *A savings deposit at a financial institution; remains on deposit for a longer time than a demand deposit. 81*

traveler's check *A check sold (for a fee of about 1.5%) by many large financial institutions, typically in denominations ranging from $20 to $100, that can be used for making purchases and exchanged for local currencies in most parts of the world. 87*

U.S. Treasury bill (T-bill) *A short-term (3-, 6-, or 12-month maturity) debt instrument issued at a discount by the U.S. Treasury in its ongoing process of funding the national debt. 93*

To access Bonus Exhibits, additional Smart Sites, Concept Checks, and more, please visit CourseMate for PFIN 3. Log in at www.cengagebrain.com.

KEY TERMS

adjustable-rate mortgage (ARM) *A mortgage on which the rate of interest, and therefore the size of the monthly payment, is adjusted based on market interest rate movements.* 122

adjustment period *On an adjustable-rate mortgage, the period of time between rate or payment changes.* 122

biweekly mortgage *A loan on which payments equal to half the regular monthly payment are made every 2 weeks.* 123

buydown *Financing made available by a builder or seller to a potential new-home buyer at well below market interest rates, often only for a short period.* 124

capitalized cost *The price of a car that is being leased.* 104

closed-end lease *The most popular form of automobile lease; often called a walk-away lease, because at the end of its term, the lessee simply turns in the car (assuming the preset mileage limit has not been exceeded and the car hasn't been abused).* 104

closing costs *All expenses (including mortgage points) that borrowers ordinarily pay when a mortgage loan is closed and they receive title to the purchased property.* 113

condominium (condo) *A form of direct ownership of an individual unit in a multiunit project in which lobbies, swimming pools, and other common areas and facilities are jointly owned by all property owners in the project.* 108

contingency clause *A clause in a real estate sales contract that makes the agreement conditional on such factors as the availability of financing, property inspections, or obtaining expert advice.* 119

conventional mortgage *A mortgage offered by a lender who assumes all the risk of loss; typically requires a down payment of at least 20% of the value of the mortgaged property.* 124

convertible ARM *An adjustable-rate mortgage loan that allows borrowers to convert from an adjustable-rate to a fixed-rate loan, usually at any time between the 13th and the 60th month.* 123

cooperative apartment (co-op) *An apartment in a building in which each tenant owns a share of the nonprofit corporation that owns the building.* 108

LEARNING GOAL SUMMARIES

LG1 Design a plan to research and select a new or used automobile.

Important purchase considerations include affordability; operating costs; whether to buy a gas, diesel, or hybrid fueled car; whether to buy a new versus a used or nearly new car; the type of car and its features; and its reliability and warranties. Knowing the dealer's cost is the key to negotiating a good price.

LG2 Decide whether to buy or lease a car.

Consider all the terms of the lease, including the annual mileage allowance and early termination penalties. The economics of leasing versus purchasing a car with an installment loan should not be considered until the price is set. The four components of the lease payment are the capitalized cost, residual value, money factor, and lease term.

LG3 Identify housing alternatives, assess the rental option, and perform a rent-or-buy analysis.

For many, renting offers convenience for their lifestyle and economic situation. The rental contract, or lease agreement, describes the terms under which you can rent the property, including the monthly rental amount, lease term, restrictions, etc. A rent-or-buy analysis will identify the least costly alternative. Also consider qualitative factors, such as how long you plan to stay in an area, and perform the analysis over a several-year timeline.

LG4 Evaluate the benefits and costs of homeownership and estimate how much you can afford to pay for a home.

In addition to the emotional rewards, other benefits of homownership are the tax shelter and inflation hedge it provides. Homeownership costs include the down payment, points and closing costs, monthly mortgage payments, property taxes and insurance, and normal home maintenance and operating expenses. Carefully consider all of these costs in estimating how much you can afford to spend on a home.

LG5 Describe the home-buying process.

Most home buyers seek the help of a real estate agent to obtain property information and access to houses. Agents split a commission, paid by the seller, upon closing. Prequalify for a mortgage before hunting for a home. A sales contract confirms all terms of the transaction. After a mortgage loan is approved, the loan is closed. A closing statement shows how much the borrower owes and the seller receives.

LG6 Choose mortgage financing that meets your needs.

Mortgage loans can be obtained from commercial banks, thrift institutions, or through a mortgage banker or mortgage broker. Although many types of mortgage loans are available, the most widely used are 30- and 15-year fixed-rate mortgages and adjustable-rate mortgages (ARMs). Sometimes interest rates will drop several years after closing, and mortgage refinancing will become attractive. The refinancing analysis considers the difference in terms between the old and new mortgages, any prepayment penalty on the old mortgage, closing costs, and how long you plan to stay in the home.

depreciation *The loss in the value of an asset such as an automobile that occurs over its period of ownership; calculated as the difference between the price initially paid and the subsequent sale price.* 101

down payment *A portion of the full purchase price provided by the purchaser when a house or other major asset is purchased; often called equity.* 111

earnest money deposit *Money pledged by a buyer to show good faith when making an offer to buy a home.* 119

FHA mortgage insurance *A program under which the Federal Housing Administration (FHA) offers lenders mortgage insurance on loans having a high loan-to-value ratio; its intent is to encourage loans to home buyers who have very little money available for a down payment and closing costs.* 124

fixed-rate mortgage *The traditional type of mortgage in which both the rate of interest and the monthly mortgage payment are fixed over the full term of the loan.* 121

foreclosure *A borrower typically cannot make scheduled mortgage payments and the lender repossesses the property in an effort to recover the loan balance owed.* 107

graduated-payment mortgage *A mortgage that starts with unusually low payments that rise over several years to a fixed payment.* 123

growing-equity mortgage *Fixed-rate mortgage with payments that increase over a specific period. Extra funds are applied to the principal so that the loan is paid off more quickly.* 123

homeowner's insurance *Insurance that is required by mortgage lenders and covers the replacement value of a home and its contents.* 116

index rate *On an adjustable-rate mortgage, the baseline index rate that captures interest rate movements.* 122

interest-only mortgage *A mortgage that requires the borrower to pay only interest; typically used to finance the purchase of more expensive properties.* 123

interest rate cap *On an adjustable-rate mortgage, the limit on the amount that the interest rate can increase each adjustment period and over the life of the loan.* 122

lease *An arrangement in which the lessee receives the use of a car (or other asset) in exchange for making monthly lease payments over a specified period.* 104

loan-to-value ratio *The maximum percentage of the value of a property that the lender is willing to loan.* 112

margin *On an adjustable-rate mortgage, the percentage points a lender adds to the index rate to determine the rate of interest.* 122

money factor *The financing rate on a lease; similar to the interest rate on a loan.* 104

mortgage banker *A firm that solicits borrowers, originates primarily government-insured and government-guaranteed loans, and places them with mortgage lenders; often uses its own money to initially fund mortgages it later resells.* 121

mortgage broker *A firm that solicits borrowers, originates primarily conventional loans, and places them with mortgage lenders; the broker merely takes loan applications and then finds lenders willing to grant the mortgage loans under the desired terms.* 121

mortgage loan *A loan secured by the property: If the borrower defaults, the lender has the legal right to liquidate the property to recover the funds it is owed.* 120

mortgage points *Fees (one point equals 1 percent of the amount borrowed) charged by lenders at the time they grant a mortgage loan; they are related to the lender's supply of loanable funds and the demand for mortgages.* 112

Multiple Listing Service (MLS) *A comprehensive listing, updated daily, of properties for sale in a given community or metropolitan area; includes a brief description of each property with a photo and its asking price but can be accessed only by realtors who work for an MLS member.* 119

negative amortization *When the principal balance on a mortgage loan increases because the monthly loan payment is lower than the amount of monthly interest being charged; some ARMs are subject to this undesirable condition.* 123

open-end (finance) lease *An automobile lease under which the estimated residual value of the car is used to determine lease payments; if the car is actually worth less than this value at the end of the lease, the lessee must pay the difference.* 104

payment cap *On an adjustable-rate mortgage, the limit on the monthly payment increase that may result from a rate adjustment.* 122

PITI *Acronym that refers to a mortgage payment consisting of principal, interest, property taxes, and homeowner's insurance.* 115

prequalification *The process of arranging with a mortgage lender, in advance of buying a home, to obtain the amount of mortgage financing the lender deems affordable for the home buyer.* 119

private mortgage insurance (PMI) *An insurance policy that protects the mortgage lender from loss in the event the borrower defaults on the loan; typically required by lenders when the down payment is less than 20 percent.* 112

property taxes *Taxes levied by local governments on the assessed value of real estate for the purpose of funding schools, law enforcement, and other local services.* 115

purchase option *A price specified in a lease at which the lessee can buy the car at the end of the lease term.* 105

Real Estate Settlement Procedures Act (RESPA) *A federal law requiring mortgage lenders to give potential borrowers a government publication describing the closing process and providing clear, advance disclosure of all closing costs to home buyers.* 120

real estate short sale *Sale of real estate property in which the proceeds are less than the balance owed on a loan secured by the property sold.* 118

rent ratio *the ratio of the average house price to the average annual rent, which provides insight into the relative attractiveness of buying a house versus renting in a given area of potential interest.* 108

residual value *The remaining value of a leased car at the end of the lease term.* 104

sales contract *An agreement to purchase an automobile that states the offering price and all conditions of the offer; when signed by the buyer and seller, the contract legally binds them to its terms.* 103

two-step ARM *An adjustable-rate mortgage with just two interest rates: one for the first 5 to 7 years of the loan, and a higher one for the remaining term of the loan.* 123

VA loan guarantee *A guarantee offered by the U.S. Veterans Administration to lenders who make qualified mortgage loans to eligible veterans of the U.S. Armed Forces and their unmarried surviving spouses.* 124

To access Bonus Exhibits, additional Smart Sites, Concept Checks, and more, please visit CourseMate for PFIN 3. Log in at www.cengagebrain.com.

KEY TERMS

affinity cards *A standard bank credit card issued in conjunction with some charitable, political, or other nonprofit organization. 137*

annual percentage rate (APR) *The actual or true rate of interest paid over the life of a loan; includes all fees and costs. 145*

average daily balance (ADB) method *A method of computing finance charges by applying interest charges to the average daily balance of the account over the billing period. 145*

bank credit card *A credit card issued by a bank or other financial institution that allows the holder to charge purchases at any establishment that accepts it. 135*

base rate *The rate of interest a bank uses as a base for loans to individuals and small to midsize businesses. 136*

cash advance *A loan that can be obtained by a bank credit cardholder at any participating bank or financial institution. 136*

credit bureau *An organization that collects and sells credit information about individual borrowers. 142*

credit investigation *An investigation that involves contacting credit references or corresponding with a credit bureau to verify information on a credit application. 142*

credit limit *A specified amount beyond which a customer may not borrow or purchase on credit. 133*

credit scoring *A method of evaluating an applicant's creditworthiness by assigning values to such factors as income, existing debts, and credit references. 144*

debit card *A card used to make transactions for cash rather than credit; replaces the need for cash or checks by initiating charges against the checking account. 138*

debt safety ratio *The proportion of total monthly consumer credit obligations to monthly take-home pay. 132*

grace period *A short period of time, usually 20 to 30 days, during which you can pay your credit card bill in full and not incur any interest charges. 136*

home equity credit line *A line of credit issued against the existing equity in a home. 140*

line of credit *The maximum amount of credit a customer is allowed to have outstanding at any point in time. 135*

LEARNING GOAL SUMMARIES

LG1 **Describe the reasons for using consumer credit and identify its benefits and problems.**

People use credit as a way to pay for relatively expensive items and, occasionally, to deal with a financial emergency. Consumer credit is also used simply because it's so convenient. Finally, it's used to partially finance the purchase of various types of investments. Unfortunately, consumer credit can be misused to the point where people live beyond their means by purchasing goods and services they simply can't afford. Such overspending can get so bad that it eventually leads to bankruptcy.

Exhibit 6.1 Minimum Payments Mean Maximum Years
Paying off credit card balances at the minimum monthly amount required by the card issuer will take a long time and cost you a great deal of interest, as this table demonstrates. The calculations here are based on a minimum 3% payment and 15% annual interest rate.

Original Balance	Years to Repay	Interest Paid	Total Interest Paid as Percentage of Original Balance
$5,000	16.4	$3,434	68.7%
4,000	15.4	2,720	68.0
3,000	14.0	2,005	66.8
2,000	12.1	1,291	64.5
1,000	8.8	577	57.7

© Cengage Learning

Exhibit 6.2 Credit Guidelines Based on Ability to Repay
According to the debt safety ratio, the amount of consumer credit you should have outstanding depends on the monthly payments you can afford to make.

| Monthly Take-Home Pay | Monthly Consumer Credit Payments | | |
	Low Debt Safety Ratio (10%)	*Manageable* Debt Safety Ratio (15%)	*Maximum* Debt Safety Ratio (20%)
$1,000	$100	$150	$ 200
$1,250	$125	$188	$ 250
$1,500	$150	$225	$ 300
$2,000	$200	$300	$ 400
$2,500	$250	$375	$ 500
$3,000	$300	$450	$ 600
$3,500	$350	$525	$ 700
$4,000	$400	$600	$ 800
$5,000	$500	$750	$1,000

© Cengage Learning

LG2 **Develop a plan to establish a strong credit history.**

Establishing a strong credit history is an important part of personal financial planning. Opening checking and savings accounts, obtaining one or two credit cards and using them judiciously, and taking out a small loan and repaying it on schedule are ways to show potential lenders that you can handle credit wisely. Be sure to use credit only when you're sure you can repay the obligation, make payments promptly, and notify a lender immediately if you can't meet payments as agreed.

minimum monthly payment *In open account credit, a minimum specified percentage of the new account balance that must be paid in order to remain current. 146*

open account credit *A form of credit extended to a consumer in advance of any transaction. 133*

overdraft protection line *A line of credit linked to a checking account that allows a depositor to overdraw the account up to a specified amount. 139*

personal bankruptcy *A form of legal recourse open to insolvent debtors, who may petition a court for protection from creditors and arrange for the orderly liquidation and distribution of their assets. 150*

retail charge card *A type of credit card issued by retailers that allows customers to charge goods and services up to a preestablished amount. 138*

revolving line of credit *A type of open account credit offered by banks and other financial institutions that can be accessed by writing checks against demand deposit or specially designated credit line accounts. 139*

reward (co-branded) credit card *A bank credit card that combines features of a traditional bank credit card with an additional incentive, such as rebates and airline mileage. 137*

secured (collateralized) credit cards *A type of credit card that's secured with some form of collateral, such as a bank CD. 138*

straight bankruptcy *A legal proceeding that results in "wiping the slate clean and starting anew"; most of a debtor's obligations are eliminated in an attempt to put the debtor's financial affairs in order. 150*

student credit card *A credit card marketed specifically to college students. 138*

unsecured personal credit line *A line of credit made available to an individual on an as-needed basis. 140*

Wage Earner Plan *An arrangement for scheduled debt repayment over future years that is an alternative to straight bankruptcy; used when a person has a steady source of income and there is a reasonable chance of repayment within 3 to 5 years. 150*

To access Bonus Exhibits, additional Smart Sites, Concept Checks, and more, please visit CourseMate for PFIN 3. Log on to www.cengagebrain.com.

Using the debt safety ratio, you can calculate how much of your monthly take-home pay is going to consumer credit payments. One widely used credit capacity guideline is that total monthly consumer credit payments (exclusive of your mortgage payment) should not exceed 20% of your monthly take-home pay.

LG3 **Distinguish among the different forms of open account credit.**

Major types of open account credit include bank credit cards, retail charge cards, and revolving lines of credit, like overdraft protection lines, home equity credit lines, and unsecured personal lines of credit. Many financial institutions issue special types of credit cards, such as rewards cards, affinity cards, or secured credit cards. Instead of using only credit cards, a growing number of consumers are turning to debit cards, which give their users a way to write checks with plastic.

LG4 **Apply for, obtain, and manage open forms of credit.**

Most types of revolving credit require formal application, which generally involves an extensive investigation of your credit background and an evaluation of your creditworthiness. This usually includes checking credit bureau reports. You should verify the accuracy of these reports regularly, and promptly correct any errors. The amount of finance charges, if any, due on consumer credit depends largely on the technique used to compute the account balance; the average daily balance method that includes new purchases is the most common today. Managing your accounts involves understanding the monthly statement and making payments on time.

LG5 **Choose the right credit cards and recognize their advantages and disadvantages.**

Before choosing a credit card, consider your spending habits and then compare the fees, interest rates, grace period, and any incentives. Read the terms of credit card agreements carefully so that you understand all the ways you can be charged interest and fees. If you pay off your balance each month, you'll want a card with low annual fees; if you carry a balance, a low interest rate is your best bet. Advantages of credit cards include interest-free loans, simplified record-keeping, ease of making returns and resolving unsatisfactory purchase disputes, convenience and security, and use in emergencies. The disadvantages are the tendency to overspend and high interest costs on unpaid balances.

LG6 **Avoid credit problems, protect yourself against credit card fraud, and understand the personal bankruptcy process.**

Keep the number of cards you use to a minimum, and be sure you can repay any balances quickly. When credit card debt gets out of control, adopt a payment strategy to pay off the debt as fast as possible by looking for a low-rate card, paying more than the minimum payment, and not charging any additional purchases until the debt is repaid or substantially paid down. Another option is a consolidation loan. To protect yourself against credit card fraud, don't give out your card number unnecessarily, destroy old cards and receipts, verify your credit card transactions, and report a lost card or suspicious activity immediately. A solution to credit abuse, albeit a drastic one, is personal bankruptcy. Those who file for bankruptcy work out a debt restructuring program under Chapter 13's Wage Earner Plan or Chapter 7's straight bankruptcy.

KEY TERMS

add-on method *A method of calculating interest by computing finance charges on the original loan balance and then adding the interest to that balance.* 172

captive finance company *A sales finance company that is owned by a manufacturer of big-ticket merchandise. GMAC is a captive finance company.* 160

cash value (of life insurance) *An accumulation of savings in an insurance policy that can be used as a source of loan collateral.* 160

chattel mortgage *A mortgage on personal property given as security for the payment of an obligation.* 165

collateral *An item of value used to secure the principal portion of a loan.* 156

collateral note *A legal note giving the lender the right to sell collateral if the borrower defaults on the obligation.* 165

consumer finance company *A firm that makes secured and unsecured personal loans to qualified individuals; also called a* small loan company. 159

consumer loans *Loans made for specific purposes using formally negotiated contracts that specify the borrowing terms and repayment.* 155

discount method *A method of calculating finance charges in which interest is computed and then subtracted from the principal, with the remainder being disbursed to the borrower.* 169

installment loan *A loan that is repaid in a series of fixed, scheduled payments rather than a lump sum.* 159

interim financing *The use of a single-payment loan to finance a purchase or pay bills in situations where the funds to be used for repayment are known to be forthcoming in the near future.* 159

lien *A legal claim permitting the lender, in case the borrower defaults, to liquidate the items serving as collateral to satisfy the obligation.* 165

loan application *An application that gives a lender information about the purpose of the loan as well as the applicant's financial condition.* 165

LEARNING GOAL SUMMARIES

LG1 **Know when to use consumer loans and be able to differentiate between the major types.**

Single-payment and installment loans are formally negotiated consumer loan arrangements used mainly to finance big-ticket items. Most of these consumer loans are taken out as auto loans, loans for other durable goods, education loans, personal loans, and consolidation loans.

LG2 **Identify the various sources of consumer loans.**

Consumer loans can be obtained from various sources, including commercial banks (the biggest providers of such credit), consumer finance companies, credit unions, S&Ls, sales finance (and captive finance) companies, life insurance companies (and other financial services organizations), and, finally, as a last resort, your friends and relatives.

Exhibit 7.1 Federal Government Student Loan Programs at a Glance

More and more college students rely on loans subsidized by the federal government to finance all or part of their educations. There are three types of federally subsidized loan programs, the basic loan provisions of which are listed here. These loans all have low interest rates and provide various deferment options and extended repayment terms. (Note: Loan rates and terms shown here are for the 2012–2013 school year.)

Loan Provisions	Type of Federal Loan Program		
	Stafford Loans*	Perkins Loans	PLUS Loans
Borrower	Student	Student	Parent
Interest rate	3.4%	5%	8.5%
Borrowing limits	*Dependent students:* $23,000 (undergrad); $65,000 (grad/professional) *Independent students:* $57,500 (undergrad) $65,000 (grad/professional)	$27,500 (undergrad) $60,000 (grad/professional)	*No total dollar limit:* Cost of attendance minus any other financial aid received
Loan fees	1% of loan origination fee (0.5% rebate up to July 2012)	None	Up to 4% origination fee
Loan term	10–25 years	10 years	10 years

*Data are for subsidized Stafford loans, and interest rates are as of mid-2012. Stafford loans can be subsidized or unsubsidized and the lifetime limits can differ. Congress passed a bill keeping the rate at this lower rate for 2012-13, which is below the previously determined 6.8%. Subsidized Stafford loans also have annual borrowing limits ranging from $3,500 for the freshman year for dependent students to $8,500 per year in graduate/professional school for independent students; likewise, Perkins loans have annual limits of $5,500 per year of undergraduate study and $8,000 per year of graduate school.
Source: http://www.fastweb.com and http://www.staffordloan.com, accessed July 2012.

LG3 **Choose the best loans by comparing finance charges, maturity, collateral, and other loan terms.**

Before taking out a consumer loan, you should be sure the purchase is compatible with your financial plans and that you can service the debt without straining your budget. When shopping for credit, it's in your best interest to compare such loan features as finance charges (APRs), loan maturities, monthly payments, and collateral requirements and then to choose loans with terms that are fully compatible with your financial plans and cash budget.

loan disclosure statement *A document, which lenders are required to supply borrowers, that states both the dollar amount of finance charges and the APR applicable to a loan.* 167

loan rollover *The process of paying off a loan by taking out another loan.* 165

prepayment penalty *An additional charge you may owe if you decide to pay off your loan prior to maturity.* 165

rule of 78s (sum-of-the-digits method) *A method of calculating interest that has extra-heavy interest charges in the early months of the loan.* 172

sales finance company *A firm that purchases notes drawn up by sellers of certain types of merchandise, typically big-ticket items.* 160

simple interest method *A method of computing finance charges in which interest is charged on the actual loan balance outstanding.* 167

single-payment loan *A loan made for a specified period, at the end of which payment is due in full.* 159

To access Bonus Exhibits, additional Smart Sites, Concept Checks, and more, please visit CourseMate for PFIN 3. Log on to www.cengagebrain.com.

LG4 Describe the features of, and calculate the finance charges on, single-payment loans.

In a single-payment loan, the borrower makes just one principal payment (at the maturity of the loan), although there may be one or more interim interest payments. Such loans are usually made for 1 year or less, and they're normally secured by some type of collateral. A major advantage of the single-payment loan is that it doesn't require monthly payments and won't tie up the borrower's cash flow. Finance charges can be calculated using either the simple interest method—applying the interest rate to the outstanding loan balance—or the discount method—calculating the interest the same way as simple interest, but then deducting it from the loan principal and getting a higher APR.

LG5 Evaluate the benefits of an installment loan.

In an installment loan, the borrower agrees to repay the loan through a series of equal installment payments (usually monthly) until the obligation is fully repaid; in this way, the borrower can receive a loan-repayment schedule that fits neatly into his or her financial plans and cash budget. This highly popular form of consumer credit can be used to finance just about any type of big-ticket asset or expenditure. Many ILs are taken out as home equity loans to capture tax advantages.

LG6 Determine the costs of installment loans and analyze whether it is better to pay cash or take out a loan.

Most single-payment loans are made with either simple or discount interest, whereas most ILs are made with either simple or add-on interest. When simple interest is used, the actual finance charge always corresponds to the stated rate of interest; in contrast, when add-on or discount rates are used, the APR is always more than the stated rate. In the end, whether it makes sense to borrow rather than to pay cash is a matter of which alternative costs less.

Exhibit 7.5 Comparative Finance Charges and APRs (Assumes a $1,000, 8 Percent, 12-Month Installment Loan)
In sharp contrast to simple interest loans, the APR with add-on installment loans is much higher than the stated rate.

	Simple Interest	Add-on Interest
Stated rate on loan	8%	8%
Finance charges	$43.88	$80.00
Monthly payments	$86.99	$90.00
Total payments made	$1,043.88	$1,080.00
APR	8%	14.45%

© Cengage Learning

KEY TERMS

beneficiary *A person who receives the death benefits of a life insurance policy after the insured's death. 197*

cash value *The accumulated refundable value of an insurance policy; results from the investment earnings on paid-in insurance premiums. 187*

convertibility *A term life policy provision allowing the insured to convert the policy to a comparable whole life policy. 187*

credit life insurance *Life insurance sold in conjunction with installment loans. 193*

decreasing term policy *A term insurance policy that maintains a level premium throughout all periods of coverage while the amount of protection decreases. 186*

disability clause *A clause in a life insurance contract containing a waiver-of-premium benefit alone or coupled with disability income. 198*

group life insurance *Life insurance that provides a master policy for a group; each eligible group member receives a certificate of insurance. 193*

guaranteed purchase option *An option in a life insurance contract giving the policyholder the right to purchase additional coverage at stipulated intervals without providing evidence of insurability. 199*

industrial life insurance (home service life insurance) *Whole life insurance issued in policies with relatively small face amounts, often $1,000 or less. 193*

insurance policy *A contract between the insured and the insurer under which the insurer agrees to reimburse the insured for any losses suffered according to specified terms. 180*

loss control *Any activity that lessens the severity of loss once it occurs. 180*

loss prevention *Any activity that reduces the probability that a loss will occur. 179*

mortgage life insurance *A term policy designed to pay off the mortgage balance in the event of the borrower's death. 193*

multiple indemnity clause *A clause in a life insurance policy that typically doubles or triples the policy's face amount if the insured dies in an accident. 198*

LEARNING GOAL SUMMARIES

LG1 Explain the concept of risk and the basics of insurance underwriting.

Adequate life insurance coverage not only protects what you've already acquired but also helps ensure the attainment of unfulfilled financial goals. The whole notion of insurance is based on the concept of risk and the different methods of handling it, including risk avoidance, loss prevention and control, risk assumption, and insurance (a cost-effective procedure that allows families to reduce financial risks by sharing losses). Through the underwriting process, insurance companies decide whom they consider an acceptable risk and the premiums to charge for coverage.

LG2 Discuss the primary reasons for life insurance and identify those who need coverage.

Life insurance fills the gap between the financial resources available to your dependents if you should die prematurely and what they need to maintain a given lifestyle. Some policies provide only a death benefit; others also have a savings component. If you have children or elderly relatives who count on your income to support them, you should include life insurance as one of several financial resources to meet their requirements. If you have no dependents, you probably don't need life insurance. Your life insurance needs change over your life cycle and should be reviewed regularly.

LG3 Calculate how much life insurance you need.

There are several ways to determine the amount of life insurance a family should have. Although the multiple-of-earnings method is simple to use, most experts agree that the needs analysis method is the best procedure. It systematically considers such variables as family income, household and other expenses, special needs, final expenses, debt liquidation, and other financial needs, which are then compared with the financial resources available to meet these needs.

Exhibit 8.1 How Much Life Insurance Do You Need?
The needs analysis method uses three steps to estimate life insurance needs.

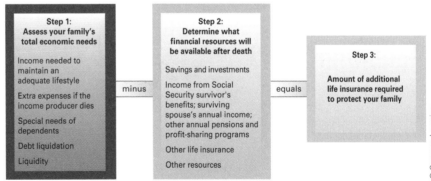

© Cengage Learning

LG4 Distinguish among the various types of life insurance policies and describe their advantages and disadvantages.

The three basic types of life insurance policies are term life, whole life, and universal life. Term life insurance provides a stipulated amount of death benefits, whereas whole life combines death benefits with a modest savings program, and universal life packages term insurance with a tax-sheltered savings/investment account that pays interest at competitive money market rates. Other types of life insurance include variable life, group life, credit life, mortgage life, and industrial life.

multiple-of-earnings method *A method of determining the amount of life insurance coverage needed by multiplying gross annual earnings by some selected number. 181*

needs analysis method *A method of determining the amount of life insurance coverage needed by considering a person's financial obligations and available financial resources in addition to life insurance. 181*

nonforfeiture right *A life insurance feature giving the whole life policyholder, upon policy cancellation, the portion of those assets that were set aside to provide payment for the future death claim. 188*

participating policy *A life insurance policy that pays policy dividends reflecting the difference between the premiums that are charged and the amount of premium necessary to fund the actual mortality experience of the company. 199*

policy loan *An advance, secured by the cash value of a whole life insurance policy, made by an insurer to the policyholder. 197*

renewability *A term life policy provision allowing the insured to renew the policy at the end of its term without having to show evidence of insurability. 187*

risk assumption *The choice to accept and bear the risk of loss. 180*

risk avoidance *Avoiding an act that would create a risk. 179*

Social Security survivor's benefits *Benefits under Social Security intended to provide basic, minimum support to families faced with the loss of a principal wage earner. 183*

straight term policy *A term insurance policy written for a given number of years, with coverage remaining unchanged throughout the effective period. 185*

term life insurance *Insurance that provides only death benefits, for a specified period, and does not provide for the accumulation of cash value. 185*

underwriting *The process used by insurers to decide who can be insured and to determine applicable rates that will be charged for premiums. 180*

universal life insurance *Permanent cash-value insurance that combines term insurance (death benefits) with a tax-sheltered savings/investment account that pays interest, usually at competitive money market rates. 191*

LG5 **Choose the best life insurance policy for your needs at the lowest cost.**

It's important not only to compare costs but also to buy the proper amount of life insurance and pick the right type of insurance policy. Carefully consider the financial stability of the insurer offering the policy, paying special attention to the ratings assigned by major rating agencies.

Exhibit 8.8 Major Advantages and Disadvantages of the Most Popular Types of Life Insurance

Major advantages and disadvantages of the most popular types of life insurance are summarized here. They should be considered when shopping for life insurance.

Type of Policy	Advantages	Disadvantages
Term	Low initial premiums Simple, easy to buy	Provides only temporary coverage for a set period May have to pay higher premiums when policy is renewed
Whole life	Permanent coverage Savings vehicle: cash value builds as premiums are paid Some tax advantages on accumulated earnings	Cost: provides less death protection per premium dollar than term Often provides lower yields than other investment vehicles Sales commissions and marketing expenses can increase costs of fully loaded policy
Universal life	Permanent coverage Flexible: lets insured adapt level of protection and cost of premiums Savings vehicle: cash value builds at current rate of interest Savings and death protection identified separately	Can be difficult to evaluate true cost at time of purchase; insurance carrier may levy costly fees and charges
Variable life	Investment vehicle: insured decides how cash value will be invested	Higher risk

© Cengage Learning

LG6 **Become familiar with the key features of life insurance policies.**

Some important contract features of life insurance policies you should become familiar with are the beneficiary clause, settlement options, policy loans, premium payments, grace period, nonforfeiture options, policy reinstatement, and change of policy. Other policy features include multiple indemnity and disability clauses, guaranteed purchase options, suicide clause, exclusions, participation, living benefits, and viatical settlements. Life insurance policy illustrations provide insight into the assumptions relied on by an insurance company and the potential performance of the policy.

variable life insurance *Life insurance in which the benefits are a function of the returns being generated on the investments selected by the policyholder. 192*

whole life insurance *Life insurance designed to offer ongoing insurance coverage over the course of an insured's entire life. 187*

To access Bonus Exhibits, additional Smart Sites, Concept Checks, and more, please visit CourseMate for PFIN 3. Log on to www.cengagebrain.com.

KEY TERMS

Blue Cross/Blue Shield plans *Prepaid hospital and medical expense plans under which health care services are provided to plan participants by member hospitals and physicians.* 207

community rating approach to health insurance premium pricing *Policyholders in a community (area) pay the same premium without regard to their personal health, age, gender, or other factors.* 211

comprehensive major medical insurance *A health insurance plan that combines into a single policy the coverage for basic hospitalization, surgical, and physician expense along with major medical protection.* 214

coordination of benefits provision *A provision often included in health insurance policies to prevent the insured from collecting more than 100 percent of covered charges; it requires that benefit payments be coordinated if the insured is eligible for benefits under more than one policy.* 216

deductible *The initial amount not covered by an insurance policy and thus the insured's responsibility; it's usually determined on a calendar-year basis or on a per-illness or per-accident basis.* 215

disability income insurance *Insurance that provides families with weekly or monthly payments to replace income when the insured is unable to work because of a covered illness, injury, or disease.* 222

exclusive provider organization (EPO) *A managed care plan that is similar to a PPO but reimburses members only when affiliated providers are used.* 207

group health insurance *Health insurance consisting of contracts written between a group, (employer, union, etc.) and the health care provider.* 205

group HMO *An HMO that provides health care services from a central facility; most prevalent in larger cities.* 206

guaranteed renewability *Policy provision ensuring continued insurance coverage for the insured's lifetime as long as the premiums continue to be paid.* 220

Health Insurance Portability and Accountability Act (HIPAA) *Federal law that protects people's ability to obtain continued health insurance after they leave a job or retire, even if they have a serious health problem.* 216

health maintenance organization (HMO) *An organization of hospitals, physicians, and other health care providers who have joined to provide comprehensive health care services to its members, who pay a monthly fee.* 206

LEARNING GOAL SUMMARIES

LG1 **Discuss why having adequate health insurance is important, and identify the factors contributing to the growing cost of health insurance.**

Adequate health insurance protects you from having to pay potentially tens of thousands of dollars of medical care out of pocket. However, many Americans are uninsured or underinsured because the cost of health insurance has skyrocketed. Trends pushing medical expenses and health insurance higher include the growth of new drugs and treatments that save lives but also cost more to provide. Administrative costs, excessive paperwork, increased regulation, and insurance fraud are also contributing to rising costs.

LG2 **Differentiate among the major types of health insurance plans, and identify major private and public health insurance providers and their programs.**

Health insurance is available from both private and government-sponsored programs. Private health insurance plans include indemnity (fee-for-service) plans and managed care plans. Indemnity plans pay a share of health care costs directly to a medical provider, who is usually separate from the insurer. The insured pays the remaining amount. In a managed care plan, subscribers contract with and make monthly payments directly to the organization providing the health services. Examples of managed care plans include health maintenance organizations (HMOs) and preferred provider organizations (PPOs). Blue Cross/Blue Shield plans are prepaid hospital and medical expense plans. Federal and state agencies also provide health insurance coverage to eligible individuals. Medicare, Medicaid, and workers' compensation insurance are all forms of government health insurance plans. The Patient Protection and Affordable Care Act became law in March of 2010 and was quickly amended by the Health Care and Education Reconciliation Act of 2010 (H.R. 4872). The legislation bars insurance companies from dropping coverage for people when they get sick and prevents exclusion due to preexisting conditions. Young adults can remain on their parents' insurance until they turn 26, and lifetime and restrictive limits on benefits are prohibited.

LG3 **Analyze your own health insurance needs and explain how to shop for appropriate coverage.**

From a health insurance perspective, most people need protection from two types of losses: (1) the cost of medical bills and other associated expenses, and (2) loss of income or household services caused by an inability to work. A good health care plan should use risk avoidance, loss prevention and control, and risk assumption strategies to reduce risk and the associated need and cost of insurance. The best way to buy health insurance is to determine your current coverage and resources and then match your needs with the various types of coverage available. When shopping for health insurance, consider the cost of coverage, its availability as an employee benefit, the quality of both the agent and the insurer or managed care provider, and your own medical needs and care preferences.

LG4 **Explain the basic types of medical expenses covered and policy provisions of health insurance plans.**

The basic types of medical expenses covered by insurance are hospitalization, surgical expenses, physician expenses (nonsurgical medical care), and major medical insurance (which covers all types of medical expenses). Some health insurers offer comprehensive major medical policies that combine basic hospitalization, surgical, and physicians expense coverage with a major medical plan to form a single policy.

The most important provisions in medical insurance policies pertain to terms of payment, terms of coverage, and cost containment. How much your plan will pay depends on deductibles, participation (coinsurance), internal limits, and coordination of benefits. Terms of coverage encompass the persons and places covered, cancellation, pregnancy and abortion, mental illness, rehabilitation, and

health reimbursement account (HRA) *An account into which employers place contributions that employees can use to pay for medical expenses. Usually combined with a high-deductible health insurance policy. 211*

health savings account (HSA) *A tax-free savings account—funded by employees, employer, or both—to spend on routine medical costs. Usually combined with a high deductible policy to pay for catastrophic care. 211*

indemnity (fee-for-service) plan *Health insurance plan in which the health care provider is separate from the insurer, who pays the provider or reimburses you for a specified percentage of expenses after a deductible amount has been met. 205*

individual practice association (IPA) *A form of HMO in which subscribers receive services from physicians practicing from their own offices and from community hospitals affiliated with the IPA. 207*

internal limits *A feature commonly found in health insurance policies that limits the amounts that will be paid for certain specified expenses, even if the claim does not exceed overall policy limits. 215*

long-term care *The delivery of medical and personal care, other than hospital care, to persons with chronic medical conditions resulting from either illness or frailty. 218*

major medical plan *An insurance plan designed to supplement the basic coverage of hospitalization, surgical, and physicians expenses; used to finance more catastrophic medical costs. 214*

managed care plan *A health care plan in which subscribers/users contract with the provider organization, which uses a designated group of providers meeting specific selection standards to furnish health care services for a monthly fee. 205*

Medicaid *A state-run public assistance program that provides health insurance benefits only to those who are unable to pay for health care. 209*

Medicare *A health insurance plan administered by the federal government to help persons age 65 and over, and others receiving monthly Social Security disability benefits, to meet their health care costs. 207*

Medicare Advantage plans *Commonly called Plan C, these plans provide Medicare benefits to eligible people, but they differ in that they are administered by private providers rather than by the government. Common supplemental benefits include vision, hearing, dental, general checkups, and health and wellness programs. 208*

group coverage continuation. The most common cost containment provisions are preadmission certification, continued stay review, second surgical opinions, waiver of coinsurance, and limitations of insurer's responsibility.

LG5 Assess the need for and features of long-term care insurance.

Long-term care insurance covers nonhospital expenses, such as nursing home care or home health care, caused by chronic illness or frailty. Coverage availability historically depended on provisions addressing type of care, eligibility requirements, services covered, renewability, and preexisting conditions. However, the Patient Protection and Affordable Care Act outlawed preexisting condition constraints. Terms-of-payment provisions include daily benefits, benefit duration, waiting period, and inflation protection. Premium levels result from differences in coverage and payment provisions, and they vary widely among insurance companies.

LG6 Discuss the features of disability income insurance and how to determine your need for it.

The loss of family income caused by the disability of a principal wage earner can be at least partially replaced by disability income insurance. Disability insurance needs can be estimated by subtracting the amount of existing monthly disability benefits from current monthly take-home pay. Important coverage terms include the definition of disability, probationary period, renewability, guaranteed insurability, and waiver of premium. Provisions pertaining to benefit amount and duration, waiting period, and cost-of-living adjustments define the terms of payment. Because these policies are expensive, you should choose as long a waiting period as possible given your other available financial resources.

optional renewability *Contractual clause allowing the insured to continue insurance only at the insurer's option. 221*

participation (co-insurance) clause *A provision in many health insurance policies stipulating that the insurer will pay some portion—say, 80 percent or 90 percent—of the amount of the covered loss in excess of the deductible. 215*

point-of-service (POS) plan *A hybrid form of HMO that allows members to go outside the HMO network for care and reimburses them at a specified percentage of the cost. 207*

preexisting condition clause *A clause included in most individual health insurance policies permitting permanent or temporary exclusion of coverage for any physical or mental problems the insured had at the time the policy was purchased. The Patient Protection and Affordable Care Act of 2010 outlawed such exclusions. 216*

preferred provider organization (PPO) *A health provider that combines the characteristics of the IPA form of HMO with an indemnity plan to provide comprehensive health care services to its subscribers within a network of physicians and hospitals. 207*

prescription drug coverage *A voluntary program under Medicare (commonly called Part D), insurance that covers*

both brand-name and generic prescription drugs at participating pharmacies. Participants pay a monthly fee and a yearly deductible and must also pay part of the cost of prescriptions, including a co-payment or co-insurance. 208*

supplementary medical insurance (SMI) *A voluntary program under Medicare (commonly called Part B) that provides payments for services not covered under basic hospital insurance (Part A). 208*

waiting period (elimination period) *The period, after an insured meets the policy's eligibility requirements, during which he or she must pay expenses out-of-pocket; when the waiting period expires, the insured begins to receive benefits. 220*

workers' compensation insurance *Health insurance required by state and federal governments and paid nearly in full by employers in most states; it compensates workers for job-related illness or injury. 209*

To access Bonus Exhibits, additional Smart Sites, Concept Checks, and more, please visit CourseMate for PFIN 3. Log on to www.cengagebrain.com.

KEY TERMS

actual cash value *A value assigned to an insured property that is determined by subtracting the amount of physical depreciation from its replacement cost. 231*

bodily injury liability losses *A PAP provision that protects the insured against claims made for bodily injury. 239*

captive agent *An insurance agent who represents only one insurance company and who is, in effect, an employee of that company. 245*

claims adjustor *An insurance specialist who works for the insurance company, as an independent adjustor, or for an adjustment bureau to investigate claims. 246*

co-insurance *In property insurance, a provision requiring a policyholder to buy insurance in an amount equal to a specified percentage of the replacement value of their property. 232*

collision insurance *Automobile insurance that pays for collision damage to an insured automobile regardless of who is at fault. 242*

comprehensive automobile insurance *Coverage that protects against loss to an insured automobile caused by any peril (with a few exceptions) other than collision. 242*

comprehensive policy *Property and liability insurance policy covering all perils unless they are specifically excluded. 232*

financial responsibility laws *Laws requiring motorists to buy a specified minimum amount of automobile liability insurance or to provide other proof of comparable financial responsibility. 244*

independent agent *An insurance agent who may place coverage with any company with which he or she has an agency relationship, as long as the insured meets that company's underwriting standards. 245*

liability insurance *Insurance that protects against the financial consequences that may arise from the insured's responsibility for property loss or injuries to others. 229*

named peril policy *Property and liability insurance policy that individually names the perils covered. 232*

negligence *Failing to act in a reasonable manner or to take necessary steps to protect others from harm. 231*

LEARNING GOAL SUMMARIES

LG1 **Discuss the importance and basic principles of property insurance, including types of exposure, indemnity, and co-insurance.**

Property and liability insurance protects against the loss of real and personal property that can occur from exposure to various perils. Such insurance also protects against loss from lawsuits based on alleged negligence by the insured. The principle of indemnity limits the insured's compensation to the amount of economic loss. The co-insurance provision requires the policyholder to buy insurance coverage that equals a set percentage of the property's value to receive full compensation under the policy's terms.

Exhibit 10.1 A Personal Property Inventory Form
Using a form like this will help you keep track of your personal property, including its date of purchase, original purchase price, and replacement cost.

Living Room

Stereo System

Brand	
Model	
Serial #	Date purchased
Purchase price $	Replacement cost $

Large-Screen TV

Brand	
Model	
Serial #	Date purchased
Purchase price $	Replacement cost $

Compact Disc Player/MP3 Player

Brand	
Model	
Serial #	Date purchased
Purchase price $	Replacement cost $

Home Theater System

Brand	
Model	
Serial #	Date purchased
Purchase price $	Replacement cost $

DVD Player

Brand	
Model	
Serial #	Date purchased
Purchase price $	Replacement cost $

Living Room

Article	Qty.	Date Purchased	Purchase Price	Replacement Cost
Air conditioners (window)				
Blinds/shades				
Bookcases				
Books				
Cabinets				
Carpets/rugs				
Chairs				
Chests				
Clocks				
Couches/sofas				
Curtains/draperies				
Fireplace fixtures				
Lamps/lighting fixtures				
Mirrors				
Pictures/paintings				
CDs				
Planters				
Stereo equipment				
Tables				
Television sets				
Other				
Other				

© Cengage Learning

no-fault automobile insurance *Automobile insurance that reimburses the parties involved in an accident without regard to negligence. 242*

peril *A cause of loss. 229*

personal automobile policy (PAP) *A comprehensive automobile insurance policy designed to be easily understood by the "typical" insurance purchaser. 238*

personal liability umbrella policy *An insurance policy providing excess liability coverage for homeowner's and automobile insurance as well as additional coverage not provided by either policy. 244*

personal property floater (PPF) *An insurance endorsement or policy providing either blanket or scheduled coverage of expensive personal property not adequately covered in a standard homeowner's policy. 235*

principle of indemnity *An insurance principle stating that an insured may not be compensated by the insurance company in an amount exceeding the insured's economic loss. 231*

property damage liability losses *A PAP provision that protects the insured against claims made for damage to property. 239*

property insurance *Insurance coverage that protects real and personal property from catastrophic losses caused by a variety of perils, such as fire, theft, vandalism, and windstorms. 229*

replacement cost *The amount necessary to repair, rebuild, or replace an asset at today's prices. 236*

right of subrogation *The right of an insurer, who has paid an insured's claim, to request reimbursement from either the person who caused the loss or that person's insurer. 232*

underinsured motorists coverage *Optional automobile insurance coverage, available in some states, that protects the insured against damages caused by being in an accident with an underinsured motorist who is found liable. 241*

uninsured motorists coverage *Automobile insurance designed to meet the needs of "innocent" victims of accidents who are negligently injured by uninsured, underinsured, or hit-and-run motorists. 241*

LG2 Identify the types of coverage provided by homeowner's insurance.

Most homeowner's insurance policies are divided into two sections. Section I covers the insured's dwelling unit, accompanying structures, and personal property. Section II provides comprehensive coverage for personal liability and medical payments to others. The most commonly sold homeowner's policies (Forms HO-2 and HO-3) cover a broad range of perils, including damage from fire or lightning, windstorms, explosions, aircraft, vehicles, smoke, vandalism, theft, freezing, and so on. Personal property coverage is typically set at 50% of the coverage on the dwelling.

LG3 Select the right homeowner's insurance policy for your needs.

Everyone should have some form of homeowner's insurance, whether you own a single-family house or a condominium, or rent an apartment. Renter's insurance covers your personal possessions. Except for the house and garage, which are covered on a replacement-cost basis, homeowner's or renter's insurance normally reimburses all losses on an actual cash-value basis, subject to applicable deductibles and policy limits. For an additional premium, you can usually obtain replacement-cost coverage on personal belongings. In Section I, internal limits are set for various classes of property. You may wish to increase these limits if you have valuable property. One way to do so is with a personal property floater (PPF). Because the standard Section II liability limit is only $100,000, it's a good idea to buy additional liability coverage, generally available at minimal cost. Choose a policy with a higher deductible to reduce premiums.

LG4 Analyze the coverage in a personal automobile policy (PAP) and choose the most cost-effective policy.

Automobile insurance policies usually protect the insured from loss due to personal liability, medical payments, uninsured (and underinsured) motorists, collision (property damage to the vehicle), and comprehensive coverage (which applies to nearly any other type of noncollision damage a car might suffer, such as theft or vandalism). Where you live, type of car, driving record, how much you drive, and your personal characteristics influence the policy premium cost. Most automobile insurers offer discounts for good driving records, safety and antitheft devices, driver's training courses, and so on. Other ways to reduce premiums are through higher deductibles and eliminating collision coverage if your car is old.

LG5 Describe other types of property and liability insurance.

Besides the major forms of homeowner's and automobile insurance, you can get other property and liability coverage, including supplemental property insurance coverage—earthquake insurance, flood insurance, and other forms of transportation insurance (mobile-home, recreational vehicle, and boat insurance)—and personal liability umbrella policies.

LG6 Choose a property and liability insurance agent and company, and settle claims.

Before buying property and liability coverage, evaluate your exposure to loss and determine the coverage needed. Also carefully select your insurance agent and insurance company to obtain appropriate coverage at a reasonable price. Equally important, make sure the agent and company you deal with have reputations for fair claims-settlement practices. Before filing a claim, decide whether the amount of damage warrants a claim. Document all claims properly and file promptly. If you have a complex loss claim, expect your insurer to assign a claims adjustor to the case.

To access Bonus Exhibits, additional Smart Sites, Concept Checks, and more, please visit CourseMate for PFIN 3. Log on to www.cengagebrain.com.

KEY TERMS

annual stockholders' report *A report made available to stockholders and other interested parties that includes a variety of financial and descriptive information about a firm's operations in the recent past. 267*

arbitration *A procedure used to settle disputes between a brokerage firm and its clients; both sides present their positions to a board of arbitration, which makes a final and usually binding decision on the matter. 265*

ask price *The price at which one can purchase a security. 259*

asset allocation *A plan for dividing a portfolio among different classes of securities in order to preserve capital by protecting the portfolio against negative market developments. 275*

bear market *A condition of the market typically associated with investor pessimism and economic slowdown; characterized by generally falling securities prices. 261*

bid price *The price at which one can sell a security. 259*

bull market *A market condition normally associated with investor optimism, economic recovery, and expansion; characterized by generally rising securities prices. 261*

discount broker *A broker with low overhead who charges low commissions and offers little or no services to investors. 263*

diversification *The process of choosing securities with dissimilar risk–return characteristics in order to create a portfolio that provides an acceptable level of return and an acceptable exposure to risk. 273*

Dow Jones Industrial Average (DJIA) *The most widely followed measure of stock market performance; consists of 30 blue-chip stocks listed mostly on the NYSE. 267*

Dow Jones Wilshire 5000 index *An index of the total market value of the approximately 6,000–7,000 or so most actively traded stocks in the United States. 268*

full-service broker *A broker who, in addition to executing clients' transactions, offers a full array of brokerage services. 263*

LEARNING GOAL SUMMARIES

LG1 **Discuss the role that investing plays in the personal financial planning process and identify several different investment objectives.**

Investing plays an important part in personal financial planning; it's the means whereby many of your financial goals can be reached. Your investment activities should be based on a sound investment plan that's linked to an ongoing savings plan. Most people invest their money to enhance their current income, accumulate funds for a major expenditure, save for retirement, or shelter some of their income from taxes.

LG2 **Distinguish between primary and secondary markets, as well as between broker and dealer markets.**

Stocks, bonds, and other long-term securities are traded in the capital, or long-term, markets. Newly issued securities are sold in the primary markets, whereas transactions between investors occur in the secondary markets; the secondary market can be further divided into broker and dealer markets. Broker markets are made up of various securities exchanges, like the NYSE as well as some smaller regional exchanges. In contrast, the dealer market is where you'll find both the NASDAQ markets (like the NASDAQ Global Select and National Markets) as well as the OTC markets (i.e., the OTCBB and Pink Sheets).

Exhibit 11.1 Broker and Dealer Markets
On a typical trading day, the secondary market is a beehive of activity where literally billions of shares change hands daily. This market consists of two parts, the broker market and the dealer market. As can be seen, each of these markets is made up of various exchanges and trading venues.

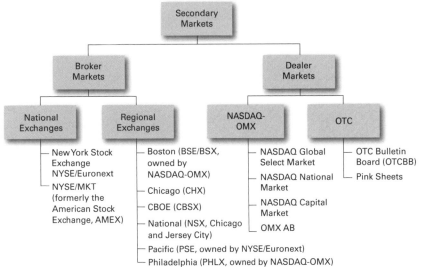

LG3 **Explain the process of buying and selling securities and recognize the different types of orders.**

The securities transaction process starts when you call and place an order with your broker, who then transmits it via sophisticated telecommunications equipment to the floor of the stock exchange or the OTC market, where it's promptly executed and confirmed. Investors can buy or sell securities in odd or round lots by simply placing one of the three basic types of orders: a market order, limit order, or stop-loss order.

LG4 **Develop an appreciation of how various forms of investment information can lead to better investing skills and returns.**

Becoming an informed investor is essential to developing a sound investment program. Vital information about specific companies and industries, the securities

© Cengage Learning

investing *The process of placing money in some medium such as stocks or bonds in the expectation of receiving some future benefit. 251*

investment plan *A statement—preferably written—that specifies how investment capital will be invested to achieve a specified goal. 254*

limit order *An order to either buy a security at a specified or lower price or to sell a security at or above a specified price. 265*

market order *An order to buy or sell a security at the best price available at the time it is placed. 265*

National Association of Securities Dealers (NASD) *An agency made up of brokers and dealers in over-the-counter securities that regulates OTC market operations. 261*

NYSE index *An index of the performance of all stocks listed on the New York Stock Exchange. 268*

odd lot *A quantity of fewer than 100 shares of a stock. 264*

online broker *Typically a discount broker through which investors can execute trades electronically/online through a commercial service or on the Internet; also called Internet broker or electronic broker. 263*

portfolio *A collection of securities assembled for the purpose of meeting common investment goals. 273*

prospectus *A document made available to prospective security buyers that describes the firm and a new security issue. 257*

round lot *A quantity of 100 shares of stock or multiples thereof. 264*

Securities and Exchange Commission (SEC) *An agency of the federal government that regulates the disclosure of information about securities and generally oversees the operation of the securities exchanges and markets. 260*

Securities Investor Protection Corporation (SIPC) *A nonprofit corporation, created by Congress and subject to SEC and congressional oversight, that insures customer accounts against the financial failure of a brokerage firm. 265*

securities markets *The marketplace in which stocks, bonds, and other financial instruments are traded. 256*

speculating *A form of investing in which future value and expected returns are highly uncertain. 251*

Standard & Poor's (S&P) indexes *Indexes compiled by Standard & Poor's that are similar to the DJIA but employ different computational methods and consist of far more stocks. 267*

stockbroker (account executive, financial consultant) *A person who buys and sells securities* on behalf of clients and gives them investment advice and information. 261

stop-loss (stop order) *An order to sell a stock when the market price reaches or drops below a specified level. 266*

To access Bonus Exhibits, additional Smart Sites, Concept Checks, and more, please visit CourseMate for PFIN 3. Log on to www.cengagebrain.com.

markets, the economy, and different investment vehicles and strategies can be obtained from such sources as annual stockholders' reports, brokerage and advisory service reports, the financial press, and the Internet. Various averages and indexes such as the DJIA, Standard & Poor's, the NYSE, and NASDAQ provide information about daily market performance. These averages and indexes not only measure performance in the overall market but also provide standards of performance.

LG5 Gain a basic understanding of the growing impact of the computer and the Internet on the field of investments.

The computer and the Internet have empowered individual investors by providing information and tools formerly available only to investing professionals. The savings they offer in time and money are huge. Investors get the most current information, including real-time stock price quotes, market activity data, research reports, educational articles, and discussion forums. Tools such as financial planning calculators, stock-screening programs, and portfolio tracking are free at many sites. Buying and selling securities online is convenient, simple, inexpensive, and fast.

LG6 Describe an investment portfolio and how you'd go about developing, monitoring, and managing a portfolio of securities.

Developing a well-diversified portfolio of investment holdings enables an investor to not only achieve given investment objectives, but also enjoy reduced exposure to risk and a more predictable level of return. To develop such a portfolio, the investor must carefully consider his or her level and stability of income, family factors, financial condition, experience and age, and disposition toward risk. Designing an asset allocation strategy, or mix of securities, that's based on these personal needs and objectives is also an important part of portfolio management. You should monitor your investment portfolio regularly to measure its performance and make changes as required by return data and life-cycle factors.

KEY TERMS

accrued interest *The amount of interest that's been earned since the last coupon payment date by the bond holder/seller, but which will be received by the new owner/buyer of the bond at the next regularly scheduled coupon payment date. 303*

agency bond *An obligation of a political subdivision of the U.S. government. 300*

beta *An index of the price volatility for a share of common stock; a reflection of how the stock price responds to market forces. 291*

blue-chip stock *A stock generally issued by companies expected to provide an uninterrupted stream of dividends and good long-term growth prospects. 291*

book value *The amount of stockholders' equity in a firm; determined by subtracting the company's liabilities and preferred stock from its assets. 290*

business risk *The degree of uncertainty associated with a firm's cash flows and with its subsequent ability to meet its operating expenses. 281*

call feature *A bond feature that allows the issuer to retire the security prior to maturity. 299*

clean price *The quoted price of a bond plus accrued interest, the total of which is the relevant price to be paid by a bond buyer. 304*

conversion premium *The difference between a convertible security's market price and its conversion value. 302*

conversion privilege *The provision in a convertible issue that stipulates the conditions of the conversion feature, such as the conversion period and conversion ratio. 301*

conversion ratio *A ratio specifying the number of shares of common stock into which a convertible bond can be converted. 301*

conversion value *A measure of what a convertible issue would trade for if it were priced to sell based on its stock value. 302*

corporate bond *A bond issued by a corporation. 301*

coupon *A bond feature that defines the annual interest income that the issuer will pay the bondholder. 298*

current yield *The amount of current income a bond provides relative to its market price. 305*

LEARNING GOAL SUMMARIES

LG1 **Describe the various types of risks to which investors are exposed as well as the sources of return.**

Although investing offers returns in the form of current income and/or capital gains, it also involves risk; the basic types of investment risk are business risk, financial risk, market risk, purchasing power risk, interest rate risk, liquidity risk, and event risk—all of which combine to affect the level of return from an investment.

LG2 **Know how to search for an acceptable investment on the basis of risk, return, and yield.**

The value, and therefore the acceptability, of any investment is a function of the amount of return it's expected to produce relative to the amount of perceived risk involved in the investment. Investors are entitled to be compensated for the risks they must accept in an investment; therefore, the more risk there is in an investment, the more return you should expect to earn. This risk-return trade-off is generally captured in the "desired rate of return," which is that rate of return you feel you should receive in compensation for the amount of risk you must assume. As long as the expected return on an investment (the return you *think* you'll earn) is greater than the desired rate of return (the return you *should* earn), it should be considered an acceptable investment candidate—one worthy of your attention.

LG3 **Discuss the merits of investing in common stock and be able to distinguish among the different types of stocks.**

Common stocks are a popular form of investing that can be used to meet just about any investment objective—from capital gains or current income to some combination of both. Investors can choose from blue chips, growth, or tech stocks; income, speculative, cyclical, or defensive stocks; and small- or mid-cap stocks. If they're so inclined, they can even buy foreign stocks by investing in ADRs (American Depositary Receipts).

LG4 **Become familiar with the various measures of performance and how to use them in placing a value on stocks.**

The value of a share of stock is largely based on performance measures: dividend yield, book value, net profit margin, return on equity (ROE), earnings per share, price/earnings (P/E) ratio, and beta. Investors look at these measures to gain insights about a firm's financial condition and operating results, and ultimately, to obtain the input needed to measure the expected return on the firm's stock.

LG5 **Describe the basic issue characteristics of bonds as well as how these securities are used as investment vehicles.**

Bonds are another popular form of investing; they're often referred to as fixed-income securities because the debt service obligations of the issuer are fixed. The coupon that the bond carries defines the amount of annual interest income that the investor will receive over time, while the par value defines the amount of capital to be repaid at maturity. Bonds may be issued with or without collateral, and most bonds allow the issuer to retire the issue before its maturity. As investment vehicles, bonds can be used to generate either current income or capital gains (which occur when market rates go down).

cyclical stock *A stock whose price movements tend to parallel the various stages of the business cycle. 292*

debenture *An unsecured bond issued on the general credit of the firm. 299*

defensive stock *A stock whose price movements are usually contrary to movements in the business cycle. 292*

desired rate of return *The minimum rate of return an investor feels should be earned in compensation for the amount of risk assumed. 286*

dirty (full) price *The quoted price of a bond plus accrued interest, the total of which is the relevant price to be paid by a bond buyer. 304*

discount bond *A bond whose market value is lower than par. 305*

dividend reinvestment plan (DRP) *A program whereby stockholders can choose to take their cash dividends in the form of more shares of the company's stock. 296*

dividend yield *The percentage return provided by the dividends paid on common stock. 289*

earnings per share (EPS) *The return earned by each share of common stock; calculated by dividing all earnings remaining after paying preferred dividends by the number of common shares outstanding. 290*

equipment trust certificate *A bond secured by certain types of equipment, such as railroad cars and airplanes. 299*

event risk *The risk that some major, unexpected event will occur that leads to a sudden and substantial change in the value of an investment. 282*

financial risk *A type of risk associated with the mix of debt and equity financing used by the issuing firm and its ability to meet its financial obligations. 281*

fixed-income securities *Securities such as bonds, notes, and preferred stocks that offer purchasers fixed periodic income. 282*

general obligation bond *A municipal bond backed by the full faith and credit of the issuing municipality. 301*

growth stock *A stock whose earnings and market price have increased over time at a rate well above average. 291*

income stock *A stock whose appeal is the dividends it pays out; offers dividend payments that can be expected to increase over time. 292*

interest rate risk *A type of risk, resulting from changing market interest rates, that mainly affects fixed-income securities. 282*

LG6 **Distinguish between the different types of bonds, gain an understanding of how bond prices behave, and know how to compute different measures of yield.**

Bonds are the publicly issued debt of corporations and various types of government from the U.S. Treasury and various agencies of the U.S. government to state and local (municipal) governments. Regardless of the issuer, the price of a bond moves inversely with market interest rates: the lower the market rate, the higher the price of the bond. There are basically two ways to measure the yield performance of a bond: one is current yield, which looks only at the coupon income on a bond; the other is yield to maturity, which provides a fully compounded rate of return that considers not only interest income but also capital gains (or loss) and interest on interest.

---

junk bond *Also known as high-yield bonds, these are highly speculative securities that have received low ratings from Moody's or Standard & Poor's. 302*

large-cap stock *A stock with a total market value of more than $10 billion. 293*

liquidity (or marketability) risk *A type of risk associated with the inability to liquidate an investment conveniently and at a reasonable price. 282*

market risk *A type of risk associated with the price volatility of a security. 282*

mid-cap stock *A stock whose total market value falls somewhere between $2 billion and $10 billion. 293*

mortgage bond *A bond secured by a claim on real assets, such as a manufacturing plant. 299*

mortgage-backed securities *Securities that are a claim on the cash flows generated by mortgage loans; bonds backed by mortgages as collateral. 300*

municipal bond *A bond issued by state or local governments; interest income is usually exempt from federal taxes. 300*

net profit margin *A key measure of profitability that relates a firm's net profits to its sales; shows the rate of return the company is earning on its sales. 290*

premium bond *A bond whose market value is higher than par. 305*

price/earnings (P/E) ratio *A measure of investors' confidence in a given security; calculated by dividing market price per share by earnings per share. 291*

proxy *A written statement used to assign a stockholder's voting rights to another person, typically one of the directors. 289*

purchasing power risk *A type of risk, resulting from possible changes in price levels, that can significantly affect investment returns. 282*

residual owners *Shareholders of the company; they are entitled to dividend income and a share of the company's profits only after all of the firm's other obligations have been met. 287*

---

return on equity (ROE) *A measure that captures the firm's overall profitability; it is important because of its impact on the firm's growth, profits, and dividends. 290*

revenue bond *A municipal bond serviced from the income generated by a specific project. 301*

risk-free rate of return *The rate of return on short-term government securities, such as Treasury bills, that is free from default risk. 285*

serial obligation *An issue that is broken down into a series of smaller bonds, each with its own maturity date and coupon rate. 301*

sinking fund *A bond provision specifying the annual repayment schedule to be used in paying off the issue. 299*

small-cap stock *A stock with a total market value of less than $2 billion. 293*

speculative stock *Stock that is purchased on little more than the hope that its price per share will increase. 292*

stock dividends *New shares of stock distributed to existing stockholders as a supplement to or substitute for cash dividends. 290*

tech stock *A stock that represents the technology sector of the market. 292*

Treasury bond *A bond issued by and backed by the full faith and credit of the U.S. government. 300*

Treasury inflation-indexed bond (TIPS) *A bond issued by the U.S. government that has principal payments that are adjusted to provide protection again inflation, as measured by the Consumer Price Index (CPI). 300*

yield to maturity *The fully compounded rate of return that a bond would yield if it were held to maturity. 305*

To access Bonus Exhibits, additional Smart Sites, Concept Checks, and more, please visit CourseMate for PFIN 3. Log on to www.cengagebrain.com.

REVIEW CARD 13

Investing in Mutual Funds, ETFs, and Real Estate

KEY TERMS

12(b)-1 fee *An annual fee that's supposed to be used to offset the promotion and selling expenses. 314*

automatic investment plan *An automatic savings program that enables an investor to channel a set amount of money systematically into a given mutual fund. 320*

automatic reinvestment plan *A plan that gives shareholders the option of electing to have dividends and capital gains distributions reinvested in additional fund shares. 321*

back-end load fund *A commission charged for redeeming fund shares. 314*

closed-end investment company *An investment company that issues a fixed number of shares, which are themselves listed and traded like any other share of stock. 312*

conversion (exchange) privileges *A feature that allows investors to switch from one mutual fund to another within a family of funds. 322*

exchange traded fund (ETF) *An investment company whose shares trade on stock exchanges; unlike mutual funds, ETF shares can be bought or sold (or sold short) throughout the day. 309*

general-purpose money fund *A money fund that invests in virtually any type of short-term investment vehicle. 319*

government securities money fund *A money fund that limits its investments to short-term securities of the U.S. government and its agencies. 319*

income (income-producing) property *Real estate purchased for leasing or renting to tenants in order to generate ongoing monthly/annual income in the form of rent receipts. 329*

international fund *A mutual fund that does all or most of its investing in foreign securities. 320*

load fund *A fund that charges a fee at time of purchase. 314*

low-load fund *A fund that has a low purchase fee. 314*

management fee *A fee paid to the professional money managers who administer a mutual fund's portfolio. 314*

LEARNING GOAL SUMMARIES

LG1 Describe the basic features and operating characteristics of mutual funds and exchange traded funds.

Mutual fund shares represent ownership in a diversified, professionally managed portfolio of securities that do not trade on stock exchanges. In contrast, exchange traded funds are investment company shares that trade throughout the day on stock exchanges. Many investors who lack the time, know-how, or commitment to manage their own money turn to these vehicles as an investment outlet. By investing in mutual funds or exchange traded funds, shareholders benefit from a level of diversification and investment performance they might otherwise find difficult to achieve.

LG2 Differentiate between open- and closed-end mutual funds as well as exchange-traded funds, and discuss the various types of fund loads and charges.

Investors can buy either open-end funds, which can issue an unlimited number of shares, or closed-end funds, which have a fixed number of shares outstanding and which trade in the secondary markets like any other share of common stock. Investors also can buy exchange-traded funds, or ETFs, which are structured like index funds and operate much like open-end funds but trade in the market like closed-end funds. There's a cost, however, to investing in mutual funds (and other types of professionally managed investment products). Mutual fund investors face a full array of loads, fees, and charges, including front-end loads, back-end loads, annual 12(b)-1 charges, and annual management fees. Some of these costs are one-time charges (like front-end loads); but others, like 12(b)-1 and management fees are paid annually.

LG3 Discuss the types of funds available to investors and the different kinds of investor services offered by mutual funds and exchange traded funds.

Each fund has an established investment objective that determines its investment policy and identifies it as a certain type of fund. Some popular types of funds are growth, aggressive growth, value, equity-income, balanced, growth-and-income, bond, money market, index, sector, socially responsible, asset allocation, and international funds. The different categories of funds have different risk-return characteristics and are important variables in the fund selection process. Many investors buy mutual funds not just for

Exhibit 13.4 Effects of Reinvesting Income*
Reinvesting dividends and/or capital gains can have tremendous effects on your investment position. This graph shows the results of a hypothetical investor who initially invested $10,000 and reinvested all dividends and capital gains distributions in additional fund shares. No adjustment has been made for any income taxes payable by the shareholder, which would be appropriate provided that the fund was held in a tax-deferred account like an individual retirement account (IRA) or a 401(k) account. This example is for the Fidelity Contrafund.

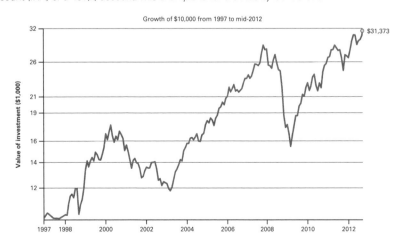

Growth of $10,000 from 1997 to mid-2012

mutual fund *A financial services organization that receives money from its shareholders and invests those funds on their behalf in a diversified portfolio of securities. 309*

net asset value (NAV) *The current market value of all the securities the fund owns, less any liabilities, on a per-share basis. 312*

no-load fund *A fund on which no transaction fees are charged. 314*

open-end investment company *A firm that can issue an unlimited number of shares that it buys and sells at a price based on the current market value of the securities it owns; also called a mutual fund. 311*

pooled diversification *A process whereby investors buy into a diversified portfolio of securities for the collective benefit of individual investors. 311*

real estate investment trust (REIT) *An investment company that accumulates money, by selling shares to investors, in order to invest it in various forms of real estate including mortgages; similar to a mutual fund, but REITs invest only in specific types of real estate or real estate–related products. 329*

socially responsible fund (SRF) *A fund that invests only in companies meeting certain moral, ethical, and/or environmental criteria. 319*

systematic withdrawal plan *A plan offered by mutual funds that allows shareholders to be paid specified amounts of money each period. 322*

tax-exempt money fund *A money fund that limits its investments to short-term, tax-exempt municipal securities. 319*

To access Bonus Exhibits, additional Smart Sites, Concept Checks, and more, please visit CourseMate for PFIN 3. Log on to www.cengagebrain.com.

their investment returns, but to take advantage of the various investor services they offer, such as automatic investment and reinvestment plans, systematic withdrawal programs, low-cost conversion and phone- or online-switching privileges, and retirement programs.

LG4 Gain an understanding of the variables that should be considered when selecting funds for investment purposes.

The fund selection process generally starts by assessing your own needs and wants; this sets the tone for your investment program and helps you decide on the types of funds to consider. Next, look at what the funds have to offer, particularly regarding the fund's investment objectives and investor services—here, narrow down the alternatives by aligning your needs with the types of funds available. From this list of funds, conduct the final selection tests: fund performance and cost—other things being equal, look for high performance and low costs.

LG5 Identify the sources of return and calculate the rate of return earned on an investment in a mutual funds as well as evaluate the performance of an exchange traded fund.

The investment performance of mutual funds and ETFs largely depends on the returns the money managers are able to generate from their securities portfolios; generally speaking, strong markets translate into attractive returns for mutual fund investors. Mutual funds and ETFs have three basic sources of return: (1) dividends, (2) capital gains distributions, and (3) changes in the fund's NAV (accruing from unrealized capital gains). Both the approximate yield and total return measures recognize these three elements and provide a simple yet effective way of measuring the annual rate of return from a mutual fund. Index-based ETF performance considers returns as well as how closely it tracks the performance of its underlying index, how consistently it pursues its investment style, how its performance compares with its peers, and how the ETF's expense ratio compares with reasonable benchmarks.

LG6 Understand the role that real estate plays in a diversified investment portfolio along with the basics of investing in real estate, either directly or indirectly.

Investing in real estate—be it raw land, income property (such as office buildings, apartments, and retail space), or even homes—provides an opportunity to earn attractive returns and further diversify an investment portfolio. Investors can buy property directly or invest in several types of real estate securities. Speculating in raw land is a high-risk type of real estate investment. Income-producing property, on the other hand, offers attractive returns from income and price appreciation as well as certain tax advantages. Investors not wishing to own real estate directly can invest indirectly through real estate mutual funds, as well as the common shares of real-estate-related companies, real estate investment trusts (REITs), mortgage-backed securities (MBSs), or real estate limited partnerships or limited liability companies. REITs, which are closed-end investment companies that invest in real estate, are the most popular type of real estate security and have a track record of solid returns.

KEY TERMS

accumulation period *The period during which premiums are paid for the purchase of an annuity. 351*

annuity *An investment product created by life insurance companies that provides a series of payments over time. 351*

annuity certain *An annuity that provides a specified monthly income for a stated number of years without consideration of any life contingency. 353*

contributory pension plan *A pension plan in which the employee bears part of the cost of the benefits. 344*

deferred annuity *An annuity in which benefit payments are postponed for a certain number of years. 352*

defined benefit plan *A pension plan in which the formula for computing benefits is stipulated in its provisions. 345*

defined contribution plan *A pension plan specifying the contributions that both employer and employee must make; it makes no promises concerning the size of the benefits at retirement. 344*

distribution period *The period during which annuity payments are made to an annuitant. 351*

Employee Retirement Income Security Act (ERISA) *A law passed in 1974 to ensure that workers eligible for pensions actually receive such benefits; also permits uncovered workers to establish individual tax-sheltered retirement plans. 343*

fixed-rate annuity *An annuity in which the insurance company agrees to pay a guaranteed rate of interest on your money. 353*

guaranteed-minimum annuity (life annuity with refund) *An annuity that provides a guaranteed minimum distribution of benefits. 352*

immediate annuity *An annuity in which the annuitant begins receiving monthly benefits immediately. 351*

individual retirement arrangement (IRA) *A retirement plan, open to any working American, to which a person may contribute a specified amount each year. 349*

installment premium annuity contract *An annuity contract purchased through periodic payments made over time. 351*

Keogh plan *An account to which self-employed persons may make specified payments that may be deducted from taxable income; earnings also accrue on a tax-deferred basis. 349*

LEARNING GOAL SUMMARIES

LG1 **Recognize the importance of retirement planning, and identify the three biggest pitfalls to good planning.**

Retirement planning plays a vital role in the personal financial planning process. It's based on many of the same principles and concepts of effective financial planning, including establishing financial goals and strategies, using savings and investment plans, and using certain insurance products, such as annuities. The three biggest pitfalls to sound retirement planning are starting too late, not saving enough, and investing too conservatively.

LG2 **Estimate your income needs in retirement and the retirement income supported by your financial plan.**

Rather than address retirement planning in a series of short-run (3- to 5-year) plans, it's best to take a long-term approach and look 20 to 30 years into the future to determine how much saving and investing you must do today to achieve the retirement goals you've set for tomorrow. Implementing a long-term retirement plan involves determining future retirement needs, estimating retirement income from known sources (such as Social Security and company pension plans), and deciding how much to save and invest each year to build up a desired nest egg.

Exhibit 14.1 Sources of Income for the Average Retiree
Social Security is the single largest source of income for the average U.S. retiree. This source alone is larger than the amount the average retiree receives from pension plans and personal wealth/investment assets combined.

Percentage distribution of sources of income for married couples and nonmarried people who are age 65 and over, 1962–2010

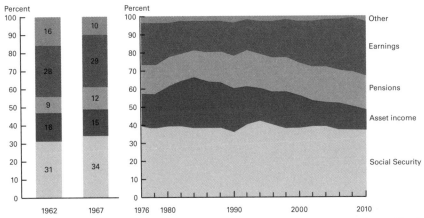

Note: A married couple is age 65 and over if the husband is age 65 and over or the husband is younger than age 55 and the wife is age 65 and over. The definition of "other" includes, but is not limited to, public assistance, unemployment compensation, worker's compensation, alimony, child support, and personal contributions. Reference population: These data refer to the civilian noninstitutionalized population.

Source: Social Security Administration, 1963 Survey of the Aged; 1968 Survey of Demographic and Economic characteristics of the Aged; U.S. Census Bureau, Current Population Survey. Annual Social and Economic Supplement, 1977–2009; http://www.agingstats.gov/Agingstatsdotnet/Main_Site/default.aspx, accessed May 2011.

LG3 **Explain the eligibility requirements and benefits of the Social Security program.**

Social Security is the foundation for the retirement programs of most families; except for a few exempt classes (mostly government employees), almost all gainfully employed workers are covered by Social Security. Upon retirement, covered workers are entitled to certain monthly benefits, as determined mainly by the employee's earning history and age at retirement.

life annuity, period certain *A type of guaranteed-minimum annuity that guarantees the annuitant a stated amount of monthly income for life; the insurer agrees to pay for a minimum number of years. 352*

life annuity with no refund (pure life) *An option under which an annuitant receives a specified amount of income for life, regardless of the length of the distribution period. 352*

noncontributory pension plan *A pension plan in which the employer pays the total cost of the benefits. 344*

profit-sharing plan *An arrangement in which the employees of a firm participate in the company's earnings. 346*

qualified pension plan *A pension plan that meets specified criteria established by the Internal Revenue Code. 346*

salary reduction, or 401(k), plan *An agreement by which part of a covered employee's pay is withheld and invested; taxes on the contributions and the account earnings are deferred until the funds are withdrawn. 347*

single premium annuity contract *An annuity contract purchased with a lump-sum payment. 351*

survivorship benefit *On an annuity, the portion of premiums and interest that has not been returned to the annuitant before his or her death. 351*

thrift and savings plan *A plan to supplement pension and other fringe benefits; the firm contributes an amount equal to a set proportion of the employee's contribution. 346*

variable annuity *An annuity in which the monthly income provided by the policy varies as a function of the insurer's actual investment experience. 353*

vested rights *Employees' nonforfeitable rights to receive benefits in a pension plan based on their own and their employer's contributions. 344*

To access Bonus Exhibits, additional Smart Sites, Concept Checks, and more, please visit CourseMate for PFIN 3. Log on to www.cengagebrain.com.

LG4 Differentiate among the types of basic and supplemental employer-sponsored pension plans.

Employer-sponsored pension and retirement plans provide a vital source of retirement income to many individuals. Such plans can often spell the difference between enjoying a comfortable standard of living in retirement or a bare subsistence. In *basic* retirement programs, all employees participate after a certain period of employment. These plans can be defined contribution or defined benefits plans. There are also several forms of *supplemental* employer-sponsored programs, including profit-sharing plans, thrift and savings plans, and perhaps most popular, salary reduction plans such as 401(k) plans.

LG5 Describe the various types of self-directed retirement plans.

In addition to company-sponsored retirement programs, individuals can set up their own self-directed tax-sheltered retirement plans; it's through such plans that most individuals can build up the nest eggs they'll need to meet their retirement objectives. The basic types of self-directed retirement programs are Keogh and SEP plans for self-employed individuals as well as various forms of IRAs, which any salary or wage earner can set up.

LG6 Choose the right type of annuity for your retirement plan.

Annuities are also an important source of income for retired people. Basically, an annuity is an investment vehicle that allows investment income to accumulate on a tax-deferred basis; it provides for the systematic liquidation (payout) of all invested capital and earnings over an extended period. There's a wide variety of annuities, including single-payment and installment-premium, fixed and variable, and immediate and deferred; there are also different payout options.

Exhibit 14.3 Types of Annuity Contracts
Annuity contracts vary according to how you pay for the annuity, how the proceeds are disbursed, how earnings accrue, and when you receive the benefits.

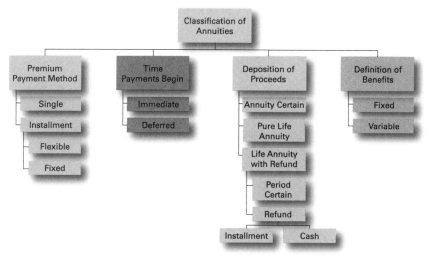

© Cengage Learning

KEY TERMS

administrator *The personal representative of the estate appointed by the court if the decedent died intestate. 369*

annual exclusion *Under the federal gift tax law, the amount that can be given each year without being subject to gift tax—for example, $13,000 in 2011. This amount is indexed for inflation. 376*

applicable exclusion amount (AEA) *Credit given to each person that can be applied to the amount of federal estate tax owed by that person at death. In 2011, the AEA was $5,000,000 per spouse. 373*

beneficiaries *Those who receive benefits—property or income— from a trust or from the estate of a decedent. A grantor can be a beneficary of his own trust. 371*

codicil *A document that legally modifies a will without revoking it. 367*

community property *All marital property co-owned equally by both spouses while living in a community property state. 370*

durable power of attorney for financial matters *Legal document that authorizes another person to take over someone's financial affairs and act on his or her behalf. 369*

durable power of attorney for health care *A written power of attorney authorizing an individual to make health care decisions on behalf of the principal when the principal is unable to make such decisions. Also called advanced directive for health care. 369*

estate planning *The process of developing a plan to administer and distribute your assets after death, in a manner consistent with your wishes and the needs of your survivors, while minimizing taxes. 359*

estate tax *A tax levied on the value of property transferred at the owner's death. 373*

ethical will *A personal statement left for family, friends, and community that shares your values, blessings, life's lessons, and hopes and dreams for the future. Also called legacy statement. 369*

executor *The personal representative of an estate designated in the decedent's will. 369*

LEARNING GOAL SUMMARIES

LG1 **Describe the role of estate planning in personal financial planning, and identify the seven steps involved in the process.**

Estate planning involves accumulating, preserving, and distributing an estate in order to most effectively achieve an estate owner's personal goals. The seven major steps to estate planning are outlined below.

Exhibit 15.2 Steps in the Estate Planning Process
The estate planning process consists of seven important steps, listed here in the order they would be performed.

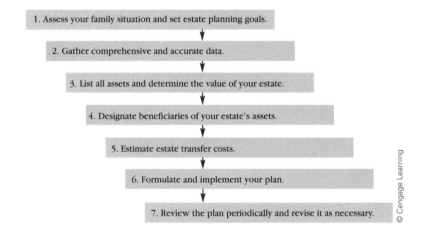

1. Assess your family situation and set estate planning goals.
2. Gather comprehensive and accurate data.
3. List all assets and determine the value of your estate.
4. Designate beneficiaries of your estate's assets.
5. Estimate estate transfer costs.
6. Formulate and implement your plan.
7. Review the plan periodically and revise it as necessary.

© Cengage Learning

LG2 **Recognize the importance of preparing a will and other documents to protect you and your estate.**

A person who dies without a valid will forfeits important privileges, including the right to decide how property will be distributed at death and the opportunity to select who will administer the estate and bear the burden of estate taxes and administrative expenses. The will should provide a clear and unambiguous expression of the testator's wishes, be flexible enough to encompass possible changes in family circumstances, and give proper regard to minimizing income, gift, and estate taxes. A will is valid only if properly executed by a person of sound mind. Once drawn up, wills can be changed by codicil or be fully revoked. The executor, named in the will, is responsible for collecting the decedent's assets, paying his or her debts and taxes, and distributing any remaining assets to the beneficiaries in the prescribed fashion. In addition to the will, other important estate planning documents include the letter of last instructions, power of attorney, living will, durable power of attorney for health care, and an ethical will.

LG3 **Explain how trusts are used in estate planning.**

The trust relationship arises when one party, the grantor (also called the trustor or settlor), transfers property to a second party, the trustee, for the benefit of a third party, the beneficiary. There are several types of trusts, but each is designed primarily for one or both of these reasons: to manage and conserve property over a long period, and to save income and estate taxes.

gift splitting *A method of reducing gift taxes; a gift given by one spouse, with the consent of the other spouse, can be treated as if each had given one-half of it. 376*

gift tax *A tax levied on the value of certain gifts made during the giver's lifetime. 373*

grantor *A person who creates a trust and whose property is transferred into it. Also called settlor, trustor, or creator. 371*

gross estate *All property that might be subject to federal estate taxes upon a person's death. 362*

intestacy *The situation that exists when a person dies without a valid will. 363*

irrevocable life insurance trust *An irrevocable trust in which the major asset is life insurance on the grantor's life. 373*

irrevocable living trust *A trust in which the grantor gives up the right to revoke or terminate the trust. 373*

joint tenancy *A type of ownership by two or more parties, with the survivor(s) continuing to hold all such property upon the death of one or more of the owners. 370*

letter of last instructions *An informal memorandum that is separate from a will and contains suggestions or recommendations for carrying out a decedent's wishes. 367*

living (inter vivos) trust *A trust created and funded during the grantor's lifetime. 372*

living will *A document that precisely states the treatments a person wants if he or she becomes terminally ill. 369*

pour-over will *A provision in a will that provides for the passing of the estate—after debts, expenses, taxes, and specific bequests—to an existing living trust. 373*

probate estate *The real and personal property owned by a person that can be transferred at death. 362*

probate process *The court-supervised disposition of a decedent's estate. 369*

revocable living trust *A trust in which the grantor reserves the right to revoke the trust and regain trust property. The grantor can serve as the initial trustee. 372*

right of survivorship *The right of surviving joint owners of property to receive title to the deceased joint owner's interest in the property. 370*

tenancy by the entirety *A form of ownership by husband and wife, recognized in certain states, in which property automatically passes to the surviving spouse. 370*

tenancy in common *A form of co-ownership under which there is no right of survivorship and each co-owner can leave his or her share to whomever he or she desires. 370*

testamentary trust *A trust created by a decedent's will and funded through the probate process. 373*

testator *The person who makes a will that provides for the disposition of property at his or her death. 364*

trust *A legal relationship created when one party transfers property to a second party for the benefit of third parties. 371*

trustee *An organization or individual selected by a grantor to manage and conserve property placed in trust for the benefit of the beneficiaries. 371*

unified rate schedule *A graduated table of rates applied to all taxable transfers; used for both federal gift and estate tax purposes. 374*

unified tax credit *The credit that can be applied against the tentative tax on estate tax base. 377*

will *A written and legally enforceable document expressing how a person's property should be distributed upon his or her death. 363*

To access Bonus Exhibits, additional Smart Sites, Concept Checks, and more, please visit CourseMate for PFIN 3. Log on to www.cengagebrain.com.

LG4 Determine whether a gift will be taxable and use planned gifts to reduce estate taxes.

Gifts of cash, financial assets, and personal or real property made during the donor's lifetime are subject to federal taxes. A gift, up to the annual exclusion amount, given to each recipient is excluded from the donor's gift tax calculation. Generally, donations to qualified charities and gifts between spouses are also excluded from the gift tax.

LG5 Calculate federal taxes due on an estate.

Federal estate taxes are a levy on the transfer of assets at death. They are unified (coordinated) with the gift tax—which imposes a graduated tax on the transfer of property during one's lifetime—so that the rates and credits are the same for both. Once federal estate taxes computed and certain credits are allowed, the resulting amount is payable in full generally within 9 months of the decedent's death.

LG6 Use effective estate planning techniques to minimize estate taxes.

Most well-defined estate plans use two estate planning techniques. Dividing involves the creation of new tax entities. It includes dividing a couple's estate into two equal parts, as well as maintaining a gift-giving program in order to use the annual exclusion applicable to gifts. Deferring gives an individual the use of money that would otherwise have been paid in taxes. Life insurance proceeds can be used to pay estate taxes and to provide beneficiaries with funds to meet their needs. While most estates are not large enough to result in a transfer tax, the potential tax exposure is a major motivation to do some estate planning. A lack of planning could result in heirs inheriting less than they would with estate planning.